AUTOCRATS *vs.* DEMOCRATS

Also by Michael McFaul

From Cold War to Hot Peace:
An American Ambassador in
Putin's Russia

AUTOCRATS

vs.

DEMOCRATS

China, Russia, America, and the New Global Disorder

MICHAEL McFAUL

MARINER BOOKS

New York Boston

HarperCollins books may be purchased for educational, business, or sales promotional use. For information, please email the Special Markets Department at SPsales@harpercollins.com.

The Mariner flag design is a registered trademark of HarperCollins Publishers LLC.

hc.com

FIRST EDITION

Designed by Chloe Foster

Library of Congress Cataloging-in-Publication Data has been applied for.

ISBN 978-0-358-67787-1

25 26 27 28 29 LBC 5 4 3 2 1

*For all the small-*d *democrats around the world fighting for democracy where it does not exist, or defending democracy where it is under assault, especially in Ukraine*

The arc of the moral universe is long,
but it bends toward justice.

Martin Luther King Jr.

Contents

Introduction

NEW COLD WAR?

THE COLD WAR ended in 1991. That year, the Soviet Union disintegrated, accelerating the appeal of democratic ideas around the world while also undermining the popularity of communist ideas and autocratic systems of government. At the time, it seemed the whole world wanted to join the democratic community of states. That year was a glorious moment to be a democrat, liberal, capitalist, multilateralist, and American. It was for me.

In 1991, I lived in Moscow doing fieldwork for my PhD dissertation and moonlighting for the National Democratic Institute (NDI), an American nongovernmental organization committed to promoting democracy. In August 1991, Russia's small-*d* democrats, led by the democratically elected President of the Russian Republic (RSFSR) Boris Yeltsin, thwarted a revanchist coup plot against Soviet leader Mikhail Gorbachev that helped trigger the dissolution of the Soviet Union a few months later. President Yeltsin and those in power in a newly independent Russia embraced democratic ideas and wanted to join the US-anchored liberal international order. As NDI's representative in Russia at the time, I was treated like a rock star.

Three decades later, great power competition is back. Some call it Cold War 2.0.[1] Others prefer Cold War II.[2] But few dispute that the United States faces new and serious threats from powerful autocracies, China and Russia, that did not exist thirty years ago. In relative terms, China and Russia have closed the power gap with the United States. The rise of these two powerful autocracies, and especially China, threatens American power and prosperity.

There is an ideological dimension to today's great power competition, too. Not only have China and Russia become increasingly autocratic at home, they also have pursued policies that aim to weaken democratic norms and institutions and strengthen autocratic regimes worldwide. The decision by autocratic Russian leader Vladimir Putin to launch a full-scale invasion of democratic Ukraine in February 2022 marked a new watershed in the conflict between democrats and autocrats in the twenty-first century.

In parallel with the rise of powerful autocrats, democratic ideas have been losing support around the world, including in the United States, since the end of the Cold War. According to Freedom House, 2024 marked the nineteenth consecutive year of a global democratic recession.[3] The eleventh year of democratic decline in the United States, 2021, was punctuated by the January 6 insurrection at the US Capitol that aimed to disrupt the peaceful transfer of presidential power through an electoral process.[4] Since then, American democracy has failed to rejuvenate, politics have become more polarized, and a growing segment of society no longer sees democracy as the best system of government. In 2022, in his final article as the coeditor of the *Journal of Democracy*, Larry Diamond soberly concluded, "This is the darkest moment for freedom in half a century."[5] In the first months of his second term, President Donald Trump has launched a bevy of attacks on democratic norms, including even hinting at his intention to run for a third term—a direct violation of the Twenty-Second Amendment of the US Constitution.

And that NDI office I helped open in 1992 in Moscow to great fanfare and praise? Putin shut it down in 2012. NDI never had a permanent office in China, but in 2019, Beijing sanctioned NDI staffers working on Asia.

Many frame this new ideological competition between great powers as a replay of the Cold War. Regarding China, the Cold War analogy is deployed in abundance.[6] China's economic rise has underwritten its military power and ideological reach, which threatens the United States and the free world more broadly. As we worried about Soviet aspirations to rule the world during the Cold War, many today believe that Chinese communist leaders seek to replace the United States as the world's hegemon. Michael Pillsbury, a China specialist and former Trump policy adviser, published *The Hundred-Year Marathon: China's Secret Strategy to Replace America as the Global Superpower*. Hoover Institution historian Niall Ferguson wrote, "When did Cold War II begin? Future historians will say it was in 2019."[7] China expert Susan Shirk started her 2022 book *Overreach* with the blunt statement "A new Cold War has already begun."[8] *New York Times* reporter David Sanger titled his recent book *New Cold Wars: China's Rise, Russia's Invasion, and America's Struggle to Defend the West.*[9] Gordon G. Chang's latest book is provocatively titled, *Plan Red: China's Project to Destroy America.*

Doctrinal statements from the first Trump administration animated this Cold War metaphor. The 2017 national security strategy rightly portrayed China as a "revisionist" power that, alongside Russia, sought "to shape a world antithetical to U.S. values and interests."[10] To underscore continuities from the Cold War, Trump's national security adviser Robert O'Brien argued, "Party General Secretary Xi Jinping sees himself as Josef Stalin's successor."[11] In one of his last major speeches as secretary of state in 2020, Michael Pompeo asserted that "the CCP regime is a Marxist-Leninist regime. General Secretary Xi Jinping is a true believer in a bankrupt totalitarian ideology. It's this ideology that informs his decades-long desire for global hegemony of Chinese communism."[12]

President Biden and his administration did not invoke the Cold War analogy with the same vigor, but their assessment of the China threat differed little from the Trump administration's. In its first significant foreign policy document, the Biden administration stated that China "is the only competitor potentially capable of combining its economic, diplomatic, military, and technological power to mount a sustained challenge to a stable and open international system."[13] In his first address to a joint session of the US Congress in 2021, Biden explained, "We're in competition with China and other countries to win the 21st Century."[14] NATO's 2024 Washington Summit Declaration warned, "The People's Republic of China's (PRC) stated ambitions and coercive policies continue to challenge our interests, security, and values. The deepening strategic partnership between Russia and the PRC and their mutually reinforcing attempts to undercut and reshape the rules-based international order are a cause for profound concern."[15]

Trump's second-term team reinvigorated the Cold War imagery. Trump's first national security adviser in his second term, Michael Waltz, warned, "I feel strongly that the Chinese Communist Party has entered into a Cold War with the United States and is explicit in its aim to replace the liberal, Western-led world order that has been in place since World War II."[16] Waltz believes that the China threat is even greater than the Soviet threat, arguing, "We're in a global arms race with an adversary that, unlike any in American history, has the economic and the military capability to truly supplant and replace us."[17] Months before taking on his new role as secretary of state, Marco Rubio echoed the same, warning that "Communist China is the most powerful adversary the United States has faced in living memory. We sometimes forget that our past enemies, including Nazi Germany and Soviet Russia, had smaller economies than we did."[18] Other analysts have suggested that the Chinese menace today is greater than the Soviet enemy. Former Australian prime minister Kevin Rudd warned, "The United States should realize that China represents the most politically and ideologically disciplined challenger it has ever faced during its century of geopolitical dominance."[19] Journalist Josh Rogin posited that the China threat "is not the same as Russia in 1950. If anything, the China challenge is orders of magnitude more difficult because of China's massive economic power and our economies' deep interconnectedness."[20] Indo-Pacific expert Michael Sobolik asserted, "Xi wants China to dominate the world . . . To the CCP, winning means exerting political dominance across the entire world."[21] In 2023, Congressman Mike Gallagher said, "This [our competition with China] is an existential struggle of what life will look like in the 21st century."[22] The Commission on the National Defense Strategy in 2024 warned ominously, "The threats the United States faces are the most serious and most challenging the nation has encountered since 1945 and include the potential for near-term major war."[23] Outpacing others in estimating the Chinese threat, Trump's former senior trade official Robert Lighthizer stated, "Now China is the greatest threat that the American nation and its systems of Western liberal democratic government have faced since the American Revolution."[24]

Analogies to a new Cold War regarding US-Russia relations appeared even earlier.[25] In 2009, British journalist Edward Lucas published *The New Cold War: Putin's Russia and the Threat to the West*.[26] Columbia professor Robert Legvold published, in 2016, *Return to Cold War*.[27] That same year at the Munich Security Conference, Russian prime minister Dmitry Medvedev invoked the Cuban Missile Crisis as a metaphor for contemporary US-Russia relations: "We are rapidly rolling into a period of a new cold war . . . I am sometimes confused: is this 2016 or 1962?"[28] Echoing Medvedev three years later, former US government officials Ernest Moniz and

Sam Nunn wrote, "Not since the 1962 Cuban missile crisis has the risk of a US-Russian confrontation been as high as it is today."[29] In 2018, President Trump declared, "Our relationship with Russia is worse now than it has ever been, and that includes the Cold War."[30] Some fault the United States for starting this second Cold War; the historian Richard Sakwa, for instance, titled his 2023 book *The Lost Peace: How the West Failed to Prevent a Second Cold War*.[31] But both sides in this blame game agree that US-Russia relations have never been as confrontational and dangerous as they are today.

What happened? How did we go from euphoria about democracy, globalization, and the West three decades ago to uncertainty about democracy, doubt about the liberal international order, and fear of powerful autocracies today? How did China and Russia pivot from pursuing reforms at home and joining the liberal international order abroad to deepening autocracy at home and threatening the liberal order abroad?

A second set of questions is what is the right way to understand the current great power competition between the United States, China, and Russia? Is our era actually a replay of the Cold War? Are we destined for war with China and doomed to conflict with Russia?[32] Or is our current era more contingent, giving agency to policymakers who aspire to reverse current confrontational trajectories?

Third, how should Americans—both leaders and citizens—respond? What is the right mix of new policies needed to advance American national interests and values in this new era of great power competition?

To answer these questions about the past, present, and future, I have divided this book into three parts, making arguments as a social scientist, a historian, and a former policymaker.

Part I explains the causes of great power competition today, using the history of US-Russia and US-China relations over the past three centuries to explain how we arrived at the tensions defining our current era. Wearing my social scientist hat in these first two chapters, I argue that three factors—power, regime types, and individuals—have interacted to produce both cooperation and conflict between the United States, China, and Russia over the last three centuries. These factors are variables, not constants; leaders are the most variable because they change more quickly and often than the balance of power or regime type. Yet, over the past few decades, all three of these factors have lined up uniquely to produce more conflict.

Part I also underscores that the United States and Russia and the United States and China are not destined for permanent conflict, let alone war, because of immutable or slowly changing factors such as culture, history, geography, and even power. The fact that earlier periods of bilateral relations were more cooperative gives hope for the possibility of cooperation again in the future. The current configuration of the balance of power, tensions exacerbated by the global contest between autocrats and democrats, and the specific leaders in office have combined to make our current era confrontational and dangerous. None of these conditions, however, are permanent. In the past, different power balances, regime types, and leaders made great power relations between the United States, China, and Russia more cooperative. That can happen again.

If part I explains the past, part II describes the present, providing a snapshot of great power competition today along three dimensions—power, ideology, and competing visions of global order. Putting my historian hat on for this section of the book, I argue that while there are some parallels between the Cold War with the Soviet Union and the present competition with China and Russia today, the differences are also great. Rigidly imposing the Cold War metaphor on our current era distorts more than illuminates current dynamics in either US-Russia or US-China relations.

The discussions of power in chapters 3, 4, and 5 reveal similarities and differences with the Cold War. This balance of power, especially between China and the United States, resembles the Cold War, with a bipolar international system dominated by the United States and China, just like the American-Soviet rivalry during the Cold War. We have also returned to an era of ideological competition between democratic and autocratic ideas and systems of government, like the Cold War. And leaders in the United States, China, and Russia have competing conceptions of the global order. The same was true between the United States and the Soviet Union during the Cold War.

Yet, as these chapters explain, the distinctions between the balance of power today and the Cold War era are also manifold. For instance, the Cold War analogy assigns China an equal superpower status to the United States. That is inaccurate. We underestimated Chinese power for too long and needed to correct our assessments. But now we have overshot the target by overestimating Chinese power and exaggerating the Chinese threat to our existence. Containing China must be a central American foreign policy objective of the twenty-first century, but China is not an *existential* threat to the United States or the free world. China does not threaten, as some claim, the very existence of the United States and our democratic allies. In the aggregate, China is not America's equal yet and may never be. When allies are included in the equation, the power gap in favor of the democratic world is even greater.

While overestimating Chinese power, many American leaders have underestimated Russian power in recent years, a claim that also cuts against the grain of conventional wisdom. Russia's full-scale invasion of Ukraine in 2022 revealed underappreciated weaknesses regarding the fighting capabilities of Russia's armed forces. In a sobering lesson to everyone trying to assess power before it is used, counting soldiers or defense spending are inexact proxies for actual military might (this lesson is essential for those trying to evaluate Chinese military capabilities today). At the same time, even with much more limited military and economic means than the United States or China, Russia has the capacity to threaten US security interests, including those of our European allies. Russia has reemerged today as a formidable adversary to the United States because (1) Putin is a risk-taker and has demonstrated a greater willingness than American or Chinese leaders to deploy Russian power in aggressive ways that directly threaten American security and the security of our allies and partners and (2) the Russian military is getting bigger and more experienced as a result of the invasion of Ukraine. Russia is much weaker than China, but the probability of a conflict between Russia and NATO allies that might drag the United States into war is as great as a conflict between China and the United States.

Regarding ideological conflict, there are also parallels and differences between today and the Cold War. The regime type—the kind of government—of great powers matters. Analyses focusing only on power to explain great power competition today are incomplete. As discussed in chapters 6, 7, and 8, there is a fundamental ideological struggle today between autocracies and democracies and between autocratic and democratic ideas. That is different from thirty years ago, when most of the world gravitated toward democracy, and more like the Cold War, when the ideological contest between the Soviet Union and the United States played a defining role in shaping international politics. Great power autocracies and democracies inherently threaten each other because they have competing narratives for their legitimacy. In addition, all three great powers—the United States, China, and Russia—seek to promote their ideologies abroad today, fueling further tensions.

However, today's ideological conflict between the great powers is less intense than it was during the Cold War. Unlike Stalin, Khrushchev, and Mao, Xi is not trying to export Marxism-Leninism or even one-party dictatorship to the entire world. China is financially and technologically supporting autocracies worldwide, but Chinese communist leaders today are not actively seeking to overthrow democracies. They put little effort into supporting their ideas in the developed world and are relatively passive, compared to the Soviets, in promoting their system of government in the developing world. Americans must be vigilant in containing Chinese ideological promotion but not frightened by it, nor overreach when trying to contain it.

Similarly, Putin's efforts to promote his brand of populist, illiberal dictatorship are not as intense or successful as the Soviet Union's promotion of communism. However, the Russian ideological threat is more significant today than many believe. Yes, Putin is corrupt and imperialist. But he is also an ideological leader who has sought to propagate his illiberal orthodox values for decades. Putin is more committed to ideological promotion than Xi is, and tragically, we must acknowledge that his ideological promotion efforts have produced some successes in many European countries and the United States. Amazingly, even after Russia launched its second, larger-scale invasion of Ukraine in 2022, many political leaders and movements worldwide—including prominent political figures and influential commentators in the United States—have maintained ideological solidarity with Putin and Putinism. Most different from the Cold War, the current leaders in Washington and Moscow embrace many shared ideas and values.

Putin has fewer means than either China or the United States to propagate his ideas, but he has demonstrated more commitment to doing so than leaders in Washington or Beijing.

Until recently, the United States has also contributed to this ideological competition with China and Russia. As discussed in chapter 6, the United States for decades has been the most ideological power of the three, unabashedly advocating for liberal democratic values worldwide, including inside China and Russia, and deploying multiple instruments to advance this normative mission. Trump has radically disrupted this longstanding tradition in American foreign policy. In his first term in office and now again today, Trump is the first US president in a century to abandon democracy promotion as a core component of American foreign policy. Whether Trump's pivot away from supporting democracy signals a permanent shift in American foreign policy or an interregnum is not yet clear. That the United States has promoted democracy in the past—and autocratic competitors therefore still perceive the United States as an ideological threat—is an observable fact. Hoping that powerful democratic states and democratic ideas do not threaten autocratic states and leaders is not realism but naïveté. The mere existence of a powerful democracy threatens the legitimacy and therefore security of powerful autocracies.

Regarding global order, China and Russia seek revision, just like the Soviets did in the previous century. As discussed in chapters 10 and 11, Xi and Putin have committed real resources to try to change the global order. Since the end of the Cold War, the United States has been committed to maintaining the global order, albeit to varying degrees, depending on who was president. That commitment has waned dramatically in the second Trump term, but again, it is too early to know whether this shift in American foreign policy is temporary or permanent. Thirty years ago, there was more consensus among all countries about what the world order should be. Today, there is more discord.

At the same time, the challenge China and Russia pose to the existing international system—sometimes referred to as the liberal international order—is not nearly as intense as the Soviet threat to the global system was during the Cold War. Soviet leaders pushed for a global revolution—the overthrow of what they called the global capitalist system anchored by the

United States. Xi seeks to reform, not destroy, the existing world order. Chinese leaders want to reshape norms within existing multilateral organizations (to varying degrees, depending on the type of institution) and grow China's influence within international institutions.* For a rising power not to try to do so would be odd—that has happened throughout history. However, these efforts should not be misunderstood as a stealth strategy to overthrow the entire established order. Unlike Soviet leaders or Mao during the Cold War, Xi and his comrades are not seeking a world revolution for a simple reason: China benefits from many of the existing norms, rules, and laws that constitute the current international system.[33] Xi and the CCP aspire to change this system to better serve China's interests (as defined by them), and they are not afraid to use all sorts of coercive methods to achieve these reforms. At times, Xi and the CCP have also ignored the rules of the existing system and used coercive power, especially economic power, because they had the means to do so.[34] That too is standard great power behavior, as the United States has demonstrated many times. But this Chinese behavior is different from the Cold War, when the Soviet Union was not even a member of some of the most important institutions of the liberal international order, did not benefit from global capitalism to the same extent that China does today, and sought to replace this American-anchored system with a communist system controlled by Moscow.

Xi has also invested in creating new multilateral organizations independent of the American-anchored international institutions. This activity is a more significant threat to American national security, prosperity, and values than Chinese efforts to modify existing global institutions. American leaders have not paid enough attention to China's success in developing new exclusionary regional organizations, many of which are at odds with American interests and values. For America's part, innovation and creativity in this arena have been in short supply.

Regarding the global order, Putin has much greater revisionist aspirations than Xi. He seeks to weaken, if not completely undermine, the liberal

---

* In this book, the terms *international institutions, multilateral institutions, international organizations,* and *multilateral organizations* will be used interchangeably. Other scholars distinguish between them.

international order created by American leadership at the end of World War II. Thankfully, Putin lacks the means to achieve his most aggressive revisionist ends, but he is not done trying.

Tragically, today, another threat to the existing international order comes from the United States. American leaders and analysts have underestimated the damage that US retrenchment and withdrawal have done to international institutions serving American purposes. Those who believe that the US is better off reverting to the isolationist traditions of a century ago or fighting alone for American interests in an anarchic global jungle are dangerously wrong but also increasingly influential in American politics, especially after Donald Trump's reelection in 2024. This threat from the United States to the liberal international order is new and different from the Cold War.

Accurately diagnosing the threats from China and Russia regarding power, ideology, and competing conceptions of the global order is critical for devising an effective, pragmatic, and sustainable US foreign policy. It certainly makes for a better television sound bite or tweet to argue that today is Cold War II or today is *not* a new Cold War. But such simplistic frameworks do not accurately describe the complex, unique dynamics of our current era of great power competition. During the Cold War, American leaders made some of their greatest mistakes when they oversimplified their analysis of international politics, which, in turn, generated ineffective foreign policies at best and disastrous wars at worst. We cannot repeat these mistakes today.

In part III of this book, I put my policymaker hat back on to propose a set of prescriptions for future American leaders. Drawing on the analysis from the previous chapters, including comparisons but also differences with the Cold War, this last part provides a blueprint for American foreign policy for the coming decades, not just the next few years. I aim to offer an American grand strategy for the twenty-first century, not just policy recommendations for the second Trump administration, organized around three themes: mistakes in the Cold War that we must avoid today, successes from the Cold War that we should replicate today, and policy prescriptions for the new challenges we face today. Understanding precisely the similarities and differences between the Cold War and now will help US policymakers learn critical lessons of both successes and failures from the Cold War for parallel issues today but also avoid applying Cold War analogies to current problems that have little to do with the previous century.

Chapter 12 details some of the mistakes American leaders made during the Cold War, predominantly driven by overestimating the Soviet power and trying to contain it everywhere. Historian Hal Brands has rightly observed, "It is a serious mistake . . . to think that America's Cold War strategy was wholly successful. The road to victory was littered with failures and higher-than-expected costs."[35] Today, we must learn from those mistakes—overreach, McCarthyism, wasteful nuclear arms races, and aiding brutal dictators worldwide—and not repeat them. Chapter 13 reviews some of our greatest successes during the Cold War, ones that American leaders should replicate today, including promoting arms control, keeping lines of communication open with adversaries to manage crises, maintaining American economic and military power, building strong alliances, promoting democratic ideas abroad, and creating and sustaining new multilateral institutions. Even if the parallels to the Cold War are inexact, there are some lessons from the previous century for our current era. Chapter 14 concludes part III with a set of prescriptions for issues that are new to our century and have nothing to do with the Cold War, like economic interdependence, geopolitical fragmentation, the China-Russia entente, and American isolationism and polarization.

I wrote most of part III before Trump's second term began. I considered amending my policy recommendations to be more aligned with and palatable to the new Trump administration but ultimately decided against it. First, doing so would betray the diagnostic analysis from the previous two sections. If what I wrote before Trump's return was accurate, it should not change now that he is once again president. Second, my hope is that the ideas I propose in part III will serve as a guide for all American presidents, all administrations, and all Americans for decades to come. If Trump and his team will not embrace my ideas for a successful American foreign policy in our new era of great power competition, I hope my recommendations will benefit future presidents and their administrations. Like the Cold War, our new era of great power competition will likely last decades.

Therefore, we need a new, bold, and enduring grand strategy to address the challenge.

I am a liberal internationalist, albeit not a traditional one, at a time when illiberal nationalism is considered in vogue. Perhaps Trump's reelection signals a permanent trajectory toward isolationism, unilateralism, and indifference to democratic values in American foreign policy. I do not know. I certainly hope not, because I am concerned that these ideas do not serve the long-term interests of the American people. Some will dismiss my worldview and policy recommendations as old-fashioned and out of date. I am okay with that. That is what critics also said about liberalism and democracy in the 1930s, when fascism was the new cool fad, or in the 1970s, when communism was being embraced as the future by many in dozens of countries around the world. And in the longer arc of history, ideas about democracy and liberalism have faded in popularity many times, but eventually came back into fashion. As long as the United States remains a democracy, I want to be in the ideological fight against illiberal nationalism and continue to make the case for why a return to internationalism, multilateralism, and support for democracy and human rights worldwide best serves American national interests. If the permissive conditions for a new embrace of such ideas reemerge in the United States, I hope part III will serve as a comprehensive blueprint for what should be done. And I want to underscore that I believe the ideas sketched in these prescriptive chapters advance *American*—not Republican or Democratic—national interests.

This book is ambitious and long. To avoid writing a book even longer and broader in scope, I deliberately left some things out. For instance, China and Russia are not the only autocracies in the world threatening American national interests; Iran and North Korea pose serious challenges too. Failed and struggling states—including Afghanistan, Libya, and Yemen—also pose security risks for the United States. Terrorists continue to threaten American security and prosperity, as do climate change and global pandemics.

This book, however, focuses on the rise of only two autocratic great powers for several reasons. First, though the international system includes hundreds of consequential state and non-state actors, great powers have reemerged again as the primary players shaping international outcomes today. China and Russia wield relatively more power than their neighbors and can influence and threaten their neighbors to a greater extent than other countries.

Second, Russia and China seek to influence international relations beyond Europe and Asia to a greater extent than other autocracies. The Chinese and Russian autocracies also share a degree of ideological tension with the democratic United States and the democratic world more generally. Iran's theocracy is the only other regime with grandiose ideological aspirations, but its reach remains regional and shows signs of diminishing. North Korea does not seek to export its ideology abroad.

Third, both autocratic challengers, Russia and China, cooperate to thwart American aims and interests. They act autonomously in their regions but often in concert with each other.[36] Sino-Russian relations, even after Putin escalated his invasion of Ukraine in 2022, are stronger today than ever before. Together, they vote at the United Nations Security Council, trade, train militarily, and cooperate closely in several new multilateral organizations. They both aid other autocracies at odds with the United States, including, first and foremost, Iran and North Korea. China and Russia also support autocrats in Venezuela, Myanmar, and Belarus.

Finally, Putin and Xi see dealing with the United States as their central foreign policy challenge. Understanding the dual threats posed by Russia and China to American national interests and devising strategies for managing relations with both great powers will remain a central concern for the makers of US foreign policy for decades to come.

Regarding the democracy camp, the United States is not the only powerful democracy in the world dealing with the challenges of China and Russia simultaneously. My original book proposal included Europe as a fourth great power on the liberal, democratic side of the ledger. Throughout the book, the European Union, NATO, and individual powerful European countries appear frequently. However, I eventually decided to treat the West, anchored but not controlled by the United States, as a single bloc, primarily due to space constraints. This analytic decision was also driven by the historical observation that the West used to act in relative unison in response to the Soviet threat. Whether that remains true in this century, especially in the Trump era, is unclear. Today, Europe also seems torn between those who want more unity and those desiring less, as well as between internationalists and isolationists. However, recent attacks by President Trump and his team in his second term against European allies could tragically trigger a deeper rift, if not a permanent split, between the United States and Europe. If Europe does begin to act as an autonomous great power influencing outcomes in the international system, independent from the United States, that historical pivot will require another book.

One could also make a case for including India as a rising great power in the democratic camp, albeit in a complicated way. On paper, India seems to have the capacity to act as a great power and influence outcomes around the world. To date, however, Indian leaders have not embraced that kind of global agenda, and India's democracy today is under duress. I hope I am wrong. The world would be better served by having more engagement from two strong democratic actors—Europe and India. For the immediate future, I fear I am right.

Part I

THE PAST

Chapter 1

COOPERATION AND CONFLICT WITH RUSSIA

WHEN IT COMES to international relations, power matters. Since there is no world government, power plays a central role in how countries interact. States with the most power have the greatest ability to threaten one another and, therefore, tend to clash. As such, power takes center stage in US-Russia tensions today—any analysis of great power relations that does not consider power is flawed.

Yet an analysis that focuses only on power is incomplete. Power is vital but so are regimes and leaders, as the history of US-Russia relations shows. For example, the Bolshevik Revolution in 1917 created a new communist government, a change that immediately triggered conflict between the United States and the Soviet Union. Later, Franklin D. Roosevelt's election in 1932 prompted the restoration of US diplomatic relations with Moscow in 1933, demonstrating the crucial role leaders can play in shaping outcomes.

This chapter traces the interaction of power, regimes, and leaders in US-Russia relations over the past two centuries, showing that the dynamic was confrontational at times but cooperative at other times. The central aim of this chapter is to demonstrate that the current tensions in US-Russia relations can shift depending on the balance of power, types of regimes, and preferences of leaders.

In broad strokes, the US-Russia relationship can be divided into five periods: (1) relative cooperation between the American democracy and the Russian monarchy in the eighteenth and nineteenth centuries; (2) even friendlier, albeit short-lived, ties between the US and Russia after autocratic breakdown and the hope of democratic transition in 1917; (3) confrontation between the US and the Soviet Union after the consolidation of Bolshevik power and the creation of the communist regime in the Soviet Union in

1918, interrupted by a brief interregnum of cooperation during World War II; (4) deep cooperation after Russia's democratic revolution in 1991; and (5) a return to confrontation today as a result of Russia's rising power and growing autocracy under Vladimir Putin.

PERIOD ONE: TSARS AND DEMOCRATS

When the new American Republic first contacted the Russian Empire, in the eighteenth century, the balance of power between the two countries was highly asymmetric. Russia was a central player in Europe and expanding its presence in Asia. The empire even had a foothold in North America, with a settlement as far south as Fort Ross in Northern California. The United States, however, was not even a regional power in North America, let alone a major world power. This acute power imbalance compelled American leaders to seek favors from the tsars in St. Petersburg, and for the most part, they were granted. For the next century, US-Russia relations were mostly cordial.

Until 1917, differences in regime type played a minor role in the bilateral relationship. While American Founding Fathers were very ideological (after all, they had led a revolution and fought a war against Britain motivated by liberal, democratic ideas), they were focused on consolidating their new republic at home. They had little capacity or intention to propagate their ideas abroad. As a weak power on the periphery of the international system, America rarely criticized the autocratic ways of tsarist Russia. After all, monarchs ruled almost everywhere at the time. US leaders wanted recognition from the autocratic great powers, including Russia, in the existing international order, not an overthrow of them. American leaders also sought powerful partners to balance against Great Britain, irrespective of regime type.

Russian tsars initially pursued a relationship with the United States as a strategy for influencing the balance of power politics in Europe, including, most importantly, weakening Great Britain. Catherine the Great expressed mild curiosity about the ideals that the rebels in the British colonies embraced, but her primary motivation in engaging with the Americans was strengthening Russia's position in Europe. During the Revolutionary War, she refused King George's request to help quell the rebellion in his colonies, instead releasing a declaration of neutrality in 1780 and offering mediating services (which were never accepted) to help end the war.[1] She blamed the revolution on King George's mismanagement of the colonies and predicted independence for them long before many of her peers. Catherine believed that an independent America would benefit Russian business interests by increasing commercial trade between Russia and the former colonies and compelling Britain to buy more goods from the Russian Empire.

However, the Russian monarchy turned coy after the American rebels won the war and established a new republic. Weakening Great Britain was good, but hobnobbing with rebels in the imperial capital of St. Petersburg was a bridge too far, at least initially. The American envoys sent to Russia struggled to gain recognition. It was not until 1809 that Alexander I finally agreed to establish diplomatic relations between the two countries, and John Quincy Adams was recognized as the first US ambassador to the Russian Empire.

The main driver of early US-Russia relations was commerce, not leaders, ideas, or power. As Alexander I made clear in 1809, "There should not be any conflicting interests or reasons for the rupture between the United States and the Russian Empire, while the trade between the two countries could be mutually beneficial."[2] Trade levels were never significant but still seen as worth pursuing by officials in both Washington and St. Petersburg.

While cooperating on trade, Americans and Russians competed for territorial control in North America along the Pacific Coast. In the nineteenth century, Russian and American leaders pursued their respective versions of Manifest Destiny. The US expanded to the west and Russia to the east, meeting but not clashing in armed conflict in California. American politicians united to push the Europeans out of North America—a policy codified as the Monroe Doctrine. As the Americans pushed farther west, war with Russia seemed inevitable. War, after all, determined the new borders between the United States and Mexico in southwest America and occurred again in Asia between Russia and Japan in 1904–5.

Strikingly, however, Russia and the United States never clashed militarily during this period. American and Russian diplomats found more cooperative ways to settle differences, including codifying borders in the

Russo-American Treaty of 1824, when Russia recognized US sovereignty over much of the Pacific Northwest, and, even more amazingly, selling Alaska to the United States for $7.2 million in a treaty signed in 1867. At the time, Tsar Alexander II thought selling would be better than fighting over this "resourceless" colony.

THE AMERICAN CIVIL WAR

Another big test of US-Russia relations emerged during the American Civil War. For President Abraham Lincoln and his secretary of state, William Seward, preventing Russia from supporting the South was a paramount goal. Worried that Great Britain and France might aid the secessionists in the southern states, they saw Russian support as a strategy to counter British and French involvement.[3] They succeeded in getting it. Similar to Russia's position regarding the American Revolutionary War, Alexander II declared Russian neutrality but informally signaled support for the North through Russian navy port calls to New York and San Francisco in 1863. US Supreme Court justice Oliver Wendell Holmes declared Alexander II to be "our friend when the world was our foe."[4]

Around the same time, Alexander II used military force to quell his own rebellion in Poland. President Lincoln supported him, at least rhetorically, by adopting a noninterventionist view on what Russian officials called the "Polish problem," even if doing so clashed with American ideals of independence and self-determination. At the time, US leaders did not try to advance normative concerns about imperialism, let alone promote democracy, when dealing with Russia; ensuring that Russia blocked foreign support for their enemies in North America, especially the rebels in the South, was far more important.

Values, however, were a positive force regarding one issue: enslaved people and serfs. Lincoln and Alexander II shared a normative bond over their commitment to liberating enslaved citizens. In 1861, Alexander II issued his Emancipation Manifesto, freeing Russia's serfs. Two years later, Lincoln signed the Emancipation Proclamation, freeing America's enslaved people.

VALUES AND IMMIGRATION

The peaceful settlement of territorial disputes in the Pacific Northwest, Russian help during the Civil War, and the freeing of the slaves and serfs in parallel did not translate into admiration for the Russian Empire by all of American society. Over time, Russia's aristocracy also began to loathe and fear US democracy. As the United States emerged to play a more prominent role in international politics, clashes in values became a growing irritant in bilateral relations. The Empire's treatment of Jews constituted the first significant confrontation over human rights in US-Russia relations.

Russia's imperial expansion westward in the nineteenth century meant that large Jewish communities were subsumed into the Empire and not welcomed by the monarchy. Around this same time, Jews from the Russian Empire started to immigrate to the United States. When St. Petersburg issued a series of anti-Semitic government decrees and sometimes encouraged violent pogroms against Jewish communities, including the deadly 1903 Kishinev pogrom, recently arrived Jewish residents in the United States used their newly acquired political rights to express outrage.[5] Criticism of Russia's inhumane rule, especially regarding the treatment of Jews, grew within American media and Congress, with parts of American society pushing for a more values-oriented American foreign policy. American Christian missionaries at the time also sought to expand their footprint in the Russian Empire and consequently became more critical of despotic tsarism and its alliance with the Russian Orthodox Church.

US government officials said and did little about human rights violations in the Russian Empire. However, the United States did welcome greater numbers of Jews fleeing persecution, taking in roughly three million immigrants from the Russian Empire between 1881 and 1924. Accepting this sizable immigrant population was both a humanitarian gesture and an intelligent strategy to expand the American workforce and power generally, underscoring that values and economic interests can support each other.

PERIOD TWO: DEMOCRATIC REGIME CHANGE

Before World War I, Russia's monarchy was already showing signs of weakness. Following Russia's defeat in the 1904–5 Russo-Japanese War, the tsar agreed, albeit reluctantly, to approve the constitution of 1906, which established a semi-independent parliament and allowed for a multiparty political system. At a time when liberal ideas were animating politics and percolating among intellectuals in Germany, Persia, and China, Russia seemed to be joining a transnational democratic movement. Over the next decade, however, the tsar rolled back many of these liberal concessions, a reactionary trajectory that helped trigger the Russian Revolution.

Throughout these tumultuous years in the Russian Empire during the first two decades of the twentieth century, US-Russia ties remained mostly cordial. For instance, in a significant expression of growing American international stature, President Theodore Roosevelt mediated the end of the Russo-Japanese War. The American president's effort produced the Treaty of Portsmouth in 1905. While Russia had suffered a military defeat, most considered the treaty's terms advantageous to Russia, underscoring the enduring cooperative ties between the Russian monarchy and the American democracy.

World War I presented the Russian monarchy with even bigger challenges. Unlike the Napoleonic Wars, which helped consolidate tsarist power, this continental war destabilized the monarchy. The United States joined this war on Russia's side only in April 1917, prompted by German submarine attacks on US merchant ships and the interception of the Zimmerman telegram (a secret German proposal about forming a military alliance with Mexico). But by the time President Wilson declared war, the February Revolution (March, according to the Gregorian calendar) in Russia had already compelled Tsar Nicholas II to abdicate his throne. That Russia looked like it was becoming a democracy made it easier for the United States to join the war, which, after the February Revolution, could be framed as a fight between democracies on one side and dictatorships on the other.

Many American liberals interpreted Russia's February Revolution as a transition from autocracy to democracy. As President Wilson argued before Congress, "Does not every American feel that assurance has been added to our hope for the future peace of the world by the wonderful and heartening things that have been happening within the last few weeks in Russia?"[6] Wilson believed that the democratic spirit of the Russian people was finally being unleashed, since "Russia was known by those who knew it best to have been always in fact democratic at heart . . . the autocracy that crowned the summit of her political structure, long as it had stood and terrible as was the reality of its power, was not, in fact, Russian in origin, character, or purpose; and now it has been shaken off and the great, generous Russian people . . . are fighting for freedom in the world, for justice, and for peace."[7] The US president quickly recognized the provisional government and pledged assistance.[8] The prime minister–chairman of the Russian provisional government, Alexander Kerensky, seemed to embrace liberal instincts, as he advocated for freedom of speech, press, assembly, and religion, adopted universal suffrage, released thousands of political prisoners, promoted equal rights for women, and called for elections for a new constituent assembly. Americans in and out of government celebrated these liberal, democratic reforms.

At this moment in bilateral relations, the United States was surging as a global power, and Russia was in decline. But this shifting balance of power did not produce a Thucydides's trap—when a rising great power threatens an existing great power, and war becomes inevitable. Ideological affinities mattered more. For a few months, regime change in Russia—from monarchy to democracy—fostered closer relations between Russia and the democratic United States.

The rapprochement did not last long. Kerensky's republic survived only a few months, weakened by his decision to keep Russia fighting in World War I—a highly unpopular war among soldiers and civilians alike. In the fall of 1917, Vladimir Lenin and his Bolshevik Party overthrew Kerensky's government in what they called the October Revolution, ending Russia's brief experiment with liberal democracy and starting a long era of communist dictatorship.

PERIOD THREE: CONFRONTATION

After seizing power in October 1917 (November, by the Gregorian calendar), Lenin and his comrades tried to construct an entirely new political and economic system in Russia in which the Communist Party owned all property, set all prices, and managed all commerce allegedly on behalf of the peasants, workers, and soldiers. At the time, Lenin aspired to export this new communist model to the entire world, threatening not just democracies but capitalist economies. Well before the Bolshevik Revolution, socialist ideas were winning popular support worldwide, especially in Europe.

Lenin's revolutionary project represented a direct challenge to the legitimacy of existing polities and economies in Europe, the United States, and Asia. Lenin wanted to establish relations between working and peasant classes that transcended national borders and, therefore, constituted a threat to all existing governments, including that of the United States. At this moment, the communist regime change in Russia, not the balance of power, played a central role in pushing US-Russia relations into a more confrontational standoff. After all, Russia emerged much weaker than the US from World War I, the Bolshevik Revolution, and the ensuing civil war. The Cold War began in 1917, not after World War II.

After the Bolsheviks seized power, President Woodrow Wilson instructed US diplomats in Russia to refrain from direct communication with the new Russian government. Wilson rhetorically criticized Russian Bolshevism and even deployed military force to undermine the new communist regime, joining Great Britain and France in invading Russia and enforcing an economic blockade in 1918, sending five thousand American soldiers to Arkhangelsk and then another eight thousand troops to Vladivostok. The mission of this military intervention changed over time. Initially, Western leaders wanted to force Russian soldiers to keep fighting the Germans on the Eastern Front. The Allied Powers worried about German-Bolshevik collusion, especially since Germany had facilitated Lenin's return to Russia.[9] The invading forces also sought to rescue the Czechoslovak Legion, which had been stranded along the Trans-Siberian railway. However, once inside Russia, the Allied Powers expanded their aims and took sides in the Russian civil war, supporting the White Army fighting the Bolsheviks' Red Army. This military intervention failed. In August 1919, after enduring over 550 casualties, the American Expeditionary Force in northern Russia disbanded, and in April 1920, the American Expeditionary Force in Siberia departed.

For sixteen years, the United States refused to establish diplomatic relations with the Bolsheviks. Lenin and his comrades adopted an equally hostile position toward the US, portraying the US military intervention in Russia as proof of American imperial ambitions and the inevitable global clash between communism and capitalism.

THE COOPERATIVE INTERLUDE

After his election in 1932, President Roosevelt sought to improve relations with the Soviet Union, mostly out of fear of German fascism and Japanese imperialism. In 1933, for the first time since 1917, the United States and the Soviet Union established diplomatic relations. The two countries did not immediately collaborate in confronting Hitler as Stalin initially sided with Nazi Germany, as codified in the 1939 Molotov-Ribbentrop pact, hoping that German armed forces would get bogged down in Western Europe and thereby allow the Soviet Union to expand farther into Eastern Europe. Stalin miscalculated. After conquering part of Poland, Hitler pivoted his armies westward and breezed to several easy victories in Western Europe. Per his agreement with Hitler, Stalin invaded Poland just a few weeks after Germany and later invaded Estonia, Latvia, Lithuania, and Finland. On June 22, 1941, however, Hitler double-crossed Stalin and invaded the Soviet Union by launching Operation Barbarossa.

After Hitler attacked the Soviet Union, the United States maintained formal neutrality, even while supplying the USSR with military and economic assistance through the Lend-Lease program beginning in October 1941. That status changed on December 7, 1941, when Japan bombed Pearl Harbor, killing over 2,400 Americans. The United States declared war on Japan the following day and three days later on Germany and Italy. As they had been during the American War of Independence, the American Civil War, and World War I, Washington and Moscow were again on the same side.

From 1941 to 1945, realpolitik considerations dominated Soviet-American relations. Roosevelt and his administration deliberately downplayed ideological rifts to project Soviet-American solidarity; they recast the communist dictator Stalin as "Uncle Joe" and, through the Lend-Lease program, provided the Soviet Red Army with over $11.3 billion in military and economic assistance (roughly $180 billion today).[10] For its part, Soviet antagonistic rhetoric about the United States also mellowed. Stalin developed a close relationship with President Roosevelt and, according to Stalin's successor Nikita Khrushchev, "always stressed [General] Eisenhower's decency, generosity and chivalry."[11] In 2013, when I traveled to Volgograd as the US ambassador to Russia to commemorate the seventieth anniversary of the Battle of Stalingrad, I met a handful of veterans—Russians *and*

Ukrainians—of that horrific fight who several decades later still expressed enormous gratitude to me for our Lend-Lease program.

During the war, tensions about strategy at times strained bilateral relations. Stalin complained bitterly about delays in opening the second front in Western Europe. In World War II, the Soviet Union suffered between twenty-four and twenty-seven million military and civilian deaths, compared to slightly over four hundred thousand American soldiers and only several thousand civilians killed in Europe and Asia. Nonetheless, throughout the war, the United States and the Soviet Union remained allies.

THE COLD WAR RESUMES

After World War II, ideological differences between the Soviet Union and the United States gradually took center stage again. Historians have examined the tactical moves of Soviet and American leaders to speculate about missed opportunities for continued collaboration and assign blame for who started the Cold War. Maybe the speed of the conflict's expansion could have been slowed; more adept diplomacy might have reduced its intensity. However, renewed confrontation was inevitable because the fundamental tension was driven not by power or leaders but by a clash of regime types and ideologies.

The United States emerged from World War II more powerful than any other country. Presidents Roosevelt and Truman and their teams deployed this power and authority to establish a set of multilateral institutions that later became known as the "liberal international order."[12] This new architecture included the United Nations, the International Monetary Fund, the International Bank for Reconstruction and Development (the World Bank), the International Finance Corporation, and the General Agreement on Tariffs and Trade, which later became the World Trade Organization. Roosevelt believed that the United States and the Soviet Union could cooperate in concert with other great powers on global issues, irrespective of regime-type differences.

At times, the Soviet Union and the United States did succeed in working together on security and humanitarian matters within this new institutional architecture. For instance, they collaborated to create the United Nations in 1945. The UN, in turn, helped coordinate American and Soviet efforts to eradicate smallpox. The superpowers also cooperated in gaining international support for the Treaty on the Non-Proliferation of Nuclear Weapons (NPT) and the United Nations Convention on the Law of the Sea (UNCLOS), although the US Senate never ratified the latter. On many other issues, however, these new multilateral organizations only marginally reduced tensions. At the UN Security Council, the Soviet Union and the United States rarely agreed. Soviet leaders refused to join the IMF, the World Bank, or GATT and rebuffed American economic assistance through the Marshall Plan. After Truman led the effort to launch the North Atlantic Treaty Organization in 1949, Stalin responded by creating his own security alliance, the Warsaw Pact, in 1955. In reaction to the American-anchored multilateral economic institutions, Moscow launched the Council for Mutual Economic Assistance (COMECON) for the communist world. The liberal international order never became global in reach. Opposing regime types and ideologies hardened the lines between these two decoupled security and economic systems.

GLOBAL IDEOLOGICAL COMPETITION

Each of these two radically different systems threatened the legitimacy of the other. Soviet leaders were not content with just building communism at home, and after World War II, US leaders did not return to American isolationist traditions. Instead, throughout the Cold War, American and Soviet leaders tried to promote their different political and economic systems abroad. At times, the aspiration of peaceful coexistence as a norm and policy held sway in both Washington and Moscow. But Soviet and American leaders ultimately devoted significant resources—including money, media, spies, and soldiers—to promote communism and capitalism, respectively, overseas. When Mao seized power in China in 1949, the People's Republic of China joined this global ideological struggle with vigor.

The Cold War was not cold. The use of force—at times overt, at other times covert—played a central role in advancing the ideological agendas of both the Soviet Union and the United States. In Europe, Stalin's main instrument for promoting communism was the Red Army. By 1948, communist regimes supported by and loyal to Moscow had taken over most of Eastern Europe, dividing the continent into two blocs for the next four decades. Stalin sought to take advantage of weak governments in Greece, Turkey, France, and Italy to promote communist revolutions through both peaceful and violent means. He unsuccessfully pushed for Libya to become a Soviet protectorate and withdrew from Iran only after tremendous pressure from the Allies. In Asia, Soviet leaders supported communist insurgents in China, Korea, Vietnam, and elsewhere.

At the end of World War II, some in Washington remained hopeful that the United States and the Soviet Union could continue to manage global security together. But Stalin's subversive, oppressive tactics in promoting communist regimes in Eastern Europe made clear that collective security cooperation between ideologically divided superpowers was utopian. Former British prime minister Winston Churchill clarified matters in his "Iron Curtain" speech on March 5, 1946, in Fulton, Missouri, when he warned that "from Stettin in the Baltic to Trieste in the Adriatic an iron curtain has descended across the Continent. Behind that line lie all the capitals of the ancient states of Central and Eastern Europe. Warsaw, Berlin, Prague, Vienna, Budapest, Belgrade, Bucharest, and Sofia, all these famous cities and the populations around them lie in what I must call the Soviet sphere, and all are subject in one form or another, not only to Soviet influence but to a very high and, in some cases, an increasing measure of control from Moscow."[13]

American diplomat George Kennan affirmed Churchill's thesis about the nature of Soviet power and offered a grand strategy in response: containment. In his famous article in *Foreign Affairs* in 1947, writing as "X," Kennan assessed that containing communism was the "greatest task our diplomacy has ever faced, and probably greatest it will ever have to face."[14] Containing communism required not just balancing Soviet military power but also joining the fight against communist ideas within countries and societies. What resulted was four decades of global conflict that included not only soldiers lost but also millions of civilian casualties in this ideological struggle.[15]

Initially, American leaders debated the scope of containment. Kennan promoted a limited strategy, arguing that the United States did not have to check every Soviet move around the world or destroy every communist movement. Kennan did not even support the creation of NATO, arguing that containment in Europe could be achieved through less provocative means, and he did not think that South Korea needed defending. Kennan believed that Western leaders in the democratic world had to avoid perpetuating, through unnecessary provocations, an image of the Soviet Union as the enemy and should instead focus on strengthening democratic and market institutions at home.[16] In Kennan's view, global enthusiasm for communism would mellow, and internal contradictions within the Soviet system would eventually bring it down. Kennan was ultimately correct, although his prediction took four decades to come true.

Kennan's recommendations for limited containment were entertained but ultimately rejected. Soviet assistance to communist insurgents in Greece fueled Truman's commitment to a more global and aggressive strategy of containment.[17] While speaking before Congress to request assistance for Greece and Turkey in 1947, in an address that codified what became known as the Truman Doctrine, President Truman framed the communist threat in existential terms: "It must be the policy of the United States to support free peoples who are resisting attempted subjugation by armed minorities or by outside pressures . . . Collapse of free institutions and loss of independence would be disastrous . . . Should we fail to aid Greece and Turkey in this fateful hour, the effect will be far-reaching . . . If we falter in our leadership, we may endanger the peace of the world—and we shall surely endanger the welfare of this Nation."[18]

The emergence of powerful communist movements in Italy and France, supported by Moscow, helped prompt the Marshall Plan, an economic and political assistance program that strengthened postwar recovery in Western Europe. To counter Soviet covert campaigns, the CIA channeled money to anti-communist leaders, parties, and trade unions throughout the world. Truman rejected the idea of distinguishing among different communist movements, believing that they were all manifestations of a Soviet grand strategy. As historian John Lewis Gaddis assessed, "The consequence [of this conceptualization] was an unnecessary proliferation of enemies in the world, an outcome very different from what the original concept of containment had intended."[19]

In 1948, after Stalin backed a coup against the democratically elected government in Czechoslovakia and imposed a blockade to try to cut off

West Berlin from West Germany, Cold War animosities intensified. Truman responded by ordering a massive airlift of supplies into the Allied-controlled parts of the city. Thankfully, this high-stakes game of chicken did not precipitate military conflict. But the standoff accelerated a deeper East-West split in Europe that lasted for four decades.

The following year, communists seized power in China, triggering fears in Washington and other capitals in the free world that historical trends were moving in favor of the communists. Bolder thinking about containment was needed.

THE KOREAN WAR

On June 25, 1950, communist North Korea invaded noncommunist South Korea. Historians still debate whether North Korean dictator Kim Il Sung made this decision independently or at the behest of Stalin. Mao's role is also debated.[20] Irrespective of who was in on this decision, the unanticipated communist invasion confirmed assumptions about Soviet global domination and compelled the United States to respond. As Truman explained, "The attack upon Korea makes it plain beyond all doubt that Communism has passed beyond the use of subversion to conquer independent nations and will now use armed invasion and war."[21]

In September 1950, Truman approved a grander strategy for containing Soviet communism, codified in National Security Council Paper 68, which stated, "The Soviet Union, unlike previous aspirants to hegemony, is animated by a new fanatic faith, antithetical to our own, and seeks to impose its absolute authority over the rest of the world. Conflict has, therefore, become endemic and is waged on the part of the Soviet Union . . . Any substantial further extension of the area under the domination of the Kremlin would raise the possibility that no coalition adequate to confront the Kremlin with greater strength could be assembled."[22] NSC-68 defined the Soviet threat as inherently expansive. Soviet leaders would not stop until the whole world had adopted their communist ideas, system of government, and economic structures or until the United States stopped them.

Because the Soviet Union was boycotting the UN then, the UN Security Council voted to approve the US-led coalition to assist South Korea. Under the command of General Douglas MacArthur, the coalition forces won several early battles in the war, prompting Mao to order his "volunteer" army to enter North Korea in October 1950. For the first time, American soldiers were engaged in direct combat with communist soldiers from North Korea and the People's Republic of China, all of whom were supported by Soviet weapons, ammunition, military planners, and even pilots, in a war over regime type. This protracted war of attrition lasted until July 27, 1953, when the Korean Armistice Agreement was signed and the demilitarized zone was established, to this day dividing the Korean Peninsula into two countries—one communist and one not.

Most American national security strategists interpreted the Korean War as a necessary act to contain communism, although the inconclusive results pleased few in American society. Soviet leaders had a different assessment. Less than a decade after the tremendous losses in World War II, Soviet leaders perceived the conflict as a major victory. Stalemate on the battlefield achieved with only minor Soviet military involvement fueled the impression of parity between communist and capitalist blocs.

THE CUBAN MISSILE CRISIS

After Stalin died in 1953, Nikita Khrushchev consolidated power by 1956. The new Soviet leader rolled back some of the most abusive features of Stalin's totalitarianism at home but added a new focus to spreading communism abroad, especially in what was then called the third world (the capitalist world being the first world, the communist bloc being the second). As Europe and the Korean Peninsula became frozen conflicts, decolonization opened up ideological competition in Africa, Asia, Latin America, and the Middle East. Nearly every national liberation struggle for independence became a locus of contestation in the global Cold War.[23]

The next major superpower ideological clash erupted in 1959 when left-leaning Fidel Castro seized power in Cuba. After President Kennedy tried unsuccessfully to overthrow Castro in a coup attempt known as the Bay of Pigs invasion, Castro and his comrades became increasingly communist in orientation and more closely aligned with the Soviet Union. Delighted to embrace a new ally only a hundred miles from the American border, Khrushchev showered Castro's regime with economic and military assistance and tried to deploy to the island nuclear weapons capable of hitting targets inside the United States. In response, in October 1962, President John F. Kennedy threatened to use a naval quarantine to stop these new deployments, propelling both countries into the most dangerous crisis of the Cold War.

Thankfully, Kennedy and Khrushchev succeeded in defusing the standoff. The two leaders subsequently realized that their countries had to develop better crisis-management and crisis-prevention mechanisms to avoid direct war, even if both continued competing in other arenas. By the 1970s, American and Soviet diplomats had negotiated several such channels of communication, including, most notably, the red phone hotline (although it is not an actual phone!).

VIETNAM

Among the many proxy wars between the US and the Soviet Union, the most tragic, unnecessary conflict was the Vietnam War. During the so-called First Indochina War, Presidents Truman and Eisenhower provided financial and military assistance to their French allies in the fight against nationalist liberation leader Ho Chi Minh and his Vietminh guerrilla army. Despite American support, the Vietminh destroyed the French forces during the Battle of Dien Bien Phu in 1954, compelling France to negotiate a hasty withdrawal agreement, which included a division of Vietnam similar to Korea's. American strategists assessed that the United States had to fill the void left by France's humiliating departure or the communists would seize control of all of Vietnam and its neighbors and, consequently, spark more communist victories throughout the world. This domino theory compelled American officials to directly intervene to try to replicate what had been achieved in Korea: a stalemate between a communist north and a capitalist south. They failed.

In 1954, President Eisenhower deployed US military advisers to South Vietnam. Under Presidents Kennedy and Johnson, the American military presence grew, eventually reaching 550,000 soldiers at the height of the war. After over 58,000 American deaths and no clear path to victory, in 1973, President Richard Nixon and his team negotiated a ceasefire with North Vietnam in return for withdrawal of US military and other foreign troops. However, two years later, the North Vietnamese army conquered

South Vietnam and marched into Saigon; in 1976, the Socialist Republic of Vietnam was established. Around the same time, in 1975, the Communist Party of Kampuchea (the Khmer Rouge) seized power in Cambodia, as did the communist Lao People's Revolutionary Party in Laos.

The American defeat in Vietnam created a strong impression around the world that communism was on the march and capitalism was in retreat. What Soviet leaders called the "world revolutionary process" seemed to be moving in their favor. Southern Africa was next.[24] The 1974 Carnation Revolution triggered a transition to democracy in Portugal and the end of its empire abroad, allowing pro-Soviet communist parties and their armies to come to power in Mozambique, Guinea-Bissau, and Angola. However, a brutal civil war fueled by the USSR, the United States, Cuba, and South Africa continued in Angola until 2002. A few years after communist victories in southern Africa, Soviet and Cuban armies intervened in the Ogaden War between Somalia and Ethiopia to assist a communist comrade in Addis Ababa, Lieutenant Colonel Mengistu Haile Mariam. In December 1979, the Zimbabwe War of Liberation ended, allowing the Chinese-backed Zimbabwe African National Union party to win the first free and fair parliamentary election in February 1980, and it has stayed in power ever since. Zimbabwe African People's Union, Moscow's client, came in second in that election, but the country still leaned toward the communist bloc. Another Soviet-backed national liberation movement, the Southwest African People's Organization, came to power in Namibia after independence in 1990.

In Central America, the collapse of Nicaragua's dictatorship in 1979 allowed another pro-Soviet and Cuban-backed socialist regime, the Sandinistas, to seize power, sparking another proxy war in which the Reagan administration supported the Contra rebels in Nicaragua and backed anti-communist groups in El Salvador and Guatemala. The ideological battle between the Soviet Union and the United States was now global, violent, and growing even in the Western Hemisphere.

DÉTENTE

At the peak of US-Soviet competition in the developing world, President Nixon and General Secretary Leonid Brezhnev surprisingly nurtured a new period of bilateral cooperation—détente. While developing ties with the

People's Republic of China to balance a rising Soviet power, Nixon also cultivated a personal rapport with Brezhnev. The strategy achieved results. During the era of détente, the US and the USSR signed the Anti-Ballistic Missile (ABM) Treaty and Strategic Arms Limitation Talks (SALT I) in 1972 and the Threshold Test Ban Treaty in 1974. The United States and the Soviet Union also expanded bilateral trade during this détente era, and the US did not try to block growing economic ties between the Soviet Union and Western Europe, especially the construction of the Druzhba (from the Russian word meaning "friendship") gas pipeline.

In 1975, the Soviet Union and the United States joined other European countries and Canada in signing the Helsinki Accords, which codified the borders redrawn by force during World War II and established an international forum—eventually renamed the Organization for Security and Cooperation in Europe (OSCE)—tasked with managing security issues in Europe. Symbolic acts of cooperation, such as the 1975 Apollo-Soyuz docking in space, punctuated this optimistic era for bilateral engagement. In the 1970s, Washington and Moscow negotiated numerous crisis-management and crisis-prevention mechanisms, demonstrating that the two superpowers could compete and cooperate simultaneously.[25] At this moment in history, in an echo of current US-China relations, there was a widespread perception that the Soviet Union was catching up to the United States regarding the balance of power, but that condition did not fuel greater conflict. Instead, new leaders, especially Nixon, negotiated a more cooperative era.

THE SOVIET INVASION OF AFGHANISTAN

Détente ended after Brezhnev invaded Afghanistan in 1979. It might have been the positive global trend in favor of communism in the 1970s, as well as the perceptions of American decline, that gave Brezhnev the false confidence to invade his neighbor to aid the communist regime there. This decision was a significant overreach and ultimately one of the indirect precipitants of the Soviet Union's collapse. The massive Soviet military presence in the country sparked a new insurgency movement—the Mujahideen—against the Soviet invaders; the soldiers were funded and armed by the United States and its partners in the Middle East. American support for the anti-communist insurgents lasted for the entire decade of

Soviet occupation, which ended in 1989 after a new reformist Soviet leader Mikhail Gorbachev, who had come to power in 1985, withdrew his forces.

PERIOD FOUR: A NEW ERA OF COOPERATION

The early 1980s marked a new peak of ideological confrontation between the Soviet Union and the United States. In response to the Soviet invasion of Afghanistan, President Jimmy Carter withdrew American athletes from the 1980 Moscow Olympics, joined the international community in levying economic sanctions against the Soviet Union, and began to arm and finance Afghan insurgents fighting Soviet occupying forces. After his election in 1980, President Reagan upped the ante by providing more significant assistance to the Mujahideen in Afghanistan as well as to movements opposing Soviet-backed governments in Angola, Nicaragua, and Cambodia. Reagan tried to pressure the Soviet economy by expanding military spending and proposing an ambitious global missile defense system, the Strategic Defense Initiative. In parallel, he sought to enhance deterrence in Europe by deploying new intermediate ballistic missiles in the United Kingdom and West Germany. In a departure from previous presidents, Reagan aimed not just to contain but to roll back communism. In the first years of the Reagan era, confrontation between Moscow and Washington increased dramatically. The Soviet Union's shootdown of Korean Air Lines Flight 007 on September 1, 1983, further exacerbated superpower tensions.

This crescendo of confrontation reversed course due to one man—Mikhail Gorbachev. In 1982, after eighteen years in power, Brezhnev died. Following brief leadership stints by Yuri Andropov and Konstantin Chernenko, Mikhail Gorbachev became general secretary of the Communist Party of the Soviet Union in March 1985. This change in leadership played the most consequential role in ending the Cold War.

Gorbachev did not plan to undermine communism or trigger the collapse of the Soviet Union. Part of a younger generation of Communist Party of the Soviet Union (CPSU) leaders, Gorbachev aimed to revitalize communism after years of stagnation in the Brezhnev era. His first reform measures were conventional—he told everyone to work harder and stop drinking so much vodka. When these small steps produced incremental results, Gorbachev rolled out a more ambitious economic reform strategy abstractly called *perestroika* (the Russian word for "rebuilding"). Under this elastic term, Gorbachev and his team introduced some limited market reforms, including decriminalizing private property, relaxing some price controls, and permitting the formation of small businesses, known euphemistically as *cooperatives*.

To accelerate his economic reform agenda, Gorbachev believed that he had to pursue political changes in tandem. He first purged the CPSU of those most diehard conservatives to try to transform this organization into a body more supportive of his reform agenda. When that did not work, or perhaps when Gorbachev grew impatient with the slow pace of change, the Soviet leader tried to revitalize state institutions as an alternative structure to the Communist Party to spearhead reforms. In 1988, Gorbachev announced that semi-free and semi-fair elections would be conducted for representatives in the USSR Congress of People's Deputies in 1989, followed by even freer and fairer elections at all lower levels of legislatures at the republic, regional, and city levels in 1990. In March of 1990, Gorbachev created the office of Soviet president, which he then occupied, to complement his Communist Party leadership role as general secretary. To stimulate pressure for change from society, Gorbachev allowed for *glasnost,* or "openness," in the press and relaxed suppression of civil society organizations, which exploded in number during the excitement of competitive elections in 1989 and 1990.

Gorbachev also initiated significant changes in Soviet foreign policy, believing that success with domestic reforms required a more benign international environment. To European capitals, he floated his idea of a "Common European Home," a vision of a united Europe stretching from the Atlantic to the Urals. To Washington, Gorbachev proposed reengagement on arms control reductions, which eventually led to the signing of the historic Intermediate-Range Nuclear Forces (INF) Treaty in 1987 and the Strategic Arms Reduction Treaty (START I) in 1991 (negotiated under Gorbachev, signed by Yeltsin)—the most significant reductions in strategic nuclear weapons ever.

Without Gorbachev, these breakthroughs with the United States would not have happened. But in diplomacy, it takes two to tango. Reagan's leadership mattered too. His courage to engage sincerely with the leader of the "evil empire" played a crucial role in improving bilateral relations. At that moment, leaders in both Moscow and Washington—not changes in the balance of power or regime types—played pivotal roles in driving these two superpowers toward a more cooperative trajectory.

Gorbachev eventually reduced support for communist regimes around the world.[26] In 1989, he withdrew Soviet forces from Afghanistan. That same year, elections in Poland and Hungary empowered political leaders who were determined to end communist rule, and Gorbachev did not try to stop them. In November 1989, protesters in East and West Berlin spontaneously joined forces to tear down the physical and political divides separating their city; massive peaceful demonstrations toppled the communist regime in Czechoslovakia, and a more violent struggle in Romania ended Nicolae Ceauşescu's dictatorship. Gorbachev did nothing to stop these democratic transitions.

DEMOCRATIC REGIME CHANGE IN THE SOVIET UNION

The partially free and fair elections for members of the USSR Congress of People's Deputies in 1989 empowered a new political institution that was more independent of the CPSU, but not in ways that Gorbachev planned. The new parliament included some members more conservative than Gorbachev but also many who were significantly more radical, among them pro-independence deputies from the non-Russian republics. In 1990, many of these anti-communist politicians won elections in legislative bodies of the Soviet republics, accelerating the push for independence in the Baltic republics, Ukraine, Georgia, and even the Russian Federation.

In the spring of 1990, anti-Gorbachev rebel Boris Yeltsin and his allies won a majority in the Russian Congress of People's Deputies. On June 12, 1990, the Russian parliament voted for a declaration of sovereignty from the Soviet Union. From that date until the final collapse of the Soviet Union the following year, when the world recognized Russia as an independent state, Gorbachev's Soviet government and Yeltsin's Russian government vied for political authority over the same Russian territory and institutions. To enhance Yeltsin's legitimacy and autonomy in an increasingly conservative Russian parliament, his team proposed and won a referendum in March 1991 to create a Russian office of the president. Yeltsin won the election as Russia's first democratically elected president in June 1991, further weakening Soviet rule within the Russian Federation.

Gorbachev tried to reconcile with Yeltsin on issues of federalism and economic reform, but ultimately, conservative critics within the Soviet government lost faith in him.In August 1991, the entire Soviet government—including the vice president, prime minister, defense minister, and KGB head—but Gorbachev (he was in Crimea under house arrest) declared emergency rule. They sent soldiers to surround key government buildings, among them the Russian parliament where Yeltsin was holed up, to stop what they believed were forces pulling the Soviet Union apart. But after a three-day standoff, Yeltsin and his supporters won. The failed coup empowered Yeltsin and anti-Soviet forces in several republics. On December 1, Ukrainians voted for independence. On December 8, 1991, Yeltsin signed a decree with his Ukrainian and Belarusian counterparts dissolving the Soviet Union.

This democratic regime change in the Soviet Union and then Russia dramatically shaped US-Soviet and then US-Russia relations. Had Yeltsin and his allies not succeeded in thwarting the coup attempt in August 1991 and dissolving the USSR several months later, the Cold War could have lingered, and maybe for a long while. The pro-Soviet coup plotters who circled the Russian parliament with tanks championed anti-liberal, anti-democratic, and anti-American views. The West's reaction to the Soviet regime's preservation would have been hostile, especially with Gorbachev sidelined, and that regime would have had to rely on violent repression to stay in power, which would have further alienated the United States and the democratic world. Instead, the coup's defeat marked the end of the Cold War. At that moment, a new set of actors—small-*d* democrats in Russia together with their ideological allies in Ukraine, Belarus, the Baltics, and the Caucasus—joined forces to dissolve the Soviet Union. That regime change ended the Cold War.

A DEMOCRATIC RUSSIA

The democratic revolution in the USSR and Russia triggered a new period of bilateral cooperation with the United States. After the collapse of the Soviet Union and the emergence of an independent Russia, President Boris Yeltsin embraced democracy, capitalism, and the liberal international order without reservation. At this moment, American leaders did not try to weaken Russia; instead, they invested in aiding market reforms inside Russia while seeking to integrate this newly independent country into American-anchored international institutions. The World Bank and the IMF both opened offices in Moscow, and the democratic world created the European Bank for Reconstruction and Development to aid market reforms in post-communist Europe, including Russia. Russian and American leaders even spoke earnestly about the possibility of an alliance.

An aspiration, however, is not an achievement. A painful and enduring economic depression that began at the exact moment as the transition to democracy undermined popular support for this new system of government. To navigate this transition, Yeltsin needed help from the West, especially the United States. If Washington aided Russia through this challenging economic period, Yeltsin and his team argued, Russia and the United States would become allies, like Germany, Italy, and Japan after World War II. It didn't work out that way.

If American leaders at the time had been concerned only with balance-of-power calculations, they would have let Russia wither, further weakening an adversary. Some realist voices in Washington pushed for just that. Within the Bush and especially Clinton administrations, however, the most senior US foreign policymakers believed that market and democratic reforms inside Russia served long-term national interests and therefore tried to help Yeltsin's cause. They just did not do enough.

YELTSIN'S MIXED REFORMS

Yeltsin's most outstanding achievement as president of independent Russia in the 1990s was managing the relatively peaceful dissolution of the Soviet Empire on his watch. There was conflict and bloodshed, including two Russian invasions of the Chechen Republic, the war between Armenia and Azerbaijan, skirmishes in Central Asia, and internal clashes in Georgia and Moldova. However, compared to the collapses of other empires, the Soviet Union's dissolution under Yeltsin was relatively peaceful.

Creating a functioning market economy out of the ruins of the Soviet command economy proved more challenging. In 1992, Yeltsin inherited a bankrupt Russian economy—no hard currency reserves, a ballooning deficit, massive foreign debt, and declining industrial production. I remember. I studied at Moscow State University from 1990 to 1991 and felt personally the consumer goods deficits and skyrocketing inflation. I was even given ration cards for bread and cigarettes (I did not use the latter) and stood in line outside for an hour and a half—in December—for a cheeseburger at the new McDonald's.

To tackle these daunting economic challenges, Yeltsin hired a team of young liberal reformers led by Yegor Gaidar. They launched an audacious plan to achieve macroeconomic stabilization, liberalization, and privatization simultaneously, earning the reform package the unfortunate label of *shock therapy*. In the first months, the strategy worked—government spending decreased, especially in the military sector, inflation stabilized, and privatization began. Gaidar's budget cuts, however, proved too challenging to enforce, as directors of state-owned enterprises demanded larger subsidies. Under pressure from this powerful interest group, at the end of the year, Yeltsin replaced Gaidar with the much more conservative Viktor Chernomyrdin, the former head of the Soviet gas enterprise Gazprom. Prime Minister Chernomyrdin pursued partial reforms with partial results, making both market reformers and communists unhappy as Russia's economy nosedived into a more profound depression.

Economic depression fueled political polarization at a time when Russia's constitution did not clearly define the division of authority between the legislative and executive branches of government. Gradually, the Russian Congress of People's Deputies turned against Yeltsin, resulting in a paralyzing constitutional crisis in the summer of 1993. Yeltsin tried to resolve the impasse by dissolving the congress with a presidential decree, but congressional leaders declared Yeltsin's act illegal and recognized Vice President Aleksandr Rutskoi as interim president. This standoff eventually escalated into a violent conflict. Rutskoi moved first, on October 3, trying to seize control of the national television station, the Moscow mayor's office, and other government buildings. Yeltsin responded the next day by ordering tanks to attack the parliament and special forces to storm the building. Yeltsin's forces arrested the coup leaders, but only after tragically killing and injuring hundreds.

After these horrific events, Yeltsin drafted a new constitution that Russian citizens ratified in a December 1993 referendum. The new constitution enhanced presidential powers. In 1996, Yeltsin won reelection by defeating the communist candidate Gennady Zyuganov in an election scarred by accusations of fraud. But for most of Yeltsin's second term, his poor health weakened his ability to govern.

Russia's economy suffered another major setback in August 1998, triggered by a global financial crisis. In response, Yeltsin felt compelled to fire his pro-market government, including Yeltsin's heir apparent, first deputy prime minister Boris Nemtsov. In his place, he named a communist ally, Yevgeny Primakov, because he was the only candidate who could win parliamentary approval at the time.[27] A year later, Yeltsin fired Primakov and replaced him with an obscure Kremlin official, Vladimir Putin; Yeltsin's inner circle decided that Putin was their best hope for holding on to the Kremlin and the property they had acquired under Yeltsin's rule. To help Prime Minister Putin win the upcoming presidential election, in a surprise televised address on December 31, 1999, Yeltsin stepped down and named Putin interim president. Three months later, Putin won the presidential election. A decade after the collapse of the Soviet Union, Russia was still a market economy and democracy, albeit a fragile and unconsolidated one.[28]

US-RUSSIA RELATIONS IN THE YELTSIN ERA

President George H. W. Bush stayed loyal to Gorbachev until the very end, believing that Gorbachev might be able to hold on to power even after the failed August 1991 attempt. Bush and most of his foreign policy team did not champion the dissolution of the USSR; they feared it. Once it happened, however, Bush embraced Yeltsin. In February 1992, the two leaders signed the Camp David Declaration, which stated boldly, "For the first time, an American President and the democratically elected President of an independent Russia met, and we did so not as adversaries but as friends. This historic meeting is yet another confirmation of the end of the Cold War and the dawn of a new era."[29] This was indeed a new era of cooperation unlike any other in American-Russian relations, caused primarily by democratic regime change in Russia.

Bush, however, did not go all in to help his new Russian friend. There was no Marshall Plan for democratic Russia, partly because the first year of Russian economic reform was also an election year in the United States, and Bush's challenger—Bill Clinton—was telling voters it was time to focus on domestic economic problems.

After winning the 1992 election, however, President Clinton pivoted, grasping the magnitude of the moment with Russia. In a 1993 address, Clinton explained, "Land wars in Europe cost hundreds of thousands of American lives in the twentieth century. The rise of a democratic Russia, satisfied within its own boundaries, bordered by other peaceful democracies, could ensure that our nation never needs to pay that kind of price again . . . We must do what we can, and we must act now. Not out of charity but because it is a wise investment."[30] Clinton believed a stronger Russia served American national security interests. A democratic Russia might even become a US ally.

To achieve his lofty goals, Clinton announced a $1.6 billion bilateral aid program for Russia and persuaded the G7 to approve an even larger multilateral package. The US government directly intervened in Russia's internal affairs at the time, providing technical assistance to government agencies and ministries on almost every issue imaginable.

While working together to consolidate market and democratic institutions inside Russia, American and Russian officials cooperated on many security issues. For instance, under the Nunn-Lugar Cooperative Threat Reduction Program, the United States provided massive financial assistance to the states in the former Soviet Union, especially Russia, to secure and destroy weapons of mass destruction. Russia and the United States also aligned on strategies for managing many international security and economic issues, among them nonproliferation efforts with Iran, the Balkan Wars, and the 1998 global financial crash.

There were some rocky moments too. NATO's decision to offer membership to three former Warsaw Pact countries—the Czech Republic, Hungary, and Poland—fueled bilateral tensions. Yeltsin criticized the idea, perceiving expansion as threatening to Russian security interests. Clinton emphasized the alliance's defensive nature and offered Russia new security arrangements, including, most notably, the NATO-Russia Permanent Joint

Council. Russia was also invited to join the G7, making it the G8. Yeltsin did not allow NATO expansion to derail US-Russia relations.

NATO's decision to bomb Serbia in the spring of 1999 to stop Serbian dictator Slobodan Milosevic's ethnic cleansing in Kosovo triggered another tense moment in bilateral relations. But again, the NATO air campaign did not permanently alter bilateral relations because Yeltsin did not want to undermine his more extensive cooperation agenda with the United States. In August 1999, Yeltsin invaded Chechnya for a second time in what he characterized then as a war against terrorism. Clinton and his team criticized the intervention, especially the military tactics, which resulted in high rates of civilian casualties. But even this tragedy did not interrupt the cooperative trajectory of US-Russia relations. Until his last day in office, Yeltsin saw cooperation with the United States and integration into the West as Russian foreign policy priorities. Clinton defined US foreign policy objectives in the same way. This was an era when shared ideas about regime type and leaders who embraced these democratic ideas played a central role in US-Russia relations.

PERIOD FIVE: A RETURN TO CONFRONTATION

Putin became Russia's second president because Yeltsin and his team selected him and then put the full force of the Kremlin electoral machine behind him. Voters ratified Yeltsin's choice. There was no groundswell of popular support for Putin's ideas at the time because voters did not know what they were. Putin was still formulating them. In his first year in office, Putin continued Yeltsin's pro-market economic policies, declaring, "The state should ensure a maximum degree of economic freedom for individuals and legal entities."[31] Putin sounded very pro-Western then, even suggesting in February 2000 that Russia should join NATO.[32] Democracy was a different matter. Putin quickly made clear his disdain for checks and balances on presidential power. He took control of Russia's two national television networks and allowed oligarchs to maintain their fortunes in exchange for support. In 2003, when Russia's richest person at the time, Mikhail Khodorkovsky, defied Putin by funding his opponents, Putin arrested him and seized his oil company, Yukos, delivering a chilling signal to

Russia's billionaires to stay out of politics. After a horrific terrorist attack on a school in Beslan, North Ossetia, on September 1, 2004, Putin ended direct elections of governors, eliminating another check on executive power. His government introduced additional measures to constrain the activities of civil society and political parties. His reelection in 2004 was not competitive. By the end of his second term in 2008, most analysts of Russian politics in the West, including me, described Russia as an autocracy.

BUSH AND PUTIN

On June 16, 2001, Putin and George W. Bush held a cordial first meeting in Slovenia, after which Bush said, "I found him very straightforward and trustworthy . . . I was able to get a sense of his soul . . . that's the beginning of a very constructive relationship."[33] US-Russia relations improved dramatically after the terrorist attacks on the World Trade Center and the Pentagon on September 11, 2001. Both countries now shared a common enemy. Putin supported the American-led war in Afghanistan, even helping the US open military bases in neighboring Uzbekistan and Kyrgyzstan. When NATO formally invited seven new countries to join the alliance at the Prague Summit in November 2002, including the former Soviet republics of Estonia, Latvia, and Lithuania, Putin expressed annoyance but not outrage and continued to collaborate with NATO Secretary-General George Robertson through the Russia-NATO Council, established in May earlier that year. The following year, Putin sided with US allies Germany and France in opposing Bush's decision to invade Iraq. However, even this significant policy disagreement did not deeply damage US-Russia relations.

More significant blows came from events on Russia's borders—the so-called color revolutions in Georgia in 2003 and Ukraine in 2004. In both countries, Putin perceived the Bush administration as promoting democratic regime change in Russia's alleged sphere of influence. He was partially correct. American NGOs did work with those who led the Rose Revolution in Georgia and the Orange Revolution in Ukraine.[34] Democratic breakthroughs in Georgia and, especially, Ukraine threatened Putin because Russia's political system at the time was becoming more autocratic. Like the Cold War, an ideological contest between Moscow and Washington was emerging again. Putin especially detested what he viewed as American intervention in the domestic affairs of other countries, explaining in his infamous speech at the Munich Security Conference in 2007, "One state and, of course, first and foremost, the United States has overstepped its national borders in every way. This is visible in the economic, political, cultural, and educational policies it imposes on other nations. Well, who likes this? Who is happy about this?"[35]

The following year, in August 2008, Russia invaded Georgia. In response to violent skirmishes between Georgians and South Ossetian separatists, Georgian president Mikheil Saakashvili tried to regain control over the breakaway region of South Ossetia by deploying the Georgian army there. Moscow struck back immediately, recapturing South Ossetia and moving deep into Georgian territory. After withdrawing its armed forces, Russia recognized the Georgian regions of South Ossetia and Abkhazia as independent countries. In reaction to Russia's blatant violation of Georgian sovereignty, Bush offered rhetorical support and economic assistance to pro-Western President Saakashvili and his government but did not provide weapons to Georgia or impose sanctions against Russia. But by the end of the Bush administration, US-Russia relations had reached a new low in the post–Cold War era.

THE OBAMA-MEDVEDEV RESET

US-Russia relations experienced another interregnum of cooperation during the Obama-Medvedev era. Since the Russian constitution barred Putin from serving a third consecutive term, he decided to step down and take the job of prime minister. Putin appointed Dmitry Medvedev as his successor, who secured victory in the 2008 presidential election. Barack Obama was elected president of the United States that same year. In 2009, the United States and Russia had new young leaders who wanted to cooperate on issues of mutual interest. Leaders—not changes in the balance of power or regime type—were driving bilateral relations in a more cooperative direction.

Obama did not seek to improve relations with Russia as a goal in and of itself, but he engaged Medvedev to advance American national security interests when his foreign policy priorities required cooperating with Russia. At the time, I worked at the White House as Obama's senior adviser for

Russia, and that is how I understood *reset*.[36] For instance, Obama wanted to reduce the number of nuclear weapons in the world but was ready to do so only if Russia did as well. So we negotiated the New Strategic Arms Reduction Treaty (New START), which Obama and Medvedev signed in 2010. That same year, the UN Security Council passed its most comprehensive multilateral sanctions package against Iran, a predicate of coercive diplomacy that helped produce the Joint Comprehensive Plan of Action (the JCPOA, also known as the Iran nuclear deal) in 2015. Through a mix of coercive and cooperative diplomacy measures, we needed to collaborate with Russia to stop Iran's nuclear weapons program, and it succeeded. During this era, the United States expanded the Northern Distribution Network (NDN), a mix of rail, air, and road routes through Russia, Central Asia, and the Caucasus into Afghanistan to reduce US dependency on the southern supply route through Pakistan. The NDN's expansion, which could be achieved only by cooperating with Russia, allowed the US to launch the Special Forces operation in Pakistan that killed bin Laden in 2011. Medvedev even shared Obama's assessment regarding the illegitimacy of autocratic rulers in the Middle East during the Arab Spring and agreed to abstain on two UN Security Council resolutions in the spring of 2011 that authorized the use of force in Libya to stop the slaughter of innocent civilians in the city of Benghazi.

PUTIN'S RETURN TO THE KREMLIN

Today, Medvedev has become one of the most odious backers of Russia's invasion of Ukraine. When I interacted with him in 2011, he expressed very different views about the United States and our two countries' shared values and common interests. I was in the room in the Kremlin in March 2011 when Medvedev told Vice President Biden that he would not veto a UN Security Council resolution authorizing the use of force in Libya. We saw Putin the next day, and he had a different view. Putin later publicly criticized Medvedev for not vetoing those UNSC resolutions, framing the NATO campaign in Libya as another case of American-supported regime change, not unlike Georgia in 2003 and Ukraine in 2004. Of course, I do not know if Putin planned all along to push Medvedev aside and become president again, but Putin did believe by 2011 that Medvedev had become too soft in dealing with the Americans. In September 2011, Putin announced his decision to run for a third presidential term. In March 2012, he won reelection.

Between these two dates, Russia held a parliamentary election tainted with levels of voting fraud common for Russian elections at the time. During this vote, however, independent election monitors used cell phones and other tools to document the outrageous instances of falsification. Subsequent circulation of this evidence of election fraud on social media sparked massive demonstrations in Russia, the largest since the collapse of the Soviet Union. These protests started with a focus on correcting the parliamentary vote but eventually led to chants of "Russia without Putin." Putin blamed Obama, Secretary of State Clinton, and me for sparking and supporting these demonstrations. When I arrived as the newly appointed US ambassador to Russia in January 2012, at the height of this popular mobilization, the Kremlin propagated the myth that Obama had sent me to orchestrate a revolution against Putin's government. They cited my 2001 book, *Russia's Unfinished Revolution*, to suggest that I had returned to Moscow to finally finish it!

Putin's return as president in combination with these popular demonstrations against him produced a profoundly negative impact on US-Russia relations. On some issues, such as the Iran nuclear deal and the removal of chemical weapons from Syria, the United States and Russia continued to work together. However, Putin's paranoia about domestic opposition to his rule compelled him to blame Washington for supporting his opponents. He recast the United States as Russia's greatest enemy. He has stuck to that line ever since.

After his reelection in 2012, Putin clamped down on independent media, opposition groups, and civil society organizations. The Russian government repeatedly arrested opposition figure Alexei Navalny and placed him under house arrest; in 2014, they jailed his brother as part of a broader effort to punish the Navalny family. The Kremlin started blocking websites and passing vague legislation on extremism that granted the authorities discretion to impede the activities of civil society organizations. The Obama administration criticized these anti-democratic trends, which, in turn, annoyed Putin. Obama's last event in Russia ever was a September 2013 meeting with civil society activists, including prominent LGBTQ+ leaders. That meeting was also the last one I attended with Obama as a member of his administration.

RUSSIA'S INVASION OF UKRAINE IN 2014

Putin's return to the Kremlin abruptly ended reset. Again, leaders matter. However, it was Putin's invasion of Ukraine in 2014 that catapulted US-Russia relations back to open animosity. In the fall of 2013, Ukrainian president Viktor Yanukovych's decision to postpone signing an association agreement with the European Union sparked massive demonstrations in Kyiv and other major Ukrainian cities. In February 2014, Yanukovych ordered sharpshooters to fire on protesters, and some shot back. European leaders attempted to mediate a peaceful resolution to this standoff, but Yanukovych eventually fled to Russia.

The United States and Europe celebrated Yanukovych's departure and the formation of a new Ukrainian government as a democratic breakthrough. Putin labeled the event an American-orchestrated "coup d'état . . . that we cannot accept."[37] As retribution, Putin annexed Crimea and supported a violent separatist movement in eastern Ukraine against the new government in Kyiv with money, guns, and soldiers. That war in eastern Ukraine festered until Putin launched his full-scale invasion of Ukraine on February 24, 2022.[38]

In annexing Crimea, Putin violated one of the most important norms of the post–World War II international system. The American and European response in 2014, therefore, was more robust than the reaction to Putin's invasion of Georgia in 2008 and included extensive sanctions on Russian companies and individuals, Russia's removal from the G8, increased economic and nonlethal military assistance to Ukraine, and agreement within NATO to increase spending and deploy more soldiers closer to the Ukrainian border.

Putin was not deterred by the Western response and took increasingly risky actions to support autocratic friends and undermine democratic foes. In 2015, Putin deployed the Russian air force to Syria to prop up its ruthless dictator, Bashar al-Assad. In 2016, Putin intervened in the US presidential election, using multiple methods—fake social media accounts, digital ads, conventional broadcast and print media outlets, and data theft—to try to help presidential candidate Donald Trump.

THE TRUMP-PUTIN RAPPROCHEMENT

The balance of power between the United States and Russia did not change dramatically in 2017. Political systems remained the same that year. However, the tone of relations changed considerably because of the new leadership in the White House. President Trump actively tried to befriend Putin even when it was considered politically unwise and opposed by many in his administration.[39] As Trump explained in a tweet on March 21, 2018, "Getting along with Russia . . . is a good thing, not a bad thing."[40] Trump never criticized Putin, never met with opponents of Putin; he tried to develop a personal relationship with the Russian autocrat. Most shocking, at a press conference with Putin in Helsinki in July 2018, Trump explained that he agreed with Putin and disagreed with his US intelligence agencies; in his view, Russia did not interfere in the 2016 presidential election. He also embraced Putin's stunning proposal of allowing Kremlin prosecutors to interrogate numerous US officials, including me, who had allegedly committed crimes against the Russian government. After this meeting with Putin, Trump refused to debrief his senior staff, telling his Russia adviser, "This is between me and my friend."[41]

Despite Trump's embrace of Putin, the Kremlin attempted to assassinate former Russian intelligence officer Sergei Skripal in the United Kingdom, murdered Chechen dissidents in Germany and Austria, poisoned Alexei Navalny with a Novichok agent, and launched cyberattacks on American companies and the US government. Trump did not convince Putin to end his war in eastern Ukraine or his occupation of Crimea.

The Trump *administration*, however, did pursue more confrontational strategies toward Russia, often without the president's blessing. The 2017 US national security strategy labeled both China and Russia as revisionist powers and stated bluntly that the two countries "are contesting our geopolitical advantages and trying to change the international order in their favor."[42] Even while Trump himself threatened to withdraw from NATO, his administration was investing in new initiatives to enhance NATO readiness. Trump's team kicked out dozens of Russian diplomats suspected of working as intelligence officers, closed the Russian consulate in San Francisco, imposed new sanctions on Russia, and supported the Countering America's Adversaries Through Sanctions Act in response to Russia's interference in the 2016 US election, violations of human rights, annexation of Crimea, and military operations in eastern Ukraine. The Trump administration also sent a modest amount of military assistance to Ukraine even as Trump personally tried to trade military aid and an Oval Office invitation to Ukrainian president Volodymyr Zelenskyy for a Ukrainian investigation of the son of his electoral opponent, Joe Biden. For suggesting this quid pro quo, Trump was impeached.

RUSSIA'S FULL-SCALE INVASION OF UKRAINE IN 2022

After winning the 2020 presidential election, President Biden changed the tone of US-Russia relations. Unlike Trump, he never praised Putin, and he signaled more support for Ukraine. At the same time, Biden initially tried to establish a "stable and predictable relationship with Russia" so that his administration could focus more on China. Biden and Putin extended the New START by another five years and held a bilateral summit on June 16, 2021, in Geneva. Putin, however, was not interested in a stable and predictable relationship with the United States, as he made clear on February 24, 2022, when he launched a full-scale invasion of Ukraine, starting the largest war in Europe since World War II. Putin's decision to invade and annex parts of Ukraine in 2022 drove US-Russia relations into their most confrontational era since the Cuban Missile Crisis in 1962.

In response to the Russian invasion, Biden mobilized NATO and other countries to provide tens of billions of dollars of military assistance to the armed forces of Ukraine, channeled similar levels of economic support to the Ukrainian government, and implemented comprehensive sanctions to reduce economic resources and technology flowing into Russia. European countries took in millions of Ukrainian refugees. The scale of American and NATO assistance to aid Ukraine in stopping the Russian invasion was unprecedented—dwarfing, for instance, American aid to the Mujahideen after the Soviet invasion of Afghanistan. Also new in this war was the specter of a nuclear conflict. When Russia's army was losing ground in the fall of 2022, Putin threatened to use tactical nuclear weapons against Ukrainian targets.

As this book goes to press, Putin has failed to achieve most of his war aims. Putin's war did not unite the imagined single Slavic nation as he had hoped and promised; instead, it catalyzed Ukrainian unity and national identity. Putin did not conquer or subjugate Ukraine. After seizing chunks of territory in the first months of the invasion, Russia lost several significant battles, including the Battle for Kyiv, the Battle of Kharkiv, and the Battle of Kherson, and by the end of 2022, Russia had lost roughly 50 percent of the territory that it had conquered at the war's outset.[43] In 2024, Russia made some incremental territorial gains in Ukraine, but so did the Ukrainian armed forces, which seized territory inside Russia in the Kursk region. Putin also failed to "denazify" Ukraine—that is, overthrow President Zelenskyy. He has not demilitarized Ukraine—just the opposite. Rather than stopping NATO enlargement, Putin's war provoked expansion when Finland and Sweden joined the alliance (ending two centuries of Swedish neutrality!), and it deepened ties between NATO and Ukraine. Putin's invasion of Ukraine has amassed significant costs for Russia's security, economy, and society, discussed in detail in subsequent chapters.

DEEPENING RUSSIAN AUTOCRACY

Following Russia's full-scale invasion of Ukraine in 2022, Putin cracked down even further on the remaining pockets of independent media, civil society, and political opposition. Independent media—TV Rain, Meduza, Proekt, *Novaya Gazeta,* Echo of Moscow, and others—were banned or labeled *foreign agents* and forced to relocate operations abroad. Opposition leaders Vladimir Kara-Murza, Ilya Yashin, and Andrei Pivovarev, among others, as well as numerous journalists and war protesters—roughly twenty thousand of them—were arrested, and thousands of websites and internet accounts, including Twitter, Facebook, and Instagram, have been blocked in the country. Hundreds of thousands of Russians fled the nation, fearing both political repression and mandatory conscription. On February 16, 2024, Putin killed Russia's most prominent opposition leader, Alexei Navalny, who was supposed to be part of the biggest ever Russia-West prisoner swap. It eventually materialized in August 2024, and several Russian opposition figures, Americans, and Germans were swapped for Russian spies and criminals. While this was a major success of Biden's diplomacy, over 1,500 political prisoners remained behind bars.

Putin's Russia is now more brutal and repressive than the Soviet Union was under most of its leaders, excluding Stalin. Putin's autocracy has more political prisoners, has killed more opposition leaders, and has tried to kill more critics abroad than, for instance, Brezhnev's dictatorship.

TRUMP-PUTIN 2.0

After his reelection in 2024, President Trump tried to rebuild his personal relationship with Putin, demonstrating once again that leaders—not just the balance of power and regime types—shape foreign policy. Trump and his new team tried to end the war in Ukraine by coercing Zelenskyy and encouraging Putin to negotiate. For Ukraine, Trump offered sticks: the threat of withdrawing military and economic aid, disruption of intelligence sharing, demand that Ukraine pay the United States back for military aid provided during the Biden administration, and pressure on Zelenskyy to concede Ukrainian territory occupied by Russian soldiers. For Russia, Trump offered carrots: the resumption of bilateral contacts, a pledge to never allow Ukraine to join NATO, hints of easing or lifting sanctions on Russian companies, reduction of American soldiers deployed in Europe, an offer to allow Russia to rejoin the G7, and alignment with Russia, North Korea, Eritrea, and other authoritarian states in voting against a United Nations resolution condemning Russia's invasion of Ukraine. Even China abstained on that vote.

To date, Trump's appeasement of Putin has not worked. Instead of agreeing to end the war in Ukraine, Putin has demanded more concessions from Trump, including a complete end of all military assistance to Ukraine from NATO, a cap on the size of the Ukrainian military, and the removal of Zelenskyy as president. As this book goes to press, the war continues. However, Trump's strategic aim of fostering closer ties with autocratic Russia and abandoning democratic Ukraine remains clear. Whether the rest of American society, the US Congress, or even some members of Trump's team will go along with this new rapprochement with Russia remains unclear. Different from Trump, according to a poll conducted in February 2025, an amazing 81 percent of Americans did not trust Putin.[44] In today's deeply polarized political climate in America, such a broad bipartisan consensus is rare. Many Americans also detest Putin's autocratic and imperial ways. In the long run, the clash between Russian autocracy and American democracy may override the individual preferences of one American president.

Chapter 2

WORKING WITH AND AGAINST CHINA

IT IS EASY, and perhaps understandable, to frame the current conflict between the United States and China as deep and enduring, rooted in immutable factors like history and culture. Some even see this confrontation as an inevitable clash of civilizations. That analytic framework is misguided. Much like the United States and Russia, over the centuries the US and China have enjoyed periods of cooperation and endured eras of confrontation shaped by variables—power, regimes, and leaders—not constants. Changes in the balance of power influenced levels of cooperation and confrontation. Periods of power asymmetry were generally more cooperative than eras of power parity. Regime change also shaped the bilateral relations. For instance, the demise of the Qing dynasty in 1911 improved US-China relations briefly because it appeared to create permissive conditions for democracy in China. Like US-Russia relations after the Bolshevik Revolution in 1917, the imposition of Communist Party dictatorship in China in 1949 profoundly shifted ties with the democratic United States in the opposite direction. A third factor—individual leaders—influenced the trajectory of US-China relations in profound ways as well. Nixon's commitment to normalizing ties in the early 1970s pushed US-China relations along a more cooperative trajectory, even though the regimes and relative balance of power of the two countries did not change at the time. Likewise, a new leader in China, Deng Xiaoping, had different ideas than Mao about market reforms at home and opening to the global economy that then pushed the two states along a more cooperative trajectory, one that another Chinese leader might not have adopted. More recently, PRC president Xi Jinping's embrace of greater state control of the economy and politics at home and adoption of a more aggressive foreign policy agenda has exacerbated tensions with the United States. A different leader might have chosen a different path for China at home and abroad. In his first term, President Trump and his team pushed US-China relations in a more confrontational direction, one that President Biden continued and President Trump intensified during his second term. None of these shifts were inevitable; they were the conscious decisions of leaders in both countries.

Like US-Russia relations over three centuries, US-China relations can be divided into five periods: (1) the century of humiliation, which included elements of cooperation and conflict; (2) increased cooperation after the autocratic breakdown in 1911 that continued through World War II; (3) major confrontation after the revolution in 1949 that placed China under Communist Party rule; (4) the rapprochement starting in the 1970s and followed by even deeper cooperation once Chinese leaders began to pursue market reforms at home and engagement with the global economy; and (5) a return to confrontation as China has become both more autocratic and more powerful under Xi Jinping, and US leaders have reacted with more strategies of coercion and containment rather than cooperation.

Consistent cooperation has not been characteristic of the past three centuries. Nor has constant confrontation. Instead, we have seen various levels of cooperation and conflict. While a new era of cooperation seems very unlikely in the near future, it is not impossible. It has happened before; it can happen again. How, when, and why cooperation did and did not occur is the subject of this chapter.

PERIOD ONE: COOPERATION GIVES WAY TO CONFLICT

Like the Russian Empire's relationship with the new American Republic, Chinese contact with the United States began in the late eighteenth century, when the US was a weak, peripheral actor in world politics and China was a regional hegemon and global economic powerhouse.[1] America's new leaders recognized this imbalance and had no intention of challenging China. The clear imbalance of power enhanced stability. Over time, however, as the United States became stronger and China became weaker, this stability eroded, giving way to confrontation between the two states during China's "century of humiliation."

Initially, Chinese rulers barely noticed the existence of the new American Republic. Beijing rejected the novel European concept of state sovereignty, preferring to see China as the center of the world (the Middle Kingdom) surrounded by tributary states. The United States was the most peripheral of these nations, several concentric circles out from China's conception of the core of the international system.

First contacts in the eighteenth century began with merchants and missionaries, what we would call "people-to-people" ties today. In 1784, a year after the Revolutionary War ended, the *Empress of China* ship departed from New York for Guangzhou (known as Canton then), bringing furs, ginseng, and Mexican silver dollars to be traded for Chinese tea, cloth, and porcelain.[2] The Americans were an increasingly attractive trading partner for China, as the East India Company's monopoly restricted British trade, and the Anglo-French War (1778–1783) and the French Revolution (1789–1799) resulted in a fading French presence in Canton.[3] For the next two centuries, albeit with periodic interruptions (especially during the first years after the communist revolution), trade has been a core and largely positive element of US-China relations. Christian missionaries from the US followed in the wake of commerce. In 1830, the Reverends Elijah Bridgman and David Abeel arrived, the first American missionaries to China to popularize Christian values and Western liberal norms.

In these initial years of contact, Chinese emperors demonstrated only passing curiosity in the American democratic experiment. American democracy was not a threatening idea; it was weak and far away. Monarchs ruled most of the world, and democracy was most certainly not a universal norm. Back then, the world was safe for autocracy.

THE CENTURY OF HUMILIATION

Contemporary Chinese history books describe the period from the First Opium War in 1839 to the founding of the People's Republic of China in 1949 as the "century of humiliation." During this era, corruption, fiscal instability, an exploding population, and bureaucratic decay eroded Chinese power, while European, Russian, and Japanese empires and the American Republic rose in strength.

This rapid and major shift in the balance of power in the world allowed the British-led European countries to coerce Chinese leaders into signing a series of what the Chinese called the "Unequal Treaties." Beijing was forced to accept unfair trade arrangements, import opium that triggered two wars, and sacrifice territory and sovereignty. The First Opium War (1839–1842) ended with the 1842 Treaty of Nanking, which forced China to hand Hong Kong to the British Empire, compelled several Chinese ports to allow trade with Europe, and granted indemnity and extraterritoriality to British subjects living in China. Following defeat in the Second Opium War (1856–1860), China signed the Treaty of Tientsin, which legalized the import of opium and gave foreigners even greater extraterritorial rights.

During this era, the Russian Empire annexed over one million square kilometers of Outer Manchuria, gains that were codified in the Treaties of Aigun in 1858 and the Treaty of Peking in 1860. After the Sino-French War of 1884–1885, France took northern Vietnam from China. In 1895, Japan defeated the crumbling Qing dynasty in the First Sino-Japanese War, annexed Taiwan and the Pescadores Islands, seized temporarily the Liaodong Peninsula, divested Beijing of its political influence in Korea, and forced China to pay significant reparations. In 1931, Japan invaded again, this time annexing Manchuria and then launching a full-scale invasion of China in 1937 that came to an end only with Japan's defeat in World War II in 1945. For China, it was indeed an era of humiliation.

During this era of European imperial exploitation, American leaders did not use military force to annex Chinese territory as others did. However, merchants from the US were eager to follow in the wake of the gunboat diplomacy of their European competitors and take advantage of Chinese weakness. They engaged heavily in the trade of Turkish opium, purchasing more than any other nation, most of which was destined for the Chinese market.[4] In 1844, the Wangxia Treaty of Peace, Amity, and Commerce finally established formal diplomatic relations between China and the United States. This treaty conferred on the United States many rights and privileges previously won by the British: most-favored-nation status, extraterritoriality, consulates, tariffs, and trade.[5] The United States joined France and Great Britain in fighting the Second Opium War, in which the Western powers compelled Beijing to accept additional concessions.

Nonetheless, American diplomats tried to carve a less imperial path than Europe and Japan had. Fearing that European powers planned to colonize China further and limit American commerce, in 1898, US Secretary of State John Hay issued a novel diplomatic note—the open-door policy. This document argued for equal access to and treatment in Chinese markets for all foreign powers in a unified and independent China. The note was issued at a time when imperial powers—including the US—were carving the world into colonies. During this era, the US took control of Cuba, the Philippines, and the Kingdom of Hawaii. American diplomats, somewhat hypocritically, committed to upholding norms of sovereignty in China as a strategy to advance American economic interests. As was the case here, norms and economic interests can sometimes reinforce each other.

SOCIETAL TIES

After the opium wars, more American missionaries came to China. American Protestant groups supported roughly 500 missionaries in China by 1890 and over 8,300 by 1920.[6] With Christianity came not only religious beliefs but also Western ideas about science, medicine, and education. Some of these ideas proved to be destabilizing. One leader, Hong Xiuquan, converted to Christianity and eventually led the Taiping Rebellion, a civil war based on Western ideas against Manchu "occupiers" in Beijing; it lasted from 1850 to 1864 and killed tens of millions before finally being subdued.[7] The Taiping Rebellion dramatically weakened the Qing monarchy and damaged the reputation of Western thought in China. During the Taiping Rebellion, foreign ideas promoted by Americans played a direct and tragic role in hindering China's political and economic development.

In the United States, Chinese laborers arrived to build American railroads, which fostered economic development and initially created a vector of win-win cooperation. Over time, however, American nationalists began to accuse Chinese immigrants of stealing jobs from white Americans and European immigrants, creating tension in the relationship between the countries. This issue was especially prevalent in California, where ethnic Chinese residents did not have electoral rights.[8]

Educational exchanges began during this era. These ties were critical to stabilizing relations then and continue to be a significant component of modern-day US-China relations. The Chinese Educational Mission (1872–1881), led by Yung Wing, a naturalized US citizen and the first Chinese recipient of an American bachelor's degree, brought one hundred and twenty young students to the United States in hopes that they would become drivers of engagement and translators of liberal ideas into Chinese society. It worked. When the students returned to China, several of them achieved considerable influence and prestige; they included the first president of the Republic of China, Sun Yat-sen; the First Lady of the Republic of China, Soong Mei-ling; successive Tsinghua University presidents; and eight ministers in the first republican government in the Republic of China.[9]

American educational programs inside China also expanded during this era, partly funded by reparations paid to the United States after the Boxer Rebellion. These programs explicitly aimed to align Chinese citizens more closely with American values and interests. By this time, Americans were no longer in awe of Chinese culture and instead were intent on changing China. As historian Michael Hunt assessed, "The decision to press the education scheme arose in part from a feeling of cultural superiority . . . Americans, in their fervor to educate the Chinese, acted on an ethnocentric conviction that China's salvation could only come through conversion to Western moral, economic, and political values."[10] Both Imperial University of Peking (founded in 1889 and now Peking University) and Tsing Hua Imperial College (founded in 1911 and now Tsinghua University) were established with significant American involvement.

THE BOXER REBELLION

Imperial intervention eventually triggered a violent backlash from Chinese society. In the 1899 Boxer Rebellion, Chinese nationalists surrounded the foreign legation district in Beijing. The Chinese government sided with the Boxers against the imperial occupiers. Empress Dowager Cixi ordered diplomats and other foreigners to leave the city. In response, President McKinley sent five thousand US troops to China to quell the rebellion and aligned the US with the Eight-Nation Alliance of Russia, Japan, Germany, Great Britain, Austria-Hungary, France, and Italy.

The imperial alliance defeated the rebels and their government allies, forcing them to sign the humiliating Boxer Protocol on September 7, 1901. The agreement compelled the Chinese government to pay over $330 million in reparations, called for the execution of numerous high-ranking officials, dismantled Chinese military installations, required the nation to provide for foreign troops stationed in Beijing, prohibited the import of weapons, and weakened the Chinese government, contributing to its collapse a decade later.

While this US military intervention is largely forgotten by the American public, that is not the case in China. A deep association between the United States and the imperial use of force lingered for decades and was especially pronounced among the founders of the Chinese Communist Party (CCP). Although Japanese and European soldiers played the leading role in repressing the Boxer Rebellion, US participation produced significant anti-American backlash in Chinese society, including boycotts of US products and businesses.

This era of feverish imperialism tilted the global balance of power away from China and toward Europe, Japan, and the United States. By the beginning of the twentieth century, the US and China were changing positions in the global order: The US was a rising power, and China was a declining power. That change in the balance of power did not start a major conventional war between the two countries, although many predict that is what such a shift would trigger today. To be sure, China's growing weakness created permissive conditions for imperial intervention. A more powerful Chinese state might have repelled these threats. The memory of Chinese vulnerability in this era has motivated the accumulation of military power in China today. Chinese leaders never want to endure another century of humiliation. However, an all-out war between the US and China did not occur then as a result of the shift in power.

PERIOD TWO: QUASI-DEMOCRATIC REGIME CHANGE

After the Boxer Rebellion, the Chinese government half-heartedly attempted reforms, but conservative inertia eventually prevailed.[11] After an uprising that began in October 1911, the corrupt and decaying monarchy finally crumbled in 1912, ending the nearly three-hundred-year-long Qing dynasty and the thousand years of imperial rule in China.[12] To avoid the state's total collapse, the Qing court agreed to create the Republic of China and allowed Sun Yat-sen to become the first provisional president on January 1, 1912. Sun was a Western-educated pioneer of liberal ideas in China. His rise to power sparked hope about the possibility of liberalism and pluralism and maybe even democracy in China. The following year, China held an election for the National Assembly in which forty million people voted for the first time.[13] Though only a fraction of the Chinese population voted in this election, the practice of holding elections for a national body nonetheless looked like a major move toward democratization in a country with thousands of years of autocratic history.

During this period of political liberalization and democratization, independent media flourished, nongovernmental organizations sprouted, the rule of law and federal reforms were embraced, and a constitution was adopted. At the time, American ideals inspired many Chinese liberals and democrats. As historian Frank Dikötter wrote, "The republican delegates who by the end of 1911 adopted a constitution for the organization of a provisional government in Nanjing clearly saw the federal government of the United States as a model to be followed."[14] For a fleeting, euphoric moment, China in 1912—like Russia in 1917—looked like it was at the beginning of a transition from autocracy to democracy.

Sun was a philosopher and intellectual, but he was not a strong leader or an effective manager. He quickly determined that he did not control the military forces necessary to hold the country together, and just three months later, in March 1912, he stepped aside to allow General Yuan Shikai to become president. Yuan emerged as a centralizing force in the new Chinese government, but he was not pursuing democracy. His primary goals were restoring the monarchy and preserving his power. He did this successfully for a short period, but eventually his strategy backfired and ushered in years of decentralization, warlordism, and civil war.

US officials responded positively to the 1911 revolution in China, as they did just a few years later when reacting to Russia's February Revolution in the spring of 1917. Fueling hope for closer relations with a democratic China, President William Taft remarked, "The natural sympathy of the American people with the assumption of republican principles by the Chinese people was appropriately expressed . . . the United States is, according to precedent, maintaining full and friendly de facto relations with the [Chinese] provisional Government."[15] After taking office in 1913, President Woodrow Wilson expressed even greater optimism about a possible Chinese democracy, seeing Sun Yat-sen as an ideological soulmate and Yuan Shikai as a necessary but temporary solution to state weakness and internal instability. He hoped the Chinese general would play a role similar to George Washington's in the founding of the American Republic. Wilson believed the US had an obligation to promote democratic practices and liberal ideas in China.[16]

These hopes were quickly dashed. After Yuan's death, the central government broke down, allowing regional warlords to fill the power vacuum, and Sun Yat-sen's commitments to liberal ideas weakened. The focus of his political party—the Kuomintang, or KMT—was no longer Chinese democracy but regaining power by any means necessary. Nine years after Sun's death, in 1925, Chiang Kai-shek took over KMT leadership, a position he held until he died in 1975.

Chiang Kai-shek was not a liberal or a democrat. While Sun's ideas were shaped by his Western education, British Hong Kong, and Japan's Meiji Restoration, Chiang's worldview was rooted in his Han identity, traditions, and culture. He embraced liberal ideas only when they were useful to nurture ties with the West and reach his ultimate goal of ruling China. Soon after taking over the KMT and its National Revolutionary Army, Chiang launched the Northern Expedition against regional warlords and achieved enough success to create the Nationalist Government in Nanjing in 1928. For a brief period, Chiang seemed to be the Chinese leader most capable of uniting the country.

In 1934, members of the Chinese Communist Party, founded in Shanghai in 1921, were forced to flee from their urban strongholds in what became known as the Long March to the north. The city of Yan'an in Shaanxi became the headquarters for the communist government in the region and a center for training party members and troops. Mao Zedong had yet to officially become party chairman, but his central role in the Long March confirmed his status as the CCP's undisputed charismatic leader. For the next several years, the CCP and KMT both claimed sovereignty over China.

Unlike in Russia, where the period of instability after the monarchy's collapse lasted only a few years, in China, the interregnum between the monarchy's collapse in 1911 and the communists' usurpation of power lasted decades. It was not until 1949 that the CCP successfully consolidated power, a period of strife prolonged by Japan's invasion of China.

REALPOLITIK AND WORLD WAR II

Not surprisingly, China's internal instability affected US-China relations. Between 1911 and 1928, diplomatic relations were interrupted twice because it was unclear which group was the legitimate government in China. Hopes among American officials for closer ties with the Republic of China based on shared liberal and democratic values quickly gave way to more immediate security considerations—dealing with an increasingly belligerent Japan. After Germany's defeat in World War I, Japan seized control of islands in the Pacific Ocean and the Chinese port of Qingdao, formerly controlled by Berlin.

Japan's efforts at regional conquest began well before World War II. In 1915, Japan issued a document known as the Twenty-One Demands that aimed to extend Japanese control over the Chinese region of Manchuria. President Wilson denounced Japan's imperial moves as violating the open-door policy, but his protests had little effect.

In 1919, the Treaty of Versailles gave Shandong Province, previously controlled by Germany, to Japan, not China, an outrageous colonial act that sparked the May Fourth Movement, a student demonstration that triggered widespread national protest. Liberals, socialists, anarchists, and communists united against the government's diplomatic failure. In 1931, Japan invaded Manchuria, allegedly in response to a Chinese attack on a Japanese railroad (the Mukden incident), renamed the region Manchukuo, and brought back Puyi, the last emperor of the Qing dynasty, to serve as the leader of this new puppet state. In 1937, Japan launched a full-scale war against the Republic of China, seizing control of several major cities and regions, including, in a brutal siege, assault, and massacre known as the Rape of Nanjing, the republic's capital. In response to Japan's invasion, the KMT and the CCP temporarily set aside their hostilities and joined forces to defeat the Japanese, although the KMT did most of the fighting.

President Roosevelt responded to the Japanese invasion by providing weapons to the Republic of China, ending American neutrality. Even before the United States declared war on Japan in 1941, a volunteer group of American pilots—the Flying Tigers—joined the Republic of China's air force. On December 7, 1941, Japan attacked Pearl Harbor in Hawaii, triggering an American declaration of war against Japan and uniting the United States and China as allies to defeat a common enemy.[17]

Just as they did for US-Soviet relations at the time, realpolitik considerations dominated US thinking about China during World War II. Victory required alliances with the leaders of any regime that could help the military cause, including communists like Stalin and Mao. Some American leaders and soldiers seemed to prefer Mao over Chiang. In 1944, the US Army Observation Group traveled to the communist capital of Yan'an to establish closer relations with the CCP and study Mao's political and military methods. Impressed by what they learned, they reported that the CCP could be a valuable wartime ally and recommended direct US assistance to the communist soldiers.[18]

American decisions during the war to ally with Stalin and nurture ties with Mao had long-term negative consequences for the Republic of China, among them, perhaps most important, US acquiescence to the Soviet invasion of Manchuria in 1945. While this Soviet campaign liberated the territory from Japanese occupation, it also enhanced Mao's military position within China at the expense of Chiang and his army.

LOSING CHINA

As discussed in the previous chapter, Franklin D. Roosevelt had ambitious ideas for a post–World War II order that included a United Nations complete with an enforcement branch, his "Four Policemen," which eventually morphed into the UN Security Council. FDR assumed that the Republic of China would be one of the great powers in this new international system. Chiang, however, failed to consolidate power in mainland China despite American assistance. In 1945, President Truman deployed his most venerated five-star general, George Marshall, to mediate talks between the KMT and CCP with the aim of forming a unified Chinese government.[19] Marshall's mission, as Truman defined it, was to help consolidate a "strong, unified, and democratic China."[20] But the effort failed; the CCP and KMT each believed it could defeat the other on the battlefield, and consequently, the civil war resumed in 1946. Washington sided with the KMT, but not enthusiastically. Unlike in Europe, there was no Marshall Plan for China.[21] Truman imposed a temporary arms embargo on the Republic of China, and American emissaries quietly tried to establish relations with Mao. With substantial support from Stalin, Mao and the CCP won in 1949. Once in power, Mao made the decision to ally with the Soviet Union in 1950.

PERIOD THREE: COMMUNIST REGIME CHANGE

On October 1, 1949, Mao announced the establishment of the People's Republic of China. Mao was a charismatic leader who generated admiration worldwide; this was especially true in the developing world, but he also had followers in Europe and the United States. Mao and Stalin forged a short-lived alliance based primarily on shared ideology, codified in 1950 in the Sino-Soviet Treaty of Friendship, Alliance, and Mutual Assistance. In Soviet parlance, the "correlation of forces" favored communism, not capitalism. A passionate debate in the United States ensued over who lost China.

For another two decades, the US continued to recognize the Republic of China—now exiled in Taiwan under KMT leader Chiang Kai-shek—as the official representative of China. Like the abrupt, negative disruption in US-Russia relations triggered by the Bolshevik Revolution in 1917, regime change in 1949 played a pivotal role in pushing ties between the US and the People's Republic of China rapidly onto a confrontational path. Mao believed his successful revolution at home was part of a global "war of liberation" against imperial subjugation worldwide. In the ideological struggle between the colonized and the colonizers and communism and capitalism, Mao viewed the US as a mortal enemy. In Washington, the feeling was mutual.

US-China relations took a nosedive during the Korean War. On June 25, 1950, North Korean communist leader Kim Il Sung invaded South Korea. Equipped with Soviet tanks, firearms, and munitions, the North Korean army quickly captured Seoul, the capital of South Korea, and advanced toward the port city of Busan, at the southern end of the peninsula. Truman, buoyed by a supportive UN Security Council resolution because the Soviet Union was boycotting the council at the time, made the difficult decision to send American soldiers to Korea to help liberate the south, an objective achieved so successfully that the American-led coalition of armed forces pushed the North Koreans back to the Chinese border.

Four months later, Mao launched a major counterattack, explaining to Stalin in a secret cable on October 2, 1950: "If we allow the United States to occupy all of Korea . . . Korean revolutionary power will suffer a fundamental defeat and the Americans will run more rampant and have negative effects for the entire Far East."[22] Chinese and North Korean forces pushed the allied forces back into South Korea, and the conflict eventually settled into a stalemate that ended only in part because of Stalin's death in March 1953. A few months later, on July 27, 1953, the warring parties signed the Korean Armistice Agreement, which created the military demarcation line and Korean demilitarized zone that has remained in place ever since.

Communist power usurpation in China was alarming enough to American strategists, but the Chinese military intervention in the Korean War was even more shocking. American and Chinese soldiers were now directly fighting each other. Some US war planners even recommended using nuclear weapons to keep the communist forces from seizing the peninsula. In addition to strengthening military ties with South Korea, American leaders deepened military relations with Japan, signed the ANZUS Treaty with Australia and New Zealand in 1951, created the Southeast Asian Treaty Organization for collective defense in 1954, and signed the Mutual Defense Treaty with the Republic of China (Taiwan) that same year.[23] In 1955, the Formosa Resolution gave Eisenhower authority to defend Taiwan and other islands near mainland China. The Second Taiwan Strait Crisis of 1958 further strengthened the American commitment to defend the island.

China's occupation of Tibet exacerbated tensions with the United States. In 1951, Mao conquered Tibet, and in 1959 he crushed the Tibetan rebellion, forcing the Dalai Lama and his government to flee to India. The US condemned the PRC's violent suppression, and in a pattern that would be repeated around the world throughout the Cold War, the CIA provided covert assistance to the Tibetan resistance as a strategy to weaken the CCP.

To counter communist expansion in Asia, the US expanded its military assistance and presence in Vietnam in what became a proxy war against both the Soviet Union and the PRC, a mirror image of the Korean War. Mao provided military support to his Hanoi comrades, first with rifles and later with antiaircraft units and military vessels.[24] In the US, Senator Joseph McCarthy aimed to eliminate what he saw as CCP influence inside the nation. From 1949 until the start of normalization talks two decades later, US-China relations were at their worst. Ideological differences, not the balance of power, were the central drivers of this animosity.

PERIOD FOUR: A NEW ERA OF COOPERATION

The pattern of US-China relations departs from that of US-Russia relations in the 1970s and 1980s. While renewed US-Russia cooperation in the late 1980s and early 1990s resulted directly from democratic regime change inside the Soviet Union and Russia, this was not the trigger for improved US-China relations. Chinese democratization never occurred. Instead, realpolitik calculations to balance the rising Soviet superpower followed by win-win economic opportunities made possible by Chinese market reforms drove this new era of bilateral rapprochement.

THE SINO-SOVIET SPLIT

The Sino-Soviet alliance did not last long. Stalin never trusted or respected Mao. He worried that Mao's alleged commitment to Marxism-Leninism camouflaged his Chinese nationalism, and, more generally, he distrusted communist movements that were beyond his direct control. Mao was an earnest communist, but he was also a nationalist and an anti-imperialist. The bitter experience of foreign intervention in China during the century of humiliation fueled a deep suspicion of outsiders meddling in China's internal affairs, and that included meddlers from Moscow. Mao eventually came to believe that Soviet-style communism was not suitable for the needs of the Chinese system. Rather than celebrating industrial workers (there were few at the time in China) as the drivers of the socialist revolution, Mao lauded the revolutionary potential of peasants. This ideological disagreement eventually produced deep divisions between Moscow and Beijing concerning the best ways and the most ideal places to promote communism worldwide.[25]

After Stalin died in 1953, Moscow's new leader Nikita Khrushchev gradually rolled out a policy of de-Stalinization. Mao despised Khrushchev's "revisionism" as an ideology and rejected his idea of "peaceful coexistence" with the capitalist West. Mao blamed Khrushchev's de-Stalinization for the anti-communist movements in East Germany in 1953 and in Hungary and Poland in 1956, and not without reason. In reaction, he sought to give the CCP more control over the economy and society, not less. In 1958, Mao launched his Great Leap Forward—a disruptive economic strategy that involved even greater state intervention as a strategy to grow industrial and agricultural production by deploying draconian techniques that resulted in tens of millions dying from starvation and disease.[26] Mao's actions were the opposite of Khrushchev's anti-Stalinist thaw. By 1960, the relationship became so strained that the USSR withdrew all aid and personnel from the PRC. Nearly a decade later, Mao's equally disastrous Cultural Revolution underscored for Khrushchev that Chinese autocracy did not always produce economic development.

Soviet and Chinese leaders also clashed on the international stage. Mao focused on supporting socialist revolutions in agrarian countries, not in the industrialized world, as prescribed by Marx and Lenin. He successfully fused decolonization and national liberation struggles with communism, seeking and winning supporters in Africa, Asia, and Latin America. CCP leaders exported their specific methods for fighting colonial powers, emphasizing the need to mobilize peasants, not workers, and capture control of the countryside before seizing the cities—the opposite of the Moscow model. An open clash between the two communist great powers erupted, pitting Soviet-backed national liberation movements against Chinese-backed national liberation movements in Angola, Mozambique, Zimbabwe, and South Africa.[27] In 1969, the two countries even fought a short war over a border dispute.

NIXON GOES TO CHINA

The Sino-Soviet split created an opportunity for improved US-China relations based on balance-of-power politics, not shared ideology. At this moment, individuals played a pivotal role in changing the dynamic of the bilateral relationship, four of them in particular: President Richard Nixon, his national security adviser and Secretary of State Henry Kissinger, Mao Zedong, and Chinese premier Zhou Enlai. To balance the Soviet Union's growing power, Nixon wanted a closer relationship with China. Mao and Zhou had similar motivations. Mao still considered the United States a capitalist imperialist foe, but now his fear of the Soviet Union was greater.

In July 1971, Kissinger secretly traveled to Beijing to meet with Zhou to prepare for Nixon's visit. He told his counterpart, "It is the conviction of President Nixon that a strong and developing People's Republic of China poses no threat to any essential U.S. interest."[28] As a concession to Beijing, Kissinger also met North Vietnamese representatives in Paris to begin negotiations for the US withdrawal from Vietnam. Eventually, on October 25, 1971, the United States abandoned the Republic of China (Taiwan) and supported UN General Assembly Resolution 2758, which recognized the People's Republic of China as the sole legal representative of China to the UN. In February 1972, Nixon became the first US president to visit the PRC. While there, he signed the Shanghai Communiqué, which outlined a road map for restoring diplomatic relations between the US and China and included opening liaison offices in Beijing and Washington. The Shanghai Communiqué codified a radically new US policy toward China and stated "its interest in a peaceful settlement of the Taiwan question by the Chinese themselves. With this prospect in mind, it affirms the ultimate objective of the withdrawal of all U.S. forces and military installations from Taiwan."[29] Nixon relaxed trade restrictions with the People's Republic of China, ended regular patrols of the Taiwan Strait, encouraged society-to-society contacts (including, most famously, ping-pong diplomacy), loosened currency controls, and eased visa restrictions on Chinese citizens. In turn, Mao relaxed the Chinese trade embargo on American goods. At this moment, shared perceptions about the balance of power by leaders in both countries drove the two closer together.

US-China relations continued to improve even after Nixon resigned in 1974. President Gerald Ford visited China in 1975, and President Jimmy Carter established formal diplomatic relations with the PRC in January 1979. Chinese vice premier and the de facto leader of the PRC, Deng Xiaoping, visited the United States shortly after that. In the next two years, dozens of treaties, agreements, and protocols were signed, and scholarly exchanges, trade, and tourism increased.

This US-China rapprochement in the 1970s ranks as one of the most dramatic shifts in bilateral relations in the twentieth century not triggered by war or revolution. Ideological differences, however, still shaped the relationship. Mao continued to support communist-leaning national liberation movements and global revolutionaries, most of whom were fighting American partners. Trade and investment did not increase for another decade. More dramatic shifts in US-China relations occurred only after domestic reforms were launched inside China.

CHINESE MARKET REFORMS

The power struggle after Mao died in 1976 resembled the factional fights in the Soviet Union after Stalin died. Deng Xiaoping eventually outmaneuvered others, ousted Hua Guofeng and the Gang of Four, and became China's new paramount leader. Deng inherited a country deeply damaged by economic dysfunction, social conflict, and discontent with the CCP. In response, he launched a comprehensive set of market reforms that required an open, cooperative approach to the global economy, especially with the United States, to succeed. At this moment, Deng's ideas about economic liberalization—not the balance of power or regime type—played the most critical role in pushing US-China relations along an even more cooperative trajectory.

Deng orchestrated one of the most extraordinary evolutionary changes of an economic system in human history. He gradually transformed China's autarkic command economy into a partial market system integrated into the global capitalist economy. Unlike Gorbachev, Deng and his successors relied on the party to implement market reforms. Ironically, the disastrous Cultural Revolution purges gave Deng the opportunity and support to rebuild the state and party with leaders more aligned with his reform agenda.[30] Under his Four Modernizations, Deng and his allies dismantled the Maoist notion of "continuous class struggle" to allow some groups in China to embrace free-enterprise practices and profit. Deng made his predilection for pragmatism over ideology clear, famously quipping, "I don't care if the cat is black or white, so long as it catches mice."

China needed access to American markets, direct foreign investment, intellectual property, and universities to achieve Deng's desired economic objectives. The US government, business community, and universities embraced China's "opening up" with great enthusiasm.[31] But Deng's government demanded concessions in return for allowing greater trade and foreign intervention, including, most important, a US commitment to a One China policy and an end to formal diplomatic relations with Taiwan, even while Beijing and Washington tacitly acknowledged that the US and Taiwanese governments, militaries, and business communities would continue cooperation. The agreement to sweep the issue of Taiwanese sovereignty under the rug served both countries well at the time.

The year 1979 was pivotal in US-China relations: Deng became the first senior Chinese Communist Party official to visit the United States; Vice President Walter Mondale reciprocated with a trip to China; the US embassy in Taipei closed; the US liaison office in Beijing was converted to an embassy; and Leonard F. Woodcock became the first US ambassador to the PRC. The two countries expanded people-to-people ties, engaging in joint research projects and student exchanges under the Agreement on Cooperation in Science and Technology. The Soviet Union's invasion of Afghanistan and its military buildup along the Chinese border further strengthened US-China relations, as Beijing and Washington found common cause against Moscow's belligerent assertion of global power. Even military and intelligence ties grew, with visits to Beijing from senior Pentagon officials and the opening of a US listening post in Xinjiang, China, to spy on the Soviet Union. In 1980, China joined the World Bank and IMF, a clear signal of intent to integrate further into the liberal international order anchored by the United States.

SUSTAINED COOPERATION

For four decades after the normalization of diplomatic relations, the American presidency flipped back and forth between parties, and new leaders succeeded Deng, but cooperation largely prevailed.

As a presidential candidate, Ronald Reagan criticized the normalization of relations with the PRC. Once in office, Reagan changed his tune. In July 1982, the Reagan administration issued the Six Assurances to Taiwan, including pledges to honor the Taiwan Relations Act.[32] But the following month, the Reagan administration signed a communiqué with the PRC to deepen normalization and reaffirm commitment to the One China policy. Reagan and Premier Zhao Ziyang made reciprocal visits in 1984, and the US government approved Beijing's purchases of American military equipment. By the end of Reagan's presidency in 1989, the United States was purchasing over one-quarter of China's total exports.

US-China engagement further deepened under President George H. W. Bush, who had served in Beijing as chief of the US liaison office (the de facto ambassador) between 1974 and 1975. Rhetorically, Bush expressed less enthusiasm for promoting democracy and freedom abroad than Reagan, making cooperation with Beijing easier. The bilateral relationship in economics gradually trended in a positive direction throughout this period.

There were strains. The most significant was the 1989 Tiananmen Square massacre. While Deng had relaxed some political controls during the early years of reform (for instance, not challenging the Democracy Wall Movement beginning in 1978, during which thousands of Chinese citizens made and put up handwritten posters on political and social issues), he responded to calls for democracy with violent repression a decade later. In April 1989, students in Beijing gathered in Tiananmen Square to commemorate the death of liberal communist leader Hu Yaobang, a movement that then swelled to "several million individuals . . . in 132 major cities, including 27 provincial towns."[33] On June 4, 1989, Chinese armed forces used brute force to clear Tiananmen Square.

Bush publicly denounced the violent massacre, suspended weapons exports, and limited the number of visitors to the US from the PRC, but he privately cautioned against an emotional overreaction that might push China back into the Soviet orbit. He sent his national security adviser Brent Scowcroft on a secret mission to Beijing to quietly communicate his desire not to disrupt bilateral relations. Deng blamed the United States for encouraging the demonstrators, telling Scowcroft, "We will never allow any people to interfere in China's internal affairs."[34] But Deng wanted to make the Tiananmen Square "incident," as Beijing called it, a hiccup, not a turning point, in US-China relations. With Bush as a partner, he succeeded.

Just months later, in the fall of 1989, Chinese leaders nervously watched the collapse of communism in Eastern Europe. Two years later, the Soviet Union disintegrated. These events only reconfirmed Deng's commitment to maintaining firm autocratic rule while implementing market reforms, a conviction that subsequent Chinese Communist Party leaders have shared.

After the collapse of the Soviet Union in 1991, the global balance of power shifted dramatically toward unipolarity as the United States became the only superpower. However, that change did not compel China to pivot toward deeper cooperation with other countries to balance against American hegemony. The opposite occurred: US-China relations deepened, mainly because leaders in both countries valued the economic benefits of increased cooperation.

In 1992 presidential candidate Bill Clinton harshly criticized Bush for being soft on Chinese dictatorship and pledged not to "coddle tyrants, from Baghdad to Beijing." Once in office, though, President Clinton deepened engagement with the PRC. American economic interests—or, more precisely, the profits accrued by American banks and corporations that traded with and invested in China—drove this strategy. To explain his policy of communist enrichment, Clinton articulated an argument that in academia is called modernization theory for why American economic engagement with China could eventually lead to democratic change.[35] As Clinton hypothesized, "The more China liberalizes its economy, the more fully it will liberate the potential of its people . . . And when individuals have the power, not just to dream, but to realize their dreams, they will demand a greater say."[36] The administration's analysis of the benefits of a democratic Russia aligned with their conclusions about the benefits of a more democratic China, assuming that democratization in Russia and China would lead to a closer partnership with the United States. In 1998, Clinton took an extensive trip to China, meeting directly with Chinese citizens and speaking firmly but politely about the importance of democratic values.

During the Clinton era, US-China relations faced challenges, especially over the status of Taiwan. Before the first free-and-fair presidential election in Taiwan in March 1996, the People's Liberation Army (PLA) conducted naval exercises and launched missile tests near the island to intimidate Taiwanese voters. In response, Clinton deployed two aircraft carriers and their accompanying ships to the region, compelling China to back down and allowing KMT leader Lee Teng-hui to win this historic democratic election. The two states averted another crisis on Clinton's watch during the NATO military campaign against Serbia when, on May 7, 1999, US jets accidentally bombed the Chinese embassy in Belgrade, killing three Chinese journalists. Chinese officials expressed outrage, and nationalist demonstrations erupted in Beijing, but no major diplomatic break ensued.

Just as in earlier eras, American critics of Chinese behavior outside the executive branch opposed Clinton's engagement strategy. The 1999 Cox Report, issued by Republican Christopher Cox and a bipartisan congressional committee, provided a scathing indictment of Chinese espionage efforts to acquire nuclear technologies.[37] Western human rights organizations highlighted Beijing's repression, especially in Tibet.[38] But deepening economic ties overshadowed these political tensions. During his last year in office, Clinton signed the US-China Relations Act of 2000, granting the PRC permanent normal trade relations status and paving the way for China's membership in the World Trade Organization.

At this moment of unrivaled American power, the United States did not need China to balance a weak, pro-American Russia or any other country. Instead of balance-of-power considerations, economic interests played a central role in shaping US policy toward China in the 1990s. Few American leaders back then were worried about great power competition with China, and Chinese leaders were not aggressively championing an alternative political model to democracy; they argued that China was developing democracy, just slowly and with Chinese characteristics. PRC leaders even allowed township and village elections and invited American and European nongovernmental organizations working on democracy and rule-of-law promotion to open offices in China.[39]

President George W. Bush mostly maintained cooperation with the CCP. Early in the Bush administration, another military accident tested bilateral relations: A Chinese fighter jet collided with an American EP-3 reconnaissance aircraft on April 1, 2001, killing the Chinese pilot. The EP-3 made an emergency landing on China's Hainan Island, where the American crew was detained. After a tense standoff, the Chinese government released the soldiers over a week later, underscoring that both governments wanted to avoid escalation. After the September 11, 2001, terrorist attacks in the United States, American attention shifted sharply toward Afghanistan, Iraq, and the greater Middle East. In parallel to the rapprochement in US-Russia relations after September 11, US-China cooperation also accelerated, as autocrats and democrats united to fight a common enemy—terrorism. Chinese leaders claimed to be facing their own terrorist challenge from alleged separatists in Xinjiang and enthusiastically adopted Bush's framework of a global war on terror. The PRC did not try to stop the American-led invasion to overthrow the Taliban and did not object to the opening of US military bases in Uzbekistan and Kyrgyzstan in China's neighborhood to help support the war in Afghanistan. Like most of the world, Beijing opposed Bush's decision to invade Iraq in 2003, but the Chinese reaction to this war was relatively muted. On other security matters, China and the United States worked together during the Bush years, including in the six-party talks seeking the end of North Korea's nuclear weapons program and cooperation at the UN Security Council to try to stop Iran from developing a nuclear bomb.

After September 11, 2001, Bush adopted the "Freedom Agenda" that aimed to promote democracy around the world. However, Bush and his team did not devote much attention to criticizing human rights abuses and autocratic rule in China. Instead, they urged Chinese leaders to embrace the role of a "responsible stakeholder" in the international system, even as a Communist Party dictatorship. Bush doubled down on the theory that economic development produces democratic change, arguing in May 2001, "Open trade is a force for freedom in China . . . Free trade has introduced new technologies that offer Chinese people access to uncensored information and democratic ideas . . . When we open trade, we open minds."[40] In 2006, the United States became China's second-biggest trading partner, and that same year, China replaced the United Kingdom as the second-largest foreign holder of US debt. Chinese direct investment in the United States expanded, while US banks, manufacturing companies, and exporters grew their businesses rapidly inside China.

Like previous periods, this expansion of economic ties was not universally welcomed, especially in the US Congress. In response to the anticipated entry of Chinese-made cars to US markets in 2005, Senators Chuck Schumer and Lindsey Graham introduced bipartisan legislation to apply a 27.5 percent tariff on these Chinese imports. The US government invoked national security concerns to block the China National Offshore Oil Corporation's bid to purchase US oil giant Unocal. In 2004, the United States filed its first WTO trade complaint case against China.[41] In the 2000s, however, leaders in both Beijing and Washington continued to frame their bilateral relations in win-win terms, especially regarding economic cooperation.[42] Neither competing regime types, antithetical ideologies, nor the global balance of power were shaping bilateral ties.

President Obama initially signaled continuity with cooperation as well.[43] In his first year in office, Obama worked closely with Chinese leader Hu Jintao to manage the 2008 global financial crisis in bilateral channels and within the newly created G20 multilateral organization. Over the next eight years, Obama and his team continued to engage with their Chinese counterparts to tackle international problems of common concern, especially within multilateral settings. Most impressive, following years of negotiations, President Obama and Xi Jinping, the new general secretary of the Chinese Communist Party, announced in 2014 that they would work together to sign what later became the Paris Climate Accords. Given that their two countries were the world's largest producers of global emissions, this landmark multilateral agreement required Chinese and American collaboration to have a real impact.[44] With other leaders of the P5 + 1 (France, Great Britain, Russia, and Germany), the United States and China joined forces in 2015 to sign the Joint Comprehensive Plan of Action, which prevented Iran from developing nuclear weapons. The US and China also found common ground in the Obama era in addressing the North Korean nuclear threat, albeit with minimal success. Significantly and surprisingly, in March 2011, China abstained from the UN Security Council resolutions authorizing the use of force against the Libyan government. The Chinese government demonstrated its commitment to international law and multilateralism by not endorsing Russia's annexation of Crimea in 2014, a stance praised by the Obama administration.

PERIOD FIVE: A RETURN TO CONFRONTATION

Today's new era of confrontation between the United States and China emerged gradually, not suddenly. It started during the Obama presidency, accelerated under the first Trump administration, and continued with Biden and in Trump's second term. Three factors combined to fuel this era of confrontation: China's rise in power, Xi's increasing autocratic policies, and Trump—that is, power, regimes, and individuals.

China's rise to approximate American power has been the central driver of friction. In September 2008, China passed Japan to become the largest US foreign creditor and emerged as the world's second-largest economy just two years later. After the 2008 financial crash, Beijing's leaders began to see America as in decline, which gave them an opportunity to become more assertive in global affairs. This perception of the balance of power in the world made Chinese leaders less willing "to show deference"[45] to the United States.

As China became more powerful, US policy toward the PRC gradually shifted to a more competitive footing. This pivot started under Obama.[46] In 2009, the Obama administration imposed a 35 percent tariff on Chinese tire imports in reaction to what Washington officials argued were unfair, state-subsidized prices.[47] As Obama warned, "Our competitors should be on notice: You will not get away with skirting the rules."[48] In 2012, the United States joined Japan and the European Union in a WTO case against China over access to rare earth materials for manufacturing high-tech products.[49] A joint US-China communiqué in 2012 made clear American displeasure with Chinese illegal and coercive methods for obtaining US technology, clarifying that China's technological cooperation "shall be decided by businesses independently and will not be used by the Chinese government as a pre-condition for market access."[50]

Chinese currency manipulation to encourage exports also became a growing source of tension, as did Chinese theft of intellectual property, digital information, and military secrets.[51] Hackers affiliated with the PLA infiltrated several prominent US corporations, stole millions of records from the US Office of Personnel Management, and obtained sensitive information on roughly one hundred fifty million Americans through cybertheft from the consumer-credit-reporting company Equifax. In response, the Obama administration adopted several measures to reduce cyber theft of data for commercial purposes, deny market economy status to China, block several Chinese acquisitions of US businesses, mobilize international pressure on Beijing to reduce excess capacity in industrial sectors, and use WTO enforcement mechanisms against unfair Chinese economic practices.[52] During this era, Beijing began the process of economic decoupling. The PRC blocked Google, Facebook, Twitter, and YouTube from operating in China, denied access to numerous Western media outlets, and generally strengthened the control of information coming into China.

A central component of Obama's pivot to Asia strategy was negotiating the Trans-Pacific Partnership (TPP), a trade agreement that included roughly 40 percent of the global economy. The Obama administration also elevated US participation in Asian multilateral organizations like the Association of Southeast Asian Nations and the East Asia Summit, signed a new free-trade agreement with South Korea, restored diplomatic relations with Burma, deepened ties with Vietnam, deployed twenty-five hundred Marines to Australia, and released new US defense guidelines stressing Asia and the Pacific as a growing security priority.[53]

Obama's policy changes did not stop Beijing from expanding its military presence in Asia, especially in the South China Sea, the world's second-most-used sea-lane, with one-third of global shipping, lucrative fisheries supplying food security, and oil and gas reserves. Competing sovereignty claims in the South China Sea spiked during this period, eventually prompting the Philippines to initiate arbitration proceedings under the UN Convention on the Law of the Sea (UNCLOS) against Chinese territorial claims in the South China Sea in 2013. In 2016, the tribunal constituted under UNCLOS decided in favor of the Philippines. Predictably, the PRC ignored the ruling. Unpredictably, Philippine president Rodrigo Duterte decided against pursuing enforcement and instead prioritized cordial relations with the growing Asian power. China began to drill for oil near the Paracel Islands, located in waters claimed by Vietnam, and started constructing artificial islands and placing military hardware on them, triggering a blunt rhetorical rebuff from Secretary of Defense Ashton Carter but not much else. By the end of the Obama era, military tensions between the United States and China over the South China Sea were more significant than ever.

Ideological tensions also grew during the Obama years. Clashes over competing values erupted most acutely when Chinese lawyer and civil rights activist Chen Guangcheng escaped house arrest in 2012 and fled to the US embassy in Beijing, where he was given refuge. Eventually, the Chinese government allowed Chen to leave the country accompanied by high-level US diplomats but blasted him as "a tool and a pawn for American politicians to blacken China."[54]

Despite the sharper points of conflict over military and human rights issues, the trajectory of US-China economic relations during the Obama era remained generally cooperative. Most government officials and analysts supported these trends, viewing economic cooperation as a net positive for American national interests.

THE XI EFFECT

If China's rise in power had coincided with PRC democratization, tensions between the US and China would have diminished or at least not have become as bad as they are today. Instead, the opposite happened: Chinese economic growth provided Beijing with greater financial resources to expand China's military and autocratic hold on power. These outcomes were not inevitable. Other countries have expanded economic development without commensurately growing military power (like Japan) or strengthening autocracy (South Korea). These results stemmed not from Chinese culture or history but from choices made by China's communist leadership and Xi Jinping in particular.[55] Like Putin in Russia, Xi has made the Chinese political system more autocratic while at the same time pursuing more aggressive foreign policies. More than any leader since Mao, Xi has negatively shaped US-China relations.

In 2012, Xi Jinping became the CCP general secretary and the chairman of the Central Military Commission. The following year, he added *president* to his list of titles. Xi aggressively tightened his control of the CCP and the state, launching a sweeping anti-corruption campaign against tens of thousands, including many well-known party officials. At the CCP twentieth party congress in October 2022, Xi populated the Standing Committee of the Politburo—the top leadership organ of the party—as well as the larger Politburo and the Central Committee with loyalists.[56] Xi spearheaded an overhaul of the PLA, again using purges of both generals and civilians to make the institution more loyal to him. Xi's most brazen consolidation of power was his instruction to the National People's Congress in 2018 to amend the constitution to eliminate presidential term limits, making him more powerful than any Chinese leader since Mao. Before Xi, one of the central features of CCP rule was a routine, regular method for the succession of leaders. That is now gone.

Xi has also extended the party's autocratic reach into society.[57] Xi expanded censorship, expelled American journalists from China, placed more draconian controls on domestic and foreign NGOs, and arrested critics who had been tolerated during the Hu era. Xi's regime also has charged critics with nonpolitical crimes to stifle dissent.[58] The CCP today does more than just censor media—it also floods social media with pro-regime messaging.[59] As USC professors Erin Carter and Brett Carter assess, "The CCP's flagship propaganda outlet is now more effusive than any point since the Cultural Revolution."[60] In the Xi era, the cocktail of human informants and powerful surveillance technologies, such as facial recognition and electronic payment systems, has deepened state control of Chinese citizens.[61] Xi also introduced a social credit-score system to encourage compliant behavior.[62] Xi's regime even uses surveillance technologies to track and harass Chinese citizens living abroad. During the COVID-19 pandemic, the space for public criticism shrank even further, and instruments for surveilling citizens grew, although the draconian lockdown also eventually sparked societal protests.[63]

Xi also has implemented several policies to enhance the state's control of the economy in what MIT professor Yasheng Huang has called "the biggest reform reversals in the history of the PRC."[64] Xi curtailed the autonomy of some of China's most successful private companies, especially in the tech sector. In 2020, Xi interrupted the $37 billion IPO of Ant Group, the financial arm of Alibaba, and subsequently directed several state-owned companies to buy significant stakes in the company. Jack Ma, the co-founder of Alibaba and at one time the wealthiest man in China, now lives in exile. Xi and his government implemented new restrictions and investigations into the rideshare corporation Didi, the internet and technology giant Tencent, the food-delivery company Meituan, and even web-based tutoring companies, actions that generated major devaluations of these publicly traded firms.

Fearful of the independent power of these companies and their owners, Xi has prioritized political control over economic growth.[65] In parallel, Xi has provided increased support for state-owned enterprises.[66] Xi also enacted many mercantilist and protectionist practices that were antithetical to Deng's "opening up." In 2015, his government rolled out "Made in China 2025," an ambitious state-led project to increase high-tech manufacturing in several sectors including electric vehicles, aerospace, robots, biotech, medical equipment, pharmaceuticals, and information technologies, including AI. Xi began decoupling from the American economy long before such policy debates in Washington started.

Xi's attacks on China's most profitable global companies, renewed support for China's state-owned enterprises, new moves against international competition, and deeper state intervention in the economy more generally have fueled speculation about his commitment to basic market principles and therefore the long-term viability of China's current economic model. Tens of thousands of China's most successful entrepreneurs have fled the country. Public-opinion polls show that the Chinese have become much more pessimistic about their economic prospects compared to twenty years ago.[67] In 2023, Xi and his new party leadership tried to reaffirm their commitment to markets and entrepreneurship to reattract investment from Chinese and foreign capitalists but with limited results.[68]

Xi also restricted regional autonomy more severely in Hong Kong, Tibet, and Xinjiang. Pro-Beijing authorities in Hong Kong passed a national security law in 2020 that criminalized previously tolerated political behavior. They arrested many prominent critics, including democratic activist Joshua Wong and media entrepreneur Jimmy Lai, and in 2021, they shut down several independent media outlets, among them Lai's *Apple Daily* newspaper and the Next Digital media company. In 2024, they jailed two more editors of the once-independent news outlet *Stand News*.[69] That same year, Hong Kong's pro-Beijing legislature passed an even more draconian national security law that gives authorities the power to arrest citizens for expressing even the most minor criticisms of the regime. In Xinjiang, the CCP has erected internment camps for mass detention, forced assimilation, and surveillance of roughly one million Uighurs and ethnic minorities, actions that have drawn comparisons to Soviet-era camps and other cultural genocide campaigns.[70] Human rights organizations have uncovered similar practices in Tibet.[71] In 2024, Freedom House ranked China one of the most repressive autocracies in the world.[72]

In parallel to increased domestic repression at home, Xi has sought to expand China's international influence dramatically. If Deng Xiaoping, Jiang Zemin, and Hu Jintao deliberately aspired to keep a low profile in international affairs, Xi brashly departed from that tradition, using methods detailed in subsequent chapters that are much more aggressive and coercive. Of course Xi was not the first leader to seek greater Chinese influence on world politics, but his aspirations and actions exceeded those of all previous CCP leaders except Mao.

THE TRUMP EFFECT

While Xi's autocratic policies at home and belligerent actions abroad during the Obama years eroded US-China relations, Trump's election in 2016 accelerated their deterioration. If Nixon was the leader who most profoundly pushed US-China relations in a positive direction, President Trump—or, more precisely, the Trump administration—might be remembered, depending on future trajectories, as the US leader who most consequentially pushed US-China relations in a confrontational direction. Senior officials from Trump's first administration agree with this assessment and are proud of that fact.

Trump himself expressed both cooperative and confrontational impulses regarding China and Xi. As a presidential candidate, Trump stated caustically, "We can't continue to allow China to rape our country,"[73] but he blamed Obama, not Xi, for the deteriorating state of US-China relations. As president-elect, Trump broke long-standing protocol and accepted a congratulatory call from Taiwanese president Tsai Ing-wen during which he allegedly questioned the US commitment to the One China policy. After his inauguration, however, Trump pivoted to court Xi, first at his resort in Florida in April 2017 and then when visiting Beijing later that year.[74]

Trump bragged that he had "developed a friendship" with Xi similar to his new rapport with Putin.[75] Over the next four years, Trump often praised Xi's leadership, never raised issues of human rights abuses inside China, rarely discussed the defense of Taiwan, and, unlike his foreign policy team, expressed no alarm about Xi's alleged efforts to dominate the world and export Marxism-Leninism.

The Trump administration, however, articulated much more bellicose views and aspired to pursue more aggressive strategies toward the PRC. Trump's 2017 national security strategy portrayed China, alongside Russia, bluntly as a "revisionist" power that sought "to shape a world antithetical to US values and interests" through its displacement of the United States in the Indo-Pacific.[76] Trump officials described the China threat in increasingly dire terms and highlighted the ideological dimension of US-China competition. In 2019, Secretary of State Mike Pompeo warned, "China wants to be the dominant economic and military power of the world, spreading its authoritarian vision for society and its corrupt practices worldwide."[77] In May 2020, a White House publication, "The United States' Strategic Approach to the People's Republic of China," asserted, "The CCP has chosen instead to exploit the free and open rules-based order and attempt to reshape the international system in its favor. Beijing openly acknowledges that it seeks to transform the international order to align with CCP interests and ideology."[78] National security adviser Robert O'Brien described Xi as Stalin's successor.[79] FBI director Christopher Wray cautioned that Chinese leaders have launched a "generational fight" to "become the world's only superpower by any means necessary."[80] These rhetorical positions marked a radical departure from previous administrations going back to Nixon.

The first Trump administration did more to describe the China threat than address it. They failed to implement a strategy of containment on the scale of their Cold War predecessors. The first Trump administration did not increase defense spending to Cold War–era levels, initiate a multilateral alliance in Asia akin to NATO, launch a foreign economic assistance program to compete with China's Belt and Road Initiative, or fund massive research and development spending at home as American presidents did to address the Soviet threat. America's first Cold Warriors also succeeded in creating a new, multifaceted set of international organizations to expand

US global power and contain Soviet influence, but Trump instead pursued disengagement and isolationism. Most detrimental, in his first term, Trump withdrew from the Trans-Pacific Partnership, undermining the potential for a united front of major trading partners to confront Chinese influence. Trump also quit numerous international agreements and treaties, including the Paris Climate Accords, the Iran nuclear deal, the UN Human Rights Council, the INF Treaty, the Open Skies Treaty, and the World Health Organization; he criticized the European Union, the World Trade Organization, and NATO, even threatening to pull out of NATO altogether. Trump even imposed new tariffs on American allies, a practice he continued with greater vigor early in his second term.

Unlike Cold War presidents, Trump devoted little energy to promoting democracy or universal values and weakened America's ability to compete ideologically with China by undermining democracy and fueling polarization at home. In his famous article for *Foreign Affairs* published in 1947, writing under the pseudonym X, George Kennan warned, "Indecision, disunity, and internal disintegration within this country [the US] have an exhilarating effect on the whole Communist movement."[81] That was precisely what Trump did during his first term, punctuated most tragically by his encouragement of the violent riot at the US Capitol on January 6, 2021, to try to interrupt the official certification of the 2020 US presidential election.

While failing to implement a new comprehensive containment doctrine or a general strategy of democratic renewal at home or abroad, Trump's first administration did implement some consequential policy changes toward China regarding bilateral trade and investment.[82] In his Section 301 report, US trade representative Robert Lighthizer spelled out China's negative impact on the US economy.[83] The Trump administration subsequently labeled China a currency manipulator and imposed tariffs on roughly half a billion dollars of Chinese imports. The Trump administration's new restrictions on trade fueled doubt in both countries about the value of free trade and direct foreign investment. In addition, the Trump administration rightly focused more attention on reducing China's illegal theft of American intellectual property.[84]

The Trump administration also banned the use of Huawei 5G technology in the United States, compelled some allies to do the same, and expanded efforts to isolate Chinese digital and communications technologies by launching the Clean Network program, which excluded Chinese telecommunication firms, apps, cloud providers, and undersea cables from internet infrastructure used by the United States and partner countries.[85] The Trump administration tightened restrictions on Huawei's access to chips made or designed with US equipment and software.[86] Trump's team scrutinized Chinese investments in the United States more vigorously, eventually reducing Chinese venture capital to a trickle.

Regarding human rights violations inside China, Trump personally never criticized Xi and allegedly even praised Xi for cracking down on Xinjiang and Hong Kong.[87] However, his administration sanctioned companies using forced labor in Xinjiang, and Secretary of State Pompeo issued a forceful statement accusing China of committing genocide in the region.[88] Beijing responded by sanctioning two dozen Trump officials, including Pompeo and national security adviser O'Brien.

During the first term, Trump's team actively sought to reduce what it believed to be harmful Chinese influence operations in the United States, pledging to respond "to CCP propaganda in the United States by highlighting malign behavior, countering false narratives, and compelling transparency."[89] The FBI launched its China Initiative, which aimed to curtail Chinese espionage and influence campaigns inside the United States. The Department of Education expanded its scrutiny of foreign gifts to US universities, and numerous Chinese students with military affiliations were banned from attending American universities. The Trump administration even suspended the Fulbright exchange program and compelled Chinese media organizations working in the United States to reduce their staff. The Chinese consulate in Houston was forced to close in 2020 over concerns that the CCP was using the facility to steal American intellectual property. During this era, some states even banned Chinese nationals from buying property. Xi responded. The Chinese government expelled a dozen American journalists, closed the US consulate in Chengdu, and sharpened its public attacks on American foreign policies in what some American specialists labeled "wolf warrior diplomacy."

Bilateral relations worsened during the COVID-19 pandemic. China delayed the release of the virus's genetic sequencing, and international research teams seeking to study the virus's origins in Wuhan, China, were denied access. Trump referred to COVID-19 as the "China virus" and blamed the CCP for its spread in the United States. Beijing, in turn, propagated outrageous lies, claiming that the US Department of Defense released the coronavirus in Wuhan. The absence of international cooperation to fight the virus, mainly due to US-China tensions, was striking and tragic.

CONFRONTATION CONTINUES

The first Trump administration succeeded in radically reframing US-China relations. By 2021, Trump's assessment of the China threat had become conventional wisdom in Washington's foreign policy circles and among Democratic and Republican policymakers. After Biden's election, Chinese officials hoped for change, speaking openly about the need for a "reset" in US-China relations. However, Biden and his new national security team showed little interest in a major policy change. Instead, they affirmed China as the paramount security challenge—as they called it, the "pacing challenge"—for the United States in the twenty-first century. When asked about this in his confirmation hearing, Secretary of State Blinken noted, "President Trump was right in taking a tougher approach to China."[90] A few months later, Blinken called the US-China relationship "the biggest geopolitical test of the 21st century" because "China is the only country with the economic, diplomatic, military, and technological power to seriously challenge the stable and open international system."[91] Biden's national security strategy affirmed bluntly, "The People's Republic of China harbors the intention and, increasingly, the capacity to reshape the international order in favor of one that tilts the global playing field to its benefit."[92]

If Biden and his team did not depart fundamentally from the Trump administration's diagnosis of the China challenge, they did pursue some different policy prescriptions. As explored in detail in subsequent chapters, the Biden administration attempted to engage and contain simultaneously, what they called their "three Cs" strategy—cooperate, compete, and confront. At his first in-person meeting with Chairman Xi, in Bali, Indonesia, on November 14, 2022, on the sidelines of a G20 summit, Biden cautioned that "this competition should not veer into conflict and underscored that the United States and China must manage the competition responsibly and maintain open lines of communication."[93] On November 15, 2023, Biden and Xi held a more extended meeting on the sidelines of the APEC summit in San Francisco, where both leaders leaned into the need for greater bilateral stability and communication. In parallel, however, the Biden administration developed an industrial policy of economic decoupling—they preferred the term *derisking*—that included more export controls on sophisticated technologies to China, new comprehensive restrictions on both outbound and inbound investment, and substantial subsidies for both American and foreign firms to stimulate new manufacturing in the United States. Biden did not retire Trump-era tariffs on Chinese goods and, in May 2024, implemented new ones on Chinese solar panels, semiconductors, electric vehicles, steel, aluminum, ship-to-shore cranes, and medical products such as syringes and surgical masks.[94] The Biden administration made several enhancements to America's deterrence posture in Asia, including signing the AUKUS agreement between Australia, the United Kingdom, and the United States to build nuclear-powered submarines jointly and enhance security cooperation more generally on emerging technologies; negotiating a new basing agreement with the Philippines; hosting the first ever trilateral Camp David summit between the United States, Japan, and South Korea in 2023; and upgrading the Quad, a nonmilitary partnership between Australia, India, Japan, and the United States, to the head-of-state level.

The dynamic of confrontation continued during the first months of the second Trump administration. In April 2025, the Trump administration imposed tariffs on almost every country in the world, the most sweeping set of tariffs ever announced in a century. After markets responded negatively to these tariffs, Trump backed down by announcing a ninety-day suspension of most duties—except for those on China, which he instead raised to 145 percent in retaliation for new Chinese tariffs on American goods. American and Chinese officials agreed to suspend these high tariff rates for a few months, but Trump's move suggested that he aims to accelerate economic decoupling between the two world's largest economies and do so at a much faster rate than he pursued during his first term. Rhetorically, Trump still held out the possibility of doing a grand bargain with China. In announcing these new extraordinarily steep tariffs, Trump said, "Xi is a smart guy and we'll end up making a very good deal."[95] Unlike senior members in his first administration, Trump does not use ideologically charged language to describe Xi or China. For instance, he has never compared Xi to Stalin.

As this book goes to press, US-China relations seem to be stuck in a deep period of confrontation. The combination of China becoming the world's second superpower, competing regime types and ideologies, and confrontational policies championed by Xi, Trump, and Biden have pushed ties between the United States and China to their lowest point in decades, probably since China's intervention in the Korean War over seventy years ago.

Part II

THE PRESENT

Chapter 3

THE END OF AMERICAN HEGEMONY

THE END OF the Cold War was the peak of American power. Both Chinese and Russian leaders at the time recognized the United States as the world's sole superpower—or, as German journalist Josef Joffe put it, an "überpower."[1] A decade later, French foreign minister Hubert Védrine still described the US as a "hyperpower" dominating "all arenas: the economic, technological, military, monetary, linguistic or cultural one."[2] America's overwhelming military and economic capabilities led analysts to characterize the international system as unipolar. The American system of democracy was admired globally too. American capitalism and US soft power won universal praise. Consumers everywhere, from Moscow to Luanda, wanted more Levi's, McDonald's, and Michael Jackson. Some celebrated American hegemony.[3] Others feared it.[4] Few, however, disputed it.

Much has changed since then. Three decades later, American power and perceptions of it at home and abroad have changed dramatically. Adversaries in Russia, China, and Iran as well as many US allies now describe our current era as one of American decline. In pursuit of "America First," the first Trump administration dampened hopes for those wanting to see the United States lead the free world and encouraged those tired or fearful of American hegemony. President Trump's reelection in 2024 has convinced many that the age of American leadership in the world is over. Some in Russia even speculated that the United States would struggle to exist as a state, comparing Trump's return to Gorbachev's rule, at the end of which the Soviet Union collapsed.[5]

Predictions of America's demise are premature. While American power has declined in relative terms since its peak in the 1990s, and Chinese and Russian power has grown in several dimensions, the US remains the most powerful country in the world. It is likely to maintain that position for the foreseeable future. As long as Trump does not permanently damage US relations with democratic allies, the balance of power will continue to be more favorable for the United States and the democratic world than for China, Russia, and the autocratic world. But the balance of power today has changed significantly since the days of American hegemony at the end of the Cold War. Crafting American foreign policies that address this new and evolving balance of power is a central challenge of our time.

WHAT IS POWER?

Before comparing the relative power of the United States, China, and Russia, we should define *power*. It is a hard challenge. Harvard professor Joseph Nye offered a simple and compelling definition: "The ability to affect others to get the outcomes one wants."[6] When the actors in question are countries, this concept of power is the ability of country A to get country B to do something that country B would not otherwise do.[7] The limits of this definition is that power can be measured accurately only after its use. Thankfully, military power is not used often, so we must measure proxies instead.

We know from history that simply counting capabilities is not the same as measuring the outcomes produced by these capabilities after use. Think about how many times we have miscalculated Soviet and Russian power over the past century. Just a decade before the Soviet Union collapsed, the CIA assessed the USSR to be twice as powerful as the United States.[8] After the Soviet Union collapsed in 1991, our assessments of Russian power swung too far in the opposite direction: Leaders and scholars thought that Russia was too weak to ever recover its great power status.[9] In May 2001, I met President George W. Bush in the White House a few weeks before his first meeting with President Putin (he even gave us a tour of his new home!). During our discussion, I told him why I rejected the conventional wisdom that Russia was a declining power, citing our inaccurate long-term projections of Soviet power after the Bolshevik Revolution and the Russian civil war. We had assumed then that Soviet Russia would be weak for a long time, but the USSR came roaring back in the 1930s when we were experiencing the Great Depression, and even more so after World War II, when the Soviet Union emerged as the world's second superpower. I worried we were making the same mistake again.[10] Bush liked the analogy. Two decades after that meeting, as discussed in detail in the next chapter, Russia reemerged as a major power in Europe, if not the world.

In 2022, we got Russian power wrong again, this time overestimating it. The Biden administration and many independent analysts predicted that the allegedly mighty Russian armed forces would occupy Kyiv, Ukraine's capital, in a matter of days after Putin gave the order to invade Ukraine on February 24, 2022. Three years later, they still have not made it to Kyiv.

And it is not just Russian military power that is hard to measure. Before the United States and its allies launched Operation Desert Storm in 1991 to liberate Kuwait from Iraq's occupation, the Iraqi army was ranked the fourth most powerful in the world. Yet the US and its allies destroyed this allegedly mighty army in just a few days. That same powerful American military, alongside allied troops, invaded Afghanistan in 2001 but with a drastically different outcome. Any rational assessment of the capabilities of the United States and its allies versus the Taliban at the time would have concluded that we had an overwhelming advantage. But twenty years later, in 2021, the United States lost the war and pulled out of Afghanistan, and the Taliban seized control again.

Quantifying and comparing power is even more complex today now that more amorphous dimensions of power, like artificial intelligence, biotechnology, quantum computing, educational systems, private sector inputs, and big data, must be added to our equations.[11]

Measuring military power without evidence from outcomes on a battlefield is especially difficult. It usually lacks precision and relies on hypotheticals and counterfactuals. In assessing the balance of military power between the United States, Russia, and China, we (thankfully) have no recent examples of great power wars. So we must instead estimate the *potential* for using military and other coercive power by assessing each side's latent capabilities, including economic resources, as the following two chapters do in detail. Chapter 4 compares Russian and American power. Chapter 5 compares Chinese and American power. These chapters also try to assess intentions to use power. Commitments to using power, ability to bluff, risk tolerance, and confidence are attributes of a leader or state that affect the ability to project power. Some leaders are more war-prone and more willing to use power than others, even with fewer capabilities. Putin falls in this category. Russia's power has grown steadily, though incrementally, since the 1990s, but Putin has demonstrated a greater willingness to use military force than his predecessors, as revealed in Chechnya in 1999, Georgia in 2008, Ukraine in 2014, Syria in 2015, Kazakhstan in 2022, and in Ukraine again in 2022. Just counting Russian soldiers, tanks, jets, population, or GDP would not have been enough to predict these wars. Intentions matter too.

Persuasion and inducements are other forms of power. In addition to coercion (military intervention, economic sanctions, and isolation), country A can get country B to do something through cooperative incentives (for example, visits to the Oval Office, votes in the United Nations, and economic payoffs). Even more so than coercive power, cooperative power is difficult to measure. While many assessments count weapons and military spending, few track metrics of persuasive diplomacy.

Tracing shifts in the balance of power over the past thirty years requires assessing the rise of China and Russia. However, it also involves analyzing actions taken by US leaders that reduced American power relative to these rising powers. Before the following two chapters compare US and Russian power and US and Chinese power today, the remainder of this chapter briefly sketches the history of American decisions and actions that weakened US power, independent of actions taken by either China or Russia.

AMERICAN UNILATERAL ACTIONS DECREASING MILITARY POWER

As the Cold War wound down and the US emerged as the world's unchallenged hegemon, the rules-based international system faced a significant challenge: a war of annexation in the Middle East. On August 2, 1990, Iraq's armed forces invaded and occupied Kuwait, a close American partner. By using military force, Iraqi dictator Saddam Hussein violated two of the central norms of the international system, codified in the United Nations Charter: the defense of sovereignty and the rejection of annexation.

So President George H. W. Bush decided the world had to respond. He successfully obtained the UN Security Council's authorization to use military force to liberate Kuwait, explaining to a joint session of Congress on September 11, 1990, "We're now in sight of a United Nations that performs as envisioned by its founders."[12]

The US-led military campaign to liberate Kuwait and defeat Iraq's armed forces was a stunning and swift military victory. The US possessed more military power than any other country but also exercised considerable persuasive power by organizing dozens of coalition partners to support this military effort. Such a robust multilateral response confirmed that the world embraced the norm of sovereignty as a foundational value of global order. Regarding military power and international legitimacy, the Gulf War marked the peak of American power.

DISARMAMENT

Soon after the end of the Gulf War in 1991, American leaders decided to reduce US military power. The Soviet Union was collapsing, and the military threat from great powers seemed small. The most dramatic decrease in American military power occurred with nuclear weapons, calibrated in concert with first Soviet and then Russian counterparts. President George H. W. Bush and Soviet leader Mikhail Gorbachev signed the bilateral START treaty in 1991, which capped the number of deployed warheads at 6,000, thereby reducing the number of deployed nuclear weapons in the world by roughly 80 percent. The Strategic Offensive Reductions Treaty (SORT), signed in 2002, lowered the number of deployed nuclear weapons to 2,200 each. The 2010 New START treaty reduced American and Russian nuclear arsenals even further, restricting each side's deployed warheads to 1,550 and delivery vehicles (intercontinental ballistic missiles, submarine-launched ballistic missiles, and bombers) to 800. The Obama administration stopped the development of new warheads, a decision the Trump administration reversed and the Biden administration amended. However, as detailed in the following two chapters, that downward trajectory is over. China is significantly expanding its nuclear arsenal, and Russia has unilaterally suspended its participation in the New START treaty. The era of nuclear arms control between great powers may now be over, at least for the foreseeable future.

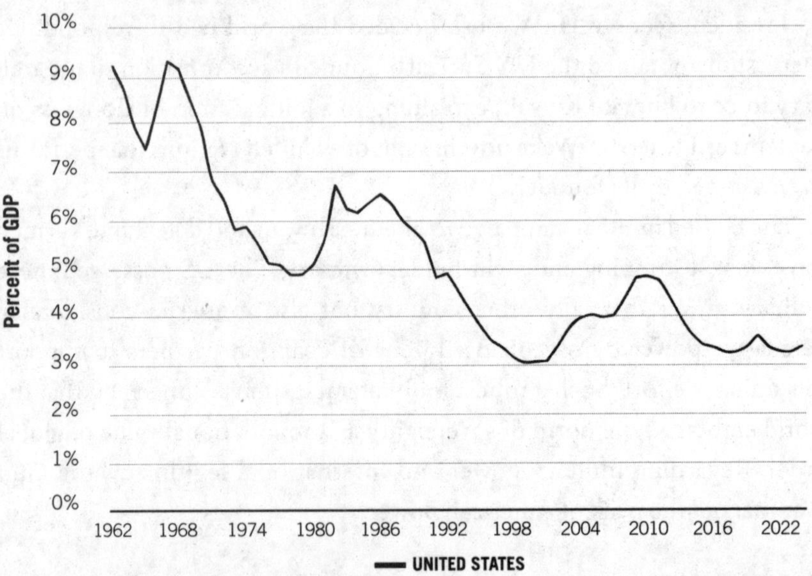

Figure 3.1 US Military Expenditures as a Share of GDP, 1962–2024

Source: Stockholm International Peace Research Institute, 2025

As they cut America's nuclear arsenal, US leaders also reduced spending on conventional forces and weapons at the end of the Cold War. During the Cold War, American military spending peaked at 9.3 percent of GDP, slightly dipped in the 1970s, then increased again in the 1980s under President Ronald Reagan. After the Cold War ended, military spending dropped dramatically, similar to the demobilization pattern after World War II.

Under both Democratic and Republican presidents, the US defense budget fell every year between 1987 and 1998 (with one exception, 1992). There was a slight uptick in 1999, followed by more cuts until 2002. President George H. W. Bush celebrated these cuts as the "peace dividend." As he explained in his January 1992 State of the Union address, "Two years ago, I began planning cuts in military spending that reflected the changes of the new era. But now, this year, with imperial communism gone, that process can be accelerated."[13] Clinton cut defense spending even further.

After al-Qaeda attacked the United States on September 11, 2001, US defense spending increased again until 2010, when the Obama administration reversed that trend. The Trump administration increased military spending again, a trend that has continued ever since, though at a modest rate that only at times has outpaced inflation. As a percentage of GDP, American acquisition spending dropped from 3 percent in the 1980s to roughly 1 percent today.[14]

Defense expert James Cunningham summarized what this "procurement holiday" meant for the US military: "From 1991 to 2006, the United States acquired, on average, just six major ships, 68 fighter and attack aircraft, and 334 tanks, artillery, and armored vehicles per year. Compare this to the average annual procurement rates in the final 15 years of the Cold War: 19 ships, 349 fighter and attack aircraft, and 2,083 tanks, artillery, and armored vehicles."[15] Despite these post–Cold War spending and procurement cuts, the United States has maintained advantages in many military domains compared to China and Russia. But these declines in spending and acquisition, particularly on naval assets, have allowed our rivals to close the gap in capabilities.

WARS OF NECESSITY AND CHOICE

Even while cutting military spending, American presidents still used hard power abroad throughout the 1990s. The United States deployed military force to overthrow President Noriega and reestablish democratic rule in Panama in 1989, liberated Kuwait in 1991, briefly intervened in a civil war in Somalia in 1992, took a leading role, including deploying armed forces, in ending wars in the Balkans in the 1990s, and led NATO in the bombing campaign against Serbia in 1999 to stop president of Yugoslavia Slobodan Milosevic's slaughter of Muslims in Kosovo.

The American use of military power abroad spiked dramatically in response to al-Qaeda's terrorist attacks on September 11, 2001. In reaction to that horrific day, President Bush launched a "global war on terror" that started first in Afghanistan in 2001 and expanded to Iraq in 2003. Bush garnered broad international support for American strikes on al-Qaeda in Afghanistan. The UN Security Council voted unanimously in favor of Resolution 1378, calling for the UN's central role in establishing a transitional administration and an international security assistance force. For the first time in history, NATO leaders invoked Article 5, which states that "an armed attack against one or more of them [NATO allies] in Europe or North America shall be considered an attack against them all."[16] Bush reframed American national security interests as the "Freedom Agenda," arguing that "sixty years of Western nations excusing and accommodating the lack of freedom in the Middle East did nothing to make us safe."[17] To implement this agenda in Afghanistan, American forces had to not only overthrow the Taliban and destroy al-Qaeda but also occupy the country, provide security, and rebuild the state until an Afghan democratic government could take root. Over the next twenty years, US soldiers, intelligence officers, diplomats, development specialists, and dozens of other multilateral actors attempted to transform Afghanistan's political system, economy, and society. These efforts were costly; over 168,000 Afghans, 2,300 US soldiers, and 1,100 allied troops were killed, and roughly a trillion was spent by the United States and another forty-nine billion by coalition allies.[18] Despite these efforts, two weeks before the United States completed its withdrawal from the country in August 2021, the Taliban seized power in a matter of days.

On March 20, 2003, the United States invaded Iraq. President Bush justified the attack as a preemptive war to stop Iraqi leader Saddam Hussein from developing weapons of mass destruction. The threat posed by Hussein's alleged arsenal turned out not to be as imminent as the US intelligence community had predicted—a fact that undermined US global credibility and thereby diminished America's persuasive power in the world. The United Kingdom, Australia, and Poland joined the United States in this war of choice. But unlike the invasion of Afghanistan, neither the UN Security Council nor NATO supported this US war in Iraq. NATO allies, including Canada, France, and Germany, joined Russia and China in openly denouncing the invasion.

This war of choice initially looked like a resounding American victory: US-led forces marched to Baghdad and toppled Hussein's autocratic regime in a matter of weeks. In May 2003, President Bush declared the end of major combat operations. However, Bush expanded the aims of this war to include democracy promotion and state-building. The new US-supported Iraqi government struggled to consolidate democracy, and the American decision to dissolve the Iraqi army spawned the formation of an array of militias that continued to fight the American occupation.

In 2008, presidential candidate Barack Obama won the Democratic Party's nomination in part by pledging to end the war in Iraq. President

Obama kept that campaign promise and completed the withdrawal of US forces from Iraq in 2011. The power vacuum left by the American withdrawal, however, allowed the terrorist organization Islamic State in Iraq and Syria (ISIS) to seize control of parts of Syria and Iraq and create a new caliphate, eventually compelling Obama to redeploy US forces to Iraq and Syria in 2014. To this day, some American Special Forces remain in the region to fight ISIS and other terrorist groups.

As it did in Afghanistan, the US war in Iraq produced mixed results for American power and national security. Two decades of war resulted in the deaths of 4,700 American and allied soldiers and over 100,000 Iraqi civilians. The US and its allies spent close to $800 billion trying to consolidate a democratic state in Iraq, but with limited results.[19] In 2024, Freedom House ranked Iraq as "not free."[20] Bush's decision to invade Iraq without UN Security Council approval also damaged America's image as a responsible actor in the rules-based international order. This legacy lingers to this day. Whenever I criticized Russian belligerent actions abroad at public events while serving as the US ambassador in Russia during the Obama administration, I often heard as a retort, "What about Iraq?"

In 2011, the United States launched a third military operation in the greater Middle East in a decade, this time in Libya. President Obama, in concert with a handful of NATO allies and Arab partners, decided to use force—predominantly airpower—to stop the perceived threat of civilian slaughter about to be launched by Libyan dictator Muammar Gaddafi against residents of Libya's second-largest city, Benghazi. The initial objective of this bombing campaign was much more limited than the aim in Afghanistan and Iraq. The goal was to stop mass killing, not democratic regime change. Like it had for Afghanistan, the United Nations Security Council endorsed this military operation; American leaders and diplomats spent months working with their Russian and Chinese counterparts to secure their abstentions. As a member of President Obama's National Security Council, I was involved in those negotiations. In March 2011, I traveled with Vice President Biden to Moscow, where he met with President Medvedev and convinced him not to veto the UN Security Council resolution authorizing the use of force in Libya. Medvedev abstained on that UN vote, a decision that Putin later lambasted in public.

For a fleeting moment, it seemed like the permanent members of the UN Security Council were working together again to provide collective security, as they had done in response to Saddam Hussein's invasion and annexation of Kuwait. The bombing campaign did accomplish the stated objective of preventing the mass killing of civilians in Benghazi—and at a small cost to the United States and with no American soldiers lost.[21] However, US-led intervention also produced unanticipated effects: Gaddafi's government collapsed; Gaddafi himself was killed, though not by the American armed forces (by Libyan rebels); and the civil war widened and dragged on for years. Over the long haul, this UN-blessed military intervention did not provide better security for most Libyans.

As had happened in Libya, peaceful protests during the Arab Spring eventually devolved into a violent civil war in Syria. Syrian dictator Bashar al-Assad used chemical weapons against civilians, triggering calls for an international intervention to stop the slaughter. This time around, however, the UN Security Council did not approve the use of force, but it did agree to the international removal of Syria's stockpile of chemical weapons.[22] Disappointed by the outcome of the military intervention in Libya and lacking the support of both the UN Security Council and the US Congress, Obama decided against significant use of force in Syria. As already mentioned, the United States did intervene in eastern Syria in 2014, but to fight ISIS, not to weaken or overthrow al-Assad's dictatorship.

American involvement in these wars in the greater Middle East had consequences for the American military and security interests. First, these conflicts depleted American hard power and distracted US strategic planners from the rise of China and Russia. How big of a distraction and how many resources were wasted is hard to calculate, but think of the counterfactual: Had the United States not been attacked on September 11, 2001, and had Bush not invaded Iraq, the United States might have focused on procuring weapons and deploying forces necessary to meet the challenge of a rising China and Russia sooner. The pivot to Asia might have happened much earlier.

Some argue that the combat experience American armed forces obtained in these wars will help the United States fight future wars with main adversaries. However, it is difficult to know how transferable these skills will be. The skills and weapons needed to fight counterinsurgency wars in Afghanistan and Iraq have little in common with those needed to fight Russia in Europe—if that war, God forbid, starts—or a future US war with China to help defend Taiwan.

Second, American wars in the Middle East damaged our reputation as the leader of the liberal international order. If the US intervention in Kuwait to repel Iraqi forces in 1991 cemented America's image as a global superpower that abided by and defended the rules-based international system, the US invasion of Iraq produced the opposite effect. Today, when American policymakers criticize other countries' violations of international norms, foreign leaders remind them of the United States' similar unilateral actions in Iraq. This whataboutism haunts American diplomacy to this day. If *power* is "the ability to affect others to get the outcomes one wants," the Iraq War diminished American power by making it harder for subsequent presidents to persuade other countries to follow the US lead regarding security and normative issues.

Third, Bush's justification for invading Iraq was to advance freedom, which blurred the lines between military intervention and democracy promotion. This conflation has harmed American and international efforts to support democracy abroad through nonmilitary means.[23] Foreign policy elites and segments of American society resist democracy promotion efforts today because they associate it with our failures in Iraq, Libya, and Afghanistan and with military intervention in general. Trump tops this list. Advocates for defending human rights and promoting democracy abroad are labeled *liberal hawks*. I know this firsthand—that label has been used to describe me pejoratively for decades, even though I was never a cheerleader for the Iraq War.[24]

Fourth, these wars were expensive. The war in Iraq, including the cost of care for war veterans and interest on debt, is estimated to have run the United States two trillion dollars.[25] The war in Afghanistan had a similar price tag, exceeding two trillion on top of the expenditures associated with reconstruction efforts.[26]

Fifth, because of American wars in the region, US engagement with many developing countries became focused on the short-term objective of combating terrorism rather than on longer-term development and governance goals. Eventually, Chinese leaders happily jumped into the developmental vacuum left by the US and started to underwrite massive infrastructure projects in Asia and Africa while we funded counterterrorist programs. These legacies linger. Today, US assistance to the developing world is still heavily focused on military aid, while Chinese assistance is more focused on economic development. In his second term, as discussed in detail in subsequent chapters, Trump dramatically cut American economic and humanitarian assistance, making the US look like it only cares about military ties. In the meantime, China continues to enjoy a reputation as a nation concerned with the welfare of other countries.

Worst of all, American-led wars in the Middle East resulted in the tragic loss of life of soldiers and civilians from the United States, its allies and partners, and Afghanistan, Iraq, Libya, and Syria. These immense losses are especially tough to justify for Afghanistan, where the war ended with the Taliban in power—just as they had been before the war began.

AMERICA'S RELATIVE ECONOMIC DECLINE

In the 1990s, the American economy had no competitors. Worries about Japan's rise dissipated. China was in only the initial stages of market reforms and global engagement. The Russian economy suffered a decade-long depression worse than the American Great Depression. American hegemony nurtured international support for free markets and private property, which served US economic interests as well. Most of the world, including China, implemented the US system—back then, it was called the Washington Consensus—regarding it as the path to prosperity. Acceptance of American ideas for reforming economies, especially in China and post-communist Europe, generated new trade and investment opportunities for American companies.[27] The collapse of communism and the expansion of democracy fueled American prosperity.

Now, three decades later, as outlined in chapter 4, Russia's economy has recovered from the hardships of the 1990s despite new costs incurred from the 2022 invasion of Ukraine. As discussed in chapter 5, China has closed the economic gap with the United States.

American leaders made decisions independent of China and Russia that allowed this gap in economic power to close. First and foremost, American foreign policies helped the Chinese and Russian economies grow. Amer-

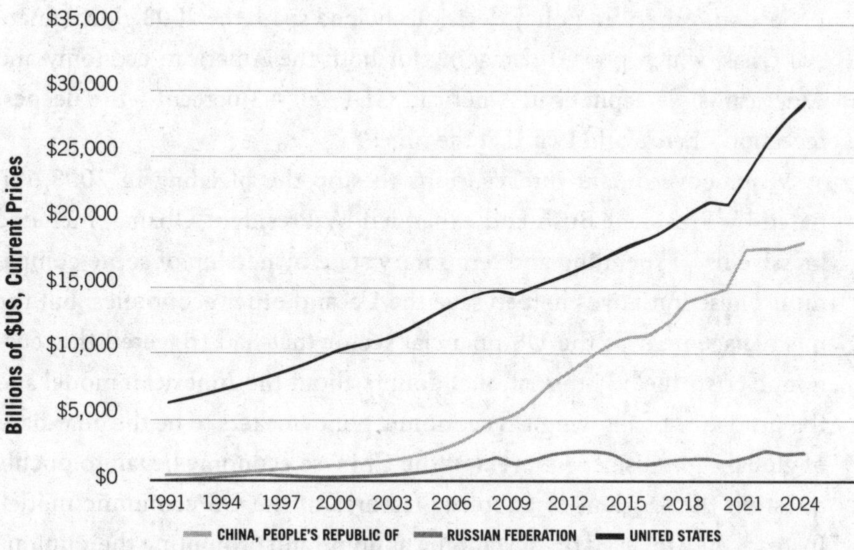

Figure 3.2 Gross Domestic Product: US, Russia, China, 1991–2024

Source: International Monetary Fund, 2025

ican leaders aided Russia's transition from communism to capitalism but paid less attention and devoted fewer resources to fostering the transition from dictatorship to democracy. Some experts at the time warned about the dangers of such a policy. As I wrote in *Foreign Affairs* in January of 1995, "The United States, in sum, has no national interest in promoting economic reforms in Russia that are not accompanied by a transformation of the political system. America's greatest national security nightmare would be the emergence of an authoritarian, imperialist Russian regime supported by a thriving market economy."[28] The same was even truer with respect to American policy decisions to spur Chinese economic growth, especially our assistance in getting China into the World Trade Organization with accompanying permanent normal trade relations status with the United States without trying more systematically to foster democratic change. At the time, guided by modernization theory, many American leaders and analysts thought that economic development in both Russia and China would lead the countries to democratize. That turned out not to be the case, at least not yet. However, US policies did help Chinese and Russian economies grow, thereby decreasing American relative economic power.

Second, American policy decisions helped spark the 2008 global financial crisis, which proved damaging for both the American economy and American-style capitalism. American GDP fell 4.3 percent—the deepest recession since World War II at the time.[29]

Major government interventions to stop the bleeding in 2008, initiated by President Bush and expanded by President Obama, included massive fiscal spending and temporary state ownership of some companies. These initiatives helped save the US and other economies, but the mismanagement of the US financial sector that had triggered this economic crisis fueled international doubts about the American model and the prudence of allowing US economic policymakers to be the guardians of global capitalism. Managers of the Chinese economy began to openly question the wisdom of adopting features of the US economic model. Instead, they focused on developing at home and promoting their unique state-led economic model abroad. In 2008, Beijing implemented what at the time was the world's most extensive stimulus package, helping China become the first major economy to recover from the global financial crisis and recording 8.7 percent economic growth in 2009 and 10.3 percent in 2010.[30] For many Chinese and foreign leaders, 2008 provided compelling evidence that the Chinese economic system was better than the American model.[31] As Vice Premier Wang Qishan told Treasury Secretary Hank Paulson, "You were my teacher, but now I am in my teacher's domain and look at your system. We aren't sure we should be learning from you anymore."[32] Paulson wrote in his memoir, "The [2008] crisis was a humbling experience, and this [conversation] was one of its most humbling moments."[33]

Third, Washington's response to the COVID-19 pandemic negatively affected the American economy. However, who benefited and lost in relative terms over the long run is still hard to assess. In 2020, the US economy contracted 3.4 percent.[34] In the first two years of the pandemic, 850,000 Americans died.[35] The COVID-19 pandemic exposed significant American dependencies on Chinese firms for drug production and other critical medical supplies. By 2021, however, the US economy had bounced back, growing by 5.7 percent. Initially, Xi Jinping's draconian lockdown policies seemed to contain the virus better and thereby prevent economic losses, but those policies proved unsustainable. Public protests, first in Shanghai and then in other major cities in the fall of 2022, triggered by a deadly apartment fire in China's Xinjiang region, compelled Xi to reverse course and lift repressive COVID restrictions overnight. In China, these severe lockdowns and underlying longer-term trends have created impediments for the economy to bounce back.

Early in his second term, President Trump initiated a series of radical, disruptive policies that could do long-term damage to American economic power. Most dramatically, in April 2025, Trump imposed what he called "reciprocal tariffs" on nearly the entire world. Trump and his economic advisers explained that they were using tariffs to fundamentally restructure the entire global economy. Global markets did not celebrate Trump's ideas, and instead crashed in response, compelling Trump to pause his tariff regime for ninety days. The enduring consequences of this dramatic change in US trade policy for the American economy are still unclear, but many financial forecasters have predicted major economic contraction. In addition, Trump 2.0 has slashed budgets for research and development, which, if continued for several years, will do major damage to American universities, a key component of the US innovation and entrepreneurship ecosystem.

ISOLATIONISM AND POLARIZATION

At the end of the Cold War, Americans were unified and confident about our place in the world. Few questioned the superiority of our democracy or market economy at home. Most also believed we had the right and responsibility to lead the world. Even Bill Clinton, whose 1992 presidential campaign slogan was "It's the economy, stupid"—an argument that President George H. W. Bush was too consumed with foreign affairs and not focused enough on Americans back home—continued many of Bush's engagement strategies. Most leaders in the Democratic and Republican Parties in the 1990s shared several core foreign policy objectives: promoting free trade, advancing democracy, and maintaining US leadership in global affairs.

Three decades later, that consensus has eroded considerably, thereby weakening America's capacity and Americans' willingness to project power abroad. Wars in Afghanistan, Iraq, Libya, and Syria—labeled *forever wars* by their critics in both political parties—fueled skepticism about America's role as the world's "policeman" and as a promoter of democracy abroad. In his first term, President Trump did not embrace the idea of America as the world's leader. Instead championing "America First," Trump pulled out of many international agreements and withdrew from global affairs more generally, and, when he did engage, often framed outcomes in zero-sum terms, even when dealing with allies.[36] The US commitment to supporting free trade withered. Trump lambasted China for stealing American jobs through, in his view, unfair trade agreements, and subsequently imposed significant tariffs on many Chinese products. Between Trump's first election victory in 2016 and his second in 2024, his voter base expanded, suggesting that these isolationist proclivities resonated with a large section of the US population. In 2023, Morning Consult's US Foreign Policy Tracker Index showed that 40 percent of Americans polled supported isolationism and only 17 percent favored engagement.[37] In 2024, this same poll revealed that only 19 percent of Americans thought that democracy promotion should be a foreign policy priority.[38] A 2024 Pew Research poll asked Americans whether President Biden should focus more on domestic or foreign policy. An astonishing 83 percent said domestic policy; only 14 percent said foreign policy.[39] After Biden's renewed emphasis on global engagement, Trump returned to the White House in 2025 with an even stronger commitment to an isolationist agenda. Trump immediately withdrew the United States from the Paris Climate Accords, the World Health Organization, and the UN Human Rights Council. He also ended funding to the United Nations' World Food Program and other health programs and threatened to slash financial support to the United Nations more generally. The second Trump administration has signaled its intent to withdraw from the World Trade Organization, reduce the US military presence in Europe, and some on the Trump team even hinted at the prospect of leaving NATO.

Parallel damage to the US's global influence has come from political polarization and challenges to democratic governance at home, punctuated most tragically by the assault on the US Capitol on January 6, 2021. Growing polarization and division between the Republican and Democratic Parties has made pursuing basic foreign policy objectives increasingly difficult. While America may still have more power than any other country, internal disagreement about how to use that power and less willingness to use it has considerably diminished America's global influence. Geopolitics abhors a vacuum, so, as outlined in subsequent chapters, the autocrats in China and Russia have taken advantage of the opportunity to reorder the world in their favor.

Chapter 4

RUSSIAN VS. AMERICAN POWER

AFTER THE SOVIET Union collapsed in 1991, many analysts and policymakers concluded that Russia had forever lost its great power status, dismissing the country as "Upper Volta with nukes," or as Senator McCain described, Russia was a "gas station masquerading as a country." This perception persisted for years after independence, especially when Russia experienced an economic meltdown in 1998 and suffered heavy losses in the second Chechen war. As a former diplomat and longtime Russia observer Thomas Graham wrote, "The precipitous decline of Russian power and influence in the world may stand as the most significant development for international relations of the last quarter of the 20th century. Never in modern history has a great power fallen so far so fast during peacetime."[1] Some even predicted the breakup of the Russian Federation.[2]

I lived in Russia in the 1990s. I was a graduate student at Moscow State University from 1990 to 1991. In 1993, I moved there again to open the Moscow office of the National Democratic Institute and was there again from 1994 to 1995 to launch the Moscow Carnegie Center, an overseas affiliate of the Carnegie Endowment for International Peace in Washington, DC. It was a chaotic, lawless time. The state seemed to have disappeared. We heard gunshots outside of our apartment at night; the trash was picked up only sporadically; and lots of stray hungry dogs chased me when I ran along the riverbank. But I believed this moment of state weakness was temporary. Russia had too many resources—educated people, minerals, oil, and nuclear weapons—to be stuck forever in some tertiary status in the global community.

In 2006, with Harvard scholar Alexandra Vacroux, I published an article called "Russian Resilience as a Great Power," explaining why Russia would eventually bounce back, just as the Soviet Union had after World War I, the Bolshevik Revolution, and the Russian civil war.[3] For me, in the 1990s and early 2000s, the more important question was whether Russia would consolidate democracy and remain inside our tent or drift back toward its long tradition of autocratic governance. A return to dictatorship would make Russia and the US adversaries, no matter how much power the Kremlin had. Tragically, that is precisely what happened.

The balance of power between the United States and Russia today has similarities with and differences from the Cold War. With China's rise, the international system is again gravitating toward bipolarity, but Russia is not one of the two poles. At the same time, Russia has emerged as a great power again, in the top three by some metrics and in the top ten by others. While Russia lags behind the United States and China by most measures of power, the Kremlin can influence international politics with its significant military, economic, cyber, and ideological capabilities, some of which the Soviet leaders did not have or did not use.[4]

Russia poses a significant threat to the United States and our allies today because of similarities and *differences* with the Cold War. First, unlike the situation during most of the Cold War, Russia is closely aligned with China today. American leaders must deal with two great powers working together, which is a serious challenge for American decision-makers.

Second, compared to Soviet predecessors and Chinese leaders today, Russian leader Vladimir Putin has demonstrated a greater willingness to deploy his government's resources to intervene in the domestic affairs of other countries in risky ways. In 2008, he invaded Georgia. In 2014, he annexed Ukraine's Crimea and supported a separatist war in eastern Ukraine. In 2015, Putin's air force rescued Syrian autocrat Bashar al-Assad, helping him stay in power for another decade. In 2016, Putin used cyber theft and disinformation to try to sway the outcome of the US presidential election in favor of Donald Trump, a candidate more sympathetic to Russia. Most boldly and tragically, Putin launched a full-scale invasion of Ukraine in February 2022 and annexed four Ukrainian regions—something that no Soviet leader since Joseph Stalin has dared to try.*

Third, Putin pursues not only security goals but also ideological objectives and revisions to the global order. As long as he remains in control, Putin will continue to deploy Russian power for revisionist purposes. Accurately assessing Russia's capabilities is an essential first step in devising effective US policies to deal with the threat the Kremlin poses today.

THE BALANCE OF MILITARY POWER

As discussed in the previous chapter, measuring military power is complicated. Before Putin invaded Ukraine in 2022, many analysts ranked Russia's military as the third most powerful in the world. That assessment seems inflated today. Measuring intangibles—the will to fight, training, and military tactics—is more complicated than counting soldiers or tanks. Quantifying new military capabilities, like artificial intelligence applications, software, and drones, is difficult too. Where wars are fought matters as well. Geographic proximity allows Russia to deploy additional assets to Ukraine and Europe quicker and more efficiently than the United States can.

The United States outranks Russia across almost all dimensions of power. Still, the gap in capabilities is narrower than many Americans believe, especially in the European theater. The image of Russia as a declining power is inaccurate. Today, Russia has the capacity to threaten American core security interests, and Putin has the will to do so.

NUCLEAR POWER

With respect to nuclear weapons, Russia and the United States have rough parity in terms of strategic capabilities, a legacy of Cold War cooperation and de-escalation. At the peak of nuclear weapons investment, the United States had an estimated 31,255 warheads, while the Soviet Union main-

---

* In this sentence, I deliberately used the phrase "full-scale invasion of Ukraine in February 2022" to underscore that February 2022 was an expansion of the Russian war started in 2014, not the beginning of a new war. To avoid repetition, however, I will not always use this exact phrase throughout the remainder of the book.

Table 4.1 Nuclear Arsenals: US vs. Russia, 2024[5]

Warheads	**United States**	**Russia**
Strategic Deployed	1,670	1,718
Strategic Reserve	1,830	1,114
Total Strategic Stockpile	3,500	2,832
Nonstrategic (Tactical) Deployed	100	0
Nonstrategic (Tactical) Reserve	100	1,477
Retired	1,477	1,150
Total Inventory	5,177	5,459
Delivery System	**United States**	**Russia**
Land (ICBM Launchers)	400	333
Sea (SSBN/Missiles)	14/280	12/192
Air (Bombers)	65	67

Source: Bulletin of the Atomic Scientists, *Nuclear Notebook, 2025. Numbers are estimates based on available open-source data as of May 2025.*

tained 40,159.[6] Over time, arms-control treaties reduced the size of both sides' arsenals while preserving relative numeric parity between the two superpowers. The most recent bilateral arms agreement—the New Strategic Arms Reduction Treaty (New START), signed by Presidents Dmitry Medvedev and Barack Obama in 2010—limited Russian and American arsenals to 1,550 deployed nuclear weapons and capped the total number of launch vehicles for these warheads at 800 for each side.

The signing of the New START treaty was an excellent day for US-Russia relations and me personally, as I helped negotiate the agreement. President Obama and a handful of us on his national security team flew to Prague, where on April 8, 2010, Obama and Medvedev signed this treaty. After we landed, I drove in Obama's presidential car—nicknamed "the Beast"—to Prague Castle and watched my boss wave to the crowds that lined the winding streets. The president was in an excellent mood that day: He was genuinely committed to reducing the number of nuclear weapons in the world. Back in Washington, we celebrated again by drinking champagne in the Oval Office after the US Senate ratified the treaty in December 2010. It is hard *to do* things in government; it is much easier *to be* in the government. But in 2010, we *did* something. We reduced the number of nuclear weapons in the world by roughly 30 percent.

Table 4.1 presents the estimated nuclear arsenals for the US and Russia in 2025. Both countries exceed the 1,550 limit of deployed warheads because the New START counts heavy bombers as only one warhead, even though American and Russian bombers are equipped to carry multiple warheads. Additionally, the treaty does not restrict non-deployed nuclear warheads (functional but kept in storage), retired warheads awaiting dismantlement, and tactical nuclear weapons, which are smaller in size and designed to target specific areas without causing mass destruction or radioactive fallout.

Together, Russia and the United States possess nearly 90 percent of the world's stockpile of nuclear weapons and remain by far the two preeminent global nuclear superpowers. According to 2025 estimates, discussed in detail in the next chapter, China maintains a much smaller but growing inventory of strategic warheads, around 600.[7] France has around 290 warheads, and the UK has 225.[8]

The New START treaty reduced the number of deployed nuclear weapons by the United States and Russia to the lowest level ever. Even after that achievement, American and Russian leaders have enough to blow up the planet with their respective arsenals, and there is growing concern that arms control may be a thing of the past. In 2019, the Trump administration withdrew from the Intermediate-Range Nuclear Forces Treaty, which banned all land-based intermediate-range missiles. In 2022, Russia suspended a vital component of the New START: on-site inspections of their deployed nuclear weapons. Russia has not formally abrogated the agreement, but the prospect of a follow-up treaty looks dim.

If the quantitative arms race of the Cold War slowed down, the qualitative arms race continued, especially in Russia. In his 2018 address to Russia's Federal Assembly, Putin unveiled five new or modernized delivery systems that could carry nuclear warheads: (1) Sarmat, an intercontinental ballistic missile capable of carrying multiple independent reentry vehicles; (2) Kinzhal, an air-launched ballistic missile; (3) Avangard, a boost-glide hypersonic vehicle; (4) Burevestnik, a nuclear-powered cruise missile; and (5) Poseidon, a nuclear-armed torpedo.[9] At around the same time, Putin announced another novel system, Tsirkon, a hypersonic cruise ship–launched missile. Putin asserted that with these weapons, "[Russia has] created offensive strike systems that the world has never seen."[10] Putin emphasized Sarmat's unlimited range, Avangard's ability to fly more than twenty times faster than the speed of sound, Burevestnik and Tsirkon's ability to evade US missile defenses, Poseidon's long-range and multiple-warhead capacity, and Kinzhal's rapid integration into Russia's air force with both nuclear and nonnuclear warheads. Kinzhal's nonnuclear version has since been used in Ukraine.[11] Only Sarmat and Avangard fall under the New START limits.[12] The Soviets had no comparable weapons. US military experts have questioned the capabilities of these weapons and delivery vehicles. For instance, the Ukrainian military has shot down several Kinzhal missiles using US-supplied Patriot defense systems, contradicting Putin's claim of an undetectable and undefeatable superweapon.[13] The bottom line, however, is that none of the new weapons contribute to a more stable nuclear balance.

US nuclear modernization has not kept pace. At the end of the Cold War, the US introduced a moratorium on nuclear testing and instituted the Stockpile Stewardship Program, which focused on extending the life of existing warheads by replacing aging materials and components.[14] In 2010 and 2015 nuclear-posture reviews, the Obama administration reaffirmed the US's commitment to the lifetime extensions of the existing nuclear infrastructure and did not propose new warhead designs. The Trump administration changed course, awarding a $13.3 billion contract to Northrop Grumman to develop a new ICBM, the ground-based strategic deterrent called Sentinel, to replace the aging Minuteman III ICBMs within a decade. However, it is undergoing extensive review and restructuring to minimize costs, which could affect the timeline for deployment.[15] The Pentagon estimates the program will cost around $141 billion, an 81 percent increase from the 2020 estimate.[16] The Biden administration expanded funding for developing a new W93 warhead, designed to be delivered by a submarine-launched ballistic missile (SLBM).[17] If funding continues, the W93 would be the first new US SLBM warhead deployed in decades.

The United States and Russia have also devoted significant resources to improving missile-defense systems. The United States is ahead, but Russian advances are closing this gap. Neither side can currently defend its territory from a whole-arsenal nuclear strike. At the beginning of his second term, President Trump proposed the construction of a "golden dome" to protect the entire country from a missile attack. Experts believe such a system would cost trillions and might not work, but the technology to deploy interceptors in space has advanced dramatically since Reagan first floated his idea for the Strategic Defense Initiative four decades ago.[18]

A final recent development in the nuclear power balance concerns new intentions to use them. More than any Soviet or American leader since 1945, Putin has talked bluntly about using nuclear weapons on the battlefield. Most alarming, when Ukraine's armed forces liberated swaths of territory previously occupied by the Russian army in the fall of 2022, Putin threatened to use "all available means to protect Russia and [its] people," including nuclear weapons, should the West continue to support Ukraine.[19] At the time, American intelligence assessed the probability that Putin would use a tactical nuclear weapon in Ukraine at 50 percent if Russian forces continued to be pushed out of Ukraine.[20] Since then, Putin has continued episodically to threaten to use nuclear weapons in response to alleged escalatory steps taken by the West in supplying Ukraine with new weapons. That is new and scary. That did not happen in the last decades of the Cold War.

CONVENTIONAL MILITARY POWER

During the Cold War, the Soviet Union and the United States maintained the two largest militaries in the world. On average, the US Army had around 2.6 million soldiers, whereas the Soviet army ranged between 2.8 and 5.3 million.[21] While the Soviet Union had an edge in ground forces, the United States maintained a lead in the air, at sea, and underwater. In this competition, no other country came close.

Following the collapse of the Soviet Union, Russian president Boris Yeltsin and his team of market reformers purposely cut military spending to try to balance the budget and reduce the military's political power.[22] While it seems hard to imagine now, US defense officials in the 1990s worried more about Russian military weakness than strength, especially fretting over the state's capacity to maintain control of its nuclear arsenal. Animated by the fear of "loose nukes," the US provided billions of dollars to the Russian government to help destroy or secure nuclear weapons. In 1996, the Russian army suffered an embarrassing defeat in the first Chechen war after two years of fighting, revealing Russian military weakness. Moscow won the second Chechen war (1999–2009) but at a tremendous cost to its army, Chechen civilians, and infrastructure. During the first decade of independence, Russia had no functional navy, and only a fraction of its air force was operational.

After becoming president in 2000, Vladimir Putin gradually changed course, allocating large percentages of the state budget to modernize Russia's military and intelligence services. In 2008, after Russia's poor but victorious performance in invading Georgia, Putin announced an even more extensive military reform: the New Look. The initiative aimed to modernize all weaponry in Russia's armed forces, create smaller but more efficient fighting forces, and introduce a contract-based system to hire professional soldiers to augment the conscripted armed forces. By 2012, the Ministry of Defense had reduced the size of the Russian army by one million service members and had made military contracts more lucrative, improving social benefits like working conditions, housing, welfare, and pensions for soldiers and their families. In 2011, Moscow adopted the State Rearmament Program with the goal of replacing or revamping 70 percent of the army's equipment. Putin also expanded his personal role in controlling the military.

In 2014, Putin used these modernized forces to occupy and annex Crimea. Western reporters described the Russian invaders as "lean and fit," "sober," and wearing "crisp and neat uniforms."[23] The following year, Putin successfully deployed his modernized air force in Syria to prop up his partner, Syrian dictator Bashar al-Assad.[24] Heavy investment in modernizing Russian capabilities seemed to be paying off, which led Putin to believe he could quickly win a war against Ukraine in 2022. He miscalculated.

As mentioned in the previous chapter, Russia's invasion of Ukraine highlighted the limitations of assessing military strength based solely on the number of soldiers and tanks, or amount of expenditures. In the first year of the war, Russia's military capabilities proved less formidable than Ukraine's much smaller and poorer fighting force. Ukrainian soldiers' strong will to fight proved to be a real advantage on the battlefield, especially given that

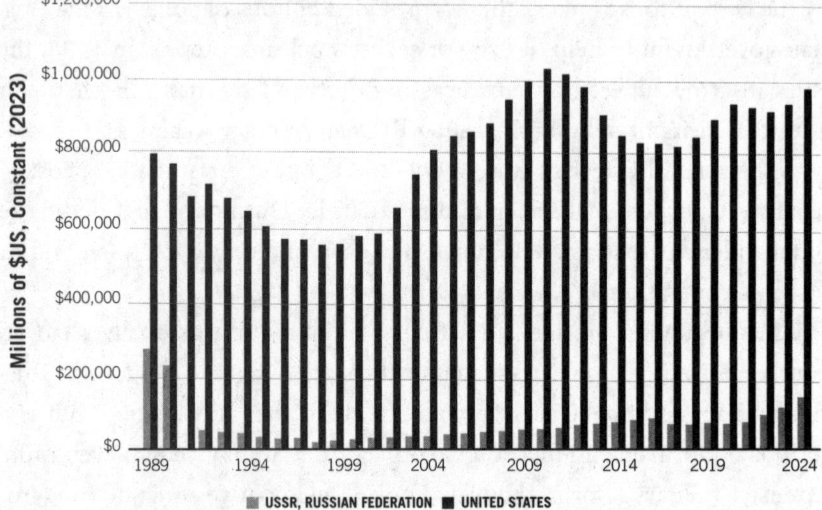

Figure 4.1 Military Expenditures: US vs. Russia, 1989–2024[25]

Source: Stockholm International Peace Research Institute, 2025

many of their Russian counterparts struggled to see the point of Putin's "special military operation." The war in Ukraine has also shown that Russia's military modernization has failed to achieve all its goals. As military expert Professor Zoltan Barany puts it, the "Russian military is a quintessential reflection of the state that created it: Autocratic, security-obsessed, and teeming with hyper centralized decision making, dysfunctional relations between civilian and military authorities, inefficiency, corruption, and brutality."[26] A few elite units did receive exceptional training, but most of the Russian army's training has been modest, especially by the standards of the world's best militaries.

As the war dragged on, however, Russia's armed forces grew in size and capability. Spending on new weapons expanded dramatically, and the Kremlin redirected massive economic resources to Russia's military-industrial complex. Russia has suffered tremendous casualties, but Putin has been able to replenish his army without triggering social unrest. As this book goes to press, optimism in Kyiv and Washington engendered by Russia's dismal military performance in 2022 is being replaced by anxiety about Russia's military renewal in 2025. Some leaders of NATO countries

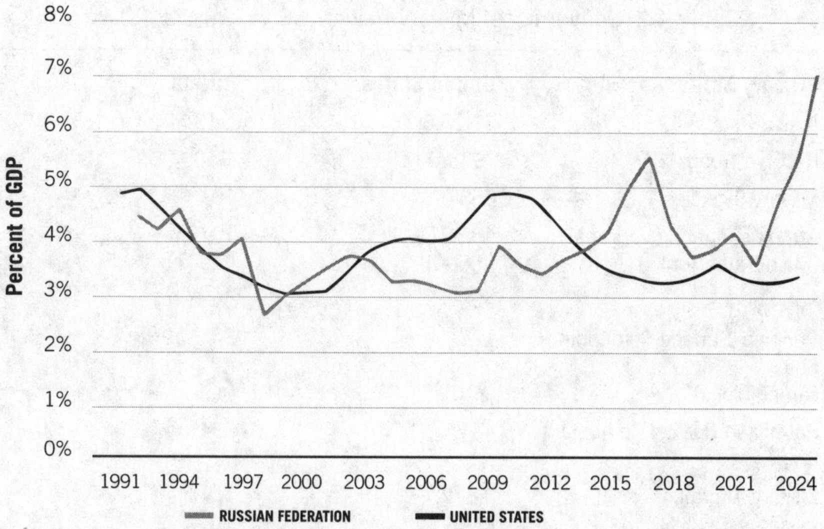

Figure 4.2 Military Expenditure of the US vs. Russia as a Share of GDP, 1991–2024

Source: Stockholm International Peace Research Institute, 2025

that share borders with Russia worry that Putin's army will emerge more capable from the war in Ukraine and present an even greater deterrence challenge for years to come.[27] Some even predict future Russian attacks on other European countries.

Regarding conventional military power, however, the United States still maintains a considerable advantage over Russia. Regarding spending, the United States remains well ahead of Russia and the rest of the world, as shown in figure 4.1.

Before invading Ukraine, Russia often spent more on its military than the United States as a percentage of GDP. After 2022, as figure 4.2 shows, Russian military expenditures have ballooned.[28] Nonetheless, even if it maintains these high levels of military spending for years to come, Russia will still not match American military power for decades to come if ever.

On another measure of military power, the number of troops, the United States is also ahead. We have maintained a larger active fighting force over the past ten years than Russia. Following Putin's 2022 invasion of Ukraine and waves of nationwide mobilization, that balance changed. The 2025 *Military*

Table 4.2 Conventional Military Power: US vs. Russia, 2024

Primary Military Assets	United States	Russia
Active Troops	1,315,600	1,134,000
Reserve Troops	797,200	1,500,000
Military Satellites	263	101
Armored Fighting Vehicles (Main Battle Tanks)	48,321 (2,640)	12,616 (2,901)
Submarines	65	51
Principal Surface Combatant Ships (Amphibious)	122 (210)	34 (43+)
Patrol and Coastal Combatant Ships	434	334
Military Aircraft	3,817	1,502
Military Helicopters (Tiltrotors)	5,581 (413)	1,101 (0)
Uninhabited Aerial Vehicles	1,264	*Data not available*
Artillery	6,540	6,215

Source: The Military Balance *2025, International Institute for Strategic Studies. Numbers are estimates based on available open-source data.*[29]

Balance report published by the International Institute for Strategic Studies (IISS) estimates that the United States and Russia had rough parity regarding the number of active troops in 2024, with the US maintaining an army of 1.3 million soldiers, sailors, and pilots and the Russian military contracting and drafting close to 1.1 million. Late in 2024, Putin ordered an increase in Russia's active service members to 1.5 million, which, if achieved, would make Russia's army the second largest in the world, behind only China.

At the same time, Russia's army continues to suffer heavy losses in Ukraine, and the nation's population was already declining before the war, constraining Putin's ability to maintain a massive army over the long run. The US does not face the same challenges: Its population is twice the size of Russia's and continues to grow, and the US is not losing giant numbers of soldiers every day in a conventional war. American soldiers are also much better trained and equipped than their Russian counterparts.

With respect to both the quality and quantity of weapons on land, sea, and air, the United States still holds major advantages over Russia.

On the ground, Russia had an advantage regarding main battle tanks (MBTs) before its 2022 invasion of Ukraine, with more than 3,000 MBTs compared to the United States' 2,645.[30] By early 2025, however, Russia had lost around 3,917 tanks of all types (2,838 destroyed, 158 damaged, 388 abandoned, and 533 captured).[31] Russian production of tanks, however, has also increased dramatically since the invasion of Ukraine and is estimated to be around one hundred each month. The IISS's 2025 *Military Balance* report estimated Russia to have 2,900 MBTs, which exceeds American numbers. However, most experts assess American tanks to be much higher quality than Russian equivalents.[32] The United States has a much larger stockpile of armored fighting vehicles than Russia, the quality of which is much better than Russia's. The protracted war between Russia and Ukraine has revealed the military utility of unmanned vehicles in the air and on the ground and the decreased effectiveness of tanks and armored fighting vehicles on open battlefields. Cheap unmanned weapons can easily target expensive tanks, destroying them for a comparatively low cost. The days of battlefield advantage being decided by numerical superiority of tanks might be over. Russia has made major advancements in drone warfare. The US military, perhaps with help from Ukrainian partners, needs to catch up.

Regarding manned aircraft, the American advantage over Russia remains vast. Moscow has improved its fourth-generation fighters, but its fifth-generation Su-57s have faced considerable delays in deployment.[33] Even with this advancement, Russia will not catch up with the US Air Force anytime soon. The American fifth-generation fighter, the F-35, is considered the most capable aircraft in history. In December 2022, the US Air Force unveiled the B-21 Raider, its first new strategic bomber in decades, an aircraft with unique stealth capabilities and longer ranges.[34] Russia is developing a next-generation strategic stealth bomber, the PAK-DA, but its production has been delayed to 2028 or 2029. Russia's long-range bombers would have difficulty avoiding US air defenses.

At sea, the United States retains considerable advantages. The United States has more and better ships, including aircraft carriers, destroyers, and submarines, to project power around the world. Russia's naval power development has been focused on enhancing coastal defense, using smaller combat ships with antiair or anti-surface weapons instead of investing in maritime warfare capabilities. Even in pursuing this mission, the Russian navy has struggled against Ukraine—a country without a navy—because of Kyiv's successful use of sea drones. Since 2022, Ukraine has destroyed an estimated twenty-eight Russian warships, compelling the Russian fleet to retreat from Sevastopol, Crimea.[35] International sanctions have hindered Russia's naval modernization, exacerbating difficulties faced by an already anemic shipbuilding industry.

Underwater, Russia has invested in improving submarine capabilities to support the Black Sea Fleet. The Russian navy has developed Borei-class submarines, which can carry up to sixteen missiles with six warheads each (though likely to carry only four warheads to comply with the New START);[36] Yasen-class submarines, allegedly capable of firing cruise missiles on both land and naval targets; and Kilo-class submarines, effective in coastal defense.[37] Russia is ahead of China in this domain, prompting some American admirals to express concern that Putin might help Xi modernize China's submarines as part of their deepening military relationship.[38] The American submarine fleet still maintains superior size and capability. According to the US Navy, this underwater fleet includes fifty-three fast-attack submarines, fourteen ballistic-missile submarines, and four guided-missile submarines.[39]

As discussed, Russia has invested heavily in developing new missiles that can be used to deliver both nuclear and conventional payloads. In November 2024, Russia used a new nuclear-capable intermediate-range ballistic missile, the Oreshnik, for the first time. Oreshnik travels at Mach 10, a speed that makes the missile incredibly difficult to sense and intercept, even for the best missile-defense systems. In response to China's buildup of short-range and intermediate-range missiles in Asia, discussed in the next chapter, the United States has been deploying more conventional missiles, especially on ships. The American military may now have to deploy more intermediate conventional missiles in Europe as well to deter Russia now that the INF Treaty, which prohibited such weapons, is no longer operable.

PRIVATE MILITARY COMPANIES

Russian private military companies (PMCs) were once an asset for Moscow to which the US had no parallel capability. Since 2013, the Kremlin has relied heavily on private military companies to pursue its foreign policy interests and project power abroad while formally denying any connection to the Russian state. Russia has roughly thirty-seven PMCs, twenty-seven of which are likely currently active.[40] The most prominent is the Wagner Group, now rebranded as Africa Corps. Putin has deployed Wagner mercenaries to, among other places, Ukraine, Syria, Libya, Sudan, the Central African Republic, Mali, Niger, and Burkina Faso to protect autocrats in exchange for mining rights and other financial concessions. Putin deployed these forces to Ukraine in 2022 to assist his conventional forces, particularly in the Battle of Bakhmut in eastern Ukraine. At the peak of Wagner's involvement in the war, this private army deployed twenty thousand soldiers in Ukraine, roughly 10 percent of the total Russian forces there.[41]

Throughout the war in Ukraine, tensions between Wagner leader Yevgeny Prigozhin and Russian generals in charge of conventional forces heightened. To eliminate the power contest and simultaneously preserve the PMC's fighting capabilities, Minister Sergei Shoigu ordered Wagner fighters to sign contracts with the Russian military, thereby bringing them under direct state control. Prigozhin resisted the incorporation of his private army into the Russian military, declined to sign the agreement, and accused Russian generals and the Minister of Defense of incompetence. In June 2023, Prigozhin launched an armed mutiny against the Russian Ministry of Defense, a dramatic showdown that ended in the negotiation of Prigozhin and Wagner's exile to Belarus. Two months later, the private plane carrying Prigozhin and his top associate Dmitry Utkin was shot down just outside of Moscow. After Prigozhin's assassination, Africa Corps is now more directly controlled by the Russian Ministry of Defense.

The Pentagon also hires private military organizations like Blackwater, now called Academi, to enhance American military capabilities. This private firm, for instance, has twenty thousand trained soldiers and over twenty aircraft.[42] The United States, however, does not rely on these private companies to advance security interests to the extent that the Kremlin does.

SPACE

During the Cold War, cooperation in space was one of the few win-win outcomes of Soviet-American diplomacy, a positive trend that continued between independent Russia and the United States for some time. In 1967, the United States and the Soviet Union signed the Outer Space Treaty, which prohibited the deployment of weapons of mass destruction in outer space.[43] In 1975, American and Soviet astronauts docked their vessels in space in a mission called the Apollo-Soyuz Test Project, which evolved into a long-term partnership at the International Space Station. In 2011, the National Aeronautics and Space Administration faced budget constraints and retired the space-shuttle program, instead relying on Russian vehicles for rides to the International Space Station.

Starting in the 2010s, however, the United States and Russia returned to more competitive rhythms in space, reminiscent of the early Cold War. In 2011, the Kremlin restored the Soviet-era global navigation satellite system (GLONASS) to its full capacity.[44] Though smaller than the US Global Positioning System, GLONASS offers Russia a degree of independence from Western-controlled satellite networks. In 2024, Russia operated 181 satellites, a significantly lower number than the United States' 5,184.[45] The US has a network of forty-nine communication satellites and fifty-six Earth-observation satellites; Russia has fifty-one and sixteen, respectively.[46] Russia has deployed a new early warning system, the Unified Space System, to better track ballistic missile launches; upgraded space-based intelligence, surveillance, and reconnaissance capabilities; and improved its hypersonic missile capabilities.

Russia's enhanced anti-satellite (ASAT) technology—that is, the ability to shoot down, jam, and spy on satellites—is especially concerning to American military planners. In 2021, Russia destroyed its own satellite in a direct-ascent anti-satellite test, producing debris that threatens to damage other satellites in orbit.[47] Since the US military relies on military and commercial satellites for communications to a much greater extent than either Chinese or Russian forces, ASAT technologies are threatening to the continuity of US military operations around the world.[48] According to US Space Force lieutenant general Nina Armagno, Russia and China will be able to put every US satellite at risk by 2025.[49] New Russian weapons can already target satellites in low Earth orbit and may soon be able to hit satellites in higher geostationary orbits. Russia has allegedly developed a nuclear weapon that, when exploded in space, produces an electromagnetic pulse that damages commercial satellites.[50]

Russia and China's advances in space have compelled the US to compete more aggressively in this domain. In 2019, the Trump administration established Space Command as the Eleventh Combatant Command and designated the US Space Force as the sixth branch of the US Armed Forces. In 2021, the Space Force submitted its first budget request for $15.4 billion and published *Space Power: Doctrine for Space Forces,* which called for the allocation of funds for a next-generation satellite system to track intercontinental ballistic missiles and increased investment in anti-satellite weapons.[51] The Space Development Agency has sought to acquire one hundred fifty satellites as part of the Proliferated Warfighter Space Architecture launched in 2023.[52] While developing new capabilities to protect existing assets in space, the US has also committed unilaterally not to conduct direct-ascent anti-satellite weapons tests and has called on other countries—especially Russia and China—to do the same.[53]

The US government has also strengthened cooperation with the private sector in space. In just fifteen years, commercial spending increased from $110 billion to $357 billion, accounting for around 80 percent of the total space economy.[54] In 2015, the Obama administration established the Defense Innovation Unit in Silicon Valley as part of the Department of Defense to encourage private innovation and military development more generally, including in space.[55] Companies like Planet, SpaceX, Axiom Space, Virgin Galactic, and Blue Origin have advanced the commercialization of space, completing trips into space with civilian crews, and companies such as Astranis have grown the commercial-satellite sector tenfold. SpaceTech Analytics has identified 5,582 US-based companies working on space technology, compared to only 8 in Russia.[56] In 2023, Russia conducted 19 orbital launch attempts; the United States carried out 109.[57]

US companies have recently developed a comparative advantage over their Russian counterparts in terms of costs of space launches. The launch cost per kilogram of payload for SpaceX is between $1,500 and $2,600, while the Russian company Proton has launch costs of $8,200 per kilogram.[58]

CYBER AND INTELLIGENCE

Assessing the balance of cyber power and intelligence capabilities is challenging, since most of these weapons, assets, and resources are classified.

The lines between intelligence gathering and malicious cyberattacks are blurred. The attacks often become evident only after an incident. While experts have only limited data to make assessments, most of them rank the United States first in cyber capabilities, with Russia and China often trading second and third places. An authoritative report published by the International Institute for Strategic Studies assessed that the US "retains a clear superiority over all other countries" both in its capabilities for defense in cyberspace and in its offensive operations.[59] In recent years, the Russian government has acquired substantial cyber capabilities and has been linked to dozens of cases of cyber-espionage.[60] Putin has dedicated immense resources to strengthening Russia's cyber power, keeping it firmly centralized in his government, unlike the more privatized American cyber ecosystem.

As with conventional military power, Putin has demonstrated a greater willingness than his American and Chinese counterparts to use cyber capabilities for malicious and belligerent purposes. In 2007, Russian hackers carried out a cyberattack against Estonia because the government in Tallinn moved a Soviet-era statue. When Russia invaded Georgia in 2008, Moscow executed distributed denial of service (DDoS) cyberattacks, flooding networks with data and overloading server capacity. In 2014, Russia used cyberattacks simultaneously with its physical operation to annex Crimea. In 2017, Russian military hackers launched one of the world's most damaging cyberattacks ever: They injected a rapidly propagating piece of malware called NotPetya into Ukraine, a program that irreversibly encrypted computers' master boot records and made many computers inoperable.[61] The disruption of global supply chains from the NotPetya attack produced billions in damages. Since invading Ukraine in 2022, Russian cyber warriors have attacked Ukrainian targets relentlessly to try to debilitate Ukraine's armed forces and the economy. Aided by the US and NATO allies, Ukrainian cyber operatives have executed defensive maneuvers to counter Russia's efforts, and they seem to have been effective. To the best of our knowledge, Ukraine has not suffered a massive digital blackout or catastrophic event triggered by a cyberattack.

Russia has also used cyber weapons against the United States. In 2022, the Department of Homeland Security's Cybersecurity and Infrastructure

Security Agency (CISA), in coordination with the FBI and the National Security Agency, took the unusual step of cautioning the American public about Russian cyber infiltration of critical American infrastructure.[62] Because US digital space is much more open, fragmented, and decentralized than Russia's, vulnerable American cyber targets are many. Russia's successful hacking of roughly two hundred and fifty government agencies and private businesses underscored how dependent the US federal government is on private companies to ensure its own cybersecurity. I myself have been attacked many times by Russian cyber agents. Of course, there might have been many Russian attacks that were not reported. However, the same is true for American cyberattacks inside Russia. Putin has little incentive to publicize these American operations.

The same opaqueness limits our ability to assess the balance of power between Russia and the United States regarding intelligence capabilities. During the Cold War, the Soviet Union and the United States had spy capabilities outpacing all others. After the collapse of the Soviet Union, resources for Russia's intelligence services dwindled, with many of the best and brightest spies flocking to the private sector, where they could translate their unique knowledge and networks, including international contacts, into wealth. Resources began to expand for Russian intelligence again when a KGB agent—Vladimir Putin—assumed the presidency in 2000. In particular, the Federal Security Service (FSB), the domestic successor organization to the KGB, grew dramatically. Though there is no published budget or number of officers, experts estimate that the FSB has over 200,000 officers.[63] Compared to the FBI or CIA, these numbers are huge; the FBI reports a staff of 35,000 and the CIA is estimated to have 21,575 employees.[64] In addition to the domestically focused FSB, Russia's other most prominent intelligence organizations include its foreign intelligence service, military intelligence, and the federal protection service, which protects senior government officials and operates their secure communications systems.

Russian intelligence officers have deeply penetrated the state under Putin. In 2015, roughly three out of four senior Russian officials were assessed to have ties to the intelligence services.[65] Intelligence officers run many of Russia's largest state-owned enterprises, including Russia's largest gas and oil companies and the military-industrial complex. Abroad, Russian intelligence agencies have become much more aggressive during the Putin era, poisoning Ukraine's presidential candidate Viktor Yushchenko in 2004, murdering former Russian Federal Security Service officer Aleksandr Litvinenko by means of a radioactive agent in London in 2006, assassinating Russian businessman Alexander Perepilichnyy with a biological toxin in Great Britain in 2012, poisoning former Russian intelligence officer Sergei Skripal with Novichok in 2018, and assassinating a Russian citizen in a Berlin park in 2019.[66] In the current era of great power competition, this kind of sinister power is unique to Russia, used only by Putin's regime and not (to my knowledge) by the American and Chinese governments.

ALLIES

The United States has many powerful military allies around the world; Russia does not. The most important military alliance for countering Russian military power is NATO. Together, the thirty-two members of this alliance spend close to one and a half trillion dollars on defense, vastly outpacing Russia.[67] In response to Russia's invasions of Ukraine, first in 2014 and then on a larger scale in 2022, NATO members committed to increasing their military spending to 2 percent of GDP, a goal most allies reached by 2024. In 2025, NATO members pledged to spend 5 percent on military and related expenditures by 2025. In reaction to Russian military interventions in Ukraine, NATO pledged to increase its high-readiness forces from 40,000 to more than 300,000 soldiers, and the United States deployed an additional 20,000 soldiers to Europe, bringing the total on that continent to roughly 100,000. When the soldiers and supporting personnel of individual armies in NATO are tallied, they amount to 3.5 million, compared to Russia's 1.5 million.[68] And if you add Ukraine's army into the mix, the balance of forces for democrats in Europe (and the United States and Canada) vastly outnumber the autocrats. NATO forces face interoperability and logistical challenges. NATO does not have a single military-industrial complex like Russia; multiple companies often make the same weapon system. After three decades of demobilization and deliberate disarmament started at the Cold War's end, codified in the Treaty on Conventional Forces in Europe, European national armies are not as well trained or as well armed as they need to be. However, in the aggregate, NATO's power is much greater than Russia's power.

To address this imbalance and, more subtly, to balance China's growing influence, Russia established the Collective Security Treaty Organization (CSTO) in 2002, a military alliance grounded in a collective defense principle like NATO's Article 5: an attack on one is an attack on all. In addition to Russia, Armenia, Belarus, Kazakhstan, Kyrgyzstan, and Tajikistan are members. Azerbaijan, Georgia, and Uzbekistan have already quit, and Armenia has threatened to do the same.[69] Together, CSTO members have only a fraction of NATO's military and economic power. The CSTO does not often act collectively; the organization did not support Russia's invasions of Georgia in 2008, Ukraine in 2014, or Ukraine again in 2022.[70] The one major collectively endorsed mission was in Kazakhstan in 2022 to support the regime there being threatened by a coup, but Russian forces were the only ones involved. And China—Russia's most important security partner—sometimes competes, not cooperates, with Russia for security relationships with countries in this alliance. At the first Central Asia–China summit, in Xian in May 2023, Xi hinted at his interest in providing an alternative security apparatus for Central Asia—China's Global Security Initiative.[71]

After invading Ukraine in 2022, Putin tried to deepen bilateral security relationships with various countries, including Iran, North Korea, and China. Soon after the war began, Iran began supplying Russia with drones and missiles and later collaborated with Russia to build the Iranian Shahed drone in Russia. After initially hesitating, Xi provided Putin with critical technologies to help rebuild Russia's military-industrial complex but has refrained from providing weapons. In June 2024, Putin and Kim Jung Un signed the Comprehensive Strategic Partnership Treaty, obliging both countries to offer immediate military assistance to each other by any means necessary if either is subjected to aggression.[72] A few months later, Kim sent more than ten thousand North Korean soldiers to Russia to fight alongside Russian forces against Ukrainian armed forces occupying Russian territory in the Kursk region. The Russian war in Ukraine has led this axis of autocracies to provide greater military assistance to one of its members, but the level of aid is nowhere near what NATO, the United States, and the European Union have provided to Ukraine.

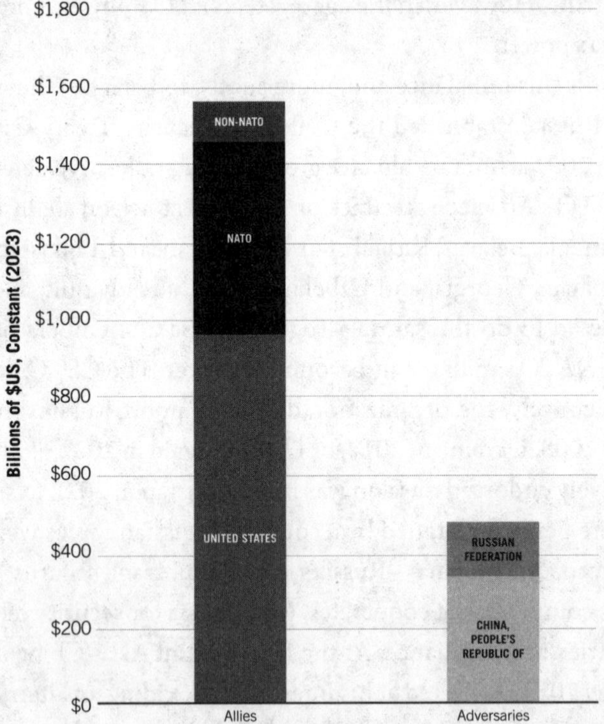

Figure 4.3 Military Spending: US Allies vs. China and Russia, 2024*

Source: Stockholm International Peace Research Institute, 2025

*This graph reflects the formal security treaties of the United States, as well as those involving both China and Russia. No state has a binding security treaty with both China and Russia, except North Korea. North Korea is excluded because military expenditure data is not publicly available. Non-NATO allies include countries that have a binding bilateral or trilateral security partnership with the United States: Australia, Japan, New Zealand, South Korea, and the Philippines. The Rio Treaty and the Southeast Asia Treaty are excluded intentionally.

THE BALANCE OF ECONOMIC POWER

Compared to most countries, Russia is a major economic power, often ranking as the eleventh largest economy in the world and even higher on other indicators. Compared to the United States and China, however, Russia is not a major economic power. On every metric of economic power, the United States remains far ahead of Russia. This gap has widened since

Putin invaded Ukraine in 2022, ending two decades of Russian integration into the global economy. Comprehensive Western sanctions in reaction to Russia's invasion of Ukraine further weakened Russia's economy and investment climate, triggered the flight of hundreds of thousands of Russia's most talented workers, and forced the Russian government to make significant shifts in investment toward the military-industrial complex. Sanctions on technology imports made the production of weapons, automobiles, internet networks, and other consumer products more costly, dramatically slowing the technology transfer needed for energy exploration in the Arctic Sea. Gazprom, the Russian energy company that analysts once speculated would become the most valuable business in the world, is now teetering on bankruptcy, in part because the company lost valuable and stable buyers in Europe. In the short term, government spending on the military-industrial complex stimulated economic growth. Rising prices of oil and gas, triggered by the beginning of the war, have helped the Russian economy too. However, in the long run, a lack of investment in the private sector, inflation, a weakening ruble, the flight of capital and talent, isolation, and growing control of the Russian economy by Putin and his cronies will constrain economic growth. In 2025, signs of that decline were already showing.[73]

Yet, even with all of Putin's policy mistakes, including the invasion of Ukraine in 2022, the Russian economy is still large and resilient. It is not the economic "basket case" that many Americans associated with the country in the 1990s. The Russian economy is unlikely to ever catch up with the United States or China, but it will remain one of the ten largest economies in the world for the rest of the century and therefore will be big enough to finance Putin's belligerent foreign policy agenda.

ECONOMIC SIZE

Even with good data, comparing economies is not an easy task. There is no perfect, one-size-fits-all metric. Institutions like the IMF, the World Bank, and national governments publish their own, sometimes conflicting, data. Putin's government has a reputation for distorting economic data that international financial institutions use for their calculations. Shortly after

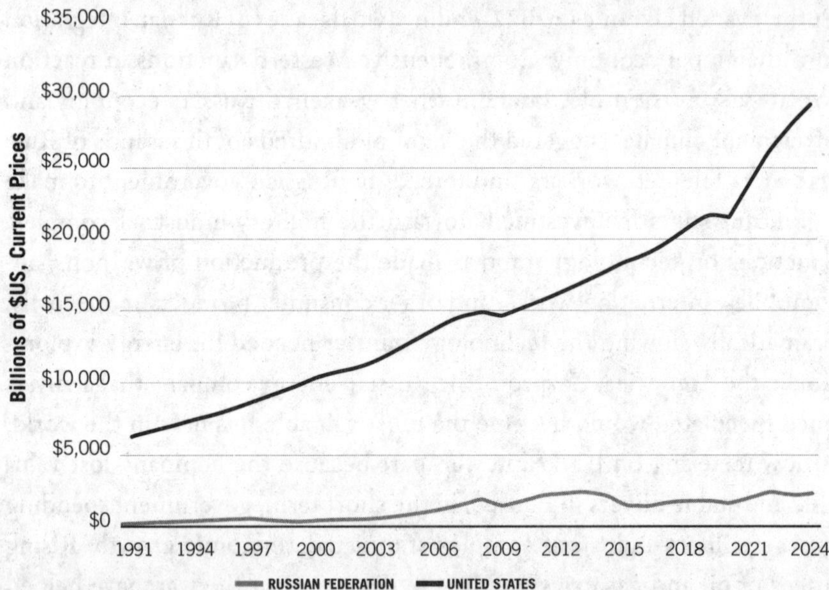

Figure 4.4 Gross Domestic Product: US vs. Russia, 1991–2024

Source: International Monetary Fund, 2025

its 2022 invasion of Ukraine, the Kremlin stopped publishing a wide range of macroeconomic and financial indicators, further complicating assessments. Despite these constraints, a comparison of several metrics shows clearly that the American economy is much more powerful than the Russian economy, but Russia's economy is neither poor nor small.

For decades, the United States has been and remains significantly ahead of Russia when comparing the most common measure of economic size: gross domestic product.

The US economy today is roughly thirteen times larger than the Russian economy. By this metric, the United States has the largest economy in the world while Russia ranks eleventh.

Purchasing power parity (PPP) is a different way to compare the size of economies. PPP calculates what goods you can buy in different countries for the same amount of money, given that prices for these goods vary between countries. Using this measure, according to the IMF estimates in 2025, Russia surges to the fourth-largest economy in the world, behind only China, the United States, and India.

GROWTH RATES

In his first presidential term, Putin embraced pro-market reforms, dramatically cutting corporate and individual income taxes and pursuing prudent fiscal policies. The combination of these policies and soaring oil and gas prices spurred the Russian economy to grow rapidly after a decade-long economic depression in the 1990s. As Swedish economist Anders Åslund wrote in 2004, "In recent years, the Russian economy has experienced an extraordinary reversal. Suddenly, it has been transformed from an apparent basket case, with steadily declining output and chronic macroeconomic instability, to one of the world's most dynamic economies, with solid macroeconomic stability."[74] The Russian economy experienced a significant decline in growth during the 2008 global financial crisis and following Putin's invasions of Ukraine in 2014 and 2022. Even before these international shocks, growing state intervention in the economy had begun to slow Russian economic growth. Since he invaded Ukraine in 2022, Putin has become even more suspicious of private-sector actors. Russian economic stagnation is likely to endure well after the war is over. Conversely, the US economy continues to grow.

GDP PER CAPITA

Russia is way behind the United States in GDP per capita. According to the 2024 IMF data, Russia's GDP per capita was at $14,795, compared to $85,812 for the United States. Even if Putin reversed course and began pursuing pro-growth economic policies again or a new Russian leader adopted such an economic strategy, Russia will not catch up with the United States on this dimension in this century, and probably never.

TRADE AND INTERDEPENDENCE

Today, Russia is much more connected to the global economy than the Soviet Union was but much less connected than the United States and China. That economic interconnectedness took a major hit after the Russian invasion of Ukraine, as sanctions impeded Russian imports and exports as well as foreign direct investment in Russia and Russia's investments abroad. Russia's total exports in 2023 plummeted by 28.3 percent to $425.1 billion.[75] That same year, American exports totaled $3 trillion. In 2023, Russian official imports totaled $285.1 billion, though the actual value is probably higher because the Russian government hides these figures to circumvent sanctions.[76] In that same year, American imports amounted to $3.8 trillion.[77] The United States maintains a significant trade deficit; Russia does not. However, what the trade deficit signals about the strength of an economy is complicated. The US can maintain large deficits because it can finance them through lending to other countries. Russia cannot do the same because few countries and individuals are willing to buy Russian treasury bonds. While less globally integrated than the United States' or China's, Russian exports play a significant role in specific sectors, including, most important, fossil fuels, but also weapons, metals, and grains. But that means that Russia is also dependent on the global economy, especially in earning hard currency from energy exports.

After Putin's full-scale invasion of Ukraine, Russian trade patterns shifted dramatically. Russia's trade with Europe—previously its largest market—plummeted but increased with China and India. Halfway through 2023, trade between Russia and China was 40 percent higher than in 2022 and over 80 percent higher than in 2021.[78] In June of 2023, Russia and China signed a multiyear economic agreement to "deepen investment cooperation in trade services," assuring agricultural exports to China and more.[79] Chinese car and tractor exports to Russia have increased significantly, with the share of Chinese cars in the Russian market exceeding 60 percent. In February 2022, brands from China accounted for only 9 percent.[80] In 2022, India emerged as a major new importer of Russian oil. In the first two years of the war, trade between the two countries increased dramatically but declined in 2024 and 2025 because of international sanctions on Russian oil exporters.[81]

Xi Jinping and India's prime minister Narendra Modi are not doing Putin a favor by purchasing Russian oil; they are taking advantage of discounted prices as a result of Western sanctions. Chinese manufacturers are gaining an advantage by selling cheap Chinese goods to Russia at inflated prices because of the country's shortage of consumer products.

Russia's growing economic isolation from Europe, coinciding with its rising economic dependence on China, reduces its influence worldwide, even in regions like Central Asia.[82] In this domain, Russia is becoming less powerful as a result of Putin's war in Ukraine.

FINANCIAL POWER

Compared to the United States, Russia has very little global financial power. Despite Putin's pressure to use the Russian ruble for economic transactions, few countries do so. Russia struggles to use the dollar because of sanctions and has been forced to rely more heavily on China's yuan.[83] Unlike China, Russia has no e-currency.

Before the invasion of Ukraine in 2022, Russia's most powerful financial institutions were expanding rapidly in the global economy, albeit in ways that often exported corruption and other malign practices.[84] Russia's banking industry had established a global footprint. Its largest bank, SberBank, had three million customers outside Russia and a 5 percent share of the international banking business. The VTB Bank Group—the second-largest bank in Russia—was active in eighteen countries.[85] However, after sanctions were imposed in 2022, SberBank's annual profit decreased by 78.3 percent from 2021, and its international presence dwindled.[86] VTB saw a similar decline. Since the start of the war in 2022, the Russian government and banks introduced strict measures to keep foreign currency in the country, capping withdrawals at $10,000.[87] Russia's financial connectivity with the outside world has dwindled substantially since the war in Ukraine expanded in 2022 and is likely to take many years to recover.

SCIENCE AND TECHNOLOGY

With the triumph of the Sputnik launch in 1957 and cosmonaut Yuri Gagarin's pioneering space flight in 1961, the Soviet Union appeared to be better at amassing resources for major scientific breakthroughs than the United States. However, as Communist Party officials channeled the country's best talent to the military-industrial complex and grew wary of technological advances that enhanced individual autonomy, like personal computers, the Soviet system failed to keep up with American technology. When the Soviet Union collapsed in 1991, Russia was well behind the United States and other European countries in science and technology and continued to fall behind in the 1990s as poor funding devastated Russia's research and development. Many of Russia's most talented scientists, mathematicians, and technologists immigrated to Israel or the United States, where they helped build some of the world's most successful tech companies.[88]

As the Russian economy recovered in the early 2000s, Russian science and technology gradually did too. The Soviet military-industrial complex sprouted a handful of successful privately owned and technologically advanced companies, and the IT market recorded growth rates of 30 to 40 percent per year in the 2000s, with offshore programming being its fastest-growing segment.[89] Kaspersky Labs, the country's most prominent cybersecurity company, gained a substantial international footprint. The search engine company Yandex competed with Google within Russia and captured a significant market share in the post-Soviet world and beyond. Russian president Dmitry Medvedev devoted special attention to facilitating growth within the Russian high-tech industry to reduce the nation's dependence on exporting fossil fuels. His most ambitious project was Skolkovo, a city created from scratch outside of Moscow that Medvedev hoped would become Russia's Silicon Valley. The Russian state funded a handful of companies in the tech sector, such as nanotechnology investor Rusnano.

After returning as president in 2012, Putin curtailed spending in these areas, tampering with high-tech growth.[90] As former deputy finance minister Sergey Aleksashenko explained, "Putin has never believed in the power of competition and private initiative."[91] Before the invasion of Ukraine, Russia devoted roughly 1 percent of its GDP to R&D, less than a third of what the US spends.[92] After the Ukraine invasion, that number decreased further in the private sector but increased in the military-industrial complex. Some pockets of innovation persisted, but overall, Russia has failed to keep pace with the United States.[93] Russian innovations in AI, for example, are far behind those of the US and China. In the 2023 Global AI Vibrancy Ranking conducted by the Stanford Institute for Human-Centered Artificial Intelligence, the United States ranked first, China second, and Russia was a distant twenty-ninth.[94]

The 2014 and 2022 invasions of Ukraine radically disrupted what little innovation was happening in the Russian high-tech sector. After the first invasion, thousands of Russia's best and brightest fled; nearly half of the emigrants worked in IT and computing, and 16 percent were senior managers.[95] High-profile tech leader Pavel Durov left Russia after losing control of his company, Vkontakte, to an investment firm closely tied to the Kremlin. Tens of thousands of other entrepreneurs followed. Russia's full-scale invasion of Ukraine in 2022 was even more disruptive to this sector, pushing many tech companies to leave Russia or split their assets and take many of the most talented scientists and technologists with them, as Russia's most successful tech company, Yandex, did. MIT pulled out of Skolkovo.[96] Not surprisingly, very few scientists or engineers are immigrating to Russia. Russia's solid education base in math and physics, a legacy from the Soviet Union, could have made the country a global leader in science and technology, but imprudent government policies—including, most disastrously, the war in Ukraine—have undermined Russia's potential. In cutting-edge science and technology, the United States and China will stay ahead of Russia for a long time.

RUSSIA'S ECONOMIC HEADWINDS

Before the Ukraine invasion, the growing role of the state in the economy was generating economic stagnation in Russia.[97] Labor productivity in private Russian firms was twice as high as it was in their state-sponsored counterparts, but as Putin became more fearful of Russia's richest citizens challenging his power, the share of the economy in private hands began shrinking.[98] In 2003, Putin seized control of Russia's largest private oil company, Yukos, and jailed its CEO, Mikhail Khodorkovsky; he was not released for a decade. Eventually, Yukos's assets ended up in Rosneft, Russia's largest state-owned oil company, run by Putin's close confidant Igor Sechin. Hundreds of Russian companies have since met the same fate.[99] After many foreign companies stopped operations in Russia in 2022, Putin seized their assets and handed them over to his loyalists, who subsequently failed to operate these enterprises efficiently. Former KGB officers are not known for their corporate management skills. Putin's personal involvement in the Russian economy is significant, with many of Russia's most valuable assets linked directly to him. The growing role of the state combined with the destruction of independent media, opposition parties, and the rule of law has produced explosive corruption throughout the Russian economy, another drag on growth.

Like China and most developed countries, Russia faces substantial demographic challenges. Since 1994, Russia's population has been shrinking, except for a brief period of growth between 2013 and 2015. Factors driving Russia's negative democratic trends include low birth rates, emigration, alcoholism, COVID-19, and massive loss of life from the war in Ukraine.

Even before the war in 2022, the United Nations projected that Russia's population would shrink by 17 percent in the next fifty years, in contrast to the expected 15 percent growth in the United States over the same period.[100] As Russia's population shrinks, so does its labor force, yet the number of retirees grows, straining the nation's pension system. In 2018, Putin was compelled to raise the retirement age to sixty-five for men and sixty-three for women—a reform met with widespread protests (two months later, he rolled women's retirement age back to sixty).[101] His government offered many economic incentives for people to have children, such as free school meals, tax breaks for large families, and cash rewards.[102] Though these efforts saw some success in the early 2000s, birth rates have declined since 2015.[103] Russia has encouraged immigration to help compensate for low birth rates, a policy that worked a little until the invasion of Ukraine.

Today, Russia continues to benefit from a robust Soviet legacy of investment in higher education, especially in STEM fields. In this dimension of power, Russia is competitive with the United States in primary and secondary education, but it still lags in university education. Russia has an outstanding literacy rate of 99.7 percent. According to international assessments, Russian high-school seniors outperform their American peers in math and physics and score similarly in reading. This success is remarkable, given that Russia spends only 4 percent of its GDP on education, compared to 5.4 percent in the US, as per 2021 data.[104] However, Russian universities cannot compete with American universities. American universities dominate the top spots of almost every list of the best universities in the world. Russia has only one university in the top one hundred, Moscow State University.

Growing inequality imposes another constraint on long-term Russian growth. According to the Gini index (a measure of income inequality in a country), the United States has the highest level of inequality of any G7 nation. The scale goes from 0 to 100 (with 0 representing perfect equality and 100 perfect inequality), and in 2021, the US's Gini index was 39.7 and 41.3 in 2022. But Russia had a Gini index of 36 in 2020 (the last year that the World Bank calculated this number for Russia), and that in an economy with many fewer resources than the United States.[105] Four of every five Russians have less than ten thousand dollars in assets, and 105 billionaires control nearly one-fifth of all household wealth.[106] Russia's richest are closely tied to the state, and their wealth often comes from personal relationships with Putin rather than expertise or entrepreneurship. This concentration of wealth intertwined with the state—oligarchic capitalism—stifles economic innovation and growth.

However, stagnating economies can endure for a long time. The Soviet Union proved that. While Russia under Putin is unlikely to grow at the impressive rates achieved in the early 2000s, given the size of the Russian economy and the abundance of natural resources in high demand around the world, Putin can support a military big enough to threaten American democratic allies and partners, especially in Europe.

Russia today constitutes a real threat to the United States not just because of its capabilities but also because of Putin's willingness to deploy Russian power—especially military power—to pursue outcomes antithetical to US interests. This challenge for American interests will remain as long as Putin rules Russia. The longer Putin has been in power, the more risky his military decisions have become. While the overall balance of power in Europe favors NATO, the balance of military forces between Lithuania and Russia or Estonia and Russia favors Moscow. Leaders in these NATO frontline states increasingly worry that Putin will attack them to test the commitment of allies to Article 5 of the NATO treaty, which states that an attack on one is an attack on all. If tempted to do so, Putin could drag the United States into a war with Russia.

This scenario is more dangerous than the last decades of the Cold War. Unlike during the Cold War, the world's second- and third-most-powerful countries—China and Russia—are close partners today. That configuration presents complex challenges to US policymakers, especially because China has more formidable military, economic, and technological resources than Russia, as discussed in the next chapter.

Chapter 5

CHINESE VS. AMERICAN POWER

FLYING FROM MOST American airports to Beijing or Shanghai makes you feel like you are traveling to the future. Getting on the train from Beijing to Shanghai only adds to the impression. It is much faster, more modern, and more efficient than the bullet train connecting San Francisco to Los Angeles. Oh, wait—we don't have one of those yet. During my visit to Beijing in the spring of 2024, I never used cash or credit cards, another feeling from the future compared to the United States. Chinese economic growth over the past several decades is genuinely miraculous, fueling the sense that China is rising as the United States is fading. And historically, economic growth usually underwrites military power. That is most certainly true with China today. Americans have good reason to fear this rising superpower. For the United States, Chinese emergence as a great power is the central national security challenge of the twenty-first century.

However, China is a country of contradictions. Flying to Beijing a few years ago, I read *The Invisible China* by my Stanford colleagues Scott Rozelle and Natalie Hell.[1] It changed forever how I think about the People's Republic of China. The invisible part of this economic and military superpower is the eight hundred million rural citizens who still live under poor conditions with limited education and health care. You do not see these poor, uneducated peasants when you are flying into Hong Kong or dining in Beijing. But they are the majority. And the subtitle of Rozelle and Hell's book, *How the Urban-Rural Divide Threatens China's Rise*, warns us of that.

There is another contradiction that I have felt personally when visiting China: the tension between economic freedom and political freedom. Many countries have achieved high levels of economic development that then spurred political change. We call it modernization theory. Today, almost all the wealthiest countries in the world are democracies. That is not an accident. Educated people who own things want to protect their property rights with the rule of law and accountable government, not just rely on the whims of monarchs, generals, mullahs, or Communist Party bosses. However, China today appears to be bucking this trend, achieving remarkable economic growth without democratizing.

Yet, I am not sure it will last. A state not constrained by the rule of law or democratic institutions can sometimes produce economic growth but also turn predatory. Since seizing power in 1949, the Chinese Communist Party has practiced both, guiding the country through four decades of prosperity, starting in the late 1970s, but also destroying vast amounts of wealth and killing tens of millions in the Mao era. These days, it is unnerving to go through passport control in Beijing, as the officer in the booth might arrest you arbitrarily. In my case, Putin might ask Xi to do so; in the case of Chinese entrepreneurs, a Communist Party official might want to seize their assets.

Today, Xi and his comrades in the CCP could continue along a path of economic development that would finance military power. But that course is not guaranteed. There are already signs that it is beginning to falter. Therefore, we Americans should practice vigilance regarding the rise of Chinese power and adopt strategies to ensure that we can achieve our core security and economic interests in a world challenged and often threatened by a second great power. At the same time, we should not overestimate Chinese power or assume that it will continue to grow forever.

Although not the only significant variable, power is the central driver of competition and conflict in US-China relations today. Think of the counterfactual: If China had the same power as Guinea-Bissau or Tajikistan, there would be much less tension in US-China relations. China's emergence as a great power second only to the United States has fueled friction with the United States. Our competition with China is exacerbated by the fact that China is the leading country in the world challenging American power. Some argue we are moving into a multipolar world with many great powers. That is not the case. The United States and China are far ahead of all other powers in the international system by most traditional metrics. The gap between these two superpowers and the rest of the world is growing, not shrinking.

Because the Cold War was bipolar as well, many quickly conclude that we have now entered a second Cold War. To be sure, bipolarity is a common feature of the Cold War and great power competition. As discussed in subsequent chapters, one superpower today is a democracy, the other is a dictatorship. That is like the Cold War too. Similar to the Cold War, both superpowers today seek to shape the entire global order in ways that advance their interests.

At the same time, regarding the balance of power, there are also significant differences between the Cold War and US-China competition today. Most important, Chinese economic power is much greater than Soviet economic power, making the China challenge a much more significant issue to manage for American leaders. Also different from the Cold War, the American and Chinese economies are highly intertwined, and the Chinese economy is deeply integrated into the global economy. The world is also less rigorously divided into two camps, populated by more midlevel powers with agency to pursue independent foreign policies. India and Brazil, for example, will not join formal alliances with the United States, but they also refuse to live in a world dominated by China. Russia and China are increasingly more aligned in opposition to the United States today. That was not true for most of the Cold War. The balance of power between the United States and China is also shifting along a trajectory favorable to China. However, the United States continues to acquire new capabilities, even if at a slower pace than China.

The framing of a zero-sum balance of power paints the picture of a rising China and a declining United States.[2] This imagery—popular in Beijing, Moscow, and with some in Washington—is misleading. Here is a different metaphor: Imagine our great power competition as a two-mile track race. (I am using this analogy because I used to run the two-mile in high school!) The US is well ahead of the field, but as the race progresses, China begins to pull away from the laggards and closes in on the US. But the US is still ahead, even if it is losing its lead. China may continue to close the gap but never catch up. That China will surpass the US in this race is a prediction, not a certainty. China may even fade, and the gap between the United States and China could widen again. This condition is fundamentally different from the Cold War, when the US and USSR were moving in opposite directions by the end of the race; as the Soviet economy slowed down, the American economy grew rapidly.

Another difference from the Cold War is that not every new dimension of Chinese power threatens American interests. Distinguishing between capabilities that threaten American security and prosperity and those that might benefit the United States, particularly regarding economic outcomes or scientific progress, constitutes a significant challenge for American grand strategists. Making such assessments requires a comprehensive accounting of the balance of power between the United States and China in many domains. This chapter now turns to that task.

THE BALANCE OF MILITARY POWER

The use of military power by great powers, especially against each other, has become rare, so estimating how latent capabilities might translate into actual use on the battlefield is an imprecise science. That the Chinese military has not fought a war in several decades adds to the difficulty of estimating the strength of the People's Liberation Army (PLA). Other factors like morale and public support are also challenging to measure, since they will not have the same impact in every military conflict.

With these caveats, we must still try to measure the balance of military power between the United States and the People's Republic of China. My bottom-line-up-front (BLUF) is that the United States still maintains a sizable advantage over China on most dimensions of military power and leads in the global balance of military power. We can keep our military advantage for decades with the proper commitment to defense planning, economic growth, and allies, as discussed in chapter 13. However, the balance of power in two more narrowly defined regions—the South China Sea and Taiwan—is more equal and trending in China's favor. That is dangerous and needs redressing.

NUCLEAR POWER

Regarding nuclear weapons, the US maintains a considerable advantage over China. The United States has more nuclear warheads, both deployed and in storage, and more and better delivery systems. Given China's practice of

Table 5.1 Nuclear Arsenals: US vs. China, 2024[3]

Warheads	**United States**	**China**
Strategic Deployed	1,670	*Data not available*
Strategic Reserve	1,830	*Data not available*
Total Strategic Inventory	3,500	600
Nonstrategic (Tactical) Deployed	100	*Data not available*
Nonstrategic (Tactical) Reserve	100	*Data not available*
Retired	1,477	*Data not available*
Total Inventory	5,177	600
Delivery Systems	**United States**	**China**
Land (Launchers)	400	712
Sea (SSBN/Missiles)	14/280	6/72
Air (Bombers)	65	20

Source: Bulletin of the Atomic Scientists, *Nuclear Notebook, 2025. Numbers are estimates based on available open-source data as of April 2025. Independent analysts disagree about the PRC's number of deployed warheads: some estimate around 24, while others argue none are deployed.*

storing warheads and delivery systems separately, none of China's strategic nuclear weapons are even considered deployed according to the definition codified in the New START treaty between Russia and the United States, giving the US another edge regarding the speed of use.

Xi and the CCP, however, are rapidly expanding their nuclear arsenal. In 2024, the *Bulletin of the Atomic Scientists* estimated China's nuclear arsenal at 500, but only a year later in 2025, the same source reported a number of 600. The US Department of Defense estimates that "the PRC will probably have over 1,000 operational warheads by 2030, much of which will be deployed at a higher readiness level and will continue growing its force to 2035."[4] In the past several years, China has built roughly three hundred new intercontinental ballistic missile silos. Although all these silos may not be armed with missiles, their mere presence will compel American strategic planners to target all of them to maintain deterrence. The PRC has upgraded its road-mobile ICBM capabilities (ICBMs carried by trucks that provide the PRC with a more survivable ground-based system), deployed more nuclear weapons on submarines and bombers, added a new longer-range missile to its submarines, and, most dramatically, tested a nuclear-capable and highly maneuverable hypersonic glide vehicle that travels much faster than other ballistic missiles.[5] General Mark A. Milley, then chairman of the Joint Chiefs of Staff, called the Chinese test of a hypersonic glide vehicle "very close" to a "Sputnik moment," referring to the Cold War moment in 1957 when Americans thought they lagged far behind the Soviets after Khrushchev successfully launched the Sputnik satellite using an ICBM.[6]

The US still retains superiority in aircraft capable of delivering nuclear weapons. China's main nuclear-capable bomber, the H-6N, and the forthcoming stealth bomber, the H-20, do not match the operational capabilities of American B-2 and B-21 aircraft.

Underwater, China has made significant strides in modernizing its sea-based nuclear-delivery systems. Its nuclear-capable and nuclear-powered Jin-class submarines, armed with submarine-launched ballistic missiles, remain vulnerable to quieter American anti-submarine weapons and earlier Chinese systems.[7] However, US defense experts estimate that China's newest nuclear-armed submarines have made remarkable improvements, warning that their deployment will have "profound implications for US undersea security."[8]

These new Chinese nuclear capabilities are disconcerting, especially if they are ever used or threatened to be used in coordination with Russia and its nuclear arsenal. This change from two to three nuclear powers represents a new security challenge for American defense planners, particularly because Chinese nuclear doctrine is not as well understood as the Russian one.[9] American strategists and diplomats have experience and relationships with arms-control negotiators in Russia but lack such a history with Beijing's decision-makers and diplomats.

Despite all these upgrades and expansion of China's nuclear arsenal, nuclear war with China is highly unlikely. I cannot imagine a circumstance in which a US president would preemptively launch a massive nuclear attack against China (or any other country) and hope that America's untested-in-battle missile defense systems would protect us from a retaliatory strike. It is even less likely that China would launch a first-strike nuclear attack against the United States, knowing that we have a substantial second-strike capability to respond. China's expanding nuclear arsenal seems designed to maintain mutual assured destruction as a strategy to deter a nuclear war, not to fight one. However, this upgraded nuclear arsenal could help the CCP leaders discourage the United States from joining a conventional war with China over Taiwan. After his full-scale invasion of Ukraine in 2022, Putin successfully used the nuclear threat to deter the US and NATO leaders from providing more lethal weapons in a timelier manner. Xi was certainly watching.

CONVENTIONAL MILITARY POWER

Regarding conventional military power, the US maintains an advantage over China, especially when adding in the capabilities of allies. However, China is catching up quickly, allocating significant resources to this cause, and in some categories and places, it is already surpassing the United States. Near Taiwan, where military conflict between the United States and China is most likely, the balance of conventional power favors China, in part because of geography. The PRC is a hundred miles from Taiwan; the US is thousands of miles away. This shifting balance of power regarding conventional weapons represents a serious threat to American national security that American leaders must urgently address.

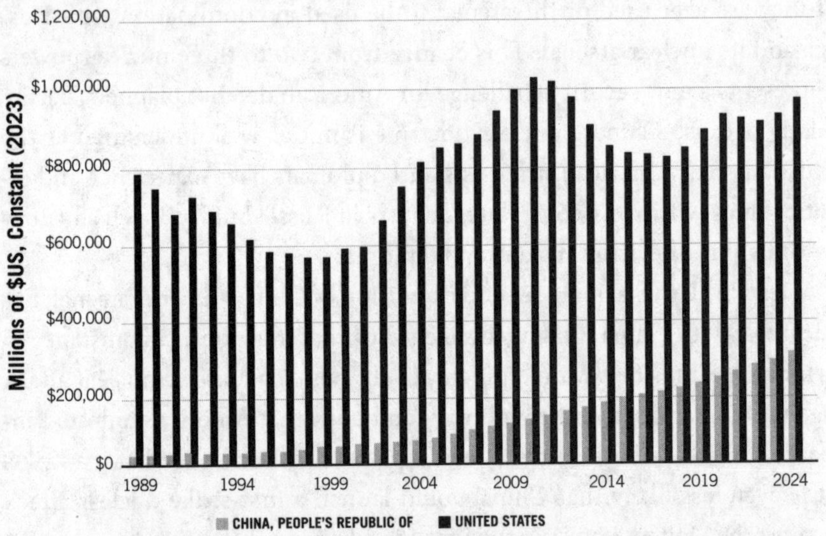

Figure 5.1 Military Expenditures: US vs. China, 1989–2024

Source: Stockholm International Peace Research Institute, 2025

Military budgets are one proxy for measuring conventional military power. In this category, as figure 5.1 shows, the US vastly outspends China.

However, comparing these figures in US dollars tells only part of the story. In China, weapons are cheaper and military salaries are lower, so the Chinese government gets a lot more from every dollar/yuan spent than the US government does. American soldiers earn up to sixteen times more than their Chinese counterparts, but these higher salaries do not make them sixteen times better at fighting.

We must remain skeptical of any data published by opaque autocracies like the PRC. The Chinese government publishes only the nominal toplines for its annual defense budget; they do not provide breakdowns of how the money is spent. This practice generates vastly different estimates of China's actual defense spending. In 2022, for instance, Beijing reported spending $229 billion on defense; SIPRI estimated the total to be $292 billion; and the IISS guessed that the figure was $242 billion. Adding to the confusion, China omits several categories from its annual defense budget, including paramilitary forces, the militarized coast guard, foreign weapons purchases, and its extensive "military-civil fusion" strategy, which aggressively adopts private technology for military purposes. When these off-budget items and differences in purchasing power between currencies are added to estimates, some assess Chinese defense spending to be closer to $700 billion.[10] Given current inflation rates in the United States, current real American spending is flat. Today, we are not spending on defense anywhere near Cold War levels.[11]

Regarding another metric of conventional military power, the number of soldiers, China has a significant advantage over the United States. According to the US Department of Defense in 2023, "The PLA is the world's largest active-duty military force and comprised of approximately 2.185 million active, 1.17 million reserve, and 660,000 paramilitary personnel for a total force of 4 million."[12] In the event of a sustained war, China's enormous population gives Beijing an edge in replenishing its armed forces. While assessing power by this metric might seem rudimentary and raw, the Russian invasion of Ukraine has reminded the world that the quantity of soldiers still matters.

Quality matters too. Because of their training and experience, American soldiers have a significant edge.[13] The PRC has not fought a war since its

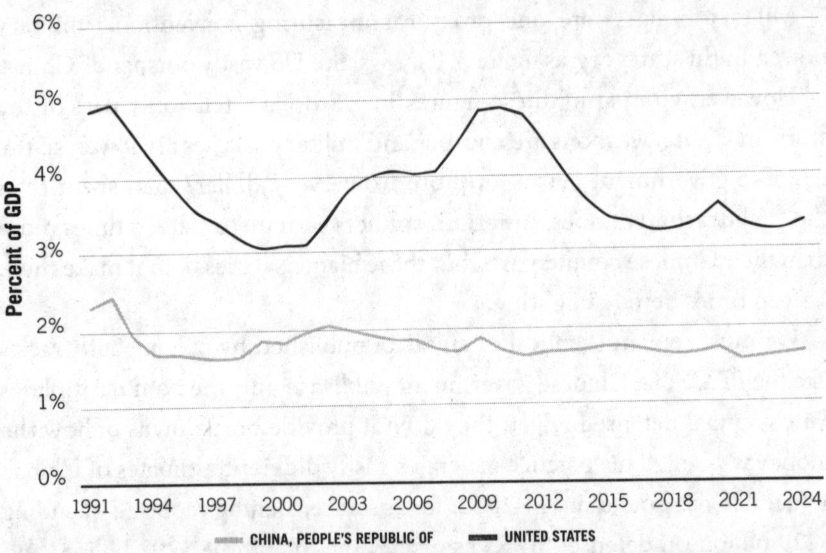

Figure 5.2 Military Expenditures of the US vs. China as a Share of GDP, 1991–2024

Source: Stockholm International Peace Research Institute, 2025

monthlong border conflict with Vietnam in 1979, compelling Xi himself to warn about what he has labeled the "peace disease."[14] By contrast, American soldiers gained extensive experience in wars in Afghanistan and Iraq, operations in Syria, and other special operations forces missions in Africa and Southeast Asia. The US military has another advantage because it empowers noncommissioned officers to make tactical decisions on the battlefield. This means that lower-echelon combat leaders can exercise initiative to make independent and responsive decisions based on the conditions they face on the battlefield rather than waiting for senior leaders much higher up in the chain of command to give orders for every tactical move. Like the Russian military, command and control in the PLA are much more hierarchical, with minimal autonomy afforded to subordinate leaders, which can impede an army's ability to conduct complex, networked, and joint military campaigns. That deficiency has been apparent regarding Russian forces fighting in Ukraine.

Comparing conventional weapons systems is another critical metric for assessing the balance of military power between the US and China.

Table 5.2 Conventional Military Power: US vs. China, 2024

Primary Military Assets	United States	China
Active Troops	1,315,600	2,035,000
Reserve Troops	797,200	510,000
Military Satellites	263	267
Armored Fighting Vehicles (Main Battle Tanks)	48,321 (2,640)	15,567 (4,700)
Submarines	65	59
Principal Surface Combatant Ships (Amphibious)	122 (210)	102 (370)
Patrol and Coastal Combatant Ships	434	714
Military Aircraft	3,817	3,263
Military Helicopters (Tiltrotors)	5,581 (413)	1,338 (0)
Uninhabited Aerial Vehicles	1,264	*Data not available*
Artillery	6,540	9,782

Source: The Military Balance *2025, International Institute for Strategic Studies. Numbers are estimates based on available open-source data.*

On the ground, China maintains a quantitative advantage over the US in artillery and main battle tanks, although when fighting vehicles are added to the equation, the United States has the advantage. Regarding quality, the US still holds the edge. The US Army's M1 Abrams outperforms China's Type 99 main battle tank. The Chinese have nothing comparable to the US Army's artillery options, including ATACMS and the High Mobility Artillery Rocket System (HIMARS). The Russia-Ukraine war has demonstrated the utility of US mobile anti-tank weapons like Javelins and loitering drones, though inexpensive commercial Chinese drones refitted for warfare have played an unexpectedly significant role in that war, especially for Ukraine's armed forces.

In the air, China remains well behind the United States. The PRC has more fixed-wing aircraft than the United States, but their quality remains lower even after recent upgrades.[15] Compared to the Chinese J-20 fighter jet (the rough equivalent of the F-16), fifth-generation American designs like the F-22 Raptor and F-35 Lightning II have superior capabilities in maneuverability, penetration, stealth, and suppression of enemy air defenses. Similarly, the new American B-21 bomber has no peer in the Chinese air force. Chinese manufacturing generally has produced amazing products, but jet engines remain one of their weak spots and one of America's comparative advantages. The US also maintains a lead in the number and quality of helicopters.

On the sea, the balance of power is becoming more equal because of massive Chinese investments in building ships and American neglect. Regarding numbers, China already has the advantage. In 2023, the DOD assessed that the PRC now had the numerically largest navy in the world, "with over 370 ships and submarines, including more than 140 major surface combatants."[16] Considering China's unmatched shipbuilding capacity, the Pentagon predicts the People's Liberation Army Navy (PLAN) fleet will expand to 400 in 2025 and 425 battle-force ships by 2030.[17] The US Navy fleet has a target of 287 battle-force ships by 2025 and a negligible plan for growth to 294 by 2030.[18] China also has the world's largest coast guard, with 546 combatant ships.[19] Xi's China has invested heavily in militarizing commercial ships, transforming fishing boats into a critical arsenal for projecting power in the South China Sea by attaching machine guns, rocket-propelled grenades, and high-velocity water cannons to commercial fishing vessels. Most of the Chinese navy is concentrated in Asia; the US Navy has missions and therefore sailors, ships, and ports all over the world.

Regarding quality, the US Navy is still ahead of China's PLAN. The eleven US aircraft carriers are bigger and better than China's three carriers. Most US aircraft carriers are equipped with advanced catapult technology for faster launch of heavier jets; China currently has three aircraft carriers, with a fourth—allegedly nuclear-powered—under construction. Two of China's three active carriers retain a more primitive steam-powered ski-jump takeoff system, although the third and most recent aircraft carrier deployed, the Fujian Type 003, is equipped with catapults powered by an electromagnetic system. But China is closing the quality gap. The Chinese built a radar system (AESA) that is on par with the US capabilities (US Aegis system). This technological advancement has made American ships, especially large aircraft carriers, easier targets. Geography gives China's navy a huge advantage in a war over Taiwan or a conflict in the South China Sea. Bases for American ships are too far away.

Under the sea, the United States maintains a huge advantage. China's nuclear-capable submarines carry less than half the munitions of current US submarines and use outdated stealth technology.[20] Chinese leaders are making considerable investments to try to close this gap. According to the Pentagon, the PLAN has built twelve nuclear submarines over the past fifteen years, with a target of eighty new submarines by 2035.[21] The US submarine fleet is not expanding at the same rate. And again, geography matters; bases for refueling and rearming American submarines are very far from Taiwan and the South China Sea. However, the success of Chinese submarine modernization is questionable. In the spring of 2024, one of the new nuclear submarines constructed by the China State Shipbuilding Corporation sank in port on the Yangtze River before ever going to sea.[22] China has also amassed the largest sea-mine arsenal in the world.

The shifting balance of power regarding long-range missiles is troubling for American national security, as the PRC has made great strides both in the quantity and quality of conventional missiles launched from land, sea, and air. Several of the PLA's new ballistic and cruise missiles can reach the island of Guam—an American territory—from land and hit US ships as far away as 2,500 miles. As part of the PRC's broader anti-access/area denial (A2/AD) doctrine—a strategy aiming to prevent adversarial forces from entering or operating within critical areas by using long-range precision weapons and defensive systems—China has developed advanced missile systems to limit the US military's ability to project power in Asia and especially in the South China Sea. The primary weapons deployed to achieve this mission are the DF-21D and DF-26B missiles, often referred to as "carrier killers." Both missiles feature maneuverable second-stage warheads that make interception difficult, forcing the US to reevaluate deploying carrier strike groups within their strike radius. Given that US military doctrine relies heavily on carrier strikes for power projection, these missiles directly challenge one of the cornerstones of US naval strategy.

US military planners have acknowledged the growing parity between the US and Chinese navies in the Indo-Pacific and have taken measures to address the threat, including increasing navy and Marine Corps spending and developing new weapons systems such as naval drones and mines. In response to the growing Chinese missile capabilities, the US Army deployed its first Long-Range Hypersonic Weapon in 2023, and the navy plans to deploy hypersonic weapons systems by 2027 as part of its Intermediate-Range Conventional Prompt Strike program. The first Trump administration withdrew from the Intermediate-Range Nuclear Forces Treaty with Russia in part to allow the US military to deploy ground-based conventional intermediate ballistic missiles in Asian countries. Since withdrawal from the treaty, however, the US has yet to find a home for these missiles because allies are not eager to host these weapons and thereby become a target of Chinese missiles in the event of a US-China war. But even without these missile systems deployed on the ground, the US maintains a large and highly accurate missile arsenal that can launch from ships and planes. The United States also maintains significant advantages regarding missile defenses, including the Ground-Based Midcourse Defense system safeguarding the US homeland, Patriot missile defense system, Terminal High Altitude Area Defense (THAAD) systems, and sea-based Aegis systems that can defend American bases as well as its allies and partners against short- and intermediate-range Chinese ballistic missiles.

When aggregating all metrics of conventional military power, the United States still maintains significant advantages over China. The PRC leads on some quantitative measures, but the United States wins most comparisons regarding quality. However, there is one critical caveat to American military superiority: US leaders seek to project power on every continent and every ocean, while to date, Chinese leaders are focused on Taiwan and the South China Sea. The balance of military power between China and the United States in this region is precariously and dangerously equal. When countries have relatively equal power, they are more likely to fight than when an asymmetric balance of power exists.[23]

SPACE

In 1967, the members of the UN Committee on the Peaceful Uses of Outer Space opened the Outer Space Treaty for signature, hoping to preserve space for peaceful purposes only. The treaty led to a series of follow-on negotiations that have lasted several decades, but divisions between states have prevented the creation of a genuinely binding agreement so far. Even proposals for narrower treaties to regulate the use of space—for example, banning anti-satellite weapon tests that permanently pollute the atmosphere with debris—have not been negotiated. This lack of international consensus has made space a rapidly emerging arena for great power competition.

The US is still ahead in space technology, but the PRC is aggressively asserting its ambition to become a leading force in space as well. In 2007, China tested its first anti-satellite weapon, producing the largest recorded amount of space debris, debris that continues to damage satellites to this day.[24] In 2019, the PRC's Chang'e-4—a crewless spacecraft—made a historic landing on the far side of the moon.[25] In a 2022 white paper, Xi emphasized that China's "eternal dream" is to "explore the vast cosmos, develop the space industry, and build China into a space power."[26] NASA chief Bill Nelson dismissed Xi's efforts to portray the Chinese space program as peaceful, asserting that the PRC's civilian space programs with supposedly benign scientific and economic goals were really secretive military projects.[27] Of course, the PRC's space program can seek to achieve multiple objectives—economic and security—at the same time.

Three indicators help us assess the balance of power between the United States and China in space: (1) the number of satellites operating in Earth orbit, measured by launch attempts; (2) payloads launched per year; and (3) the mass of payloads. Out of 7,560 active satellites in orbit as of May 2023, 5,184 belong to the United States, 628 to China, and 181 to Russia.[28] This increase, however, exaggerates American military capabilities in space, as satellites launched by private companies are generally small, low Earth orbiters with limited military applications. Regarding launches per year, Jonathan's "Space Report 2023" counted that SpaceX was responsible for 98 out of 109 for the United States, 95 of which were commercial and 3 for foreign governments.[29] The US government accounted for only 11 launch attempts, a much smaller figure than the PRC's 67. Regarding payloads launched yearly, the US leads overall but has parity with China in military terms. Of the 2,232 total launches for the United States, business and commercial satellites comprised 97 percent of total payloads.[30] As for defense-specific payloads, the US launched 29, 32, and 43 from 2021 to 2023, compared to China's 39, 45, and 42, respectively.[31]

In a war, the United States can attack Chinese space targets using ICBMs and ASAT capabilities. The creation of the Space Force allows the US to centrally coordinate a response to threats in space from foreign adversaries and helps prevent Chinese preeminence in this domain. But China can attack our satellites too, and the US armed forces rely much more heavily on satellites for communications and targeting than either China or Russia.

CYBER AND INTELLIGENCE

As mentioned in the previous chapter, outside analysts have a difficult time assessing countries' cyber and intelligence capabilities because these assets are hidden and classified. That said, most expert estimates of cyber capabilities rank the US first, China second, and Russia third.[32] In a comprehensive assessment in 2021, the International Institute for Strategic Studies concluded that "US offensive cyber capabilities are more developed than those of any other country."[33] American defensive capabilities are also improving rapidly. US assistance to Ukraine in the cyber world has demonstrated indirectly these improvements. Russia has been relentless in attacking Ukrainian targets in the cyber world but has had minimal success.

At the same time, the United States is much more open than China, creating easier targets for cyberattacks in the event of war. Chinese malware on American systems is deep and worrisome. In 2024, the US government admitted that it had identified but failed to remove Chinese hackers from American communication networks.[34] During a war, Chinese cyber penetration could influence the physical balance of power. Successful cyber hacks can alter GPS data to misdirect a drone strike, override safeties within natural-gas distribution stations, and even disrupt air traffic control systems to change flight paths. Suppose open conflict breaks out between the United States and China. In that case, Chinese cyber warriors can sabotage our cloud computing, chip infrastructure, and data centers, constituting a major threat to our economy as well as the economies of our allies. The United States has these capabilities too. Hopefully, mutual assured destruction will deter the worst-case uses of these kinds of weapons against civilian targets.

The United States is the world's leader in spying. Expert estimates rank the United States above China regarding international intelligence-gathering capabilities in both the physical and cyber worlds.[35] The US also has intelligence cooperation agreements with the United Kingdom, Canada, Australia, and New Zealand (the so-called Five Eyes), arguably the most powerful international intelligence partnership in history. More generally, the extensive network of military bases and alliances of the United States provides the US with greater intelligence capability than China and its partners. Now and then, we get a glimpse of these capabilities, such as when Robert Mueller indicted Russian agents in 2018 for interfering in the 2016 presidential election or when President Biden declassified intelligence to prove to the world that Putin was planning to launch a massive invasion of Ukraine on February 24, 2022. Most US intelligence successes, however, are never revealed. The same is true for China's.

At the same time, anecdotal evidence suggests that China is catching up. Beijing has focused special efforts on stealing military and economic secrets. As early as 2001, if not earlier, Chinese hackers began to infiltrate NASA networks, Pentagon internal systems, and major US military contractors—most notably Lockheed Martin and Boeing—to steal designs of critical US military technologies, including US space shuttles, F-35 fighters, military jet engines, and cruise and supersonic missiles. A Defense Science Board report identified over two dozen such instances.[36] In 2012, Chinese hackers gained access to the Office of Personnel Management's systems, and in 2014 and 2015 Chinese hackers stole over twenty million data files of government employees, including their Social Security numbers and fingerprint information. Dyadic Cyber Incident and Campaign Dataset in 2022 found China to be the most aggressive actor in economic espionage, targeting US firms with over a hundred malicious cyber campaigns, at least ninety of which were linked to espionage campaigns.[37] As of 2023, China is implicated in 224 reported instances of espionage and more than 1,200 lawsuits over intellectual property theft.[38] In our new era of AI competition, access to data is critical to training sophisticated AI models, therefore, the theft of terabytes of data and IP worth billions of dollars is the "equivalent of every ship in the navy sinking each year."[39]

While the United States maintains real advantages regarding signals intelligence (for example, tapping phones, accessing email, and so forth), the CCP enjoys some advantages regarding human intelligence (human spies).

For instance, unlike the United States, China can use its large overseas Chinese population to help acquire data about critical technologies. Conversely, the explosion in the number of surveillance cameras and AI-driven facial-recognition programs in China has made American human spying in the country much more difficult.

ALLIES

When assessing the global balance of military power between the United States and the PRC, allies and partners must be added to the equation. After doing so, the US surges ahead of China as the most powerful country on the planet. In Europe, the US is part of NATO, the world's largest and most enduring military alliance, one that recently grew even stronger with the addition of Finland and Sweden. In Asia, the United States has formal alliance treaties with Australia, Japan, South Korea, New Zealand, the Philippines, and Thailand and close military partnerships with other countries in the region, including Singapore and Vietnam. Japan's considerable naval forces could be game-changing in the event of war over Taiwan.[40] Australia's capabilities—advanced naval shipbuilding, long-range strike missiles, and advanced air combat technologies—could also make a difference in such a conflict.[41]

India is formally nonaligned but leans toward the US on military matters. In the Middle East, Israel is the closest US ally, but Washington maintains military relationships with Bahrain, Egypt, Jordan, Kuwait, Morocco, Qatar, Saudi Arabia, and Tunisia. Under a special designation of Major Non-NATO Allies, the US has defense, trade, and security cooperation arrangements with many countries, including Argentina, Bahrain, Brazil, Colombia, Egypt, Jordan, Kuwait, Morocco, Pakistan, Qatar, and Tunisia.[42] Additionally, the US Department of Defense has nurtured close ties with partners in Africa and Latin America through weapons sales, training exercises, anti-terrorist operations, and basing agreements. Given all these security partnerships, it is not surprising that American allies outspend China and Russia together.

The PRC has a formal and binding defense agreement with only one country, North Korea, a legacy of the Cold War. Few today assess this treaty as a net positive for China. The PRC has developed close military partner-

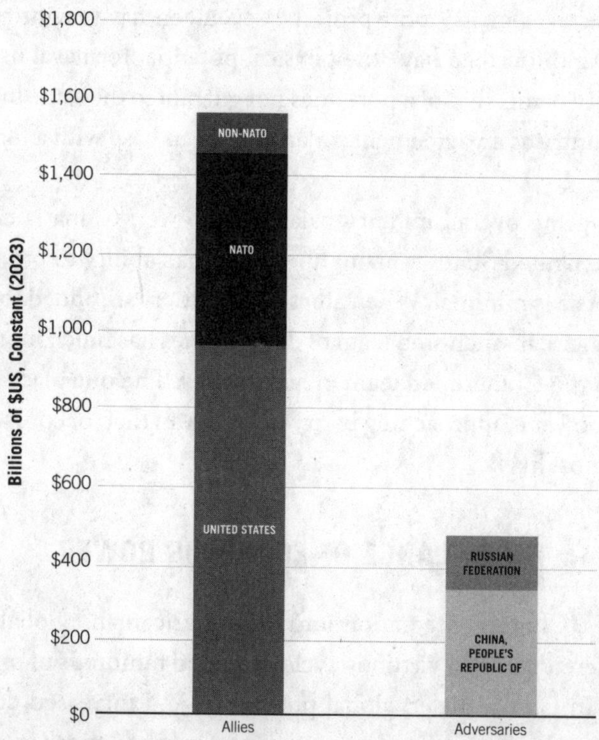

Figure 5.3 Military Spending: US Allies vs. China and Russia, 2024*

Source: Stockholm International Peace Research Institute, 2025

*This graph reflects the formal security treaties of the United States, as well as those involving both China and Russia. No state has a binding security treaty with both China and Russia, except North Korea. North Korea is excluded because military expenditure data is not publicly available. Non-NATO allies include countries that have a binding bilateral or trilateral security partnership with the United States: Australia, Japan, New Zealand, South Korea, and the Philippines. The Rio Treaty and the Southeast Asia Treaty are excluded intentionally.

ships with Russia and Pakistan but have no formal alliances. The military cooperation with Pakistan is more of an obligation and a liability than a force multiplier for Beijing. Subsequent chapters discuss the China-Russia entente in greater detail.

In addition, the United States also has roughly seven hundred fifty military bases and facilities in eighty countries. China has only one formal overseas base, in Djibouti. Informally, however, the PRC has secured base access through partial or full ownership of dual-use ports as an alternative strategy to constructing overseas bases.[43] Beijing has acquired equity ownership or operational stakes in 129 port projects; seventeen have majority Chinese ownership, and fourteen have the physical potential for naval use.[44] However, majority ownership of a port does not guarantee the same buy-in from the host country as an agreement for an American base with a foreign partner does.

Regarding the overall military balance of power, China is closing the gap, but the United States remains ahead. China's ability to project power outside of Asia is minimal. When allies and partners are added to the equation, the American-anchored team of democracies has much more military power than the Chinese-led team of autocracies. The one place where the balance of power is approaching parity is Asia. And that, of course, is where conflict is most likely.

THE BALANCE OF ECONOMIC POWER

For decades, Chinese integration into the American and global economy was considered part of a virtuous cycle: It pulled hundreds of millions out of poverty in China, fueled global prosperity, and increased demand for American goods and services among the members of China's growing middle class. However, at the same time, the growth and integration of Chinese firms into the global economy gradually displaced American companies and workers. The precise impact of the Chinese economic expansion on American manufacturing jobs remains a debate in academic circles.[45] But it is not a debate among blue-collar workers in the Midwest, as the 2016 and 2024 presidential victories of Donald Trump showed. This group attributes the decline of American manufacturing jobs to the growth of Chinese competition. Today, Republicans and Democrats alike question the wisdom of having helped the Chinese economy grow exponentially. For many, China's economic rise is now seen as a major threat to American national interests.

Regarding economic power, China is the most significant competitor the United States has faced in the past century, far greater than the Soviet Union. No American adversary—Nazi Germany, Imperial Japan, or the Soviet Union—has ever come as close as China in terms of economic parity with the United States. Though recent indicators show China's economic growth slowing, China will remain an economic superpower for decades, if not longer.

At the same time, a striking difference from the Cold War is that the People's Republic of China is both an economic competitor and a partner of the United States. In the past century, the Soviet Union was mainly a competitor. American companies and investors and those of our allies engage profitably with the Chinese economy in ways that Soviet leaders discouraged. For example, through sales to China, Boeing, Apple, Nvidia, and American farmers have earned enormous profits and supported thousands of American jobs. American consumers have similarly benefited from lower-priced products imported from China. In parallel, Chinese companies trade with and invest in American companies, Chinese scholars conduct collaborative research with American universities, Chinese students study in the United States, and Chinese financial institutions buy American bonds to degrees Moscow and Washington did not allow during the Cold War.

This economic entanglement presents both challenges and opportunities for American policymakers. Because the United States had few ties with the Soviet economy during the Cold War, American presidents could pursue a strategy of economic containment with little cost to American companies and consumers. That is not true today; economic containment policies toward China hurt not only the Chinese economy but also the American economy and the economies of US allies and partners. Consequently, we must carefully assess the implications of a robust Chinese economy for American security interests, recognizing that all Chinese economic power does not translate seamlessly into military power or political influence or automatically threaten American national interests. To make such careful assessments, measuring Chinese economic power accurately is the first step.

ECONOMIC SIZE

Comparing economies is challenging, even with accurate data. It is even more complex with inflated, distorted, or hidden data—the kind we often get from China.[46] Despite these measurement challenges, few would dispute that the United States and China constitute the two largest economies in the world, a condition that will endure for decades.

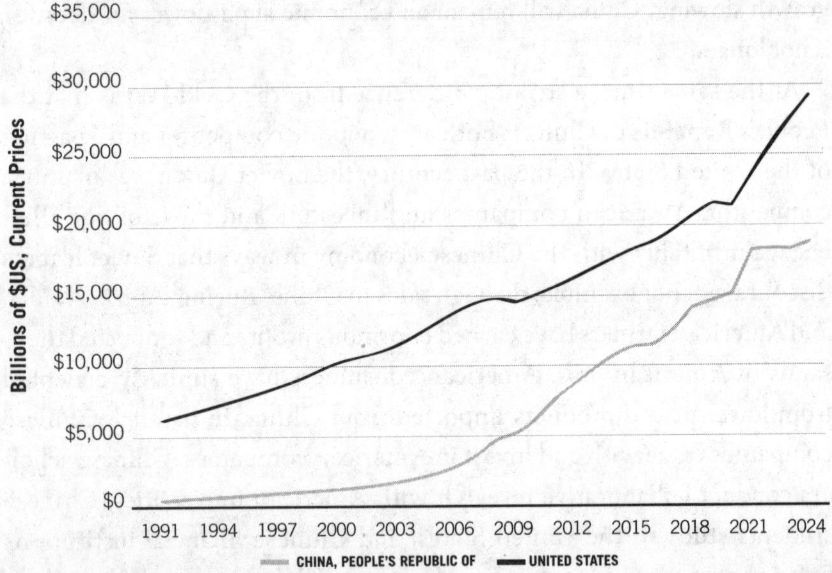

Figure 5.4 Gross Domestic Product: US vs. China, 1991–2024

Source: International Monetary Fund, 2025

The most basic and widely cited metric of economic size is gross domestic product. By this measure, the US remains ahead of China on a nominal basis.

In 2024, the IMF assessed the GDP of the United States at $29.18 trillion (26 percent of the world economy) compared to China's $18.75 trillion (17 percent of the world economy).[47] The American share of the global economy has remained remarkably steady for the past forty years at about 25 percent. Statements about rapid American economic decline from Beijing communists or Washington politicians are inaccurate. By contrast, China's share has skyrocketed from barely 2 percent forty years ago to 17 percent today. China has closed the gap primarily by speeding ahead of other economies, not by reducing the American share. Chinese success in expanding manufacturing capacity has been especially impressive, now surpassing that of the United States by roughly a two-to-one margin.

Purchasing power parity—PPP—is another metric used to compare the size of economies. PPP measures the price ratio of the same goods in different countries. If prices are lower in country A than in country B, you can purchase more with the same amount of money. By this accounting measure, the Chinese economy in 2024 was about 30 percent larger than the American economy: $38.15 trillion versus $29.18 trillion, respectively.[48]

It is disputed which metric more accurately captures the size of an economy. PPP is probably more relevant when comparing total economic strength because it represents a government's purchasing capacity to buy components of national power, be it infrastructure to support the economy or weapons to support the military. By both measures, however, the US and China are the world's two biggest economies, well ahead of the rest of the world.

GROWTH RATES

In 1978, two years after Mao Zedong's death, Deng Xiaoping introduced market reforms that radically accelerated Chinese economic growth. From 1992 to 2002, the Chinese economy expanded at an annual average rate of 10.3 percent, compared to 3.4 percent for the United States. This fantastic pace of economic expansion dramatically reduced the gap between the Chinese and American economies.

Chinese leaders, however, could not sustain such a high level of growth forever. In 2019, Chinese GDP growth fell to 6 percent—the lowest rate since 1990. The following year, COVID-19 hit, and Xi implemented draconian lockdowns to contain the disease. These lockdowns, combined with other structural factors, reduced growth to 2.2 percent. In 2021, the Chinese economy bounced back, growing at 8.4 percent compared to the previous year, but it tapered again to 3 percent in 2022.[49] The era of 10 percent annual growth rates in China is over; even 5 percent will prove difficult to sustain. In 2025, the IMF projected China's economy to grow by 4 percent.

Meanwhile, at least until President Trump's disruptive economic measures in the spring of 2025, the American economy has continued to grow much faster than most other developed economies in the world.[50] It recovered from the COVID-19 pandemic faster than any major industrialized country. In 2023, the US economy soared above all others in Europe, recording 2.9 percent real GDP growth, compared to 0.6 percent in the EU.[51]

GDP PER CAPITA

When comparing the balance of economic power in terms of GDP per capita, competition between the United States and China is not close. Even

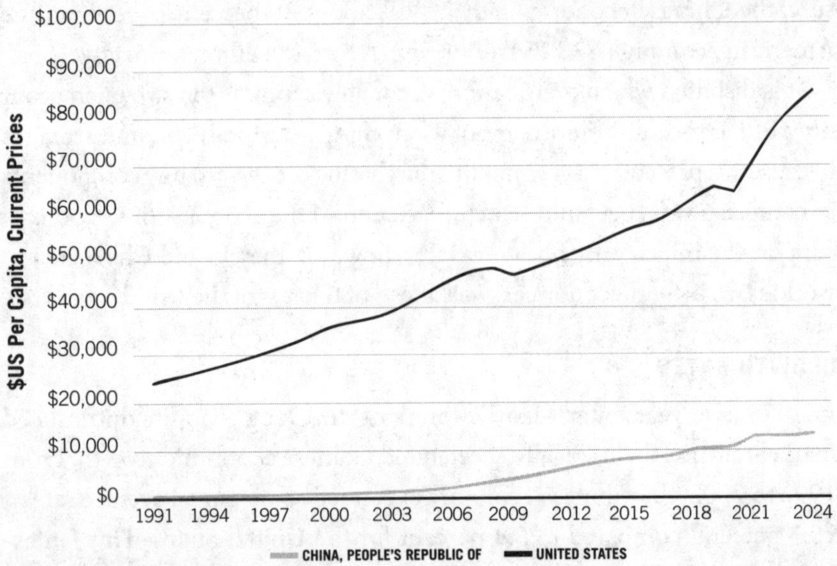

Figure 5.5 GDP per Capita: US vs. China, 1991–2024

Source: International Monetary Fund, 2025

if Xi's economic advisers find a way to sustain growth at 5 percent for the next several decades, the Chinese will not become as wealthy as Americans in this century.

Americans are roughly six times richer than the Chinese.[52] The gap is widening as US income levels rise while Chinese incomes are showing signs of stagnation. According to the 2024 IMF data, the US is seventh in the world in terms of GDP per capita at $85,812, while China ranked a distant seventy-fourth at $13,313. As measured by GDP per capita, almost all the most affluent countries are democracies and either formally allied or partnered with the United States. China's one major partner, Russia, ranks sixty-eighth at $14,795.[53]

GDP per capita matters because it shows potential problems for Chinese leaders. The transition from an upper-middle-income economy—a status China achieved only in 2010—to a high-income economy is rare. It often generates political instability in autocracies and sometimes prompts democratic breakthroughs, as we saw in South Korea and Taiwan. Very few countries leap from a middle-income to an upper-income economy.

TRADE AND INTERDEPENDENCE

Over the past several decades, as already mentioned, the American and Chinese economies have become deeply intertwined. In recent years, both Chinese and American leaders have adopted policies of "dual circulation" (the Chinese concept) or "reshoring" (the American slogan) to disentangle, decouple, or "de-risk" their economies from each other in both trade and investment. In 2023, US imports from China fell 20.4 percent compared to 2022.[54] The following year, they began to grow again, but marginally, from $426.9 billion in 2023 to $438.9 billion in 2024.[55] In 2020, US foreign direct investment (FDI) in China reached roughly $125 billion. That same year, China's FDI in the US was approximately $38 billion.[56] In 2023, however, the investment climate in China sharply deteriorated. Coupled with US sanctions, structural and industrial inefficiencies, and onerous domestic regulations, China's net foreign direct investment plummeted by over 90 percent in 2023 compared to its 2021 peak, falling to its lowest level in three decades.[57] Investment into China from American private equity funds shrank by a staggering margin, from $140 billion in 2019 to $4 billion in 2023.[58] At the beginning of his second term, President Trump seemed determined to accelerate decoupling through the use of high tariffs on Chinese goods complemented by comprehensive restrictions on investment flows. Xi seems ready to match Trump's efforts tit for tat. Despite these recent trends and new aspirations, however, China remains the third-largest export market for US goods (after Canada and Mexico), and the US is the largest export market for Chinese goods.[59]

The economies of these two superpowers are highly intertwined not only with each other but with the rest of the world. In 2013, China surpassed the US as the world's largest trading country when the PRC emerged as the top trading partner for nearly one hundred countries.[60] When China joined the World Trade Organization in 2001, roughly four-fifths of the globe traded more with the United States than China. Today, only about 30 percent of all countries have a larger trade volume with the US than China.[61] The United States remains the world's second-largest trading partner.

This level of economic entanglement between two rival great powers is not unique in world history but it is very different from the Cold War. China's embrace of global trade and investment enables the CCP leaders to pull levers of power that their Soviet counterparts never had. China wields considerable economic leverage against other countries, including key American allies in Asia—Japan, Australia, South Korea, and the Philippines—that rely on China's large consumer market. Apart from gas exports in Western Europe, the Soviet Union had no significant coercive economic power available to use against US allies during the Cold War. China, on the other hand, did not hesitate to restrict the sales of rare earth elements to Japan during the intensified territorial conflict in the East China Sea, banned the import of Australian coal as retaliation for demanding an investigation to discover the origin of COVID-19, imposed punitive measures against South Korean firms following Seoul's decision to deploy American Terminal High Altitude Area Defense systems, and stopped the import of bananas from the Philippines after its territorial dispute in the South China Sea. The global reliance on China's production of critical minerals needed to manufacture semiconductors, smartphones, batteries for electric vehicles, jet engines, and satellites poses a serious security threat to the United States and its allies. At the same time, this level of interdependence limits the PRC's potential to behave disruptively in the international system. Chinese leaders have much more to gain from peace and stability and much more to lose from conflict and war than their counterparts in Moscow do today or had during the Cold War.

FINANCIAL POWER

While China has sprinted ahead of the US in global trade, the US maintains a considerable lead in global finance as the world's largest debtor nation. This status is mainly attributable to the US dollar's central role in the international financial and monetary system. Gloomy predictions regarding the collapse of the US dollar and the rise of the Chinese renminbi (RMB) as the new global currency have not yet materialized. As Goldman Sachs executive Jared Cohen assessed in 2024, China's Cross-Border Interbank Payment System "handles a reported 25,900 [transactions] a day," while the US equivalent—the US Clearing House of Interbank Payments System—does "500,000 daily transactions totaling $1.8 trillion in value."[62] In March 2023, for the first time, the RMB became the most used currency in China's cross-border transactions, and Beijing has already launched a digital currency—the digital yuan, or e-CNY—despite serious debate about the merits of electronic currencies.[63] To date, Xi's rhetorical calls for currency diversification, including central-bank digital currencies, significantly outpace reality. The dollar remains the world's currency of choice, with an overwhelming proportion of global foreign exchange reserves still held in US dollars.[64]

Serving as the world's banker has drawbacks. American financial and monetary dominance makes US manufacturing costly, creating long-term adverse effects for American workers and companies.[65] As much as Xi and other Chinese officials tout the need for less global reliance on the dollar, the status quo serves them well by allowing them to keep the value of their currency low and thereby encourage exports.

US Treasury bonds continue to be a trusted international investment everywhere, including in Beijing, which maintains the world's largest foreign exchange reserves, worth roughly $3 trillion. Because a significant portion, $860 billion, is held in US Treasuries denominated in dollars, Xi has limited ability to coerce the US through economic power.[66] Chinese leaders may aspire to reduce their dependence on US Treasury bonds, but better investment options are unavailable, especially in China's own bond market.[67]

Chinese companies are outpacing their American counterparts in cashless payment systems. Ant Group's Alipay and Tencent's WeChat Pay have rapidly transformed banking, finance, and other transactions inside China and are gaining market share globally.[68] However, with these super-apps comes super-surveillance, which has mellowed enthusiasm for adopting e-currencies in democratic countries. Who will ultimately win this arena of competition remains uncertain.

SCIENCE AND TECHNOLOGY

Technological advances have long played a key role in augmenting military power. For instance, during the Cold War, America's ability to harness computing power more effectively than the Soviet Union, especially in semiconductor technology, was critical to US victory.[69] In this arena of competition, China is a much greater challenge than the Soviet Union was. China is home to some of the world's best tech companies. In 2023, the Australian Strategic Policy Institute estimated China was ahead in thirty-seven of forty-four critical technologies, including 5G communications, electric batteries, and autonomous systems operation technology.[70] China is also racing ahead in electric vehicles, high-speed rail, drones, solar panels, pharmaceuticals, robotics, hypersonic missiles, commercial nuclear power, low-end chips, and liquid crystal displays. In recent years, Xi's assertion of state control of some of China's most successful companies slowed growth in this sector, but Xi's new focus on "high-quality development" suggests he still understands the necessity of investing in emerging technologies.

Regarding spending on education, the US remains ahead, but less so than three decades ago. Comparing fundamental research and education, the *Times Higher Education*'s World University Ranks 2025 placed twenty-two American universities in the top fifty compared to six in China (and two are in Hong Kong), but China's top universities are trying to catch up. But on this metric of power, China has a very long way to go to close the gap with the United States, and it will likely never do so, unless the US government cuts funding for research universities in a dramatic and sustained way as President Trump started to do in the first year of his second term. When allies are added to this comparison, the world's democracies vastly outpace China and Russia: eighty-seven for the democratic camp to thirteen for the autocratic one, among which five are in Hong Kong and may not stay in the top one hundred in the wake of Beijing's crackdown there.[71]

After the Soviet Union collapsed, the US government dramatically cut budgets for research funding, but increases in private investment have enabled the US to hold on to its R&D lead.[72] According to the Organization for Economic Cooperation and Development (OECD), US gross domestic R&D spending reached about 3.4 percent of GDP in 2022 (over $892 billion).[73] Chinese R&D investments have increased dramatically, from less than $3 billion in 1991 to $458 billion in 2023 (3.3 trillion yuan), but they are still well below American spending.[74] Regarding spending on fundamental research (science and engineering) as a percentage of overall R&D spending, the United States is still well ahead of China, 15 percent compared to 6 percent in 2021.[75] In his second term, however, Trump radically cut research and development funding in truly irrational ways; these cuts were so counter to American long-term national interests that one hopes the democratic system of checks and balances in the United States will reverse these funding cuts and continue to support this major American advantage.[76]

The quality and quantity of research output are other critical indicators of technological and scientific leadership. The conventional wisdom was that China won on quantity and the United States on quality. That now is changing.[77] Eight years ago, the Chinese Academy of Sciences (CAS) was the only Chinese institution in the top ten global leaders in scientific publications; the United States claimed more spots than any other nation, with three universities—Harvard, Stanford, and MIT—on the list.[78] In 2024, eight of the top ten institutions producing high-quality scientific research are based in China. Only one in the top ten is in the US (Harvard).[79] In the past ten years, CAS has surged ahead of all competitors in producing high-cited STEM papers, publishing 17,262 in 2022 compared to 8,504 for the University of California system and 5,176 for Harvard University.[80] CAS has also played a leading role in China's production of AI research.[81] CAS is a government entity overseeing 115 institutes and two universities, so comparing CAS output to individual American universities may be unfair. However, there should be no question that Xi and his CCP comrades are spending heavily to compete with the United States in this critical arena of great power competition. Beijing is devoting more attention and resources to research and development at a time when many conservative American politicians are questioning the utility of research universities because of their alleged "wokeness" and are threatening to cut government funding for basic research.

TECH COMPANIES, AI, CHIPS, AND QUANTUM COMPUTING

Regarding tech firms, the majority of the top twenty world's most valuable companies are American; China has one or two. While valuations change often these days, in part in response to Trump's tariffs and export controls, Alphabet, Amazon, Apple, Meta, Microsoft, and Nvidia continue to tower above their Chinese competitors in value, profitability, and product quality. China is catching up and even moving ahead in some tech sectors, especially when manufacturing is involved. China's DJI, for instance, is the largest producer of commercial drones. China's Hikvision Digital Technology is the world's leading video-surveillance equipment supplier. China also leads the world in producing robots and then installing them in factories, and is also outpacing the world in electric vehicle production, solar panels, batteries, and nuclear reactors. In the aggregate, the American tech sector's total value still outpaces China and every other country in the world, but the gap is closing.

Xi's distrust of tech companies has slowed China's progress in this domain. The CCP's crackdown on some of the country's most successful tech companies, including Jack Ma's Alibaba and the ride-hailing platform Didi, and its stifling of Hong Kong as a global center of finance and entrepreneurship show that in Xi's China, politics trumps economics, science, and technology.[82] Whether these anti-market, anti-innovation actions are a temporary blip or the beginning of a long-term state crackdown is not clear. Artificial intelligence, in particular, creates challenges for regimes trying to limit the flow of information, since most AI models depend on massive datasets and Chinese AI companies censor sensitive information about the People's Republic of China.

Because AI enhances so many other fields, such as neuroscience, biology, and quantum computing, as well as autonomous weapons systems, surveillance capabilities, cyber technologies, and command-and-control systems, who wins this race is especially critical.[83] So far, the United States is ahead according to several metrics. In 2024, private investment in American AI ventures grew to $109.1 billion, nearly twelve times the size of investment into Chinese AI ventures, $9.3 billion.[84] Stanford University's annual AI Index assessed that "in 2023, 61 notable AI models originated from US-based institutions, far outpacing the European Union's 21 and China's 15."[85] The AI Index ranks the United States first, China second, and all others far behind. American tech giants Meta, Microsoft, Nvidia, and Amazon—as well as newer companies like Open AI and Anthropic—seek to make multibillion-dollar bets to dominate the market. In terms of money spent and raised, they are ahead of their Chinese competitors.

China holds an edge on some measures. Stanford's AI Index report in 2024 stated that "disaggregated by geographic area, the majority of the world's granted AI patents are from China (61.1%) and the United States

(20.9%)."[86] Chinese researchers also outpace their American counterparts in AI publications, reaching parity in the share of highly cited AI publications.[87] The Chinese state assists AI development more directly than the US government, providing subsidies, preferential tax treatments, and close cooperation with state-run research institutions. For example, China's giant search engine Baidu collaborated with Tsinghua University's Institute for AI Research to develop Baidu's autonomous driving system based on China's 5G network, and China's online retail powerhouse Alibaba has cooperated with CAS to develop upgraded cloud platforms, algorithm software, and consulting services.[88] Chinese tech companies like Lenovo and iFlyTek have also benefited from deeply intertwined collaboration and ownership arrangements with CAS.[89]

The Biden administration tried to slow China's AI development by restricting the export of high-end chips and EUV lithography machines and putting constraints on China's ability to obtain American data.[90] Initial assessments suggested that these chip-export restrictions were hampering Chinese AI development.[91] It is too early to assess how effective these constraints will be over the long term, both because of leakage of chips through third countries and because these restrictions are compelling Chinese leaders and firms to accelerate the production of their own chips, their own chip-making equipment, and new ways to achieve mass computing power without using the most sophisticated chips made by non-Chinese companies.[92]

The assumption that the United States was way ahead in AI development was radically challenged in January of 2025 when China's AI company DeepSeek released a new model with performance capabilities similar to the best American models that was developed at a fraction of the cost, used much less computing power, and was not constrained by US export controls on high-end chips. DeepSeek's R1 model is also much cheaper to use, meaning that fast adoption, especially in the developing world, is likely. Some compared the release of DeepSeek's new AI model to a Sputnik moment, as the American giant lead in the AI race with China appeared to vanish overnight. Stocks of American companies involved in AI production, including, most dramatically, Nvidia, the producer of the high-end chips needed for AI, plummeted after the release of DeepSeek's new product. Nvidia's single-day loss in market value of $600 billion was the largest ever for a US company.[93] Alibaba's Qwen 2.5 AI product, released a few days after DeepSeek R1, claims to perform as well as DeepSeek and the best American models.[94] Several other less well-known Chinese AI companies are quickly closing the gap on their American and French competitors.

Similarly to AI, quantum technology has emerged as a pivotal area of US-China technological competition. Unlike ordinary computers, quantum computers can process significantly more information and perform complex calculations much faster. Quantum computers enable breakthroughs in fields that require immense computational power.[95] For example, in medicine, quantum computers could accelerate drug discovery and testing of potential treatments, developing drugs in minutes rather than years. In materials science, quantum simulations could lead to the creation of stronger and lighter materials by modeling atomic structures with unprecedented precision. Quantum computing will also have a transformative impact in the military and security domains, where quantum's potential to unlock encryption could give our enemies all our secrets (and access to all our bank accounts!).

Not surprisingly, therefore, the US and China have invested billions in developing this technology. Regarding government spending, China is ahead. In 2023, China invested $15.3 billion in quantum technology, including support for the world's largest quantum research facility in Hefei, compared to the US government's $3.8 billion.[96] However, America's private-sector spending on quantum computing, estimated to be over $3.3 billion of investment between 2001 and 2023, is ahead of China's.[97] Companies like Google and IBM are investing in specialized infrastructure and pioneering research networks to make quantum computing commercially viable. In 2022, IBM unveiled a 433-qubit processor, setting a new benchmark in quantum hardware.[98] Regarding research, American authors retain a narrow lead in the quality of quantum-computing research papers, but Chinese scientists are closing the gap.

CHINA'S ECONOMIC CHALLENGES

While China has been closing the economic gap with the United States for decades, its model also shows signs of running out of steam. A combination of policy decisions and structural factors has slowed growth. New leadership or a change in thinking can produce new policies to spur more innovation and productivity gains, but structural factors are much harder to change in the short term.

Xi's economic policies present the most immediate challenge to growth. As discussed in chapter 2, the CCP's expanding control and ownership of the economy have spurred large-scale capital flight out of China. Thousands of China's wealthiest businesspeople have also left. CCP leadership continues implementing policies that encourage investment, manufacturing, and individual savings but suppress consumer spending. This strategy is not sustainable. Unproductive investments in state-owned enterprises and underperforming infrastructure projects overseas through the Belt and Road Initiative (BRI) have resulted in massive debt and nonperforming loans at government-related organizations and within firms. China's debt is now estimated to be nearing 300 percent of its GDP.[99] China's real estate sector is particularly troubled by overinvestment, ballooning debt, and falling housing prices.[100] In 2021, property giant Evergrande defaulted on its loans with $300 billion in liabilities.[101] Trouble in this sector means trouble overall, since real estate accounted for a staggering 60 to 70 percent of China's household wealth in 2022.[102] By comparison, home equity accounted for only 28.5 percent of American household wealth in 2021.[103]

China has a second significant problem constraining growth: a shrinking workforce. Over the past four decades, the Chinese economy grew rapidly in large part because the country's gigantic workforce continued to expand and became more productive, especially when prodded by Deng Xiaoping's reforms to move tens of millions from village farms to city factories.[104] In 2022, however, China reported its first population decline since the 1960s, when the disastrous Great Leap Forward caused mass famine. By 2100, China could have five hundred million fewer people than it did in 2023, and a larger share than ever will be over sixty-five.

Similar demographic changes are affecting most of the developed world, but the Chinese population is less wealthy than their counterparts in Europe, the United States, Japan, South Korea, and Taiwan and is aging faster than their income is increasing, which translates into a significant drag on future growth. China's One Child Policy also produced massive distortions in the gender ratio; China has thirty-five million fewer women than men, meaning there are thirty-five million fewer potential couples who could have children.[105] Strict limits on immigration have further constrained the growth of the population and labor force. China has one of the world's lowest shares of immigrants—only 1.4 million individuals, or 0.1 percent of its total population, according to the 2020 census. Chinese law denies foreign nationals an easy road to citizenship and the ability to remain in the country after retirement. From 2012 to 2021, China experienced a steady outflow of people, highlighting challenges in attracting and retaining foreign talent. A shrinking labor pool increases wages and reduces the tax base needed to support an aging society. Without significant reforms, Chinese society will get old before it gets rich.

The US faces demographic challenges too—particularly declining birth rates—but has three significant advantages over China. First, birth rates in the United States are higher than in China. Second, unlike the PRC, America saw tremendous GDP per capita growth before its society grew old. Third, despite a recent rise in anti-immigrant sentiment and policies, especially during the first and second Trump administrations, the US has historically attracted massive numbers of new workers from abroad. From 2012 to 2025, US net migration averaged 1.44 million annually.[106] In 2023, the US was home to 47.83 million immigrants, 14.3 percent of its population.[107] If reinvigorated again, immigration will be one of America's greatest advantages over China in the twenty-first century.

In addition to bad policies and demographics, human capital is a third constraint on growth in China. Despite significant investments in education, China still has one of the world's least-educated populations of middle-income countries.[108] Chinese students from high-income provinces like Beijing, Shanghai, Jiangsu, and Zhejiang score above their American counterparts.[109] China outpaces the rest of the world in educating its college students in STEM fields and produces more than eight times the STEM graduates the US yields.[110] In addition, roughly three hundred thousand Chinese students studied in the US in 2022.[111] Despite these efforts, eight hundred million Chinese people in rural areas do not receive an education comparable to those in urban areas. Even after decades of urbanization, a much larger percentage of Chinese students than American students live in rural areas, where only one in ten Chinese adult workers have a high-school degree (compared to one in four in cities).[112] China's rural labor force has one of the lowest education levels of any middle-income country.[113] Among the high-income OECD countries, 80 percent of the labor force has obtained a high-school education. For the US, it is around 92 percent. China is at 36.6 percent.[114] Even with the best policies and investments, reaching current averages for OECD high-school education will take China decades. This large and undereducated segment of rural society impedes China's graduation from a middle-income to a high-income country.[115]

Regarding human capital, the US has its problems too. American high-school students perform at approximately the same level or worse than the same group did twenty years ago on basic subjects like reading, mathematics, and science. However, the US is still ahead of China in this critical measure of economic power and potential. The United States still maintains a sizable lead over China regarding not only high-school education but college as well. Roughly half of Americans receive some college education, compared to only 18.5 percent of Chinese.[116]

Inequality is a fourth constraint on growth. Economic growth in the post-Mao era dramatically increased income and wealth inequality.[117] In 2021, the World Bank estimated China's Gini index at 35.7, which, despite official rhetoric about the values of socialism and equality, is higher than most developed countries, though not yet as high as the United States.[118] (As a reminder from the previous chapter, a ranking of 0 represents absolute income equality, and a ranking of 100 is complete income inequality.) Moreover, experts question the validity of China's reported numbers and suggest that actual inequality levels might be much higher. Inequality hinders long-term economic growth, prevents countries from becoming high-income economies, and heightens the potential for political instability. In response to this very anti-socialist trend, Xi launched in 2021 his initiative for "common prosperity"—a campaign committed to wealth redistribution. The following year, he called for a more significant commitment to "high-quality" growth. So far, measurable results from these new policies have been limited.

GLOBAL ECONOMIC POWER: AUTOCRATS VS. DEMOCRATS

As with its military power, the United States has many wealthy allies and friends compared to China. Aggregate economic power worldwide is concentrated in the hands of the US and its democratic allies and partners. Globally, nine of the ten largest economies are democracies: the US, Germany, Japan, India, the United Kingdom, France, Brazil, Italy, and Canada[119] (China is the one exception). Six of these top-ten economies are US allies, and the other two have closer relations with the US than with China. Among the top twenty economies, seventeen are democracies, all leaning toward the United States. (The three autocracies in the top twenty are China, Russia, and Saudi Arabia, and the last still leans toward the US too.) And if just US democratic allies are included, Asia experts Kurt Campbell and Rush Doshi calculated that they combine for $60 trillion of economic activity compared to $18 trillion for the PRC.[120]

Comparisons of GDP per capita skew even more dramatically in favor of the democrats and against the autocrats. Of the twenty wealthiest countries in the world in terms of GDP per capita, eighteen are democracies closely tied to the United States, and the two autocracies on this list—Qatar and Singapore—lean toward the US, not China. If the Chinese leaders aim to shift the economic balance of power in favor of autocracies and against democracies, they have a long way to go.

CONCLUSION

In the aggregate, American military power outpaces Chinese power today. The PRC is closing the gap and already has some clear advantages regarding, for instance, the number of soldiers and ships as well as high-quality missiles, but the United States in the aggregate is poised to remain ahead for decades. The only variable that could undermine this trajectory is self-inflicted wounds from American leaders who pursue new, catastrophic policies that damage economic growth and military power. Tragically, President Trump is experimenting with just that in his first months in office, but the long-term implications of his new policies, especially regarding tariffs and cuts in R&D budgets, are still not clear.

Disturbingly, however, the balance of military power in Asia is more equal while geography gives the PRC a home field advantage, and that is the region where a conflict between the United States and China is most likely. The PRC lacks the military means to push the US out of Asia, let alone establish Chinese hegemony in the region. Chinese leaders would have to devote a substantially more significant percentage of the national budget to military spending than they are doing now to achieve this goal. Trying to do so could produce imbalanced domestic spending and overreach abroad—the very kind of policies that accelerated the Soviet Union's collapse. But compared to American military assets deterring them, the PRC already has the military capabilities to believe that they could win a quick war to seize Taiwan. They could be very wrong in that assessment, as Putin was in thinking he could conquer Ukraine in weeks. But the increasingly equal balance of capabilities in the region between the United States and China today could tempt miscalculation.

American strategists must also be careful to estimate China's economic prowess accurately. China's economy is much greater and more intertwined with the world than the Soviet Union's economy ever was, giving Xi the capacity to shape global politics in ways Soviet leaders could only dream of. Since becoming a great power, the United States has never faced an economic competitor as formidable as China. However, translating economic capacity into influence is not easy; using economic power to persuade or coerce other nations to take actions for China's benefit is difficult. Recent PRC attempts to use economic coercion to achieve foreign policy objectives have backfired.[121] Moreover, as just discussed, the Chinese economy faces significant structural and demographic challenges, exacerbated by Xi's recent poor economic policies that will limit Beijing's capacity to use economic power for international influence. Finally, US leaders should not perceive all Chinese economic capacity as a zero-sum threat to American interests. The idea that the US should try to weaken the overall Chinese economy is misguided. We should not want to impoverish the Chinese people—nor could we if we wanted to. Our era's fundamental foreign policy challenge is figuring out the delicate balance between economic engagement and containment.

To get that policy balance right, we need to not only assess Chinese power but also determine for what purposes the PRC intends to use this power—the subject of chapters 8 and 11.

Chapter 6

THE WANING OF DEMOCRACY AS A UNIVERSAL VALUE

AT THE END of the Cold War, democracy emerged as the most legitimate and popular system of government in the world. After the fall of the Berlin Wall in 1989, nearly every European country under communist dictatorship transitioned to democracy. Two years later, leaders of the fifteen newly independent states that emerged from the collapse of the Soviet Union signaled a desire to build democracy (at least rhetorically). Some new leaders were more committed to the task than others; most had not consolidated democratic systems of government a decade later.[1] But no leader or movement in the region or the world was promoting an alternative. Even Xi's top ideologist today, Wang Huning, wrote in 1986, "In today's world, democracy has become the goal of political development . . . Without a highly democratic political system, there can be no talk of standing tall as a modernized, powerful country among the world's advanced nations."[2] South Africa's shift from apartheid to democracy occurred around the same time, anchoring a wave of democratization throughout Africa and a hopeful time for democracy worldwide.

Some autocrats dug in. In this same era, leaders of the Chinese Communist Party violently repressed peaceful pro-democracy protesters in Tiananmen Square in the summer of 1989. But even so, most autocrats argued that their countries were either following their particular forms of democracy or slowly transitioning from dictatorship. They were not advocating for a different type of government. Except for some fanatic theocrats in Iran and jihadi terrorists along the Afghanistan-Pakistan border, most of the world was embracing liberalism as an ideology and democracy as a system of government as the only games in town. As political scientist Francis Fukuyama accurately wrote then, "The triumph of the West, of the Western *idea*, is evident first of all in the total exhaustion of viable systematic alternatives to Western liberalism."[3]

The leaders of the United States—one of the oldest and best-functioning democracies in the world then—proudly proclaimed their indispensable role in advancing democracy globally and readiness to provide resources to help other countries consolidate democracy. As Americans pushed for individualism and free markets over collectivism and communism, people worldwide admired and embraced what many equated with American values at the time.

Back then, I was already an enthusiastic champion of democracy and an optimistic supporter of democracy promotion. From 1990 to 1991, I worked in the Soviet Union as an adviser for an American democracy promotion nongovernmental organization, the National Democratic Institute (NDI). I returned to Moscow in 1992 to open NDI's first office in a newly independent and democratic Russia. President Yeltsin's government, Russia's parliament, and civil society leaders welcomed me and my NDI colleagues with open arms. Few questioned whether democracy was the best system of government. Building democracy was considered an engineering problem, not a normative debate. In the 1990s, other democracies and even the United Nations expanded their democracy promotion efforts too. Some scholars, including myself, suggested democracy promotion had become a universal value.[4]

Today, this optimism about democracy's universal appeal is gone. As an idea, democracy no longer enjoys the hegemonic place it did thirty years ago. Past waves of democratization have overreached and receded, so we should have expected the same for our era.[5] Democratic breakthroughs failed to consolidate in several major countries, including Russia, Turkey, and Egypt. In addition, as discussed earlier, autocratic countries are becoming more powerful than they were thirty years ago. Older democracies, including the United States, do not perform as effectively as they did politically and economically. In his second term, President Trump has sought to expand executive power in ways that threaten democracy within the United States.[6] In parallel, democracy promotion has become controversial as a foreign policy objective in the United States and around the world, considered imperial by some, ineffective and a waste of money by others. In his first term, Trump was not a supporter of democracy promotion. In his second term, Trump has been openly hostile to this idea.

The rise of two powerful autocracies, China and Russia, is to blame for some of the democratic decline in the world, trends explored in detail in the following two chapters. However, the decline of democracy as a universal value is not just a story of rising autocracies. Two other factors contributed: (1) US foreign policy decisions over the past three decades and (2) the erosion of the quality of democracy within older liberal democracies, especially in the United States. Before examining how Russia and China aspire to undermine democratic governance and ideas around the world in chapters 7 and 8, this chapter traces the evolution of American democracy promotion efforts since the end of the Cold War and the uneven practice of democracy within the United States, especially in recent years.

WHAT IS IDEOLOGY?

Before reviewing this history of decline regarding ideas about democracy and the growing ideological struggle between democrats and autocrats in the world today, we should define *ideology*. It is a challenging task. Some defenders of democracy reject calling democracy an ideology, preferring to label it strictly as a particular form of government. There is some wisdom in calling democracy and autocracy not ideologies but systems of government. But there are norms, ideas, and ideological frameworks that accompany and are generated by these two systems of government. As international relations scholar Mark Haas explains, "Political ideologies are the principles upon which a particular leadership group attempts to legitimate its claim to rule and the primary institutional economic and social goals to which it swears allegiance. Ideologies are, in short, particular visions for ordering *domestic* politics."[7]

Liberalism strongly correlates with democracy. Illiberalism strongly correlates with dictatorship. If no one disagrees that liberalism is an ideology, then illiberalism must also be considered an ideology. Of course, there is a range of more specific ideologies that leaders have used to justify a variety of regime types, especially on the autocratic side of the ledger, including communism, fascism, Islamic fundamentalism, and monarchy. If these ideas legitimating dictatorship are considered by most to be ideologies, then the ideas legitimating democracy must be labeled as an ideology as well.

Many scholars of international relations believe that ideas, ideologies, and regime types do not matter in explaining world politics, and that power is the only driver of relations between great powers. Such accounts are incomplete. Of course all analyses of great *power* relations must start with power, as this book did. However, the balance of power does not explain everything in international politics. Regime type and the ideas that support different systems of government matter too. Countries with democratic systems of government that espouse liberal values get along better with each other than countries with opposing systems of government supported by different ideologies. Democracies do not go to war with each other. Autocracies do. Autocracies and democracies have often fought too, and they most certainly have competed over the centuries. They are competing now. Ideas and ideological frameworks also influence how leaders understand the world and, in response, shape their foreign policies.[8]

In today's world, the United States (at least until Trump's second term), Russia, and China all promote their ideas abroad. They are all ideological powers. Leaders of countries with limited military or economic capabilities must focus on security and rarely promote their ideas abroad. Leaders of great powers have the luxury, or face the temptation, of venturing beyond worries of survival and therefore are more likely to promote their ideas about governance, economics, and international relations to other countries. Great powers make mistakes when they overreach with their ideological missions in ways that undermine their core security and economic interests.[9]

The very existence of a powerful democracy threatens autocracies, in that such a country challenges the legitimacy of dictatorships. Likewise, the very existence of a powerful autocracy threatens democracies. In addition, great powers can feel threatened by small powers and non-state movements with different ideological orientations. That was true in nineteenth-century Europe.[10] And it is true today. Leaders of the powerful democratic United States feel threatened by autocratic Iran and North Korea. Putin, the leader of a powerful autocratic Russia, feels threatened by democratic Ukraine.

Xi, the leader of a powerful autocratic China, feels threatened by democratic Taiwan. Even tiny, liberal, and democratic Hong Kong was too much for Xi to tolerate. He felt compelled to use repressive measures to shut it down.

Of course, ideology is just *one* of the factors generating great power conflict today, just as it was during the Cold War. However, ignoring Putinism, Xi Jinping's Thought, or American liberalism is an analytic mistake. And understanding why American ideas about democracy and liberalism have faded in appeal over the past three decades is critical for crafting US strategies for succeeding in the ideological competition between great powers today.

AMERICAN OVERREACH

During the Cold War, the American democratic system of government was not ideal, nor was progress toward a more perfect union linear. While the civil rights movement and political campaigns to advance rights for women and the LGBTQ community produced tangible democratic advances, these successes also generated backlashes and moments when American democracy seemed to be fracturing and political polarization was becoming more acute. After Martin Luther King Jr. and Bobby Kennedy were assassinated in 1968 and National Guardsmen killed four students at Kent State in 1970, it was hard to be inspired by American democracy. The crimes and corruption of President Richard Nixon and his team, culminating in Nixon's resignation in 1974, also tarnished the global image of American democracy. Like the voices of the Chinese and Russian governments trumpeting the US decline today, Soviet propagandists seized on these struggles to argue that the "correlation of forces" (to use the Soviet term) was moving against the democratic United States and toward communism. And yet, despite these struggles, the United States remained a democracy.

At times during the Cold War, other democracies questioned certain American foreign policy decisions. France left NATO's military command structure for a while. European leaders and societies loudly criticized the American involvement in the Vietnam War. Antinuclear activists in West Germany and elsewhere demonstrated against Reagan's decision to deploy new missiles in Europe. However, these disagreements never developed into lasting fissures, let alone the breakup of the democratic world, in addressing the Soviet threat. At the end of the Cold War, democratic unity and admiration for American democracy were more robust than ever.

Toward the end of the Cold War and right after, US leaders took advantage of America's unprecedented power and universal admiration for its values to try to promote democracy abroad with greater vigor. Inspired by President Reagan's 1982 speech to the British parliament, the US Congress established the National Endowment for Democracy two years later, along with its four affiliated organizations—the National Democratic Institute for International Affairs, the National Republican Institute (later renamed the International Republican Institute), the Center for Independent Private Enterprise, and the American Center for International Labor Solidarity—all of which were tasked with advancing democratic ideas and practices around the world. After the Soviet Union collapsed, these organizations expanded their work to help consolidate democratic breakthroughs in the post-communist world as well as in Africa, Asia, and Latin America, and eventually the Middle East. In 1992, the US Congress passed the Freedom Support Act to provide new resources to the US Agency for International Development (USAID) and its implementing partners to foster democratic and market development in post-communist Europe and the former Soviet Union. Other organizations in the democracy promotion business, such as the International Foundation for Elections Systems, Freedom House, Internews, IREX, the Asia Foundation, the Eurasia Foundation, the Carter Center, and the Open Society Institute, were created or expanded around the same time.

President Clinton leaned into this glorious moment for democracy worldwide, declaring in his January 1993 inaugural address, "Our greatest strength is the power of our ideas, which are still new in many lands. Across the world, we see them embraced, and we rejoice. Our hopes, our hearts, our hands, are with those on every continent who are building democracy and freedom. Their cause is America's cause."[11] Clinton and his administration considered NATO's expansion a tool for consolidating democracy in Eastern Europe.

Clinton could press for democracy-assistance programs in countries around the world and push for enlarging NATO because the United States was the world's only superpower at the time. Autocrats in the 1990s did not have the means to push back. Yet even with hegemonic power, American leaders often chose to work within the multilateral organizations to advance principles of sovereignty and human rights, as they did with the US-led military coalitions to oust Iraqi soldiers from Kuwait in 1991 and the Taliban and al-Qaeda from Afghanistan in 2001. Advancing democracy abroad and supporting the liberal international order were considered synergistic missions.

At times, however, these two missions clashed. For instance, after failing to get UN Security Council support for the use of force against dictator Slobodan Milosevic to stop his slaughter of Muslims in Kosovo, Clinton turned to NATO for support for this military campaign in 1999. In bombing Serbia, Clinton thought he was defending human rights, but others around the world perceived this American-led military intervention as an act of unilateralism in defiance of international law and the liberal international order.

President George W. Bush took that defiance to a new level when he decided to invade Iraq in 2003 without UN Security Council or NATO endorsement. In the run-up to the war, Bush and his administration advanced security arguments to gain support for invading both Afghanistan and Iraq. But after American soldiers and their allies had toppled the Afghan and Iraqi dictatorships, the mission changed to democracy promotion, consistent with Bush's embrace of his new Freedom Agenda after al-Qaeda attacked the United States on September 11, 2001. As Bush explained at the end of his second term, "It's in our national interest to continue liberty's advance—because we know from history that the advance of freedom is necessary for our security and for world peace."[12]

Both wars initially did topple dictatorships and produce more freedom in Afghanistan and Iraq, but the absence of a UN mandate or even support from democratic allies in Iraq fueled the perception that the United States had again acted against the rules of the liberal international order. Over time, the failure of democracy to take root in Afghanistan and Iraq further eroded global support for American democracy promotion.

Senator Barack Obama did not support the decision to invade Iraq. After his election in 2008, President Obama pledged to stop using military force as a means for democratic regime change. Obama did not abandon the cause of supporting democracy abroad but tried to introduce a more nuanced, long-term strategy. He explained in numerous speeches (some of which I helped write) his unequivocal support for democracy, human rights, and the rule of law abroad for both security and moral reasons but shunned the use of military force for regime change, advocating instead for peaceful, incremental change. He aimed to frame democracy promotion as an international mission in support of universal values, not just an American project.[13] More than Clinton or Bush, Obama was committed to multilateralism to advance both American interests and universal values.

In the spring of 2011, Obama faced a major challenge to his principles when deciding whether to use military force in Libya to save civilian lives in Benghazi, which was on the verge of being attacked by government forces. Obama eventually opted to use force, but only if the UN Security Council blessed the idea and on the condition that the United States would not occupy the country to try to build a democracy there. Because Russia and China abstained, Obama won UN Security Council approval for this NATO-led bombing campaign that contributed to the ouster of Libyan dictator Muammar Gaddafi, even if that was not the goal of military intervention. However, the collapse of Libyan autocracy in 2011 resulted not in a transition to democracy but instead a civil war. This disappointing outcome in Libya and other failed attempts at democratic transition throughout most of the Arab world, including a horrific civil war in Syria, further fueled negative perceptions of the United States as an effective democracy promoter.[14]

In his first term, President Trump devoted no attention or energy to promoting democracy in the Middle East or anywhere else. When the Saudi dictatorship killed journalist Jamal Khashoggi, Trump said nothing and actively courted the monarchs in Saudi Arabia and the region. Trump was the first American president to meet North Korean dictator Kim Jong Un and never raised that country's human rights abuses during their conversations. With great enthusiasm, Trump embraced Putin, never criticizing the Russian dictator for his repressive ways, even as some in his administration held more critical views of Russian autocracy.[15] After Putin tried to kill Russian opposition leader Alexei Navalny in 2020, Trump was silent. Trump was even at odds with his administration about autocratic China. While many Trump officials made bold statements criticizing China's communist dictatorship and Xi's autocratic rule, Trump himself avoided doing so directly. He focused instead on unfair trade policies and did not endorse a Treasury Department's plan to sanction officials connected to human rights violations in Xinjiang.[16] More than any president in the past century, Trump in his first term demonstrated shocking deference to autocrats.[17] His administration stood up the State Department's Commission on Unalienable Rights, but Trump himself never seemed interested in this work.[18] Trump promoted the live-and-let-live theme. As he explained in a 2018 speech at the UN General Assembly, "I honor the right of every nation to pursue its own customs, beliefs, and traditions. The United States will not tell you how to live, work, or worship. We only ask that you honor our sovereignty in return."[19] Those are themes easily found in the speeches of both Putin and Xi.

Trump criticized many democratic leaders, including Canadian prime minister Justin Trudeau, French president Emmanuel Macron, and German chancellor Angela Merkel, and he berated democratic clubs, including most aggressively NATO. Trump showed zero interest in helping democratic Ukraine.[20] He never tried to leverage his relationship with Putin to negotiate an end to the Russian-supported war in eastern Ukraine, which continued throughout his entire first term. Instead, Trump attempted to condition the provision of military assistance to his reelection efforts, a "quid pro quo" proposal that resulted in his first impeachment.

Paradoxically, the US Congress increased budgets for democracy assistance during the Trump era. In 2019, the US Congress raised the annual budget for the National Endowment for Democracy from $180 million to $300 million.[21] In 2020, the NED provided more grants to democratic activists worldwide than any year during its thirty-six-year history.[22] However, these bigger budgets did not offset Trump's anti-democratic foreign policies. After four years of Trump in office, America's reputation as a force for democracy and human rights was greatly diminished.

President Biden tried to rekindle an American focus on democracy promotion. At the 2021 virtual Munich Security Conference, the new president affirmed, "Democracy doesn't happen by accident. We have to defend it, fight for it, strengthen it, renew it."[23] In April 2021, Biden told Congress, "America will not back away from . . . our commitment to human rights and fundamental freedoms and to our alliances."[24] Biden often framed international politics as a battle between democrats and autocrats; he convened democracy summits and rolled out new policy instruments for promoting good governance, especially to fight corruption. After autocratic Russia invaded democratic Ukraine in February 2022, Biden forged a coalition of democracies to provide weapons and economic aid to help Ukraine and played a leading role in organizing a coalition of democratic countries to impose sanctions on Russia. In response to threats from autocratic China, Biden increased military support for democratic Taiwan.

Biden's commitment to supporting democracy in the Middle East was more muted, as his administration openly courted deeper ties with Arab monarchies as a strategy to contain Iran and later try to help end the war in Gaza triggered by Hamas's horrific terrorist attack against Israel on October 7, 2023. The massive loss of civilian life in Gaza resulting from Israel's military intervention fueled new accusations of American hypocrisy regarding human rights, damaging once again America's reputation as a promoter of democracy, especially in the developing world. The American withdrawal from Afghanistan on Biden's watch underscored the US failure to build democracy there.

And then Trump won reelection in 2024, ushering in what promises to be another era of indifference about democracy and human rights. In his first months in office, Trump and his team, led by billionaire Elon Musk, dramatically slashed budgets for many American instruments of ideological promotion, including USAID and its implementing partners involved in democracy promotion; NED and its affiliated organizations (although some of NED's funding was later restored); the State Department's Bureau of Democracy, Human Rights and Labor, which also funds democracy promotion programs; several US government-funded media organizations, including Voice of America, Radio Free Asia, Radio Free Europe, Radio Farda (which broadcasts into Iran), Radio Martí (which broadcasts into Cuba), and Alhurra (working in the Middle East); and many international educational exchange programs, including the Fulbright Program. No US president has ever moved so quickly to cut funding for democracy promotion.

In addition, Trump immediately picked fights with democratic allies like Canada, Denmark, and Panama, threatening to make Canada the fifty-first US state, annex or buy Greenland, and take control of the Panama Canal. With scathing statements about democratic rollback in Europe, new tariffs, and threats to reduce US military presence in Europe, Trump and his team also fueled major tensions with our European allies and NATO. Equally dramatically and abruptly, Trump switched sides in the war in Ukraine, giving many concessions to Putin's Russia without securing any reciprocal gains for Ukraine and the West more broadly. In the global clash between autocrats and democrats before Trump, the United States was generally on the side of the democrats. Today, it is not so clear.

Trump's return to the White House coincided with record lows for domestic support for promoting democracy abroad. A 2024 poll conducted by the University of Maryland revealed that only a third of Americans surveyed "believe that spreading democracy globally should be a goal of American foreign policy"; a third responded that democracy promotion should not be a goal, and a third did not know.[25] Other polls of Americans revealed that democracy promotion was not a high priority compared to other foreign policy concerns.[26]

Few recent wins in advancing democracy, the return of Trump to the White House, and low public support for promoting democracy abroad combine to make the ideological competition with China and Russia more challenging today than competition with the Soviets was during the Cold War. During the Cold War, US presidents never flirted with joining sides with our ideological adversaries. In courting Putin and fighting with democratic allies, that is exactly what Trump is doing today.

THE DAMAGED MODEL OF AMERICAN DEMOCRACY

Democracy's recent struggles in the United States have become an additional factor benefiting the autocrats and undermining the democrats worldwide. The practice of American democracy at home has faltered and therefore has been losing its appeal abroad as a model for others to emulate. Between 2010 and 2020, the US system of government became less democratic, according to Freedom House assessments.[27] The weakening of political parties, the explosion of unregulated campaign financing, gerrymandering of congressional districts, and general societal polarization are anti-democratic trends that started many years ago but accelerated during Trump's first term as president.[28] Trump's attacks on the independent media and on truth more generally, the politicization of the US legal system, and the use of public office for personal gain were highly corrosive to the American system of democracy. During his presidency, leading international watchdogs—Freedom House, the Economist Intelligence Unit's Democracy Index, V-Dem, and Reporters Without Borders' press freedom index—showed significant decline in the United States' democratic standing.[29] In 2021, for the first time, the Stockholm-based International Institute for Democracy and Electoral Assistance added the United States to its list of backsliding democracies that had fallen "victim to authoritarian tendencies itself."[30]

Before 2020, some analysts worried about the potential breakdown of American democracy.[31] At no time since the Civil War, however, did American democracy come as close to collapse as it did after the 2020 presidential election when Trump refused to recognize election results, launched dozens of legal challenges, and inspired an armed insurrection against the US Congress on January 6, 2021, to disrupt the peaceful transfer of power to the newly elected president, Joseph Biden. For his role in inciting this violence, Trump became the first president in American history to be impeached twice. Autocrats worldwide expressed glee. Supporters of democracy—both elected leaders in democracies and opposition activists in autocracies—wondered if American democracy would survive.

Biden's 2020 election victory marked a moment of democratic renewal. More Americans voted for Biden than any other presidential candidate in US history, animated partly by their desire to remove Trump from office. That is how democracy is supposed to work. But even President Biden expressed doubts about the future of American democracy, wondering out loud in his first State of the Union address, "Can our democracy deliver to the most pressing needs of our people? Can our democracy overcome the lies, anger, hate, and fears that have pulled us apart?" To unite a Congress still reeling after the assault on the Capitol on January 6, 2021, Biden added that "America's adversaries—the autocrats of the world—

are betting we can't" and challenged lawmakers to prove the autocrats wrong.[32]

Assaults on American democracy continued during the Biden era, with several state legislatures passing laws to increase voter suppression and changing election administration procedures to bolster partisan involvement in the election process. Dozens of political officials and candidates embraced anti-democratic ideas of election subversion and justified partisan violence.[33] Although he ran for president for a third time in 2024, Trump still refused to accept the results of the 2020 election. By consolidating control over the Republican Party during his renewed campaign in 2024, Trump succeeded in transforming a large segment of the American population into an anti-democratic force. Reflecting this shift, a 2022 poll found that roughly 34 percent of Americans believed that violent action against the government could sometimes be justified.[34]

Donald Trump's decisive electoral victory in 2024 helped ensure a peaceful, democratic transfer of presidential power in January 2025. That was good news. The bad news is that President Trump has continued to espouse anti-democratic ideas and dramatically escalated his challenges to democratic norms and institutions. On his first day in office, Trump pardoned all those involved in the violent insurrection at the Capitol on January 6, 2021. In just the first weeks of Trump's second term, Elon Musk and the new administration fired dozens of officials across many departments, froze funding, and threatened to shut down multiple different agencies without any input from Congress. These purges included military officers relieved of their duties without cause. As democracy specialist Larry Diamond explained and warned, "Pressing his claim to imperial power (through the theory of the 'unitary executive'), Trump has moved to assert absolute control over all federal regulatory bodies, including the Securities and Exchange Commission, the Federal Trade Commission, and the Federal Communications Commission. This not only hobbles their capacity to act independently in the public interest but opens the door to massive corruption."[35] Trump also has tried to end birthright citizenship, guaranteed in the Fourteenth Amendment of the US Constitution. Most egregiously, invoking the Alien Enemies Act of 1798, the Trump administration has arrested and deported American residents, including annulling (but then restoring) hundreds of visas for international students, without any due process.[36] Judges around the country temporarily stopped many instances of executive overreach, but as this book goes to print, Trump and his team of self-described revolutionaries continue to challenge laws and norms of checks and balances between different branches of government that have helped American democracy endure for so long.

Based on intuition, not data, I remain optimistic that American democracy will survive a second Trump term. American democratic institutions are resilient; civil society supporting democracy is strong; and most citizens support democracy. Voters elected Trump to bring the price of eggs down, not to foment a revolution. That said, just maintaining democracy is not the same as practicing democracy in a way that inspires others around the world. To a far greater extent than during any period of the twentieth century, including the Cold War and the Vietnam War, democracy has lost its universal appeal within American society, while polarization among political elites has made the possibility of democratic renewal less likely.

These conditions at home have significantly constrained America's ability to defend and support democracy abroad. The US political system today looks unstable and uninspiring, allowing autocrats to promote their system of government as more stable and effective. More generally, political polarization, erosion of democratic practices, and decline in public support for democratic ideas at home have weakened the US ability to compete abroad much more than during the Cold War. Today, we have returned to an era of great power competition between autocrats and democrats like the last century. But this time around, America's status as the leader of the free world is not as strong as it was when we fought the Cold War.

AMERICAN INSTRUMENTS OF IDEOLOGICAL EXPORT

As mentioned earlier, President Trump began his second term showing little interest in supporting democracy abroad and great inclination to weaken, if not completely dismantle, many of the tools of ideological promotion that previous US presidents used during the Cold War and the post–Cold War era to win the battle of ideas against our autocratic adversaries. As the following two chapters document, Putin's Russia and Xi's China are not shutting down their instruments to promote their respective brands of autocracy and undermine democracy. If the United States under President Trump continues to disarm from this ideological competition with China and Russia unilaterally, other democratic countries, especially in Europe, as well as democratic movements within autocracies will continue to fight without us. But without the United States in the contest, the balance of ideological power will shift dramatically toward the autocrats. That would be a terrible outcome both for the world and for American security and economic interests.

Because the United States is a democracy, the debate about the purpose of American power in the world will continue during the second Trump administration and beyond. If future presidents want to reinvigorate our participation in the global ideological struggle between autocrats and democrats, there is a comprehensive toolbox to advance democracy abroad that can be revitalized or rebuilt from scratch if some of these instruments do not survive Trump's second term.

PARTY-TO-PARTY TIES

Compared to China, party-to-party ties are not a significant feature of American ideological promotion. Instead, the US government has established a complicated hybrid model for fostering relations with political parties abroad. When the NED was created, two party-focused organizations were established too: the International Republican Institute, affiliated with the Republican Party, and the National Democratic Institute, affiliated with the Democratic Party. These organizations operate in confusing ways, blurring the lines between government, nongovernment, and political parties. Although both IRI and NDI boards are composed of Republicans and Democrats, these parties do not control NDI or IRI, and NDI and IRI do not function as their international departments. The US government—Congress through NED and the executive branch through USAID and the State Department—funds both (although Trump ended that financial support in 2025). IRI and NDI work in dozens of countries, seeking to promote the development of political parties as a critical institution of democracy. However, both are nonpartisan and do not take instructions from the White House or the State Department. NDI and IRI tend to work with multiple political parties, not just a single party with a shared ideological affiliation. They have expanded beyond party development to include election observation, polling, and civil society support more generally. Unlike Chinese Communist Party training programs, which promote the CCP system of government, IRI and NDI promote democratic ideas, institutions, and organizations generally, not *American* democracy specifically. As this book goes to press, IRI and NDI remain intact, though the future of their work remains unclear given Trump's reduction in foreign aid, executive actions affecting international programs, and the administration's orientation away from democracy promotion abroad.

NONGOVERNMENTAL ORGANIZATIONS

Other American nongovernmental organizations aim to foster the development of civil society and democratic institutions. For instance, Internews and IREX focus on nurturing independent media, the International Foundation for Electoral Systems aids election administration, the Solidarity Center promotes trade unions, and the Center for International Private Enterprise (CIPE) encourages the development of business associations. Dozens of American NGOs foster the development of civil society. Many of these American organizations have received money from US government sources, including USAID and the State Department, at least until the second Trump administration started cutting budgets for such work. Some Trump supporters have claimed that these organizations are corrupt and "woke," but there are few data to support such hypotheses. Enhancing transparency in US funding and increasing accountability, through rigorous independent evaluations of programs' effectiveness and impact, would certainly improve the work of these NGOs. Eliminating them entirely, however, would be a gift to Putin and Xi, crippling America's ability to compete effectively in the arena of ideas with autocratic Russia and autocratic China.

US-FUNDED INTERNATIONAL MEDIA

At the end of the Cold War, many assumed that American ideas and values did not require continued support, as they seemed to be taking root everywhere. The US government got out of the business of studying and countering propaganda from anti-democratic countries. Public diplomacy faded from favor. In 1999, the US Congress mandated President Clinton to shut down the United States Information Agency, whose mission had been "to understand, inform and influence foreign publics in promotion of the national interest, and to broaden the dialogue between Americans and US institutions, and their counterparts abroad." By the end of the twentieth century, that mission was considered accomplished.

Until Trump's return to office in 2025, US government-funded media remained active, and the growth of Chinese and Russian state-owned media worldwide compelled the United States to up its game regarding government-funded global media. For fiscal year 2025, Biden requested $950 million to fund the work of the US Agency for Global Media (USAGM),[37] which runs several broadcasting stations, including Voice of America, Radio Free Europe / Radio Liberty, Radio y Televisión Martí (Cuba), Alhurra (the Middle East and North Africa), Radio Sawa (the Middle East), and Radio Free Asia. The agency also financed the Open Technology Fund, an independent NGO committed to advancing global internet freedom. With the second Trump administration's budget slashes for USAGM, it is unclear which of these media organizations will still be functioning by the time this book comes out. As of April 2025, all abovementioned broadcasting stations remain operational, though in a significantly limited capacity with ongoing legal efforts.

One can argue that the prospects of USAGM shutdown are not that significant. After all, dozens of private American companies create content and disseminate information abroad, among them news organizations with international reach and, especially, social media companies. However, the USAGM has consistently maintained a clear ideological mission: "to inform, engage, and connect people around the world in support of freedom and democracy." VOA, the largest USAGM network, in addition to reporting news, has had an explicit mission to explain American foreign policy and the United States more generally to foreign audiences. USAGM networks function as surrogate media in countries with limited press freedom, and many of their journalists want to be viewed as independent reporters.

Measuring the impact of these American media organizations in supporting or advancing democratic ideas is difficult. That China and Russia are so committed to limiting the reach of these companies into their societies suggests that they must be making substantive contributions to the ideological struggle between autocracies and democracies. That China and Russia are also investing heavily in their versions of Voice of America underscores their recognition of the strategic value these tools hold in competing with the United States and the rest of the democratic world.

ECONOMIC AID

Until Trump's return to the White House in 2025, the US was one of the world's largest providers of bilateral economic assistance. In addition to advancing security and economic objectives, this aid served as a critical instrument for promoting US ideological goals. Since its creation in 1961, USAID has functioned as the leading provider of development assistance from the US government. President Biden's budget request for USAID for fiscal year 2025 was $42.8 billion.[38] In his second term, however, Trump radically downsized USAID and placed it under direct control of the State Department, dramatically weakening America's ability to compete with China in this dimension.

In addition to USAID, the US government has utilized other tools to promote development and democracy simultaneously. In 2004, the Bush administration established the Millennium Challenge Corporation (MCC), a bilateral aid agency that provides funds to countries meeting both economic and governance conditions. Democracy and accountability metrics are explicitly built into MCC loan decisions. In 2011, President Obama launched the Open Government Partnership, a voluntary multi-stakeholder initiative to elicit government pledges for transparency. In 2019, the US Congress and the first Trump administration worked together to merge the Overseas Private Investment Corporation and USAID's Development Credit Authority to create the Development Finance Corporation (DFC), with a mandate to compete with China's Belt and Road Initiative. At the G7 meeting in 2021, President Biden rolled out a multilateral initiative called Build Back Better World, later renamed Partnership for Global Infrastructure and Investment, making the link between economic assistance and democratic values explicit.

Describing all American economic assistance as solely ideologically driven would be inaccurate. While coordination exists between USAID's economic and democratic programs, USAID's core mission, as its budget shows, has remained economic development and humanitarian aid rather than democracy promotion. Some assistance aims to incentivize countries to purchase American goods, including arms. Other packages, such as aid to Israel and Egypt, are tied directly to security goals. Over the past two decades, the US government has provided financial assistance to governments to combat terrorist organizations with little focus on advancing democratic ideas. But values matter as well. For instance, the Biden administration provided both weapons and financial aid to democratic Ukraine to help it survive the invasion from autocratic Russia. In his second term, Trump has signaled no desire to continue this vital aid for the defense of democratic Ukraine.

America's most powerful agents of development—and, indirectly, of American values—often come from the private sector, including private American foundations. American companies abroad support American ideas, especially about individualism and entrepreneurship, which have a corresponding, albeit not direct, relationship with individual human rights and political freedoms. It is no coincidence that the wealthiest countries in the world are also the most democratic. The reach of American musicians, actors, and athletes far exceeds that of any NED grant or IRI party-training program. In this dimension of soft power competition, Americans have outpaced their Chinese and Russian counterparts.

ACADEMIC EXCHANGES

American research universities attract the best students and scholars from all over the world—including from autocracies. Foreign students and researchers who can find jobs or academic positions play a significant role in stimulating the American ecosystem of technological development and innovation. Although student-exchange programs were interrupted by the COVID-19 pandemic, a million international students are once again studying in American universities. Washington funds a fraction of these scholars and students, though most come without US government support. US government scholarships do not have an overt ideological agenda, but US officials believe that exposure to the United States makes these students more friendly to the United States and more receptive to democracy. As Secretary of State Tony Blinken argued, "By welcoming international students to the United States, we can share the core values of our democracy, including the free expression of ideas, open and spirited debate, and civic engagement."[39] More international students want to study in the United States than in China or Russia. As an instrument of soft power, our universities and research institutions remain a critical comparative advantage for the United States when competing with our adversaries.

Unfortunately, this tool of American soft power is also under assault during the second Trump administration. As already mentioned, government funding for US academic exchanges such as the Fulbright Program has been cut. Even more detrimentally, US funding to universities for research has been dramatically reduced, decreasing support for faculty but also for their doctoral and post-doctoral students, many of whom come from abroad. These cuts are making American universities less attractive destinations for foreign students. Additionally, the Trump administration's decision (later suspended) to revoke more than a thousand student visas in just a matter of weeks due to alleged threats to American national security has greatly dampened enthusiasm for the world's best and the brightest to enroll in US universities. The same is true of Trump's attempt to prevent international students from enrolling at Harvard.

COERCIVE ECONOMIC POWER

The US government has used coercive economic tools such as sanctions and export controls to advance ideological goals to a much greater extent than the Russian and Chinese governments have. Sometimes, sanctions aimed to weaken autocratic regimes for security reasons; other times, ideological goals and even regime change have been explicit objectives. In many cases, these goals are intertwined. Only in a small handful of cases, such as deploying sanctions against apartheid South Africa to induce political change, was the primary goal overtly ideological.

In recent years, the United States has imposed sanctions on several autocratic regimes, among them Russia, China, Iran, North Korea, Cuba, and Venezuela. For instance, the first Trump administration enacted new sanctions on Chinese firms, impeded Chinese investments in the United States, and incentivized many American companies to decouple from Chinese suppliers. Trump's team encouraged companies based in democracies to disengage from specific sectors of the Chinese economy, especially 5G and semiconductors. The Biden administration kept these sanctions in place and, in 2024, expanded them, adding new export and investment controls. To the best of my knowledge, the aim of these actions was not to foment a democratic revolution in China but to weaken China as an economic and ideologically antagonistic power.

Similarly, the US has sanctioned Russian companies and individuals and implemented export controls in response to Putin's illegal and antidemocratic actions abroad: the annexation of Crimea, Russian interference in US presidential elections, and, most dramatically, Putin's full-scale invasion of Ukraine in 2022. The weakening of Russia's autocracy through sanctions strengthens democracy, most directly in Ukraine but indirectly in the countries neighboring Russia. Not surprisingly, most democratic forces in Belarus, Georgia, and even Russia (or, more accurately, Russian democratic leaders living in exile) support American sanctions against Putin's dictatorship.

American sanctions on North Korea and Iran have been implemented primarily for security reasons—to prevent Tehran from obtaining a nuclear weapon and to stop the expansion of North Korea's nuclear weapons program. During the Trump era, some senior officials suggested that sanctions should be designed and implemented to foster regime change in Iran, but that aspiration was retired during the Biden administration. At times, US leaders have implemented sanctions against Cuba and Venezuela to trigger regime change or at least to punish autocratic behavior, though obviously with limited success so far.

In the past, the United States has also imposed sanctions in response to human rights abuses. For instance, the Magnitsky Act, signed into law in 2012, explicitly seeks to punish human rights abusers within Russia. That is an ideological mission. Four years later, Congress passed the Global

Magnitsky Act, which aims to hold human rights abusers around the world accountable. These laws seek to weaken the power of autocratic regimes indirectly. The United States has encouraged other democratic countries to impose sanctions on human rights abusers too. To those being sanctioned by Washington for abuses of human rights, the United States looks like a very ideological power. Again, however, that era may be ending or at least put on pause during the second Trump administration. President Trump has not expressed a desire to use economic sanctions to promote liberal or democratic values.

MILITARY INTERVENTION

As already discussed, American leaders have used force to weaken and even overthrow regimes that they disliked, both during the Cold War and after. During the Cold War, the United States carried out covert actions for ideological purposes, sometimes even to overthrow democratically elected leaders of leftist orientation or to repress national liberation movements with the "wrong" ideological orientation. US presidents almost always justified using overt military force to pursue security objectives and rarely to promote democracy. The one possible exception might be the US intervention in Panama. After invading or occupying a country, however, American soldiers and civilians have rarely left without attempting to install a democracy.[40] By my count, starting with the Spanish-American War in 1898, only five out of seventeen US military interventions produced democratic regime change: Germany, Italy, Japan after 1945, Grenada after 1983, and Panama after 1992. (South Korea eventually became a democracy, but only three decades after the war ended in 1953.)

US covert operations in pursuit of ideological objectives are more complicated for academics to track and evaluate than overt actions, but some have become publicly known. During the Cold War, the CIA played an enduring role in trying to weaken communist regimes. At the same time, US involvement in coups in Iran and Chile helped autocracy. After the Cold War, CIA support for Serbian opposition forces helped topple Slobodan Milosevic in October 2000 and ushered in a more democratic era there. Because these missions are classified, we will not learn for decades whether the US intelligence community is now active in weakening autocratic adversaries. What we know for sure is that our adversaries think they are being targeted by the CIA.

WHAT WE *DON'T* DO ANYMORE

During the Cold War, the United States and the Soviet Union actively participated in proxy wars around the world that were often motivated by ideological goals. Since the end of the Cold War, the United States and China have not engaged in a significant proxy war. That is good news, since the Cold War and its proxy wars were far from cold. The same was true of the US and Russia until 2022, when Putin launched a full-scale invasion of Ukraine, and the United States and dozens of democratic allies and partners responded by supplying military assistance to Ukraine's armed forces. That American weapons have been used to kill Russian soldiers in Ukraine and even inside Russia marks a unique new threshold in US-Russia confrontation reminiscent of the Cold War standoffs. That Chinese soldiers were discovered in 2025 fighting alongside Russia in its war against Ukraine is also an ominous sign of escalation. Whether the war in Ukraine is the beginning of a new era of proxy wars between the United States and Russia and China or an aberration remains unclear.

IMPACT

The list of instruments of democracy promotion just reviewed suggests that the United States has been trying to promote democratic ideas abroad since the end of the Cold War, or at least that was the case until Trump's return in 2025. In fact, in the first weeks of his second term, Trump has aggressively cut resources for many of these instruments of ideological programs, the first president ever to do so. Yet before these Trump disruptions, tracing the effectiveness of individual American programs and initiatives to support democracy in the vast sea of factors pushing against democratic governance was difficult. That said, the macro trend lines are clear. After an explosion of democratic advances in the 1980s and 1990s, democracy has been in retreat over the past two decades. According to Freedom House, 2024 was the nineteenth consecutive year of declining freedom internationally. In 2025, the number of people living under autocracy—or "not free" countries, as defined by Freedom House—exceeds the number living under democracy, or "free" countries; the ratio is 40 percent to 20 percent.[41]

Many countries have regressed in the face of intensifying corruption, breakdowns in the rule of law, and fierce challenges from populist forces that target minorities and reject the principle of the separation of powers. Russia and then Hungary suffered the most significant reversals in Europe and Eurasia, but other new democracies in the region have had troubling trajectories, including Georgia, Mongolia, and Serbia. The rise of national populist movements in older democracies has disrupted decades of democratic stability. In addition, a wave of recent coups d'état has rattled the African continent. India has seen departures from democratic norms through its creation of a controversial register of citizens, threats to freedom of expression, suppression of protests, and revocation of Indian Kashmir's autonomous status.[42] Nearly all the democratic gains from the Arab Spring that began in 2011 have been erased, even in Tunisia, which held on the longest, and the erosion of democracy in Turkey adds to the trajectory of democratic decline in the region.

Obviously, the United States cannot be blamed for all these democratic failures. However, US democracy promotion efforts have often fallen short in slowing these autocratic trends, and in some cases—Afghanistan and Iraq in particular, but also during the Arab Spring—have achieved only limited results. Most alarming, democracy is under threat at home in the United States more than it has been at any time since the Civil War. As Larry Diamond wrote in 2022 in his final article as the coeditor of the *Journal of Democracy*, "Democracy in the United States has begun to deconsolidate and is at serious risk of breaking down in the next presidential election."[43] Trump's decisive election victory in 2024 ended worries of a replay of January 6, 2021, because Trump and his supporters might not have recognized the results of a Kamala Harris victory. Yet, his reelection has triggered new concerns about the gradual erosion of American democratic institutions. The speed at which the second Trump administration has moved to expand executive authority in ways that usurp legislative and judicial powers has been stunning.

Nonetheless, US actions have sometimes facilitated democratic breakthroughs, especially in Serbia in 2000, Georgia in 2003, and Ukraine in

2004. More recently, Washington coordinated the free world's response to Putin's full-scale invasion in February 2022. Without US help, democracy in Ukraine would most likely have collapsed. The EU's decision in 2022 to offer Ukraine and Moldova a path toward membership will help consolidate democratic rule in both countries. The US military and diplomatic support for Taiwan has helped preserve democracy on that island.

While American efforts at supporting democratic ideas worldwide may be less effective than they have been, they continue to threaten autocracies. We know this fact from the nervous statements that Xi and Putin consistently make about US democracy promotion efforts. And China and Russia are not yet filling the vacuum with a string of successes in promoting dictatorship. The current recession is also not as deep as the previous anti-democratic waves. Just a hundred years ago—between two World Wars—fascism and communism seemed to be the future, yet that anti-democratic wave did not last. At the height of the Cold War, dozens of countries claimed to be communist, including two of the largest countries in the world, the Soviet Union and the People's Republic of China, and many revolutionary movements in the 1950s and 1960s espoused Marxist-Leninist and Maoist ideas. By the 1970s, communist victories in Southeast Asia, southern Africa, and Latin America and domestic turmoil in the United States had created the impression of Soviet autocratic ascendancy and American democratic decline. As we know, those trends did not last either. Across southern Europe and Latin America, especially after the Soviet collapse, dozens of countries abandoned dictatorship in favor of democracy. The Arab Spring produced only temporary democratic gains, but societal demand for democratic change in the region has not been fully extinguished.

In their careful assessment of long-term trends, democracy experts Steven Levitsky and Lucan Way conclude that "the last quarter-century remains by far the most democratic in history."[44] And when you look back across centuries, the trajectory in favor of freedom is even more impressive. Just a few hundred years ago, there were no democracies.

Societal demand for democratic ideas also remains strong. In autocracies and countries where democratic institutions are under pressure, civic movements continue to mobilize in small, incremental ways, with nonviolent civic resistance occurring daily. They form, mobilize, engage, and push for democratic renewal. Popular mobilization has exploded episodically in autocracies—the Green Revolution in Iran in 2009, the Arab Spring in 2011, Russia in 2011 and 2012, Hong Kong in 2014 and 2019, Belarus in 2020, and Venezuela in 2024—and there have also been pro-democratic uprisings in Burma, Algeria, Sudan, and Thailand.[45] Journalists working in highly repressive environments continue to expose government transgressions. Human rights activists in Russia, Iran, China, and Venezuela go to jail every day, but that such people exist at all shows the enduring appeal of democratic ideas. Pro-democratic lawyers fight to get them out of jail, and sometimes they also get arrested. Small-*d* democrats, often living in exile, continue to press their liberal democratic ideas on social media platforms against their autocratic foes.

No commensurate popular forces are mobilizing in favor of autocracy. Popular uprisings in support of Chinese one-party rule, Iranian theocracy, or Putinism do not occur. When people take to the streets to protest for political change, they never call for the creation of the Chinese or Russian model. Seldom do we see pro-Putin or pro-Xi activists protesting for autocracy in democracies. It is hard to identify a single country that has flipped from liberal democracy to Leninist-party rule.

In addition, according to the polls, most *people* in the world, while frustrated by the performance of their democracies, still prefer democracy to other systems of government.[46] Despite Chinese efforts to push their system at the expense of the United States, more people hold favorable views of the United States than of China.[47] International demand for American leadership to help check the expansion of Chinese and Russian ideas remains robust.

Whether the United States will continue to try to meet that demand is uncertain—more uncertain than ever after Trump's reelection. Alarmingly, many of Trump's ideas sound eerily similar to anti-democratic populists in other countries. When Vice President J. D. Vance gave his first major foreign policy speech at the Munich Security Conference in February 2025, he claimed (wrongly, in my view) that the greatest threat to Europe was not Russia or China but the practice of democracy in Europe itself, such as censorship and migration. In doing so, he clearly aligned his government with illiberal populist parties in Europe, which many democracy scholars view as threats to democracy. The fight between autocrats and democrats today is not only between countries but also within them. Some democratic leaders in Europe worry about which side Trump's America is on.

The United States, however, is still a democracy. That Trump leans authoritarian and some in his circle actively seek to weaken democratic institutions at home and abandon democracy promotion abroad does not necessarily mean that the United States will exit forever the ideological contest to promote democracy and resist autocracy. Four years from now, a new president could pivot back to this long-standing American tradition. I hope so, because Russia and China are not shutting down their efforts to promote autocracy, as the next two chapters discuss.

Chapter 7

EXPORTING PUTINISM

MY FAMILY AND I arrived in Moscow over the Martin Luther King Jr. holiday weekend in January 2012. The long weekend gave us all a few days to recover from jet lag before stepping into our new assignments, mine being the new US ambassador to Russia. I had never worked as an ambassador before but was excited by the challenge. As President Obama's senior adviser on Russia at the White House for the previous three years, I had been involved in several tough negotiations with Russian government officials, so I felt prepared to do the same in this new role. I thought diplomacy would come naturally to me. After all, I spoke Russian and had lived in Russia many times before. And I was a contributor to Obama's reset of US-Russia relations, so I assumed I would get friendly treatment from my hosts. I was wrong.

On the weekend I arrived, even before I had the chance to report for duty at the embassy for my first day of work, Russia's largest television station ran a detailed hit piece on me, warning Russians that I was an expert on revolution whom Obama had sent to Russia to foment regime change against Putin. I was shocked. I knew the television commentator who produced and narrated the clip. He surely didn't believe such nonsense, did he? And why was the Kremlin attacking me before I had done anything? Over the next several weeks, I heard some reassuring comments from Kremlin officials, including directly from Russian president Dmitry Medvedev. They explained that these attacks were just standard campaign stuff, as Prime Minister Putin was running for reelection as president at the time. The attacks would fade away after he was reelected, so I was reassured.

But they did not. The central myth Putin and his propagandists advanced was that I was a fomenter, an agitator, an orchestrator of color revolutions who had been sent to Russia to do what other American agents had pulled off in Serbia in 2000, Georgia in 2003, and Ukraine in 2004. The fact that I had written about these post-communist democratic breakthroughs and had also written a book titled *Russia's Unfinished Revolution* was twisted as evidence to prove my passion for regime change in Russia. While working at the White House, I had explained to Obama that Putin did not really believe these conspiracy theories about the United States. He simply used them to mobilize domestic support. I left Moscow in 2014 with a very different view. Putin did genuinely believe that the US aimed to overthrow him.

If power and the balance of power between countries were all that mattered, Putin would have had no reason to portray me to his people as a revolutionary. But in world politics, ideas matter too. And when the ideas legitimizing different kinds of governments are antithetical to each other, like democracy versus autocracy, they cause tensions between great powers. As was the case during the Cold War, an ideological clash exists between the United States and Russia today. As Russia has become more autocratic during Putin's reign, tensions have increased. That is a pattern, not a spurious correlation. Over the past century, powerful autocracies have tended to clash with the democratic United States. Moreover, Putin seeks to both consolidate his brand of conservative, populist dictatorship at home and promote these ideas abroad. His international efforts to promote Putinism have often clashed with American global support for liberal ideas and democratic practices. Putin has focused on promoting his ideas within old democracies, especially in Europe and the United States, making the front line of this current ideological struggle within countries, not just between them. And Putin has had some successes, courting like-minded leaders and movements in several European countries and even the United States.

Ideological competition between the United States and Russia today is not as intense as it was between Washington and Moscow during the Cold War. Putinism lacks the global appeal of communism, and Russia has fewer resources for ideological promotion than the Soviet Union had. Nonetheless, Putin's ambition to promote his ideas abroad is deep—much deeper than Chairman Xi's or President Trump's. Unlike Xi and Trump, Putin has demonstrated a willingness to use all means at his disposal, including, most tragically, the Russian military, to advance his ideas. For too long, American policymakers ignored or downplayed this ideological dimension of Russian power, wrongly casting Putin as a purely "transactional" leader or someone focused only on preserving power at home. In fact, Putin can be both these things *and* an ideologue with global ambitions at the same time. (Stalin was both a thug and an ideologue too.) While Putin remains in power, the promotion of Putinism worldwide will remain a component of conflict between the United States and Russia.

GLOBAL PUTINISM

If Beijing's primary ideological difference with the West centers on an alternative model of economic development, Moscow today focuses more on identity politics. Putin champions a virulent variant of illiberal, orthodox, and nationalistic ideas emphasizing identity, culture, and tradition. The core components of Putinism for export are advancing conservative values and attacking democratic values, supporting a strong state, defending autocracy through promoting sovereignty, nurturing a positive image of Russia, and undercutting truth itself.

PROMOTING CONSERVATIVE ORTHODOXY, ATTACKING LIBERAL DEMOCRACY

Conservatism is the core tenet of Putin's ideology. Conservatism, of course, is a very elastic term, meaning very different things to different people. Putin uses the concept in ways that might sound alien to self-described conservatives in other countries. (That was true for socialism during the Cold War too.) In his view, conservatism is the only ideology consistent with Russian culture.

Putin defines his brand of conservatism in opposition to Western liberalism, which he berates as decadent, immoral, and dangerous. He invokes orthodox ideas to distinguish Russians from liberal Europeans and Americans, arguing that Russians "have a different genetic, cultural and moral code."[1] Putin regularly lambasts the Western liberal notion of "universal values" as antithetical to conservative traditions in Russia and many other countries. Russia's 2021 national security strategy explicitly codified "the defense of traditional Russian spiritual and moral values, culture, and historical memory" as national security priorities.[2] This ideational cleavage is not defined in Marxist economic terms between owners and workers but along cultural and identity divides. Putin has fused Soviet themes of greatness on the international stage with his new brand of conservatism: readopting the Soviet national anthem, transforming May 9—Victory Day in the Great Patriotic War—into a quasi-religious holiday, and even resurrecting Joseph Stalin as a Russian hero, even though Joseph Vissarionovich Dzhugashvili was Georgian. As Russian experts Maria Snegovaya, Michael Kimmage, and Jade McGlynn explained, "Putinism gradually rehabilitated Stalin as a 'state-builder'"—the role Putin often ascribes to himself.[3]

If Xi and the CCP focus on exporting their ideas to the developing world, Putin channels most of Russia's energies for ideological promotion toward the developed world, especially Europe. Putin believes that Western leaders have lost their way morally but that Russia can help rescue their societies. Putin desires to fuse rather than separate church and state, in direct contrast to most Western democracies. Putin and his team see ideological soulmates in advanced industrial countries where resentment is rising due to globalization and immigration. Putin fancies himself as the strongest and most important conservative leader in the world; his mission is to aid weaker leaders and movements that share his values. In August 2024, Putin even signed a decree offering asylum in Russia to foreigners who embrace "traditional Russian spiritual and moral values" and want to escape countries espousing "neoliberal ideology."[4]

Putin has devoted obsessive attention to issues of sexual orientation, blaming the West for promoting homosexuality and other practices he considers deviant. As he bluntly claimed, "Many of the Euro-Atlantic countries are actually rejecting their roots, including the Christian values that constitute the basis of Western civilization. They are denying moral principles and all traditional identities: national, cultural, religious, and even sexual. They are implementing policies that equate large families with same-sex partnerships, belief in God with the belief in Satan."[5] In 2013, Putin signed legislation to constrain the activities of gay rights organizations inside Russia, then amended the Russian constitution to ban same-sex marriage;

he later banned LGBTQ+ books, movies, and events and made it illegal for anyone to acknowledge same-sex marriage as "normal."

In pushing these draconian laws, Putin claims to be defending conservative, collective values, arguing that one individual's happiness "must not be allowed to overshadow the culture, traditions, and traditional family values of millions of people making up the core population."[6] Putin chastises individualism as another decadent Western idea that has undermined traditional values and led to the degradation of many societies in Europe and North America. Putin is ready to help these societies get back on track. Putinism is fundamentally Russian, constraining the international appeal of Putin's orthodox ideas.[7] Ideologies based on ethnic or national identity are almost by definition not as transferable across national boundaries as ideas based on individual or class identities, such as liberalism or Marxism. Putin and his ideological surrogates address this issue by stressing the global appeal of conservative ideas, of which Russian Orthodoxy is just one variant. In the Kremlin's view, American evangelicals, Orthodox Jews, and traditional Muslims share a similar normative orientation.

Putin is not just playing defense. He has developed an offensive game against liberal ideas and democratic governments. The Russian state has actively intervened in democratic countries to support illiberal nationalists and weaken liberal democrats. Fomenting societal polarization in democracies weakens them, a goal that Putin is not afraid to pursue even in the most powerful democracy in the world, the United States.[8]

THE STRONG STATE

In his first years in power, Putin went to great lengths to prop up a Potemkin facade of democracy within Russia, complete with elections, multiple parties, a parliament, and a judiciary. (The Soviet Union held elections too.) Putin claimed to promote a particular kind of Russian-style democracy, using qualifying adjectives such as *managed*, then *sovereign*, and later *illiberal* to distinguish Russia's brand of democracy from the West's. It was *liberal* democracy that Putin allegedly rejected. As Russian ambassador Mikhail Ulyanov argued with me on X on February 4, 2023, "The distinction [between liberalism and democracy] is evident for me. Liberals are very much authoritarian, in my view. Democracy is something different, Ambassador."[9] Liberal rights and democratic institutions correlate with each other closely, as Freedom House assessments have shown for decades. But Putin wants you to believe otherwise—that you can have democracy without individual human rights. It is a narrative that Russia and China share today, as underscored by the joint essay published in 2021 by Russian and Chinese ambassadors to the United States, titled "Respecting People's Democratic Rights."[10]

Over time, Putin's passion for selling his regime as a democracy faded. His surrogates have openly defended censorship as a necessary tool for maintaining state power. Russian ideologues close to Putin have promoted monarchy and empire as admirable systems of government, arguing that they are more aligned with Russian values. Putin's embrace of Russian imperial traditions became even more apparent after he launched his full-scale war against Ukraine in 2022. Putin no longer feigns embarrassment when called a tsar, instead encouraging comparisons to Peter the Great and Catherine the Great. At the same time, Putin, his inner circle, and his propagandists label Russians pushing for actual democracy as "fifth column" traitors and American agents whose elimination is a "necessary self-purification of society that will only strengthen [Russia]."[11] To help purify Russian society and rid it of illiberal, democratic ideas, Putin's regime killed two of Russia's most famous democratic leaders, Boris Nemtsov in 2015 and Alexei Navalny in 2024, and jailed or exiled many others.

Putin champions the need for a "strong state" as a euphemism for dictatorship. For Putin, a state constrained by checks and balances or independent political and economic actors is a weak one, and weak states are antithetical to Russian tradition. Amendments to the Russian constitution adopted in 2020 extending Putin's possible rule until 2036 included language about the need for a "strong state stability." His image-makers have devoted considerable effort to portraying Putin as a strong, masculine leader, showing photos of him riding horses and fishing without a shirt, piloting a military jet, practicing martial arts, and diving for ancient treasures.

SUPPORTING AUTOCRACY BY DEFENDING SOVEREIGNTY

As Putin is an autocrat himself, it is not surprising that he defends other autocrats around the world. This support for autocrats is often dressed up as a defense of sovereignty—another central tenet of Putinism. Putin portrays the United States as a global hegemon seeking to dictate how "vassal" states around the world should behave. He has repeatedly berated American and European efforts to promote democracy as violations of sovereignty aimed at overthrowing the regimes they disliked. As he explained in February 2023, "[The United States and its allies] behaved just as shamelessly and duplicitously when destroying Yugoslavia, Iraq, Libya, and Syria. They will never be able to wash off this shame. The concepts of honor, trust, and decency are not for them. Over the long centuries of colonialism, diktat and hegemony, they got used to being allowed everything, got used to spitting on the whole world."[12] Putin saw a sinister American hand behind pro-democratic social uprisings in what he defined as Russia's "near abroad" in Serbia in 2000, Georgia in 2003, Ukraine in 2004, Kyrgyzstan in 2005, Belarus in 2006, Ukraine again in 2013 and 2014, Russia in 2011 and 2012, Armenia in 2018, and Belarus again in 2020.

Putin has most loudly championed the narrative of American imperial interference regarding Russia's internal affairs. In December 2011, after electoral fraud in Russia's parliamentary elections sparked protests, Putin chastised Secretary of State Hillary Clinton for providing a "signal" to Russian opposition leaders to mobilize against his regime. Of course, Russians mobilized themselves, but Putin could not believe that Russians could organize independently against his regime. The American deep state, especially the CIA, had to have been involved. It was during those protests that I landed in Moscow as the new US ambassador to Russia and was repeatedly accused of fomenting revolution against Putin's regime.[13]

After Russia escalated its war against Ukraine in 2022, Putin's attacks on the United States as a usurper of sovereignty became even more virulent. Putin argued that American support for "Nazis" in Ukraine was intended to weaken and ultimately "finish us [Russia] once and for all."[14] According to Putin, "They [the West] were the ones who started this war, while we used force and are using it to stop the war . . . The United States and NATO quickly deployed their army bases and secret biological laboratories near Russian borders . . . The people of Ukraine have become hostages of the Kiev regime and its Western handlers, who have in fact occupied that country in the political, military and economic sense and have been destroying Ukrainian industry for decades now as they plundered its natural resources . . . The current Ukrainian regime is serving not national interests, but the interests of third countries."[15] For Putin, Ukrainians are merely Russians with accents, unnaturally divided from ethnic Russians by first the Bolsheviks after 1917 and then the West, following the dissolution of the Soviet Union. In Putin's framing, therefore, Russia must liberate their Slavic brothers and sisters from the American-backed Nazi regime. Because Putin does not consider Ukraine a separate nation from Russia, he portrays his invasion as an opposition to "unification."

Putin claims that Russia is the world's strongest defender against American imperialism. This framing has echoes of the Cold War when the Soviet Union claimed to be fighting for independence and decolonization against the European imperial powers. Different from the previous century, however, Putin is not promoting progressive, socialist ideas for the liberated but instead allegedly helping defend them from "attempts to impose pseudo-humanistic or other neoliberal ideological views that undermine traditional spiritual and moral values and integrity."[16]

POSITIVE IMAGE OF RUSSIA

Like many other countries, the Kremlin has engaged in a seemingly more benign objective of promoting a positive image of Russia. Under Putin, however, this effort has taken on an imperial edge for those countries that used to be part of the Russian Empire or the Soviet Union. Putin argues that "Russia is not just a country, but a distinct [Eurasian] civilization thanks to its rich traditions, multiethnic character, and numerous cultures and faiths,"[17] which transcends Russia's borders. In making this claim, Putin and his ideologues invoke the idea of what they call "Russian World" (Russkiy Mir) and Eurasianism. Initially, following the collapse of the Soviet Union, with many Russian-speaking émigrés scattered across Eurasia, Russian World was a "social network" of those "thinking and speaking in Russian" that offered Russian companies and cultural figures market and influence opportunities.[18] With time, however, Russian World acquired a religious (Russian Orthodoxy) and then colonial character to the countries on Russia's borders, especially those with large Russian-speaking communities.[19] The Kremlin celebrates Russian culture as a positive force in the world compared to the ills that come from Western culture.[20]

UNDERMINING TRUTH

Another aim of Putin's global ideological mission is to weaken the very idea of truth.[21] Russian agents in the broadcast and digital space frequently do not try to win an argument but instead promote the idea that there is no objective truth or independent facts. Everything is relative. This ideological campaign against truth contrasts with Moscow's Cold War ideological agenda, when Soviet propagandists pushed a positive agenda about the benefits of communism. Putin's propagandists focus on a negative and deliberately confusing message that every idea, person, and country is bad, or at least no better than anything, anyone, or anywhere else. Whataboutism is frequently deployed. As American historian Anne Applebaum observed about autocrats worldwide today, including in Russia, "They don't offer their fellow citizens a vision of utopia. And they don't inspire them to build a better world. Instead, they teach people to be cynical and passive because there is no better world to build."[22] Russia might be flawed, but the United States is no better—or so the argument goes. If everyone around the world adopts this analytical framing, then Putin's sins are no different from those committed by democratic leaders.

RUSSIAN INSTRUMENTS OF IDEOLOGICAL EXPORT

If Putin aimed to promote his ideas only within Russia, tensions with the United States and the rest of the democratic world might not be so acute. However, Putin aims to propagate his ideas abroad, just as most American leaders (before Trump) and organizations have sought to advance democracy abroad. These competing missions exacerbate tensions between autocratic Russia and the democratic West. Putin and his propagandists believe that Putinism has global appeal because Russia is a global power, but they have concentrated their efforts on ideological promotion in Europe and the United States.

To transmit ideas and concepts of Putinism worldwide, the Russian government has reconfigured several Soviet-era tools for ideological promotion and developed a few new methods. The very existence of this expansive toolkit is evidence that competition between the United States and Russia is not shaped only by power. Putin's Russia is back in the ideology promotion business just like the Soviets were, even if the content of this ideology has changed since the Cold War.

PERSONAL DIPLOMACY

Putin has devoted considerable energy to forging personal relationships with ideologically aligned leaders, especially in the former Soviet Union and Europe but also in the United States. Many of these leaders, though not all, are autocrats like Putin. But all of them, including those who are in power or who are trying to achieve power in democracies, share Putin's conservative, populist ideology. Thirty years ago, few leaders in the world embraced illiberal nationalism; most celebrated liberal internationalism. Today, that is no longer true. Tragically, Putin has many ideological soulmates in power or striving to take power.

In the former Soviet Union, Putin has supported Belarusian dictator Aleksandr Lukashenko for decades. Especially after massive demonstrations erupted in Belarus following a fraudulent 2020 presidential election, the Russian dictator leaned in to help his autocratic neighbor. To return the favor, Lukashenko allowed Putin to use Belarus as a staging ground for Russia's invasion of Ukraine in 2022. In Georgia, Putin has courted billionaire Bidzina Ivanishvili, whose Georgian Dream political party has undermined democratic institutions and pulled Georgia away from Europe; in November 2024 Georgia suspended accession talks with the European Union for four years.[23] In Ukraine, Putin publicly endorsed and funded Viktor Yanukovych's 2004 presidential campaign, stood with him against demonstrators in 2014, and continued to support anti-democratic groups in Ukraine after Yanukovych fled.[24] Putin also backed former Moldovan president Igor Dodon, who expressed his intent to cancel Moldova's trade agreement with the EU during his first state visit to Russia.

The list goes on. In 2023, when autocratic Azerbaijan seized Nagorno-Karabakh from the more democratically leaning Armenia, Putin did nothing to stop the assault despite Armenia's continuous requests for military support from the Russia-led Collective Security Treaty Organization (CSTO), of which Armenia was a member. In Central Asia, Putin has nurtured close relations with most of the autocrats ruling in the region except for Uzbekistan. In 2022, Putin sent twenty-five hundred "peacemakers" to

Kazakhstan to help defend the embattled autocracy there from what Putin called a "foreign-backed terrorist uprising."[25] Putin has similarly courted Mongolian president Khurelsukh Ukhnaa, who consciously imitates Putin's "strong man" image, complete with bare-chested photos.[26]

In Europe, Putin's closest ideological ally is Hungary's prime minister Viktor Orbán—the only EU leader who did not condemn Putin's 2022 invasion of Ukraine and subsequently tried to block EU aid to Ukraine and sanctions against Russia. The Putin-Orbán relationship is not just transactional; it is ideological, evident in the kind of ideas both leaders propagate within their countries as well as in their shared disdain for American "imperialism" and European liberal values. No European leader has done more to weaken the EU than Orbán, and weakening the EU is precisely what Putin wants.

In France, Putin has cultivated ties with an illiberal nationalist leader, Marine Le Pen. In 2017, Putin provided financial assistance for her presidential campaign and met her at the Kremlin in a public show of support for her political party right before that election. In turn, Le Pen expressed support for the Russian dictator, arguing, "The model that is defended by Vladimir Putin, which is one of reasoned protectionism, looking after the interests of his own country, defending his identity, is one that I like, as long as I can defend this model in my own country."[27]

In Italy, Putin has nurtured personal ties with illiberal nationalist leader Matteo Salvini. Secret audio recordings revealed that Salvini's Lega Nord allegedly participated in backroom deals with Russian operatives to receive funds from a Russian state-owned company.[28]

In the United Kingdom, Nigel Farage is a longtime Kremlin favorite due to his disdain for the EU. When asked which world leader he most admired, Farage answered "Putin."[29] While measuring causal impact has proven elusive, Putin's media did try to support Farage's successful campaign to push Great Britain out of the European Union.[30]

Ideological affinities have also undergirded Putin's relationship with Serbian president Aleksandar Vučić, Czech prime minister Andrej Babiš, Slovenian prime minister Janez Janša, Slovak prime minister Robert Fico, Geert Wilders and his Party for Freedom in the Netherlands, nationalist conservative party leaders in Austria, Bulgaria, and Germany, and Romanian presidential candidate Călin Georgescu in 2024. In 2021, sixteen right-wing European leaders and the leaders of populist parties signed a joint declaration in defense of conservative values; it declared, "The EU is becoming more and more a tool of radical forces that would like to carry out a cultural, religious transformation and ultimately a nationless construction of Europe, aiming to create a European Superstate, destruct or cancel European tradition, transform basic social institutions and moral principles . . . The cooperation of European nations should be based on tradition, respect for the culture and history of European states, respect for Europe's Judeo-Christian heritage and the common values that unite our nations."[31] These are precisely the ideas Putin espouses, demonstrating how the fight between liberalism and illiberalism in Europe is both between and within countries.

Some of Putin's relationships with these European populist nationalists were interrupted by his invasion of Ukraine. Strikingly, Italy's populist conservative prime minister Giorgia Meloni did not side with Putin but pledged continuity in Italy's support for Ukraine. But even as the war dragged on, there were already signs of repair with Putin's ideological partners in several European countries. In the June 2024 elections for the European parliament, pro-Putin, right-wing parties made significant gains.

Regarding the United States, Putin has used personal diplomacy to push his ideological agenda, including most aggressively with President Trump. As discussed below, Russia used multiple means to try to assist Trump's first presidential election campaign in 2016. While Trump was president the first time, Putin openly embraced the American leader as an ideological soulmate. When Trump tried to stay in power by encouraging insurrectionists to interrupt the peaceful transfer of political power on January 6, 2021, Moscow defended the action. A Russian history book stated bluntly and falsely that the 2020 presidential election was rigged against Trump.[32] After Biden won the election in 2020, Putin's state-controlled media openly advocated for the return of Trump. When Trump won in 2024, Russia's state-controlled media channels celebrated his victory.

In the Middle East, Putin has personally cultivated relations with several autocrats who also champion conservative values. Putin has nurtured a deep relationship with the supreme leader of theocratic Iran, repeatedly defending the Iranian dictatorship against American threats and criticizing Trump's bombings of Iran in June 2025. After Russia invaded Ukraine, Iran's theocrats showed their support for Putin by selling drones and missiles to Russia. Putin has courted deeper ties with the monarchs in the Middle East, including most notably with Saudi leader Mohammed bin Salman (MBS). When the rest of the world chastised MBS or avoided contact with him after his apparent involvement in the assassination of Saudi journalist Jamal Khashoggi in 2018, Putin went out of his way to signal support for the Saudi monarch.[33] After Russia invaded Ukraine in 2022, MBS returned the favor by maintaining significant Saudi investments in Russia when hundreds of companies from the democratic world pulled out.[34] In November 2022, in defiance of the Biden administration, MBS and Putin led the OPEC+ cartel to reduce oil exports to drive global fuel prices up, which helped Putin fund his war. In December 2023, MBS welcomed Putin to Saudi Arabia, one of the few countries Putin visited after invading Ukraine.

Despite being on opposing sides in numerous geopolitical conflicts, especially in Syria and Libya, Putin and Turkey's president Recep Tayyip Erdogan share an ideological commitment to strong-man rule, limits on democratic practices, and conservative values. Even though Erdogan sold drones to Ukraine against Putin's wishes, Turkey—a NATO ally—also paid $2.5 billion to purchase Russia's S-400 missile system in a deal finalized in 2019, a decision that outraged Washington at the time.

In Asia, as described in more detail in subsequent chapters, Putin has devoted special attention to cultivating his personal relationship with Xi Jinping. Putin has claimed that he and Xi "enjoy an unprecedentedly high level of trust and cooperation."[35] In turn, Xi has described Russia as a "sincere and like-minded partner"[36] and praised Putin as his "best friend."[37] The Chinese dictator certainly does not need Putin's support to sustain his autocratic rule at home, but the Kremlin's pro-Chinese rhetoric helps create the perception of an anti-American coalition of great powers.

Russia's war in Ukraine strained relations between the two leaders. Just days before the 2022 Russian invasion, Putin and Xi signed a comprehensive joint statement in Beijing that affirmed many strong ideological affinities. However, in public, Xi has used tepid language to support his partner in Moscow. In Putin and Xi's first in-person meeting following

Russia's invasion of Ukraine, Putin publicly acknowledged that China had "some questions and concerns" about the war but then repeatedly endorsed China's claim to Taiwan.[38] Xi, however, did not reciprocate by endorsing Putin's annexations in eastern Ukraine. To date, China has not provided direct military assistance to Russia but has increased imports of Russian fossil fuels and vastly expanded exports of critical technologies to Russia's military-industrial complex. In April 2025, however, President Zelenskyy reported that dozens of Chinese soldiers were fighting alongside Russian soldiers inside Ukraine, although whether the Chinese government was directly involved in their recruitment and deployment remains uncertain.[39]

While other forces, explored in subsequent chapters, are at play in strengthening China-Russia ties, Putin's personal role in cultivating relations with Xi based on a shared set of ideas has played a central role in bringing the two countries close together.

Elsewhere in Asia, Putin has cultivated ties with autocratic leaders in North Korea, Vietnam, and Laos. In June 2024, Putin visited Pyongyang for the first time in two decades to sign a security agreement. A few months later, Kim Jung Un sent ten thousand soldiers to Russia to fight against Ukraine.

Despite the differences in their regimes, Putin has even nurtured close personal ties with Indian prime minister Narendra Modi. Modi has claimed to have "special chemistry" with Putin and classifies Russia as an "integral friend and trustworthy partner."[40] In turn, Putin awarded Modi the Order of St. Andrew the Apostle, the highest state decoration of Russia, for promoting bilateral ties. After Putin invaded Ukraine in 2022, India stayed neutral and emerged as one of the biggest buyers of Russian oil, and Modi was one of the few world leaders to visit Moscow. A year after Russia's invasion began, 51 percent of Indians considered Russia a country "that shares our interests and values," and another 29 percent thought of Russia as "a necessary partner—with which we must strategically cooperate."[41] By comparison, only 35 percent of polled Chinese citizens identified Russia as an ally, and another 44 percent considered Russia a "necessary partner."

In Latin America, Putin has courted several dictators, although these relationships are based less on shared conservative ideology and more on shared anti-Americanism. Most aggressively, Putin has helped Venezuelan president Nicolás Maduro stay in power. Many democracies, including the United States, recognized opposition leader Juan Guaido as the country's interim president after Maduro stole the presidential election in 2019, but Russia's foreign minister Sergey Lavrov accused Washington of "publicly setting a course for illegal regime change."[42] When Maduro stole the presidential election again in 2024, Putin recognized the falsified election results immediately and sent private Russian soldiers to help Maduro repress protests. In Cuba, after Soviet assistance dried up, Putin restarted support for the island, forgave its billions of debt to Russia, and, in the summer of 2024, sent Russian warships to the island for a port call. In return, Cuba recognized Russia's annexation of Ukraine's Crimea and voted repeatedly against UN General Assembly resolutions denouncing Russia's invasion of Ukraine after 2022. Putin has also courted leftist autocrats Daniel Ortega in Nicaragua and Evo Morales in Bolivia while embracing the nationalist and populist president of Brazil Jair Bolsonaro when he was in power.

Of course, Putin pursued Russian national interests of varying sorts, as he defined them, when cultivating these personal relationships with these leaders. All heads of state do that. But Putin has favorites—ideological friends—in these countries, which he has made clear. Whether Putinism has contributed to the rise of the populist nationalists or whether these kinds of leaders have popped up independently of each other is hard to know. The transnational populist movement in Europe and the United States most likely would have arisen without Putin in power in Russia. However, what is clear is that the ties between these leaders are not based only on economic or security interests but also have a clear ideological component. And within the global club of populist, nationalist, and conservative leaders, Putin is an admired and central figure.

PARTY-TO-PARTY TIES

Compared to the Communist Party of the Soviet Union or today's Communist Party of China, Putin's political party, United Russia, is relatively weak at home and inactive abroad. However, Putin's efforts to nurture party-to-party ties as an instrument of ideological promotion are much stronger today than they were thirty years ago. For instance, in 2004 and 2010, the

Kremlin provided substantial assistance to the campaigns of Ukrainian president Viktor Yanukovych. Even after 2014, the Kremlin and its proxies maintained deep contact with pro-Russian parties and actors in Ukraine until their activities were suspended after Putin's 2022 full-scale invasion of Ukraine. In Estonia, Latvia, and Lithuania, Moscow has cultivated ties with political parties representing ethnic Russian minorities. United Russia has initiated agreements with the Austrian Freedom Party and Italy's Lega Nord party, the leaders of which were implicated in scandals for allegedly trying to take money from Russian sources. In 2014, a Kremlin-tied bank lent $9.8 million to French presidential candidate Marine Le Pen and her political party.[43] The Young Guard of United Russia has partnered with the right-wing Alternative for Germany. Most nationalist, populist, anti-EU parties in Europe have some relationship with their ideological allies in Russia. The Communist Party of China and United Russia have nurtured formal ties for decades. In 2024, after a meeting between the chairman of the United Russia Party, Dmitry Medvedev, and Liu Jianchao Liu, the head of the International Department of the CPC Central Committee, the CCP press release stated that "the Russian side regards the Chinese side as a priority cooperation partner, and that the current Russia-China relationship is at its best in history."[44] However, compared to the international activities of the Chinese Communist Party and the global programs run by US National Democratic Institute and the International Republican Institute, United Russia and its affiliates are much less active.

PEOPLE-TO-PEOPLE TIES

Russian nongovernmental organizations (NGOs) have also played a growing role in advancing Putinism abroad. Like their Chinese counterparts, Russian operatives loyal to Putin studied how the US government funds American NGOs to promote liberalism and democracy and are now trying to use these same methods to promote illiberalism and autocracy.

Putin's most powerful nongovernmental organization in this ideological promotion project is the Russian Orthodox Church. Putin has underwritten efforts by the Russian Orthodox Church to connect with other Orthodox faiths and like-minded ideological groups. The Russian idea that Moscow is the "third Rome" (after Rome and Constantinople) for the

Christian faith allegedly endows Russia with a special relationship with the rest of the Orthodox world. Putin personally fostered ties between the "White Church"—the Orthodox Church leaders in the United States—and the Orthodox Church in Moscow, which eventually led to the signing of the Act of Canonical Communion in May 2007. That union later helped Putin win endorsement of his annexation of Crimea from many in the Russian diaspora.[45]

The Russian Orthodox Church has nurtured relationships with evangelical churches in Europe and the United States, bonding over their shared positions on marriage, abortion, and anti-LGBTQ rights. In June 2013, Brian Brown of the National Organization for Marriage traveled to Moscow and gave a speech opposing the adoption of children by same-sex couples.[46] After Putin signed a law sharply limiting the adoption of Russian children by single individuals or unmarried couples from countries allowing same-sex marriage, American conservative commentator Rush Limbaugh remarked on his radio show, "I have to tell you that it freaks me out that Vladimir Putin is saying things I agree with."[47] The brainchild of two Russian professors and American Allan Carlson, the World Congress of Families has grown into an international anti-LGBTQ and anti-abortion coalition. In 2015, Patriarch Kirill of the Russian Orthodox Church hosted Franklin Graham, the CEO of the Billy Graham Evangelistic Association, who praised Putin for "protecting Russian young people against homosexual propaganda."[48]

Putin surrogates have also nurtured relationships with American and European populist nationalists. In 2013, American politician Patrick Buchanan praised Putin as a spiritual leader, claiming that the Russian leader "is seeking to redefine the 'Us vs. Them' world conflict of the future as one in which conservatives, traditionalists, and nationalists of all continents and countries stand up against the cultural and ideological imperialism of what he sees as a decadent West."[49] A year later, Buchanan argued, "The new ideological struggle is between a debauched West led by the United States and a traditionalist world Russia . . . it is Russia that is on God's side."[50] In 2019, Fox News anchor Tucker Carlson remarked, "I think we should probably take the side of Russia if we have to choose between Russia and Ukraine." On the eve of Putin's invasion of Ukraine, Carlson asked, "Why is it disloyal to side with Russia but loyal to side with Ukraine?"[51] Two years after the war began, Carlson traveled to Moscow to conduct a friendly interview with Putin, listening quietly to Putin's lengthy retelling of centuries of history that, in his view, justified his invasion, occupation, and annexation.[52] During this trip, Carlson did segments praising the Russian shopping centers and the Moscow Metro. For years, Russian conservative nationalist Alexander Dugin has cultivated ties with ideological partners in the United States, becoming a darling of right-wing American influencers such as Alex Jones and Steve Bannon. For instance, advertising his interview with Dugin on X on February 19, 2025, Alex Jones tweeted, "Top Russian Strategist Alexander Dugin Says The World Has Just Witnessed The 2nd American Revolution & That The Globalist System Has Been Defeated."[53] Dugin, in turn, celebrated Trump's reelection in 2024 as the end of global liberalism and regularly cheers on the MAGA movement, including Elon Musk's assault on what Dugin calls the "deep state." When Kash Patel was confirmed as Trump's new FBI director, Dugin on X called it a "huge success. Trump shows who is the absolute master in the house. That is real day of thunder. Revolution doesn't stop for a while. New day new blow. It is excellent. ALL key figures are now put in the key positions."[54]

To advance Putin's ideological agenda, the Kremlin has also funded numerous parastatal organizations, including the Russia World Foundation, which supports Russia Houses around the world (Russia's rough equivalent of China's Confucius Institutes), the Gorchakov Fund, the Foundation for National Values Protection, the Strategic Culture Foundation, the International Anticrisis Center, and the Association for Free Research and International Cooperation, all of which aim to connect with like-minded individuals and groups.[55] Pro-Kremlin NGOs have organized conferences and cultivated ties with extremist conservative and racist groups. The Valdai Forum, an annual conference that brings together Russian and international scholars and journalists and at which Putin always speaks, is another mechanism for Putin to spread his ideas.

The geographical focus of Russian nongovernmental actors promoting illiberalism and autocracy is Europe and the United States, but a few groups are active elsewhere. For instance, the Association for Free Research and International Cooperation (AFRIC) has operated mainly in Africa, monitoring elections to subvert credible election observation, indirectly organizing protests, and publishing opinion polls to influence electoral preferences.[56] In 2021, the United States sanctioned AFRIC and the Foundation for National Values Protection as punishment for their subversive ideological work.[57]

Courting, coercing, and silencing the Russian diaspora is another component of Russian engagement with nongovernmental organizations abroad. After the collapse of the Soviet Union, roughly twenty-five million ethnic Russians suddenly lived in newly independent states outside of Russia's borders. After years of neglect in the 1990s, Putin and his proxies have sought to cultivate ties with these communities through targeted media, foundations, NGOs, and religious organizations. Russia's Federal Agency for the Commonwealth of Independent State Affairs, Compatriots Living Abroad, and International Humanitarian Cooperation (Rossotrudnichestvo) has right in its title the specific mission of aiding "Compatriots Living Abroad." Putin has offered citizenship to ethnic Russians living abroad and issued passports to ethnic Russians living in territories occupied by the Russian army.[58]

Additionally, Putin actively seeks to silence Russian critics living abroad, using Interpol to try to chase down opposition leaders (and Western critics) in other countries[59] and, most frighteningly, poisoning and at times even killing Russians living abroad who criticize Russia's dictatorship. Labeling them as extremists and terrorists, the Kremlin has issued arrest warrants and convicted in absentia prominent Russian opposition leaders and cultural figures living abroad, such as Yuliya Navalnaya, chess champion Garry Kasparov, and novelist Boris Akunin.

PROPAGANDA AND DISINFORMATION

Putin's government has invested considerable resources in developing broadcast, print, and social media platforms to promote Putinism and subvert liberal values both at home and abroad. After mainly playing defense inside Russia during his first years in power, Putin went on the offensive in the information space, expanding multiple media instruments to advance his ideological agenda worldwide.

Within the former Soviet Union, Putin's state-controlled television and radio channels have increased their reach. Numerous oligarchs and politicians, including those loyal to Putin in Ukraine (until the 2022 invasion), Georgia, and Moldova, own or control significant media assets. Russian artists, musicians, athletes, and social media personalities play a major role in shaping public opinion in Russia's neighboring countries, where millions still speak Russian.

Pro-Western democratic actors in the region have pushed back. Leaders in Lithuania, Latvia, and Estonia have restricted Russian-state broadcasting in their countries. In Ukraine, pro-Russian oligarch Viktor Medvedchuk controlled three top television stations until President Volodymyr Zelenskyy sanctioned him and took these stations off the air. After Russia invaded Ukraine in 2022, Zelenskyy and his government devoted even greater resources to combat Russian propaganda. Putin, in turn, cut off Ukrainian media in occupied territories and allowed only Russian media outlets to operate there. In the rest of the former Soviet Union, however, Russian television channels play a pivotal role in propagating Putin's ideas.

Beyond the Russian-speaking world, Putin's flagship propaganda asset is Russia Today, an information agency that controls the television network RT and the multimedia platform Sputnik International to provide "alternative news" to Western sources. For 2022, RT's annual budget was $310 million.[60] RT broadcasts and provides digital content in over one hundred countries in six languages: Arabic, English, French, German, Russian, and Spanish (strikingly, not Chinese). RT often uses cable bundles and hotel contracts to reach foreign audiences and has developed a substantial footprint on US-owned social media platforms. RT became the first television news channel to reach one billion views on YouTube. After invading Ukraine in 2022, Putin banned Twitter, Facebook, and Instagram inside Russia, but RT continued to propagate content on all three platforms for two more years until Meta—the parent company of Facebook and Instagram—banned RT from its platforms in September 2024.[61] Twitter, now owned by Elon Musk and renamed X, still allows RT, Sputnik, and other Russia state actors to operate on its platform. In September 2024, the United States finally sanctioned RT and its affiliates.[62] Russian actors also operate television, broadcast, and social media in Madagascar, Sudan, Mozambique, Libya, the Central African Republic, and the Democratic Republic of Congo.[63]

Russian international television and radio have similarities and differences with Soviet-era methods. On the similarities side, RT unapologetically promotes the Kremlin's viewpoint on Russian and global affairs. As RT's editor in chief Margarita Simonyan explained, "Since RT receives budget from the state, it must complete tasks given by the state."[64] After Russia invaded Ukraine, Simonyan stated even more bluntly, "There is no objectivity . . . When Russia is at war, we are, of course, on the side of Russia."[65] RT is not the BBC. RT and Sputnik are instruments of Putin's regime.

Regarding differences with the Cold War, RT and its partners have greater resources and a more modern, professional staff compared to Soviet global media. RT's production quality is first-rate and often includes native speakers as foreign-language broadcasters. In contrast to the heavy-handed, boring Soviet propaganda, RT and Sputnik cleverly mix entertainment, news, opinion, and disinformation. RT and Sputnik have blended into media ecosystems worldwide, echoing and amplifying perspectives from like-minded local media outlets. Messages are targeted more regionally. Generally, audiences in Europe and the United States receive conservative populist messaging, while people in the developing world receive more anti-imperialism, left-of-center content that echoes Soviet-era themes.

However, the biggest difference with the Cold War is the wealth of new opportunities for propaganda offered by the internet, possibilities that Soviet predecessors could only have dreamed of. Without setting foot in a target country, Russian actors can deploy a myriad of digital instruments to propagate Putinism and undermine democratic values. Unlike what happened in the Cold War, American companies have played an essential role in supporting Russian propaganda efforts today. To a greater degree than any other national government, the Kremlin and its proxies use fake accounts, public figures, and digital disinformation to advance ideological goals on social media platforms owned by Americans.[66]

Their efforts to shape American public opinion were most notable during the 2016 presidential election. The Internet Research Agency, a Russian-funded organization founded by Putin's then-friend Yevgeny Prigozhin, had a monthly operating budget of one million dollars to carry out an array of tactics to influence American electoral preferences, including the creation of thousands of fictitious accounts to push targeted messaging, and "posing as US persons and creating false US personas, operated social media pages and groups designed to attract US audiences, . . . [using] the stolen identities of real US persons . . . to reach significant numbers of Americans for purposes of interfering with the US political system."[67] Twitter reported over 2,700 IRA-controlled accounts and 36,700 Russia-linked accounts that had generated approximately 1.4 million election-related tweets, receiving 288 million impressions.[68] Facebook identified 470 IRA-controlled accounts that collectively made 80,000 posts during this period.[69] IRA employees in St. Petersburg even contacted Americans directly and organized physical rallies in the United States. According to the US Senate Select Committee on Intelligence, "The IRA sought to influence the 2016 US presidential election by harming Hillary Clinton's chances of success and supporting Donald Trump at the direction of the Kremlin."[70] In parallel, RT and Sputnik International pushed messages in the United States for Trump and against Clinton.[71]

They tried again during the 2020 US presidential election. As the Director of National Intelligence Avril Haines assessed, "Putin authorized, and a range of Russian government organizations conducted, influence operations aimed at denigrating President Biden's candidacy and the Democratic Party, supporting former President Trump, undermining public confidence in the electoral process, and exacerbating socio-political divisions."[72] In addition, according to the US intelligence community, "Russia's online influence actors sought to affect US public perceptions of the candidates, as well as advance Moscow's longstanding goals of undermining confidence in US election processes and increasing sociopolitical divisions . . . online influence actors sought to amplify mistrust in the electoral process by denigrating Mail-in ballots, highlighting alleged irregularities . . . online influence actors generally promoted former president Trump and his commentary . . . [and] sought to discourage US left-leaning audiences from voting by suggesting that neither candidate was a preferable option."[73] After the 2020 election, Kremlin-controlled media outlets and social media actors continued "to promote narratives questioning the election results and disparaging President Biden and the Democratic Party."[74] In 2024, Russian propagandists pushed anti-Harris and pro-Trump messaging.[75] No scientific study has ever proven that these Russian state media campaigns influenced the outcome of any of these elections. That Putin's agents were trying to do so is clear.

The United States is not the only country in which Russian media has tried to sway electoral outcomes. In Europe, Africa, and Latin America, the Kremlin has deployed traditional and digital media to compete ideologically with their liberal foes in democracies during elections and referenda, such as the vote for independence in Scotland in 2014, the vote in the United Kingdom to exit the European Union in 2016, and parliamentary and presidential elections in numerous European countries.[76] In Romania during the 2024 presidential election, the scale of Russia's social media support for pro-Russian, anti-NATO candidate Călin Georgescu was so overwhelming in the first round that the Romanian supreme court made the extraordinary decision to annul that result before the second round of this vote took place.[77]

SPYING, STEALING, AND DOXING

The Russian government has aggressively engaged in cyber theft and then publication of stolen data—doxing—to advance ideological objectives. Russia's most audacious execution of this kind of influence operation occurred during the 2016 US presidential election when the Main Intelligence Directorate of the General Staff of the Russian Army (GRU) penetrated the computers and networks of the Democratic National Committee, the Democratic Congressional Campaign Committee, and Clinton's campaign staff, and then published what they had stolen.[78] The publication of this stolen content generated a narrative in the US media that the DNC had mistreated presidential candidate Bernie Sanders and fueled an image of Clinton as corrupt. Thousands of stolen emails were published continuously, which Clinton called "a drip, drip, drip" against her campaign.[79] Russian agents penetrated the digital networks of both political parties but published data only from the Democrats. Again, whether this Russian operation influenced the outcome of the election has never been proven definitively, but they most certainly were attempting to do so.[80]

The Kremlin has used similar methods in other countries.[81] CyberBerkut—a group connected to the Russian military intelligence—hacked into the Ukrainian election system. In Germany, Russian hackers targeted the

Bundestag and the Christian Democratic Union Party.[82] A successful operation was executed in 2017 against French presidential candidate Emmanuel Macron and his En Marche! political movement.[83] The release of stolen data amplified by bots and organic online actors was designed to help Le Pen, Putin's ideological ally.[84] In the United Kingdom, Russian digital spies compromised the email account of Defense Secretary Liam Fox and then released the stolen documents to help the Labor Party's campaign.[85] During the 2020 Polish presidential election, a Russian-linked organization hacked into several websites to try to influence the election.[86]

The Kremlin has also deployed human agents—intelligence officers, surrogates, and intermediaries from third countries—to advance ideological objectives. During the 2016 US presidential election, a Russian delegation led by lawyer Natalia Veselnitskaya met with Trump campaign officials to offer them compromising materials on Clinton.[87] Four years later, Russian actors met with Trump associates to try to spread disinformation about "corrupt ties between President Biden, his family, and other US officials and Ukraine."[88] Kremlin agents "provided materials to Trump administration-linked US persons to advocate for formal investigations; hired a US firm to petition US officials; and attempted to make contact with several senior US officials."[89]

Russian intelligence officers and their agents have played direct roles in other countries to advance Putin's ideological agenda of weakening ideological foes, strengthening like-minded allies, and generally fostering societal polarization and division in democracies. Russian intelligence officers also have been assigned to autocracies close to Russia to help them learn how to control social movements.[90] Since Putin's full-scale invasion of Ukraine, Russian agents have carried out sabotage operations in European democracies to frighten these societies and thereby discourage them from supporting democratic Ukraine.[91]

LOBBYING, PHILANTHROPY, AND CORRUPTION

Putin and his associates have hired lobbyists in many countries, including the United States, to advance both economic and ideological objectives. Most famously, the Kremlin purchased the services of former German chancellor Gerhard Schroeder by inviting him to serve as the chairman of the

Rosneft board of directors and to sit on the Nord Stream II board. Schroeder defended and advanced many of Putin's foreign policy positions in Germany before resigning from the Rosneft board in 2022. Former Austrian foreign minister Karin Kneissel, who famously danced with Putin at her wedding in 2018, joined Rosneft's board and eventually ended up in Russia after the 2022 invasion of Ukraine to "teach." Russian money in British politics has been extensive and well documented. As a British parliament report summed it up, "Illicit financing and money were invested in extending patronage and building influence across a wide sphere of the British establishment—PR firms, charities, political interests, academia, and cultural institutions were all willing beneficiaries of Russian money, contributing to a 'reputation laundering' process . . . Lawyers, accountants, estate agents, and PR professionals have played a role, wittingly or unwittingly, in the extension of Russian influence, which is often linked to promoting the nefarious interests of the Russian state."[92] In the United States, Russian companies have employed lobbyists and PR firms to advance their companies' economic interests but also to promote a positive image of Russia more generally.

Like Chinese and American business leaders, a handful of wealthy Russian executives and magnates have engaged in international philanthropy to improve Russia's image. In the United States, individual Russians and their foundations have provided significant gifts to the Kennedy Center, the Kennan Institute in Washington, DC, Fort Ross in Northern California, and several universities. Some efforts seem closely coordinated with Putin's ideological agenda, others less so.

ECONOMIC INSTRUMENTS

Russia has fewer economic resources available for ideological promotion than the United States and China. That said, Putin has increased assistance programs and demonstrated a greater willingness to leverage economic power to pursue ideological objectives.

Before invading Ukraine in 2022, Putin did not aggressively use trade and investment to advance his ideological agenda abroad. Russia sold oil, gas, and other raw materials to both democracies and autocracies; there was no discernible correlation between foreign direct investment inside Russia or Russian investment abroad and Putin's global objectives. In the early years of Putin's presidency, the Kremlin focused on attracting investment primarily from democracies, including the United States. Even a decade later, when I was the US ambassador to Russia, Putin actively cultivated American investment, personally negotiating the multibillion-dollar deal between ExxonMobil and Rosneft. Back then, the US government encouraged Russian direct investment in the United States.

In parallel, Putin pursued some ideologically motivated economic deals. For instance, Putin subsidized energy exports to Belarusian dictator Aleksandr Lukashenko for decades and extended even more financial assistance after 2020 when mass protests threatened to topple the Belarusian autocrat. Likewise, Moscow has provided generous economic aid and subsidized energy to the separatist Georgian territories of South Ossetia and Abkhazia, which Russia recognized as independent countries after invading in 2008. Venezuela is another place where ideology shapes Russian investment decisions.

After Putin invaded Ukraine in 2014 and more dramatically after 2022, ideological objectives have played a more significant role in shaping Russian economic activity abroad. After 2014, the Kremlin poured massive resources into Crimea and the separatist regions in eastern Ukraine to try to win hearts and minds there. After 2014, Russian exports shifted toward the autocratic East and then accelerated even further after the democratic world imposed comprehensive sanctions on Russian companies in response to Putin's invasion of Ukraine in 2022. In 2023, Russia-China trade increased dramatically, reaching $240 billion, the highest level ever. At the same time, hundreds of companies with headquarters in democratic countries exited Russia, sometimes leaving behind significant investments that they sold to Russian actors at substantially reduced prices or that were confiscated by the Russian state. That was not true just a decade ago, let alone twenty years ago, when Boris Yeltsin and democratic Russia were keenly focused on integrating their economy into Europe and the democratic community of states and aggressively seeking to attract foreign direct investment into Russia from the democratic world. Today, the decoupling of Russia and the democratic world has been much more dramatic than the decoupling of China and the democratic world so far.

In parallel to strengthening economic ties with autocracies, Putin has occasionally deployed coercive economic instruments to try to undermine democracies. In response to the Rose Revolution in Georgia in 2003, Putin blocked wine and mineral imports. After invading Georgia in 2008, the Kremlin put in place even greater economic restrictions, which were then lifted when a more Russian-friendly, less democratic government came to power. After the Orange Revolution in 2004 and again after the Revolution of Dignity in 2014, the Kremlin banned many Ukrainian imports and blocked their transit to Central Asia.[93] After Putin escalated his war in Ukraine in 2022, Russia deployed its air force, rockets, and ships to try to destroy the economy of democratic Ukraine.

During the Cold War, the United States and the Soviet Union used economic aid as a major tool of ideological promotion. After the Soviet Union's collapse, Russian leaders exited this competition and focused on addressing their economic woes, becoming a net recipient of aid. More recently, however, Russia has reentered the assistance competition. In 2008, the Russian government established a revamped aid agency, Rossotrudnichestvo, to "increase the effectiveness of governance in the field of international cooperation."[94] In 2019, Moscow established the International Agency for Sovereign Development to assist developing countries in restructuring their debt. Budgets for these aid organizations are small compared to Beijing's BRI and Washington's USAID.[95] Briefly, the COVID-19 pandemic allowed Moscow to play a more significant role in the aid contest between great powers because Russia succeeded in developing an effective vaccine before China and the United States. However, disbursement problems, accusations of overpricing, and corruption did not generate the hoped-for soft-power payoffs.[96]

COVERT AND OVERT MILITARY INTERVENTIONS

During the Cold War, the United States and the Soviet Union deployed coercive instruments—covert action, military assistance for guerrilla groups, and at times direct military intervention—to support or undermine ideological movements and regimes. After the Cold War ended, democratic Russia stopped using such tactics abroad. Autocratic Russia under Putin resurrected these methods, both to weaken democracies and strengthen autocracies. In 2007, Putin ordered a major cyberattack against democratic

Estonia. In 2010, Russia helped incite a popular revolt to oust Kyrgyz president Kurmanbek Bakiyev and replace him with a more pro-Russian government.[97] Russian military intelligence was behind the 2014 explosion of the Bulgarian arms firm EMCO that killed two Czech workers.[98] In 2023, Russian intelligence officers helped the Serbian government subdue protesters who challenged the freeness and fairness of a parliamentary election. More audaciously, Putin deployed intelligence officers to help plot a coup against Montenegrin prime minister Milo Đukanović and take control of parliament as a means to try blocking Montenegro's membership in NATO.[99]

Putin's Russia has also deployed military power to advance ideological objectives, most notably in Ukraine where the Kremlin explicitly seeks the overthrow of the democratically elected president and his government. But Putin has run a similar military playbook in other countries to weaken democracies and support dictatorships. In 2008, the Kremlin invaded Georgia and then recognized South Ossetia and Abkhazia as independent countries to weaken democratic Georgia. In 2015, Putin deployed his air force in Syria to help defend Bashar al-Assad's dictatorship, killing thousands of innocent civilians. In 2022, in an echo of Soviet interventions in Hungary in 1956 and Czechoslovakia in 1968, Putin deployed soldiers into Kazakhstan to prop up the ruling autocratic government.

In Syria, Ukraine, and a dozen other countries, Putin has also deployed private paramilitary mercenaries, the Wagner Group, to aid autocrats and undermine democrats. These guns-for-hire have undertaken significant combat operations in the civil war in Syria and in Putin's invasion of Ukraine but have also been active in the African Sahel and bordering countries—Burkina Faso, Sudan, Mali, Niger, and the Central African Republic—to fight terrorist groups and secure minerals and other economic benefits for Russia, although always in the service of autocrats, never democrats.[100] Another private Russian security contractor, the RSB Group, has conducted operations in parts of Libya controlled by Russian partner field marshal Khalifa Haftar. After the Wagner Group's leader Yevgeny Prigozhin led an unsuccessful rebellion against Moscow in the summer of 2022, Prigozhin was assassinated, and the Wagner Group was renamed the Africa Corps (and various other titles when working elsewhere), but it continued to conduct missions in support of dictators—in Niger after the coup in 2023 and in Venezuela to help autocrat Maduro stay in power after a falsified presidential vote in 2024.

Putin's use of military power to defend autocracies and undermine democracies is both similar and different to the Cold War practices. In Hungary in 1956, Czechoslovakia in 1968, and Afghanistan in 1979, Soviet armed forces intervened to save autocratic allies under duress—as Putin's Russia did in Syria and Kazakhstan. After World War II, however, Soviet leaders never invaded countries to colonize or annex territory, which is what Putin has attempted to do in Ukraine since 2022. That is new. Putin's invasion of Ukraine has more in common with European conflicts before the Cold War, including Hitler's invasions and annexations, and wars of imperial conquest in earlier centuries.

IMPACT

This ideological mission is not some marginal project for Putin. It is fundamental to who he is and what his regime is. Like leaders in the United States and China, Putin uses the toolkit just described to pursue multiple objectives—security, economic, and ideological goals—at the same time, but some of them are primarily aimed at pursuing ideological ends. That Putin is prepared to spend so much in lives and treasure, especially in Ukraine, underscores how ideologically motivated he has become. Russia's security and economic objectives in Ukraine could be achieved through much less costly means than invasion and occupation, as they were achieved, after all, before 2022. Compared to Xi, Putin has demonstrated a more profound commitment and a greater willingness to take risks to erode democracy and support his ideological allies abroad.

That Putin has ideological goals is clear. Whether he is achieving them is harder to know. First, it is nearly impossible to disaggregate ideological, security, and economic motivations, so measuring the ideological successes independently is hard to do. Second, Putinism as an ideology is not as well defined as communism or liberalism (although we have assigned more logic and consistency to these ideologies than they deserve). Third, Putin's message in Europe and the United States is different than Putin's message in Africa and other parts of the developing world. In the West, Putin and his regime have focused on promoting illiberal, orthodox, and conservative values. In the developing world, Putinism sounds much like messages from the Soviet era with a heavy dose of anti-imperial Americanism. Fourth, current Russian resources devoted to ideological promotion are smaller than what the Soviet Union marshaled. Measuring their causal effect on concrete outcomes in other countries, therefore, is difficult because so many other factors are in play. Finally, Putin's invasion of Ukraine has interrupted his international ideological effort. We still don't know if this moment signals a lasting rupture or a temporary setback.

With all these caveats and constraints on measurement in mind, some of Putin's successes are clear and should concern American policymakers. Most crudely, there has been a correlation in the twenty-first century between the rise of Russian autocratic power and the demise of democracy worldwide. A similar correlation exists between the rise of Chinese autocratic power and the erosion of global democracy. Untangling what is cause and what is effect is challenging. However, some autocratic gains and democratic losses in the world resulted at least in part from Putin's actions.

SUSTAINING AUTOCRACY

Most consequentially, Putin has helped autocrats stay in power. In 2015, Putin's decision to intervene in the Syrian civil war saved al-Assad for many years. Without Russia's air force, that dictatorship would have fallen a decade ago instead of in 2024. In addition, Russian economic, intelligence, and diplomatic assistance played a pivotal role in saving Lukashenko's dictatorship from falling to massive, pro-democratic protests in 2020. In a more democratic neighborhood, Lukashenko would not have survived. Putin's assistance to Nicolás Maduro in Venezuela also has proved essential. After the coup and violent repression of democratic forces in Myanmar, the United States and Russia lined up again on opposite sides, but so far, Russia's autocratic allies have prevailed.

In Africa, Putin's provisions of economic assistance, diplomatic cover, military arms, and contract soldiers have helped to support authoritarian regimes and coup plotters. In the Central African Republic, a former Russian defense intelligence official, Valery Zakharov, even became Faustin-Archange Touadéra's national security adviser. In Mali and Niger,

Russian mercenaries combined with Moscow's diplomatic, economic, and military support have helped consolidate the power of the military juntas that seized power there in 2022 and 2023, respectively. Russian actions in Africa are much more aggressive in supporting autocrats than Chinese activities on the continent. In Central Asia, Russia has helped to keep the region safe for autocracy for decades, including intervening militarily in Kazakhstan in 2022 and using energy exports and other economic tools to support strongmen in Kyrgyzstan, Mongolia, and Tajikistan.

Not all Russian efforts to help autocrats have succeeded. Putin and his proxies have intervened directly with special forces, intelligence operatives, and contract soldiers to win allies in Libya, but with limited success. In Sudan, as many as five hundred Wagner Group soldiers helped defend dictator Omar al-Bashir, but that regime was toppled in 2019. In 2015, Putin's military intervention in Syria kept al-Assad in power for many years but not forever. In 2024, the Syrian dictatorship collapsed, and al-Assad fled to Russia. Russian autocratic allies Iran, Hezbollah, and Hamas are much weaker today than just a few years ago. Putin could do nothing to prevent Trump from bombing his autocratic allies in Iran in June 2025.

In addition to helping autocrats, Putin has succeeded in weakening some democracies and democrats. In Europe, Putin's courtship of illiberal leaders has helped to weaken democracy, especially in Hungary, but also in Serbia, Georgia, and Slovakia. Putin's ties to far-right movements in nearly every European democracy have helped to sow polarization and division in these societies. The illegitimacy and brutality of Putin's war in Ukraine have compelled some populist nationalists in Europe, such as Italian prime minister Meloni, to reconsider their affinities with Putin, but not all. Hungary's Orbán refused to condemn Putin's invasion, pushed for the lifting of EU sanctions, and delayed assistance packages to Ukraine. After being reelected, another Putin ideological kindred spirit, Prime Minister Robert Fico of Slovakia, argued that bringing Ukraine into NATO would trigger World War III. Putin's influence efforts in Georgia have been especially consequential, both in eroding democracy and exacerbating tensions between the government of Georgia and the European Union. By remaining neutral, Putin implicitly backed Azerbaijan's short war against Armenia in 2020, which damaged the reputation of the democratic-leaning government in Armenia that had come to power in 2018 through a peaceful uprising. Putin's greatest failure in his efforts to undermine democracy in Europe is Ukraine. After more than three years of full-scale invasion, Ukrainian democracy remains intact.

In the United States, the record of Russian ideological promotion is mixed. Putin's efforts to sway election outcomes did not produce traceable effects but did help to catalyze anti-Putin sentiment in the Democratic Party. At the same time, Russia's invasion of Ukraine in 2022 strained but did not break his ideological affinities with American politicians and television commentators. Donald Trump did not condemn Putin's invasion and continued to call Putin a strong leader at the top of his game. Other Americans who shared Putin's ideological agenda have falsely accused Zelenskyy of corruption and pushed to end US aid to Ukraine. In the fall of 2023, conservative Republicans held up aid to Ukraine for six months, a delay that directly assisted Russia's war efforts. After Trump's reelection, future US support for Ukraine has become very uncertain. These are tangible benefits for autocratic Russia and blows for democratic Ukraine.

A POSITIVE IMAGE OF RUSSIA

Putin's efforts to resurrect Russia's image as a positive force in the world achieved some limited successes. A Pew Research Center public-opinion poll in thirty-five countries in 2024 reported that "a median of 65% of adults in the surveyed countries have an unfavorable view of Russia, while 28% have a favorable view."[101] But when broken down between developed and developing countries, Russia enjoys a much better reputation in the Global South than in the Global North. After Putin invaded Ukraine, Russia's image took a nosedive in Europe and the United States, but the longer-term effects are still hard to predict.[102]

Trump's embrace of Putin has produced a significant positive change toward Russia among Republican politicians and voters, a complete reversal from the Cold War. In Africa, protesters supporting the coups in Mali, Burkina Faso, and Niger as well as anti-government protesters in northern Nigeria waved Russian flags.[103] That is new too.

More generally, Putin's perceived global fight against alleged American hegemony has won favor in some societies in the developing world, a lingering legacy of the Cold War. Strikingly, both governments and societies in many postcolonial countries rejected the framing of Putin's invasion of Ukraine as a colonial or imperial action. Most countries in Africa, Asia, Latin America, and the Middle East did not impose sanctions on Russia after the invasion of Ukraine, and some, including most notably, India, have increased imports from Russia. Many of these countries have allowed themselves to act as intermediaries for the shipment of technology into Russia. A year after Putin invaded Ukraine, polling data from India, China, and Turkey showed much more support for Russia there than in the United States, the EU, and Great Britain.[104] Israel's military intervention in Gaza in response to the Hamas terrorist attack on October 7, 2023, helped to recast the United States and Israel as the "colonizers" and deflected attention away from Putin's imperial war and crimes against humanity in Ukraine.

Autocratic leaders worldwide have found a powerful and intentional friend in Putin. Even rulers of regimes with close ties to the United States—such as Mohammed bin Salman in Saudi Arabia and Recep Erdogan in Turkey—have developed relations with Putin in ways that would have been unimaginable during the Cold War.

Within democracies, the battle between autocrats and democrats, or liberal and illiberal forces, is much more acute than any parallel contest between communism and its critics during the Cold War. In the previous century, communism posed a serious threat to many European democracies during the Cold War in the early years, but those faded with time and were never acute in the United States. By contrast, the challenges to liberal democracy from within supported by Russia are much greater today, even within the oldest and most powerful democracy in the world, the United States. That is different from the Cold War, and it is not changing anytime soon.

Chapter 8

EXPORTING XI JINPING THOUGHT

IN THE SPRING of 2024, I taught a short course on great power competition at Stanford's center at Peking University in Beijing. It was my first time back in China since the COVID-19 pandemic—a five-year absence—and my first time meeting with Chinese officials and academics since the pandemic began. During one session with a Chinese government–affiliated think tank, the conversation became heated. Echoing Xi, my Chinese colleagues insisted that American acceptance of their doctrine of "mutual respect" would improve US-China relations.

I asked what exactly *mutual respect* meant, and they explained that it meant acceptance of their system of government—that is, of Communist Party dictatorship. I countered that showing respect for their system of government—dictatorship—would be at odds with American traditions of liberalism and democracy. Asking American foreign policy leaders to stop talking about human rights and democracy would be just as impossible as American officials asking Chinese leaders to stop mentioning socialism or "Xi Jinping Thought" in their diplomacy. I proposed that although US officials could not stop talking about democracy altogether, they could refrain from calling for a democratic revolution in China. To me, this felt like a compromise.

This discussion reaffirmed for me the existence of ideological competition as a fundamental component of the relationship between the US and China today. Chinese autocracy and American democracy can coexist peacefully, but the existence of two fundamentally different, powerful, and opposing systems threatens the leaders and societies of both countries. No number of win-win dialogues, diplomatic reassurances, or track-two conferences will eliminate this tension completely.

In the past, countries with different regime types and opposing ideologies have learned to cooperate and coexist, or at least avoid war. As explored in chapter 2, US-China ideological tensions were not always as sharp as they are now. Several new factors have exacerbated more recent clashes. Most important, China has grown more powerful. American leaders are not generally as threatened by weak dictatorships as they are by strong ones.

Second, the success of China's economic model threatens the legitimacy of democracy globally; the Chinese communist system under Mao was less threatening to US interests because it did not produce similar economic results.

Third, Xi Jinping emphasizes ideological themes—making public pronouncements on Marxism-Leninism, socialism, and communism—more frequently than any Chinese leader since Mao. Xi is not Mao 2.0.[1] He aims to fuse elements of Maoism with Deng's "Reform and Opening Up" that have proven successful for development. Nonetheless, his ideological reorientation is radical enough to have fueled greater tensions with the democratic world and especially the United States, affirming that individual leaders—not just power alone—can profoundly influence a country's role in international affairs.[2]

A fourth source of the heightened ideological tension is Xi's anxiety about the spread of liberal democratic ideas inside China, Hong Kong, and Taiwan. In Xi's view, if democratic ideas gain more popularity in China, they could prompt a color revolution, toppling the CCP's authoritarian rule. The party's anxieties about American democracy promotion were revealed in a leaked 2013 memo, which bluntly concluded that the goal of American foreign policy was "to undermine the Party's leadership, abolish the People's Democracy, negate our country's constitution as well as our established system and principles, and bring about a change of allegiance by bringing Western political systems to China."[3] A few years later, Chinese leaders blamed "external foreign forces" for orchestrating and funding the 2019 protests in Hong Kong and accused Americans of attempting to destabilize Tibet and Xinjiang as part of a broader strategy to split up China. Beijing has long identified American support of democratic Taiwan as a threat to its political system. More generally, CCP leaders see internal societal mobilization against any autocratic regime as America's doing.

The first Trump administration's amplification of the communist threat from China was a fifth factor exacerbating ideological tensions. In 2019, Trump's secretary of state, Michael Pompeo, argued, "We're finally realizing the degree to which the Chinese Communist Party is truly hostile to the United States and our values."[4] The China threat did not need to be framed this way; the administration could have chosen to talk about it primarily in security or economic terms. They chose the opposite, emphasizing the ideological dimension of the China challenge, a departure from the previous Obama administration.

Though he did not use the good-versus-evil imagery characteristic of the first Trump administration, Biden also framed the rivalry with China in ideological terms. He often cited the dichotomy between autocracies and democracies as a major driver of global competition, including with China. Biden once told reporters, "Your children or grandchildren are going to be doing their doctoral thesis on who succeeded, autocracy or democracy, because that is [what's] at stake . . . We have got to prove democracy works."[5] Congress did too. The House of Representatives created a Select Committee on Strategic Competition between the United States and the Chinese Communist Party (not the People's Republic of China) in 2023. In unapologetic ideological terms, the organization stated it was "committed to working on a bipartisan basis to build consensus on the threat posed by the Chinese Communist Party and develop a plan of action to defend the American people, our economy, and our values."[6] The former chair of the Select Committee on the CCP Congressman Mike Gallagher warned that US-China competition was "an existential struggle over what life will look like in the 21st century."[7]

In the first months of Trump's second term, it remains unclear how prominently the new administration will highlight ideological differences. As already mentioned in the introduction, Trump's new secretary of state Marco Rubio clearly thinks about the China threat in ideological terms, calling "Communist China . . . the most powerful adversary the United States has faced in living memory."[8] So far in his second term, Trump has avoided using such language. Instead, Trump frames the China threat in economic, not ideological, terms. No matter what Trump thinks personally, however, the ideological dimension will remain a component of US-China competition as long as China remains an autocracy and the United States a democracy and as long as both countries devote resources to promoting their competing ideas abroad.[9] While Trump may be pulling back on supporting democracy promotion, Xi is not dismantling his instruments of ideological promotion and soft power.

At the same time, today's ideological clash between the US and China differs from the Cold War in several ways. First, while Chinese leaders have devoted considerable attention and resources to advancing their ideas abroad, their commitment to the export of socialism or even autocracy has never come near Soviet levels. Chinese leaders are more focused on promoting their ideas at home to stay in power, not propagating them abroad. Second, Chinese methods of ideological promotion so far have been demonstrably less violent and coercive than Soviet, Russian, or even American strategies. Rather than threatening to overthrow or weaken democracies, Chinese leaders today focus more on defending existing autocracies.[10] Third, there is no coherent "China model" available for easy emulation because Beijing's governance and development model has changed over time. Deng's model of development and Xi's model are different. Moreover, Chinese leaders have been content to let the developing countries they assist pick and choose which elements of the Chinese system to import rather than seeking to export a comprehensive economic and governance package as Soviet Communist Party leaders did.[11] For example, a country can request Chinese assistance in developing surveillance systems without instituting Communist Party rule. This method of autocracy promotion might be more threatening to American interests than the Soviet assistance system, which tended to be costly and disruptive. Fourth, "Chinese-style modernization" today is more attractive than the Soviet communist system was during the Cold War's final years precisely because it is not as ideologically rooted: the Chinese development system, after all, has some features of market economies. Fifth, CCP leaders today are expanding their influence at a time when global support for democracy and capitalism is softening and the American commitment to investing in these values around the world is waning, especially in Trump's second term. Paradoxically, while less intense, overt, and confrontational than the Soviet ideological challenge to the United States and the free world in the last century, China's more subtle and softer methods of ideological promotion could be more successful in the long run, especially as the United States under President Trump retreats from supporting democratic ideas.

XI'S IDEAS FOR THE WORLD

Beijing aims to advance the Chinese economic development model, defend autocracy by promoting sovereignty, champion traditional Chinese values, and, more generally and not uniquely, promote a positive image of China abroad.[12] However, this commitment is not nearly as time- or resource-intensive as the Maoist and Soviet efforts to promote communism, socialism, and Marxism-Leninism. The ideological struggle between the United States and China is a central driver of great power competition today, but it is not as intense or confrontational as the Cold War.

THE CHINESE ECONOMIC MODEL

Xi pitches the "Chinese model" or "Chinese-style modernization" as an attractive alternative to the Western economic model for developing nations to emulate. Unlike the Cold War, his model is not diametrically opposed to Western market systems. The Chinese model of a state-planned command economy championed by Mao is dramatically different from the strategy that post-Mao leaders adopted. Still, it is not the same model of development supported by the United States and the West more generally.

Some scholars have identified parallels between the development trajectories of post-1978 China and Japan, South Korea, and Taiwan.[13] The adoption, not rejection, of the Western model initially spurred Chinese economic development. These reforms were enacted through the alliance of Chinese liberal economic reformers, Western academics, businesspeople, and multilateral economic institutions.[14] While the PRC's centralized power structure empowered Deng Xiaoping to implement market reforms quickly, the growth that emerged from Deng's policies should not be attributed to the presence of an autocratic system.[15] When people point to the success of the Chinese economy to argue that autocracies are better at generating economic growth than democracies, they forget that Mao's authoritarian regime failed to produce economic development or individual prosperity for decades. Further, while the consolidated power in the Chinese system allowed Deng to quickly initiate reforms, it was actually partial decentralization that drove economic growth; among other things, it shifted incentives and created competition between regional governments.[16] Eventually, a decade later, the lack of political liberalization constrained what could have been even greater Chinese economic growth, a phenomenon that then accelerated under Xi.[17]

Chinese leaders became more confident in their hybrid economic model after the 2008 global financial crisis. The Chinese economy weathered the crisis better than American and European market economies, which led Beijing to begin promoting the China model as superior to the West's Washington Consensus.[18] Under Xi, the PRC has expanded the state's role in the economy even further, moving farther away from the neoliberal policies promoted by the United States, the IMF, and the World Bank. Instead of allowing the private sector to lead development, Xi trumpets that "the Party leads everything."[19]

In spreading their message about the benefits of state-led economic development and autocratic governance, China's leaders primarily target the developing world. No one has ever heard Xi say that Germany or Japan should adopt the China model. By contrast, Soviet leaders pushed their communist model everywhere, including in wealthy democracies, consistent with Marx's theory that socialist revolutions would occur in the most advanced capitalist countries first. Rather than promoting revolution in the developed world, Beijing has looked for trade and investment there.

Some Chinese and Western scholars have argued that developing countries will struggle to adopt the Chinese development model because the essential features of the model that have generated economic growth are not easily replicable.[20] At times, Xi himself has cast doubt on the possibility of exporting the Chinese model because it is "characterized by features that are unique to the Chinese context."[21] China has a strong state capable of implementing this strategy effectively, which many developing countries lack. The Chinese economy also relies on massive industrial capacity that helps Chinese exports undercut competitors. Smaller countries cannot replicate that strategy.

SUPPORTING AUTOCRACY BY DEFENDING SOVEREIGNTY

Chinese leaders defend autocratic regimes by championing "sovereignty" and "noninterference" in the internal affairs of other states as the most critical norm in international politics. Xi and other Chinese leaders frequently use the phrase *mutual respect* to signal to Western democracy promoters that they should stop lecturing their Chinese colleagues and other autocrats around the world on how to govern. When China uses its UN Security Council veto, it is often in support of sovereignty as a method to camouflage the defense of autocracy. Like Putin's Russia, Xi's China typically defends the sovereignty of regimes over the freedoms and liberties of individuals. Chinese diplomats never challenge the electoral results in other countries, no matter how fraudulent they may be.

In 2022, Xi launched the Global Security Initiative in an attempt to institutionalize and popularize existing Chinese security practices, specifically a commitment to sovereignty and noninterference in internal affairs and opposition to alleged American unilateralism and hegemony.[22] A year later, he introduced the Global Civilization Initiative, a kind of live-and-let-live document that "advocates the respect for the diversity of civilizations, the common values of humanity, the importance of inheritance and innovation of civilizations, and robust international people-to-people exchanges and cooperation," which he contrasted with his perception of the American desire to impose its norms and values on other countries.[23]

Regarding respect for sovereignty, Chinese behavior often contradicts its rhetoric. Xi has blatantly violated the sovereignty of India and Southeast Asia countries in the South China Sea and did not denounce Russia's brazen violations of Ukrainian sovereignty in 2014 and 2022. However, the sovereignty script has generally worked well for Beijing as a strategy for defending dictatorships, especially in parts of the world that were previously colonized by imperialist powers.[24]

PROMOTING CHINESE VALUES AND A POSITIVE IMAGE OF CHINA

All leaders with the means to do so promote a positive image of their country's culture and values. Xi has focused much more than previous leaders on portraying Chinese traditional values as worthy of emulation. One of Xi's staunch supporters, Chinese businessman Eric Li, wrote, "Among all top Chinese leaders since the beginning of the People's Republic, Xi is the first and only one to place Chinese traditional culture front and center of the party's political program."[25] Previous communist leaders emphasized shared economic interests and class identities with their counterparts in the developing world as a means of aligning themselves with the developing world in contrast to the allegedly exploitative developed world. Xi has not abandoned those themes, but simply added Chinese values to his messaging.

Just as Putin does, Xi casts his country's national ideas as anti-Western. For instance, CCP ideologists have argued that Confucius's ideas about harmony and deference to authority can help guard against the decadent and destabilizing Western ideas of liberal democracy. In another parallel to Putinism, Chinese ideologues celebrate the collective over the individual. PRC scholars have suggested that Chinese values hold universal appeal. Some go so far as to predict that Chinese Confucian thinking will eventually subsume liberal values. As Renmin University professor Wang Yiwei put it, "The specialness of China originated in China but belongs to the world."[26]

Nonetheless, Xi is more focused on deepening traditional values within China than promoting them abroad. He often emphasizes Chinese uniqueness and exceptionalism—themes targeted at a domestic, not international, audience.[27] Unlike Wang Yiwei, other Chinese scholars argue that Xi's emphasis on Confucianism proves his lack of interest in exporting ideology, since Chinese concepts, norms, and practices associated with Confucianism are not transferable.[28] This emphasis on uniqueness contrasts sharply with the Soviet multinational, multicultural, and transnational framework used to argue that all societies could implement a Soviet system. Lenin and Brezhnev never promoted "Marxism-Leninism *with Russian characteristics*."

EXPORTING COMMUNISM?

Some believe that Xi is exporting communism, socialism, and Marxism-Leninism. As discussed in earlier chapters, many senior officials in the first Trump administration certainly believed so. After he left government, Trump's US trade representative Robert Lighthizer wrote a book warning about the China menace, arguing explicitly that "China is the great threat that the American nation and its system of Western liberal democratic government has faced since the American revolution" because China is "spreading its anti-American, anti-democratic, Communist system."[29] Lighthizer might be right. We in the US must all acknowledge our limited insight into Xi's thinking.

However, judging from PRC *actions*, Xi has not devoted considerable resources or attention to promoting communism, socialism, and Marxism-Leninism globally. Xi's ideological framing of Chinese foreign policy is much more aggressive than that of his recent predecessors, but it is still nowhere near as revisionist and threatening as those of Stalin, Khrushchev, Brezhnev, Mao, or even Putin. To date, Xi has never used or even threatened to use military power to impose the Chinese political system on another country. Beijing's coercive subjugation of Hong Kong resembles the Soviet communist takeovers in Eastern Europe, but the analogy is imperfect—Hong Kong was never a sovereign country. A PRC invasion of Taiwan would more closely resemble Soviet or American methods of using force for regime change, but again, the analogy is inexact, given Taiwan's complicated sovereignty status.

Xi's priority remains the preservation of his regime at home, not promoting socialism abroad. *National* rejuvenation remains Xi's core goal, not international conversion to a Chinese system. Given the list of difficult domestic challenges Xi faces at home and the memory of the Soviet Union's ultimate collapse, we should not be surprised that domestic control is Xi's highest priority. Compared to Putin, Xi has acted much more conservatively in promoting his ideas abroad.

CHINESE INSTRUMENTS OF IDEOLOGICAL EXPORT

The most compelling evidence that Xi seeks to export his ideology is the number of tools the CCP has developed for this objective. Like American and Russian efforts, these Chinese instruments are used to pursue multiple objectives—security, economic, and ideological goals—simultaneously. However, ideological aims are most certainly a part of many foreign policy tools and the main focus of a handful of these instruments.

PERSONAL DIPLOMACY

Xi personally plays a very active role in Chinese foreign policy. He frequently travels abroad and hosts foreign leaders in Beijing.[30] Not all these engagements have an ideological component, but many do. In his meetings with foreign leaders, Xi looks to sow division between the United States and its allies and partners, warning American partners in Asia not to choose sides and encouraging those in Europe to become more independent from American hegemony, an argument that has become easier to make in Trump's second term. For example, during a European trip in the spring of 2024, Xi visited France (which has championed most actively an independent European foreign policy under President Macron), then stopped in Serbia and Hungary, two countries with leaders very distant from Washington. When meeting with leaders from Saudi Arabia and Vietnam—two autocracies with close ties to the United States—Xi leans into themes of mutual respect to signal his support for their autocratic systems of government.

While Xi has provided a general defense of autocracy when meeting with most foreign dictators, he has played a very personal and direct role in supporting Putin. Though the leaders promote different kinds of autocracy, their relationship has become increasingly close. Putin champions illiberal conservative populism targeted primarily at leaders and societies in the developed world, and Xi touts a state-led socialist model of economic development focused much more on leaders and societies in the developing world. However, Xi and Putin have bonded over their shared defense of autocracy and animosity toward the United States.

As discussed in the previous chapter, Putin embraced ideological competition with the US much earlier than Xi. Over time, though, Putin and Xi have gradually begun to coordinate their anti-American, anti-democratic actions. The two leaders have met dozens of times since Xi came to power in 2012. Putin calls Xi his "good old friend"[31] while Xi describes Putin as "my best, most intimate friend."[32] The most comprehensive public expression of their deep bond was a lengthy joint statement published in February 2022—just weeks before Putin invaded Ukraine—during Putin's visit to China to open the Winter Olympics. The joint declaration trumpeted that "friendship between the two States has no limits, there are no 'forbidden' areas of cooperation." It underscored the ideological unity between the PRC and Russia and criticized "certain states" that imposed their democratic system on others.[33]

Putin's invasion of Ukraine in 2022 strained but did not break this ideologically anchored entente. Xi has never publicly endorsed Russia's invasion of Ukraine. For instance, in March 2022, China did not join Russia and the small handful of other countries—Belarus, Eritrea, Syria, and North Korea—that voted against the first UN General Assembly resolution denouncing the Russian invasion, instead choosing to abstain. Unlike North Korea and Iran, Chinese officials have consistently said they are not providing arms to Russia, though this policy of military restraint was called into question by the discovery of over a hundred Chinese soldiers fighting in Ukraine on Russia's side. After Putin invaded Ukraine in 2022, Chinese officials dropped the phrase "no limits" from their statements. At the same time, Xi and other senior PRC officials blamed the United States and NATO for fueling the conflict by arming Ukraine, and they have provided Russia with concrete assistance by purchasing Russian fossil fuels to help Putin finance his war and sent vital technology to Russian military enterprises to build new weapons.[34]

PARTY-TO-PARTY TIES

During the Cold War, Soviet and Chinese communist parties aggressively nurtured ties with socialist and communist parties in other countries to advance the "world communist revolution." The collapse of the USSR interrupted Moscow's work, but Chinese efforts to cultivate party-to-party ties that started during the Cold War have continued. The CCP International Department (also called the International Liaison Department) boasts positive relationships with over 160 countries and subnational provinces and more than six hundred political parties.[35]

Rather than interacting with only left-leaning parties, as was the case during the Cold War, the CCP now focuses on creating partnerships with parties in power. Over 70 percent of CCP contacts are with government parties, compared to roughly 28 percent with opposition parties, irrespective of ideological orientation. None of the opposition parties are pursuing revolution or regime change. As a legacy of the Cold War, the CCP maintains special ties to ruling communist and socialist parties in Laos, North Korea, Cuba, Zimbabwe, and Vietnam (despite tense governmental relations with Hanoi).[36]

In a striking parallel to Soviet practices, the CCP provides direct assistance and training programs to political parties.[37] Leftist and socialist parties in Africa actively participate in extensive party-training programs with CCP counterparts. In 2022, the CCP invested forty million dollars to establish an overseas party-training center, the Julius Nyerere Leadership School, in Tanzania, in partnership with the ruling political parties from the region. American and Russian political parties do not have similar facilities abroad. The themes of these training sessions include the advantages of one-party rule, the virtues of socialism, party governance, party discipline, anti-corruption methods, and Xi Jinping Thought.[38] Beijing uses party-to-party channels and training programs not only for ideological promotion but also to advance Chinese security and economic interests and promote a positive image of China in general.

The CCP is the most aggressive in their party-to-party influence campaigns in Taiwan. Despite fighting a brutal civil war with the Kuomintang (KMT) last century, the CCP now intervenes directly in the domestic affairs of Taiwan to support the KMT and shun the Democratic Progressive Party (DPP) because the KMT is less supportive of independence than the DPP. After DPP candidate Lai Ching-te won Taiwan's presidential election in 2024, Xi hosted former Taiwanese president Ma Ying-jeou from the KMT in Beijing to underscore the CCP's ties with pro-unification forces on the island.

The CCP also sponsors training programs for government officials, primarily from the developing world. The ideological content of these contacts varies and is hard to quantify. At the Baise Executive Leadership Academy, controlled by the Guangxi Communist Party, the Chinese government pays officials from Southeast Asia to study the Chinese model.[39] Political scientist Maria Repnikova found that training offered in several African countries promotes general introductions to China and its economic development model but these initiatives "don't present a coherent model of Chinese governance that can be adopted in other contexts."[40] Some curricula explicitly seek to promote repressive techniques. China expert Elizabeth Economy has written about PRC seminars under the auspices of the Belt and Road Initiative "on how to conduct online censorship and surveillance for officials from other countries, such as the Philippines, Saudi Arabia, the UAE, and Thailand."[41]

NONGOVERNMENTAL ORGANIZATIONS

In China today, the label *nongovernmental organization* is a misnomer; many independent NGOs in the PRC have been shut down or co-opted by the regime. Most of those still operating are funded or supported by the government. As such, programs described as having people-to-people ties are often actually government-to-people or party-to-people ties. The well-funded United Front Work Department leads these efforts to build relationships with nongovernmental organizations abroad.[42] The United Front's work abroad is similar to Soviet practices during the Cold War in that nongovernmental partners in other countries are often unaware of their Chinese counterparts' direct ties to the CCP. The United Front has funded student groups (including the Chinese Students and Scholars Associations) and trade organizations abroad that have protested policies considered hostile to CCP interests.[43] The United Front also has focused on cultivating ties with the millions of ethnic Chinese living abroad and state-owned media has developed a special mission of targeting the Chinese diaspora around the world. Those living abroad but using Chinese social media like WeChat remain in the PRC-censored media sphere.[44]

Not all Chinese programs supporting contacts with foreign societies promote CCP ideology. Exchanges between Chinese and foreign physicists and biologists generally lack ideological content. On more sensitive topics like politics, economics, and international relations, state influence and coercion has compelled Chinese scholars to self-censor in public settings. That does not mean, however, that every Chinese professor is acting on behalf of the CCP, as their private remarks often make clear.

GLOBAL MEDIA

Like Moscow and Washington, Beijing has invested heavily in broadcast, print, and social media in recent years as another instrument to propagate ideology and advance state interests. The PRC does not publish an annual budget for global media, but experts estimate annual media spending is roughly ten billion dollars.[45] If it is an accurate estimate, that is significantly more than the annual budgets of all US government media outlets, including Voice of America and Radio Free Asia, which tragically Trump's second administration gutted. The China Global Television Network (CGTN) broadcasts in over one hundred fifty countries in six languages. China Radio International has nearly seventy overseas stations and reports in over sixty languages, and Xinhua, the Chinese government's leading news agency, has almost one hundred eighty bureaus around the world and publishes in several languages.[46]

The Chinese state media apparatus has taken advantage of the economic challenges that media companies around the world face by providing content at free or subsidized rates. Xinhua has signed cooperation and content-sharing agreements with media organizations in many countries, often providing free text and photos.[47] The PRC's English-language newspaper, *China Daily*, has deals with over two dozen newspapers around the world to place *China Daily* inserts in these foreign publications.[48] The Chinese media company StarTimes controls a large share of Africa's cable and satellite television market, providing CGTN programming at lower rates than the BBC and CNN. Chinese companies close to the state have acquired partial or complete ownership of foreign media organizations in Hong Kong, Taiwan, South Africa, and the Czech Republic—all of which have resulted in editorial changes to make content more sympathetic to the CCP.[49] As the economics of news and data change in ways that make it harder to maintain the traditional reporter/subscription model, state-owned entities that do not need to generate profit have a great advantage. They can flood the pages of African newspapers, the search engines Google, Baidu, and Yandex, and the Metaverse with content from a particular viewpoint.

Beijing has successfully cultivated a powerful presence on American and Chinese social media platforms around the world through the activity of Chinese diplomats, government officials, and journalists working for state-run media organizations. Chinese diplomats have become active and aggressive on social media in English, using whataboutism to counter pro-Western talking points and spreading disinformation with such vigor that they earned the nickname of "wolf warrior diplomats."[50] This wolf-warrior diplomacy became so ferocious that Xi decided to rein in these diplomats in 2021 out of fear that the strategy was backfiring.

The CCP runs multipronged, regionally diversified information *and* disinformation campaigns on social media platforms.[51] In 2019, Twitter disclosed that it had taken 936 accounts offline and suspended another 200,000, all of which were part of a "state-backed" disinformation campaign to undermine the credibility of Hong Kong protesters.[52] Chinese information and disinformation campaigns are especially aggressive in targeting Taiwanese audiences, especially during elections.[53]

All these media outlets produce content criticizing the United States. Chinese outlets often portray the United States as a declining power in contrast to rising China. They have devoted special attention to the inefficiency of American democracy, which, they allege, has produced inequality, racial tensions, and crumbling infrastructure. The assault on the US Capitol on January 6, 2021, provided Chinese media outlets with fresh material for lambasting the American model. Chinese media also aims to sow division within democratic societies. The CCP can exploit the openness of democracies while guarding itself against foreign influences by blocking most American social media platforms at home. Like their Russian counterparts, Chinese content producers do not always seek to win arguments or advance specific ideas; instead, they want to raise doubts about facts.

The Chinese-owned company TikTok is another powerful tool for disseminating CCP views abroad while blocking content critical of PRC policies.[54] In response to pending US legislation banning the app in the United States, TikTok instructed millions of users to call their congressional representatives and urge them to "stop a TikTok shutdown."[55] The effort failed, and the law passed, although President Trump then delayed its enforcement. Still, in conducting this campaign, TikTok revealed why its operation in the United States was dangerous, a lesson for other democracies that still allow TikTok to function freely, not constrained by transparency or content-moderation regulations. The US government does not have a comparable means to instantly reach tens of millions of Chinese citizens.

As you would expect, Chinese state-owned and state-controlled media defend China, portraying China's benevolence as a civilization, culture, and international partner, trumpeting the regime's legitimacy and performance, and rebutting critics.[56] In Xi's words, the central objective is to "tell China's stories well."[57] At the same time, the PRC represses what journalists from democratic countries write about China to protect the state's image abroad. Inside China, authorities regularly use travel restrictions, monitoring, and harassment to limit foreign reporting.[58] In response to the Trump administration's decision to limit the number of Chinese journalists within the United States working for government media outlets, Beijing expelled reporters from the *New York Times*, the *Wall Street Journal*, and the *Washington Post*.

Artificial intelligence, especially large language models (LLMs), which require big datasets to function effectively, provides the PRC with another tool for influencing the informational contest between autocrats and democrats. AI models trained by Chinese companies are increasingly used in the democratic world. In January 2025, the Chinese company DeepSeek released its R1 model, which became instantly popular worldwide because it achieved near state-of-the-art performance for a fraction of the cost of its American competitors. However, sensitive topics—including anything critical of the Chinese Communist Party or Xi—yield limited or no results. If Beijing can produce data about the PRC and the world informed by a CCP perspective that is then consumed by these LLM models, they can shape how AI products portray the Chinese regime, system of government, culture, values, and development model. And of course, CCP content producers will have a special advantage in shaping AI models being trained in Mandarin.

LOBBYING AND MOVIES

The CCP uses the openness of the United States to shape ideological competition. For instance, lobbying is one mechanism available to PRC actors in the United States that American actors do not have in China. A comprehensive study by China expert Erin Baggott Carter of public records of the Foreign Agent Registration Act revealed over ten thousand lobbying activities undertaken by the Chinese government and affiliated firms between 2005 and 2019, an influence operation well beyond anything ever undertaken by Soviet agents.[59] Carter's study concluded that American legislators targeted by Chinese lobbying efforts were twice as likely to sponsor legislation favorable to Chinese interests. The United States does not have a similar network of lobbyists walking the hallways of the National People's Congress in Beijing.

Chinese propagandists are also active in shaping Hollywood films. By purchasing stakes in movie production companies, denying visas to actors and directors, and threatening to block the distribution of American movies to the massive Chinese audience, the CCP has shaped the content of American films, not only for movies shown in China but worldwide.[60] For instance, the movie *World War Z* originally had a Chinese virus threatening the world, but it was changed to a North Korean virus.[61] Likewise, the remake of the 1984 Cold War classic *Red Dawn* initially cast China as the new villain, but that role was ultimately changed to North Korea as well. American director Judd Apatow lamented, "Instead of us doing business with China and leading to China becoming more free, what has happened is a place like China has bought our silence with their money."[62]

EDUCATION, RESEARCH, AND CULTURE

Chinese investments in education, research, and culture are another vehicle the PRC uses to shape the images of China and the US to governments and societies abroad. In 2004, Beijing began to construct a vast network of public educational organizations called Confucius Institutes to promote the study of Chinese language, culture, history, and literature abroad through the lens of the CCP. By 2021, Confucius Institutes had footholds in 158 countries, including the US.[63] The Soviet Union had no similar network of organizations in the United States or other democracies. American analysts and government officials have disagreed over the exact ideological mission of these organizations. Critics—including the US government—claim that American universities with Confucius Institutes on their campuses and private individuals affiliated with these organizations are exercising self-censorship of anything criticizing the PRC.[64] Others argue that the influence of these organizations on American college campuses has been exaggerated. Scientific studies designed to measure the influence of these programs are few and inconclusive.[65] Nonetheless, concern about political influence has compelled over one hundred Confucius Institutes in the United States to close.[66] In the fall of 2024, the US House of Representatives passed a bill—HR 1516, the DHS Restrictions on Confucius Institutes and Chinese Entities of Concern Act—that barred American universities with a Confucius Institute on campus from receiving federal funding, but a companion bill has yet to pass the Senate.[67]

The Chinese government has provided financial support for academic research around the world. Nearly two decades ago, the CCP created the Thousand Talents Plan (TTP) to attract scientists and engineers from overseas to China. The plan fosters collaboration with Chinese scientists, bolstering Chinese research and development and helping the country meet the goals of the Made in China 2025 initiative, which aims to make China a world leader in a dozen key technology sectors. The CCP established the China Association for Science and Technology (CAST) in the United States to attract talent. CAST has sixteen chapters and ten thousand members in the United States.[68]

The US government eventually determined that TTP was used illegally to obtain critical technologies from labs at American universities and corporations. Independent researchers have identified technology transfers to the People's Liberation Army from the program.[69] American academics have been found guilty of not disclosing financial support from the Chinese government.[70] Through its China Initiative, started in 2018, the Justice Department exposed a network of Chinese researchers who had applied for US visas without disclosing their affiliations with the People's Liberation Army.[71] In 2019, a US Senate committee declared TTP a threat to US national security interests.[72] Fears about TTP success also fueled overreach by US law enforcement officials. Some academics were falsely accused and later acquitted.[73]

Beijing provides scholarships for international students, particularly from developing countries.[74] China is the second-most-popular destination for all African students studying abroad, behind only France.[75] Beijing places a special emphasis on recruiting students from Central Asia to win support for Chinese foreign policy goals in these countries, including the Belt and Road Initiative.[76] The PRC wants to bring future leaders from all over the world, not just developing countries, to study in China. In

2015 and 2016, China's top two universities, Peking University and Tsinghua University, established the Yenching Academy and the Schwarzman Scholars programs respectively, the rough Chinese equivalents of Oxford's Rhodes Scholarship. When Xi met with Biden at the sidelines of the 2023 APEC meeting in San Francisco, he pledged to attract fifty thousand American students to study in China in the next five years.

Like other soft-power instruments, the CCP pursues multiple objectives when promoting education and research worldwide. One clear motivation is improving China's image abroad, shaping a favorable narrative about China and its government while defending the regime against criticism. A second objective is acquiring intellectual property for commercial and military purposes. The goal of promoting Xi Jinping's Thought, let alone communism, does not seem to be a central part of this mission, especially when compared to the more blunt efforts of the Soviets during the Cold War. The story of who is learning from whom in CCP education initiatives is complex. For example, the Confucius Institutes and the Yenching Academy support the study of the Mandarin language and Chinese culture—but such study can enhance American knowledge of China, helping our leaders advance our security and economic interests. Many American students who studied in the Soviet Union became analysts, professors, and policymakers of the USSR and later Russia. I was one of them. In addition, not all Chinese government funding for foreign academics supports espionage, intellectual property theft, or the Chinese military and Chinese Communist Party. Chinese government funding for basic scientific research is largely motivated by a longer-term agenda of strengthening Chinese research and development by subsidizing cooperation with advanced labs and universities in the United States and elsewhere. That is an agenda more tied to economic growth than ideological promotion. It is also an agenda that is not necessarily antithetical to American interests.

ECONOMIC INSTRUMENTS

During the Cold War, the United States and the Soviet Union each used trade, investment, and aid to promote its ideologies and contain the ideas of the other superpower. However, the relationship between foreign economic policy and ideological promotion was not tightly correlated and varied from place to place over time. Sometimes, economic goals drove trade and investment policies; other times, political and security goals were more salient. The same is true today for China. Xi's government pursues policies of economic statecraft that enhance profits and the well-being of Chinese companies and citizens, but it also uses economic tools to pursue noneconomic objectives, including ideological goals.

Trade and Investment

Since 1978, CCP leaders have prioritized engagement with the global economy to spur Chinese economic development. The strategy worked amazingly well, at least for the first four decades.[77] Chinese trade with the outside world exploded, making China the number-one trading partner for most countries. Chinese leaders subsequently redirected hard-currency surpluses from trade to finance construction projects abroad and purchased companies all over the world. The scale of Chinese economic engagement with the global economy was historic—$2.4 trillion, including roughly $945 billion on construction projects and $1.4 trillion in asset purchases and investments.[78] A portion of this economic activity eventually became a component of the Belt and Road Initiative, but the financing and building of large infrastructure projects and asset purchases overseas began before the BRI's launch.

The paramount objective for Chinese economic activity abroad is stimulating economic growth at home. However, it also has other aims, including promoting the CCP's ideological and security goals. Assessing the role of Chinese trade and investment in promoting these two noneconomic objectives is challenging. Chinese trade and investment have helped autocracies keep their grip on power in Asia and worldwide.[79] In these countries, China's ideological and economic goals work to reinforce each other. At the same time, many of China's biggest trading partners today are not autocracies. A significant portion of PRC trade is with wealthy democracies, including the United States, European Union member states, Taiwan, Japan, and South Korea, but no one argues that the CCP is using Chinese economic resources to support democratic stability abroad. A focus on fostering trade and development with the wealthiest countries in the world—countries that are also democracies—was not an accident. As the CCP prioritized domestic economic growth, Chinese firms were most interested in trading with and investing in rich democracies because that is where opportunities for the most significant profits were.

Chinese trade and investment aims in the developing world are more complicated. State-owned enterprises (SOEs) controlled by the party carry out most of these economic activities. These companies are not driven solely by profits for their firms and shareholders but also act as agents of the state. That said, there is no strong correlation between the level of Chinese investment and regime type. Even in developing countries where the Chinese are more likely to have ideological influence, the PRC is not rigorously prioritizing investment in autocratic regimes over democratic regimes.

In addition, it is challenging for the CCP to direct the ideological promotion of Chinese firms through overseas trade and investment. Not all Chinese companies, including even state-owned enterprises, behave alike, and most certainly not all Chinese companies act as loyal instruments of CCP ideological aims. Some SOEs investing abroad have closer ties to local and regional governments than they do to Beijing, making them more likely to prioritize activities that result in increased local government tax revenues rather than those that advance the central government's interests, including especially ideological goals.[80] Chinese economic interactions with the outside world remain decentralized despite Xi's effort to increase central control. The CCP has even less control over private companies operating abroad, which prioritize profits and market share over advancing socialism and Xi Jinping Thought. If Alibaba and Tencent were supposed to be instruments of CCP communist ideology, they have done a lousy job of it.

There is one group of autocracies that Chinese firms are explicitly instructed to help sustain—enemies of the United States. As already discussed, Russia is a clear example.[81] Iran is another. In 2021, China signed a sweeping twenty-five-year four-hundred-billion-dollar deal with Iran, trading investment in Iran's nuclear power, ports, and fossil fuels for energy and military-technology transfers. Chinese economic ties with North Korea help sustain the anti-American dictatorship there. In Central Asia, Chinese trade and investment help to keep in power autocracies and threaten to undermine Mongolia, the region's sole but weakening democracy. Chinese trading practices also support Maduro's autocracy in Venezuela, offsetting the effects of American sanctions and Western pressure more broadly. The same is true of Chinese economic ties with Cuba and Nicaragua. In these countries, Chinese exports play a direct and consequential role in support of autocracy in one sector specifically: technology to help states surveil and collect data on their citizens.[82]

Belts, Roads, and Banks

Not long ago, China was a major recipient of economic aid from Western countries and international financial institutions. Today, the PRC has become one of the largest international aid providers. Between 2000 and 2021, Chinese government institutions and state-owned entities spent $1.34 trillion on over 20,000 foreign aid projects in 165 countries worldwide.[83]

The PRC has provided direct bilateral assistance to developing countries for decades, but these activities expanded dramatically after Xi launched the Belt and Road Initiative in 2013. BRI projects aim to connect China by land (the belt) and sea (the road) to these countries. Projects that fall under the BRI umbrella are not charity projects and are not even coded by most as bilateral aid. Instead, BRI is a hybrid model of assistance and investment, though more the latter than the former. Recipient countries partly (and sometimes mostly) pay for BRI infrastructure projects. For Xi, BRI is one of his most important foreign policy initiatives, if not *the* most important. Xi and his supporters frame BRI as China's leading project of deepening globalization or "re-globalization" at a time when the United States is portrayed as seeking to decouple, deglobalize, and disengage.[84] In 2017, Xi enshrined BRI in the Chinese constitution.

Because of BRI's broad and loosely defined mandate, hundreds of Chinese projects have been labeled or recast as components of BRI and its derivatives (like the Digital Silk Road and the Health Silk Road).[85] Chinese companies and local governments eagerly slap the BRI label on almost any foreign economic engagement to help secure state financing. By 2023, 149 countries, including some American allies and close partners, had signed BRI cooperation agreements with China.[86] China's roughly one-trillion-dollar pledge to BRI projects is about seven times what the US spent on the Marshall Plan after World War II.[87]

Another relatively new instrument of Chinese economic statecraft is the Asian Infrastructure Investment Bank (AIIB). Launched in 2016 with a mission of "financing the Infrastructure for Tomorrow—infrastructure with sustainability at its core," AIIB is China's nearest equivalent to the World Bank. Although founded and anchored by the Chinese government, AIIB has deliberately aspired to become an independent, multilateral development bank. AIIB has a capitalization of over one hundred billion dollars and garners the highest credit ratings for most of its projects.[88] In 2016, the Obama administration declined to become a member and tried to dissuade other countries from joining, but with minimal success—the AIIB now has over one hundred members, including several democratic allies of the United States, such as Australia, France, Germany, the United Kingdom, and Canada, though Canada suspended its participation in 2023. After China, the European bloc is the most influential actor within the bank. AIIB often co-finances projects with other multilateral development banks, including the World Bank and the Asian Development Bank. Ironically, democratic India, which has an adversarial relationship with China, is the largest recipient of AIIB funding. Surprisingly, AIIB has rarely funded BRI projects.[89] They are too risky.

China is also a major partner in the New Development Bank (NDB). Headquartered in Shanghai and founded by the leaders of Brazil, Russia, India, China, and South Africa (BRICS), this multilateral development bank aims to support public and private partnerships through loans, equity participation, and other economic instruments.[90] Unlike the AIIB, the NDB focuses on developing infrastructure with fewer resources in a much narrower geography. Because China's voting shares in the NDB are not greater than that of any other BRICS member—including its rival India—the NDB is less attractive to Beijing than BRI or AIIB as a way to provide development aid and carry out economic statecraft more generally.[91]

The primary aim of all of these Chinese economic instruments of aid and investment is to benefit the Chinese economy. Beijing uses BRI to develop poorer western regions of China, diversify energy import routes, and offload overcapacity, especially in construction and steel production.[92] Stimulating economic development in partner countries through BRI projects and AIIB loans creates new economic opportunities for Chinese companies and banks. Beijing also uses economic assistance—bilateral aid, BRI projects, and AIIB loans—to secure energy and other raw material supplies, as other powerful states often do.[93] Chinese leaders—like their American and Russian counterparts—usually claim to pursue more altruistic goals with their investment and assistance, like alleviating poverty and suffering. Not surprisingly, given the mixed composition of its members, among which are many European democracies, the AIIB acts more like other multilateral development banks and less like a promoter of Chinese interests and CCP ideas.

However, Chinese economic growth is not the only aim of China's foreign economic assistance and investment, especially in the developing world. Xi also seeks to use these economic instruments to counter American influence worldwide. If the US enjoys a comparative advantage in providing security assistance to other countries, China has a comparative advantage in delivering infrastructure projects. Before BRI's launch, some Chinese officials and academics were calling for rebalancing China's western frontiers to offset the US pivot to Asia on China's eastern borders. BRI has helped to achieve this geopolitical shift. The conditions that countries must meet to receive BRI funding differ from those of the World Bank or other Western lending institutions. State-owned policy banks such as China Development Bank and Export-Import Bank of China are the primary funders of BRI projects.[94] They take their instruction from the CCP and are not guided solely by market forces or strict development goals. Chinese loans and projects do not have the restrictions on environmental impact and the labor protections that are often attached to Western loans and even many AIIB projects. Human rights concerns that sometimes block or slow economic assistance from democratic countries and their international financial institutions play no role in Chinese aid projects. Therefore, Chinese companies can move much faster than their American or European counterparts. However, they are also more prone to investing in projects that are not economically viable.

Xi has leveraged economic assistance projects to also achieve security objectives. The most infamous example was China's acquisition of the Hambantota Port in Sri Lanka. After the Sri Lankan government could not keep up with debt payments to their Chinese creditors, they gave Beijing a controlling stake in the port and a ninety-nine-year lease. This Chinese acquisition triggered international alarm about Beijing's use of a new kind of coercive economic mechanism—"debt-trap diplomacy"—as part of a more extensive campaign to obtain other assets overseas for military purposes. However, to presume a comprehensive strategy of debt-trap diplomacy from the Sri Lanka case or a handful of other coercive plays would be premature.[95] Bad publicity from the Hambantota Port transaction damaged China's global image. Future Chinese attempts to coercively leverage debt for security objectives will be challenging for Beijing to carry out. Moreover, there is no strong evidence that the PRC is pursuing debt-trap schemes, preferring instead to restructure loans more consistent with Western norms as a less-than-ideal means to get some money back from debtor nations.[96]

Whether China can afford to continue using these economic statecraft tools for security, economic, or ideological gain is uncertain. As Chinese growth has slowed, domestic criticisms of BRI and other economic-assistance programs have risen. Many countries that initially embraced BRI projects and financing now face liquidity problems. In 2022, roughly 60 percent of China's overseas loans were held by financially distressed countries, triggering conversations in Beijing about the need to allocate BRI funds more conservatively.[97] A 2023 joint study by the Kiel Institute and AidData showed that Chinese banks increased their foreign bailout lending to help BRI countries service their debt.[98] In 2019, Chinese officials began acknowledging governance and corruption risks associated with BRI lending and spending. Xi himself called for launching a "Clean BRI" that would be free of corruption.[99] Xi's enthusiasm for a rapid BRI expansion around the world allowed and sometimes compelled Chinese banks and companies to invest in financially unsound projects. There were prudent financial reasons that led Western financial institutions to avoid investment in similar projects. Now, Chinese economic actors are bearing the costs.

At the third BRI summit, in October 2023, there was a new emphasis on smaller and greener projects, a move away from large infrastructure projects like roads and dams, and a new emphasis on cheaper digital initiatives for e-commerce, consistent with Xi's new focus on "high-productive" investments at home.[100] After dipping during COVID, BRI investments and financing have rebounded, estimated at $74.5 billion in 2022 and $92.4 billion in 2023.[101]

Tracing a direct causal connection between BRI investment and the CCP's ideological aim is difficult. BRI could help Xi and the CCP foster a positive image for China in the developing world for years, if not decades, to come, especially when the United States is offering few alternatives. Trump's decision to radically scale back USAID offers Beijing all sorts of new opportunities to look good with its foreign aid and investment programs. Whether BRI advances more ambitious ideological objectives, like support for autocracy, the Chinese model of development, and socialism, is harder to discern.

Economic Sanctions

China's economy is big enough to withstand the economic sanctions imposed by other countries while also being able to inflict costly sanctions on smaller countries and foreign companies. Beijing has begun to use economic power as a coercive tool more frequently to deter criticism of Chinese autocracy and Chinese foreign policy. For instance, Beijing issued travel bans and asset freezes targeting individuals that criticized Chinese actions in Hong Kong and Xinjiang.[102] After Australia called for an independent inquiry into the origins of the COVID-19 virus, the PRC imposed significant tariffs on Australian imports.[103] When PRC leaders perceived Lithuania as violating the One China principle by strengthening ties with Taiwan, they attempted to impose a complete trade embargo on this small Baltic country.[104] The Chinese government stopped television broadcasts of NBA basketball games after an NBA team owner tweeted out criticism of China's crackdown in Hong Kong, explaining on its state-controlled television network, "Any speech challenging a country's national sovereignty and social stability is not within the scope of freedom of speech."[105] The Chinese government has increasingly punished foreign companies in China for even small slights to the party.[106]

China has also developed various countermeasures to protect their economy from Western sanctions and tariffs. When Western democracies tried to sanction China for human rights violations in Hong Kong and Xinjiang, Beijing instituted the Anti-Foreign Sanctions Law to deter future sanctions. This law is part of a more extensive legal apparatus Chinese leaders have built up to respond to foreign sanctions and regulations that affect China, a suite of policies that includes the Foreign Investment Law, the Export Control Law, and the Unreliable Entity List.[107] Beijing even arrested Canadians Michael Kovrig and Michael Spavor on alleged espionage claims in retaliation for the arrest of Huawei CFO Meng Wanzhou in Vancouver. (Meng had been detained in Vancouver at the request of the US for allegedly circumventing sanctions with Iran.) In 2021, Beijing released the two Canadians, but only after Canada allowed Meng Wanzhou to return to China. The CCP has studied how the United States, Europe, and other democracies implemented sanctions against Russia after Putin invaded Ukraine in 2022 and taken steps to insulate the Chinese economy from such coercive economic measures in the future.[108]

Vaccine Diplomacy

After the global COVID-19 outbreak in 2019, Chinese medical aid and vaccines became a new instrument in Beijing's toolkit for promoting a positive image of China and its development model. As China expert Bethany Allen explained, "The Chinese Communist Party used the conditions of the pandemic to push its national interests, often in a manner incompatible with open democratic values."[109] The United States and China failed to cooperate in combating this global health threat, partly because Trump blamed Beijing for the virus and partly because PRC leaders calculated that they could cultivate better diplomatic and public relations by helping other countries without coordinating their aid with the United States. During the first year of the pandemic, Chinese state media boasted about the superiority of China's COVID response and, by extension, the Chinese model of governance. They contrasted their response to the alleged inept reaction of the United States and other democratic countries. The PRC also provided relief assistance and sold and donated billions of vaccines. Chinese billionaire Jack Ma donated five hundred thousand test kits and a million surgical masks to the United States, and the Chinese telecommunications company Huawei sent aid to New York, earning public thanks from Governor Andrew Cuomo.

Over time, however, China's international image as a do-gooder in the fight against COVID-19 faded. Chinese global vaccine distribution lagged well behind pledged timelines. The Sinovac vaccine performed poorly compared to American, European, and Russian vaccines.[110] Xi's draconian commitment to his "zero-COVID" policy further damaged China's global image as a humane country. When Xi suddenly lifted repressive restrictions in response to public pressure, an estimated 80 percent of the Chinese population became infected—an outcome that challenged the wisdom of China's multiyear lockdowns.

IMPACT

While China is undoubtedly an ideological power today, Chinese ideological promotion is more defensive than offensive. Xi focuses on defending existing autocracies, not creating new ones. Moreover, while Xi and the CCP are trying to propagate their ideology abroad, this does not necessarily mean their efforts have been effective. As American promoters of democracy know well, aspirations and big budgets do not always produce outcomes. Targeted governments, societies, and individuals have the agency to repel or embrace China's ideological promotion efforts.[111] To date, the evidence shows that China has a mixed record of achievement regarding ideological promotion.

EXPORTING COMMUNISM AND SUPPORTING AUTOCRACY

As already discussed, there is weak evidence to support the hypothesis that Xi seeks to export communism, socialism, and Marxism-Leninism or pursue what former Secretary of State Pompeo called a "decades-long desire for the global hegemony of Chinese communism."[112] But if I am wrong, and Xi and the CCP actually are trying to promote communism abroad as an "existential threat" to the free world, they have failed miserably, at least so far. The CCP's training programs, global media investments, and economic assistance have not produced a single new communist or Marxist-Leninist regime since the end of the Cold War. No mass movement has emerged in the twenty-first century demanding the creation of a socialist regime or clamoring for the adoption of China's system of one-party autocratic rule. Conversely, we have seen the emergence of new democracies in this century, often aided by the United States, and the formation of mass movements inspired by democratic ideas, not communist ideas, even in very repressive regimes.

The expansion of Chinese instruments for exporting ideas has coincided with the global democratic recession over the past two decades, but it isn't easy to disentangle the causal relationship between these trends. In the post-Mao era, the CCP has rarely adopted strategies to try to replace democracies with autocracies. Beijing's approach is much more conservative than that of communist proselytizers during the Cold War, focusing instead on defending autocracies already in place rather than seeking to change regimes from democracies to dictatorships. In this preservation mission, they have achieved results, helping to prop up dictatorships in Russia, Iran, North Korea, Venezuela, and Myanmar.

In addition, the CCP has not scored many wins in weakening democracies. Notable exceptions are Xi's engagement—including economic aid, trade, and investment—with Orbán in Hungary and Vučić in Serbia, which has helped these leaders undermine democratic practices in both countries. CCP disinformation campaigns have also helped to confuse people around the world about what is true and what is not in a similar manner to Russian campaigns. The long-term effects of algorithm manipulation on platforms like TikTok to weaken support for liberal democratic norms are still unknown, but we have not seen any clear-cut victories for democracy erosion by the CCP. In Taiwan, Beijing propagandists have tried their hardest to influence electoral preferences but with limited results. Pro-democratic, anti-PRC candidates from the DPP keep winning elections there, including the most recent presidential election in 2024.

Tracing the impact of Chinese ideological promotion on individuals around the world is more challenging, but there is no compelling evidence to prove that Chinese ideological promotion has changed global attitudes about communism or socialism. That may be partly because propaganda takes decades of consumption before producing attitudinal changes. If so, then a decade from now, we may finally discover that trillions of TikTok videos have subtly advanced communist ideas or the embrace of China's dictatorship. But such trends are not apparent today. Trying to trace ideological impact presents a real chicken-and-egg problem because those who sign up to participate in CCP training programs or who read government-controlled Chinese media outlets may have already been inclined toward socialist ideas or the Chinese model. To date, however, the CCP has not successfully fueled a global demand for socialist ideas because the Chinese Communist Party is not trying very hard to promote socialism. This condition is very different from the Cold War, when the Soviet Union devoted major resources to explicitly promote communism globally and achieved some tangible results. During the Xi era, the world has not witnessed waves of communist regimes coming to power as we saw throughout the Cold War, especially in the 1940s in Eastern Europe and China and then again in the 1970s, when communists seized power in Southeast Asia, southern Africa, Nicaragua, and Afghanistan. And while the world has experienced a recession in democratic practices over the past two decades, in no country in the world did autocrats seize power by destroying democratic institutions with the help of the CCP.

And it even may be that Chinese efforts to promote socialism, to the extent that CCP officials are trying, are having the opposite effect. An important lesson from the Cold War is that many Soviet programs and instruments to cultivate Marxism-Leninism eventually produced a backlash. For instance, some Africans who studied in the Soviet Union became committed communists, but many became capitalists. In the 1980s, I studied in Moscow with several of them. Similarly, heavy-handed Soviet propaganda and subjugation in Eastern Europe and the Baltic states made many citizens in these countries virulently anti-communist. There are already signs that Beijing's most aggressive effort to impose its system of rule on a free society—Hong Kong—is backfiring. Once citizens have lived under freedom, it is difficult for them to grow accustomed to and accept autocracy.

EXPORTING THE CHINESE MODEL OF DEVELOPMENT

Xi has a most powerful instrument for promoting the Chinese model of development—the success of the Chinese economy. What that model is today, however, is confusing. The Chinese economy today has many elements, such as markets and private property, that are also elements of the Western mode of economic development. The PRC model gives a much greater role to the state than the neoliberal model celebrated by the Washington Consensus in the 1990s, but the latter is also changing—converging more toward Chinese practices—including the American economic model during the Biden administration that sought to use the state to stimulate domestic manufacturing.[113] Other governments in the developed and developing worlds have increased the state's role in running their economies. What is unique about the Chinese development model is becoming increasingly harder to identify.

That said, it is still unclear if China's global economic engagement efforts have won it more fans. In a Pew Research Center poll conducted in thirty-five countries in 2024, "a median of 54% of adults in these nations have a favorable view of the US, while a median of 35% see China favorably."[114] Whatever positive attitudes for the China model BRI or CGTN programming created have been offset in many countries by adverse reactions to other Chinese belligerent foreign policies.

To be sure, when global aggregate polling numbers are divided between developing and developed countries, China's economic model and economic aid, trade, and investment activities are perceived much more positively in the developing world than in the developed world.[115] At the same time, there is also growing evidence of a backlash against Chinese foreign economic policies in the developing world. Debt buildup from BRI-recipient countries has compelled many leaders to rethink their financial ties with Beijing.[116] As already discussed, the Chinese acquisition of the port in Sri Lanka scared leaders and societies in the developing world. Critics in Africa complain that Chinese firms employ too many Chinese workers and transfer too many of the economic benefits to China.[117] Chinese business practices of bribing government officials have sparked backlashes in democratic countries where these practices have been exposed. Electoral candidates in democracies in the developing world now even run on anti-Chinese platforms.

Moreover, China's economic model is not performing as well as it did in previous decades. Xi's decision to expand state control over the economy has slowed growth. An overheated real estate sector, mounting youth unemployment, and overproduction in the manufacturing sector are all signs of growing economic troubles. Combined with an aging and declining population and the fact that it is much harder to grow as a middle-income country than a low-income country, Chinese economic growth will almost certainly never again experience the glory days of the Deng, Jiang, and Hu eras. If the Chinese economy begins to falter, the appeal of the Chinese model will fade too.

FOSTERING A POSITIVE IMAGE OF CHINA

Chinese leaders have achieved some success in promoting China's image abroad, particularly in the developing world. In Africa, poll respondents in South Africa, Kenya, and Nigeria reported a more favorable view of China than the United States.[118] In Nigeria, 80 percent of respondents had a favorable view of China, compared to 74 percent expressing a favorable view of the United States. And Nigeria is a democracy. In Ethiopia, one careful study has shown that Confucius Institutes have succeeded in fostering a positive image of the PRC.[119] In Malaysia, Indonesia, and Thailand, China recorded a significant boost in support in recent years, where majorities reported that, if forced to align with either China or the United States, they would side with China.[120] Since the outbreak of war in Gaza triggered by the Hamas terrorist attack against Israel on October 7, 2023, surveys conducted in five Arab countries show that the standing of the United States among citizens has declined dramatically while attitudes toward China have warmed, reversing a half-decade trend of weakening support for China in the Arab world.[121] Trump's return to the White House will likely fuel more positive attitudes toward China and negative feelings for the United States, as occurred in many countries during Trump's first term.

Chinese leaders also have partly succeeded in containing criticism of their anti-democratic practices. Many governments with large Muslim populations that trade with China do not criticize the PRC's human rights abuses in Xinjiang. One rarely, if ever, hears Saudi leaders speak out in support of Muslim people in detention centers in Xinjiang. Foreign companies doing business in Hong Kong refrain from commenting on the CCP's crackdown on independent media and democratic activists there.

However, as already mentioned, the net effect of these efforts to promote a positive image of China is mixed globally. As budgets for their media and other soft-power programs ballooned, negative views about China reached historic highs.[122] The percentage of Americans with an unfavorable view of the PRC has jumped from 35 percent in 2005 to 47 percent in 2017 and 81 percent in 2024.[123] In most high-income countries (with the exception of Singapore), the US is viewed more favorably than China, although again, these numbers could change as a result of the second Trump administration.[124] (Of course, these negative ratings might have been even higher without Chinese efforts to promote a positive image of their country.)

Research projects seeking to identify a causal relationship between Chinese foreign media and China's global image have produced mixed results. Social science experiments that expose participants to Chinese messages show improved perceptions of the CCP as a result.[125] However, in the real world, when other factors intervene to shape attitudes, the rise in Chinese spending on international media or BRI projects has not produced a decisively positive jump in China's global image. And despite massive investments, Chinese global media has not made significant gains in market share.[126] CGTN still lags far behind CNN in viewership. Even in Asia, CGTN ranks only tenth in popularity among television networks.[127] Some countries are cracking down on these Chinese instruments of influence: The UK revoked CGTN's license to broadcast, India banned TikTok, WeChat, and other Chinese apps, and the US is trying to force the Chinese owners to divest from TikTok. Already, several democracies are considering bans of products from Chinese AI company DeepSeek because of obvious political biases that have surfaced in its latest model.

However, the ideological contest between China and the United States will be a long one. Recent setbacks in the CCP's ideological promotion efforts should not fuel complacency in the West and the United States in particular. In industry, Chinese firms have demonstrated a remarkable capacity to compete, learn, adapt, and improve. We should expect similar adjustments from competition regarding those Chinese actors involved in ideological promotion.

Chapter 9

THE DECLINE OF THE LIBERAL INTERNATIONAL ORDER

AFTER THE SOVIET Union collapsed, the US-anchored international system—the "liberal international order"—had no serious competitors. The Warsaw Pact was gone, and so was the Soviet economic bloc. For the first time since the liberal international order's creation, its leaders aspired to make the system truly global. No one seriously sought to challenge this international system; almost everyone sought to join it.

Three decades later, this international liberal order is breaking down. Some say it is already dead. As discussed in the next two chapters, the rise of autocratic Russia and China has challenged this global order. But China and Russia are not the only threats to the international system today. Over the past three decades, changes within the liberal democratic world have weakened the appeal of this system, including for many Americans. President Trump has catalyzed that sentiment to now seriously challenge, if not destroy, the future of this system. Before tracing the external challenges to today's international order, we must first understand the threats from within that have festered and grown over the past three decades.

WHAT IS INTERNATIONAL ORDER?

Some readers will scoff at the notion that there is, can, or should be an "international system" or "global order," especially one anchored by rules, norms, laws, and institutions. For instance, self-described realists argue that anarchy is a natural and enduring condition of world politics. No higher authority can tell countries what to do. In their view, there is no international law, just the law of the jungle.[1] State power is all that matters, and consequently, countries must do everything they can to increase their power. The balance of power among states—nothing else—determines how countries deal with each other.

That analysis is partially correct, but it is not the whole story. Of course, state power is a central driver of international politics, but it is not the only factor that matters. As discussed in previous chapters, regime type, ideology, and individuals also shape patterns of cooperation and competition between countries, including the United States, Russia, and China. There is also an additional set of forces that under certain conditions can influence state-to-state interactions: international institutions. Countries do not exist in total global anarchy all the time. They belong to an international system with rules, norms, treaties, and multilateral organizations and institutions that can sometimes influence their behavior. Some scholars, myself included, believe that multilateral institutions can foster cooperation between nations to provide public goods and win-win outcomes.[2] Agreement on mutually understood rules and norms can make every country better off.[3] Multilateral institutions can also act as forums where leaders can voice their opinions and be better understood by peers and competitors, helping avoid misperceptions. Most minimally, agreement on rules can enable coordination that makes everyone better off, like laws instructing everyone which side of the road to drive on.

Like traffic laws at home, multilateral institutions in global affairs can facilitate win-win outcomes without all participants embracing the same norms, values, and ideologies. By establishing routine patterns of behavior and interaction, international institutions can take on a life of their own, shaping relations between states in unanticipated ways distinct from the balance of power that led to their creation.[4] The United Nations is a good example. Although created initially by the United States, Soviet Union, France, the UK, and China in 1945, today the UN does not act exclusively in the interests of these founding members and sometimes even acts against their interests.

Some American scholars and policymakers question the utility of multilateral organizations for advancing US interests abroad, arguing that they constrain American power. They argue that the United States is better off going it alone. President Trump most certainly leans in this direction. I disagree. Generally, though not always, the institutions supporting the global order have advanced American interests. The subset of multilateral organizations binding together the free democratic world is even more beneficial to the United States; we are more powerful (and our interests are better served) than we would be acting alone.

China and Russia invest significant resources in shaping existing international institutions and creating new ones. Why would they do so if these multilateral institutions were powerless or insignificant? Instead of pretending that these international institutions do not matter, we should try to understand how China and Russia want to use and shape these structures to increase their influence abroad and then develop a new American strategy to respond to these challenges. To do so requires first understanding how the global consensus about the value of the liberal international order from thirty years ago collapsed to such an extent that some predict the imminent end of this global system today.

PEAK LIBERAL INTERNATIONALISM

The end of the Cold War renewed hope about the possibility of collective security and a genuinely global liberal order, not one limited to the West. The 1990 UN Security Council (UNSC) authorization of the use of force in Kuwait was especially inspiring, as the world united in defense of Kuwait's sovereignty after Iraq invaded. Even Soviet leader Mikhail Gorbachev joined other UNSC members in endorsing this major military operation, partly because Gorbachev was seeking greater integration of the Soviet Union into the liberal international order. President George H. W. Bush described this moment as the onset of "a new world order" in which for "the first time, the United Nations Security Council, free from the clash of cold war ideologies, functioned as its designers intended—a force for conflict resolution in collective security."[5]

After the collapse of the Soviet Union, the government of newly independent Russia sought, even more vigorously than Gorbachev, to join all US-anchored international clubs, including NATO.[6] The possibility of a genuinely international liberal order finally seemed within reach. Chinese leaders at the time took a more cautious approach, adopting a more cooperative attitude toward international *economic* institutions but without aspiring to join Western-anchored security institutions and passively resisting the efforts of multilateral organizations that promoted human rights and liberal democratic norms. At the time, American leaders were okay with China's partial integration in just international economic clubs because many believed in modernization theory—that democratic change within China would eventually follow economic development nurtured by market reforms. In the 1990s, US leaders believed Russia and China could become responsible stakeholders in the liberal international order. Most countries in the 1990s embraced market-oriented policies supported by the United States. Back then, the bundle of economic reforms needed to integrate and prosper in the global economy as recommended by the World Bank and IMF was touted as the Washington Consensus. The moment created the conditions for institutions anchored by the United States to dictate the economics and, at times, politics of individual countries to a greater extent than ever before.[7]

This consensus did not last. Gradually political leaders, especially in the developing world but also Russia, began to push back against the set of economic policy reforms recommended by the Washington Consensus. Governments under pressure from the IMF and World Bank berated what they called draconian, neoliberal, and even neo-imperial reforms, even as these programs were producing economic growth and reducing poverty.[8] Nonetheless, the Chinese economy, and eventually the Russian economy for a while, benefited from market reforms at home and integration into the international economic order.

A similar convergence emerged briefly regarding norms about governance and human rights. In 1948, the Soviet Union and other communist countries joined theocratic Saudi Arabia and apartheid South Africa in abstaining from signing the Universal Declaration of Human Rights, seeing it as a US instrument of ideological promotion. This perception prevailed in many parts of the world until the end of the Cold War. Russia's first post-Soviet leader, Boris Yeltsin, wholeheartedly embraced these liberal democratic ideas and pushed for Russian integration into international organizations focused on democracy and human rights. Yeltsin and his government even invited many of the world's most prominent human rights organizations to open offices in Russia. In the summer of 1992, I opened the headquarters of one of them, the National Democratic Institute, in Moscow. At the time, leaders in Washington wanted to help Russia's new democracy consolidate; they provided technical advisers and millions in aid to redesign political institutions according to democratic principles.

Chinese leaders at the time flirted, albeit cautiously, with these liberal, pluralistic principles and also invited international nongovernmental organizations supporting soft-democratic and rule-of-law agendas to operate inside China.[9] Democracy seemed to emerge as a universal value. Some autocracies back then, such as the communist regime in China, claimed they were on a long, slow path toward democracy. To this day, many autocratic leaders around the world, Putin and Xi among them, claim to be practicing democracy, even while emphasizing their non-Western, unique ways of doing so. For instance, the lengthy joint statement on cooperation issued by Russia and China in February 2022 stated that the two "sides share the understanding that democracy is a universal human value . . . and that its promotion and protection is a common responsibility of the entire world community."[10] Rhetorically, the language of democratic governance is still more popular globally than its alternatives.

THE DECLINE

Three decades later, global consensus about the utility of international security, economic, and political institutions has eroded considerably. The UN Security Council has acted collectively on nonproliferation, support for military intervention and reconstruction in Afghanistan after September 11, 2001, and the use of force in Libya in 2011, but these instances are anomalies. The more prevalent practice today in the UN Security Council is deep division like the Cold War, pitting the two autocracies on the council (Russia and China) against the three democracies (France, the United Kingdom, and the United States). UN votes about Israel are the one exception; the United States usually stands alone in its support for Israel regarding the Israeli-Palestinian conflict. Cooperation within multilateral bodies governing the global economy has eroded too. The United

States and China are increasingly decoupling from each other, seeking instead to get the rest of the world to line up into two camps.[11] Multilateral economic institutions supporting global capitalism, including, most notably, the World Trade Organization, are on life support. Some analysts have already declared globalization dead.[12] International cooperation within multilateral organizations about political norms like democracy and human rights now rarely occurs.

Several factors have contributed to the decline in the liberal international order, but two are most salient: the rise of new great powers uncommitted to the existing system and doubt among American leaders and the public about the utility of continuing to participate in, let alone lead, this global order, the subject of the rest of this chapter.

ERODING AMERICAN ENTHUSIASM

The decline of the liberal international order cannot be entirely blamed on the rise of China and Russia. American leaders, especially in the Trump era, have wavered in their commitment to the international order that the US created at the end of World War II.

Policy debates in the United States over the utility of multilateral institutions and interdependence have been fierce for a long time, even throughout the Cold War. Rarely in American history have US presidents supported constraints on American sovereignty. However, immediately after the Cold War, a bipartisan consensus did emerge for a while about America's role in leading this "new world order." Presidents George H. W. Bush, Bill Clinton, George W. Bush, and Barack Obama all supported the system, at least rhetorically. In practice, though, these presidents did not always adhere to its rules. Clinton's decision to bomb Serbia in 1999 without the UNSC's blessing damaged America's reputation as a defender of the rules-based international system. George W. Bush's decision to invade Iraq in 2003 delivered an even more significant blow to America's standing as an advocate for international law and multilateralism. American allies France and Germany sided with Russia and China against the Iraqi invasion, which fueled reputational costs for the US that linger to this day. Tragically, Putin's blatant disregard for international law when invading and annexing Ukraine in 2022 is frequently compared to the American invasion of Iraq.

When I speak or write about Putin's invasion of Ukraine, I hear this whataboutism all the time, and not only from Russian trolls on X.

Even some successful collective security initiatives produced unexpected adverse effects. Most of the world united in support of the US-led invasion of Afghanistan in 2001. However, by the time of the American withdrawal from Afghanistan in 2021, which allowed the Taliban to return to power, the perception of the morality and efficacy of that long war had dwindled in the international community.

The costs of American-led multilateral military interventions have not been only reputational. While the stated aim of UN-endorsed military intervention in Libya in 2011 was well intended and one I supported as a White House official at the time—prevention of civilian slaughter in Benghazi—the result was a collapsed state without a suitable replacement, which plunged the country into prolonged civil war. The lack of sufficient post-conflict planning—about what would happen after Gaddafi's regime was toppled—curbed enthusiasm for future collective security efforts in Syria and elsewhere. While the United States, Russia, and other UN Security Council members did unite to support UN Security Council Resolution 2118 in September 2013 to authorize the elimination of chemical weapons stockpiles in Syria, the UN Security Council did nothing to stop the brutal civil war there; it continued for over a decade until Bashar al-Assad's barbaric rule came to an end in December 2024.

The greatest challenge to America's commitment to the liberal international order has not come from foreign critics of these military interventions but percolated up from within. Some US policymakers still believe that the US can advance American power, interests, and values through international institutions. Obama most certainly thought that multilateral institutions such as the United Nations, NATO, the World Bank, and the IMF were force multipliers, reducing the need for the US to act alone and helping to restrain the actions of other states in ways that contravene American interests, be they security, economic, or moral.[13] Different from Bush, Obama used military force only when he had UN Security Council backing, as he obtained before bombing Libya. Other leaders do not have the same perspective regarding the utility of international institutions. A growing share of American policymakers—mainly in the Republican Party, but across the aisle as well—believe that global institutions constrain Washington's ability to pursue national interests effectively.

President Trump is the most important voice among them. During his first term, Trump told the UN General Assembly, "We will never surrender America's sovereignty to an unelected, unaccountable, global bureaucracy."[14] Trump championed a return to the American isolationism of the 1930s, echoing a slogan of that era: "America First."[15] As international relations scholar Kyle Lascurettes observed, "While the Obama team framed international order as a central component of American strength, President Trump's NSS [national security strategy] doesn't even mention the term."[16] Trump saw just the burdens, not the benefits, of playing a leading role in international organizations.[17] He framed interactions with other countries in transactional, zero-sum terms. He withdrew from several international agreements, including the Trans-Pacific Partnership, the Paris Climate Accords, the Iran nuclear deal, the Intermediate-Range Nuclear Forces Treaty with Russia, the Open Skies Treaty, and the World Health Organization. Trump debilitated the WTO by not appointing judges responsible for dispute settlements to its appellate body—the WTO's equivalent of a supreme court.[18] He raised serious doubts about his commitment to NATO and American allies in Asia. As European Union president Donald Tusk pointed out at the time, the rules-based international order was being challenged "not by the usual suspects, but by its main architect and guarantor, the US."[19]

The Biden administration attempted to renew America's commitment to multilateralism by rejoining the Paris Climate Accords and the World Health Organization, rhetorically committing to cooperation with the United Nations, and reassuring allies in Europe and Asia of the American commitment to joint security. However, Biden did not rejoin or renegotiate the Iran nuclear deal or revive the Open Skies or INF Treaties. Biden was even less enthusiastic about reviving international economic institutions. As a candidate, Biden sharply criticized Trump's protectionist policies. Yet, once elected, he did not attempt to rejoin the Comprehensive and Progressive Agreement for Trans-Pacific Partnership (CPTPP). His administration instead launched a new organization for a dozen American partners in Asia—the Indo-Pacific Economic Framework (IPEF).[20] However, IPEF lacks the comprehensive trade liberalization, market access, and economic benefits that the CPTPP would have provided and may survive a second Trump term.

Biden also did not repeal Trump 1.0–era tariffs against China but instead expanded restrictive economic policies, including a 100 percent tariff on Chinese electric vehicles, far-reaching export controls on the sale of many technologies to China, and subsidies and incentives for producing semiconductors within the United States. While these disruptions to free trade may be necessary for containing China's economic power, as discussed in detail in later chapters, they also undermined the spirit, if not the laws, of the liberal economic order. Washington was violating its own Washington Consensus then. When WTO officials criticized the Biden administration's policies for violating the organization's standards, the administration essentially told the WTO "to take a hike," as Princeton economist Paul Krugman colorfully put it.[21] The Biden administration invoked national security to claim that the WTO had no authority to tell the United States what to do.[22]

Not everything Biden did to counter China's growing economic power was antithetical to multilateralism. For instance, Biden, with the other G7 leaders, launched a six-hundred-billion-dollar multilateral effort—the Partnership for Global Infrastructure and Investment—to offer infrastructure financing to developing countries as an alternative to China's Belt and Road Initiative. Even here, though, the focus of most of Biden's efforts at fostering economic cooperation was regional, not global. Most projects aimed to support countries in Southeast Asia, South Asia, and Latin America.

Biden also tried to renew the American tradition of trying to lead multilateral political institutions to advance human rights. Biden often framed US competition with China and Russia as being between democracy and autocracy. Secretary of State Antony Blinken championed internationalism as well, calling for its revitalization: "We want not just to sustain the international order that made so much of that progress possible, but to modernize it, to make sure that it represents the interests, the values, the hopes of all nations, big and small, from every region."[23] Biden and his team convened Summits for Democracy, signaling a renewed commitment to democratic governance worldwide, and published the first ever United States

Strategy on Countering Corruption with new multilateral streams of work. The Biden administration also initiated efforts for multilateral cooperation on artificial intelligence safety.

But even Biden's commitment to multilateralism regarding democracy, human rights, and the rule of law was not absolute. Under his administration, Congress passed legislation to sanction officials of the International Criminal Court after the court indicted Prime Minister Netanyahu of Israel for war crimes. The United States has never joined the ICC, but seeking sanctions against its leaders was a new step in American anti-multilateralism.

Biden's four years in office did not quell the public debate within American society about the utility of international engagement or participating in international organizations—something the Trump campaign exploited during the 2024 campaign. Candidate Trump was explicitly skeptical of multilateralism and supportive of isolationism. His election victory reflected a growing skepticism about multilateralism and global engagement more generally among Americans. After decades of wars in the Middle East, many American politicians, civil society organizations, and citizens advocate for pulling back, arguing that the United States can no longer serve as the world's policeman. Although the US withdrawal from Afghanistan was abrupt and poorly executed, few Americans criticized Biden's decision to leave. After Putin invaded Ukraine in 2022, the United States provided Ukraine with more military assistance than any other country did, accompanied by substantial economic aid, but it did so without the full support of the US Congress or the public. Many American politicians questioned the US's decision to engage in a so-called proxy war with Russia. Republican voters are more skeptical than Democratic supporters about the value of engagement.[24] But these impulses are growing within the Democratic Party as well.

Growing skepticism in American society about the value of multilateralism extends to economic issues. A vigorous chorus of critics now contends that free trade, global investment, and interdependence supported by economic multilateral organizations have done more harm than good to American economic interests. Today, almost no American politician, Democrat or Republican, defends the World Trade Organization. The debate about the utility of interdependence with China is fierce. If a few decades ago, most US leaders championed the benefits of trade and investment with China, the opposite is true today. The new conventional wisdom in Washington is that trade and investment with China enriched and empowered the Communist Party of China at the expense of American workers.[25] Many now say it was a mistake to have let China join the WTO, and some have even argued that China's permanent normal trade relations status should be revoked.[26] Even with other democratic countries, Biden and his team devoted little attention to expanding free trade agreements and fueled economic tensions with allies, especially South Korea and Japan.[27]

This growing isolationist sentiment in American society is in part what helped Trump win reelection in 2024. Almost immediately after returning to the White House in 2025, Trump accelerated America's disengagement with multilateral institutions and global engagement. Trump quickly pulled out of the Paris Climate Accords, the World Health Organization, and the UN Human Rights Council, underscoring his commitment to isolationism. Trump and his team want to act alone, unconstrained by allies, multilateral organizations, and international norms. As Trump's senior adviser, Elon Musk, declared emphatically in December 2024, "We should not have any international treaties that restrict the freedom of Americans."[28]

Trump levied his greatest assault against the international *economic* order, announcing the most expansive set of tariffs in American history on both autocratic adversaries and America's closest democratic allies in April 2025 (Russia was strikingly excluded). In doing so, Trump signaled his disdain for the World Trade Organization and previously signed trade agreements, including one—the United States–Mexico–Canada Agreement (USMCA)—that he himself negotiated during his first term. Stock market crashes and bond market volatility compelled Trump to retreat, first regarding the tariffs on allies and then on high-tech Chinese imports. But as this book goes to press, Trump's universal tariff of 10 percent on every country worldwide is still in place, new major tariffs on Chinese goods also remain, and general uncertainty and anxiety about Trump's future actions in trade is still acute. Most disruptively, Trump imposed these new tariffs in the name of national security without consulting US Congress, making this moment, according to economic historian Douglas Irwin, a "big break with history."[29] The liberal economic order established after World War II has never been under more serious stress, and the main revisionist is not Putin or Xi, but Trump.

In the first weeks of his second term, Trump also challenged America's commitment to international security organizations. Soon after being sworn into office, his new secretary of defense, Peter Hegseth, warned NATO to prepare for American troop withdrawals from Europe. Vice President J. D. Vance exacerbated tensions within NATO by scolding European allies in a speech at the Munich Security Conference for allegedly practicing censorship and allowing dangerous immigration. I attended that conference and watched Europeans feel deeply insulted by his remarks. They immediately began discussing a future of European defense disconnected from the United States. Trump's embrace of Putin also alienated many democratic allies in Europe, especially those most threatened by Russia.

Most unexpectedly, Trump even threatened the sovereignty of several American allies and partners, undermining one of the core norms of the international system established after World War II. He repeatedly referred to Canada as the fifty-first US state, claimed that US security interests required the United States take back the Panama Canal, and, most aggressively, emphasized the need to annex Greenland. In March 2025, Vice President Vance even led a high-profile US delegation to the American military base in Greenland to advocate for annexation, despite polling data indicating that a large majority of Greenlanders have expressed no enthusiasm for an American takeover.[30] In June 2025, Trump bombed Iran without seeking, let alone obtaining, support from the UN Security Council or NATO.

Today, Trump seems eager to exit, if not dismantle, many of the multilateral organizations that undergirded the liberal international order. The US president, however, does not wield complete control over American foreign policy. Members of Congress, business groups, investors, the media, civil society, and professors (like me!) will resist Trump's pivot to greater isolationism and unilateralism. It is too early to tell whether Trump's preferences today represent an enduring trajectory in American foreign policy, or a short-term departure from nearly a hundred years of American commitment to internationalism. Perhaps a deep American and global recession, triggered by Trump's irrational and unpredictable tariff policies, could revive support for rules-based international economic policies of the past. But over the next four years, Trump's United States could easily emerge as a greater threat to liberal internationalism than Putin's Russia or Xi's China.

Chapter 10

RUSSIAN GLOBAL (DIS)ORDER

DURING THE 1990–1991 academic year, I was a Fulbright Scholar at Moscow State University, working on my dissertation on external influences on national liberation movements in southern Africa but moonlighting as an adviser to the National Democratic Institute. At the time, as an American nongovernmental organization dedicated to promoting democracy abroad, the NDI did not have permanent staff in the Soviet Union, so I played the role of adviser when delegations visited. One day, I accompanied a prominent American group on a visit to Russia's "foreign minister," Andrey Kozyrev. I put *foreign minister* in quotation marks because at the time, the Russian Federation was one of fifteen republics that constituted the USSR and therefore had no formal diplomatic relations with other countries.

But on June 12, 1990, the Russian parliament adopted the Declaration of State Sovereignty, a key step toward Russia's full independence from the Soviet Union. Russian leader Boris Yeltsin decided he needed a foreign minister. Yeltsin was formally the chairman of the Congress of People's Deputies but acted as the de facto chief executive of the Russian Republic, a status ratified by Russian voters in June 1991 when they elected him as president. The US government did not exactly approve of our visit to Kozyrev's office because, at the time, the Bush administration did not recognize Russia as an independent country. But we went anyway in a show of solidarity with the Russian officials who had been elected recently in free and fair elections.

While researching my dissertation, I had read a few of Kozyrev's articles. Before joining Yeltsin, he was a rising star in the Soviet Ministry of Foreign Affairs. He had a reputation for his creative "new thinking"—a term

Gorbachev coined—about Soviet foreign policy, especially regarding relations with what was called back then the third world. However, as we sat in his modest office in a drab building on the city's outskirts, I was shocked by Kozyrev's downright revolutionary ideas about international relations, which sounded just like ours. In flawless English, Kozyrev explained that he and his boss wanted Russia to become a full member of the West. He wanted Russia to join all the West's clubs, including NATO, without any special treatment or relaxed conditions. There was none of the usual insistence that would grow with time in Russia about the need for the US to recognize Russia as a great power with a unique history and special traditions. Kozyrev believed that Russia would be better off—richer, freer, and more secure—just as a normal, regular member of the West.

I walked out inspired by his convictions but also sobered by the fact that he was the foreign minister of a country that did not exist. Then, amazingly, just a few months later, Russia became an independent country, Kozyrev became foreign minister, and his ideas were suddenly shaping Russian foreign policy. President Boris Yeltsin, Foreign Minister Kozyrev, and their new pro-Western team sought to consolidate democratic and market institutions at home and integrate the newly independent Russian Federation into the liberal international order.[1]

Because he sought a complete break from the Soviet past, Yeltsin embraced the entire suite of security, economic, and political international institutions that undergirded the US-anchored global order, including commitments to human rights, democracy, and liberalism. As Kozyrev wrote in his memoir, "I was convinced that the interests of democratic Russia were opposite to those of the interests of the Soviets, who defied the democratic West; wasted national resources on the arms race; supported rogue regimes, like Assad's in Syria or Saddam Hussein's in Iraq; and dreamed of restoring an anti-American alliance with communist China."[2] At the time, Russia and the other former Soviet republics were more interested in integrating with the West than in re-creating Soviet-era multilateral institutions.

That era is now over. But it did not end quickly. In the 1990s, Russia joined the G7, making it the G8, and the Council of Europe, and the following decade deepened cooperative relations with NATO through the creation of the NATO-Russia Council. When I worked at the White House in the first years of the Obama administration, one of our projects was helping Russia join the World Trade Organization, a task that was completed in 2011 after nearly two decades of negotiations. However, momentum toward integration slowed dramatically after Putin annexed Crimea and supported a secessionist war in eastern Ukraine in 2014; it stopped entirely after Putin invaded Ukraine with even more soldiers in 2022. By 2014, Putin was done joining Western-dominated clubs, and the democratic world was equally tired of trying to integrate Russia into the liberal international order.

Putin now aims to weaken, if not destroy, the liberal international order, join China-anchored clubs, and create multilateral organizations of his own. In Putin's view, "The [Biden] administration and practically the entire collective West [are] attempting to maintain their global dominance. They continue to impose their so-called rules on the international community, which they change time after time, juggling them as they see fit."[3] That is why Putin wanted Trump back in the White House in 2024. Putin is most interested in going back to the nineteenth-century norms, where great powers act independently, are not constrained by international law or international organizations, and can pursue their interests as they see fit. He thinks Trump shares this view. He may be right. Putin is particularly enamored with resurrecting spheres of influence for the great powers, including subjugating states on Russia's borders. Ukraine, of course, tops his list of countries Putin wants to control. Today, Russia is the most revisionist great power in the world, outpacing all others in seeking to undermine core tenets, norms, and institutions of the post–World War II order.

MULTILATERAL SECURITY INSTITUTIONS

Today, the only multilateral security institution that Putin likes is the UN Security Council. Putin would be delighted to see other multilateral security institutions fall apart. His one attempt at creating a multinational security organization—the Collective Security Treaty Organization (CSTO)—has produced minimal results. Putin prefers bilateral approaches over multilateral arrangements to advance Russian security interests, as he defines them.

UN SECURITY COUNCIL AND EUROPEAN SECURITY ORGANIZATIONS

Since intervening in Ukraine in 2014 and again in 2022, Putin has adopted a very hypocritical set of positions regarding collective security. On the one hand, the Russian autocrat has brazenly defied some of the UN's core norms that even Soviet leaders did not violate: recognizing Abkhazia and South Ossetia as independent countries, annexing Ukrainian territory, and committing crimes against humanity. On March 17, 2023, the International Criminal Court issued a warrant to arrest Putin for war crimes. At the same time, Putin does not want to undermine the power of the UN Security Council entirely because he values Russia's veto there. Russia continues to participate in some multilateral security treaties, including those that ban the production of chemical and biological weapons, as well as the Non-Proliferation Treaty.

To distract from Russian abuses of global security laws, rules, and norms, Putin and his surrogates frequently invoke whataboutism. What about the US-led invasion of Iraq in 2003, the NATO bombing campaigns in Libya in 2011 and Serbia in 1999, and the US intervention in Syria to defeat ISIS in 2014? At the Munich Security Conference in 2007, for instance, Putin declared that the United States' "unilateral and frequently illegitimate actions have not resolved any problems" but have "caused new human tragedies and created new centers of tension," and "the United States has overstepped its national borders in every way."[4] In that same speech, Putin implied that American imperialism in this century was even worse than it was during the Cold War, when "there were at least some rules that all participants in international communication more or less adhered to or tried to follow. Now, it seems that there are no rules at all."[5] A decade later, Putin declared, "They [the West] behaved just as shamelessly and duplicitously when destroying Yugoslavia, Iraq, Libya, and Syria. They will never be able to wash off this shame . . . they got used to being allowed everything, got used to spitting on the whole world."[6] According to Putin, it is the United States, not Russia, "that destroyed the international security system . . . pushing the whole world into a global conflict."[7]

In berating alleged American unilateralism and imperialism, Putin often has a kindred spirit in Xi. As they pledged together after their meeting in Beijing in February 2022, "Russia and China stand against attempts by external forces to undermine security and stability in their common adjacent regions and intend to counter interference by outside forces in the internal affairs of sovereign countries under any pretext, oppose colour revolutions, and will increase cooperation in the aforementioned areas."[8] Xi may not completely support Putin's invasion of Ukraine, but he stands beside his comrade in Moscow in expressing disdain for the United States.

After the Soviet Union collapsed, Russia initially continued participating in regional security-focused organizations and treaties concluded during the Cold War, including the Organization for Security and Co-Operation in Europe (OSCE), the Treaty on Conventional Armed Forces in Europe (CFE), and the Vienna Document. However, Moscow's enthusiasm for the OSCE and CFE waned after it invaded Georgia and Ukraine. In Europe, Putin's project regarding multilateral security organizations is destruction, not construction, especially concerning NATO, so that Russia can pursue its security interests on the continent with individual countries. Putin's record of success has been mixed. By invading Ukraine in 2022, Putin triggered two powerful countries, Finland and Sweden, to join NATO. At the same time, Putin's courtships of conservative populist leaders in several NATO countries, especially Hungary and Slovakia, have weakened alliance cohesion. Putin's courtship of Trump has yielded dividends for him too. Trump's threat to withdraw American forces from Europe coupled with his disdain for Ukraine has fueled significant tensions within NATO.

THE COLLECTIVE SECURITY TREATY ORGANIZATION

Like Xi, Putin has invested in creating alternative security structures independent of the United States and the West, including, most notably, the Collective Security Treaty Organization. Created in 2002, the CSTO united several countries that were once Soviet republics—Armenia, Belarus, Kazakhstan, Kyrgyzstan, Russia, and Tajikistan. Putin hoped that the CSTO would become a counterweight to NATO, like the Warsaw Pact was during the Cold War, complete with the same collective security guarantee that an attack on one was an attack on all. In practice, however, the CSTO has functioned more as an instrument of Russian influence in the post-Soviet region, dedicated to supporting pro-Russian autocrats and keeping other great powers out of what Putin considers Russia's sphere of influence. Russia provides most of the soldiers and funding for a CSTO alliance.[9]

As discussed earlier, the CSTO's most audacious operation occurred in Kazakhstan in January 2022, when Russian armed forces intervened, with the CSTO's rubber stamp, to assist President Tokayev in thwarting a coup attempt. The successful operation fueled the perception that Russia had reemerged as the regional military hegemon in the former Soviet space.

The following year, however, Russia and the CSTO did not come to the aid of Armenia. In 2023, when Azerbaijan deployed massive military force to seize control of Nagorno-Karabakh, a region held controversially at the time by Armenia, the CSTO failed to respond to Armenia's multiple requests for assistance. This was not the first time the CSTO failed to respond to Armenia's requests for military aid; the same had happened during another flare-up in Nagorno-Karabakh in 2020. In 2023, Armenian prime minister Nikol Pashinyan asked France, a NATO member, to supply defensive weapons to thwart possible future attacks from Azerbaijan, and in 2024, he froze Armenia's participation in CSTO.[10] Joint membership in the CSTO has not reduced tensions between Kyrgyzstan and Tajikistan, a simmering conflict that has occasionally escalated into direct fire between their two armies. The CSTO did not act collectively in response to the alleged threat to Russia from NATO. When Putin invaded Ukraine in 2022, he did so alone, without either rhetorical endorsement or material aid from the CSTO. The solidarity within NATO for Ukraine (despite Ukraine not being a NATO member) is much greater than CSTO unity behind Russia.

Russia also actively participates in the Shanghai Cooperation Organization (SCO), which Russia and China founded in 2001 with Central and South Asian states to pursue collective economic and security objectives. The SCO is more of a Chinese project than a Russian one; therefore, it will be discussed in detail in the next chapter.

BILATERAL SECURITY INITIATIVES

While China, Russia, Iran, and North Korea cooperate comprehensively on giving each other military support, Russia has few formal military allies. Russia has alliances with the territories of Abkhazia and South Ossetia in Georgia and Transnistria in Moldova, but these enclaves provide almost no tangible security benefit to Russia. Russia maintains military bases in Armenia, Kyrgyzstan, Tajikistan, and occupied Ukraine, but the utility of these military assets is limited, and the Azerbaijani invasion of the Nagorno-Karabakh region in 2023 has fueled doubts about the future of Russia's base in Armenia. Russia's naval losses in the war in Ukraine, even though Ukraine does not have a navy, have compelled the Kremlin to move ships from occupied Sevastopol in Crimea to Novorossiysk in Russia. After the fall of al-Assad in late 2024, Russia lost its bases in Syria too.

Putin seeks to enhance Russian security (as he defines it) mainly through unilateral measures and bilateral ties, not through multilateral organizations or formal allies. Putin is old-school, preferring fluid nineteenth-century balance-of-power arrangements between great powers rather than formal multilateral organizations or treaties. As Putin quipped in 2015, "I would like to remind you Alexander III, our emperor, once said that Russia has just two allies, the armed forces and the navy."[11] Some people—me, for instance!—fear going back to the anarchic, Hobbesian jungle of international politics we had leading up to the First and Second World Wars. Putin yearns for it.

THE CHINA-RUSSIA ENTENTE

As discussed throughout this book, a central difference between the Cold War and great power relations today is Russia and China's deep security, economic, and ideological partnership. Once Putin came to power in 2000, relations between Russia and China gradually improved. Xi's ascent in 2012 accelerated relations to become even closer.

Regarding military ties, Russia and China have engaged for years in regular naval drills and joint military exercises. The PLA has taken part in annual strategic exercises inside Russia, and Russian forces have participated in regular Chinese military exercises. In July 2024, Russian and Chinese bomber jets flew together in an exercise off the coast of Alaska.[12] After Putin invaded Ukraine in 2022, Russian and Chinese military enterprises have become more integrated, as Chinese firms have become critical suppliers of components to Russian military enterprises that build drones, missiles, and transport vehicles.[13] And as mentioned earlier, in April 2025, Zelenskyy announced the discovery of 150 Chinese soldiers fighting alongside Russian armed forces in Ukraine.

Russia, in turn, has been China's primary foreign supplier of advanced aerospace and nuclear technologies. In addition, Russia and China coordinate closely within global organizations regarding security issues, often voting in tandem in the UN Security Council.

However, this bilateral relationship does have limits regarding security matters, much to Putin's disappointment. China did not recognize Abkhazia and South Ossetia as independent countries, did not endorse Russia's annexation of Crimea in 2014, and has not publicly supported Putin's invasion or annexation of parts of Ukraine after 2022. Rather than joining Russia in voting against UN General Assembly resolutions condemning these acts of Russian belligerency, China has abstained. At the same time, Xi does not want his friend to fail in Ukraine and therefore has continued to purchase more Russian energy exports and provide technological components for Russia's military industries.

A formal military alliance between China and Russia is unlikely.[14] And some security interests clash, especially in Central Asia and Africa. In the coming years, however, Moscow and Beijing will act as close partners on many security, economic, and ideological matters as long as Putin and Xi are in power. Despite strains from Putin's war in Ukraine, China and Russia remain firmly united by their opposition to the United States and its democratic allies. Compared to Xi, Putin is much more strident in his anti-Americanism and rejection of the liberal international order in general. However, both leaders lean the same way in solidarity against shared adversaries, including, first and foremost, the United States.

THE REST OF ASIA

Beyond his close partnership with Xi and China, Putin has played only a marginal role in disrupting existing security arrangements and organizations in Asia, and he has failed to create anything new in the region. Regarding Asia's other major powers, Japan and South Korea, Putin maintained limited relationships with both countries until he invaded Ukraine in 2022, after which both Asian democracies joined the international sanctions coalitions against Russia and provided significant economic assistance to Ukraine. The Russo-Japanese relationship is still marred by a dispute over the Kuril Islands, which the Soviet Union seized during World War II and Japan wants back.

After Putin invaded Ukraine in 2022, Russia's relations with North Korea greatly expanded. The countries started moving closer when Russia began to purchase vast quantities of ammunition from Pyongyang.[15] In September 2023, Kim Jong Un spent a week in eastern Russia and had a meeting with Putin, after which North Korea trumpeted a "fresh heyday" in bilateral relations. In June 2024, Putin traveled to North Korea for the first time in decades and signed with Kim the "Treaty on the Comprehensive Strategic Partnership," which, among other areas of deeper security cooperation, committed both countries to providing military assistance to the other if either was attacked. Because of Putin's deeper embrace of Kim Jong Un, Russia is no longer cooperating with China and the United States to limit the development of North Korea's nuclear weapons program. In March 2024, Russia vetoed a UN Security Council resolution for the renewal of the UN Panel of Experts tasked with monitoring the implementation of UN sanctions against North Korea. And, most surprisingly, in the fall of 2024 Kim Jong Un sent ten thousand North Korean soldiers to fight alongside Russian soldiers against Ukraine's armed forces. A decade ago, when I was in the US government, Russia cooperated with the United States and China in multilateral settings to try to slow North Korea's nuclear weapons program. That era is over now.

RUSSIA IN THE MIDDLE EAST AND NORTH AFRICA

Through bilateral, not multilateral, initiatives, Putin has sought to reassert Russia as a pivotal player in security matters in the Middle East and North Africa. Russia's most important partner in the region is Iran, a relationship that deepened when Tehran started to provide Moscow with military assistance—especially drones—to fight its war in Ukraine. Iran is a highly disruptive actor in the region. In pursuing nuclear weapons, Iran could trigger nuclear proliferation in the Middle East, starting with Saudi Arabia. Iran's theocrats have deployed Iranian militias and their Hezbollah allies in Syria to prop up al-Assad for a decade, fought proxy wars in Lebanon by supporting Hezbollah, in Yemen by backing the Houthis, and in Palestine by providing aid to Hamas. After the Hamas terrorist attack against Israel on October 7, 2023, Iranian proxies began to attack American military units stationed in the region as well as ships. Putin today seems just fine with all these provocative actions—a stark contrast from Russian policy toward Iran just a decade earlier, when Russia voted together with the United States in the UN Security Council to impose sanctions on Iran, then cooperated closely with American diplomats to negotiate the Iran nuclear deal.[16] Those days of great power cooperation to advance regional security in the Middle East are over.

Moreover, for nearly a decade, Putin actively supported al-Assad in Syria, repeatedly defying collective initiatives in the UN Security Council aimed at facilitating a negotiated end to the civil war there and in 2015 deploying the Russian air force to keep the Syrian dictator in power. Thankfully, Putin's autocratic ally in Syria lost power in 2024.

Putin has also expanded Russia's involvement in security matters in North Africa. Following the NATO-led intervention in Libya in 2011 that helped topple the Gaddafi regime there, Putin tried to fill the power vacuum and propel Field Marshal Khalifa Haftar into power. Far from facilitating any peace agreement in the country, Russian mercenaries fueled chaos through village raids, indiscriminate bombing, and executions.[17]

With more stable autocratic regimes in the Arab world, Putin has pushed hard to court leaders formerly aligned with the United States. His most significant success has been with Saudi Arabia. When the Saudi Crown Prince Mohammed bin Salman was shunned globally for apparently ordering the assassination of Saudi journalist Jamal Khashoggi in Istanbul, Putin signaled solidarity with his fellow autocrat. The two leaders have worked together closely on coordinating their exports of oil to maintain higher prices, much to the chagrin of American leaders. When the United States and Russia restarted bilateral relations in February 2025, Riyadh hosted the first high-level meeting between Secretary of State Rubio and Foreign Minister Lavrov. Putin has also nurtured cooperative ties with the Gulf monarchies, especially the UAE, overcoming the damage to Russian relations with the Arab world from the Chechen wars. In Egypt, Putin has cultivated new ties with autocratic leader Abdel Fattah el-Sisi after he seized power in the 2013 coup. Even Russian-Iraq relations have improved. None of Putin's relationships with Arab leaders were seriously interrupted by his invasion of Ukraine.

Putin has also developed a close personal relationship with Israeli prime minister Benjamin Netanyahu and cultivated societal ties with the country's large Russian émigré community. Strikingly, Israel did not join other liberal democracies in providing military and economic assistance to Ukraine or imposing sanctions against Russia, even though President Zelenskyy is Jewish. The Hamas terrorist attack on Israel strained but did not break bilateral relations. Putin tried to support both sides, first condemning the Hamas terrorist attack, then denouncing the Israeli military's response and the treatment of civilians in Gaza. Given Russia's close connections with both Israel and Hamas, Putin could have played the role of mediator in this conflict, but he did not. Whether Putin's support for Hamas and its principal benefactor, Iran, will result in a longer-term rupture or a temporary hiccup is not clear. What is clear is that the war in Gaza distracted the world from Russia's invasion of Ukraine, and that served Putin well. In 2025, Putin condemned Israel's bombing of Iran but with little vigor.

RUSSIAN GUNS FOR HIRE IN AFRICA

After a near complete departure from Africa after the Soviet collapse, Russia returned to the continent to play a significant role in security matters, primarily in defense of autocrats. Russia's infamous Wagner Group, now the Africa Corps, has been deployed or hired to provide security to numerous autocrats on that continent.[18] Russian soldiers supported the coup plotters who took over in Mali and Niger. In Niger, Russians showed up when American armed forces that were there to fight terrorist groups were asked to leave. After the coup in Mali had been aided by Russia, the new military junta, led by Lieutenant Colonel Assimi Goita, voted against a UN General Assembly resolution condemning Russia's invasion of Ukraine. Russia recently signed dozens of military cooperation agreements with sub-Saharan countries, making Russia the continent's largest arms supplier.[19]

RUSSIA IN LATIN AMERICA

In Latin America, Putin again used bilateral relations, not multilateral forums, to expand Russia's presence, bolster support for autocrats, and weaken American influence. Since 2006, when populist dictator Hugo Chávez signed a $2.9 billion arms agreement with the Russian Federation, Russia has become one of Venezuela's most significant partners.[20] In exchange, Chávez promised the Kremlin exclusive access to Venezuelan oil and drilling assets at below-market prices. After Chávez's death, the Kremlin intervened to prop up his successor, Nicolás Maduro, first in 2017 by bailing out Venezuela in a restructuring deal worth roughly three billion dollars and later providing weapons worth approximately ten billion, then again in 2024, when most countries in the world recognized Maduro's defeat in the presidential election but Russia did not. To help Maduro manage protests after the falsified vote, Putin sent his soldiers from the Wagner Group.[21]

Moscow has also strengthened old Cold War ties to left-leaning autocracies in Cuba and Nicaragua. President Daniel Ortega rewarded Putin's support by voting (with only a handful of other nations) against the UN resolutions that condemned Putin's annexation of four Ukrainian regions.[22] Cuba, surprisingly, abstained.

In all these regions just briefly surveyed, except Central Asia, Putin has focused more on promoting *bilateral* security ties than on working with *multilateral* institutions. Only in the former Soviet Union has Russia tried to develop a multilateral security organization, the CSTO, but with limited success.

MULTILATERAL ECONOMIC INSTITUTIONS

For most of the twentieth century, Soviet leaders aspired to construct an alternative international economic system to the US-anchored liberal international order. Their most significant achievement was the Council for Mutual Economic Assistance, which fostered ties among communist states in Europe and around the world. After the Soviet collapse in 1991, newly independent Russia tried to maintain economic relations with the other independent countries in the former Soviet space by creating the Commonwealth of Independent States, but that project failed. Russia and the other newly independent nations were more interested in joining Western clubs than in creating their own.

During the first two terms of his presidency, Putin continued this Western trajectory, more or less. He cherished Russia's role in the G8 and pushed to join the WTO. After the 2008 financial crisis, President Medvedev played an active role in the G20 and elevated Russia's pursuit of WTO membership, which was finally achieved in 2011. Russia played a central role in the Asia-Pacific Economic Cooperation (APEC), hosting the organization's annual summit in Vladivostok in 2011.

Over time, however, Putin lost interest in Western economic organizations and focused on strengthening Russia-anchored regional organizations, including, most important, the Eurasian Economic Union (EEU), created in May 2014 by Russia, Kazakhstan, and Belarus; Armenia and Kyrgyzstan joined later. Putin's aim, however, was to bring all the former republics of the Soviet Union except for the Baltic states into his new economic club. Like the CSTO, which is supposed to be an answer to NATO, the EEU is the Russian counter to the European Union. Putin defined this competition for membership in zero-sum terms: A country could not be a member of both economic organizations. While I was ambassador to Russia, from 2012 to 2014, it seemed that launching the EEU, with Ukraine as a member, was Putin's highest foreign policy objective, on par with Xi's obsession with expanding his Belt and Road Initiative.

The EEU has succeeded in creating a functioning single market through harmonized tariff policies, technical regulations, and labor mobility. Russia dominates the union, accounting for the lion's share of the body's GDP. The EEU also integrates cross-regional political activity, providing an alternative authoritarian club to the democratic governance norms of Western-created bodies such as the EU. Criticizing the EEU, Secretary of State Hillary Clinton accused Moscow of attempting "to re-Sovietize" the Eurasian landmass, which generated sharp rebukes from Putin and Foreign Minister Lavrov. As the US ambassador to Russia, I was the personal recipient of one of these rebukes from Lavrov. While denying any interest in restoring the USSR, Putin has made no secret of his broader goals for the EEU, saying that "close integration—based on new values, politics, and economy—is the order of the day."[23] American officials talk about multilateral cooperation with "like-minded nations." Putin does too.

As testimony to the importance of the EEU to Putin, the Kremlin pledged to provide billions to Ukrainian president Yanukovych in 2013 to persuade him not to sign an accession agreement with the European Union.[24] Yanukovych's decision to delay signing that EU agreement triggered the 2014

Revolution of Dignity and subsequent Russian intervention in Ukraine, including the annexation of Crimea.

Russia's invasion of Ukraine in 2022 significantly interrupted progress toward greater cohesion within the EEU, halting its expansion. Ukraine and Moldova, once Kremlin targets for candidacy in the EEU, are now firmly focused on joining the EU, not the EEU. Uzbekistan—Central Asia's most populous state—has refused to participate. Even Tajikistan, despite being highly dependent on remittances from labor migrants in Russia, has repeatedly resisted pressure to join. Putin's long-term ambitions for this economic organization remain hamstrung by Russia's limited economic clout. Except for Lukashenko in Belarus, leaders and citizens across Eurasia seek to diversify ties, not narrow them exclusively to Russia.

In addition to the EEU, Russia has played a leadership role in BRICS. The multilateral economic organization originally consisted of Brazil, Russia, India, China, and South Africa (hence the acronym), then expanded to include Egypt, Ethiopia, Iran, Saudi Arabia, and the United Arab Emirates. Initially, BRICS focused on fostering the growth of their emerging market economies. Over time, however, growing tensions between China and the United States and between Russia and the United States transformed BRICS into an institutional counterweight to American-led multilateral economic organizations such as the G7. As discussed already, BRICS also created the New Development Bank. Thus far, however, BRICS has yet to wield collective economic power; its bank is a marginal player in international development finance, and the level of economic policy coordination within the group does not match what happens in the G7.[25] Within this organization, Russia is China's junior partner.

Putin has continued to participate in some economic institutions in which the US also participates, including the G20, APEC, and WTO, often using Russia's membership to blunt the influence of the United States, sometimes with success. For example, in 2023, Putin succeeded in blocking the G20's condemnation of his invasion of Ukraine.[26] Russia's influence in these multilateral economic organizations is still limited because the Russian economy is weak. While Chinese participation in these economic clubs may influence them from within, Russia does not have that capability, even if Putin has that desire.

ECONOMIC INTERDEPENDENCE

For the first two decades after the Soviet Union's collapse, not unlike the first decades of "opening up" with China after the death of Mao, Russian and American leaders collaborated to deepen Russian integration in the global economy, nurture bilateral trade, and encourage American companies to invest in Russia and some Russian companies to invest in the United States. A handful of Russian-American partnerships produced remarkable outcomes, the largest of which was the Rosneft-ExxonMobil joint venture, which had an estimated value of over five hundred billion dollars. Boeing sold billions of dollars in planes to Aeroflot and other Russian companies. Boeing's Moscow Design Center employed hundreds of Russians until Boeing suspended its operations after Russia's 2022 invasion of Ukraine, and Russian engineers worked at Boeing facilities in the US. Other collaborations included Ford's venture with the Russian automotive company Sollers, the Pfizer-NovaMedica joint venture to create a new pharmaceutical plant and transfer technology, and Pepsi's purchase of the Russian dairy company Wimm-Bill-Dann. Trade and investment between the two countries rose considerably between 2009 and 2013. Trade with and investment from many European countries, especially Germany, also expanded during these years.

Economic interdependence, however, did not stop Putin's Russia from invading Ukraine twice. The US ambition to encourage economic integration, trade, and investment waned after Russia annexed Crimea in 2014 and ended completely after Putin invaded Ukraine in 2022. The United States joined other democracies in imposing significant sanctions on the Russian government, companies, and individuals in response to that invasion, and over a thousand Western companies quit Russia altogether, further decoupling the Russian economy from the economies of the democratic world. The US embassy in Moscow even urged Americans to leave the country. Some stayed; the profits were too large to abandon. But the American companies most valued by the Kremlin such as ExxonMobil and Boeing quit and are unlikely to come back. As aerospace consultant Richard Aboulafia colorfully speculated, "If given the choice between reentering Russia and drinking bleach, I'm sure that the glass of bleach is looking mighty good."[27]

After Putin's wars in Ukraine, a similar story of economic disengagement unfolded between Europe and Russia. Trade and investment in Russia declined after 2014, but Russia and Europe remained sizably connected, particularly in the energy sector. After Russia's second invasion of Ukraine, the EU took decisive and economically painful measures to radically reduce Russian gas and oil imports. For now, Putin has offset the economic consequences of this decoupling by expanding Russian oil and gas exports to China, India, and other non-European markets. However, the loss of Europe as the market for hydrocarbon exports has decreased Putin's revenues for fighting his war and had a devastating impact on Russia's largest gas producer, Gazprom. Two decades ago, some analysts predicted that Gazprom would become the most valuable company in the world. Today, the company is teetering on bankruptcy. The decoupling of the Russian economy from the West after the war in Ukraine damaged many other Russian multinational corporations that had developed growth strategies based on integration into the global economy. That possibility of growth is over for the near term.

In response to international sanctions, Putin confiscated Western assets in Russia or allowed his cronies to purchase them at rock-bottom prices when companies headquartered in democracies sought to exit Russia quickly after the 2022 invasion of Ukraine. The long-term effects of a change in these firms' ownership will further drag down the Russian economy. Before 2022, corruption, the absence of the rule of law, and crony capitalism had made Russia a tough place for Western investors to run profitable enterprises. With these assets transferred from profit-oriented managers to Putin cronies, they will become even less effective at fostering economic growth. The momentum for decoupling between Russia and the West is strong and unlikely to slow anytime soon.

MULTILATERAL POLITICAL INSTITUTIONS

After the collapse of the Soviet Union in 1991, Russians enthusiastically joined all political clubs based on democratic values, most notably the Council of Europe. During the 1990s, many international human rights organizations opened offices in Russia, among them Human Rights Watch, Amnesty International, Greenpeace, and Transparency International.

Gradually and then abruptly, the Kremlin's enthusiasm for these international organizations committed to advancing democracy and human rights faded after Putin became president. For Putin, the least valuable part of the liberal international order has always been those organizations supporting liberalism, democracy, and human rights. Putin sees these multilateral organizations as an extension of US hegemony. As prime minister, Putin did not object to Russia joining the rest of the democratic world in 2011 in approving and implementing the UN Security Council Resolution 1975 that sent two thousand UN peacekeepers to Ivory Coast and imposed sanctions to help restore democracy there. That same year, however, Putin publicly condemned Medvedev for abstaining on UN Security Council resolutions authorizing the use of force against the Libyan government for humanitarian purposes. Ever since, Russia has blocked any attempts by the United States and other democracies to use the United Nations to sanction autocrats or defend human rights, especially resolutions aimed at ending the civil war in Syria or criticizing Russia's invasion of Ukraine.[28]

Putin has used Russia's presence within UN agencies and councils to dilute democratic norms, particularly concerning human rights, internet freedom, and the rule of law. In 2021, the General Assembly shockingly elected Russia to the UN Human Rights Council for a three-year term, enabling Russia to work closely with China to undermine the global human rights regime. That ended in 2022, when the UN expelled Russia from the UNHRC following its invasion of Ukraine. In 2022, Putin campaigned, though unsuccessfully, to elect Russian Rashid Ismailov as secretary general of the International Telecommunication Union, a UN regulatory agency vital to sustaining internet freedom. The Russian-Chinese tag team for Ismailov failed; an American, Doreen Bogdan-Martin, won instead. Still, this advocacy demonstrated how much Russia seeks to dilute global norms on internet freedom.

Russia's relationship with European-based multilateral organizations focused on human rights and the rule of law gradually and then radically deteriorated under Putin. The Council of Europe granted Russia membership based on an optimistic proposition that integration would be better than isolation.[29] Russia joined the council's European Convention on Human Rights (ECHR). Russian human rights activists and their international supporters tried to seek justice and override Russian legal decisions within the European Court of Human Rights (also known as the Strasbourg Court), initiatives that generated Kremlin hostility toward this European body. The Council of Europe suspended Russia in March 2022 in response to Putin's invasion of Ukraine, and six months later, Russia quit the ECHR. Russia under Putin developed a contentious relationship with the OSCE as well, especially those parts of the organization responsible for election monitoring, human rights, and the rule of law. After the Russian invasion of Ukraine, Russia remained an OSCE member, but just barely. There are no procedures in the organization for expelling members. In 2016, Putin withdrew from the Rome Statute, which governs the International Criminal Court, after the ICC ruled that Russia's activity in Crimea amounted to an "ongoing occupation" and armed conflict.[30] (In 2000, Russia signed the Rome Statute but it had never formally ratified the treaty.) In March 2023, the ICC issued an arrest warrant for Putin, alleging that the Russian leader had committed war crimes. The ICC indicted Maria Lvova-Belova, Putin's commissioner for Children's Rights, for the same crimes. It was the first time that the ICC had taken such an action against the leader of a UN Security Council member. Not surprisingly, Putin ridiculed the indictment and lambasted the action as an illegal violation of sovereignty. Putin has zero interest in these kinds of multilateral organizations. While having limited means to damage them, Putin eagerly seeks their destruction.

Chapter 11

CHINA AND THE GLOBAL ORDER

IN 2009, I traveled to Singapore with President Obama as a member of his National Security Council. Obama's primary purpose on that trip was to participate in the ASEAN summit, but while there, he met with Russia's President Medvedev for another round of negotiations on the New START treaty. That is why I was on the trip. In briefings on that trip, my colleague at the NSC who was responsible for international economics, Mike Froman, used the acronym TPP, which I had never heard before. We all thought that Mike was a little too obsessed with this funny-sounding abbreviation. Many of us at the time did not understand the significance of the Trans-Pacific Partnership (TPP), especially compared to the nuclear treaty negotiations with Russia with which I was involved. What could be more significant than reducing the number of nuclear weapons in the world?

Over time, however, I learned why TPP was significant, and potentially even more important than the New START treaty. Beijing was aggressively inventing new multilateral institutions to enhance economic cooperation, especially with developing countries. The United States had to propose alternatives to its allies and partners in Asia and Latin America. Back then, TPP (now CPTPP) was the key initiative in this effort, constituting a free trade agreement among the Pacific countries that deliberately excluded China. It was precisely what the United States needed in order to strengthen its economic ties with friendly countries in the region and limit China's growing economic influence there. Several years later, however, presidential candidate Donald Trump called Obama's TPP a "rape of our country."[1] Once in office in 2017, Trump pulled the United States out of the agreement.

That Trump decision was a huge mistake. In the US-China competition, no fight is more important than the battle over who will shape the contours of the international order—in particular, who will decide the rules, norms, and institutions that govern the global economy. Xi Jinping is implementing a sophisticated strategy in this space to stake out a leadership role for China in the twenty-first century similar to the one the United States played in the twentieth century. As Xi asserted boldly, China must "lead the reform of the global governance system," as "China is "moving closer toward the world's center stage."[2] Xi predicts "great changes unseen in a century" that will usher in a new era of Chinese influence in the world as America's role in the global order declines.[3] And he is achieving some successes, often underestimated by American leaders.[4]

Regarding multilateral security institutions, Xi mostly wants to affirm the status quo, which serves China's interests well, but he also seeks changes to reflect Chinese interests better. And like other great powers over the past two centuries, China ignores multilateral institutions that it perceives as damaging to its national security interests. For instance, in 2016, the PRC ignored the Permanent Court of Arbitration's decision on a sovereignty dispute in the South China Sea because accepting it would have limited China's ability to assert its control in the South China Sea.

Regarding multilateral economic institutions, Xi is more aggressive in seeking to change them to better accommodate his definition of Chinese interests. Many in Washington believe Xi aims to destroy the existing international economic order and unseat the United States as the dominant power in the global economy. To date, Xi's actions regarding international economic institutions have been more evolutionary than revolutionary, but even those initiatives challenge American interests.

As for multilateral political institutions, Beijing is the most disruptive.[5] The Chinese communist regime rejects outright Western claims of the universality of human rights and liberal democracy, instead championing Chinese values and the principle of sovereignty. Xi has not quit these organizations but has fought for China to take on a more significant role in them to impede the promotion of liberal, democratic values.

While seeking change within existing structures, the PRC has simultaneously created new China-anchored multilateral institutions that exclude the United States. These clubs bolster China's independence from the US-centered organizations founded after World War II. Xi and his CCP comrades have taken advantage of global discontent with the existing liberal international order anchored by the United States to offer new clubs, especially for countries in the developing world. As China specialist Elizabeth Economy observes, "Dissatisfaction with the current international order has created a global audience more amenable to China's proposals than might have existed not long ago."[6] Some have likened this effort to develop an alternative world order to the old Chinese system of *tianxia* ("all under heaven"), in which Imperial China—the Middle Kingdom—was the center of the world with lesser, "tributary" states around its periphery.[7]

Regardless of the parallels to the past, American leaders should be alarmed by this Chinese project of inventing and anchoring parallel multilateral organizations.[8] Of course any rising great power will be inclined to challenge the existing economic order to allow its economy to expand and support its broader goals, just as the United States did at the end of the nineteenth century.[9] We saw the same pattern with a rising Japan in the 1980s when that nation sought a more significant role in international economic institutions.[10] The challenge from China today, however, is different from the rise of the US or Japan because the PRC is an autocracy, a very powerful one. China's rise as a member within existing multilateral liberal institutions creates challenges for those committed to preserving the *liberal* international order. The transition from British to American hegemony a century ago was relatively smooth because it was a shift from one liberal power to another. If Beijing were to replace the United States as the leader of the current global system, the transition would be profound and damaging to US interests.

Given China's opaque regime, it is hard to know precisely what Xi aspires to achieve concerning revisions to the global order.[11] In actions and words, Chinese leaders to date have demonstrated more modest aims at disrupting the global order than Soviet leaders during the Cold War did. However, this more modest and evolutionary challenge—a boiling-frog strategy—might be more difficult for American policymakers to thwart. Other countries do not see the dangers that Americans do or should see. And those countries might be right. Maybe some of China's reforms to the existing order and new clubs outside of the existing order could be beneficial to other nations' interests, especially when the United States in the Trump era is pulling back from existing multilateral institutions, not proposing a new set of liberal-centric reforms, and offering little to nothing regarding new security and economic clubs exclusively for democracies. Moreover, the China challenge varies by domain, so the US responses cannot be blanket restrictions or protections. Oversimplifying or exaggerating the Chinese strategy makes it harder for American leaders to convince other countries to stand with us. Getting right this diagnosis of China's threat to the global order is a necessary condition for formulating a successful prescriptive strategy for the United States.

MULTILATERAL SECURITY INSTITUTIONS

Ever since the PRC took over China's seat in the United Nations in 1971, Beijing has valued its position as a permanent member of the UN Security Council and an influential member of the United Nations. Regarding this multilateral security institution, China is a status quo defender. Despite rhetorical calls for reform of the global security system—like Xi's vague Global Security Initiative—CCP leaders have no intention of undermining the UN system.[12] As one of the P5—the five permanent members of the UNSC—the PRC wields a powerful veto that prevents the UN from acting contrary to China's security interests (as defined by Xi). Like every other P5 leader, Xi does not want to lose his power. In this domain of global order, China seeks continuity, not change.

Beijing values the United Nations more than the United States and Russia, expanding its cooperation with United Nations organizations over recent decades. Beijing has pursued and secured leadership roles in UN bodies such as the Food and Agriculture Organization, the International Telecommunication Union, the UN Industrial Development Organization, and the International Civil Aviation Organization.[13] At one point, a Chinese official, Meng Hongwei, headed Interpol, although Xi later recalled and arrested him, which was not a great look for someone leading an international police organization. The PRC has become the second-biggest financial supporter of the United Nations, behind only the United States, and that could change in Trump's second term. Moreover, the PRC has vastly expanded its participation in UN peacekeeping missions, providing more soldiers than any other UN Security Council member.[14] China cooperates with UN entities on climate change, development, and the Arctic and has worked with the United States on UN-backed efforts to stop nuclear proliferation in North Korea and Iran.[15]

The PRC is usually opposed to authorizing military intervention against sovereign countries, but Beijing has supported or abstained from UN Security Council resolutions that allowed the use of force, led by the United States, against Iraq in 1990, Afghanistan in 2001, and Libya in 2011. In many ways, China's behavior is more consistent with United Nations norms and practices than that of Russia and the United States. Both Russia and the United States have launched invasions of countries without the blessing of the UN Security Council. To date, China has not.

That said, China's record of engagement with the UN is cluttered with contradictions. China has increasingly demonstrated a willingness to wield its veto power to advance its interests at the expense of collective security. For instance, despite Syria's proven record of gross human rights violations, the PRC vetoed UN resolutions condemning the al-Assad regime's violent crackdowns on its citizens and the use of chemical weapons, as well as a resolution authorizing cross-border humanitarian aid to Syrian civilians.[16] The PRC also vetoed UN resolutions condemning the Myanmar military regime's abuses after the 2021 coup d'état because of Myanmar's importance for China in securing energy supply routes. By protecting tyrannical regimes that violate human rights in North Korea, Myanmar, Sudan, and Zimbabwe, China seeks to weaken the UN's powers to defend universal values.[17] In 2024, China reversed its long-standing support of the UN panel monitoring the implementation of sanctions against North Korea's nuclear program and instead backed a new Russian proposal for annual assessments.[18] That was a step away from collective security and a step in support of Russia, which increasingly relies on North Korea for ammunition and soldiers for its war in Ukraine.

China has also demonstrated hypocrisy regarding the norm of sovereignty, one of the core values of the UN and the international system that Chinese leaders frequently celebrate.[19] China supported Kuwait during

Iraq's invasion and Iraq during the US-led invasion, did not endorse Russia's interventions in Georgia and Ukraine, and voted for the creation of a sovereign and independent Palestinian state. At the same time, China brazenly defied the UN Convention on the Law of the Sea (UNCLOS) by claiming sovereignty in the South China Sea within what it calls the "nine-dash line"—an arbitrary sea border it drew unilaterally. In 2013, in response to these illegal Chinese territorial claims, the Philippines lodged a formal complaint at the Permanent Court of Arbitration in The Hague. The court ruled in favor of the Philippines, but Beijing ignored the verdict, arguing that the court did not have the authority to decide China's territorial claims, directly contradicting the rules the PRC had agreed to abide by when signing UNCLOS.[20] Seeking Chinese investment, loans, and aid and wanting to avoid escalating tensions with his great power neighbor, Philippines' president Rodrigo Duterte decided not to pursue enforcement of this decision. This episode demonstrates how China leverages its economic clout to enforce political preferences on its neighbors and undermine international norms when compliance proves inconvenient.

To secure a buffer zone around the Chinese mainland and make future military power projection easier throughout the region, the PRC has continued to ignore the maritime sovereignty claims of other countries in the South China Sea. Instead of respecting the two-hundred-nautical-mile exclusive economic zones of different countries, Xi has pursued extensive land-reclamation projects in the South China Sea, constructing military installations on artificial islands and continuously harassing vessels in these waters despite their right of freedom of navigation. In 2022, China violated India's sovereignty by unilaterally deploying forces along the disputed border in India's northeastern state of Arunachal Pradesh.[21]

As the PRC has grown more powerful, its disregard for international security arrangements has become bolder. China's introduction of the 2020 Hong Kong National Security Law blatantly violated the principle of "one country, two systems" that was developed by Deng Xiaoping in the early 1980s and embedded in the 1984 Sino-British Joint Declaration as well as Hong Kong Basic Law adopted by the National People's Congress of China in 1990. Beijing's crackdown in Hong Kong heightened concerns around the world about an imminent invasion of Taiwan.[22] In his speech at China's

Communist Party Congress in 2022, Xi threatened, "We will continue to strive for peaceful reunification with the greatest sincerity and the utmost effort, but we will never promise to renounce the use of force, and we reserve the option of taking all necessary measures."[23] Consistent with Xi's ominous statements, Chinese armed forces have performed more aggressive maneuvers against Taiwan in recent years, carrying out dress rehearsals for a blockade in response to Speaker Nancy Pelosi's 2022 visit to the island, and after the inauguration of Lai Ching-te as Taiwan's new president in May 2024, and then again on an even larger scale in December 2024 and April 2025.[24]

American leaders have demonstrated similar hypocrisies regarding sovereignty. The US-led invasion of Iraq in 2003 is the most obvious example. However, US violations of the norms of multilateral security institutions should not be misunderstood as an aspiration to undermine the global security system. (In his second term, Trump may actually seek that kind of change, but as this book goes into publication, it is too early to tell.) The same is true of China. Despite the dramatic buildup of military and economic capabilities, Beijing has not launched a full-scale invasion of another sovereign country in the post–Cold War era (as both the United States and Russia have) and has not annexed territory (as Russia has). Compared to the Soviets during the Cold War, Xi and his Chinese communist comrades are much more supportive of existing multilateral security institutions. As Xi explained, "The current international order is not perfect, but there is no need to overthrow it or start anew."[25] That is because these multilateral security organizations serve Chinese security interests. Unlike the Soviet leaders during the Cold War, Xi is not seeking revolutionary change to the global security architecture, just incremental change to better accommodate China's interests and permission to violate the rules occasionally, as the other great powers do.

NEW SECURITY ORGANIZATIONS

While working within existing multilateral institutions, Beijing has created a few new independent clubs to advance China's global security vision. For instance, Xi launched the Global Security Initiative, which aspires to leverage "Chinese wisdom and solutions" allegedly for the good of all countries seeking peace.[26] To date, the GSI has not generated many results and sounds more aspirational than operational, consistent with a Chinese pattern of deploying general concepts and initiatives—one Chinese expert calls it "Slogan Politics"—often thin in content.[27] Beijing has organized multilateral security conferences, such as the China-Africa Defense and Security Forum and the China-Africa Peace and Security Forum. However, these are mostly talk shops that do not commit China or other members to concrete actions.[28]

Beijing also anchors the Shanghai Cooperation Organization (SCO), an economic and security initiative created with Russia and Central and South Asian states. Formally, SCO's security agenda focuses narrowly on coordinating efforts to combat extremism, separatism, and terrorism. Members also commit to upholding the norm of "non-interference in internal affairs" and have signed generic documents affirming their support for "cybersecurity," a euphemism for control of digital data within their borders. This club, however, has made few tangible contributions to advancing the PRC's security goals.[29] The organization facilitates joint military exercises that Chinese troops participate in and has allowed the PRC to grow a military presence in Central Asia; China now has an outpost in Tajikistan and performs joint counterterrorism patrols at the China-Tajikistan-Afghanistan border.[30] However, the SCO is not a formal military alliance, and it will likely never be one, since SCO members Russia and China, as well as India and Pakistan, have divergent security interests. Even if other member states were to agree to such a framework, the PRC is wary of formal alliances.[31] Today, China has only one formal military alliance, with North Korea, and it only exists as a legacy from the Cold War. This bilateral relationship is fraught with complexity and cannot be considered of military benefit for Beijing. Outside of that agreement, the PRC has a long-standing tradition of avoiding binding alliances that dates back to Mao-era principles of non-alignment.

When Chinese leaders look for partners, they frame their engagement as seeking to deepen and expand "global partnerships," not create alliances. Beijing officials celebrate their independent foreign policy, at times hinting that allies can be more of a burden than a benefit (maybe that is what you have to say when you don't have any real allies). Like Russia and the United

States, China does cooperate with multiple partners on security issues such as arms sales, port-access agreements, military-to-military dialogues, joint training exercises, military-student exchanges, and export of technologies for "domestic security." But these are mostly tools to cultivate security cooperation on a bilateral, not multilateral, basis.

CHINA'S SPECIAL AND COMPLICATED SECURITY PARTNERSHIP WITH RUSSIA

Regarding security, China has one special partner: Russia. While the two countries share membership in several multilateral organizations, the security component of their work together is mostly conducted through bilateral channels. As discussed earlier, Xi and Putin have developed a close personal rapport after dozens of meetings over the past decade. Their shared disdain for the United States and their common defense of autocracy forms the core of this bilateral partnership.[32]

As already discussed, Putin's decision to invade Ukraine in 2022 complicated this partnership. Regarding international security institutions, Putin is much more rogue than Xi. While Xi seeks revision of multilateral security organizations to better support Chinese interests, Putin wants to tear them down. So far, Xi has tried to chart a delicate balancing act of supporting his radically revisionist friend in Moscow without abandoning China's position in the old global security architecture.

On the assistance side, as discussed in the previous chapter, China has helped Russia undermine the effectiveness of Western sanctions by buying more Russian fossil fuels and supplying directly or acting as an intermediary to help Russian enterprises secure critical technologies needed for weapons production.[33] In 2023 and 2024, trade volumes between Russia and China reached all-time highs of $240 billion.[34] At crucial moments, Xi has signaled public support for Putin. For instance, in March 2023, just three days after the International Criminal Court issued a warrant for Putin's arrest for war crimes, Xi met with Putin in Moscow. Xi and other Chinese officials have blamed the United States and NATO for fueling the conflict by supplying weapons to the Ukrainian army. Putin's invasion of Ukraine did not interrupt bilateral security cooperation, which includes numerous joint military exercises on land and sea.[35] When Russia launched Ocean-2024, its largest naval exercise in thirty years—it included over 400 warships, 120 aircraft, and 90,000 military personnel—China played a pivotal role.[36] In 2024, Chinese and Russian jets even entered Alaska's air defense identification zone together for the first time during a joint aerial patrol.[37]

At the same time, Xi has shown little enthusiasm for Putin's imperial war. In February 2022, a joint statement of the two countries proclaimed there were "no limits" to their partnership. In May 2024, that phrase was dropped from a statement about China-Russia cooperation.[38] China's ambassador to the EU publicly dismissed this "no limits" phrase as "nothing but rhetoric."[39] Beijing also was not pleased when Putin invited over ten thousand North Korean soldiers to fight against the Ukrainian soldiers in the Kursk region of Russia in the fall of 2024.[40]

Careful actions followed China's cautious statements. Unlike Trump's America in 2025, the PRC did not vote against but has abstained on UN resolutions condemning Russia's invasion of Ukraine. Unlike leaders in Iran and North Korea, Xi has not provided Putin with weapons. While German chancellor Olaf Scholz was visiting Beijing in November 2022, Xi publicly criticized Putin for threatening to use nuclear weapons, stating, "The international community should . . . oppose the threat or use of nuclear weapons."[41] At the time, US officials appreciated this warning, since that was the moment when American intelligence had assessed the highest probability of Putin's using nuclear weapons on the battlefield in Ukraine. Xi has tried to maintain cordial ties with Kyiv, as Ukraine had emerged as a major grain exporter to China before the war started. In return, Ukrainian president Volodymyr Zelenskyy has muted his criticism of China, hoping to expand economic ties after the war. Following US threats of secondary sanctions on Chinese companies, Chinese banks began halting transactions with Russia, freezing tens of billions of yuan in payments and increasing transaction costs for Russian firms using intermediaries.[42] In the second quarter of 2024, due to payment difficulties, the Bank of China decreased its assets in Russia by 37 percent, and the Industrial and Commercial Bank of China reduced theirs by 27 percent.[43] In the energy sector, despite Putin's continuous push to build the Power of Siberia 2 pipeline between Russia and China, the project has still not started because of disputes over pricing and other concessions sought by Beijing.[44] These delays have generated resentment in Russia, where some now believe that China is taking advantage of Russia's increasing isolation instead of showing comradely support. And while trade overall between the two countries increased significantly after Putin invaded Ukraine, the volume is still comparatively modest. As French economist Agathe Demarais observed in 2024, "Chinese companies export as much to Russia as they do to the Netherlands, an economy almost 2.5 times smaller than Russia's that does not share a long border with China. At $111bn, Chinese exports to Russia are lower than those to Vietnam."[45] Rather than booming, trade ties between Russia and China are catching up from an abnormally low prior base.

Tensions in Sino-Russian relations are not new.[46] For example, in 2017, Xi rejected all forty transportation projects proposed by Putin's Eurasian Economic Union for BRI funding.[47] In Central Asia, Russia and China compete for economic influence more than they cooperate, and China is winning that contest.[48] Beijing is increasingly willing to engage Central Asia without Russians in the room, and the PRC is the top trading partner for all Central Asian countries except Kazakhstan. Even in Kazakhstan, where Xi initially launched BRI and where China invests heavily, Beijing is rapidly closing the gap with Russia for dominance in trade.[49]

Xi's refusal to fully endorse Putin's invasion of Ukraine reflects a fundamental divergence between Russian and Chinese conceptions of global security. As discussed in the previous chapter, Putin no longer seeks to play a cooperative role in the liberal international order. He wants to maintain Russia's veto in the UNSC, but beyond that, he is pursuing radical revision, if not outright destruction, of most existing security arrangements. Putin is especially fixated on undermining NATO. And in these endeavors, Putin wants Xi to join him. According to Chinese officials, Russia has offered to act as the ice-breaking ship and then allow China to follow in its wake.[50] To date, however, Xi has not demonstrated a desire to return to the laws of the jungle. In the short run, Putin's invasion of Ukraine has distracted American and European leaders from the Asian theater, which benefits Xi. In the long run, however, Chinese officials worry privately—and a few Chinese experts on Russia in public—that Putin's war in Ukraine will drag on for years with inconclusive results and thereby weaken Russia as a partner against the West.[51]

MULTILATERAL ECONOMIC INSTITUTIONS

Xi's true intentions regarding the economic global order are hard to know. The best Sinologists in the world argue intensely about them.[52] Some warn that Xi aims to take over the global economy.[53] Others contend that Chinese leaders wield economic statecraft primarily to maintain Chinese domestic economic growth and not to pursue hegemonic domination of the entire world.[54] Those of us who are not members of the CCP's Politburo Standing Committee must admit that we do not know what Xi is plotting behind closed doors. The reason the academic debate about Xi's preferences is so divided and intense is that the data to support alternative hypotheses are so thin.

So instead, we should focus on what Xi does. In this domain, he is doing a lot. Compared to their actions regarding security institutions, Xi and his agents are far more innovative and revisionist, threatening the status quo regarding many multilateral economic organizations. However, compared to the Soviet playbook during the Cold War, China's actions are not nearly as aggressive, destructive, or confrontational. Soviet communist leaders were not seeking a voice in the IMF, the World Bank, or other US-anchored organizations—they wanted to destroy these organizations. It is the opposite for Chinese leaders. Xi wants a greater say in how these institutions operate so that he can tilt them in favor of China's preferred policies. Xi does not want to destroy them because they are too beneficial to the Chinese economy. After Mao's death, new leaders like Deng Xiaoping and Hua Guofeng abandoned the rigid dichotomy of planned versus market economy, embraced market reforms, pursued integration into the global economy, and sought to cooperate with multilateral economic institutions. Over two decades, these efforts culminated in China joining the World Trade Organization in 2001. No other country has benefited more from the WTO or the liberal international economic order than communist China. Why would Chinese leaders want to destroy something that has supported China's prosperity so much?

As Beijing continues engaging with multilateral economic institutions, however, Xi wants to insulate Chinese economic power from this US-led architecture and coercive American economic statecraft. Part of his strategy for doing so is what he calls "dual circulation," a set of policies aimed at decoupling the Chinese domestic economy from the international one. Another part of his strategy is the creation of *new* multilateral economic organizations independent of American influence. Cleverly, the CCP does not require exclusivity as a condition for countries to join its international economic organizations. That allows states to have one foot in the old institutional order created long ago by the United States and another in the new architecture anchored by China.

This Chinese dual-pronged strategy of changing existing multilateral economic organizations while also creating new economic clubs independent from the United States is much more nuanced and sophisticated than the more blunt, aggressive challenge to the liberal international order posed by the Soviet Union during the Cold War. Regarding its new economic clubs, China today can offer significantly greater economic incentives to participants than anything provided by Moscow during the Cold War. That makes this part of the Chinese strategy most dangerous to American national interests.

REVISING THE STATUS QUO

For decades China benefited from the global economic architecture created by the United States at the end of World War II. But then the 2008 global financial crisis cast doubt in Beijing on the resilience of the American economic model at home and its international institutions supporting capitalism abroad. The Chinese economy weathered this storm much better than its peers in the West, which offered the PRC opportunities to assume a more significant leadership role in the governance of the global economy, especially within the newly created G20—a multilateral institution made up of representatives from the world's twenty largest economies. Advocates for the Chinese model argued that the world needed a "reglobalisation process" under Chinese leadership.[55]

Since the 2008 crisis, Beijing has advocated for the G20 to take on a more significant role in global economic governance. At the G20's creation, many in the West predicted that it would replace the G8 (now the G7 again after Russia's departure) as the most consequential body governing the global economy. In 2010, CCP leader Hu Jintao argued that the G20 needed to become the "premier platform for advancing international economic cooperation."[56] At the G20 summit in Hangzhou in 2016, Xi asserted that "it is necessary to transform the G-20 from a crisis-responding mechanism to a long-term governance mechanism."[57]

The PRC's desire to elevate the G20 was part of a broader push to change international economic institutions to better reflect the new balance of economic power in the world. At the World Economic Forum in Davos in 2017, Xi argued, "There is a growing call from the international community for reforming the global economic governance system . . . Emerging markets and developing countries deserve greater representation and voice."[58] In 2024, Xi brazenly claimed that China was the only country capable of leading this global governance system reform. He said, "Among the world's major countries, China has the best track record with respect to peace and security . . . Every increase of China's strength is an increase of the prospects of world peace."[59]

China has achieved some results in reshaping the old international economic order. For instance, Xi successfully advocated for greater Chinese influence in the IMF, including increased use of China's currency, the renminbi.[60] Xi has tried to assert more influence in international standards-setting bodies, especially those focused on emerging technologies and big data, pressing all the time for the adoption of Chinese standards.[61] In addition, Beijing has played an active role in expanding Chinese influence in the World Health Organization, using its new leverage to evade accountability for the COVID-19 pandemic. The WHO's director general Tedros Ghebreyesus consistently downplayed the seriousness of the virus and deflected Chinese responsibility for the virus's spread. Chinese officials have also assumed leadership roles in the International Civil Aviation Organization, the International Telecommunication Union, the Food and Agriculture Organization, the Industrial Development Organization, and Interpol to bend these international organizations to better support Chinese interests. With some success, Xi and Chinese diplomats have positioned China as a more responsible stakeholder within the United Nations than the United States in pursuing the UN's seventeen sustainable development goals.[62] Xi even tried to inject some CCP socialist ideas into discussions of global economic governance, asserting, for instance, that "facts have repeatedly told us that Marx and Engels's analysis of the basic contradiction of capitalist society is not outdated, nor is the historical materialist view that capitalism will inevitably perish and socialism will inevitably triumph outdated"[63] and claiming China wanted to "make the global governance system more fair and equitable."[64] Deng never said such things about global capitalism when he was pursuing opening up.

As with China's contradictory actions regarding adherence to international security institutions, China often displays hypocrisy regarding multilateral economic institutions. Xi and other Chinese leaders delivered stirring speeches about the virtues of responsible global economic governance at Davos, but in practice, Chinese firms cut corners, ignore rules, and wield political power for financial gain in ways that violate core tenets of the WTO and the liberal international economic order more generally.[65] Intellectual property theft, industrial espionage, forced technology transfer, subsidized support for state-owned enterprises, trade retaliation, and restricted market access prove that Chinese leaders and their economic agents frequently abuse the system they claim to be respecting and reforming.[66]

Violating laws, rules, and norms of international institutions does not necessarily mean that a country seeks their destruction. If that were the case, we would have to conclude that the United States seeks the destruction of the liberal international order because US leaders have also ignored the multilateral bodies that undergird this system many times. So far, Xi and the CCP are acting as muddling reformers, not militant revolutionaries, regarding the existing global economic system. Xi and his inner circle still recognize that multilateral economic institutions provide permissive conditions for China's economic development. They also understand that China's domestic economic challenges cannot be addressed through complete decoupling from the global economy or destroying the existing international economic order.

No country would suffer more from rapid disengagement than China. Even the breakdown of the US economy would damage Chinese economic interests. During the first rounds of the 2025 tariff war between the United States and China, Xi imposed substantial tariffs on American goods in response to Trump's new tariffs on Chinese goods, but also signaled that

China did not want this tit-for-tat pattern to escalate indefinitely. Soviet communist leaders aspired to destroy the world capitalist system; CCP leaders seek to maintain the benefits they accrue from participation in the world capitalist system while leveraging China's growing economic power to change the system in ways even more favorable to the PRC's economic interests. In this domain of US-China competition, the Cold War metaphor distorts our understanding more than it illuminates.

A PARALLEL ECONOMIC ORDER

The 2008 financial crisis sent a powerful signal to CCP leaders about the need to create their own multilateral economic architecture outside the American-led system.[67] Since 2008, Chinese leaders have launched new initiatives and created new economic clubs that directly link parts of the world, especially the developing world, to the Chinese economy. This network of organizations is vast and includes most prominently the Shanghai Cooperation Organization, the Regional Comprehensive Economic Partnership, and BRICS. Chinese leaders proclaim proudly that collectively, the BRICS economies represent a more significant share of the global economy than the American-anchored G7. In Europe, China also anchors the 17 + 1 (now the 14 + 1, after the departure of three Baltic countries), which is China's confab for structuring economic and cultural cooperation with Central and Eastern Europe. Elsewhere in the world, they have established the Forum for China-Africa Cooperation, the China–Arab States Cooperation Forum, the China and the Community of Latin American States, the Conference on Interaction and Confidence Building Measures in Asia (CICA), and the China–Central Asia Summit. China takes a leadership position in all these organizations, and the US is not a member of any of them.[68] While most of these organizations focus on economic cooperation, some have security components as well, among them the SCO as well as the CICA.[69] As described already in chapter 8, the CCP has created new major multilateral assistance and investment organizations independent of the US, including the Belt and Road Initiative, the Asian Infrastructure Investment Bank, and the New Development Bank affiliated with BRICS. The aim of these economic networks and clubs is to create what Beijing calls a "Community of Common Destiny" that excludes the United States and other high-income countries.[70]

Another component of the PRC's strategy to foster global economic autonomy from the United States is promoting the international adoption of the RMB to weaken the dollar's dominance in the global financial system.[71] The Chinese-backed Cross-Border Interbank Payment System provides an alternative to the European-based Society for Worldwide Interbank Financial Telecommunication (SWIFT), which facilitates global bank transactions.[72] China launched the e-CNY (otherwise known as "digital RMB") to facilitate financial transactions outside of the existing international system, thereby reducing dependence on the West. By establishing these systems outside Western control, the PRC can more easily evade sanctions and expand its influence over Western companies working within China and with Chinese firms in third countries.[73] Chinese traders increasingly require that partners conduct transactions in RMB and use their banks for financing. In March 2023, the RMB became the most used currency in China's cross-border transactions.[74]

This independent Chinese economic architecture is distinct from the Soviet-anchored system of global economic order in two respects. First, countries are not forced to choose one side only. Second, there is no strict ideological requirement for a regime to interact with Chinese-led institutions. During the Cold War, countries generally had to join the economic clubs of one superpower only. Today, Chinese leaders allow countries to participate in both the US-anchored liberal international order and their emerging suite of organizations. That policy is more lenient than Putin's conditionality regarding his Eurasian Economic Union, which does not allow its members to join the EU. Countries can obtain financing from both the AIIB and the World Bank. Countries that accept BRI projects are not pressured to stop working with the IMF. Participants in China's multilateral economic world are not required to be dictatorships or adopt a Chinese governance model. Many democracies, and even some American allies, were founding members of AIIB. Recipients of AIIB funding and BRI projects are a mix of democracies and autocracies.

This flexible Chinese approach makes it more challenging, if not impossible, for the United States to oppose or weaken China's new economic clubs, especially as democratic countries and American allies benefit from association with these systems, and in the second Trump term, the United States increasingly threatens its economic partners with tariffs and other coercive measures (including, in the case of Panama, Denmark, Canada, and Gaza, even annexation). Some of Beijing's agreements are actual win-win outcomes. The fact that the United States is not offering attractive alternative economic clubs for potential partners worldwide (as with the TPP) makes the challenge of constraining the influence of these Chinese-anchored organizations harder. It is difficult to beat something with nothing.

More recently, however, China has begun to overreach, especially when using its own coercive economic instruments. After China tried to strong-arm Lithuania for being too supportive of Taiwan, all three Baltic countries quit China's 17 + 1 initiative. Some European democracies have already quit or radically reduced their engagement in BRI. Conversely, the sudden expansion of BRICS to include several countries with close ties to the United States along with the BRI's growing reach has sparked new debates in Washington about ways to contain the expansion of these Chinese economic clubs. Just weeks into Trump's second term, his administration compelled Panama to quit BRI. Over the next four years, we should expect more pressure on countries from Trump and his team to choose sides.

ASPIRATION VS. IMPACT

Chinese leaders complain about American hegemony in the world economy but have not articulated a clear alternative.[75] If they ever do, they still lack the capabilities to construct a new global economic order. Chinese achievements in a handful of new, independent economic clubs like SCO and BRICS should not be interpreted yet as the seeds of a new international system. As China continues to grow as a great power, it is not inevitable that it will push the United States out of its leading role in the global economy. I think it is unlikely.

My biggest reason for optimism, as long as Trump does not dismantle it, is America's extensive network—much more significant than China's—of powerful, wealthy economic allies who share our vision for maintaining the *liberal* international order. Nine of the world's ten largest economies are democracies, and none of these nine are interested in a global economic order dominated by China. These countries are not using Chinese RMB for all financial transactions, saving their reserves in Chinese banks, or defending property rights in Chinese courts. The US dollar remains the currency of choice for most countries. Should China ever attempt to unilaterally destroy the current system, other powerful actors will resist. While many lower-income countries complain about American hegemony, they also have signaled little enthusiasm for a Chinese-dominated international economic order. Despite developing countries' criticism of the IMF, the World Bank, and the WTO, few of them want to see these institutions disappear.

It is too early to judge the long-term impact of China's new multilateral economic organizations. The BRICS' rapid expansion could trigger more significant internal tensions—among the new members are bitter rivals such as Saudi Arabia and Iran. The BRICS bank—the NDB—has struggled with transparency, fund disbursement, and turmoil among member countries. The SCO has failed to generate a positive economic agenda, partly because of the Russian-Chinese rivalry in Central Asia. While AIIB functions efficiently like other multilateral development banks, Xi's signature initiative—BRI—is in trouble, overextended, and triggering backlashes in several countries. In 2022, the World Bank estimated that 60 percent of BRI loans were to countries in financial distress.[76] Strikingly, AIIB rarely finances BRI projects because they are too risky. Chinese aspirations to build an alternative global economic system may already have exceeded capabilities.

THE ENDURING CONDITION OF ECONOMIC ENTANGLEMENT

The size of the Chinese economy and its connectivity with the rest of the world are unprecedented, even as the latter has recently declined. Because of rising income levels, Chinese domestic consumption has begun to account for a larger share of the national economy, thereby reducing reliance on exports.[77] Great power competition has driven decoupling, as both US and Chinese leaders now challenge the wisdom of overreliance on the other. The Trump and Biden administrations accelerated these trends by imposing tariffs, restricting Chinese investment in the United States, incentivizing supply chain diversification, and placing greater controls on technology and data transfers to China. China's leaders have responded by imposing tariffs of their own, providing subsidies to domestic manufacturers of electric vehicles, solar panels, and many other products, placing restrictions on foreign investors to push foreign car makers out of the Chinese market, and imposing restrictions on the sale of critical minerals to the United States. This trajectory of decoupling between the two largest economies will likely continue for decades. In his second term, Trump seems determined to accelerate it.

And yet, despite these pressures and increasingly restrictive policies, the American and Chinese economies remain intertwined—a condition that will also likely endure for decades. The value of goods traded between the two countries has increased in all but three of the past twenty-five years.[78] The US remains China's most important individual trading partner. China ranks as the third-highest importer of American goods, after only Mexico and Canada. In the wake of Xi's COVID-19 restrictions and amid political pressure for supply chain diversity, many US firms started to rethink their investment strategies in China. Still, few companies already operating in China want to leave the Chinese market altogether. The market is just too big and valuable. And they most certainly do not want to see their competitors worldwide fill the void. American tech companies are especially concerned that export restrictions on their products will help their European and Asian competitors while doing little to slow Chinese technological development.

Even if Chinese and American leaders wanted to decouple completely, it is not obvious that they *could*. China and the US remain intertwined through debt financing. China is the second-largest holder of American debt, with almost $784 billion in US Treasury bonds by February of 2025.[79] This imbalance might suggest that the US government is highly dependent on China. Still, the dependence goes both ways: Beijing needs to park money in US Treasury bonds as a means for depressing the value of the yuan, a key policy instrument for expanding Chinese exports, and as a hedge against Chinese economic volatility. Any sudden Chinese divestment from these US Treasury bonds big enough to damage the US economy would also derail the Chinese economy. Interdependence is a two-way street. The same is true of global supply chains. Apple products are designed in the US but mostly manufactured in China. American and European pharmaceutical companies depend heavily on components from China. The robotics industry is also deeply intertwined between the US and China. The biggest global producers of microchips operate factories inside China, obtain inputs from China, and sell to Chinese firms—even after American and Western initiatives, like the CHIPS Act, created incentives to decouple this sector. This level of integration cannot be changed overnight without doing serious damage to both economies.

Many American analysts assume that interdependence with China is always a liability. But interdependence, if appropriately managed, can be a source of stability too.[80] Soviet leaders did not have to factor in trade or investment losses, supply chain disruptions, or energy embargoes when deciding to invade Hungary in 1956, Czechoslovakia in 1968, or Afghanistan in 1979. Compared to China, the post-Soviet Russian economy was far less integrated into the global economy when Putin decided to invade Georgia in 2008 and Ukraine in 2014 and 2022. After witnessing foreign investor flight and Western sanctions in response to Putin's invasion of Ukraine in 2022, Chinese leaders must know that an invasion of Taiwan will generate even more severe negative consequences for their economy.

We also should not assume that entanglement benefiting China always harms the United States. The economic exchange between the two countries is often still win-win, not zero-sum. The US economy represents 24 percent of the global economy, a percentage that has stayed roughly the same for decades. China's share of the global economy has been rising, but not at America's expense. China's economy grew faster because of interactions with the US economy and integration into the global economy, but the US economy benefited from China's economic rise as well. Specific individuals in the American economy, especially American workers in manufacturing jobs, suffered from China's rise, triggering a political backlash that helped Trump win the presidential elections in 2016 and 2024.[81] It is not obvious, however, that a strategy to suppress and isolate the Chinese economy would have saved those blue-collar jobs. Other rising economies would have likely filled the void. In addition, recent studies of the "China shock" on American jobs have shown that increased services-related employment offset losses in manufacturing jobs.[82] And while workers in manufacturing jobs certainly suffered—and should have received more support in transitioning to new, high-quality opportunities—American consumers also benefited from lower prices of goods made in China. To argue, as some American politicians now do, that economic interaction with China was a disaster for the American economy is inaccurate. During this period of growing US-China trade and investment, the American economy grew more rapidly than any other developed economy, bringing the US to seventh place in the world regarding GDP per capita.

Despite policy pushes from Beijing and Washington to strengthen economic independence and accelerate decoupling, some interdependence will remain for a long time. Neither country has enough economic power to isolate the other, let alone destroy or subjugate it. The United States will not become a tributary state subservient to the Middle Kingdom. The PRC will not be excised from the global economy. Learning how to further benefit from or at least manage economic entanglement will remain a challenge for American leaders for decades. How to do so more effectively is discussed in the final prescriptive section of this book.

MULTILATERAL POLITICAL INSTITUTIONS

Chinese leaders have pursued a more antagonistic approach to multilateral institutions supporting liberal democratic values.[83] When China was weaker, Beijing paid lip service to values promoted by the West. But as China has become more powerful, leaders have increasingly challenged the idea that Western ideas of democracy and liberalism are universal values. In the Xi era, Chinese officials publicly signal support for the international order, but they do not pledge allegiance to the *liberal* international order. Beijing rejects the notion that the US should have, what they call, the unilateral power to define the concepts of democracy and human rights, framing US-led campaigns promoting these ideas as imperial projects. As Chinese diplomat Yang Jiechi argued in 2021, "I don't think the overwhelming majority of countries in the world would recognize the universal values advocated by the United States or that the opinion of the United States could represent international public opinion."[84] Xi argues that there are many forms of democracy that do not conform to the American definition, among them the CCP's new favorite phrase—the PRC's "whole-process people's democracy."

Much like Putin, Xi abhors US democracy promotion efforts, accusing the US of fomenting color revolutions in Serbia, Georgia, and Ukraine and funding pro-democracy movements in Burma, Hong Kong, and across

Southeast Asia in the Milk Tea Alliance. Beijing stresses the failures of US regime-change actions, especially the invasion of Afghanistan and Iraq and the US-led military intervention in Libya to protect—allegedly, in Beijing's view—civilians in Benghazi. As former vice deputy foreign minister Le Yucheng argued regarding alleged American-led interference during the Arab Spring, "Were they really [aiming] to protect human rights in these countries? I think they openly produced human rights disasters."[85]

Chinese leaders seek to gain respect for Chinese values (as defined by them), such as the importance of patriotism, sovereignty, and meritocracy. Beijing officials prioritize the interests of the state and society over the interests of the individual.[86] Rhetorically, current Chinese leaders also prioritize general economic development over individual rights. Rather than emphasizing the ideological differences between autocrats and democrats, Chinese leaders focus on the divide between the Global North and the Global South, which pits the "exploited" China and the developing world against the alleged imperial developed world.

Xi and his government aspire to neutralize the international system's ability to hold national governments, including China's, accountable for domestic human rights violations.[87] To achieve this objective, Beijing has pursued leadership positions within multilateral organizations focused on human rights to dilute their effectiveness.[88] For example, China joined the UN Human Rights Council to hinder the group's criticism of autocracies.[89] Following a letter from nearly two dozen UN members criticizing Chinese repressive policies in Xinjiang, Beijing countered with a statement of support from over fifty backers lauding China's "remarkable achievements in the field of human rights," deflected calls for an independent investigation into abuses in Xinjiang, and blocked the Office of the UN High Commission for Human Rights from having a presence inside China. CCP leaders have maintained a loose alliance of roughly fifty countries called the "Like-Minded Group of Developing Countries" to coordinate collective responses to alleged attacks from countries in the developed world.[90] Xi expects countries benefiting from Chinese investments not to criticize their domestic human rights abuses within international forums; he demands silence from Arab countries about China's repression of Muslims in Xinjiang. Strikingly, after China helped to rebuild the Piraeus Port in Athens, the Greek government split ranks with other European democracies and refrained from criticizing China's human rights record at the United Nations.[91]

Chinese efforts to shape international political norms have been especially aggressive in the digital space. In the name of "cyber sovereignty," PRC leaders have pressed the international community to recognize their prerogative to control the flow of information within their country as well as their right to store and control data generated by people and companies within their borders.[92] These arguments have gained support from many other dictatorships, especially those within multilateral organizations anchored by China. China's assertion of sovereignty over the Chinese internet has helped to erode internet freedom globally, effectively segmenting a system that once aspired to be open and universal. Chinese companies closely tied to the state, like TikTok, have taken advantage of more laissez-faire American data collection norms and laws, allowing them to harvest massive amounts of data on US citizens. In contrast, American companies are blocked from doing the same in China.[93] However, that imbalance may be ending, as American leaders increasingly see the risks of allowing Chinese-owned social media companies to operate freely in the United States.

In these battles against liberal values within multilateral institutions, China has an ideological ally in Russia. In 2021, the two countries released a joint statement that emphasized shared views on global governance and rejected the West's definition of human rights, declaring that "there is no single standard of democracy."[94] The following year, Putin and Xi released a joint manifesto on shared values for global order, stating that "certain States' attempts to impose their own 'democratic standards' on other countries . . . prove to be nothing but flouting of democracy and go against the spirit and true values of democracy."[95] China and Russia have worked closely within multilateral organizations to assert their claims to sovereignty on the internet.

Chinese cooperation on international norms regarding artificial intelligence may be more promising. In March 2024, China endorsed a US-sponsored resolution at the United Nations General Assembly called "Seizing the Opportunities of Safe, Secure, and Trustworthy Artificial Intelligence Systems for Sustainable Development."[96] UN General Assembly resolutions have little binding authority. Still, the fact that the US and China supported general principles of AI use was a small step in what will be a long process of trying to govern the use of this revolutionary technology.

Efforts like this are small examples of a larger trend: Xi and his comrades can work to move China "close to the world's stage" without removing the United States from that same stage. As Xi suggested in 2022 after a meeting with President Biden, "The world is big enough for the two countries to develop themselves and prosper together."[97] He said something similar when meeting with Secretary of State Blinken in April 2024 in Beijing: "China is happy to see the confident, open, prosperous, and thriving United States. We hope the US can also look at China's development in a positive light."[98] Like most autocratic leaders, Xi is concerned first and foremost with maintaining his regime's power and legitimacy, which to date has required cooperation with the US-led existing international order, not its destruction. That is different from the Cold War. Whether that Chinese approach is easier or more challenging to manage for the United States, however, is a more complex question, one tackled at length in the final section of this book.

Part III

THE FUTURE

Chapter 12

LEARNING FROM COLD WAR MISTAKES

WINNERS GET TO write history, so we Americans have triumphantly penned a heroic role for ourselves in defeating communism and ending the Cold War. That narrative is partially true. American leaders, their allies, and their partners in the democratic world pursued several successful policies that helped the United States and democratic world prevail over the Soviet Union and the communist world, as discussed in the next chapter. At the same time, pro-democratic movements in communist countries in Eastern Europe and the former Soviet Union played the pivotal role in defeating communism, an essential lesson for decision-makers in Washington when they are devising new policies for dealing with autocratic China and Russia today. While winning the long game, however, US policymakers also made mistakes during the Cold War—errors that resulted in millions of deaths, wasted economic resources, and damaged America's reputation as a champion of liberal, democratic values.[1] In our new era of great power competition, we cannot afford to make such costly mistakes again; we have fewer resources and less will to contain China and Russia than we had during the Cold War. We must learn from our errors in the Cold War, so we don't repeat them today.

OVERESTIMATING THE ENEMY

After the Cold War ended, the Soviet Union's defeat looked inevitable. In hindsight, some claimed that the Soviet Union was never a significant threat, Soviet technology was always inferior, the Soviet economy was perpetually in shambles, and communism worldwide was not popular. This revisionist history has made it easier for some policymakers and analysts today to claim that the Chinese threat is much more dire than the Soviet challenge ever was. This assessment is wrong.

Many have either forgotten or never knew that for most of the second half of the twentieth century, US leaders and the American people were truly frightened by Soviet military power, technology, allies, and communist ideas. These fears sometimes led them to overestimate Soviet capabilities and misallocate resources.

First and foremost, US leaders and society overestimated Soviet military power. For instance, the Soviet Union's successful launch of Sputnik in 1957 scared Americans into believing that we were woefully behind in military technology, specifically intercontinental ballistic missiles. US leaders believed (or claimed to believe) there was a "missile gap" with the Soviets and therefore expended vast resources to build up launch systems for nuclear warheads—intercontinental ballistic missiles in particular—to "catch up" with the Soviet Union. Moscow responded in turn, resulting in a massive, expensive, dangerous, and unnecessary arms race. With a more accurate assessment of the Soviet Union's missile capabilities, the United States could have pivoted to arms control or developed more survivable delivery systems much earlier. In retrospect, the United States should have deployed more nuclear weapons on submarines and airplanes and fewer in ground-based silos, which are usable only as first-strike weapons and cannot survive a Soviet attack. But because the Soviets had so many ICBMs, American leaders thought we needed them too. To this day, we are still irrationally bound to a norm of precise parity with Moscow regarding nuclear weapons. Just because they have 1,550 deployed nuclear warheads, do we need the same number? Wouldn't we be just fine with 1,500?

Second, we overestimated the size and strength of the Soviet economy until the waning years of the Cold War. Foreshadowing debates about the China economic model today, some analysts speculated that the Soviet centralized command system was better at producing technological breakthroughs than our decentralized market system. Soviet dictators could channel more resources into the military-industrial complex than American leaders, who were constrained by voters' preferences, or so the argument went. American academics and intelligence analysts even forecast that the Soviet economy would eventually overtake the American economy.

Nobel laureate Paul Samuelson wrongly predicted in his famous textbook *Economics: An Introductory Analysis* that the Soviet economy would reach parity with the US economy in the 1980s.[2] As he wrote in the 1961 edition of this classic text, "The Soviet economy is proof that, contrary to what many skeptics had earlier believed, a socialist command economy can function and even thrive."[3]

As in the 1930s, when the US endured a crushing depression while Stalin's communist system generated fantastic growth, American economic woes in the 1970s compelled some to argue that the United States needed to grow the state's role in managing the economy. A Republican president, Richard Nixon, introduced wage and price controls. We now know that these assessments about the vigor of the Soviet economy were wrong and state interventions in the market economy unnecessary. Today, we are having a similar debate about whether the United States needs to adopt Chinese economic methods—including protectionism and subsidies for some sectors—to compete effectively with the PRC over the long haul.

Third, Americans exaggerated the appeal of communism. In the 1970s and early 1980s, communism seemed to be on the march, and democracy appeared to be in decline. In that decade, Marxist-Leninist regimes seized power in Vietnam, Laos, and Cambodia in Southeast Asia; Angola, Mozambique, and Zimbabwe in southern Africa; in Afghanistan in South Asia; and even in America's backyard, in Nicaragua. In 1979, the US lost a critical ally in the Middle East, Iran's shah, Mohammad Reza Pahlavi, to conservative theocrats, which the Soviets framed as a victory for their side.[4] In the late 1960s and early 1970s, the practice of American democracy at home faced multiple challenges: violent clashes around the civil rights movement and anti-war demonstrations, multiple assassinations of prominent political leaders, the proliferation of radical groups like the Weathermen and Black Panthers, and the resignation of President Nixon. In 1979, President Jimmy Carter delivered an alarming speech "about a fundamental threat to American democracy . . . It is a crisis of confidence. The erosion of our confidence in the future is threatening to destroy the social and the political fabric of America."[5] In retrospect, we know that these estimates of the popularity of communism and the decline of democracy were inaccurate. Just several years later, the Soviet Union collapsed.

ASSESSING CHINA—ACCURATELY

As we did with the Soviet Union, we risk overestimating the threat of China today. When rising powers challenge incumbent great powers, miscalculations driven by fear occur often. For decades, of course, we made the opposite mistake. American leaders underestimated China's economic and military power rise and naively hoped the Chinese Communist Party would gradually democratize. Leninist parties do not do that, as we should have learned while observing the disruptive, revolutionary transitions from communism to democracy in Eastern Europe and the Soviet Union at the end of the 1990s.[6] A correction was needed regarding assessments of the Chinese military, economic, and ideological threat.[7] And vigilance is still needed regarding accurate net assessments of Chinese power and intentions.

However, we have now overshot the target. There has been too much groupthink in the opposite direction. China is not "the greatest threat that the American nation and its system of Western liberal democratic government have faced since the American Revolution."[8] China is not an "existential threat" to the United States. Xi does not seek nor have the power to eliminate the United States from the planet (that is literally what an existential threat is). China does not seek to export its communist dictatorship to the entire world. China does not aspire to destroy the current international system and replace the United States as the world's only hegemon, anchoring a coercive communist global order run by Beijing. China does not seek "nothing less than world domination."[9] These overstatements about Chinese intentions and capabilities echo similar exaggerations of Soviet power and aims during the Cold War. American strategy for dealing with the real China challenge will be more successful if we do not make the Cold War mistake of overestimating the threat again.

Without question, as previous chapters have discussed in detail, the PRC represents the most significant challenge by far to American security and economic interests in the twenty-first century. Containing that threat effectively must be the paramount objective of American foreign policy for the next several decades. China's rising military power is real and threatening. Alarmingly, the PRC already has some military advantages over the United States, such as the number of soldiers, ships, and missiles. Every week, or so it seems, the Chinese military is announcing the successful construction of a monstrous amphibious assault ship, testing a new sixth-generation fighter jet, and deploying an accurate anti-ship ballistic missile.[10] China is closing the gap with the United States in almost every other dimension of military power, including in new emerging technologies such as AI, quantum computing, and synthetic biology. In Asia, the military balance of power is reaching parity between China and the United States and our allies. Yet overestimating the Chinese military threat will produce bad American policy responses and scare Americans into devoting our limited resources to unnecessary projects.

Today, some analysts argue that Chinese military spending is twice its reported size, hovering around seven hundred billion dollars.[11] Is that true? Or are these numbers meant to frighten Americans and our allies into spending more on defense?[12] We need to get this assessment right, free of partisan politics. The same is true regarding China's nuclear buildup. We must hedge for the possibility that they are seeking parity with us but not assume they want to or will achieve that goal quickly. Some scholars argue that Xi does not aim to reach parity with the United States.[13] Who is right? Again, we must make this assessment with as much precision as possible. Engaging in a nuclear arms race with China today like we did with the Soviet Union during the Cold War will be costly and unnecessary. Likewise, American evaluations of China's AI, quantum computing, synthetic biology, autonomous weapons, hypersonic missiles, and other cutting-edge technologies must be done precisely and soberly, devoid of the hyperbole and fear during the Cold War that cast the Red Army and the Soviet military-industrial complex as way more capable than they turned out to be.

We also should not underestimate our capabilities. China is closing the military gap, but the United States is still significantly ahead regarding nuclear weapons, defense spending, the quality of weapons and soldiers, and emerging technologies. When allies are added to the equation, the balance of power tilts even more significantly toward the United States.[14] In addition, the American global military footprint—including bases, arms sales, and military-to-military agreements—is vastly greater than China's international reach. Even the assumption that China is more powerful in Asia should be interrogated, especially when America's allies and partners in Asia are included in the assessment.

Latent capability also is not actual power. When assessing Chinese capabilities for invading Taiwan, we should remember how wrong our initial calculations were regarding Russian military power in Ukraine—we counted the number of soldiers and the rubles spent on defense and concluded that the Russian invading army would conquer Ukraine in a few weeks. Chinese soldiers have not fought in decades. Chinese weapons have never been tested in battle. And maybe Chinese defense spending is not as efficient as many assume.

As discussed in the next chapter, American policymakers and our allies rightly spent significant percentages of their GDP on our military to contain the Soviet Union. We must do so again. Defense-spending levels in the democratic world today are way too low. However, overspending on defense and diverting resources from other vital elements of American power, such as education and infrastructure, must also be avoided. There is a Goldilocks equilibrium that will allow us to deter Chinese power without wasting resources on unnecessary military weapons.

Regarding the economic balance of power, the Chinese economy is much bigger and more successful than the Soviet economy. That is a scary reality, maybe the most frightening fact of our new era of great power competition in contrast to the Cold War. China's scientific and technological capabilities have outpaced anything the Soviets achieved (even if we did not know so precisely at the time). Already, Chinese manufacturing capabilities vastly surpass American manufacturing capabilities. That never happened during the Cold War or even during World War II. Some Chinese open-AI models may be as good as the best released by American companies.[15] China already dominates global markets for solar and batteries and is likely to do the same in many other high-tech sectors, including electric vehicles, chips, and display screens.

At the same time, we should not overestimate Chinese economic prowess, especially in the long term. For instance, we should not assume that the Chinese economy will overtake ours, as many predicted for the Soviet economy during the Cold War. We made the same mistake regarding the Japanese threat in the 1980s and early 1990s, when Japan's share of the global economy reached roughly 18 percent, including 22 percent of the world's manufacturing, which is roughly where China is today.[16] Some even predicted war between the "declining" United States and the "rising" Japan.[17] Sound familiar? We should also remember that the Chinese economy grew fastest when CCP leaders aggressively implemented market reforms.[18] Xi is now moving in the opposite direction, expanding the state's role in the economy, stifling entrepreneurship, repressing domestic consumption, and limiting the role of market forces and foreigners in the Chinese economy. These policy decisions are slowing growth. Moreover, China faces a monumental demographic crisis: Its population is growing slower, becoming older, and is unable to acquire the skills required for high-tech industries that would help China escape the middle-income trap. China's rural residents lack the education and health care needed to help push China from a middle-income to a high-income economy.[19] Overproduction, underconsumption, ballooning debt (especially at the regional government level and in real estate), growing inequality, and youth unemployment impede growth. As demonstrated by capital flight, emigration of businesspeople, the faltering consumer confidence index, and stagnant Chinese stock markets and bond prices, many Chinese nationals and foreign investors are now worried about the long-term performance of the Chinese economy.[20] More generally, recent public opinion polls in China show a big jump in the number of respondents who think they are poor because of unequal opportunities and an unfair economic system.[21] This is new and destabilizing.

We also should not underestimate our economic capabilities. As discussed in the next chapter, the American economy faces real challenges, especially with some imprudent and irrational economic policies of Trump's second administration. However, so far, compared to the rest of the developed world, US growth has remained robust. American companies—especially high-tech firms—are way more valuable, the US stock market outpaces all others, American financial markets are second to none, the dollar is still the world's currency, and US universities continue to lead the world. As currently constructed, the Chinese model is not outperforming the American model and faces many significant constraints for maintaining future growth.[22]

When assessing the Chinese threat accurately, we also should not assume that all Chinese economic growth adversely affects American national interests. Framing economic power in Manichaean zero-sum terms is counterproductive and unnecessary. Over the past four decades, the American economy has grown in part because of Chinese economic development, and vice versa.

In parallel to assessing military and economic capabilities accurately, we must try to understand Chinese intentions as best as we can, anchoring those assessments on Chinese actions and not just interpretations of speeches and statements. Our scholars and intelligence community must remain vigilant in trying to understand accurately Xi's preferences that threaten the United States and the free world but also not overestimate Chinese aspirations, like we sometimes did regarding the Soviet Union during the Cold War, for political purposes. We can and should take heart that, thus far, their efforts to promote communism globally are minimal, and even their actions to support autocratic regime change in other countries have been limited. Xi and the CCP are helping autocrats already in power and they devote significant resources to pursuing that objective. However, they have not yet used military force to overthrow a democracy and install an autocracy, let alone a Communist Party dictatorship. American leaders must realize that Xi and his comrades are focused first on using Leninist methods to hold on to power at home and are not trying very hard to export communist ideology.[23] While Xi has ruthlessly suppressed independent media, free and fair elections, and opposition movements and civil society in Hong Kong, and he has brazenly violated human rights in Xinjiang and Tibet, these actions are within the PRC's borders. This is different from Putin's military aggression abroad and different from Soviet belligerent behavior abroad too.

Unlike the Communist Party of the Soviet Union, Xi and the CCP are not devoting significant efforts to undermining democracy and capitalism in the developed world. Xi wants to weaken these democracies, especially the United States, but not overthrow them. Different from the Soviet autarkic command economy, the Chinese economy today needs successful capitalist economies (the US, Europe, Japan, South Korea, and so on) to continue to fuel domestic development. China is not trying to destroy the entire liberal international order because China benefits from that system.

I might be wrong. Xi and his comrades might secretly be plotting to transform all countries into communist regimes and rule the world by subjecting free countries to their repressive international institutions, dethroning the United States as the world's most powerful nation. When Xi was a young man, his worldview was shaped by Marx, Lenin, and other nineteenth-century Russian revolutionary writers, leading some to conclude that Xi remains a true revolutionary, committed "to undermine—and ultimately displace—Western ideas and institutions."[24] Over time, these alleged radical aspirations could drive China to undertake more revolutionary actions. As some have predicted, Xi could someday become the next Stalin.[25] However, if Xi does seek to transform all countries into Marxist-Leninist regimes or to rule the globe by replacing the United States as the world's sole hegemon and destroying the liberal international order, he is hiding his preferences extremely well and achieving few results. So far, observable CCP *actions* do not suggest a threat to global democracy and capitalism commensurate to the Soviets' stated goals and sometimes successful actions in expanding the communist autocratic world and undermining the capitalist democratic world. As discussed previously, Soviet-backed communism spread throughout the world in the 1970s. There is no parallel wave of Chinese-supported communism or even dictatorship advancing on every continent today.

ASSESSING RUSSIA—ACCURATELY

Our challenge in estimating Russian power in the twenty-first century is akin to our mistaken underestimations of Chinese Communist Party intentions and power at the beginning of the Cold War.[26] Back then, American leaders were surprised by the PRC's decision to intervene in the Korean War because they did not believe that the newly created People's Republic of China had the means to do so or that Mao had the will. Like our underestimates of Chinese power and intentions in the early years of the Cold War, American leaders made similar mistakes in underestimating Russian capabilities and Putin's belligerent intentions in the past two decades.

We then made the opposite mistake of overestimating Russian power in the run-up to Russia's invasion of Ukraine in February 2022, when American analysts inside and outside of the government wrongly assessed that it would be a matter of days or weeks before Russian soldiers reached downtown Kyiv.[27] The Biden administration evacuated our embassy in Kyiv and blew up our communications equipment there because they did not think we would be back anytime soon. That assessment proved incorrect. The Biden administration and the rest of the world also underestimated Ukrainian military power at the time, underscoring the limits of counting soldiers, guns, and spending as measures of military power without estimating intangibles like the will to fight.

Three years after Russia's tragic and barbaric invasion of Ukraine, the challenges of accurately estimating Russian power remain. Russia's military forces have suffered over seven hundred thousand casualties as well as massive losses in tanks, ships, and other weaponry.[28] However, because of the Kremlin's heavy investment in military spending and soldier recruitment, the Russian army is bigger and better armed than it was at the beginning of 2022. In 2024, Russian defense spending rose by an estimated 6.7 percent of Russia's GDP, a post-Soviet record high, making the war "the main driver of Russia's economic growth."[29] Putin claimed to have created half a million new jobs in the military-industrial complex, employing an estimated 3.5 million Russians, or 2.5 percent of the population.[30] To evade sanctions, supply chains were reconfigured and rerouted to secure key technological components through third countries.

If measuring Russian capabilities accurately remains challenging, Putin's intentions should never be underestimated again. In the early years of the Cold War, Mao lacked the means of his Soviet counterparts but still had an intense will to use those capabilities to pursue violent, ideological, revolutionary ends, including entering the Korean War, to the surprise of Washington officials. Putin is like Mao, a leader with more limited means than the other autocratic great power today but with much more will to use that power. Had we understood Putin's intentions more accurately in the 2000s, we could have expanded NATO faster or at least armed Ukraine earlier to deter Russian invasions in 2014 and 2022.

OVERREACH

In the long run, as discussed in the next chapter, the American strategy of containment during the Cold War succeeded. But along the way, US leaders defined this strategy in radically different ways and sometimes made costly mistakes in its implementation. At first, the US defined the containment mission too narrowly, and that emboldened our enemies to invade South Korea. After that mistake, however, we overcompensated and defined the containment mission too expansively. In reaction to the Korean War, advocates for global containment won over those promoting a more constrained scope.[31] In doing so, US strategists sometimes failed to distinguish nationalism from communism. As a former colony that fought a war of independence against an imperial power, the United States could have sided more aggressively with national liberation leaders in the era of decolonization that accelerated after the end of World War II. We should have been the natural allies for movements fighting for independence. After all, the Soviet Union was an empire that had conquered and colonized Estonians, Latvians, Ukrainians, Georgians, Tatars, Chechens, Tuvans, et cetera. However, because the Soviet Union often supplied liberation movements with weapons, training, and propaganda, many insurgents embraced communist ideas, at least rhetorically, and embraced communist parties as allies. Their commitment to communist ideas and their promoters was often shallow initially, but some of our overreactions helped deepen them.[32] Too many American presidents and national security strategists simplistically perceived nationalist liberation movements as communist surrogates.[33] As Michael Green observed regarding Vietnam, "A US strategy based on principles of self-determination and the Atlantic Charter might well have succeeded in Indochina as it had in Yugoslavia."[34]

Tragically, the exaggeration of the communist threat to American security interests resulted in the US fighting and prolonging an unnecessary war in Vietnam and giving military assistance to "freedom fighters" from Angola to Nicaragua. These actions of overreach were not necessary to win the Cold War. We must learn the bitter lessons of overreach and not repeat them today, especially regarding China. We need a measured and calibrated containment strategy for China and Russia. Knowing when to contain, when to ignore, and when to engage these autocratic powers, and having the wisdom to know the difference, will be a central challenge of effective US policymaking for decades to come.

Given the resource constraints of our current era and a population less enthusiastic about international engagement generally, US strategists must better distinguish between essential national security interests and peripheral concerns. American core interests are (1) to protect American territory, (2) to deter attacks on our allies globally, (3) to stop Russian annexation and imperial conquest in Europe, (4) to prevent war with the PRC over Taiwan, and (5) to preserve freedom of navigation in the South China Sea. Of course, the United States has many other security and economic interests around the world, but leaders in Beijing and Moscow must understand clearly our priorities. If everything is a priority, nothing is a priority. Signaling credible commitments to these strategic imperatives is critical to a successful strategy for containing China and Russia in the twenty-first century. Just as stopping Soviet actions everywhere and all the time was not necessary to win the Cold War, containing every Chinese action worldwide is not feasible or necessary today. Trying to do so will only distract us from our paramount goals and lead to the misallocation of resources. As Hal Brands has correctly observed, "Middle-ground approaches like containment are inherently unsatisfying. But in a long struggle, a strategy that gradually advances while avoiding disasters is probably good enough."[35] A Goldilocks strategy of containment, guided by our core interests, is what should be pursued now.

For starters, pursuing policies of imperial overreach such as annexing Greenland, Canada, the Panama Canal, or Gaza should be taken off the table immediately. We do not need to seize any of these territories to effectively contain China and Russia, and the very pursuit of these annexations would drain scarce resources, damage relations with allies, and seriously tarnish America's image abroad.

Choosing our battles wisely regarding economic competition with China is also critical. During the Cold War, the United States had substantial economic advantages over the Soviet Union and therefore could afford to spend money on supporting corrupt anti-communists and inefficient aid programs and still be okay. Today, we do not enjoy the same resource advantages over China as we did over the Soviet Union. Hence, we cannot frame every Chinese trade deal and investment project abroad as a threat to *vital* American security interests. In deciding when to contain, where to engage, and when to signal indifference, we must distinguish between Chinese economic activities purely for profit and those for political influence or ideological promotion. Does the adoption of Huawei technologies by NATO allies threaten US security? Yes, and thus it should be blocked. Does the installment of 5G Huawei technologies in Rwanda threaten US security? No, and thus it does not need to be blocked by all means necessary.

We should apply similar logic when deciding when and how to counter Xi's Belt and Road Initiative. Of course, US strategists should worry about Chinese investments in ports and infrastructure worldwide that can be used for military missions, and do their best to block their expansion. However, even regarding ports, not all Chinese investments are alike. The Chinese state-owned enterprise COSCO Shipping, which became the largest shareholder of Greece's biggest container port and Europe's busiest passenger port of Piraeus, facilitates commerce beneficial to Greeks and other American allies without exporting communism or autocracy or expanding the reach of the Chinese navy (yet). Many BRI projects aim to increase revenue for Chinese firms, and some even generate economic benefits for American partner countries. New roads in Asia and new airports in Africa do not inherently threaten US vital national interests. In addition, some BRI projects are bad investments with no hope of success. The American response to those kinds of projects should be to just get out of the way and let the Chinese fail on their own. When providing American economic assistance, if Trump does not completely shut down all forms of foreign aid, we must be careful not to let the containment of China override prudent economic practices. In pursuing global containment during the Cold War, American leaders misallocated economic assistance in ways that propped up alleged anti-communists but did not spur economic development or promote democratic reform.[36] We should learn that lesson from the previous century and not repeat it today.

Different from the Cold War, the American economy and the economies of our allies and partners sometimes benefit from interacting with the Chinese economy. Cutting off all trade and investment with the PRC—trying to return to the Cold War structure of two rigid and separate economic blocs—would produce catastrophic economic consequences for American companies and consumers. And attempting to tell countries to choose between the American bloc and the China bloc could easily expose American weakness, an outcome that would not advance American interests. If we try to pressure countries to join our bloc and cut off ties with China, countries like Indonesia, India, Brazil, Saudi Arabia, South Africa, Singapore, and Mexico will resist taking sides. For many US allies—Australia, Japan, and South Korea in Asia and many European allies—economic ties with China are too deep to be severed entirely. Spending diplomatic capital to achieve an unrealistic objective damages America's global standing. Again, a Goldilocks strategy of containment means not forcing all countries to choose sides regarding economic relations with us versus China but focusing more narrowly on containing Chinese economic activity abroad only when and where US vital national security interests are at stake.

As for Russia, the paramount component of a successful containment strategy should remain helping Ukraine stop Putin's army and then arming Ukraine sufficiently to deter a future attack. As discussed in more detail in the next chapter, American leaders must enhance NATO's military capability to strengthen deterrence. Pulling American soldiers out of Europe or leaving NATO altogether would be a catastrophic mistake and make future military conflicts with Putin's Russia, or even with NATO allies, more likely. But trying to contain every Russian military operation in Africa, the Middle East, the Caucasus, and Central Asia is not necessary. Letting the Russians fail on their own in these regions is part of an intelligent American strategy too. Russian indifference to Azerbaijan's conquest of Nagorno-Karabakh produced a real backlash from the Armenian population. That is good for the United States. The Wagner Group, a Russian mercenary army closely tied to the Kremlin, achieved some initial successes in helping autocrats in Africa. However, the backlash within some African countries has begun to grow in response to financial windfalls that these Russian agents received.[37] That is good for the United States too. Regarding competition between Russia and China in Central Asia, the United States should again get out of the way, let them clash, and look for new opportunities after leaders and citizens in the region tire of both Russian and Chinese coercive methods. The Russian retreat from Syria after Putin's puppet al-Assad fled to Moscow in the fall of 2024 served American national interests without us playing a significant role.

During the Cold War, Moscow's overreach in promoting Marxist-Leninist regimes worldwide weakened the Soviet Union. The invasion of Afghanistan proved exceptionally costly, but support for communist regimes in Cuba, Angola, Mozambique, Nicaragua, and Eastern Europe placed burdens on the Soviet economy as well, accelerating the end of the Cold War. Focused on expanding influence abroad, Soviet leader Leonid Brezhnev neglected his domestic economy, and the sustained period of stagnation—*zastoi*—eventually doomed the Soviet Union. Today, both Xi and Putin are overreaching, just like Brezhnev did, regarding using military force and providing economic assistance abroad while neglecting domestic economic problems.[38] We should let them continue to overreach, and make it more costly, without practicing overreach ourselves.

In retrospect, we know that stopping communism everywhere in the world was not necessary to win the Cold War. We did not have to try to contain communism in Cuba, Vietnam, or Angola. The dominoes metaphor animating our efforts to stop communism in the jungles of Vietnam to avoid it spreading to the streets of Berlin and San Francisco did not play out.[39] That is an important lesson to remember today. We can prevail in our competition with China and Russia without stopping or trying to stop their every move around the world.

AVOIDING McCARTHYISM

Another tragedy of containment overreach was the overexuberant search for enemies from within: McCarthyism. Too many innocent Americans were wrongly persecuted during this era. Some of the most talented Americans in the movie industry, science and technology, and the State Department were jailed or blacklisted. America's reputation as a free society also took a massive hit because of this witch hunt. The US government, including elected officials in Congress, acted just like their Soviet counterparts. We could have skipped this chapter of American history and still won the Cold War.

Today, we must avoid a replay of McCarthyism, especially regarding Americans of Chinese and Asian descent but also Russian immigrants. We cannot allow the suppression of free speech through deportations or cancellations of visas for international students. Some American politicians and commentators have even called for the banning of Chinese students in the United States. Some US states have already limited what properties

Chinese citizens can own, citing vague security concerns as justification. One American senator even called for limits on "Communist Chinese garlic" because it was allegedly "grown and produced with sewage and other unsanitary practices," a claim that turned out not to be true.[40] American leaders should not fear Chinese and Russian immigrants but encourage talented citizens from both countries to immigrate to the United States. The bigger the brain drains from both countries, the better. Of course, the FBI must increase its vigilance regarding spies, including those engaged in economic espionage. However, we want people to move to the free world, preferably with their financial resources and talented employees if they are from the private sector. As discussed in chapter 14, we must avoid using federal executive power to stifle debate among Americans over legitimate policy issues. If we deploy nondemocratic means to fight among ourselves, we have less focus and energy for China and Russia.

AIDING DICTATORS

During the Cold War, American leaders often prioritized the containment of communism over the support for democracy. In their fight against communists, American presidents and their administrations propped up dictators and supported the overthrow of leaders—sometimes even democratically elected leaders—who were considered too pink. In the name of containment, Washington maintained ties with and provided resources to dozens of very repressive dictatorships, including South Africa, Rhodesia (now Zimbabwe), Zaire (the Democratic Republic of the Congo), Chile, Brazil, Argentina, Saudi Arabia, Iran, Iraq, Vietnam, Indonesia, and even the People's Republic of China. At times, US policymakers directly undermined legitimate governments, such as when they supported coups against leaders in Iran in 1953, Guatemala in 1954, Brazil in 1964, Indonesia in 1965, and Chile in 1973.[41] The US also provided military and economic support to insurgents who had little or no affinity for democratic ideas in Angola, Cambodia, Nicaragua, El Salvador, and Afghanistan. Tragically, these policies sometimes helped precipitate the emergence of extreme, anti-democratic, and anti-American regimes, like the theocracies in Iran and Afghanistan. Perhaps not coincidentally, global democratic development during the Cold War slowed compared to earlier and later periods.[42]

In retrospect, we know that we did not have to prop up right-wing dictators or support coups against alleged anti-American leftists to win the Cold War. The Bay of Pigs—the US-supported operation to try to overthrow Fidel Castro in Cuba—was a mistake that helped to push Castro and his comrades toward a closer relationship with Moscow. We most certainly did not have to support the reprehensible apartheid regime in South Africa and the many ruthless generals and strongmen in Africa, Asia, Europe, and Latin America. These autocrats scared American leaders into believing that their demise would allow communist regimes loyal to Moscow to seize power. At times, that scenario did unfold, as in Vietnam, Cambodia, Laos, Angola, Mozambique, and Nicaragua. But much more often, it did not. Transitions to democracy in Spain, Portugal, and Greece did not bring to power anti-American communists. In Chile, the Philippines, and South Korea in the 1980s, autocrats with very close ties to Washington were all eventually pushed out of power, but the emergence of democracy in these countries did not allow communists to take over or undermine core US national security interests.[43] Likewise, the transition from apartheid to democracy in South Africa did not threaten US security or economic interests, even though Nelson Mandela and his African National Congress party had at the time deep ties to the Communist Party of South Africa and the Soviet Union.

In addition, military intervention, indirect assistance, covert operations, and support for coups in the name of communist containment undermined America's reputation as the leader of the free world. A different strategy to support decolonization, as Senator Kennedy proposed in 1957, that did not prop up anti-communist dictators might have helped end the Cold War sooner.[44]

These Cold War scars of hypocrisy still shape how some people, especially in the developing world, perceive the United States. For instance, Russia's invasion of Ukraine is an act of imperialism and recolonization, but American diplomats have failed to persuade many elites and societies in the developing world to accept this framework. As a champion of national liberation movements and decolonization during the Cold War, Moscow is given a pass for its imperial mission in Georgia and Ukraine from too many in Africa, Asia, Latin America, and the Middle East.

In our new era of great power competition with China and Russia today, the long-term costs of propping up dictators in the name of short-term containment benefits need to be calculated more precisely. We should not prop up autocrats just because they claim to be anti-Chinese or anti-Russian. Selling arms to Saudi Arabia and turning a blind eye to the killing of journalist Jamal Khashoggi sustains autocracy. So does deepening security ties with Vietnam while US officials pretend that its ruling Communist Party is reforming. All sorts of American companies sell products, including surveillance equipment and website-blocking tools, that aid autocrats, and they also purchase products from dictatorships, including China, which bolsters their hold on power. Tragically, too many American companies continued to operate in, pay taxes to, and trade with Russia after Putin invaded Ukraine in February 2022.[45] These companies are directly underwriting Putin's dictatorship in Russia and funding his war in Ukraine. US officials also failed to criticize coups in Egypt or Sudan. Demonstrating indifference to the most egregious anti-democratic act—a coup d'état—undermines America's reputation as a defender of freedom. And in America's contest with China and Russia, our nation's democratic values constitute one of our greatest advantages.

When we rightly tell the world to worry about the PRC's support of pro-Chinese autocracies but then support pro-American autocrats, the rest of the world sees our hypocrisy. That hypocrisy undermines our credibility when we press for the human rights of journalists in Iran, opposition leaders in Russia, and religious organizations in China. A wise first step for containing Chinese and Russian support for autocracy would be to get out of the same business. In our new age of great power competition, we are compelled again to engage with autocrats for some core security and economic reasons.[46] But we should do so only when absolutely necessary to advance the pursuit of essential interests and without pretending these autocratic leaders are reformers, closet democrats, or emerging liberals. We should also remember that liberal democracies—not dictatorships—have been and will remain our most reliable and enduring allies. Dictators either fall from power or change their minds quickly, unconstrained by democratic institutions and voting.

When American presidents and diplomats engage with autocratic leaders in Beijing and Moscow, they should also meet with civil society actors in or from these countries—dual-track diplomacy. Reagan perfected this strategy when he engaged with both Soviet government officials and societal leaders in his visit to Moscow in 1988, a historical analogy that should be emulated today.

POLITICIZING DEVELOPMENT AID

As discussed earlier, to help contain communism during the Cold War, the US developed extensive international economic-assistance programs, including the flagship United States Agency for International Development (USAID), founded by President John F. Kennedy in 1961. American aid providers did not attach strict conditions to aid for fear that the recipients would turn to the other side. This was a mistake. Subsequent research has demonstrated that this politicized aid did not foster economic development but often instead propped up corrupt autocrats.[47]

When American aid was used for development goals during the Cold War, it focused mostly on economic growth, not political reform, animated by modernization theory, which suggests that rising standards of living must precede democratization.[48] People must become more affluent, urban, and educated before they pushed for democratic change, or so it was believed. This sequencing sometimes did play out but more often did not, partly because geopolitical priorities trumped even a focus on using aid strategically to stimulate economic development.[49] Aid was often just a bribe to dictators to stay close to the United States and away from the Soviet Union. In addition, economic growth did not automatically trigger demand for democratic institutions; it sometimes strengthened autocracies. For instance, the United States provided economic assistance to China and Russia in the 1980s and 1990s, which may have helped support economic growth but ultimately it inadvertently also facilitated autocratic consolidation.

Modernization does not always produce democracy, but democratization does facilitate modernization. Recent research has demonstrated that democratic reforms facilitate economic growth.[50] Studies also show that economic assistance tied to short-term geopolitical goals has rarely produced sustained development outcomes.[51] Therefore, direct aid should be conditioned to pursue both development and democratic objectives.[52] When competing, especially with China today in the developing world, American leaders should bundle aid to support market reforms and democratic governance together and not go back to Cold War practices of assisting pro-American, anti-Chinese dictators or focusing first on economic development and waiting for democratic change later.

To compete effectively with China, the US government must devote more resources to foreign aid, which before Trump 2.0 constituted only 1 percent of the federal budget, and now is being slashed to minuscule levels. This push to cut foreign aid is a colossal mistake that will drastically limit America's ability to compete with China in the developing world. Reform of USAID and other aid providers is needed; destruction is not. While we outpace China and Russia in military spending, the PRC has sprinted ahead of the United States regarding expenditures for economic assistance. To build greater support for aid among taxpayers, American leaders must reframe how citizens think about the terms *aid* and *defense. Aid* sounds like a gift to recipient countries. That is the wrong imagery. Aid should benefit the governments and organizations that receive it, but it should also be understood as an essential tool for advancing American security, economic, and ideational objectives abroad. One way to shift this understanding for leaders and the American public would be to include economic assistance packages in the National Defense Authorization Act. To foster deeper commitment to foreign aid, the US Congress should mandate more comprehensive evaluations of effectiveness, greater transparency regarding contracts with implementing partners, and no longer allow foreign aid deliverers to make a profit.

It will not happen during Trump's second term. But future presidents more committed to winning this century's new era of great power competition could collaborate with the US Congress to create a new Department of Sustainable Development. Kennedy created USAID in 1961 to compete more effectively with the Soviets. We need similar innovation today to compete more effectively with the Chinese. Whatever is left of USAID after Trump's second term would constitute the core of this new department. Parts of the Departments of Defense, State, Treasury, Justice, Agriculture, and Commerce engaged in the development of the rule of law could be integrated into one new department. For instance, the State Department's

Bureau of Conflict and Stabilization Operations, the Office of Foreign Assistance, the Middle East Partnership Initiative, the Open Technology Fund, the Millennium Challenge Corporation, and the US International Development Finance Corporation could be merged into this new department, signaling to the world that the United States is serious again about using foreign assistance to advance our security, economic, and ideological goals. The future secretary of this department would be a cabinet member. And the mandate of this new department would be an unambiguous focus on aligning long-term strategic development and democracy goals.

After Trump, future presidents and their administrations should also press the international aid community to create global standards for greater transparency about development assistance and government contracting to undercut corrupt actors in this domain. Citizens and nongovernmental organizations, trade unions, and political parties in recipient countries would be especially empowered. Currently, the Chinese government and Chinese firms provide minimal details about the terms of their contracts with and loans to developing countries.[53] Russian agreements are also opaque. American diplomacy, technical assistance, and agenda-setting power in multilateral institutions might help countries receiving PRC aid and investment compel Chinese interlocutors to acquiesce to greater transparency, more competition, and better environmental standards.

LOSING THE PEACE

Americans won the Cold War, but not alone. Courageous democratic leaders and movements inside the communist world did most of the heavy lifting. Poles, Hungarians, and East Germans, then Czechs, Slovaks, and Romanians, and later Estonians, Latvians, Lithuanians, Ukrainians, Georgians, and Russians played the lead role in undermining communism, the Warsaw Pact, and, finally, the Soviet Union. Without these popular, largely nonviolent social movements inside the communist bloc, the United States and the democratic world would never have emerged victorious in the last century's era of great power competition.

Reformers within communist governments also played a critical role, if at times accidentally. Most consequentially, Gorbachev introduced domestic reforms that helped weaken the Soviet Union and end the Cold War. A different leader could have implemented incremental economic reforms to generate growth and maintain stability without collapse, as happened in China. In Poland, General Jaruzelski's willingness to join roundtable talks with the opposition helped accelerate the demise of communism there, and Hungarian communist reformers played a similar role in unraveling dictatorship in 1989.[54] Another former senior Communist Party leader in the Soviet Union, Boris Yeltsin also played a central role in dismembering the Soviet Union and, at least for a decade, oriented Russia toward democracy, markets, and the West.[55]

The Chinese and Russian people—not external actors—will play the leading roles in determining the future of their political systems. Today, dictatorships in both countries are deeply entrenched. However, the surprising history of political change in the communist world in the 1980s should remind us that our ability to understand societal preferences in autocracies is imperfect as are our tools for predicting revolutions. Change can happen fast. Social scientists already have uncovered signs of social discontent in both China and Russia.[56] The lesson from the Cold War is that the United States has few effective instruments and limited resources to trigger democratic revolutions inside China and Russia, but can support democratization once it begins. Trying to promote revolution from without could produce the opposite result: greater autocracy. And obviously, today, neither Xi nor Putin are like Gorbachev.

If democratization does begin in Russia or China in the future, the United States and the democratic world need to be ready to foster its success more effectively than we did at the end of the Cold War. Our record of winning the peace after the collapse of communism in Europe and Eurasia was mixed. We pursued some successful policies, including providing a package of reforms and aid that helped consolidate democracy in Eastern Europe. NATO and the European Union also offered membership to these post-communist countries if they succeeded in implementing market and democratic reforms. That helped consolidate democracy too. While the paths of democratic consolidation varied, and some countries—notably Hungary—have recently backslid, the project was mostly successful, in large part because solid majorities in these countries celebrated their liberation from Soviet imperialism, embraced democratic ideas, and wanted to join the West.

Except the Baltic states, Western efforts to help consolidate democracy were less successful in the former Soviet Union. In Russia, they failed. Multiple factors—predominantly domestic variables—combined to undermine Russian democracy.[57] And some bad luck did not help either. For instance, the 1998 global financial meltdown was a major blow to Russia's democratic future by compelling the reformist government, including first deputy prime minister Boris Nemtsov, Yeltsin's heir apparent, to resign. The ensuing political chain of events eventually led Yeltsin (or, more accurately, his entourage, since Yeltsin was often incapacitated due to health issues at the time) to appoint Putin, first as prime minister and then in 2000 as acting president, a title that the Russian electorate made permanent in an election later that spring. The selection of Putin by Yeltsin's entourage was a disastrous decision for the future of Russian democracy. Even so, the United States and the democratic world could have done much more to help consolidate democracy in Russia in the 1990s so the 1998 financial crisis would not have been such a consequential event for Russia's democratic future.

Most important, the United States and the rest of the free world should have provided Russians with greater economic resources to help them endure the economic depression that all post-communist countries experienced in transitioning from communism to capitalism. In 1992, we needed to do it fast. As a condition of greater assistance, we could have pressed Yeltsin to dismantle Soviet-era institutions of repression, including, most important, the KGB, and dissolve the Communist Party of the Soviet Union and its successor, the Communist Party of the Russian Federation, because of its crimes against humanity. Putin, after all, used the FSB—the domestic successor organization to the KGB—to gradually stifle political opposition and undermine democratic institutions. We also could have offered membership in—or at least a pathway to joining—democratic institutions such as NATO and the European Union to several countries, especially those on Russia's borders like Georgia and Ukraine. Additionally, we could have provided much greater military assistance to deter Russian invasions if democracy ultimately failed in Russia, as it did. We failed to do so because we thought it was, as American political scientist Francis Fukuyama put it, the "end of history," meaning all countries would inevitably and organically adopt market and democratic institutions without our involvement. That was a flawed assessment. The next time around, our efforts to help failed autocracies become democracies need to look more like 1945 than 1991.

Today, Ukraine is paying the heaviest price for the consequences of us not winning the peace after the Cold War. Putin's barbaric invasion of Ukraine would never have happened had democracy taken root in Russia in the 1990s. The people of Georgia, Moldova, and Belarus are suffering too. Everyone living under tyranny in the post-Soviet space today could have been freer and more prosperous had we succeeded in helping Russia consolidate democracy in the 1990s. At the same time, we could have hedged against the failure of Russian democracy by fostering closer military ties with Russia's democratic neighbors. If we get a second chance with Russia or a first chance with China to assist democratic consolidation and integration with our liberal international institutions, we must learn from our past mistakes and not fail again.

Chapter 13

REPLICATING COLD WAR SUCCESSES TODAY

THE PREVIOUS CHAPTER chronicled Cold War mistakes to avoid in our new great power competition with China and Russia. At the same time, American leaders achieved some fantastic successes during the Cold War. Even though the parallels between the Cold War and today are inexact, we can still learn from our past successes to guide our policy today.

Regrettably, President Trump started his second term by attacking and weakening some of our most successful Cold War instruments of deterrence, democracy promotion, and international cooperation. He has fueled tensions with many of our allies, gutted foreign assistance, including funding for organizations dedicated to supporting democratic ideas, dismantled US-funded global media, decreased resources for diplomacy, courted autocrats, assaulted the norms and practices guiding global trade, cut spending for research and development, and purged the US government of many of its most talented public servants. Trump's irrational and unpredictable economic policies, especially his sweeping tariffs, might inflict long-term damage to one of America's greatest Cold War achievements: a thriving, growing, and innovative economy that outpaced our adversaries'. These moves play directly into the hands of Putin and Xi, who are not cutting their budgets for foreign aid, global media, or diplomacy; radically disrupting trade and investment practices; or picking fights with each other or other autocracies. China, in particular, is well-positioned to take advantage of Trump's unilateral disarmament regarding America's toolkit of influence abroad. These short-sighted disruptions won't just harm American soft power, they also undermine America's ability to project hard power. It is hard to negotiate access to a new military base without diplomats, foreign aid, or a positive image of America. Coercion has its limits.

President Trump personally might not be interested in learning and applying lessons of success from the Cold War, but other elected officials, the American people, and future presidents might and, as the rest of this chapter tries to demonstrate, should be.

DETERRENCE AND ENGAGEMENT

The term *Cold War* reflects our central achievement of the era: the avoidance of a major *hot* war between the United States and the Soviet Union. We had close calls, of course, but American leaders ultimately succeeded in preventing World War III. Champions of the Cold War metaphor for today's great power competition often focus on the success of American confrontational strategies from the previous century. However, US policies that were effective in stabilizing our relationship with the Soviet Union used a mix of isolation and engagement, deterrence and cooperation, and competition and negotiation. We should pursue and perfect a similar multifaceted strategy today.

ENHANCE DETERRENCE

Maintaining a credible deterrent was central to the American strategy for avoiding war with the Soviet Union. Leaders in Moscow were not willing to attack the United States or its allies, because they did not have the means to do so. They also did not want to risk stumbling into war with us in a third country, in part because they feared that such a conventional war could quickly escalate to a nuclear war. We need to maintain, if not strengthen, this posture today so that Russia and China see a war with the United States as not only undesirable but unwinnable. Doing so does not imply a return to American hegemony. We cannot aspire to reach the level of preeminence of thirty years ago, which, as Trump's defense strategist Elbridge Colby wrote, "could be crippling, seriously stressing the US economy, the ultimate source of America's military strength."[1] We should instead focus on maintaining a level of military capacity sufficient to prevent war with China and Russia.

A successful deterrence strategy begins with the modernization of our nuclear arsenal to maintain mutual assured destruction. Today, we must deter two major nuclear powers instead of just one. That is a bigger challenge than we faced during the Cold War. This goal is achievable, and with the appropriate suite of policies, we can accomplish it without triggering a new and wasteful arms race. To do so, US military planners should focus on developing more survivable weapons, like submarine-launched ballistic missiles (SLBMs), instead of vulnerable land-based weapons, like intercontinental ballistic missiles (ICBMs). Biden took steps in this direction by continuing to develop the new W93 nuclear warhead for deployment on submarines. As SLBMs are the most survivable leg of the nuclear triad, it is essential that we modernize our SLBM capabilities to ensure operational readiness. Still, we cannot ignore the other legs of the triad: We need to maintain land- and air-based nuclear capabilities to hedge against future breakthrough technologies, like high-powered quantum sensor technology and gravimeters, that might make submarines easier to track. This is most efficiently accomplished in the air; we should at least maintain and preferably expand the numbers of our modernized nuclear-armed bombers even as we invest primarily in greater SLBM capabilities.

After World War II, the United States dramatically demobilized its army and cut military spending. That spending honeymoon ended when the Cold War began. Today, the post–Cold War honeymoon needs to be over too. The US must return to higher military spending levels akin to Cold War levels so that the American military is competitive with the technologically sophisticated and massive armies of China and Russia. The only way to prevent great power wars is to be prepared to fight them.

The US must begin by building more ships and submarines. Chinese naval power is surging while the US shipbuilding industry has slipped far behind.[2] Given this disparity, American leaders should contract with Japan and South Korea to meet demand by jointly producing or purchasing their domestically produced boats.[3] Alone, we will never catch up with China. Our domestic production should focus on areas that we have a comparative advantage in, and for shipbuilding, that is submarines.

The US military also needs a much higher volume of missiles—especially long-range fires—deployed on sea, air, and land platforms in Asia. China has invested heavily in these weapons—both in quantity and quality—to try to prevent American ships from supporting Taiwanese forces in the event of a PRC invasion. In this missile-arms race in Asia, the United States is behind. In particular, our limited capabilities to strike moving Chinese ships cannot adequately deter a PRC attack of Taiwan. We must focus on developing these capabilities, including insulating our supply chains from China for the components needed to produce these missiles.[4]

The Pentagon must also spend more on small, cheap, maneuverable weapons platforms, most of which should eventually be unmanned aircraft, sea vessels, and land vehicles.[5] The development of mixed systems—partly operated by humans, partly unmanned—should be an interim step, as the air force is doing with its Collaborative Combat Aircraft program.[6] In the air, on the land, and at sea, we have witnessed the advantages of small, inexpensive swarms of precision weapons in the war between Russia and Ukraine. Nothing can move on the battlefield in Ukraine—not ships, tanks, artillery, or even soldiers on motorcycles—without being attacked by drones. Today, the United States relies on large, expensive unmanned vehicles when we should be focused on acquiring low-cost, disposable drones. In the not-so-distant future, we should even buy from or form joint ventures with Ukrainian drone companies. In Asia, the more fast, small, swarming unmanned vehicles we have to use, the better.

Russia's invasion of Ukraine has also demonstrated the need for volume. We need to produce a much larger number of old-school weapons as well—howitzers, anti-tank Javelin missiles, Stinger man-portable air-defense systems, missile defense interceptors, and ammunition—lots of ammunition. The US expended a significant portion of our available stockpile in Ukraine. We need to replenish our stores today to avoid facing a conflict with "empty bins," a phrase coined by defense scholar Seth Jones to describe the disastrous result of insufficient investment in the defense manufacturing base.[7] As with shipbuilding, our efforts to enhance our industrial capacity for weapons and ammunition should be carried out in coordination with allies. The Biden administration took a step in this direction with revisions to the US implementation of the Missile Technology Control Regime in January 2025, which should allow the US to coordinate more closely with allies and partners to build out our entire bloc's defense capabilities.[8] But that is just a first small step; greater integration of the free world's military industries is necessary to maintain a sufficient deterrent in this century.

The US should also forward-deploy more soldiers in Asia and Europe, not fewer, as President Trump and his team have suggested.[9] In response to Putin's invasion of Ukraine in 2022, Biden prudently redeployed thousands of American soldiers to Europe. They should stay there. In Asia, the Biden administration secured access to several military bases in the Philippines close to Taiwan. We must maintain basing access and deploy more American soldiers, sailors, and pilots in Asia. Having a larger number of regional bases and volume of forces makes a strike on any single American base far less effective in degrading American capabilities for China during a future conflict.[10] Greater pre-deployment of weapons and ammunition throughout the border areas of Russia and China is also necessary.

To better deter Beijing and Moscow, the US must also make more significant investments in technological innovation, just as US policymakers did during the Cold War to offset the Soviet Union's numerical advantage in conventional military power. US strategists should focus on developing better hypersonic glide vehicles, more accurate anti-ship missiles as well as defensive interceptors, faster drones, and more advanced sensors. We should not discard weapons we have already purchased; instead, we should upgrade existing platforms with enhanced capabilities that leverage technological breakthroughs, especially with artificial intelligence.[11] We must also improve our cyber capabilities, including system resilience, critical infrastructure, and offensive cyber weapons to deter attacks.

The combination of more mobile platforms in the air, underwater, and on land—armed with more accurate and longer-range weapons, and connected by resilient communications—will increase the survivability of America's armed forces, especially in Asia. It is a major shift in American military strategy and traditions, as American strategists Andrew Lim and James Fearon write, away from the "current stock of fixed and visible assets" and toward more "elusive forces in multiple domains."[12] But it is the only way to keep the peace in Asia.

The US must also maintain a resilient space architecture to prevent either China or Russia from disabling our communication, sensing, and positioning satellites during a conflict. Both countries continue to build counterspace capabilities and anti-satellite weapons systems.[13] While it would have been best to create a multilateral agreement to prevent the militarization of space altogether, space is a warfighting domain. In space, we cannot afford to fall behind the Chinese. American military strategists worry that US space capabilities—such as the Global Positioning System—would be among the first targets in a conflict over Taiwan. Maintaining our ability to communicate and see from space during wartime requires building innovative commercial alternatives to aging space infrastructure as part of the Resilient Global Positioning System,[14] Tactically Responsive Space Program,[15] and the Proliferated Warfighter Space Architecture. These initiatives improve the redundancy, resilience, low latency, and global coverage of US space assets.[16] The US should also build a Civil Reserve Space Fleet (CRSF), modeled after the successful Civil Reserve Air Fleet, which enables commercial airlines to support the military during national emergencies.[17]

Staying ahead of China in developing synthetic biology and resilience against bioweapons should also be a greater focus in American defense policy. Threatening mutually assured destruction does not work in this domain, in part because American leaders could never credibly commit to using these classes of weapons. We must instead build up our defense capabilities to make a biological attack less lethal.[18] The United States and our allies have a long way to go to create a stockpile of enough protective gear, transmission-slowing technologies, and vaccines to deter a biological attack.

To more quickly integrate emerging technologies into our fighting forces, the Pentagon must make it easier to contract with high-tech firms and smaller companies.[19] According to Michael Brown, the former director of the Defense Innovation Unit at the US Department of Defense, five large companies—often referred to as the "primes"—"receive about 70 percent of defense contracts . . . [while] in just the last five years, the defense industrial base has lost 17,045 independent companies."[20] That is not a winning strategy for maintaining, let alone enhancing, deterrence against China and Russia. There is some successful innovation happening in defense acquisitions already; for example, in the CIA's In-Q-Tel venture capital enterprise, the Pentagon's Defense Innovation Unit in Silicon Valley, and the DOD's Open Data and Applications Government-Owned Interoperable Repositories program.[21] In 2024, Meta announced it would allow the DOD and defense companies to use its Llama AI models.[22] The Biden administration also launched Replicator, a new program to purchase cheap, expendable drones. These initiatives are a good start, but not enough. Replicator, for example, made up 0.059 percent of the DOD's 2024 budget and only 0.16 percent of the department's acquisitions budget.[23] Much of the research, development, and innovation for military purposes today occurs in the private sector, not the US government or its affiliated national laboratories—a stark difference from the Cold War. Consequently, the Pentagon, CIA, and other government agencies involved in defense and intelligence must strengthen their ability to interface with the most innovative companies in the private sector. American leaders also must design new programs to attract tech talent into the defense and public sectors, such as providing opportunities to serve in government for a few years rather than a lifetime, and offer more competitive compensation packages to attract the most talented AI and quantum experts into public service.

I understand that my proposals in this section might sound like a costly laundry list. Ethically, there is also something unsettling for me about advocating for more defense spending. I would rather the US government spent more on scholarships than weapons. I am also scared to death of wars fought with unmanned, AI-enhanced autonomous drones. A better strategy would be for great power leaders to sign treaties limiting the use cases of these weapons. However, those diplomatic opportunities are not available at this moment, so the United States must keep investing in its deterrent in every dimension of warfare. During the Cold War, we avoided World War III by maintaining the best military in the world. We must do so again.

DEEPEN ALLIANCES

One of the greatest successes of American foreign policy during the Cold War was the creation of our fantastic system of alliances. Once it became clear that the UN Security Council could not live up to its aspiration of providing collective security, American leaders joined Canada and ten European countries to create the North Atlantic Treaty Organization in 1949. The United States signed bilateral security treaties with several Asian allies soon after. In a foreshadowing of our debates about the organization's expansion today, some American strategists—most notably George

Kennan—worried that the creation of NATO would provoke the Kremlin. Others bristled at the idea of signing treaties with former enemies (Germany, Italy, and Japan). And the NATO alliance was not without controversies after it was established. There were disputes with European allies during the Suez Canal crisis in 1956; France withdrew from NATO's integrated military structure for a while in 1966; and tensions emerged between Washington and European societies in the 1980s when Reagan pushed for the deployment of Pershing missiles in Europe. Our European allies worried about whether the United States would come to their rescue if the Soviets invaded. In Asia, the United States has also had issues with alliance cohesion, especially during the periods of democratization in South Korea and the Philippines. Some Cold War alliances even failed—the Southeast Asia Treaty Organization and the Central Treaty Organization collapsed and have faded from memory. In the long run, though, American alliances largely endured and played a vital role in helping us keep the peace during the Cold War. They must play a similar role now as we work to avoid war with Moscow and Beijing. The second Trump administration's assault on alliance cohesion—the threats to annex Greenland and Canada, lectures about imperfections in European democracies, hints of reducing the number of US soldiers in Europe and Asia, and voting with Russia, North Korea, Belarus, and the like on UN resolutions about the war in Ukraine—has undermined American national security interests. As Winston Churchill said, "There is only one thing worse than fighting with allies, and that is fighting without them." Having strong, loyal allies was our greatest advantage during the Cold War. In dealing with China and Russia in this century, we must maintain that advantage.

Strengthen NATO

A major war between Russia and NATO allies is unlikely today. However, this nightmare scenario is more probable than it was during the final decades of the Cold War because of Putin's high level of risk-taking. In addition to his invasions of Georgia and Ukraine and launching cyberattacks and various other sabotage operations against NATO, Putin also has nurtured divisions within the alliance along ideological lines and courted illiberal, anti-NATO populists in Hungary, Slovakia, Croatia, Romania, Italy, France, Germany, and the United States.[24] Putin wants the alliance to dissolve. NATO allies on the borders of Russia are especially worried about Putin's provocations that might test NATO's unity and resolve.[25] Maintaining a strong NATO deterrent against Russian aggression in Europe, therefore, must remain a paramount US national security objective. Pulling back, as Trump and his new team have hinted, will make conflict between Russia and NATO allies more likely, not less.

US leaders must continue to encourage NATO members to increase spending on military defense. Two percent of national budgets for defense—a goal reached by twenty-three NATO allies in 2024—must be a floor, not a ceiling. Five percent is a long-term target better suited for today's threat environment. US leaders also must push for greater interoperability between allied armed forces. Mobility bottlenecks degrade military capacity within the alliance, especially in railway infrastructure and airlift capacity. With Finland and Sweden joining as new members, fortifying the most northern borders of the alliance merits greater attention and resources, especially in the Baltic Sea, where Russian ships sabotaged undersea cables.[26] Permanently stationing combat forces in all allied countries bordering Russia would bolster signaling that acts of aggression against any member of the alliance will trigger a unified response. NATO allies must also commit to joint defense production of tanks, long-range fires, air-defense systems, and ammunition. Maintaining non-standardized production lines of a dozen types of tanks, infantry fighting vehicles, and howitzers is economically inefficient and inhibits military interoperability.[27] As former Italian prime minister Mario Draghi argued in a study on EU competitiveness, fragmentation "means that the [defense] industry lacks scale, which is essential in a capital-intensive sector with long investment cycles" and "leads to serious issues related to a lack of standardisation and the interoperability of equipment."[28]

The militaries of all NATO countries must innovate collectively to address new security challenges from AI, cyber weapons, quantum computing, and synthetic biology. Existing programs like the NATO Innovation Fund and NATO's Defense Innovation Fund for the North Atlantic's ongoing work in these critical areas should be continued and expanded. US leaders should celebrate intra-European security initiatives, like Permanent

Structured Cooperation and the European Defense Fund. Independent European security initiatives that do not include the United States help us achieve our shared mission of deterring Russia.

NATO must also continue to deepen its integration with Ukraine. Once the war is over, Ukraine should be invited to join the alliance immediately. Putin should not get a say in who joins *our* alliance. NATO membership is the only credible security guarantee for Ukraine and the best way to keep peace on the Russia-Ukraine border. Moscow has never attacked a NATO country. NATO has never attacked the Soviet Union and will never initiate an unprovoked war against Russia. The armed forces of Ukraine are now one of the best-trained, best-armed fighting forces in Europe and will significantly enhance the alliance's capabilities. With sophisticated drones, sensors, and other new weapons systems, Ukrainian soldiers could be stationed in other NATO countries bordering Russia and someday maybe even replace American soldiers in these frontline states. Ukraine could also become a joint production partner with European and American firms in manufacturing armaments, especially unmanned air and sea vehicles, for the entire alliance.

Strengthen Alliances in Asia

American leaders must also continue to strengthen alliances in Asia to deter China from launching a war. China's military capabilities are expanding so our collective capabilities with our allies must expand too. As discussed previously, Biden and his team smartly expanded American bilateral security cooperation with Australia, Japan, the Philippines, and South Korea to respond to China's increasingly assertive posture in the region. In September 2021, Biden and his British and Australian counterparts launched an "enhanced trilateral security partnership" called AUKUS to increase military-to-military cooperation, including, most important, the sharing of American nuclear-powered submarine technology with the Australian navy. AUKUS must develop other lines of collective effort more rapidly, including AI and cyber technologies for military applications. In August 2023, Biden hosted a trilateral summit with leaders from Japan and South Korea during which the three leaders signed the Camp David Principles, deepening trilateral security cooperation. This was a significant step in the right direction in overcoming lingering animosities between Japan and South Korea. AUKUS and US–Japan–South Korea cooperation should now be institutionalized, complete with a secretariat, regular meetings, and annual outputs. In 2024, American and Japanese leaders agreed to create a joint force headquarters co-commanded by American and Japanese generals. Secretary of Defense Lloyd Austin described this as "the most significant change to US Forces Japan since its creation, and one of the strongest improvements in our military ties with Japan in 70 years."[29] The faster this joint command gets up to full capacity, the better. Recent Japanese decisions to allocate more resources to defense should be applauded as a model for other American allies in Asia. More generally, any policy that enhances the military, industrial, and technological capabilities of our alliances in Asia—what Asian security experts Kurt Campbell and Rosh Doshi called "capacity-centric statecraft"—must be pursued, as collective power is the only way to keep pace with China in the region.[30]

The high degree of military cooperation must extend into the intelligence community. For several decades, Australia, Canada, New Zealand, the United Kingdom, and the US have shared intelligence under a cooperative agreement informally called "Five Eyes." The rise of China as a threat requires that Five Eyes be expanded to a group of Seven Eyes, with the addition of Japan and South Korea.

Biden's upgrading the Quadrilateral Security Dialogue ("Quad") to a head-of-state-level summit between Australia, India, Japan, and the US was also a positive step. To date, Quad leaders have focused on increasing cooperation in supply chain security, climate-disaster and pandemic prevention, and high-tech and space advancements. Gradually, the organization should expand its focus to include cooperation on security, including upgrading shared cybersecurity capabilities, deterring biosecurity threats, and conducting joint military training exercises. American leaders should encourage the Quad to become the "Quint" by inviting South Korea to join.

In parallel, American leaders should enhance cooperation with Malaysia, Indonesia, Vietnam, and other ASEAN countries to maintain a free and open Indo-Pacific region. None of these countries will join the US in a military alliance, but they could cooperate on economic issues with military implications. For instance, the US should initiate a new agreement with

ASEAN countries to secure supply chains of critical minerals, thereby denying China the opportunity to control this market.

A New Military Alliance in Asia?

Could existing security arrangements and partnerships provide the components for a new multilateral alliance in Asia, like NATO? Probably not, and certainly not anytime soon. During Trump 2.0, such a radical idea is a non-starter. However, in track-two dialogues and off-the-record meetings between allies, the idea should be explored, if for no other reason than to signal to China about potential for collective action if Beijing escalates its threats against our allies and partners in Asia. A new multilateral alliance—the Pacific Alliance Treaty Organization, or PATO—could begin with Japan, South Korea, Australia, and New Zealand and later expand to include other democracies in the region, as well as small but strategically significant states like the Freely Associated States, made up of the Federated States of Micronesia, the Republic of the Marshall Islands, and the Republic of Palau.[31] Over time, given their interests and ties to the region, the United Kingdom and France could also join.

PATO would serve as a multilateral forum to strengthen member states' national defense and coordinate collective security by increasing information exchange, creating joint weapons production ventures, and orchestrating regional military exercises and training. Like NATO, this new alliance would be exclusively defensive. PATO would need to credibly commit to never carrying out a first attack on China, instead taking military action only in response to an attack on an ally. As we witnessed in Europe during the interwar period and, more recently, in Georgia and Ukraine, small countries without strong allies are vulnerable to great powers on their borders. In Europe, NATO has helped keep peace. In Asia, PATO could do the same.

It will prove extremely difficult to create such an organization during peacetime, but American leaders should lay the groundwork now to launch PATO in response to a major provocative military move by China. Just as the Soviet-orchestrated coup in Czechoslovakia in 1948 accelerated NATO's institutionalization in 1949, Chinese leaders should know that a Chinese invasion of Taiwan would immediately trigger a collective response.

Communicating this plan beforehand might help prevent war over the island.

Avoid War Over Taiwan

A monumental achievement during the Cold War was the avoidance of war between the US and China over Taiwan. Keeping the peace should continue to be a top priority for American leaders today, even as the PRC modernizes and expands its military force and Xi signals his goal of ending the century of humiliation and "reunifying" China. If Xi decides to invade or blockade the island, the US could be dragged into a war without winners—all sides would suffer significant casualties and face catastrophic economic consequences. American leaders, therefore, must do everything they can to prevent an attack on Taiwan. As Trump's former deputy national security adviser Matt Pottinger rightly observed, "If just one lesson could be drawn from Russia's invasion of Ukraine, it must be that deterrence would have been a lot cheaper than war."[32]

A comprehensive strategy for preventing war over Taiwan begins with maintaining policies that have proven effective, including, first and foremost, reaffirming "strategic ambiguity" about the US response to an act of aggression by the PRC against Taiwan. There is little to gain from departing from this policy because such a change would give Xi an excuse to escalate. American leaders should convince allies (especially Japan) to adopt the same strategy. Multilateral strategic ambiguity would be better than American unilateral ambiguity.

American leaders should also learn lessons from the outcome of our actions in the lead-up to the Russian invasion of Ukraine. NATO and the US began to provide significant military assistance to Ukraine only after Russia launched its full-scale attack. That was a mistake. They should have provided weapons and training to Ukrainian soldiers years before Putin invaded to help deter the invasion altogether, and once Russia launched an attack, they should have given Ukraine what they needed at the outset of the invasion rather than increasing assistance incrementally.[33] Stockpiling more weapons and munitions in Taiwan now is especially urgent because shipping military supplies to the island during an invasion will be much more complicated than it is in Ukraine.[34] Expanding training at this point is also imperative. NATO countries share borders with Ukraine. An ocean separates Taiwan from its military partners and is far from most US military bases.

In addition, American officials must continue to persuade Taiwan's leaders to increase their defense spending. Since the early 2000s, Taiwan has spent roughly 2 percent of its GDP on defense. After Putin invaded Ukraine, Taiwanese officials expanded their military defense budget to nineteen billion dollars, a 7.7 percent rise from the previous year, but still not nearly enough given the growing military threat from Beijing.[35] Given the current threat environment, Taiwan should allocate at least as much as Poland—4 percent of its GDP—on defense; it would be even better if they reached Israel's levels of 5 percent. American officials could make higher defense spending levels by Taiwan a precondition for additional US military assistance. In 2024, mandatory military service for men in Taiwan increased from four months to one year, but at least two years of service are needed for greater readiness, ideally with increased training and interaction with US military instructors. Taiwan's government should also devote more resources to homeland resistance and territorial defense, including education, training, and preparation for civic resistance tactics and urban guerrilla warfare operations. Territorial defense units in Ukraine were essential in slowing Russia's invasion.

US leaders must encourage their Taiwanese counterparts to invest in asymmetric capabilities: "a large number of small things."[36] Taiwanese officials devote a disproportionate percentage of their resources to acquiring large and costly conventional platforms (like fighter aircraft and diesel submarines) and too few to mobile, unmanned, smaller weapons systems that could survive the early stages of an attack from Beijing. As former State Department official James Timbie and retired Admiral James Ellis argue, "Effective short-range anti-air and anti-ship defenses could increase the risk that an invasion attempt would fail or be substantially delayed either in the water or on the island."[37] More smart sea mines that can be activated and deactivated, coastal defense cruise missiles, and Joint Air-to-Surface Standoff Missiles are also essential for deterring a PRC invasion.[38] In addition, Taiwan needs better air-defense capabilities, including portable weapons like Stingers, as well as redundant, simpler systems of communication that can survive electronic warfare attacks. If PLA soldiers do make it onto the island, Taiwan will need a large number of the anti-tank Javelins that have proved so effective against Russian armor in Ukraine. US leaders should greenlight American and Taiwanese companies to cooperate on the joint production of weapons systems.[39]

In addition to weapons and ammunition, US officials should encourage their Taiwanese counterparts to stockpile critical resources. Most of Taiwan's energy supply comes from imported fossil fuels, making the country very vulnerable to an energy blockade in a conflict. Taiwan's leaders must pursue a higher degree of energy independence through investments in renewable energy and the reintroduction of nuclear power on the island to better withstand a blockade.

To enhance deterrence, US national security leaders must move more American forces and weapons closer to Taiwan and make them more resilient to PLA attacks. American diplomats should secure permission from Japan to use the US air base in Kadena and navy base that is home to submarine activities in Yokosuka if a conflict breaks out over Taiwan. Alongside regional allies, we must increase the number of stations for rearming and refueling submarines throughout the Indo-Pacific region. Hawaii and Guam are too far away to be effective options for submarine resupply. In the Philippines, the current right to rotate American armed forces through military bases should be upgraded to permanent basing permissions with cross-service access—multiple branches of the US military, not just the army, should have access to these bases.

As mentioned above, these moves must be accompanied by improvements in American long-strike capabilities deployed on more mobile platforms in the Asian theater to offset the Chinese growing anti-access/area denial (A2/AD) capabilities that make forward American deployments vulnerable. If the PRC does invade Taiwan and the US responds by helping to defend the island, the US military will have to rely on submarines and long-range bombers to avoid Chinese missiles, but too many of these planes and subs are not ready for combat today. As US defense policy analysts Robert Haddick, Mark Montgomery, and Isaac Harris assess,

"One third of the navy's attack submarines are idle at depot maintenance shipyards," and only roughly half of long-range bombers were designated "mission capable" in 2022.[40] That needs to change.

While the American military's possible response to a future invasion should remain ambiguous, American leaders should outline the nonmilitary consequences of an invasion or blockade clearly. For instance, the American president could state publicly that the United States would recognize Taiwan's independence in response to a Chinese invasion. Or, as already mentioned, an invasion could trigger the creation of PATO. In coordination with allies and partners, American leaders should spell out the economic costs of war to Beijing: a comprehensive package of sanctions, the freezing of Chinese assets abroad, and an energy embargo. Given the state's reliance on global trade for economic growth and dependence on energy imports, China is much more vulnerable to sanctions than Russia. Having studied Western sanctions used against Russia in the wake of Putin's invasion of Ukraine, Chinese leaders are adopting measures to reduce their exposure to potential sanctions.[41] However, even with these measures in place, the high degree of Chinese dependence on the global economy, especially in energy and finance, will likely continue for decades.

American officials should coordinate with the Taiwanese government and the private sector to ensure that Beijing understands there will be no spoils of conquest—after an invasion, a devastated Taiwanese economy will remain. The specialized skills of employees in Taiwan's high-tech companies are not easily replaceable. As former Taiwan Semiconductor Manufacturing Company (TSMC) chairman Marc Liu explained, "Nobody can control TSMC by force . . . If you take a military force or invasion, you will render TSMC's factory not operable because this is such a sophisticated manufacturing facility . . . So, if you take it over by force, you can no longer make it operable."[42] PRC leaders must understand that similar patterns of destruction would occur in all of Taiwan's major industries. Xi may be willing to pay a very high economic price to be remembered as the Chinese leader who completed reunification. Other Chinese leaders and elites might hold a different view of the return on investment of an invasion. Making sure they understand the full costs of invasion enhances deterrence.

American officials also must reaffirm that the US will not recognize Taiwan as an independent country unless China invades. If Taiwanese leaders take steps toward independence, they should know they cannot rely on the US for defense.

Avoid War in the South China Sea

In the South China Sea, Xi is pushing to undermine the laws, norms, and protocols established under the UN Convention on the Law of the Sea. Xi's claims over this entire body of water are illegitimate and destabilizing. Therefore, the US, together with allies and partners, must strengthen its commitment to maintaining the status quo in the South China Sea. The US cannot stop the PRC from building islands in the South China Sea, but we can maintain freedom of navigation and work toward settling disputed territorial claims.[43] If American diplomats help the other claimant countries (the Philippines, Taiwan, Vietnam, Brunei, and Malaysia) reach an agreement about rights to the islands and exclusive economic zones, it will be easier to pressure China to accept the status quo and allow continued freedom of navigation.[44]

RENEWING ARMS CONTROL

During the Cold War, American and Soviet leaders wasted resources on developing their nuclear arsenals that they could have allocated to domestic, welfare-enhancing programs. At the peak of the nuclear arms race, the United States had an estimated 31,255 warheads, while the Soviet Union maintained 40,159.[45] Early arms-control agreements were able to slow the pace of the arms race, and later treaties—the START, SORT, and New START treaties—dramatically reduced the number of deployed nuclear weapons and their delivery vehicles. American and Soviet leaders signed the Anti-Ballistic Missile Treaty in 1972 to limit the deployment of missile defenses as a way to guarantee that each side remained vulnerable to a nuclear strike by the other. Soviet and American leaders also signed treaties to limit the testing of nuclear weapons and to eliminate a whole category of weapons in Europe—intermediate-range ballistic missiles. Moscow and Washington also cooperated in the creation of multilateral arms-control treaties, including the historic 1968 Non-Proliferation Treaty that sought to prevent further spread of nuclear weapons. American and Soviet leaders cooperated to enhance transparency and share information about their respective arsenals to increase stability; sophisticated verification regimes were embedded in arms-control treaties. Reagan used to say "Trust but verify" when negotiating agreements with the Soviets. While working in the US government on the New START treaty, I amended Reagan's words to "Don't trust, only verify." Signed in 2010, the New START treaty had the most comprehensive inspection regime of any treaty ever. We need that today with China and Russia.

Unfortunately, many arms-control treaties have not survived our new era of great power competition. The ABM, INF, and Open Skies treaties are gone. Russia has suspended participation in the New START treaty, which expires in 2026. This trend needs to be reversed. American leaders should try to bring arms control back, even while recognizing that negotiating new agreements, let alone signing and implementing them, will be a long and challenging process with China and Russia. If it is going to be a long journey, it is best to start taking the first steps now.

US diplomats could start by pursuing new measures to give all great powers more information about one another's nuclear capabilities. Uncertainty about the nuclear capabilities of adversaries compels military strategists to develop war plans based on worst-case scenarios. To enhance transparency with Russia, American leaders should look for ways to reengage Russia in the New START treaty. Next, American and Russian diplomats must negotiate a follow-on treaty extending the limits and inspection regime from the current New START treaty before its expiration. In the distant future—probably in the post-Putin era—US diplomats should engage their Russian counterparts in a new agreement that would place limits on these new long-range nuclear weapons–delivery systems not currently covered in the New START treaty and on nonstrategic and tactical nuclear weapons. These talks will drag on for years, but the very exercise of having these conversations is stabilizing.

Arms control talks with Beijing will be even more difficult to start because the American nuclear arsenal is much larger than China's. Chinese officials have made clear that they are not interested in agreeing to numerical limits until they reach parity. The gap that Beijing invokes in this argument is quickly closing, though.[46] As Chinese leaders become more confident in the survivability of their retaliatory capability, they may become more ready to start discussions on limits before reaching parity.[47] Just beginning a sustained conversation about nuclear arms control—including exchanging information about their respective nuclear arsenals—will be stabilizing because it will allow the states to better understand one another's nuclear doctrines.[48] If a bilateral or trilateral format with China or Russia or both proves impossible, US national security leaders should not be afraid to encourage allies like France and Great Britain to engage in multilateral arms control talks with us and these two autocratic nuclear great powers.

American leaders should also pursue new multilateral treaties to increase conventional weapons transparency. There is too much uncertainty about the quality and quantity of conventional arsenals around the world, especially in Europe and Asia. An agreement to provide global transparency about weapons deployments, training exercises, and military sales would be incredibly valuable. There already is one in Europe, the Vienna Document, although it has not functioned effectively since Russia's invasion of Ukraine in 2014. We need something similar for the whole world today. A more ambitious proposal for the far future would be to negotiate limits on the deployment of conventional weapons. Limitations on the deployment of weapons could eventually extend to artificial intelligence, synthetic biology, autonomous weapons, cyber weapons, and space-based weapons. These efforts should start with a ban on tests of anti-satellite weapons that produce debris damaging the space commons for all countries.

In the context of the current global threat environment, proposing such arms control agreements will sound naive to some. I get it. However, the fact that we accomplished this goal before should inspire hope that we should at least try to do it again. The Conventional Armed Forces in Europe Treaty, signed in 1990, reduced the number of deployed conventional armaments between the Atlantic Ocean and the Ural Mountains before Russia suspended its implementation of the agreement in 2007 and ultimately withdrew in 2023. Resurrecting the norm of arms limits and starting a new multilateral dialogue could help slow today's explosion of arms deployment around the world. Advocates of arms control in the early years of the Cold War were also ridiculed as idealistic and naive. But after years of failure, they achieved unexpected breakthroughs that enhanced American national security.[49] If we succeeded with arms control against an assertive ideological enemy during the Cold War, we should at least try again with China and Russia. Nothing is lost in trying. In fact, the very act of signaling support for arms control is beneficial for America's reputation especially when US diplomats pursue nuclear nonproliferation efforts with other countries. We have less credibility in stopping Iran from acquiring a nuclear weapon or slowing the development of North Korea's nuclear weapons program if we have joined a new arms race with China and Russia.

MANAGE AND PREVENT CRISES

During the Cold War, the dangers of poor bilateral communication channels became obvious during the 1962 Cuban Missile Crisis. It proved to American and Soviet leaders that both sides would benefit from developing practices and mechanisms to manage and prevent crises. The metaphor of a red-phone hotline connecting the White House and the Kremlin emerged as a symbol of the willingness to communicate openly to prevent conflict based on accidents and misperceptions. By the 1970s, US-Soviet relations were more stable and predictable, a result of the perception of a symmetric balance of power that came from increased transparency and routine lines of communication.[50]

That isn't to say there were no communication problems between Washington and Moscow during the later stages of the Cold War. Though the hotline remained open, the Soviet invasion of Afghanistan disrupted relations; during the first two years of the Reagan administration, communications with Moscow were few. But in 1982, Reagan's new secretary of state George Shultz restored regular bilateral contacts, even as the US and Soviet Union continued to clash on fundamental issues.[51] From Shultz's time until Putin's invasion of Ukraine, communications between the US and the USSR (and subsequently Russia) were regular and routine.

During and after the Cold War, American and Chinese leaders developed regular channels for bilateral dialogue, most expansively in the Obama-Hu years under the auspices of the 2009 US-China Strategic and Economic Dialogue. In his first term, Trump ended this pattern of engagement. According to Tsinghua professor Yan Xuetong, "Under the Obama administration, there were more than 90 official channels for dialogue between the two governments. By the end of Trump's first term, there were none."[52]

Cold War successes in crisis management and prevention must be replicated today. The US, China, and Russia will continue to have significant, irreconcilable disagreements. Despite these disagreements, conflict should never emerge because of poor information or a misperception of the other side's actions or intentions. Maintaining regular communication channels, especially between military and intelligence officials, is essential for avoiding war. In particular, American and Chinese military leaders must create routine protocols with urgency to help avoid accidental sea conflict. As former secretary of state Condoleezza Rice warned, "Alarmingly, the United States and China still have none of the deconfliction measures in place that the United States and Russia do."[53] That needs to change.

AN ORGANIZATION OF SECURITY AND COOPERATION IN ASIA

In the 1970s, the US, USSR, Canada, and dozens of European countries in NATO and the Warsaw Pact participated in negotiations that produced the Helsinki Final Act and, subsequently, the Organization of Security and Co-operation in Europe (OSCE). The Helsinki Accords focused primarily on security, codifying recognition of existing European borders redrawn after World War II, including Soviet annexations.[54] Because concrete Soviet annexations were recognized in exchange for vague language about human rights, many criticized Helsinki as a diplomatic coup for Moscow. But over time, the accords proved useful for democratic activists in Soviet-annexed countries; it gave human rights organizations across Eastern Europe the ability to press for the rights codified in Basket Three of the document.

Putin's disregard for European security norms and treaties has undermined the efficacy of European security organizations, including the OSCE. However, because the PRC is not as belligerently revisionist as Russia today, an Organization for Security and Cooperation in Asia (OSCA) could be stabilizing for the region. And, as with the OSCE, the United States would benefit from membership in the OSCA. Helsinki was designed to address border disputes and ambiguous sovereignty issues—such as the division of Germany—and that could be helpful in Asia today to freeze ambiguous sovereignty arrangements on the Korean Peninsula, in the South China Sea, and between Taiwan and the PRC. The principle of only peaceful means for unification could be codified, accompanied by a pledge from signatories not to recognize any change to Taiwan's status. Beijing will never agree to such a norm, but getting other countries in a new multilateral security organization to do so would have a stabilizing effect. Even discussion of such a concept would be beneficial. In addition, OSCA could develop crisis-management procedures to mediate and resolve sovereignty disputes. The new organization would also provide a forum for countries without established bilateral relations, like North Korea and the United States, to meet and engage on issues. A recurring regional security conference would compel politicians to develop an agenda for each summit, as institutionalized meetings have the advantage of set dates and regular participants. A permanent organization would also create institutions with helpful expertise. The OSCE, for example, has developed a superb election-monitoring capacity that could be replicated in Asia.

Starting a Helsinki-like process or creating an OSCE-like organization in Asia would be extremely difficult, but the same was true when it was done in Europe. Twentieth-century Europe had deeper ideological divisions, ethnic tensions, and territorial disputes than Asia today. Overcoming the challenges that divide Asian countries today would be no more difficult than creating a security organization in the 1970s that included former enemies (France and Germany) and existing adversaries (the Soviet Union and the United States). If nothing else, beginning a negotiation process would create regular interaction between competing countries that would have stabilizing effects even if no new organization ultimately emerged.

KNOW THY ENEMY

During the Cold War, the US government incentivized scholars and students to study the Russian language, history, and culture as well as the languages and cultures of other communist countries. When I was a student at Stanford, the US government gave me a scholarship to study Polish. Learning Polish, including two summers at the Jagiellonian University in Krakow in the 1980s, gave me a less Russia-centric perspective on Eastern Europe and a greater appreciation for the nations captive to Soviet imperialism, a valuable framework back then and one still helpful in understanding the relationship between Ukraine and Russia today.

Just as we did in the previous century, the US government should invest more in understanding the intentions and actions of our biggest rivals.[55] We need to expand programs that focus on not only security but also politics, economics, ideology, climate change, digital technologies, and artificial intelligence. We must encourage American students to develop linguistic and cultural expertise by expanding programs like Boren, Fulbright, Critical Language Scholarship, and the Department of Education's Title Six and Foreign Language Area Studies programs. Trump's decision to cancel the Fulbright Program with China in his first term and Biden's failure to restore it were mistakes. In his second term, Trump has threatened to make even deeper cuts to student exchange programs worldwide. That would be a catastrophic mistake, deeply damaging our country's ability to understand not only our adversaries but also our friends. After US students return from studying in China (there are no American exchange programs in Russia now), they should be incentivized to use their knowledge to serve our country and not be sidelined from government careers because of counterintelligence concerns.[56] These exchanges should go both ways: More resources should be devoted to attracting students and scholars from China and Russia to come study in the US. The more opportunities we can create to make their "Americanologists" smarter about our country, the better.

American scholars and analysts also must study the impact of Chinese and Russian foreign policies on third countries. We have armies of experts reading the tea leaves of Xi's intentions but significantly less research is being done on the impact of Chinese actions in the developing world. We must cultivate new specialists in Chinese-Ghanian relations, Russian-Malian relations, Chinese-Tajik ties, and Russian-Kazakh ties. We also need to invest in the study of deterrence, arms control, and nuclear weapons through the lens of emerging technologies. We must nurture new knowledge held by experts focused on AI policies, quantum computing, synthetic biology, and other emerging technologies. We did that during the Cold War when the "emerging technology" was nuclear weapons; we should do it again now.

ADVANCE DEMOCRACY ABROAD

American support for democracy around the world during the Cold War was imperfect, hypocritical, and sometimes ineffective. At times, especially after the communist takeover in China in 1949 and again in the 1970s, communism appeared to be winning the contest of ideas. But the trend eventually reversed. By the end of the Cold War, more people and countries embraced democratic ideas. US policies and programs contributed positively to this phenomenon. They can again today. The good news is that the ideological threat from the PRC and Russia is not nearly as intense or global as the Soviet ideological challenge. The bad news is that democratic forces have achieved very few outright victories in the past decade. Globally, we have endured two decades of democratic recession.[57] The challenges of democratic backsliding are compounded by the perception, especially in the developing world, of a well-performing Chinese economic model. Putin's brand of orthodox nationalist populism has attracted millions of followers in the older democracies of Europe and the US. There is also a growing perception that democracy both new and old is not delivering. Perhaps most disturbingly, President Trump and many of his supporters embrace Putin's illiberal nationalism. In the struggle between autocrats and democrats in the twenty-first century, some have begun to wonder which side the United States is on.

President Trump, some in his administration, and some outside analysts have concluded that the US should get out of the business of supporting democracy abroad and focus on realpolitik balance-of-power interests.[58] That would be a mistake. Trump's assault on America's tools for advancing democratic values in the early months of his second term is unilateral disarmament. Of course, agencies like USAID and Voice of America require reform and restructuring to ensure greater efficiency. In addition, American instruments for democracy promotion should be adapted for today's new ideological contest between autocrats and democrats. But abandoning this project altogether is short-sighted and self-defeating.

Democracy promotion was a vital part of America's strategy for winning the Cold War and will be essential for competing effectively with China and Russia today. In the current era of great power competition, the superiority of our democratic ideas is one of our most significant advantages. China may outperform us in making electric vehicles. Russia has many more military mercenaries than we do. But both are far behind the United States and our democratic allies in the contest of ideas. When was the last time you saw tens of thousands protesting in the streets to demand a one-man dictatorship or Communist Party rule? Even during the past two decades of democratic decay, mass protests in support of democracy still happen frequently in repressive countries like Iran, Belarus, and Venezuela. People go to jail for years or are killed for supporting democratic ideas. Two of my friends—Boris Nemtsov and Alexei Navalny—were killed in Russia for holding the audacious belief that the Russian people should elect their leaders. Jails in Hong Kong, Xinjiang, and other Chinese cities are filled with brave people with similar beliefs.[59] No one goes to jail in democracies today for supporting communism or Putinism.

There is a reason why people are inspired by democracy. It is a better system. As Churchill said, "No one pretends that democracy is perfect or all-wise. Indeed it has been said that democracy is the worst form of Government except for all those other forms that have been tried from time to time." Democracy is more effective in representing the interests of citizens because they can hold their leaders accountable. Mao, Stalin, Hitler, and Pol Pot slaughtered millions of their citizens and people in neighboring countries. Mass killings, including famines, do not happen in democracies. On average, democracies outperform autocracies in economic development, health, education, and security.[60] It is no accident that the wealthiest countries in the world are also the most democratic in the world. Nine of the world's ten largest economies are democracies, and democracies dominate the top of the list of countries in terms of both GDP per capita and the World Bank's Human Development Index. On average, democratic breakthroughs produce higher growth rates than the previous dictatorships.[61] In addition, public-opinion polls show that most people in the world prefer democracy to other forms of government.[62] Most dictators pretend to be democrats, another indicator of democracy's global appeal.[63] Advocates for democracy worldwide—ministers in democratic governments and human rights activists fighting against autocratic regimes—want to see the US in the business of supporting democracy.

The spread of democracy also advances American security and economic interests. Almost every American adversary has been a dictatorship. Not every past or present autocracy is an enemy of the US, but every American enemy has been an autocracy. All of America's adversaries today—China, Russia, Iran, North Korea—are autocracies. The deadly cocktail of autocracy and power has consistently threatened American security—in World War I, World War II, the Cold War, and today. Conversely, the expansion of democracy has enhanced our security. Democratic transitions created new American allies in Germany, Italy, Japan, and Eastern Europe. The expansion of democracy has opened markets for American business and given US companies new investment and trade opportunities.

US efforts to advance democracy have achieved limited results in the past two decades. But we succeeded during the Cold War in advancing democratic ideas. American leaders should learn from our past successes to more effectively support democracy today.

GET OUR OWN HOUSE IN ORDER

American democracy endured real challenges during the Cold War, especially in the 1960s and early 1970s, but nothing like today. If American leaders want to win the ideological contest with China and Russia in this century, we must devote more attention to improving our democratic system of government at home. That project should include automatic voter registration, better management and funding of polling places, fewer restrictions on voter participation, and making Election Day a national holiday. American democracy also desperately needs campaign-finance reform to provide transparency about candidates' funding sources and more ambitiously limit the sums individuals can provide candidates. Our elections need better protection from foreign interference, including cybersecurity, transparency about foreign media, and a ban on in-kind support from international actors.[64] Partisan redistricting for congressional elections must end. Primaries controlled by political parties that promote extremist candidates should be replaced by open primaries where the top four candidates reach the second round of voting irrespective of party affiliation.[65] States that have adopted this system have already chosen less extreme officials. Ranked-choice voting improves democratic performance.

Where it is practiced, including in New York and Maine, ranked-choice voting has punished extremist candidates and rewarded those seeking broader support.[66]

The undemocratic practice of taxation without representation for residents of the District of Columbia and American territories such as Puerto Rico should also end. Better border security and additional resources to support legal immigration would improve American democracy. Increased transparency about methods social media companies use to curate their content and new regulations for artificial intelligence, including requirements to tag deepfakes and regulations for testing of new AI models for safety, would strengthen American democracy as well.[67] Most ambitiously, American believers in a more representative democracy should support the passage of legislation to end the Electoral College. This eighteenth-century artifact denies American voters the ability to elect the president of the United States directly.

Most urgently, the assaults on democratic practices launched by Trump in his second term must be slowed and reversed. As outlined in chapter 6, Trump tried to dramatically expand the power of the executive branch in 2025, including shutting down entire federal agencies without any input from the US Congress. He has also invoked national security to impose the most sweeping set of tariffs in a hundred years, again without any involvement of the US Congress, even though the US Constitution assigns this power to the legislative branch. Most alarmingly for the future of the rule of law and the system of checks and balances—foundations of American democracy—the Trump administration wrongly jailed and deported an immigrant with legal protected status to El Salvador.[68] As already mentioned, Trump and his team have also signaled intentions that violate two constitutional amendments: the Fourteenth Amendment, which guarantees birthright citizenship, and the Twenty-Second Amendment, which bars presidents from running for a third term.

This list of democratic reforms and defenses is only partial and contains sweeping *shoulds* and *musts* that are easy to list and hard to achieve.[69] Some readers might read my list of reforms as partisan. That is not my intention. Instead, I aim to suggest reforms that would strengthen American democratic institutions—the rules of the game of democracy—without wading into policy debates between Republicans and Democrats or conservatives and liberals. US foreign policymakers must understand the connection between improving democracy at home and pursuing national interests abroad. The US cannot claim to be the leader of the free world if antidemocratic practices in our system are ignored, let alone allowed to grow.

STRENGTHEN THE US ECONOMIC MODEL

The success of the US economy was America's best instrument for promoting democracy during the Cold War. With China today, the competition between economic models is much more formidable than it was during the Cold War. The Chinese system has produced fantastic growth over the past four decades. Even with recent setbacks, the Chinese economic model is Xi's most effective tool in the ideological competition with the United States.

American leaders, therefore, must innovate, reform, and renew American capitalism to outperform China. The Biden administration took some steps to invest in America's economic renewal, including new incentives to promote domestic manufacturing, subsidies for adopting clean energy, and much-needed infrastructure investments, but more needs to be done. To support the AI revolution and benefit from its potential, we must prioritize increasing our energy supplies, including nuclear energy. Policies that support entrepreneurship need to be refined—prudent tax rates, laws to promote competition (especially in high-tech fields), and the proper ecosystem to stimulate long-term private investment. The American economic model would benefit greatly from better health care, childcare, and elderly care, improved K-12 education, more housing, better transportation infrastructure, and successful climate-change policies.[70] These reforms would help reduce inequality, which in turn would stimulate economic growth and nurture support for democracy. Lower levels of inequality and a vibrant middle class were critical features of our Cold War economy that inspired emulation around the globe. We must regain that status again.

During the Cold War, American investments in education made US universities the best in the world. Our ability to attract the best students from around the world to study, work, and immigrate to the US was a significant advantage we maintained over the Soviet Union. We still have this advantage over China and Russia today, but we must expand it, not weaken it as the second Trump administration has done early in the term by implementing dramatic cuts to our research universities. The US and its allies are home to the world's top research universities. China has only six (two are in Hong Kong); Russia has none.[71] In research on AI, American companies and universities have a lead over China, but to maintain that edge, we must enact regulations to deepen competition in the private sector and provide additional resources to research universities. US strategists must also devise better incentives to retain foreign talent, as international graduates fill critical talent gaps in our high-tech labor market.[72] The second Trump administration's policy of revoking student visas without any due process and its attempt to ban international students from attending Harvard will scare away the world's best and the brightest from coming to the US. These irrational practices must be stopped as quickly as possible.

Our economy also needs creative policy changes to take advantage of the opportunities of the post-industrial, information-driven, AI-enhanced world that is emerging. This requires changing some of our past practices, including the introduction of some new industrial policies to facilitate new domestic manufacturing of critical technologies. However, we will not outpace the Chinese by becoming like them. Just as FDR introduced some government interventions in the private sector in the 1930s without embracing communism, US leaders today must make moves to restructure our economy without trying to emulate the Chinese model.

DEMOCRACY PROMOTION *WITHOUT* THE MILITARY

Despite the myths propagated by our adversaries, the United States has rarely used military force to promote democracy. Apart from the US intervention in Panama, every use of American military force was initiated to pursue security objectives—even the invasion of Iraq in 2003.[73] It was only after using force to achieve security objectives that American presidents sought to promote democracy in Germany, Japan, Afghanistan, Iraq, and elsewhere. Our record of success in consolidating democracy after military intervention is not impressive (five for seventeen, by my count). To make clear that military force should never be conflated with democracy promotion, every national security strategy written by future American presidents should state that we will not use our armed forces for democratic regime change.

SHORE UP NEW DEMOCRACIES

In the ideological struggle today between autocrats and democrats, our priority must be defense, not offense—strengthening new and fragile democracies. Instead of giving aid to semi-autocratic governments in hopes they will eventually democratize or expending resources to try to undermine consolidated dictatorships, US leaders should help newly elected leaders in emerging democracies like Sri Lanka, Zambia, Malawi, Guatemala, Armenia, and Moldova consolidate their democratic gains. Democracy expert Larry Diamond assessed that only two out of twenty countries that recently experienced democratic breakthroughs successfully consolidated a democratic system of government over the longer term.[74] That is an abysmal record. We need to reverse it.

Conversely, when autocracies break down, the United States must lead in helping democratic institutions take root. The Biden administration launched the Democracy Delivers Initiative to aid democratic "bright spots" and leveraged private philanthropy to pledge over five hundred million dollars to this effort.[75] Trump is unlikely to be interested in continuing this program. But hopefully, future American leaders will expand (or reinstitute) Democracy Delivers while also establishing a "Democracy Consolidation Fund" within it—a Marshall Plan for new democracies—to keep funds in reserve that can be transferred immediately to societies that achieve a democratic breakthrough. Had such a fund been available to Russian democrats in 1991, they might have succeeded in consolidating democracy. Ukrainian democratic forces that led the Orange Revolution in 2004 could also have benefited from a quick infusion of financial support. When resources for democracy promotion are limited, US programs must focus on strengthening those institutions and organizations that constrain executive power, such as independent media, anti-corruption agencies, parliaments, judiciaries, and nongovernmental organizations, to stop democratic backsliding.[76]

In the global struggle between democracy and autocracy today, Ukraine is on the front lines. After the war ends, American leaders must galvanize the free world to invest in Ukraine, not only with massive military assistance and NATO membership to deter a future Russia attack, but also in strengthening Ukrainian democratic institutions. During the war, Zelenskyy and his team felt compelled, with good reason, to concentrate political power in the executive branch. After the war ends, parliament and regional governments must become stronger, space for independent media should open, and civil society must have a greater say in policy deliberations. A thriving democracy in Ukraine will inspire democratic forces in Russia, Belarus, Georgia, and Armenia. A failing democracy in Ukraine will embolden autocrats in these places and the rest of the world.

American leaders must devote more effort to preventing backsliding in established democracies. During Trump's second term, this issue is unlikely to be a priority, as many of the backsliders, such as Viktor Orbán in Hungary, are ideological kindred spirits of Trump and his MAGA movement. After Trump, however, future Americans should lead NATO in adding a provision to the treaty allowing for the temporary suspension of allies that are no longer democracies.

DIRECT SUPPORT TO DEMOCRATIC ACTIVISTS

US leaders should seek more effective ways to support democracy and human rights activists directly. There are too many middlemen in the democracy business, meaning that too many resources are spent on the salaries and overhead of American and European "implementing partners," leaving less for the democrats we should be helping. The second Trump administration has rightly focused on disrupting this system but tragically seems committed only to ending, not reforming, foreign assistance in support of democracy. If a window of opportunity after Trump opens again to implement effective reforms, a revised strategy should include more direct grants to civil society organizations, greater resources to provide more access to information to people living in autocracies, and increased legal assistance, visas, infrastructure support, and both physical security and cybersecurity for journalists and opposition leaders living in exile. In fragile autocracies, elections still provide the best opportunity for democratic breakthroughs.[77] Assistance programs that enhance the transparency of elections, including election-monitoring organizations, exit polls, and parallel vote tabulations, should be supported with more vigor. And after civil societies prove that autocrats stole an election, the United States must act more aggressively alongside the rest of the democratic world to try to tip the balance in favor of democratic breakthroughs. This will require sanctions, asset freezes, and arrest warrants for those involved in the falsification operation. The 2024 presidential election in Venezuela was one such moment to adopt these policies; it offered a real chance for a democratic breakthrough, but the democratic world failed to apply enough pressure on the autocratic regime to allow the actual winner of this election to take power. When future opportunities for democratic breakthroughs emerge, the United States and the rest of the democratic world must be more prepared to act.

A straightforward way to expand more direct aid to democrats would be to increase the budget of the National Endowment for Democracy (NED). With more funding, NED could provide more resources directly to democratic activists and fund US nongovernmental organizations supporting global democracy.

US government officials in cooperation with Congress could take a second, bolder step and establish new foundations focused on supporting specific institutions and functions of democracy—civil society, the rule of law, women's rights, independent media, and anti-corruption. Funds previously allocated to the State Department and the USAID for democracy promotion—now ended by the second Trump administration—could be restored in the future, not through these government bodies but instead through new independent foundations. This approach would create more separation from the US government and could attract funding from other governments and private foundations. It is dangerous for some democracy activists and groups to take money directly from the State Department. That is why Trump's plan to incorporate all USAID into the State Department is the wrong move. These new foundations would operate like the World Bank but for democracy instead of development.

In the Trump era, increased funding for NED or support for creating new government-funded foundations seems unlikely, meaning we need another innovation independent of the US government—an International Platform for Freedom. The IPF could function as a secure platform to connect activists to funders, ideas, and infrastructure. Think of IPF as an eBay, Craigslist, Amazon, PayPal, and Coursera all in one, curated by experts to channel the flow of information about democracy and funding for democratic organizations to small-*d* democrats worldwide.[78] Grandmothers in Montana could use the IPF to send thirty dollars to a women's NGO in Pakistan. Youth leaders in Zimbabwe could use the platform to obtain knowledge about successful democratic transitions led by young people in Serbia. Stanford professors could give lectures on the platform about the pros and cons of different electoral systems to new democratic leaders in Sri Lanka. Creating this nongovernmental platform would allow more private individuals and NGOs to support democracy activists directly and quickly. AI companies could also provide information on democracy—a large language model devoted just to democracy—to all small-*d* democrats of the world.

INTERNATIONALIZE DEMOCRACY PROMOTION

The autocrats of the world are united. China, Russia, Iran, and North Korea coordinate their activities on a wide range of issues. The democratic side needs to do the same. During the Cold War, ideological solidarity in the "liberal West" proved essential for containing and defeating the "communist East." We need to renew that ideological solidarity again.

As a first step, the US must create stronger ties among democratic governments. The G7 should coordinate not only on economic issues, but also on democracy, human rights, and free speech on social media platforms.[79] South Korea and Australia (not Russia, as Trump proposed) should be invited to join the organization.

More broadly, small-*d* democrats in democracies and autocracies, including those living in exile, should be connected and united in conferences, clubs, and organizations. Illiberal nationalists around the world regularly interact with one another, sharing lessons from both their successes and failures. Liberal internationalists must do the same. At a minimum, organizations like the World Movement for Democracy should be expanded to foster greater global collaboration in support of democratic values.

The US should also be comfortable leading from behind in the global struggle for democracy. Activists from newer democracies understand the democratic transition process better than their counterparts in older democracies. As democracy experts Thomas Carothers and Frances

Brown explain, "Innovation with newer, non-Western democracies makes the case for treating democracy building as a mutual learning exercise rather than an export business."[80] International learning about nongovernmental election monitoring, from the Philippines to Chile to Serbia to Ukraine, is an example of a success story of transnational knowledge sharing in which the United States did not play a central role. Democratic leaders living in exile from Russia, Belarus, Venezuela, Burma, China, and Iran should learn from each other. American organizations could facilitate this learning by supporting transnational networks but they should do so without leading them. Given the challenges to democracy within the United States during the second Trump administration, European democracies must step up and take on a more prominent leadership role in the global struggle between autocracies and democracies.

COUNTER AUTOCRATIC DISINFORMATION

President Eisenhower created the United States Information Agency (USIA) to inform overseas audiences about the United States. The theory was simple: The more international audiences knew about the United States, the more they would like us. It worked. I remember my weekly visits in the 1980s to the USIA office in downtown Harare, Zimbabwe, where I was doing research for my doctoral dissertation at Oxford. Entering the building was like stepping into America, complete with a daily broadcast of ABC's *World News Tonight* with Peter Jennings, delayed by one day. The place made America look good and feel good, making me proud of my country. I loved seeing Zimbabweans engage with the office's resources. During the Cold War, Radio Free Europe and Radio Liberty also reached large audiences in the communist world.

After the Cold War ended, US policymakers lost interest in these projects. In 1999, Congress compelled President Bill Clinton to integrate USIA into the State Department. That was shortsighted. USIA was more effective as an independent agency. Equally imprudent was Trump's decision to defund the media organizations under the umbrella of the United States Agency for Global Media (USAGM) in 2025. To counter the growing influence of information from China and Russia, the US government must not shut down, but restructure, reform, modernize, and expand its media organizations.

The best strategy for countering Russian and Chinese disinformation is accurate, independent reporting from credible journalists, both those from democracies and professional journalists from China, Russia, and other autocracies, including those working in exile. Today's reporters need more support from democratic countries; they need financial assistance, visa support, legal defense, short-term training opportunities, yearlong fellowships at American universities, and internships at US and European media organizations. Dedicated funds are also needed for investigative journalists and their servers abroad, including aid in hiding the identities of these journalists and their sources.

In the past several years, many American social media companies introduced reforms to increase transparency about content on their platforms produced by state-owned or government-controlled media, including labeling content, banning certain advertisement purchases, and adjusting algorithms. Journalists working for RT, Sputnik, and CGTN were labeled as foreign agents. In 2024, Meta banned RT and other Russian state-owned media outlets from Facebook and its other platforms.[81] The second Trump administration has encouraged these companies to roll back such policies. That is a mistake. Social media companies operating in democracies can and should do more to combat foreign-sponsored disinformation, labeling deepfakes and de-amplifying grossly false content produced by hostile governments.[82] Putin and Xi cannot be allowed to use American social media to spread disinformation.

The US Congress should respectfully oppose President Trump and allocate more resources to support US government-funded international media organizations, not fewer.[83] As former Radio Free Europe and Radio Liberty president Jeff Gedmin wrote, "The current budget of $750 million for all US media costs roughly what we spend on eight or nine top-shelf fighter jets."[84] At the same time, American leaders in the executive and legislative branches of government should work together to restructure these US-government-funded media organizations to give most of them more autonomy from the US government. Most media organizations within the USAGM—Radio Liberty, Radio Free Asia, Radio y Televisión Martí (Cuba), and the Middle East Broadcasting Networks (MNB)—should become completely independent from the federal government with nonpartisan boards and independent sources of funding. New independent media organizations for Africa and Latin America also should be created by spinning off VOA Africa and VOA Latin America into independent media companies. The sole mission of these organizations should be independent journalism, following the model of the BBC, a publicly funded but independent and highly credible news organization.

At the same time, after these spinoffs gain autonomy, the remainder of VOA, if Trump succeeds in shutting it down, needs to be first resurrected and then more closely aligned with the United States government to provide officials with a platform to explain their policies. VOA's current multiple-headed mission—to "serve as a consistently reliable and authoritative source of news," "represent America, not any single segment of American society," and "present the policies of the United States clearly and effectively"—is impossible to pursue. A restructured VOA should focus solely on the third objective, presenting the policies of the United States clearly and effectively, and leave independent reporting to the other entities described above.

MORE CLUBS FOR DEMOCRACIES

Even before World War II ended, US officials started planning for the creation of multilateral institutions to sustain a new international economic order in what became known as the Bretton Woods system. After the war, the US led the creation of a new global security order, including, most important, the United Nations. Some of these institutions were successful; others were not. The deep divide between the Soviet Union and the United States often prevented the UN Security Council from effectively providing global security, even if Washington and Moscow did at times cooperate in multilateral settings to produce positive collective outcomes, including on the Non-Proliferation Treaty, the Biological Weapons Convention, the elimination of smallpox, the Helsinki Accords and its Organization for Security and Co-operation in Europe, the UN Convention on the Law of the Sea, and the Chemical Weapons Convention.

During the Cold War, the liberal international *economic* order united the capitalist world and excluded the communist world. A clear and positive lesson from the Cold War is that international economic organizations by and for democracies contributed to Soviet containment and ultimately helped the West prevail. These kinds of organizations need to be created and strengthened again to unite the democratic world today. China has invested heavily in creating its own economic clubs that exclude the United States. The democratic world needs to do the same.

In the post–Cold War era, we made the mistake of extending membership in multilateral economic institutions to autocratic countries that were not qualified or resisted adopting the norms, laws, and procedures of the liberal economic order, eventually straining the system. For instance, the EU extended membership to some countries from the former communist world that resisted implementing market reforms and a few—most notably Hungary—that rolled back democratic practices after getting into this club. China joined the World Trade Organization without fully committing to the rules of the game, which later produced adverse economic outcomes for the factories and workers in developed countries that traded with the PRC, including the United States. Trump won two elections partly because he capitalized on anger among American voters about what they saw as unfair globalization.

In reaction, as former US trade official Michael Beeman observed, "America is walking out on the very trading system it helped establish, shape, and promote."[85] The withdrawal process, which began during Trump's first term, has accelerated in his second, most notably through the imposition of tariffs on goods from nearly every country, including substantial tariffs on Chinese products. These actions prompted Beijing to retaliate with new tariffs on American goods and restrictions on exports of rare minerals critical for the production of semiconductors, batteries, and other essential components for US high-tech products. This is a mistake. Autarky, protectionism, unilateralism, and isolationism are ineffective strategies for our current era. Trade, international investment, and engagement with the global economy, especially between democratic countries, still advance American economic interests.[86]

Instead of walking away, the United States should strengthen American leadership in existing multilateral organizations in which autocratic countries like China and Russia are members, especially those dealing with economic issues. Withdrawing would further weaken America's ability to address challenges posed by China and Russia. Rather than pulling out of multilateral organizations or trying to kick China out of international organizations, American leaders should mobilize democratic allies to reform existing multilateral organizations to better advance our interests and values.

Reengaging and reforming the existing architecture, however, are not enough. As discussed in chapter 11, Beijing is busy creating new multilateral organizations, especially ones working on economic issues. To a much lesser extent, Russia is doing this as well. US leaders must do the same—create new clubs, especially for economic matters, whose members are only democracies. We did that during the Cold War. We should do it again now.

RENEW AMERICAN LEADERSHIP IN EXISTING MULTILATERAL ORGANIZATIONS

President Trump does not believe in multilateralism and is especially skeptical about international economic organizations. Trump and his team have rightly observed that Chinese communist leaders have used their membership in these organizations to their unfair benefit, frequently ignoring the laws, rules, and norms of these clubs. That said, walking away is not the prudent American response. American leaders must get back in the fight, at a minimum, to check bad Chinese and Russian behavior within these organizations.

During the Cold War, the United States led the free world in reducing tariffs between capitalist countries through bodies like the General Agreement on Trade and Tariffs, which then became the World Trade Organization. After the Cold War ended, we encouraged former communist countries, including China and Russia, to join. In retrospect, the bar for admission for these two countries and other autocracies should have been higher. However, the solution is not to abandon the WTO altogether, as Trump has suggested, but to engage with greater vigor and push for reform. The US still benefits from competition and free and fair trade. The expansion of trade in the past several decades has helped to reduce poverty, slow carbon emissions, and generate global economic growth, including in the United States.[87] The WTO played a positive role in supporting these desired outcomes. With reform, the WTO can still play a positive role in supporting the growth of the American economy and the economies of our democratic allies.

American leaders rightly want fair trade, especially with China. Xi cannot use subsidies and regulations to help Chinese firms, suppress domestic consumption, and manipulate currency to expand exports—China expert and economic analyst Liza Tobin colorfully labels these practices "brute force economics"—and then berate the US government for no longer supporting free trade.[88] At the same time, American leaders sound hypocritical when complaining about Chinese overcapacity leading to flooded markets of cheap electric vehicles, solar panels, and batteries around the world while they also protect American companies with tariffs, give subsidies to American firms to open factories domestically, and provide American consumers with financial incentives to buy EVs made in America. If they continue, these unilateral tit-for-tat moves by Washington and Beijing will generate a race to the bottom where both sides (and the world) will lose. We did that in the 1930s, producing a global depression. We should not repeat that mistake today.

The WTO is barely functioning today. By the time this book is published, it may be dead. That would be a bad outcome for American long-term economic interests. The US and China still need independent referees to distinguish between subsidized overcapacity and cheaper, better products resulting from innovation and competition. Instead of giving up on the WTO, American leaders must adopt a strategy for reinvigorating this multilateral body, even if the scope of its mandate should be more limited. Despite flawed enforcement procedures, the WTO remains the most powerful dispute-settlement structure for global economic issues. Even while Chinese leaders seek ways to subvert WTO norms and practices, WTO membership has made the Chinese economy more open and compelled Chinese actors to participate in dispute settlement hearings in Geneva.[89]

To improve the WTO, the United States should stop blocking the appointment and reappointment of judges to the WTO's Appellate Body and allow this organization to do its work resolving disputes.[90] US leaders should also press to expand WTO stakeholders to include environmentalists, workers, and consumers. Many rules and regulations codified in the

US-Mexico-Canada Agreement could serve as a road map.[91] American officials should also lead an effort within the WTO to address new challenges of the digital economy, including new regulations for protecting intellectual property and data, since current WTO rules were designed for a world without smartphones, cloud computing, digital commerce, digital currencies, and AI.[92] American trade negotiators should also rally other countries to pressure China to abide by WTO rules, including filing a multilateral case against China within the WTO.[93]

In addition, American leaders should strengthen the IMF and World Bank to help the free world better compete with Chinese state-owned banks and PRC foreign loans and assistance. The IMF and World Bank need more money and a deeper commitment to fostering the development of democratic institutions. These organizations should not bail out countries that have signed bad financial deals with Chinese lenders. US leaders should work with other democracies to expand the OECD's Blue Dot Network, "the first global certification framework for quality infrastructure projects."[94] Better information about infrastructure projects will help leaders in the developing world make prudent decisions about which deals from China to accept and which ones to avoid.

In collaboration with democratic allies, the US must take a more assertive role in existing standard-setting organizations, like the World Customs Organization, the World Intellectual Property Organization, and the International Labor Organization. Beijing and Moscow, to a lesser extent, long ago recognized the importance of these standard-setting groups and pushed for greater leadership within them. In UN bodies and expert groups, these autocratic countries aggressively block progress on cyber and digital norms in the name of sovereignty and nonintervention. We must push back to establish constructive laws and standards for an open internet and greater individual control over personal data.[95] The US could lead the world in establishing a new treaty and international organizations to create standards and norms for using artificial intelligence and other emerging technologies. President Trump is unlikely to seek this kind of leadership, but future American leaders should.

Finally, the United States cannot give up on the United Nations. While cooperation in pursuit of collective security is improbable today within the UN Security Council because of deep divisions between the autocrats (China and Russia) and the democrats (France, Great Britain, and the United States), the UN continues to provide collective goods on various other American interests, including climate change, norms to guide the use of AI, peacekeeping, humanitarian assistance, and, more generally, management of the commons. The UN resolution "Seizing the Opportunities of Safe, Secure, and Trustworthy Artificial Intelligence Systems for Sustainable Development" adopted in the spring of 2024 signaled American leadership on shaping norms about AI in ways beneficial for open societies, including our own.[96]

To strengthen our leadership in the UN, American officials could ratify the United Nations Convention on the Law of the Sea, a treaty establishing rules of engagement on the world's oceans. Doing so would enhance American leverage in dealing with China in the South China Sea and Russia in the Arctic Sea and eliminate the hypocrisy of pressuring countries to adhere to an agreement we have not yet ratified.[97] Ratifying this treaty would also provide greater predictability for American companies to conduct deep-seabed mining of rare-earth minerals, thereby reducing our dependence on China.[98] In addition, the US Senate should ratify the Convention on the Elimination of All Forms of Discrimination against Women (CEDAW). President Carter signed this treaty in 1980, and nearly 97 percent of all countries worldwide have ratified this uncontroversial agreement. America's absence is embarrassing and undermines our reputation as an advocate for human rights. The US must rejoin and then engage more assertively in the UN Human Rights Council to check Chinese, Russian, and other autocratic influences. In 2020, fifty-three countries signed a statement in support of China's new security law for Hong Kong, while only twenty-seven on the council criticized it.[99] That is outrageous.

STRENGTHEN INSTITUTIONAL TIES BETWEEN DEMOCRACIES

China is creating new clubs for autocracies. The United States must create new clubs for democracies. Some new multilateral security organizations (including, most ambitiously, the Pacific Alliance Treaty Organization) have already been suggested, as have some new multilateral institutions for uniting the free world to advance democracy abroad (the International

Platform for Freedom). We also need creativity in uniting the democratic world on economic issues to match China's initiatives in this domain. US leaders could expand the G7 to become the G10 or even the G15. Other democracies on the list of the largest economies in the world should be invited to join—South Korea, Spain, Australia, and Mexico, then India, Brazil, and Indonesia. Just as China expanded BRICS, we should expand the G7 and have it evolve into a more authoritative body to deepen trade and investment between the free-world economies, creating new rules and norms on technology regulation, finance, data sharing, competition policy, supply chains, and access to critical minerals for the free world. An expanded G7 could adopt explicit norms against imposing tariffs on other member states and blocking investments within member states. We should want to encourage more investment, trade, technology development, and research collaboration between democracies and less between autocracies and democracies. We want to reduce Chinese access to data from Americans and other citizens of democracies, but we also want to increase the flow of data between democracies as a necessary condition to compete with Chinese tech companies, especially on AI.[100] This larger group of democracies could become the focal point for defending new democratic norms by adopting shared practices to regulate AI, quantum computing, and other emerging technologies. If democracies do not unite to navigate the ethical, economic, and security issues of these new technologies together, China will win.[101]

In his first term, President Trump made a mistake in withdrawing from negotiations to join the Trans-Pacific Partnership. The TPP offered a new multilateral framework to address China's rise. Instead of trying to explain this agreement's security and economic benefits to the American people, the Biden administration gave up and offered instead a more modest Indo-Pacific Economic Framework for Prosperity that has not gained much traction. After the United States withdrew from the TPP, the remaining nations prudently negotiated a new trade agreement without us: the CPTPP, now one of the largest free-trade organizations in the world.[102] Current members have kept the door open for the US to join. We should walk through it. Trump won't do that, but future American leaders should. They would have to explain more convincingly to the American people why US membership in CPTPP would serve our interests in dealing with unfair Chinese trade and investment policies more effectively because CPTPP members have expanded production networks, built interconnected innovation systems, increased collaborative manufacturing, and developed mutual trust in supply chains.[103] Changing its name and introducing reforms, like the first Trump administration did with NAFTA, could be part of a strategy for eventually getting the United States back in.

Building on the US-EU Trade and Technology Council launched during the Biden era, American leaders—most likely in a post-Trump era—should revisit the ambitious but prudent idea of negotiating a comprehensive trade agreement with the European Union. In the competition between autocrats and democrats, we want to deepen our economic ties with the most powerful bloc of democracies in the world, the European Union.

As this book goes to print, the second Trump administration is just starting to implement a foreign policy agenda antithetical to many of the successes from the last Cold War. This makes recommendations for stronger alliances, more money for democracy promotion, greater engagement with existing international organizations, and the creation of new clubs for democracies sound out of touch with our time. I am very aware that many of the policy recommendations outlined in the chapter may not resonate with Trump and his team. However, the lessons from the Cold War are clear. These policies and organizations helped us win the Cold War and can help us again today. Conversely, retreating from them will make competing effectively with China and Russia much harder. If Trump and his team do not appreciate this fact, hopefully future American leaders and American society as a whole will.

Chapter 14

NEW POLICIES FOR NEW CHALLENGES

THE PREVIOUS TWO chapters discussed Cold War successes to repeat and mistakes to avoid in our current era of great power competition. There is also a third category—dimensions of great power rivalry today that have nothing in common with the Cold War. First, the degree of economic interdependence between China and the United States, fueled in part by the size and success of the Chinese economy as described in chapter 5, has no parallel in the Cold War. Second, compared to the previous century, the world is more fragmented, with enough other rising powers to compel some analysts to describe the current international system as multipolar. Third, the China-Russia partnership is deep and scary; they were divided during the Cold War. Fourth, the United States, especially under President Trump, has gravitated toward isolationist and unilateral policies that US Cold War presidents rarely espoused. Fifth, America's polarized division at home coupled with the erosion of democratic institutions and norms are greater than in any period during the Cold War. Speaking at the Munich Security Summit in February 2025, Vice President Vance said, "The threat that I worry the most about vis-à-vis Europe is not Russia, it's not China . . . what I worry about is the threat from within, the retreat of Europe from some of its most fundamental values—values shared with the United States of America."[1] Vance was wrong about European democracy; its erosion is not a greater threat to the continent than Russia or China. But the threat from within the United States could very well metastasize into a greater threat to American national security than either China or Russia. Most alarmingly, in the first year of Trump's second term, in today's struggle between autocrats and democrats, it is not always clear which side the United States is on. That is new and different from the Cold War. In fact, in all American history, that ambiguity has never been as salient as it is today.

ECONOMIC INTERDEPENDENCE

During the Cold War, the United States anchored the international capitalist system, while the Soviet Union headed a separate global communist bloc. This feature of the Cold War has no parallel today; the Chinese economy is now deeply embedded in the global system and intertwined with the American economy and our allies. Similarly, the Russian economy is more integrated with the global economy today than it was during the Cold War, although that weakened after Russia invaded Ukraine. Unlike the previous century, economic interdependence between the great powers is a feature of today's international system.

SELECTIVE, NOT TOTAL, DECOUPLING

Some American strategists, including several close to President Trump, do not like the interdependence of our era and advocate for a sharp, if not complete, decoupling from the Chinese economy. Massive tariffs on Chinese goods implemented in the first months of Trump 2.0 suggest that Trump might be serious about pursuing complete decoupling. That is imprudent. Should American foreign policymakers pursue such a strategy, the US economy would lose more than one trillion dollars in sales over the next decade and greatly damage its long-term global competitiveness.[2] Trying to disentangle just one sector of the global economy—the semiconductor industry—would adversely affect American companies and firms located in countries with close ties to the United States, including, first and foremost, Taiwan. Likewise, companies like Apple that rely on China for assembly and inputs would be devastated. So would Boeing and American farmers who depend on access to the Chinese market. Thousands of small businesses in the United States rely on inputs from China to make their products, and would face bankruptcy from even the pursuit of complete decoupling. The service industries that foster bilateral trade—shipping and distribution companies, marketing firms, banks and accountants, dockworkers, and the like—would all suffer massive losses from decoupling. Even in more sensitive fields, such as artificial intelligence and drug research, the global ecosystem benefits the most from some level of interaction between American and Chinese researchers, rather than two entirely disconnected blocs. More broadly, it is not in America's long-term interests to try to reverse the course of economic development at home or abroad. Do we really want to try to "onshore" the production of tennis shoes or the assembly of phones? Who would be willing to do those kinds of jobs? And would American consumers be prepared to pay significantly more for these products if they were made in the US with our higher-cost labor force? The American economy is outperforming its peers' in the developed world largely due to the productivity gains driven by a dynamic and skilled workforce—by better jobs, not cheaper ones. That momentum would be slowed if we tried to resurrect industries reliant on low-wage workers to produce low-value products. The American economy is also fueled by services, including some low-paying sectors, but also many high-paying industries. Shifting back toward producing more cheap goods within our borders will slow labor productivity and, in turn, economic growth.

Rather than pushing for more protectionism to insulate the American economy, American leaders should continue to seek better ways to benefit from trade and investment with China and other countries. At the same time, they should stimulate American manufacturing in high-tech industries that create and support high-paying, high-productivity jobs, while simultaneously pursuing targeted policies that limit Chinese acquisition of technology that threaten US security interests. That is a complicated formula, but it offers the most promising path forward.

Complete decoupling is also not feasible. Even when the economic ties between communist and capitalist blocs were weak during the Cold War, some interdependence developed, especially between Europe and the Soviet Union over gas supplies that American leaders could not stop.[3] China's economic entanglement with the entire world is much deeper. Developing countries reliant on goods and investment from China will not embrace a Manichaean realignment into blue and red economic blocs. If Chinese firms offer less expensive electric vehicles to buy or cheaper AI models to use, or provide funding to build roads and airports in Africa, Asia, and

Latin America, lectures from Washington about the communist menace will fall on deaf ears, especially if we are not offering alternatives. If we try to decouple from China, the rest of the world will not follow us.

In addition, Chinese dependence on the global economy is not all bad. This condition makes any action that might disrupt trade and investment, such as an invasion of Taiwan, more costly. If China were completely independent from the American economy, Chinese leaders would have less to lose from launching such a war. Economic interdependence does not guarantee peace but it does increase the costs of conflict.[4] Moreover, the United States is less dependent on the Chinese economy than China is on the global economy. Xi needs trade and investment with the outside world to maintain economic growth at home more than American leaders do. For instance, China imports vast amounts of fossil fuels, and much of it is transported by ships that can be interdicted during wartime. The same would be true for imported components, on which Chinese manufacturing depends heavily.

Attempting—and failing—to decouple or isolate the Chinese economy would also damage the United States' credibility. If we and our democratic allies could not decouple from and isolate the much smaller Russian economy after Putin invaded Ukraine, we should have modest expectations about our capacities to do so with China in peacetime. If Xi were to invade Taiwan, we should worry about our ability to convince the world to impose effective sanctions to achieve China's economic isolation.

While we cannot go back to the Cold War when the global economy was divided into two blocs, we also cannot continue to engage with the Chinese economy in ways that help the Chinese military modernize or give Chinese companies unfair advantages. The same is true for Russia. The prudent strategy is selective decoupling. American leaders should continue to pursue decoupling in domains where our core security and economic interests are threatened, but they should maintain, if not expand, engagement in areas where our economic interests are advanced. That is a challenging Goldilocks balancing act, but it is the only rational course.

Some core US interests require complete decoupling. For instance, and most obvious, the US must stop the Chinese exports of ingredients for making fentanyl to Mexico, where the drug is produced and then illegally brought into the US, contributing to an explosive opioid crisis.[5] Preventing Chinese military and intelligence officers from studying in the United States is another domain in which complete decoupling should be the goal. Curtailing the export of the most sophisticated chips to China—like chips essential in developing artificial intelligence that could give the PLA military advantages—is also a worthy objective, but also difficult to calibrate correctly. The Biden administration started to do that, even though it prompted the CCP to devote more resources to developing China's chip industry and triggered Chinese trade restrictions on the United States.[6] The second Trump administration expanded bans of exports to China of even lesser sophisticated chips, such as Nvidia's H20 chip, which some analysts at the time warned, "simply hands the Chinese AI market over to Huawei."[7] On this debate, it will be years before we know who was right.

More generally, American leaders must be more aggressive in stopping all technological transfers, investments, and research collaborations that help modernize Chinese and Russian military capabilities.[8] American companies cannot be assisting Chinese breakthroughs in AI and quantum computing that strengthen the Chinese military. The US government should provide permissive conditions to stimulate competition among AI companies, including those developing open models, as the only strategy for competing with Chinese AI companies around the world, but it should do so in ways that do not benefit PLA targeting and CCP data collection on Americans, our allies, and our partners.

In parallel, building on the first international meeting of artificial intelligence safety institutes held in San Francisco in November 2024, the free world must continue to expand its efforts to ensure artificial intelligence is being used safely.[9] Bilateral attempts to limit AI development in the United States and China are likely to fail, but the United States and China do have a mutual interest in preventing the proliferation of AI-enabling technologies—high-performing chips in particular—to rogue states or terrorist organizations that could use such capacity to construct threatening weapons, such as synthetic viruses or sophisticated cyber hacks.[10] As the Soviet Union and the United States led the world on nuclear nonproliferation during the Cold War, leaders in Washington and Beijing could construct a regime for tracking and then preventing the proliferation of dangerous AI technologies, including assigning digital unique identifiers for all of the world's most sophisticated chips.[11]

The first Trump and Biden administrations smartly expanded the capabilities and power of the Committee on Foreign Investment in the United States (CFIUS) to provide more scrutiny of Chinese investments in American companies developing and producing sensitive technologies. In August 2023, President Biden signed an executive order that empowered the US government to stop or give greater scrutiny to American investment in Chinese companies producing military-related technologies, such as semiconductors, quantum computing, and artificial intelligence.[12] This suite of new policies—greater export controls, restrictions and greater transparency on inbound investment from China to the United States, and limits and more transparency on outbound investment from the United States to China—provides US policymakers with a better toolkit to stop helping the modernization and development of China's military. Early in his second term, Trump signaled his commitment to expanding these policies by signing the "American First Investment Policy." Now they must be used with greater vigor.

More selective decoupling in telecommunications is also necessary. The free world needs to keep Chinese information and communication companies from penetrating its societies, since this infrastructure can be used for intelligence gathering and, in times of war, disruption. For security reasons, American allies cannot use telecommunication products made by Chinese firms such as Huawei and ZTE.[13] At the same time, the United States cannot compel non-ally partners, especially in the developing world, to stop buying these Chinese products if we do not offer alternatives. The democratic governments of the world must provide better incentives for its companies, such as Ericsson and Nokia, to build more information and communications technology (ICT) capacity to reduce dependence on Chinese technology and hardware.[14] To start, Washington should embrace the effort launched by the United Kingdom to create a D10 club of democracies to coordinate the development of an alternative ICT infrastructure and forge a private-public partnership to provide a price-competitive alternative to Chinese companies, complete with government-backed financing.[15]

More decoupling is also needed regarding American technological components used by Chinese surveillance companies. That is simply unacceptable. No American components should be used in the manufacturing of Chinese products of repression. The US government must also restrict the export of American surveillance technologies to other authoritarian regimes. We have no credibility in berating the Chinese for exporting surveillance technologies to support autocrats if we allow American companies to do the same.

To underscore, *selective* investment and export controls of technology transfer, not comprehensive limits, is the prudent strategy. While restricting the export of high-end chips and limiting the use of open-source AI models for the People's Liberation Army, American strategists must remember that AI has many nonmilitary applications, including in health care and education, that US leaders should not impede in China or any country. In fact, the US should encourage Chinese citizens to use products like ChatGPT as a way to subvert the Chinese digital wall reducing the flow of information into China. The same is true for Russia. The Chinese Communist Party and Putin have successfully blocked media and social media platforms from reaching Chinese and Russian citizens. We do not want to help them achieve similar success in blocking information that might come from AI products. More generally, open-source AI models are an essential element of a robust, innovative ecosystem for AI development in the United States and the rest of the world. Although it is a difficult balance to achieve, we must preserve that ecosystem without helping the militaries of our adversaries.

The same principle must be applied to American investments in the PRC and Chinese investments in the United States. (Today, investments between the United States and Russia have rightly been reduced to a trickle.) Investments that directly strengthen the Chinese military must be stopped. Those that do not should be left alone. Should a Chinese investment in a start-up that aims to produce AI products that help military targeting be blocked? Of course. Should the construction of a battery factory in the United States by a Chinese private company be stopped? If not controlled by the CCP and not the sole producer of batteries in the US, then maybe not. We need batteries, and we want the intellectual property transfer, just as China has successfully done for decades in attracting foreign direct investment. Should Chinese investors be allowed to take equity positions in US drone companies? No. Should all Chinese foreign direct investment in the United States be outlawed? No. Should American mutual funds hold equity positions in sanctioned Chinese companies? No. Should American mutual funds be prohibited from investing in all Chinese firms? No. Will this be complicated to regulate and police? Yes. Impossible to find a Goldilocks solution? No.

Regarding disruption of Chinese economic activity with third countries, US policymakers should also adopt a selective strategy, not a maximalist approach. The construction of Huawei 5G infrastructure in the United Kingdom—a US ally—is detrimental to US security interests. The same system in Uzbekistan does not produce similarly harmful consequences for American security. The United States does not need and should not try to contain all Chinese economic activity around the world, especially because all-out global economic warfare against Chinese companies will fail. Even attempting to do so may make Chinese firms stronger. When sanctioning Huawei, the Trump administration thought they were pushing this Chinese telecommunications company out of business. Today, Huawei is stronger than ever, and countries that Washington coerced to sever ties with this Chinese firm resented the American pressure.[16]

The best way to reduce Chinese sales and investments in other countries is not through coercion but through competition. We cannot expect governments in the developing world to refuse Chinese trade and investment if we do not offer alternatives. In some sectors, such as electric vehicles, 5G, batteries, and solar panels, Chinese firms may already be too far ahead for American companies to compete with. But in AI, 6G, chips, finance, the dollar, computers, phones, airplanes, pharmaceuticals, medical equipment, agriculture, energy, and even automobiles, the United States has much to offer the rest of the world if we can maintain a level playing field—an international rules-based order for managing trade and investment—with Chinese competitors.

The sanctions coalition of four dozen countries that Biden helped assemble in response to Putin's invasion of Ukraine in 2022 to reduce Russian war funding was a noble objective, even if too much money, mainly generated from the export of fossil fuels, and too many technology components, primarily from China but also from democratic countries, still made their way to Russia.

However, the current government architecture for implementing these policies of economic statecraft against China and Russia is too small, decentralized, and underfunded. The US agencies and actors involved in enacting these policies are scattered among Treasury, Commerce, State, Defense, the National Security Council, and the intelligence community, and they lack sufficient capacity to do their jobs effectively.[17] Rarely does creating a new deputy national security adviser or signing a new executive order solve a coordination problem. But a unique feature of our new era of great power rivalry is economic and technology competition with China, so our national security apparatus should reflect this new reality. The National Security Council was created at the dawn of the Cold War. Now is the moment to create a new agency or council for economic statecraft.

American efforts to expand control on exports of sensitive technologies to China and Russia should also be internationalized and institutionalized among the democratic community of states. That was the case during the Cold War when the United States took the lead in establishing the Coordinating Committee for Multilateral Export Controls (CoCom) to limit the transfer of goods and technologies of military value to the Soviet Union and other communist states.[18] CoCom was hard to enforce but produced positive results, in large part because the organization was international. Today, we need a new CoCom for the free world—one that limits the transfer of military and dual-use technologies to China and Russia, while also coordinating sanctions policies among democracies. The current architecture is too balkanized, leaky, and ill-equipped to address twenty-first-century challenges, such as stopping financial flows to malicious actors through cryptocurrencies.

In parallel, US controls on American investments in companies producing military technologies in China and Russia must be internationalized within the community of democracies. Investment controls in democracies, limits on sensitive technologies, and transparency around investment outflows to autocracies could be consolidated into a single new international organization composed of democracies. It could be called the International

Committee on Foreign Investments in Democracies, modeled after the US Committee on Foreign Investment in the United States.[19] Given that the US has more capacity than other democracies to review foreign investment and real estate transactions for national security reasons, we could share this intelligence with our allies and partners through this new organization. This body could designate certain companies and their intellectual property as critical to security. Once a company obtains such a designation, a set of incentives to firms from democratic countries could automatically kick in to keep these assets within the democratic community and away from autocratic adversaries.

In addition to monitoring and stopping investments in sensitive technologies from autocracies, the democratic world must collaborate more effectively to expand joint investments in critical technologies and scientific cooperation.[20] Technological cooperation among Taiwan, the United States, and other democracies regarding the development of semiconductors is especially urgent. The CHIPS and Science Act of 2022 should be a first step, not the last initiative, toward deeper integration of this industry in the democratic world. Greater scientific collaboration between democracies is also needed. To bolster US research on artificial intelligence, Stanford professors John Etchemendy and Fei-Fei Li proposed the creation of a national AI research resource (NAIRR) to "provide academic and non-profit researchers with the compute power and government datasets needed for education and research."[21] The Biden administration launched a pilot NAIRR.[22] The next step should be the creation of an *international* AI research resource shared and financed by a coalition of democratic allies.[23]

Finally, impediments to investment and scientific collaboration between individuals and companies based in democracies must be kept to a minimum. To compete with the autocratic world, we need more economic connectivity between countries in the free world, not less. For instance, the Biden administration mistakenly blocked Nippon Steel's purchase of US Steel because of alleged national security concerns. That purchase would have led to the transfer of technology from Japan to the United States, which would have made US Steel a more efficient and profitable company, produced modern steel needed for American firms, and sustained quality jobs in the United States. Hopefully in Trump's second term, this investment collaboration between companies located in democratic countries can be resurrected.

LIMITING TARIFFS

American leaders should use tariffs only as a last resort and as sparingly as possible. Trump's decision early in his second term to impose tariffs on virtually every country in the world was unnecessary and dangerous. Most detrimental, these tariffs impose a burden on US consumers at a time when inflation poses a significant challenge for middle-class Americans. Tariffs are also unfair; they hurt lower-income Americans much more than rich Americans.[24] In addition, for every tit, there is a tat. In the first months of the second Trump administration, major tariffs on Chinese imports to the United States triggered new tariffs on American products exported to China. While tariffs theoretically might benefit some workers in import-competing industries, they hurt workers in sectors that rely on foreign inputs and those in exporting industries. Invoking security concerns too expansively to justify market distortions will have long-term adverse consequences for the American economy and America's reputation as the leader of the free world.[25] We should learn the bitter lessons of the 1930s tariff wars to avoid repeating these same mistakes today.

More generally, competition, if fair, makes our companies more efficient and our products more desirable. State interventions in the form of tariffs, subsidies, and non-tariff barriers create opportunities for corruption and bring the government into picking winners and losers, a job better done by private investors and consumers. The United States will compete most effectively with China over the coming century if we lean into our strengths—competition, innovation, markets, private equity—and not try to use Chinese methods of state intervention in the economy. Exorbitant tariffs on Chinese products will not save American companies or seriously damage Chinese companies; they will push cheaper Chinese exports to other markets in the developing world. We might succeed in walling off the American economy from Chinese competition but lose the rest of the global economy.

Imposing tariffs on our allies is especially damaging and should be considered only when national security interests are at stake. Tariffs on steel and aluminum imports imposed on democratic allies by the first Trump administration were a clear example of when he went too far. In response, Canada imposed tariffs on assorted US steel products, and the EU and Mexico targeted an expansive list of goods, including cosmetics, fruits, pork, cotton, and other consumer goods.[26] These costs were borne almost entirely by American households and firms, not foreign exporters. In his second term, President Trump quickly threatened to impose new tariffs on many democratic allies. Such a policy is highly counterproductive. To compete effectively with the Chinese economy in this century, we need more economic interaction and less friction between democratic countries.

DIVERSIFY SUPPLY CHAINS

US policymakers should continue to offer more incentives to American companies to diversify without pushing for complete decoupling of supply chains. *Homeshoring* and *friend-shoring*—relocating supply chains to the US and our partners—is laudable, but diversity is the higher imperative. The US CHIPS and Science Act incentivized chipmakers to build new plants in the United States. The world's largest producer of chips—Taiwan's TSMC—committed to building new factories in the United States and Germany but without shutting down all its plants in China and Taiwan. South Korea's Samsung did too, but without leaving China. That is smart diversification without complete decoupling. If Trump does not impose imprudent, damaging tariffs on Mexico, our southern neighbor promises to become a significant new player in the supply chains that produce semiconductors and other products.[27] That serves American security and economic interests. In the past several years, American companies making smartphones, medicines, medical devices, and textiles have begun diversifying supply chains.[28] American leaders must encourage greater diversification of supply chains so that China cannot impose costly sanctions on the United States in the event of an escalated conflict or war. In particular, US policymakers must pursue policies that reduce American reliance on Chinese-made components critical to producing American arms and weapons, especially rare earth minerals needed to build jet engines, lasers, and radars.[29] A parallel supply diversification strategy must be expedited to reduce Chinese chokeholds on rare earths needed for commercial components such as batteries and magnets, as well as ingredients needed to produce pharmaceuticals.

As with decoupling, too much government-led diversification of supply chains is counterproductive. Markets, not bureaucrats, should drive decisions about where production facilities should be located. Many companies are doing just that without Washington's guidance. Bad economic outcomes occur when bureaucrats in the US federal government decide which American companies get subsidies and which do not.[30] American government programs aimed at attracting production back home risk adversely affecting companies located in allied countries. The CHIPS Act has already triggered increased friction with our allies in Europe and South Korea. ASML, the very successful company in the Netherlands that exports equipment to make high-end chips, worries that American policies will reduce its sales in China and thereby cut into its research and development budgets.[31] In Taiwan, not all political leaders are pleased with TSMC's decision to make significant investments in the United States because that means fewer jobs at home and weakens what they call the "silicon shield"—the production of chips essential to the American economy, which compels American national security decision-makers to defend the island out of economic necessity. Likewise, leaders at Nvidia, the American chipmaking company and the most valuable company in the world at the time of this writing, have expressed a similar worry about losing market share in the very lucrative Chinese economy because of excessive US government restrictions on their exports. Some industrial policy today is necessary. Too much industrial policy threatens economic growth and stifles innovation.

American policymakers should not overreact to existing economic entanglements and dependencies on China but quietly and deliberately reduce them by deploying a strict cost-benefit analysis of every move for the entire American economy. In theory, coercive economic leverage sounds like a powerful tool of diplomacy. In practice, however, it is tough to use effectively, especially with a giant economy like China's, that relies on trade as a driver of economic growth.[32] Xi and his government have tried to punish countries using economic sanctions in response to alleged political slights, but with limited success. As economists Matthew Reynolds and Matthew Goodman assessed, "A careful analysis of eight case studies of Chinese economic coercion since 2010—against Japan, Norway, the Philippines, Mongolia, South Korea, Australia, Canada, and Lithuania—reveals that the most salient characteristic of China's economic coercion is that it simply is not very effective."[33] If Chinese leaders have achieved few results from coercive economic actions against these smaller economies, their ability to damage the giant American economy is even more limited.

The US approach to Russia should be more aggressive. Putin's violation of the fundamental norms and laws of the international system requires keeping in place long-term economic sanctions until the Kremlin pays the requisite reparations needed to rebuild Ukraine. The US also remains too dependent on Russia for titanium and nuclear fuel, which probably explains why Russian state-owned enterprises VSMPO-AVISMA Corporation, the world's largest titanium producer, and Rosatom, the supplier of nuclear fuel, have not been sanctioned.[34] That needs to change. There are other sources available.[35] As long as Russia's invasion of Ukraine continues, greater isolation of the Russian economy—more sanctions and better controls on technology going to Russian defense firms—must continue as well.[36] After the war ends, containing Russian coercive economic power, especially regarding the use of fossil fuel exports, should remain an American foreign policy priority. Reducing the resources Putin has at his disposal to go to war or coerce countries should remain a strategic objective of the United States and the free world well after the war ends.

ENCOURAGING AMERICAN INVESTMENT ABROAD

In the countries and sectors in which Chinese economic investment threatens US core security interests, the US must devote more resources to offering alternatives. For instance, regarding the building and finance of physical infrastructure, the scale of American resources remains a fraction of what Beijing offers. We will succeed in convincing countries to turn down Chinese projects only by providing financing and construction alternatives.

Since 2020, the federal government has utilized the new Development Finance Corporation (DFC) to compete with China's BRI; in 2024, the DFC committed over twelve billion dollars to roughly 189 projects.[37] That is real progress but still not nearly enough to compete with BRI, now estimated to total around a trillion dollars. Unlike Chinese state entities, the DFC lends only to private companies, not governments, with the aim of mobilizing the private sector to make investments that advance US foreign policy goals. That is smart. However, the DFC's budget is inadequate to compete with China's state-owned banks and multilateral lenders. Congress should relax restrictions to allow the DFC to compete with China in middle-income countries, not just low-income countries.

The Partnership for Global Infrastructure and Investment, a G7 initiative to offer developing countries an alternative to China's BRI, must also be implemented and expanded. The aspiration to invest six hundred billion dollars, mostly by attracting private capital, far exceeds actual commitments.[38] At the same time, US leaders should not try to compete with China by emulating them; instead, they should play to American comparative advantages. Building roads, railways, and stadiums is not America's strong suit, especially when such projects require financing from state-owned banks, which the United States does not have. Instead, US government financing is most effective when catalyzing, not replacing, American private-sector investment. The United States also should focus on investing in service industries, another comparative strength. More should be done to develop digital, data, cloud, and AI infrastructure, especially in democracies in the developing world, seeking an alternative to Chinese technology. China's vast investments in information and communications technology (ICT) in the developing world over the last two decades give Chinese AI companies and products a head start in capturing market share in Africa, Asia, Latin America, and the Middle East.[39] The United States has to catch up. Doing so will require exporting "good enough" or "second best" AI products and services, not just the most cutting-edge and therefore the most expensive.

At the same time, US policymakers should not fear *all* Chinese investments abroad. Some of these projects produce economic growth for countries without turning recipients into vassals of the Chinese Communist Party. American leaders also should not try to stop bad Chinese investments abroad, since many Chinese financing and investment projects have triggered backlashes, making future plays unlikely. China's experience in Sri Lanka is a good example. When the government struggled to pay back what it owed China to build the Hambantota Port, it leased the facility to Beijing for ninety-nine years. That decision proved unpopular among Sri Lankans and triggered global outrage, and the blowback created the opportunity for the US Development Finance Corporation to make a $553 million investment in a container terminal in Sri Lanka's Port of Colombo.[40] China is now severely overleveraged. Chinese banks are holding lots of bad, non-performing loans. Beijing cannot afford future defaults on these loans, which limits its capacity to pursue debt-trap diplomacy even if Xi wanted to do so. Infrastructure projects do not generate significant returns on investments, which explains why US companies are less involved in building and financing them.[41]

In addition, US leaders must adopt more effective mechanisms to encourage trade with developing countries. Citizens in these countries want our investment, but they also want access to our domestic market. The United States has such a program, the Generalized System of Preferences (GSP), but it has lost bipartisan support.[42] GSP needs renewal and modernization to include new provisions about worker rights, digital issues, and environmental concerns. GSP helps us compete with China while aiding in diversifying supply chains.

In providing foreign direct investment (FDI) to other countries, the United States is significantly ahead of China. At the end of 2023, the United States held a cumulative foreign direct investment around the world of $9.23 trillion compared to China's $2.9 trillion.[43] In 2023, American companies accounted for $394 billion of worldwide foreign direct investment compared to $185.3 billion for China. In terms of attracting FDI, the US is similarly ahead, attracting $352.9 billion to the United States in 2022 and $288.7 billion in 2023, compared to China's inward flows of $190.2 billion in 2022 and $42.7 billion in 2023. Estimates for 2024 suggest that FDI in the US continued to expand and FDI in China continued to contract. In this arena of competition with China, the United States is winning. US leaders should do all they can to maintain this advantage.

SLOW HARMFUL CHINESE DECOUPLING

Beijing made the first move in the decoupling game when it blocked Google, Meta, Twitter, and various other international news organizations. Under the euphemism of "dual-use circulation," Xi continues to follow a sophisticated strategy of reducing China's exposure to international markets in many sectors. The prudent American response to these decoupling moves is not tit-for-tat blocking of Chinese companies but pressing China to lift bans on American companies and nongovernmental organizations. Even if this pressure campaign has little immediate effect, it will signal to the rest of the world that the US is committed to open markets. We will not compete successfully against China by becoming more like them.

The US government and American firms must work together to combat more subtle forms of Chinese decoupling and censorship. For example, the NBA cannot signal fear about its owners or players criticizing Chinese policies. Hollywood cannot be afraid of casting a Chinese villain occasionally. US diplomats must defend these kinds of actions more vigorously. The US government also must not tolerate expulsions of American journalists and scholars and should continue to make their return a central talking point in every bilateral meeting. At the same time, we should not expel Chinese journalists and scholars without cause, and we should not harass them once they arrive in our country. We should not behave like the Chinese Communist Party. The Trump administration rightly compelled Chinese journalists working for Chinese government entities in the US to register under the Foreign Agent Registration Act (FARA) but wrongly expelled them and limited their work. Denying visas to Chinese professors, think tank scholars, entrepreneurs, and students—if they are not spies and abide by our laws—is not the American way and does not advance American national interests. Asking universities to report to the federal government about Chinese students, or international students from any country, is also wrong and unnecessary. We want Chinese students and scholars to understand the United States better. Instead of following China down the rabbit hole of more decoupling, protectionism, and less interaction between our economies and societies, we should push for the opposite.

CHINESE AND RUSSIAN ACTIVITIES IN THE UNITED STATES

During the Cold War, very few Soviet citizens studied in the United States, owned companies or houses in the United States, or traveled freely back and forth between the United States and the Soviet Union. Brezhnev obviously did not control social media companies operating in the United States or produce content in Moscow circulated by American companies.

Today, Chinese citizens undertake all these activities. On a smaller scale, Russians do too. Until Russia invaded Ukraine in 2022, millions of American households, including mine, had Russia's RT television station bundled into their cable services. Russian and Chinese state-controlled propagandists still actively use social media platforms to push their ideological messages in the United States. These are unique features of our current era of great power competition with no parallels to the Cold War. Therefore, we need new policies.

As a first step, US leaders must enact rules and pass legislation for greater transparency about Chinese government-sponsored activities within the United States—"constructive vigilance"—as experts Larry Diamond and Orville Schell labeled it in their important study of such behavior.[44] While more limited, similar measures are needed for Kremlin-sponsored and Kremlin-controlled activities inside the United States. For instance, building on recent reforms that require Chinese firms listed on our stock exchanges to adopt American accounting standards, there is a need for greater transparency regarding the internal governance, ownership, and accounting procedures of both Chinese and Russian firms operating in the United States. Chinese government grants and contracts with American research organizations also require more transparency. More resources for the FBI and our intelligence agencies to investigate and stop such malign activities are needed too. Most obviously, agents of the Chinese Communist Party should not be allowed to stifle debate and academic freedom on college campuses, as has tragically occurred in the past.[45] And Beijing cannot be allowed to run a secret police station in New York City![46]

At the same time, measures for greater transparency should not produce discrimination against Chinese or Russian citizens, a topic already discussed in chapter 12. Chinese and Russian students on American campuses must be treated like all other students. It is the responsibility of the federal government, not university officials, to keep Chinese spies out of classrooms and labs. Blocking Chinese nationals seeking to purchase homes or property in the United States serves marginal US security interests while damaging America's image abroad.[47]

Officials and businesspeople tied to the Kremlin or the CCP cannot be allowed to hide their wealth in the United States illicitly. The United States should adopt better laws to eliminate anonymous ownership of corporations and real estate and the transfer of funds abroad through law firms.[48] American financial and law firms that assist in these money-laundering schemes for Russian and Chinese oligarchs must be deterred from doing so.[49]

Also different from the Cold War, Chinese and Russian malicious actors are everywhere in the digital world. When the US government detects malicious activity by Chinese or Russian cyber spies, they should expose them immediately.[50] The US government needs greater resources to identify cyber spies like the infamous Chinese Salt Typhoon group, which hacked into eight American telecom companies, but it also needs the capability to remove Chinese malware from our systems.[51] Regarding Chinese and Russian government disinformation operations in digital spaces, the United States government should compel the labeling, if not the outright ban, of Chinese and Russian state-sponsored actors on American-owned social media platforms. Trump's decision to close or defund government agencies tasked with tracking and reducing such disinformation being propagated by China and Russia was a mistake. We can guarantee the First Amendment rights of Americans on social media without extending that right to Xi's bots and Putin's trolls.

To augment these domestic efforts, the US must encourage the free world to adopt similar laws and regulations requiring greater transparency of Chinese and Russian investments and actors in their countries. Russian media penetration is exploding inside the countries of some of our allies in Europe, as demonstrated by the 2024 presidential election in Romania. As discussed in chapter 8, Chinese activities inside democracies, including in the United States and Taiwan, are expanding on many fronts. These efforts must be exposed, and the malicious activities stopped.

ATTRACT CHINESE AND RUSSIAN TALENT TO THE UNITED STATES

American leaders should create more permissive conditions to attract the best and the brightest from China and Russia to study, research, and work in the United States. Putin's invasion of Ukraine triggered a mass exodus of talented Russian workers, especially in the tech sector. The US needs to implement a much more aggressive strategy to reach these people. A similar comprehensive plan should be implemented to bring Chinese entrepreneurs fleeing Xi's oppressive autocracy to the United States. National security experts Diamond, Ellis, and Schell argue that "H-1B visas be made available to all international students who complete a graduate program in science or engineering at an accredited US university, without numerical visa caps."[52] The bolder step would be to give every Chinese and Russian student who receives an advanced degree in STEM a green card. During World War II and the Cold War, the most talented scientists from around the world came to the United States. We need to not only welcome but aggressively recruit such people again. In our great power competition with China and Russia today, attracting talented immigrants is one of America's most significant comparative advantages. The second Trump administration's policy of cancelling visas of international students without cause or due process has done real damage to America's standing and needs to end immediately.

RUN FASTER

As discussed in the previous chapter, a successful US strategy for competing with China must include not only policies to slow China's military, economic, and technological development but also new ideas to speed up American military, economic, and technological development. While the threat is less acute with Russia, the same is true. Defense is only part of a successful strategy. America needs more offense: policies promoting education, innovation, investment, economic growth, and scientific achievement. As Biden's Secretary of Commerce Gina Raimondo rightly reflected in her last weeks in office, "The only way to beat China is to stay ahead of them . . . We have to run faster, out innovate them. That's the way to win."[53] Policies to help our economy run faster, in turn, would promote greater dependence on the American economy and more interdependence among all economies but especially democracies. That is a good outcome, not one to be feared.

LIVING WITH FRAGMENTATION

During the Cold War, Soviet and American leaders tried to persuade or pressure every country in the world to join their red or blue teams, and they had some success in doing so. That rigidity is gone today and is not coming back. Regarding the distribution of power in the twenty-first century, the international system is gravitating again toward bipolarity dominated by the United States and China, not multipolarity.[54] But several midlevel powers have emerged with enough resources to play a more autonomous role in global affairs than those countries in the nonaligned movement could during the Cold War.[55] A handful of countries are economic powerhouses, and that enables independence from China and the United States. Another group of countries today have unique resources or products in the global economy that empower them to avoid economic coercion from either Beijing or Washington. Some possess critical rare minerals or energy resources; others have accumulated significant capital assets (usually generated from the sale of fossil fuels); and a third group fulfills unique niches in global supply chains. Strikingly, even many American allies in Europe and Asia have demonstrated an unwillingness to follow Washington's command to decouple from China. In the first weeks of his second term, Trump ridiculed and threatened allies, which further undermined unity in the democratic bloc, fueling greater global fragmentation. In the future, triggered in part by Trump's belligerent policies, Europe might emerge a fourth great power, independent of the United States.

Already, Indian prime minister Modi is maintaining cordial relations with both Russia and the United States. Biden hosted the Indian leader for a state dinner in Washington in June 2023, and Modi received the Order of St. Andrew—the highest civilian decoration in Russia—while visiting Putin in Moscow the following year. During the Cold War, Saudi Arabia was firmly aligned with the United States against the Soviet Union. Today, the kingdom courts American, Chinese, and Russian leaders simultaneously. Brazil is following a similar path, still trading with and seeking investments from the United States but also courting economic ties with China and is an active member of BRICS. A Communist Party still rules Vietnam, but leaders in Hanoi are managing a delicate balancing act to maintain cordial ties with Washington, Beijing, and Moscow. During the Cold War, Angola was firmly entrenched in the Soviet bloc. Today, Angolan president João Lourenço insists that "the world is a rainbow . . . It's not made of two colors."[56] Even Taiwan trades and invests in the People's Republic of China.

Smaller pro-Western countries—Singapore is an excellent example—reject pressure from Washington to choose sides. Hungary is a member of NATO and the EU, but Prime Minister Orbán courts friendly ties with Russia and pursues investments from China. During the Cold War, that would have been impossible. Because the ideological struggle between the People's Republic of China and the United States is not as intense as the US-Soviet rivalry, it is easier for countries to avoid aligning firmly with one ideological camp. If Trump veers even farther from the democratic camp and continues to embrace the autocrats, fluidity in the international system will grow even more.

American policymakers must learn to live with these new conditions and avoid trying to pressure countries to choose sides. Some countries will not acquiesce to such loyalty demands because they are economically independent or need to maintain economic ties with China and Russia. We do not need them to cut off all relations with China and Russia to achieve our security objectives. If we try too hard to force them to join our team and stop interacting with the autocratic team, our efforts could backfire and produce the opposite result.

LIMITING THE CHINA-RUSSIA ENTENTE

As discussed already, the Chinese and Soviet communists split during the Cold War, and that division—initiated by them, not us—benefited American national interests. Their differences offered American leaders an opportunity to cultivate relations with both countries that were stronger than those countries' relations with each other.[57] The American courtship of the People's Republic of China in the 1970s was especially successful in preserving division with the communist bloc. That feature of the Cold War does not exist today, and it is not coming back until there is democratic change in Russia or China. Therefore, the challenge of dealing with two great autocratic powers, not just one, is another fundamental difference with the Cold War. Together, China and Russia have considerable military and economic power. Both are nuclear powers, and Putin has threatened to use nuclear weapons in ways that Soviet leaders never did.[58] That is new too. Also different from the Cold War, the United States will soon have to deal with two nuclear superpowers, not just one, as Beijing rapidly expands its nuclear arsenal. China and Russia both have ideological appeal too. Putinism is especially attractive in the developed world, while the Chinese economic model has its greatest number of followers in the developing world.

To slow China's rise, some American politicians and analysts have recommended peeling away the junior partner, Russia, just as we did with China during the Cold War. The anonymous author of the "The Longer Telegram: Toward a New American China Strategy"—a direct attempt to echo Kennan from the Cold War—argued that "the United States must rebalance its relationship with Russia whether it likes it or not . . . It is in the United States' enduring interest to prevent further deepening of the Moscow-Beijing entente."[59] In the first weeks of his second term, Trump seemed to be actively pursuing such a strategy, forging close ties with Putin even at the expense of American relationships with allies and partners in Europe.

In the abstract, courting Russia to balance against China might sound appealing. In reality, it is not achievable, and the US will waste valuable international leverage and prestige in pursuing this unobtainable objective. Most different from the Cold War, today there is no China-Russia split for Trump or American diplomats to exploit. By the time national security adviser Henry Kissinger made his first secret visit to Beijing in 1971, the Sino-Soviet split was several years old. Kissinger did not need to convince Premier Zhou Enlai to distance China from Moscow. Zhou and Mao had already done so. Today, Putin sees Xi Jinping as his most important partner in the world and the United States as his greatest enemy. He will never abandon China. Although Russia and China are not formal allies, their military cooperation—including arms sales, support for each other's defense industries, coordinating mechanisms, and joint exercises—has been robust for decades. Putin's dependence on China deepened after he dramatically expanded his invasion of Ukraine in 2022, especially regarding revenues raised from increased exports of fossil fuels to China and imports of technology from China to Russia's military-industrial complex.[60] According to Secretary of State Antony Blinken in December 2024, "70 percent of the components going into things that Russia needs to make for the war" and "90 percent of the microelectronics" were coming from China.[61] Why would Putin give up that direct, tangible, and reliable support for his budget and military enterprises for some vague promise of improved relations with the United States? Putin can rely on his autocratic friend in Beijing for many years to come. Trump cannot guarantee support beyond 2028. Efforts by Trump or future American leaders to peel Putin away will fail and therefore damage America's reputation, especially among democracies, including those in Europe most directly threatened by Russia. Trump will also struggle to sell his rapprochement with Russia at home. In February 2025, 81 percent of Americans did not trust Putin; only 9 percent did.[62]

In the improbable event that a strategy of peeling Russia away from China succeeded, rapprochement with Russia would bring few benefits to the United States and its allies. China needs Russia's energy exports; the United States does not. Putin will never deploy Russian soldiers, missiles, or ships to contain China in Asia. Although it is hard for me to imagine, maybe Putin could help isolate China at the UN Security Council and other international forums. But Beijing has its own veto. And if Putin did agree to pivot back toward the West, he would demand unsavory concessions, including recognition of his annexed parts of Ukraine and indirect control over the rest of the country. Closer relations with the Russian autocrat also would undermine what should be America's aspiration to unite the free world. Trump might not be interested in the mission, but many other American leaders are, and hopefully future US presidents will be too. Someday, the United States should seek a deeper partnership with Russia to compete with China, but only with a democratic Russia, not an autocratic Putin.

In the long run, American leaders have a better chance to work with their Chinese counterparts to temper their support for Moscow. Xi has consistently expressed his admiration for Putin. As discussed throughout this book, China has aided Putin's war effort in Ukraine. And Xi and Putin share a common enemy: the United States. At the same time, Xi has not gone all in to support his friend in Moscow. The war in Ukraine has shown again and again that China is unwilling to directly support Russia, despite their close partnership. Unlike Iran and North Korea, China has not provided weapons to Russia, and Xi even limited the export of civilian drones.[63] Beijing was not pleased when Putin asked for and received from Kim Jong Un in the fall of 2024 over ten thousand North Korean soldiers to fight in Russia's war against Ukraine. Unlike Trump's United States, Xi's China has never voted against UN resolutions condemning Russia's invasion of Ukraine.

Furthermore, since 2022, many Chinese companies have limited their interactions with Russian firms to avoid sanctions from Western countries. To reduce Russia's influence operations in the United States, the Chinese social media company TikTok even banned some accounts from Russia's state-owned media companies RT and Sputnik.[64] Some Chinese experts have publicly expressed their reservations about Russia as a reliable partner.[65] When I met with Chinese academics and think-tankers in Beijing in the spring of 2024, I heard lots of skepticism about the wisdom of Putin's invasion of Ukraine. Researchers working at institutions connected directly to the Chinese government do not express such concerns about Russia without some approval from above. More generally, Chinese businesspeople, academics, and the elites admire America more than Russia.

Compared to Putin's Russia, Xi's China today benefits more from engagement with the United States and working within the current international system. US leaders should remind their counterparts in Beijing of this fact. Many today have ridiculed the Bush administration's idea of encouraging Beijing to become a "responsible stakeholder." However, it is premature to give up on the notion that China could play a more constructive role as a status quo power rather than an aggressive revisionist one like Russia. Quietly, persistently, and with low expectations for success, American leaders must remind their Chinese counterparts that China is better off as a major player in the existing global order than it would be as a rogue state like Russia. In one of his last interviews before leaving office, Secretary Blinken did just that, arguing that China "aspires to leadership, and in aspiring to leadership it also has to, I think, assess how its own reputation is seen around the world" when supporting Russia's war.[66] American diplomats need to keep making this argument. Trump's new tariff war with China makes such efforts unlikely in the short term, but future American presidents should revisit such a strategy.

The sober reality is that the United States has few instruments to disrupt this autocratic axis. The more realistic aspiration is to prevent China-Russia relations from deepening further. That can best be done by persuading Chinese leaders to reduce their affiliation with and support for Russia, not the other way around.

REVERSING AMERICAN ISOLATIONISM

We should not romanticize the degree of unity among American foreign policy elites and society during the Cold War. There were real divisions, especially during the Vietnam War. Containment was an elastic concept that Cold War presidents stretched to mean everything from the rollback of communism to détente, making it easy to agree on such a strategy because it meant very different things to different people. At the end of World War II, the American isolationist tradition gained momentum again, especially in the Republican Party, and was tempered only by Eisenhower's election in 1952. Thereafter, elites and most of society were united in the belief that the United States had to lead the free world to pursue American security and economic interests and advance American values. Regarding the Soviet threat, most accepted that the United States needed to confront the communist challenge by active participation in world affairs. Internationalism gained broad bipartisan support.

That is gone today. Instead, deep currents within the Republican and Democratic Parties aspire to pull back from global engagement. Many yearn for old-fashioned isolationism—a long tradition in American history before the Cold War.[67] As Georgetown professor Charles Kupchan observes, "America's sustained enthusiasm of international engagement is . . . the exception, not the rule, across the nation's history."[68] These isolationist ideas are back in vogue, especially now after Trump's reelection.

The appeal of isolationist ideas started growing soon after the Cold War ended.[69] Republican presidential candidate Pat Buchanan brought these ideas to national debates when challenging one of our most internationalist presidents, George H. W. Bush, in the 1992 election. Two decades later, in 2016, presidential candidate Donald Trump catalyzed this disengagement spirit within the Republican Party with his "America First" slogan—a direct and unapologetic echo of the isolationist America First Committee from the 1930s.[70] In his first term, President Trump followed campaign pledges with isolationist actions, withdrawing from numerous multilateral agreements, such as the TPP and the Paris Climate Accords. In his second term, President Trump has pledged to do even more to isolate the United States from the rest of the world, including pulling out of the WHO, UN Human Rights Council, and Paris Climate Accords again, threatening to quit the WTO, imposing major tariffs on everyone, withdrawing American soldiers from Europe, and maybe even leaving NATO altogether.

Such isolationist moves will benefit China. As Tsinghua professor Yan Xuetong wrote in December 2024 on the eve of Trump's second term, "Trump's dubious commitment to US allies will encourage other countries to hedge their bets, building ties with Beijing to offset the unpredictability of Washington."[71] Tragically, Yan is right. Russia also benefits from a retreating America. It is the central reason why the Kremlin was cheering for Trump's return to the White House.

Trump, however, is not the only leader in the Republican Party who advocates for isolationist ideas. Allies, trade, and multilateral organizations have become unpopular among a large segment of the GOP. Nothing gets a bigger applause line in a campaign speech than proclaiming that the United States should not serve as the world's policeman. Segments of the Republican Party even want to limit legal immigration. The isolationist GOP today has little in common with the internationalist Republican Party of the Reagan, Bush 41, and Bush 43 eras.

When Trump engaged in the world during his first term, he preferred acting alone rather than with allies or in accordance with the rules and norms of international institutions. He was already an unapologetic unilateralist then. Buoyed by a second electoral mandate, Trump's unilateral proclivities are likely to grow even more in his second term. As his financial backer and close political adviser Elon Musk declared soon after Trump won reelection, "We should not have any international treaties that restrict the freedom of Americans."[72] When Trump bombed Iran in June 2025, he did so without endorsement from the United Nations, NATO, or the US Congress. Trump's threats to buy or seize Greenland, the Panama Canal, Gaza, and even Canada are clear contradictions to Trump's commitment to isolationism.

While the isolationist and unilateralist tendencies are strongest in the Republican Party, isolationism also has admirers in the Democratic Party.

Critics of American engagement on the left start by denouncing "liberal interventionism," wrongly conflating a policy of advancing democracy abroad with support for American wars. Strong forces within the Democratic Party now reject trade and global economic engagement more generally, preferring protectionist tariffs and other barriers to limit economic activity crossing American borders. President Biden and his administration did little to promote trade, even with allies. As former US trade official Michael Beeman assessed, "Since coming to office, the Biden administration has turned down all opportunities and proposals to join new reciprocal tariff-cutting negotiations, along with placing a much lower priority on efforts to remove non-tariff barriers."[73] There are no signs that these anti-trade proclivities within the Democratic Party will abate in Trump's second term. More generally, support for restraint in American foreign policy has grown in popularity among both self-described progressive foreign policy elites and voters. Within the DC think tank world, a "restrainer" movement has exploded in recent years, funded by both conservative and progressive foundations.

This growing commitment to isolationism today had no parallel during the Cold War. Unilateralism is also more salient today compared to the previous century. These new dimensions of our current era of great power competition are dangerous for American security, economic, and moral interests, especially because Xi and Putin are not pulling back. Instead, these autocrats are taking advantage of our dwindling enthusiasm for international engagement from Africa to Central Asia to the United Nations. As China expert David Shambaugh assessed, "China's power and position in the world has never been greater."[74] China's global reach will only grow if the US pulls back. As American politicians and analysts lambast the evils of globalization, their Chinese counterparts celebrate its virtues and China's role in revitalizing it.[75]

American strategists must stop this dangerous drift toward isolationism. They must explain to the American people why retreating from the world will produce more security threats and less economic prosperity for the United States down the road, just as it did in the 1930s. They must explain how we can commit to not using military force to promote democracy without abandoning engagement with the outside world and pursuing policies to advance democracy abroad through peaceful means. We can seek to amend trade agreements and reform international trade organizations to make them more beneficial for American workers and companies without abandoning trade and multilateral economic institutions altogether.[76] The Atlantic and Pacific Oceans do not protect us from international threats as they did in the past when isolationism worked as a foreign policy doctrine. Russian missiles and Chinese malware can penetrate our borders in minutes. The hope that wars in Europe or Asia can start and go on without eventually affecting American security and economic interests—without eventually dragging us into them—is naive. We tried that in the 1930s, and it didn't work.[77] It is even less likely to work today when the world is much more intertwined.

When we do engage, we are more effective when acting in concert with allies than when going it alone. The increasingly popular idea within Trump circles that we are better off acting unilaterally, not constrained by allies or multilateral institutions, is dangerous and flawed. The United States is more secure with strong, democratic allies. Tearing down or withdrawing from international organizations to allow the United States more freedom to maneuver may feel liberating in the short term but will have long-term negative consequences for American national interests, especially as the US faces strategic competition with China and Russia in the next several decades.

REDUCING DOMESTIC POLARIZATION

During the Cold War, the ideological struggle was primarily fought between countries. Today, the ideological contest between autocrats and democrats also occurs within countries, including the most powerful democracy in the world—the United States. Today, the greatest threat to American security, prosperity, and democracy comes not from China or Russia but from within the United States. This is new and different from the Cold War.

Most alarmingly, a segment of American society is no longer committed to democratic governance. In the global fight between autocrats and democrats, we now have some Americans, including at times the president of the United States, on the autocratic side. In his first term, Trump fueled disdain for American democratic traditions most damagingly by falsely claiming that the 2020 presidential election was rigged and then encouraging his followers, on January 6, 2021, to disrupt the peaceful transfer of power from one democratically elected president to another. Whatever they believed privately, a shocking number of Republican Party leaders publicly refused to acknowledge the results of the 2020 presidential elections.[78] As historian Robert Kagan wrote, it "proved that Trump and his most die-hard supporters are prepared to defy constitutional and democratic norms, just as revolutionary movements have in the past."[79] In the 2022 midterm elections, according to journalist Zack Beauchamp, "the Republican Party nominated roughly 370 candidates for federal and statewide office who rejected or questioned the legitimacy of Biden's 2020 win."[80] In 2024, presidential candidate Trump continued to perpetuate the myth that the 2020 election was stolen, calling it the "big lie," a false claim many prominent conservative politicians and major media outlets amplified. An alarming percentage of Americans across the political spectrum now lack confidence in the freeness and fairness of elections.[81]

When citizens do not accept the results of free and fair elections, democracies break down. In 2024, a growing percentage of Americans—45 percent—expressed dissatisfaction with how American democracy represented the people, and a shocking 76 percent thought American democracy was under threat.[82] Trump's campaign statements in 2024 fueled that fear. Echoing autocrats from Stalin to Hitler to Putin, Trump talked incessantly about the "enemy from within" on the campaign trail, people whom he vowed to arrest if reelected. Mr. Trump also promised to "launch the largest deportation in American history."[83] And then Trump won, guaranteeing that debates about the democratic rules of the game will endure for years. As discussed in the previous chapter, Trump's barrage of executive orders at the beginning of his second term coupled with the funding stoppages and purges throughout the federal government have already tested the Constitution's division of power among three branches of government. Leaders of the Democratic Party pushed back, helping to fuel even greater polarization in American society than during Trump's first term.

Trump, however, is not acting alone in weakening our democratic system of government. State legislatures have passed laws that worsen voter suppression and increase partisan authority over election processes.[84] Dozens of political officials and candidates openly embrace election subversion and justify partisan violence.[85] Over 90 percent of Republicans and those independents who lean toward the Republican Party expressed concerns that "social media sites intentionally censor political viewpoints that they find objectionable."[86] Conversely, progressives assert that right-wing media—especially social media—fundamentally distorts the truth and propagates disinformation that amplifies similar content produced by autocratic adversaries, including, first and foremost, Russia.[87] Conservative Americans express deep concerns about alleged government's infringement on their personal liberties.[88] They also believe that illegal immigrants are straining the welfare capabilities of federal, state, and local governments to which American citizens, voters, and taxpayers—not those in our country illegally—should have access. For them, this is an issue of democratic governance too. This is all new. During the Cold War, we never had such assaults on or doubts about our democratic system from within.

A related unique feature of our current era is that a large segment of the American population has expressed ideological affinity with one of our autocratic adversaries: Vladimir Putin. The most prominent of these Americans is President Donald Trump. During his first term in office, Trump praised Putin, but those rhetorical flurries had only minor impacts on US foreign policies. In the beginning of his second term, Trump pivoted immediately toward supporting Putin and attacking President Zelenskyy, blaming the Ukrainian president for starting the war—a blatant falsehood—calling him a dictator, and offering Russia all sorts of concessions as an inducement to end the Russian invasion of Ukraine without asking Putin for any concessions in return. It was an extraordinary, unprecedented reversal of American foreign policy. During the Cold War, some Americans supported communist ideas, the Soviet Union, and the People's Republic of China, but they were marginal groups. Today, those who embrace Putin's illiberal, conservative ideas constitute a significant segment of the population, and one of them is the president. That is new. During the Cold War, we had fringe figures, not popular pundits like Tucker Carlson, who traveled to Russia to conduct sycophantic interviews with Putin, Stalin, or Khrushchev and then praised Moscow's Metro system and shopping centers as being better than ours. Many American conservative leaders and even some businesspeople admire populist nationalist parties and movements in Europe with close ties to Putin, including, most alarmingly, the extreme nationalist AfD party in Germany. In the 1930s, some prominent American business leaders and social movements admired the fascist movements in Europe, especially the Nazis in Germany, and even sometimes collaborated directly with them.[89] Those kinds of activities ended during the Cold War, when Americans' open support for communists in Europe and Asia was very rare. This solidarity between illiberal national populists in the US and Russia is new. Thankfully, Xi Jinping Thought has few admirers inside the United States.

Relatedly, domestic political polarization has also increased compared to the Cold War. As former Secretary of State Condoleezza Rice colorfully wrote, "The New Four Horsemen of the Apocalypse—populism, nativism, isolationism, and protectionism—tend to ride together, and they are challenging the political center."[90] Dissatisfaction with elites and the status quo has fueled deep divisions in American society. The gap between rich and poor has exploded and now approximates the Gilded Age of the late nineteenth century.[91] We did not have such income inequality during the Cold War, which helped American society remain united in confronting a common enemy. The extreme divide between political parties makes achieving basic national security objectives difficult.[92] We cannot pass a long-term defense budget but must rely on continuing resolutions, making strategic military planning and procurement challenging.[93] Polarization also damages America's image worldwide. During the Cold War, societies on every continent, especially those living under tyranny, were inspired by the vibrancy of American capitalism and democracy. That is less true today. Our polarized political fights, including tragic moments like January 6, 2021, inspire no one committed to democracy.

Our adversaries clearly understand the benefits of our domestic disunity and at times have meddled in American politics to exacerbate these divisions, as Russia did in the 2016 and 2020 US presidential elections. Our adversaries understand that if Americans are fighting with each other, they are less likely to fight against them. The senseless six-month delay in approving new aid to Ukraine in 2024 benefited Putin's army in achieving gains on the battlefield. While visiting Taiwan in the summer of 2022 and spring of 2025, I heard leaders worry that a divided and polarized America might be unable to come to their aid if Xi invaded their island. As former Trump officials and China specialists Matthew Pottinger and Matthew Turpin bluntly warned, "American disunity may encourage China's leadership to conclude that US politics are too fraught to forge a consensus to intervene in Taiwan."[94] President Trump's reelection has already exacerbated domestic polarization, making it more difficult for the United States to act confidently and united in global affairs. If we are fighting at home about the deportation of immigrants or debating whether to invade Canada, we are not focused on enhancing deterrence against China and Russia. Using the American military to execute domestic policies, as Trump has started to do on the US-Mexico border, is damaging to our defense readiness and morale. So, too, are witch hunts in the Pentagon for alleged "woke" generals or purges in the CIA of alleged "DEI" agents.

There are no silver bullets for reducing American polarization. Democratic reforms spelled out in the previous chapter—ending partisan redistricting for congressional seats, eliminating primaries that reward extremist candidates, and enhancing campaign-finance transparency—would help. Policies that reduce economic inequality would also help. Anything that reduced the salience of identity politics—a central driver of polarization—would help.[95] In experimental settings, social scientists have identified a long list of interventions centered on better information that might reduce polarization.[96] However, operationalizing these findings in the real world is difficult. The good news is that societal preferences have not changed significantly in the past several decades. The elites and the institutions they control—like media and campaign financing—are the ones changing more profoundly. As American electoral expert Professor Larry Bartels has written about populism in Europe and the United States, "The gains of populist and far-right forces have less to do with a genuine shift in political beliefs among the public than they do with changing elite politics."[97] In my home state of Montana, Barack Obama won 47 percent of the vote in 2008. It is hard to believe that Montanans have radically shifted their fundamental beliefs in just a few electoral cycles.

The other good news is that we recovered from past eras of polarization.

We overcame divisions in the 1960s and 1970s and renewed American democracy. We overcame the deep divisions during the Gilded Age of the nineteenth century.[98] It took a long time, but we eventually healed after our tragic Civil War. Renewal in America is not only possible but, as history suggests, probable.

What is most needed to reduce polarization is principled, patriotic American leadership. Sincere US leaders need to describe accurately to American citizens the threats we face from China and Russia and then explain that we can address them only through greater unity. If we can get our own house in order—recommit to observing the democratic rules of the game even while fighting fiercely over policy issues and reducing polarization—we will prevail and even prosper in a new era of great power competition with China and Russia. If we cannot, we will lose.

Epilogue

DON'T BET AGAINST AMERICA JUST YET

THE GLORY DAYS of American hegemony, democracy as a universal value, and a global commitment to the liberal international order are over. Great power competition between autocrats and democrats is back. It is a perilous and challenging moment for American security and prosperity. As discussed throughout this book, America's current competition with Russia and China has similarities with the Cold War: bipolarity between the US and China, ideological competition between autocracies and democracies, and rival visions for global order. But there are also differences. In some ways, today's great power competition feels even more dangerous than the Cold War. For instance, it is easier to imagine scenarios that could precipitate major conventional wars between Russia and the United States or China and the United States. During the Cold War, we thought that the advent of nuclear weapons would prevent the possibility of an all-out war between the Soviet Union and the United States. The emergence of two nuclear superpowers was considered stabilizing because nuclear weapons were better at preserving the status quo (through mutually assured destruction) than changing it.[1] Russia's full-scale invasion of Ukraine in 2022—the first major conventional war in Europe since World War II—and Putin's explicit threat to use tactical nuclear weapons in battle—another first since the invention of nuclear weapons—make the specter of great power war feel more likely than during the Cold War. The possibility of a major war between the United States and China over Taiwan also feels more probable today than ever before, especially since some military planners believe that a major war with the PRC can be fought without going nuclear. That is different from the Cold War, when American strategists assumed that a major conventional war with the Soviet Union could easily become nuclear and, therefore, did all they could to avoid escalation. Some even forecast an exact year—2027—of military conflict between the United States and China.[2] That is not that far in the future! More frightening than the Soviet Union during the Cold War, China has massive economic power today, especially manufacturing capability, which has no peer, but also technological prowess that rivals American competitors in several domains. America's domestic polarization and new isolationist impulses fuel the impression of an American decline, another new and unnerving condition not as present during the Cold War.

And then came Trump . . . again. Trump's second term, at least its first months, has weakened America's ability to compete with China and Russia. Today, in contrast to the Cold War, America's greatest threats come not from China or Russia but from within. In chapter 13 especially, but also in other sections of this book, I have identified several major American successes that helped us prevail during the Cold War. Trump has weakened or destroyed almost all of them.

First, allies. Allies constituted one of America's most significant advantages over the Soviets in the last century and, until this year, remained one of our superpowers compared to China and Russia. Collectively, the US and its allies had more military and economic power than the Soviet Union and its allies in the last century, and China and Russia in this century. Trump, however, is now destroying this advantage. Within weeks of returning to the White House, Trump sparked new and unnecessary divisions with several of our NATO allies. Most irrationally, he expressed imperial ambitions to make Canada the fifty-first state and take Greenland away from Denmark. Who gets in a fight with Canadians? Or Danes, for that matter? In February 2025, Vice President J. D. Vance delivered a shocking speech at the Munich Security Conference in which he claimed wrongly that the poor practice of democracy in Europe was a greater threat to the continent than Russia or China.[3] I was there. Our European allies were insulted and shocked. Many predicted that we were witnessing the beginning of the end of the special transatlantic relationship between democracies that had endured for nearly a century. Subsequent hints from Trump administration officials of plans to withdraw American soldiers from Europe fueled anxious speculations about the end of NATO. Trump's embrace of Russian dictator Putin and withdrawal of support for democratic Ukraine further strained relations between the United States and the rest of NATO and the European Union. Compared to Europe, US alliances in Asia have remained stable, but leaders there worry that they will be next. In Taiwan in March 2025, I heard many worries from senior government officials and business leaders about Trump's commitment to their security.

Second, ideas. During the Cold War, the United States had better ideas about democracy, human rights, and the rule of law to offer to the world than the Soviet Union's communism. Until recently, that was an advantage that carried over to our new era of competition. In this century, democracy has remained a more popular form of government worldwide than dictatorship, including both Putinism and Xi Jinping Thought. Trump, however, seems committed to throwing away this tremendous American advantage. As discussed in earlier chapters, Trump's assault on many democratic norms and institutions in the first months of his second term has rapidly undermined the appeal of the American system as one to be emulated. Trump's aggressive consolidation of executive power, especially at the expense of the judicial branch, the rule of law, and individual human rights, has triggered the most significant constitutional crisis in the United States since the Civil War. In addition, as demonstrated most dramatically in the changing of sides in the Russia-Ukraine war, Trump has also embraced dictators and disparaged democratic leaders. Shockingly, the Trump administration has voted against UN General Assembly resolutions criticizing Russia's invasion of Ukraine, aligning with Russia, North Korea, Belarus, Nicaragua, and other rogue dictatorships. Even China abstained. The second Trump administration also dismantled some of America's most successful instruments for supporting democratic and market ideas abroad during the Cold War. The Trump team radically reduced funding to the US Agency for International Development (USAID), and thereby, many American democracy promotion organizations financed by USAID. What was left of USAID was incorporated into the State Department and instructed to work only on humanitarian assistance. Following the withdrawal of USAID funding to projects worldwide, Chinese assistance officials have tried to step in to fill the void.[4] Trump's team cut the budget of the State Department's Bureau of Democracy, Human Rights, and Labor, thereby ending thousands of grants and contracts for dozens of organizations promoting human rights, democracy, independent media, and the rule of law around the world. They also slashed funding for the US Agency for Global Media, and thereby the media organizations supported by USAGM, including Voice of America, Radio Free Europe, Radio Free Asia, Radio Farda (for Iran), Alhurra (for the Arab world), Radio Martí (for Cuba), and Open Technology Fund (promoting internet freedom in repressive environments). The second Trump administration dismantled the network of US government organizations in the State Department, the FBI, and Homeland Security, fighting foreign-funded disinformation campaigns in the United States and worldwide. Trump even gutted financial support for student exchanges, including the US flagship Fulbright Program. Of course, China and Russia have not cut their foreign assistance and media outlets promoting their brands of autocracy or their student exchange programs.

Third, international institutions. As discussed in earlier chapters, another major American asset during the Cold War was the liberal international economic order, supported by the American dollar, the IMF, World Bank, and GATT, which later became the WTO. This economic system was not global. It excluded the communist world. But capitalist countries within this system became more prosperous, including the United States, while the Soviet Union and its economic partners fell behind. After the Cold War ended, this system expanded, and in retrospect, probably too far and too fast. However, even with its problems, the global system of trade, investment, and finance anchored by the United States was still providing benefits to the United States, its allies, and partners. But then Trump's second administration imposed tariffs on nearly every country in the world (strikingly, Russia was excluded), including massive tariffs on Chinese goods, thereby threatening to destroy the global capitalist system erected in the aftermath of World War II that was, in part, built to help avoid World War III. Even the American dollar, which served for decades as the world's currency, is now being undermined by Trump's erratic foreign economic policies.

As discussed throughout this book, multilateral security and political institutions created after World War II, such as the United Nations, did not work as well as international economic organizations dedicated to supporting capitalism. However, the UN did facilitate cooperation on nuclear nonproliferation, global health, and climate change while establishing important norms for sovereignty and decolonization, and against annexation and imperialism. American participation in these international institutions and adherence to these norms served US national interests. In his second term, Trump has undermined these institutions and norms in two somewhat contradictory ways. First, Trump has accelerated his first-term isolationist practice of pulling out of international agreements and organizations. At the same time, Trump's imperial ambitions to acquire Greenland, Canada, the Panama Canal, and even Gaza, if ever realized, would undermine the norm against annexation that endured, with minor exceptions, throughout the Cold War. Putin loves Trump's neocolonial statements (they are still just that; stated desires, not actions), as they normalize Putin's annexation projects in Ukraine and Georgia. Xi's goal of seizing Taiwan is also made easier in a world without norms against sovereignty, where each great power dominates its respective sphere of influence.

Finally, American power. Another great American advantage in the Cold War was a capitalist economy that outperformed the Soviet communist system, which in turn supported an innovative and powerful military that also outpaced the Red Army and the Soviet military-industrial complex. In today's new era of great power competition, maintaining an edge over China in the economic and military domains constitutes the biggest challenge for the United States. Thankfully, Trump has not *yet* significantly damaged the American economy and has signaled a commitment to increasing defense spending. However, even in this area, warning signs have emerged in the early months of Trump's second term.

As already mentioned, Trump's irrational and ideological obsession with tariffs could do severe damage to the American economy. Equally troubling are Trump's moves to damage the scientific, research, and innovation ecosystem that was vital for America's winning the Cold War—and will be essential for outcompeting China in the twenty-first century. At the top of this list of self-inflicted wounds are Trump's cuts to American research universities, allegedly in the fight against antisemitism and "woke-ism." If they continue, such an assault on one of America's greatest advantages over China and Russia will have devastating consequences. In the highly competitive economic and technological race with China, there could be no bigger gift to Beijing than weakening our best universities.[5]

In addition, the Trump administration's decision to randomly revoke over 1,500 visas (a practice that was then temporarily suspended) for international students and refuse visas to international students at Harvard University are catastrophic blows to America's ability to recruit the world's best and brightest. That was a great advantage the United States maintained over the Soviet Union—and, until just a few months ago, over China and Russia as well. Moreover, many international students have stayed, then started or led some of America's most successful and innovative companies, emerged as academic leaders, provided medical care in our hospitals, and, more broadly, become productive members of American society. If we lose these talented people because they are too afraid to study in Trump's America and attend Cambridge in Great Britain or Tsinghua in China instead, the long-term damage to American research, innovation, and economic prosperity will be deep.

Furthermore, in his first months of his second term, Trump purged many US departments and agencies of some of their most talented people. Experienced generals were dismissed without explanation. The Department of Education was gutted. Diplomats were asked to retire early. The budgets of most government bodies were radically reduced. The cuts of government employees were deepest among the youngest. These people might never come back to public service. Without question, the US federal government needs reform, and no one likes waste. However, Trump's "burn it to the ground" strategy could eventually have negative consequences for the American economy. It is hard to sustain economic growth without a functioning state and effective bureaucracy.

In addition to undermining these successful policies from the Cold War, Trump is flirting with repeating some American mistakes from the last century. The cancellation of visas of international students who protested for the "wrong" causes has strong echoes of McCarthyism. So, too, does the rise in attacks from government policies and societal actions against citizens of Chinese descent and Chinese citizens living in the United States. In addition, Trump's embrace of autocrats—Putin in particular—to allegedly help balance against China has echoes of our courtships of evil dictators in the Cold War to help contain the Soviet Union. As a student during the

Cold War, I was appalled by America's close relationship with apartheid South Africa and protested against it on the campuses of Stanford and Oxford. I am equally disgusted by Trump's rapprochement with Putin, which, as discussed earlier, will never help us contain China but instead taint America's reputation. Finally, Trump's dream to enlarge the United States, even if done with treasure and not soldiers, sounds again like overreach. Just as the United States did not have the resources to contain communism everywhere and all the time during the Cold War, we cannot afford Trump's imperial projects today.

The return of great power competition between autocrats and democrats would have been challenging for even the most innovative US president committed to strengthening alliances, promoting democracy, building multilateral institutions, especially those undergirding global capitalism, and renewing America's economic and military power. However, the challenge of great power rivalry for American security and prosperity has been exacerbated by President Trump's self-inflicted damage to American power and influence in the world, at least in the first months of his second term. Trump is not making America great again. He is making America weak, precisely at a moment in history when we cannot afford to make such mistakes. China is rising, and Putin is unlikely to stop in Ukraine.

And yet, over the long run, I remain optimistic about America's potential to prevail in this new great power rivalry, even if the next few years might be rocky. The challenges are profound. Yet, I would much rather be on "team democracy" than "team autocracy." I would rather be the next president of the United States than the leader of China or Russia. Today, compared to China and Russia, the United States has more military and economic power, stronger allies, and better ideas about domestic governance and global order. Compared to the Cold War, the Chinese and Russian challenges in the aggregate regarding power, ideas, and threats to the global order are less intense. Trump is weakening these advantages but has not yet destroyed them. If we can hold on to them for the next few years and then strengthen them in the longer term, we will be all right. We will prevail.

Regarding military capabilities, the democrats—the United States and our democratic allies and partners—still have more power than the autocrats. The United States and Russia are the only two nuclear superpowers in the world, and China is catching up. While China has more soldiers and ships than the United States, the Pentagon outspends China annually by a wider margin and maintains qualitative advantages regarding most weapon systems and warrior readiness. Xi and Putin are well aware of the US military superiority. When allies are added to the military balance of power equation, the democrats have the advantage over the autocrats. As long as we do not squander these relationships in NATO by threatening to annex Greenland or Canada or pull our soldiers out of Europe or Asia, the US has dozens of strong military allies in Europe and Asia. China and Russia only have each other, and their ties are not nearly as deep as those between the United States and our allies, and a few other actors, such as Iran and North Korea.

Regarding economic power, with Russia far behind (though much stronger than thirty years ago), there are two global leaders: the United States and China. Different indices measure Chinese and American economic power in varying ways, with some ranking China first and others placing the United States at the top. While the United States is still ahead in the aggregate, China is catching up and, in some sectors, has already surpassed the US. For instance, China's manufacturing is second to none, and its rapid development of AI, quantum computing, and biotechnology is concerning. That said, the American dollar remains the world's dominant currency, and American financial power and US Treasury bonds have no peer, as long as Trump does not undermine them. America has the largest concentration of the world's top universities, as long as Trump does not gut them. American companies continue to dominate the list of the most valuable companies and remain at the forefront of technological innovation, as long as Trump's tariffs do not trigger a recession. The claim that the Chinese economy will outpace the American economy is a hypothesis, not a certainty. The jump from a middle-income country to a high-income economy is hard and occurs rarely.[6] The Chinese economy faces many structural challenges, as evidenced by its already slowing growth. The American economy has problems, too, and Trump is exacerbating them, but the Chinese economic challenges are deeper. And again, when allies and partners are added to assessments of the balance of economic power, the democracies remain ahead by a wide margin. Nine of the top ten economies in the world are democracies. Only autocratic China breaks into the top ten.

Regarding ideological competition, the challenges China and Russia pose to the world are formidable. China's economic model of state-led development appeals to the developing world—Africa, Asia, Latin America, and the Middle East. Putin's conservative populism has won the hearts and minds of millions in the developed world, especially in Europe, the United States, and parts of the developing world. In this twenty-first-century ideological struggle between democrats and autocrats, democrats have recorded few wins lately. Liberalism and democracy are under assault in the oldest democracies, including in the United States.[7] Most disturbingly, Trump has shown no commitment to advancing democracy abroad or maintaining it at home.

And yet, liberal, democratic ideas are still more popular worldwide than illiberal, autocratic ideas. As public opinion polls show, most people globally still agree with Churchill that "democracy is the worst form of Government except all those others that have been tried from time to time." Even though the last two decades have marked a period of democratic recession and coups d'état in West Africa and Myanmar have brought military leaders to power, mass protests in support of communism, fascism, theocracy, or monarchy have not taken place in our era. Most mass demonstrations in the last two decades—including those that have not succeeded yet, such as in Belarus, Hong Kong, Iran, Russia, or Venezuela—have pushed for democratic change, not autocratic rule. No one organizes popular movements to advance Xi Jinping's Thought or Putinism. While there is an alarming rise of autocrats and their followers in old democracies, there are also democrats in Russia and China, as well as Iran, Venezuela, Myanmar, Belarus, and other autocracies. And in response to Trump's recent assault on democratic and rule-of-law institutions, there are already signs of a new social movement in support of democracy taking shape.

When our current tumultuous era is situated in a broader historical context—spanning centuries rather than just a few decades—the trend toward democracies and away from autocracies is even more apparent. Compared to 1776, the 1930s, or the 1970s, there are far more democracies today. The long arch of history has moved slowly and irregularly, but it has steadily moved toward democracy and against dictatorship. Democratic United States, if it survives a second Trump administration, and I think it will, is on the right side of history. Leaders in autocratic China and Russia are not.

Regarding competing conceptions of global order, China and Russia are pushing for new ideas and changes in the international order that undermine American interests and values. Putin seeks the complete destruction of the current global order. Thankfully, he has limited means to advance his assault and offers little in the way of a constructive alternative. That said, Putin's willingness to challenge what he and many others worldwide see as unfair American hegemony attracts supporters. Putin has demonstrated a strong will, including using military force, to achieve his anti-multilateral ends. The Chinese threat to the liberal order is more subtle but potentially more dangerous in the long run since Beijing has more capabilities than Moscow. Xi offers ideas for reforming existing international institutions in ways that benefit China (as he defines them), but the Chinese Communist Party chairman is also creating new multilateral organizations independent of the American-anchored liberal economic order. More alarmingly, these attract followers. China's rising power makes the CCP's alternative vision of global order increasingly attractive, especially when the United States under Trump seems to be abandoning the old international order it created and anchored for several decades. Some even argue that the United States has adopted many Chinese economic statecraft practices. As Obama's former US trade representative, Michael Froman, assesses, "The United States is now operating largely in accordance with Beijing's standards, with a new economic model characterized by protectionism, constraints on foreign investment, subsidies, and industrial policy—essentially nationalist state capitalism."[8] As Trump pulls the United States back from global engagement, China is filling the void, especially in Africa, Asia, Latin America, and the Middle East.[9]

At the same time, China is nowhere near as revisionist as the Soviet Union. Xi is not trying to make every country in the world communist and then submit to a new international order dominated by Beijing. That was the Soviet project. That is not Xi's agenda. In this dimension of great power competition, the Cold War analogy is inexact. Or, let me posit more humbly: if Xi and his comrades genuinely want to subjugate the world under communist rule, they have done a great job concealing their plan in words. And in actions, so far, they have achieved few results. Nonetheless, challenges to the existing order from a radical revisionist like Putin and the successful efforts of the Chinese to construct alternative multilateral organizations independent of the United States are real.

The American-created international system is not dead yet but is facing its greatest challenge ever in the second Trump term. Tragically, Trump does not believe in the value of multilateralism. He wrongly thinks that the United States is better off going it alone. Hopefully his brand of unilateralism will be an interregnum in the history of American foreign policy, not a new long-term trajectory. Many leaders and societies worldwide still value international institutions that the United States established or helped create at the end of World War II—the United Nations, the IMF, the World Bank, and then GATT (now WTO), as well as multilateral organizations like NATO, the G7, and the OECD, and newer configurations in Asia such as AUKUS and the Quad. Many complain about American hegemony and unilateralism, but few want to see the United States withdraw from international affairs altogether or let China take over. When there are international crises, the first call has still been to Washington, not Beijing or Moscow, even in the first months of Trump's second term. If the United States were to retreat even further, China would not have the capacity to fill the void. The result would not be Chinese hegemony but anarchy. That is why most of the world fears and does not celebrate the current American isolationist tradition in American politics, led by President Trump but also embraced by many on both the left and right.

In all three arenas of competition—power, ideology, and competing visions of the global order—the United States still maintains advantages over China and Russia. However, this is not the time for complacency, especially given current trends in American domestic politics. As outlined in part III of this book, American leaders must adopt new policies to increase American power, promote democratic ideas more effectively, and strengthen multilateral institutions that advance American interests and values. To prevail against our autocratic rivals, America needs a new grand strategy.

I understand that many policy recommendations suggested in part III are challenging to implement. Some critics will dismiss them as naive. Others will say they are too ambitious for our current era or obsolete and out of touch with today's zeitgeist, given our new isolationist, unilateralist, realist times. I disagree. Times of great challenge require boldness and creativity. If our current moment is the dawn of a long era of great power competition, we need big, new ideas like those embraced at the beginning of the Cold War.

I also understand that Trump and his administration will not agree with many, if not most, of my recommendations. That is okay. Democracies get stronger because they create the permissive conditions for big debates. If Trump's isolationist, unilateral policies produce greater security and prosperity for the American people, I will praise his revolutionary vision in my next book. But if Trump's approach to foreign policy and national security fails to produce lasting benefits for the American people, there will be a window of opportunity for new ideas—like those outlined in this book—as well as the revival of some old ideas that worked in the past and could work again, with amendment and updating. As long as we remain a democracy, I will continue to explain why liberal internationalism better serves American national interests than illiberal nationalism. Albeit not perfectly, the strategy produced positive results for American security and prosperity for the last hundred years. This approach can do so again with revision, reform, and innovation.

Adopting the prescriptive ideas proposed in this book, however, will require two necessary conditions currently in short supply: confidence and unity.

Right now, the United States is not a confident nation. We are polarized. We are fearful. The way some politicians talk about American decline and Chinese prowess, you would think we are just a few years away from being colonized by Beijing! That is the wrong mindset. The Chinese are not ten feet tall. Americans must be less fearful about global challenges and more confident in our country: our power, our ideas, and our global allies, partners, and organizations. The perception of decline itself can be dangerous; in the past, it has even compelled anxious countries to launch preemptive wars against rising powers.[10] We do not need that. Instead, Americans should have greater confidence in our current strengths and ideals and greater faith in our ability to renew and strengthen them in the future. To repeat, when comparing Chinese and Russian advantages to ours, I would rather be on the democratic team than the autocratic team. Historically, in contests between great powers, democracies have generally outperformed autocracies.[11]

We have endured but recovered from periods of pessimism and apparent decline before. The 1930s were the darkest hours for the democratic world in the last century, but we eventually prevailed in World War II and gradually reinvigorated the free world. Democracy around the world also seemed in deep decline in the late 1960s and early 1970s, when communist regimes seized power in Southeast Asia, Southern Africa, Latin America, and Afghanistan. At home, American society back then was also deeply divided, traumatized by violence during the civil rights and anti-war movements, political assassinations, and the first and only resignation of a US president. But we eventually recovered. Just two decades later, the Soviet Union collapsed, communism receded as a global force, the United States reemerged as more powerful and united than ever before, and the whole world seemed to gravitate toward democratic and market ideas—that is, American ideas. This story of renewal is one of America's greatest strengths—one of democracy's greatest strengths.

To stimulate a new era of renewal, American leaders need to express greater confidence in democracy as a superior normative idea and a better system of government. They need to understand and explain to the American people that developing countries may want Chinese infrastructure investments, desire more trade with China, or find Chinese financing less expensive while simultaneously wishing to maintain or pursue democracy domestically and deepen ties with the United States and the free world. American leaders should also have more confidence in our unique model of capitalism and not try to compete with the Chinese by becoming more like them. The paranoid notion that the Chinese economy will surge past the United States anytime soon is ill-conceived. The scary idea that China will take over the world is flawed. None of these outcomes is inevitable. And we need not sit on the sidelines and passively watch these trends unfold. We have agency to shape them.

As I learned from coaching third-grade basketball, confidence has a power of its own. American leaders in government, business, and society must rekindle a more resolute belief in our comparative advantages. A confident, steady, fearless United States will inspire other countries to align with us. A nervous, erratic, and frightened United States will compel other nations to hedge against us. In a world divided once again between autocrats and democrats, we are still on the right side of history. The sooner we remember this fact, the quicker it will become a self-fulfilling prophecy.

In addition to confidence, a second necessary condition for the United States to succeed in today's era of great power competition is unity. Americans must stop fighting each other, hating each other, and practicing polarizing politics. Of course, Americans should continue to debate policies about taxes, trade, abortion, and immigration. And of particular concern to me, Americans need a more substantive but respectful debate about foreign policy and national security. For too long, elites in Washington, New York, Cambridge, and Palo Alto—Democrats and Republicans alike—assumed they knew what was best for the rest of the country regarding foreign policy and national security. The disconnect between foreign policy and the American public has been growing for decades, creating space for Trump to come in with his radical, disruptive agenda. Few Americans lamented the dismantling of USAID or VOA, because no one in decades had bothered to explain why and how these government organizations advanced the welfare of ranchers in Montana or teachers in Wisconsin. That must change. People like me need to take on this project. That is one reason why I wrote this book. And when I do a book tour after its release, I plan to spend most of my time in the middle of America, not on the coasts.

However, we can only have such debates by committing to play by the basic rules of the democratic game and showing basic decency to our fellow Americans—all Americans, regardless of party affiliation, religion, race, or ethnicity. Today's greatest threat to our security and prosperity is not China or Russia, but our divided selves. If we can get our act together at home—if we can break this fever of extreme polarization—we will prevail and prosper again, as we did during the Cold War.

As stressed throughout this book, structural factors like power, wealth, and regime type shape but do not determine history. Individuals matter too. The United States is endowed with many resources that should give Americans confidence when addressing the new challenges from China and Russia today. However, victory in this new era of great power competition is not guaranteed by innate forces; it is a responsibility to be assumed by individuals—American citizens, acting *together*—once more. We have done it before; we can do it again.

Acknowledgments

The inspiration for this book began a decade ago, during a summer I spent learning about the Chinese economy and political reform at the Stanford Center at Peking University (SCPKU) as the Distinguished Mingde Faculty Fellow. I am not an expert on China. However, as someone who has spent most of his life studying Marxist-Leninist regimes, I approached the then-popular optimism about the prospects of the Chinese Communist Party reforming, let alone democratizing, with skepticism. This kind of path had rarely occurred in the communist world. In the late 1980s, Soviet experts engaged in similar debates, and some were hopeful that the new Soviet Communist Party leader, Mikhail Gorbachev, could impose evolutionary democratic change from above. I was in the other camp, convinced that only the breakdown of the Communist Party of the Soviet Union would create the permissive conditions for genuine democratization. I thought a sobering book about lessons learned from the Soviet transition experience applied to the debate on Chinese reform would be a useful contribution.

But back then and still today, I had a demanding day job, leading the Freeman Spogli Institute for International Studies, teaching at Stanford, and various other commitments that left me with little more than an hour here and there for this book idea. And then the debate on China moved on. By the time I spent a second summer at SCPKU in Beijing in 2019, the pendulum had swung—especially in Washington—toward a new consensus: we had entered a new Cold War with another communist regime, the People's Republic of China. In my view, this was an important analytical correction to earlier optimism. However, conventional wisdom then overshot the target, and groupthink began to suppress a much-needed debate about the true drivers of conflict in US-China relations. So, I shifted my focus too, believing that my contribution could be to draw lessons from the original Cold War to inform how to navigate our relations with China today—an idea I first explored in an article for *The Washington Quarterly* in 2020. The book grew.

Around the same time, I also began to feel like American national security strategists were rightfully focused on the China threat but wrongly ignoring the Russia threat. Putin's Russia did not have the same capabilities as Xi's China, but Putin himself had stronger intentions to challenge the United States and the liberal international world more broadly. So Russia had to be added to a book on great power competition—the book grew longer. And then, Putin launched his full-scale invasion of Ukraine in 2022. The book had to expand again.

Soon after, I decided to add introductory chapters explaining the origins of confrontation with China and Russia, because I kept reading too many accounts that treated these rivalries as inevitable or immutable. That, too, required more space. And after explaining and describing this new era of great power competition, some of my initial readers of the manuscript asked what I would do about it. So I added a chapter on policy prescriptions, which eventually turned into three chapters. The book got even longer. In fact, by the time I finished the first complete draft of this book, it totaled twelve hundred pages with over five thousand footnotes. As the book's scope kept expanding, so did the timeline for writing it. And things kept changing! Donald Trump's reelection alone required an expansion and rewrite of several sections.

The book you bought and maybe will read (it is still around five hundred pages, so I am just grateful you picked it up!) is a radically condensed version of the original draft. I hope that it reads as a synthesis of historical analysis and a lot of literature. I fear that for some experts on Russia, China, or the United States, it will instead read like an oversimplification. In trying to maintain the full scope of the book, with a storyline beginning in the eighteenth century and ending with the first months of Trump's second term, that is a risk I ultimately decided to take. While individual experts on Russia, China, or the United States may not learn anything new in the chapters devoted to their area of specialization, I hope they will find value in the comparisons and insights offered in chapters on which they are not specialists. To all those experts, especially in the China field, from whom I learned a lot while writing this book: thank you. And also, my apologies for having to cut so many endnotes referencing your work!

That said, I wrote this book with another audience in mind, extending beyond experts on Russia, China, or American foreign policy. My biggest hope is that this book will be read by nonexperts, especially in the United States, which will help us as a country to have a more informed debate about America's place in the world. I worry about the American public's lack of engagement with foreign policy issues. And when that engagement does happen, it is often oversimplified, reduced to slogans and bumper stickers, or stops at the statement of an objective without a feasible strategy for achieving it. I am all for making America great again, or keeping America great. However, how to pursue that goal in foreign policy is the harder question in our new era of great competition, which is unlike any period we have lived through before. The real world is complex, in many ways more complex than the Cold War. To succeed in this new era, American leaders and society must understand that complexity, which sometimes requires reading long and complicated books like this one. If long and complex, I also aspired to write a readable book that is thin on jargon and references to theory (although international relations scholars will quickly recognize the theoretical scaffolding embedded in the book).

Writing such a big book over such a long period required a lot of help. First and foremost, I want to thank those who read parts of the book in draft. Reading someone else's work in draft is the most generous act in academia. Honestly, I rarely have the time to do so, which is why I am so grateful for those who made the time to offer this gift to me: Mike Brown, Larry Diamond, Jim Fearon, Tarek Ghani, Jim Goldgeier, Elliott Zaagman, Alex Lennon, Isobel Porteous, David Shambaugh, Gustavs Zilgalvis, and Cole McFaul (yes, he is my son, and he is the real specialist on China in the family, unlike me!).

The community of scholars studying China, Taiwan, South Korea, Japan, and Asia more broadly at Stanford University, including Erin Carter, Elizabeth Economy, Don Emmerson, Tom Fingar, Chenjian Li, Hongbin Li, Oriana Mastro, Curtis Milhaupt, Jean Oi, Jennifer Pan, Scott Rozelle, Gi-Wook Shin, Dan Sneider, Kharis Templeman, Glenn Tiffert, Kiyo Tsutsui,

Andy Walder, Chenggang Xu, and Yiqing Xu, has been very generous with their time in helping educate me about all things Asia. Outside of Stanford, I am especially grateful to China experts Jude Blanchett, Weitseng Chen, Karl Eikenberry, Taylor Fravel, Yasheng Huang, Evan Medeiros, Minxin Pei, Matt Pottinger, Orville Schell, and David Shambaugh, from whom I have learned immensely through conversations and interactions over the years. I also want to thank academic colleagues at Peking University and Tsinghua University for the generosity of their time over many years in helping me learn about US-China relations.

My learning curve on China was especially steep, but I also had new things to learn about Russia and American foreign policy while writing this book. At Stanford, I am especially grateful for conversations and interactions over the years with Chip Blacker, Brett Carter, Larry Diamond, Jim Ellis, Jim Fearon, Joe Felter, Niall Ferguson, Frank Fukuyama, Timothy Garton Ash, Jim Goldgeier, Anna Gryzmala-Busse, Eric Jensen, Colin Kahl, H. R. McMaster, Condoleezza Rice, Scott Sagan, George Shultz, Ken Shultz, Kathryn Stoner, Harold Trinkunas, and Amy Zegart. And for my continuing education about Russia, I am also indebted to my Ukrainian colleagues in government, civil society, and academia, too many to mention here.

As already noted, this book has been a long time in the making. The great advantage, however, of researching and writing a book for this long is that I got the opportunity to work with many talented research assistants at Stanford, including Michael Alisky, Lucas Beissner, Isabel Cai, Kaidi Dai, Hitsch Daines, Sharon Du, Kyle Duchynski, Dakota Foster, Hannah Freeman, Devin Fung, Maya Guzdar, Janpal Singh LaChapelle, Chubing Li, Marianne Lu, Anna Manafova, Vaughn Nahapetian, Seungpo Sohn, and Yifan Xu. In the final year of writing, Hannah Freeman's detailed and rigorous work on the entire manuscript as well as insightful suggestions on conceptual issues played an especially vital role in getting this book across the finish line.

I am also thankful to Jingfu Chen, Chubing Li, and Peggy Zou for their terrific assistance during my fieldwork in China in 2015, 2019, 2024, and 2025.

In addition, I want to thank the students who participated in my seminar on *A New Cold War? Great Power Relations in the 21st Century*, which I taught at Stanford from 2021 to 2025, and once as a minicourse with both Stanford and Peking University students in the spring of 2024. I learned a lot from them. I, too, hope they learned from me and their peers in these seminars. More generally, I always learn from teaching at Stanford. It is one of the great blessings of my life. So, to all my students, not just those in this course, thank you.

I also wanted to thank Matt Harper at HarperCollins, who gave me terrific advice on the big-picture themes of this book throughout its evolution; my agent Jay Mandel at WME, whose wisdom and optimism helped me immensely along the way; and excellent editorial assistance from Marina Krakovsky in the early phase of the book and Tracy Roe in the final phase.

A few more people made extraordinary contributions to the research and writing of this book. During the early years of research and writing, Bronte Kass was my superstar research assistant, editor, muse, and all-around great colleague who helped with every facet of this book and much more, including TAing my classes and helping me write and edit hundreds of other essays and articles. I also benefited tremendously from having Laura van Megen join our research team for a year. Laura is a real expert on China and dramatically improved all the China chapters as well as the arguments of the book more broadly. And for the final push—one that I thought would last months, but stretched out for years—Anastasia (Nastya) Guzenko was my intellectual partner, providing excellent research assistance, fantastic rewrites of almost every sentence in this book, and theoretical and analytic contributions well beyond the formal duties of her job description. While finishing this book with me, Nastya also served as a teaching assistant for my courses; edited everything else I wrote, from academic articles to Substack essays; and provided constant intellectual stimulation. Of course, neither Nastya nor anyone mentioned in this section is responsible for the analysis and arguments of the book. That I own by myself. But more than anyone else, Nastya helped shape the final manuscript. I am deeply indebted to her.

I also want to give special thanks to my executive assistant, Mahlorei Bruce-Apalis. The title "executive assistant" does not fully capture the depth and breadth of support Mahlorei has provided me over the years. To help me get this book done, Mahlorei triaged dozens of daily requests—from faculty, students, deans, FSI Council members and staff, MSNBC producers, White House officials, Ukrainian government leaders, senators, donors, and more—all while still trying to carve out bits of time for researching and writing this book. Add to that reserving space on my calendar for family and friends, and you now understand that Mahlorei has a very demanding job! But Mahlorei does it with the utmost professionalism, calm, and grace. I would never have completed this book without her.

I also want to thank my senior leadership team at the Freeman Spogli Institute—Ari Chasnoff, Megan Gorman, and Michelle Townsend—for never thinking of this book as a distraction from my day job but instead stepping in and up for me every day to help carry the responsibility of leading this fantastic institute. I want to thank the FSI Advisory Council, too, which provided me with the research support to complete this book.

I also want to thank my wife, Donna, and my sons, Cole and Luke, for joining me on research trips to China during the summers of 2015 and 2019—and for patiently listening to my endless complaints about having to work on "the book" when I should have been doing more fun things with them. Thank you, Donna, Cole, and Luke, for also thoughtfully discussing the ideas in the book with me. I am extremely fortunate to have such sharp, analytical thinkers in my own family! I am especially grateful to Donna for allowing me too many weekends to "get a little work done on the book" because I had no time during the week. But I am most appreciative of Donna's support for everything I do, far beyond just this book.

I am also very grateful to my siblings Pat, Christie, Shawn, and Tim for always supporting the work I do, be it writing this book or standing up for democratic values at home and abroad. They are always in my corner. That gives me tremendous strength.

Finally, I want to thank my parents, Helen and Kip McFaul, for instilling in me a deep appreciation for learning and a commitment to trying to make the world a better place. I know I learned a lot from writing this book. I hope its publication will help make the world more secure, prosperous, and democratic.

Notes

Introduction: New Cold War?

1. George Takach, *Cold War 2.0: Artificial Intelligence in the New Battle Between China, Russia, and America* (New York: Pegasus, 2024).
2. Niall Ferguson, "Cold War II," *National Review*, December 3, 2020, https://www.nationalreview.com/magazine/2020/12/17/cold-war-ii/.
3. Yana Gorokhovskaia and Cathryn Grothe, "Freedom in the World 2025: The Uphill Battle to Safeguard Rights," Freedom House, February 2025, https://freedomhouse.org/sites/default/files/2025-02/FITW_World_2025_Feb.2025.pdf.
4. Sarah Repucci, "Reversing the Decline of Democracy in the United States," Freedom House, 2022, https://freedomhouse.org/report/freedom-world/2022/global-expansion-authoritarian-rule/reversing-decline-democracy-united-states.
5. Larry Diamond, "Democracy's Arc: From Resurgent to Imperiled," *Journal of Democracy* 33, no. 1 (January 2022): 176, https://www.journalofdemocracy.org/articles/democracys-arc-from-resurgent-to-imperiled/.
6. Dmitri Alperovitch with Garrett Graff, *World on the Brink: How America Can Beat China in the Race for the 21st Century* (New York: Public Affairs, 2024); David Sanger, *New Cold Wars: China's Rise, Russia's Invasion, and America's Struggle to Defend the West* (New York: Crown, 2024); Michael Sobolik, *Countering China's Great Game: A Strategy for American Dominance* (Annapolis, MD: Naval Institute Press, 2024); Michael Doyle, *Cold Peace: Avoiding the New Cold War* (New York: Liveright, 2023); Bob Davis and Lingling Wei, *Superpower Showdown: How the Battle Between Trump and Xi Threatens a New Cold War* (New York: HarperCollins, 2020); Robert Kaplan, "A New Cold War Has Begun," *Foreign Policy*, January 7, 2019, https://foreignpolicy.com/2019/01/07/a-new-cold-war-has-begun/.
7. Niall Ferguson, "The New Cold War? It's with China, and It Has Already Begun," *New York Times*, December 2, 2019, https://www.nytimes.com/2019/12/02/opinion/china-cold-war.html.
8. Susan Shirk, *Overreach: How China Derailed Its Peaceful Rise* (Oxford: Oxford University Press, 2022), 1.
9. Sanger, *New Cold Wars*.
10. "National Security Strategy of the United States of America," White House, December 2017, https://trumpwhitehouse.archives.gov/wp-content/uploads/2017/12/NSS-Final-12-18-2017-0905.pdf.
11. Robert O'Brien, "The Chinese Communist Party's Ideology and Global Ambitions," White House, June 24, 2020, https://trumpwhitehouse.archives.gov/briefings-statements/chinese-communist-partys-ideology-global-ambitions/.
12. Michael R. Pompeo, "Communist China and the Free World's Future," US Department of State, July 23, 2020, https://2017-2021.state.gov/communist-china-and-the-free-worlds-future-2/.
13. Interim National Security Strategic Guidance, White House, March 2021, https://bidenwhitehouse.archives.gov/wp-content/uploads/2021/03/NSC-1v2.pdf.

14. Joe Biden, "Address to a Joint Session of Congress at the U.S. Capitol," April 28, 2021, accessed on April 15, 2023, https://www.whitehouse.gov/briefing-room/speeches-remarks/2021/04/29/remarks-by-president-biden-in-address-to-a-joint-session-of-congress/.
15. "Washington Summit Declaration," NATO, meeting of the North Atlantic Council in Washington, DC, July 10, 2024, https://www.nato.int/cps/en/natohq/official_texts_227678.htm.
16. Edward Wong and Ana Swanson, "Despite a Cabinet Stocked with China Hawks, Trump May Be Cautious," *New York Times*, November 22, 2024.
17. Wong and Swanson, "Despite a Cabinet Stocked."
18. Marco Rubio, *The World China Made: "Made in China" Nine Years Later* (Washington, DC: Project for Strong Labor Markets and National Development, Office of Senator Marco Rubio, September 9, 2024), 2.
19. Kevin Rudd, "The World According to Xi Jinping: What China's Ideologue in Chief Really Believes," *Foreign Affairs* 101, no. 6 (November/December 2022): 21.
20. Josh Rogin, *Chaos Under Heaven: Trump, Xi, and the Battle for the 21st Century* (New York: Mariner, 2021), 190.
21. Sobolik, *Countering China's Great Game*, 3–4.
22. Michael Gallagher, "Chairman Gallagher's Opening Remarks at the Select Committee on the Chinese Communist Party," Select Committee on the CCP, February 28, 2023, https://selectcommitteeontheccp.house.gov/media/press-releases/chairman-gallaghers-opening-remarks.
23. Jane Harmon, chair, Commission on the National Defense Strategy (Washington, DC: Rand, July 2024), v.
24. Robert Lighthizer, *No Trade Is Free: Changing Course, Taking on China, and Helping America's Workers* (Northampton, MA: Broadside, 2023), 90.
25. Simon Shuster, "Exclusive: Gorbachev Blames the U.S. for Provoking 'New Cold War,'" *Time*, December 11, 2014, https://time.com/3630352/mikhail-gorbachev-vladimir-putin-cold-war/; Alina Polyakova, "Are U.S. and Russia in a New Cold War?," Brookings Institution, January 20, 2019, https://www.brookings.edu/opinions/are-u-s-and-russia-in-a-new-cold-war/.
26. Edward Lucas, *The New Cold War: Putin's Russia and the Threat to the West* (New York: St. Martin's, 2009).
27. Robert Legvold, *Return to Cold War* (New York: Polity Press, 2016).
28. Dmitry Medvedev, "Munich Security Conference," Russian government, February 13, 2016, http://government.ru/en/news/21784/.
29. Ernest J. Moniz and Sam Nunn, "The Return of Doomsday: The New Nuclear Arms Race—and How Washington and Moscow Can Stop It," *Foreign Affairs* (September/October 2019), https://www.foreignaffairs.com/articles/russian-federation/2019-08-06/return-doomsday.
30. Donald J. Trump, Twitter, April 11, 2018, https://twitter.com/realDonaldTrump/status/984032798821568513/.
31. Richard Sakwa, *The Lost Peace: How the West Failed to Prevent a Second Cold War* (New Haven, CT: Yale University Press, 2023).
32. Graham Allison, *Destined for War: Can America and China Escape Thucydides's Trap?* (Boston: Houghton Mifflin Harcourt, 2017).
33. Boris Ponomarev, *Lenin and the World Revolutionary Process* (Moscow: Progress Publishers, 1980).
34. Liza Tobin, "China's Brute Force Economics: Waking Up from the Dream of a Level Playing Field," *Texas National Security Review* 6, no. 1 (Winter 2022/2023): 82–98.
35. Hal Brands, "America's War for Global Order Is a Marathon," *Foreign Policy*, January 25, 2022, https://foreignpolicy.com/2022/01/25/americas-war-for-global-order-is-a-marathon/.

36. Anne Applebaum, *Autocracy, Inc.: The Dictators Who Want to Run the World* (New York: Doubleday, 2024).

1. Cooperation and Conflict with Russia

1. Frank A. Golder, "Catherine II and the American Revolution," *American Historical Review* 21, no. 1 (Fall 1915): 93–94.
2. "Russia Established Diplomatic Relations with USA," Boris Yeltsin Presidential Library, November 5, 1809, https://www.prlib.ru/en/history/619690.
3. Thomas A. Bailey, "Notes and Documents: The Russian Fleet Myth Re-Examined," *Mississippi Valley Historical Review* 38 (Summer 1951): 81.
4. Marshall B. Davison, "A Royal Welcome for the Russian Navy," *American Heritage* 11, no. 4 (June 1960): 38.
5. Philip Ernest Schoenberg, "The American Reaction to the Kishinev Pogrom of 1903," *American Jewish Historical Quarterly* 63, no. 3 (Spring 1974): 263.
6. Woodrow Wilson, speech to US Congress in Washington, DC, April 2, 1917, https://millercenter.org/the-presidency/presidential-speeches/april-2-1917-address-congress-requesting-declaration-war.
7. Wilson, speech to US Congress.
8. George F. Kennan, *Russia and the West Under Lenin and Stalin* (Boston: Little, Brown, 1961), 25–26.
9. Margaret MacMillan, *Paris 1919: Six Months That Changed the World* (New York: Random House, 2003), 69.
10. US Embassy and Consulates in Russia, "World War II Allies: U.S. Lend-Lease to the Soviet Union, 1941–1945," https://ru.usembassy.gov/world-war-ii-allies-u-s-lend-lease-to-the-soviet-union-1941-1945/.
11. Edward Crankshaw, *Khrushchev Remembers* (Boston: Little, Brown, 1970), 220.
12. G. John Ikenberry, *A World Safe for Democracy: Liberal Internationalism and the Crises of Global Order* (New Haven, CT: Yale University Press, 2021), 178.
13. Winston Churchill, "'Iron Curtain' Speech," March 1946, National Archives, https://www.nationalarchives.gov.uk/education/resources/cold-war-on-file/iron-curtain-speech/.
14. George F. Kennan [X, pseud.], "The Sources of Soviet Conduct," *Foreign Affairs* (July 1, 1947), https://www.foreignaffairs.com/russian-federation/george-kennan-sources-soviet-conduct.
15. Paul Thomas Chamberlin, *The Cold War's Killing Fields: Rethinking the Long Peace* (New York: HarperCollins, 2018), 12.
16. John Lewis Gaddis, *Russia, the Soviet Union, and the United States: An Interpretive History* (New York: John Wiley and Sons, 1978), 183.
17. Robert Beisner, *Dean Acheson: A Life in the Cold War* (Oxford: Oxford University Press, 2006), 55.
18. Harry S. Truman, "Address of the President to Congress, Recommending Assistance to Greece and Turkey, March 12, 1947," Harry S. Truman Library and Museum, https://www.trumanlibrary.gov/library/research-files/address-president-congress-recommending-assistance-greece-and-turkey.
19. Gaddis, *Russia, the Soviet Union, and the United States*, 196.
20. Zhihua Shen and Yafeng Xia, *A Misunderstood Friendship: Mao Zedong, Kim Il-Sung and Sino–North Korea Relations 1949–1976* (New York: Columbia University Press, 2018), 27–34.
21. Statement issued by the president, Office of the Historian, US Department of State, June 27, 1950, https://history.state.gov/historicaldocuments/frus1950v07/d119.
22. "NSC 68: United States Objectives and Programs for National Security: A Report to the President Pursuant to the President's Directive of January 31, 1950," April 14, 1950, https://fas.org/irp/offdocs/nsc-hst/nsc-68.htm.

23. Odd Arne Westad, *The Cold War: A World History* (New York: Basic Books, 2017).
24. Michael McFaul, "Southern African Liberation and Great Power Intervention: Towards a Theory of Revolution in an International Context" (PhD diss., Oxford University, 1991).
25. Alexander George, *Managing US-Soviet Rivalry: Problems of Crisis Prevention* (Boulder, CO: Westview, 1983).
26. Michael McFaul, "The Demise of the World Revolutionary Process: Soviet-Angolan Relations Under Gorbachev," *Journal of Southern African Studies* 16, no. 3 (Spring 1990): 165–89.
27. Leon Aron, *Yeltsin: A Revolutionary Life* (New York: St. Martin's Press, 2000), 657–58.
28. Michael McFaul, *Russia's Unfinished Revolution: Political Change from Gorbachev to Putin* (Ithaca, NY: Cornell University Press, 2001).
29. "The President's News Conference with President Boris Yeltsin of Russia," George Bush Presidential Library and Museum, February 1, 1992, https://bush41library.tamu.edu/archives/public-papers/3898/.
30. Bill Clinton, "A Strategic Alliance with Russian Reform," *U.S. Department of State Dispatch* 4, no. 13, April 5, 1993, 189–94.
31. Vladimir Putin, "Interview with ORT and RTR TV Channels and the Nezavisimaya Gazeta Newspaper," President of Russia, December 25, 2000, http://en.kremlin.ru/events/president/transcripts/21149.
32. David Hoffman, "Putin Says 'Why Not' to Russia Joining NATO," *Washington Post*, March 5, 2000, https://www.washingtonpost.com/archive/politics/2000/03/06/putin-says-why-not-to-russia-joining-nato/c1973032-c10f-4bff-9174-8cae673790cd/.
33. Caroline Wyatt, "Bush and Putin: Best of Friends," BBC News, June 16, 2001, http://news.bbc.co.uk/2/hi/europe/1392791.stm.
34. Michael McFaul, "Ukraine Imports Democracy: External Influences on the Orange Revolution," *International Security* 32, no. 2 (Fall 2007): 45–83.
35. Vladimir Putin, "Speech and the Following Discussion at the Munich Conference on Security Policy," President of Russia, February 10, 2007, http://en.kremlin.ru/events/president/transcripts/24034.
36. Michael McFaul, *From Cold War to Hot Peace* (Boston: Houghton Mifflin Harcourt, 2018), Chapter 6: Launching the Reset.
37. "Direct Line with Vladimir Putin," President of Russia, April 16, 2015, http://en.kremlin.ru/events/president/news/49261.
38. David Marples, ed., *The War in Ukraine's Donbas: Origins, Contexts, and Future* (New York: Central European University Press, 2022).
39. H. R. McMaster, *At War with Ourselves: My Tour of Duty in the Trump White House* (New York: HarperCollins, 2022), 187–89.
40. McMaster, *At War with Ourselves*, 311.
41. Adam Entous, "What Fiona Hill Learned in the White House," *New Yorker*, June 22, 2020, https://www.newyorker.com/magazine/2020/06/29/what-fiona-hill-learned-in-the-white-house.
42. "National Security Strategy of the United States of America," December 2017.
43. "Russian Offensive Campaign Assessment, February 24, 2025," Institute for the Study of War, February 24, 2025, https://www.understandingwar.org/backgrounder/russian-offensive-campaign-assessment-february-24-2025.
44. Elizabeth Crisp, "8 in 10 Say Putin Should Not Be Trusted," *The Hill*, February 19, 2025, https://thehill.com/policy/international/5153611-quinnipiac-poll-russia-putin-trust/.

2. Working with and Against China

1. John Pomfret, *The Beautiful Country and Middle Kingdom: America, China, 1776 to the Present* (New York: Picador, 2016), 11.
2. John Haddad, *America's First Adventure in China: Trade, Treaties, Opium, and Salvation* (Philadelphia: Temple University Press, 2013), 8.

3. Stephen R. Platt, *Imperial Twilight: The Opium War and the End of China's Last Golden Age* (New York: Knopf, 2018), 71.
4. Platt, *Imperial Twilight*, 20.
5. Ping Chia Kuo, "Caleb Cushing and the Treaty of Wangxia, 1844," *Journal of Modern History* 5, no. 1 (March 1933): 34–54.
6. Paul A. Varg, "Sino-American Relations Past and Present," *Diplomatic History* 4, no. 2 (1980): 102.
7. Stephen Platt, *Autumn in the Heavenly Kingdom: China, the West, and the Epic Story of the Taiping Civil War* (New York: Knopf, 2012).
8. Erika Lee, *At America's Gates: Chinese Immigration During the Exclusion Era, 1882–1943* (Chapel Hill: University of North Carolina Press, 2003), 41.
9. Madeline Y. Hsu, "Chinese and American Collaborations Through Educational Exchange During the Era of Exclusion, 1872–1955," *Pacific Historical Review* 83, no. 2 (2014): 322.
10. Michael S. Hunt, "The American Remission of the Boxer Indemnity: A Reappraisal," *Journal of Asian Studies* 31, no. 3 (May 1972): 556–57.
11. Lucien Bianco, *Origins of the Chinese Revolution, 1915–1949* (Stanford: Stanford University Press, 1971), 6.
12. Yuhua Wang, *The Rise and Fall of Imperial China: The Social Origins of State Development* (Princeton, NJ: Princeton University Press, 2022), 198.
13. Frank Dikötter, *The Age of Openness: China Before Mao* (Berkeley: University of California Press, 2008), 19.
14. Dikötter, *The Age of Openness*, 9.
15. William Taft, "December 3, 1912: Fourth Annual Message," University of Virginia Miller Center, December 3, 1912, https://millercenter.org/the-presidency/presidential-speeches/december-3-1912-fourth-annual-message.
16. Eugene Trani, "Woodrow Wilson, China, and the Missionaries, 1913–1921," *Journal of Presbyterian History* 49, no. 4 (Winter 1971): 332.
17. Rana Mitter, *Forgotten Ally: China's World War II, 1937–1945* (Boston: Houghton Mifflin Harcourt, 2013).
18. John S. Service, "Desirability of American Military Aid to the Chinese Communist Armies," September 28, 1944, *Foreign Relations of the United States, 1944, China*, vol. 6 (Washington, DC: US Government Printing Office, 1967), 600–601, https://history.state.gov/historicaldocuments/frus1944v06/d453.
19. Daniel Kurtz-Phelan, *The China Mission: George Marshall's Unfinished War, 1945–1947* (New York: W. W. Norton, 2018).
20. Michael Green, *By More Than Providence: Grade Strategy and American Power in the Asia Pacific Since 1783* (New York: Columbia University Press, 2017), 255.
21. Frank Dikötter, *The Tragedy of Liberation: A History of the Chinese Revolution 1945–1957* (London: Bloomsbury Press, 2013), 15–16.
22. Seth Faison Jr., "Mao's Cable Explains Drive into Korea," *New York Times*, February 26, 1992, https://www.nytimes.com/1992/02/26/world/mao-s-cable-explains-drive-into-korea.html.
23. Harry S. Truman, "The President's News Conference," National Archives, Harry S. Truman Library and Museum, January 5, 1950, https://www.trumanlibrary.gov/library/public-papers/3/presidents-news-conference.
24. Chen Jian, "China's Involvement in the Vietnam War, 1964–69," *China Quarterly* 142 (June 1995): 379, https://doi.org/10.1017/S0305741000034974.
25. Jeremy Friedman, *Shadow Cold War: The Sino-Soviet Competition for the Third World* (Chapel Hill: University of North Carolina Press, 2015).
26. Andrew Walder, *China Under Mao: A Revolution Derailed* (Cambridge, MA: Harvard University Press, 2017).
27. Michael McFaul, "Southern African Liberation and Great Power Intervention: Towards a Theory of Revolution in an International Context" (PhD diss., Oxford University, 1991).

28. "Memorandum of Conversation," Office of the Historian, US Department of State, July 9, 1971, https://history.state.gov/historicaldocuments/frus1969-76v17/d139.
29. "Joint Statement Following Discussions with Leaders of the People's Republic of China," Office of the Historian, US Department of State, February 27, 1972, https://history.state.gov/historicaldocuments/frus1969-76v17/d203.
30. Andrew Walder, "Bending the Arc of Chinese History: The Cultural Revolution's Paradoxical Legacy," *China Quarterly* 227 (September 2016): 613–31.
31. Julian Gewirtz, *Unlikely Partners: Chinese Reformers, Western Economists, and the Making of Global China* (Cambridge, MA: Harvard University Press, 2017).
32. "The 'Six Assurances' to Taiwan," Taiwan Documents Project, July 1982, http://www.taiwandocuments.org/assurances.htm.
33. Minxin Pei, "China: The Doomed Transition Moment of 1989," in Kathryn Stoner and Michael McFaul, eds., *Transitions to Democracy: A Comparative Perspective* (Baltimore: Johns Hopkins University Press, 2013), 378.
34. "Memorandum of Conversation," July 2, 1989, *The Wire China*, https://www.thewirechina.com/wp-content/uploads/2020/06/Deng_Scowcroft_July_2_1989_Meeting.pdf.
35. Henry Rowan, "The Short March: China's Road to Democracy," *National Interest* 45 (Fall 1996): 61–70.
36. "Clinton's Words on China: Trade Is the Smart Thing," *New York Times*, March 9, 2000, https://www.nytimes.com/2000/03/09/world/clinton-s-words-on-china-trade-is-the-smart-thing.html.
37. *U.S. National Security and Military/Commercial Concerns with the People's Republic of China*, US House of Representatives Select Committee, January 3, 1999, https://china.usc.edu/sites/default/files/article/attachments/cox-report-1999-us-china-military-security.pdf.
38. "Human Rights Violations in Tibet," Human Rights Watch, June 13, 2000, https://www.hrw.org/news/2000/06/13/human-rights-violations-tibet.
39. Sungmin Cho, "Why Non-Democracy Engages with Western Democracy-Promotion Programs: The China Model," *World Politics* 71, no. 4 (2021): 774–817.
40. George W. Bush, "Remarks to the Los Angeles World Affairs Council in Los Angeles, California," American Presidency Project, UC Santa Barbara, May 29, 2001, https://www.presidency.ucsb.edu/documents/remarks-the-los-angeles-world-affairs-council-los-angeles-california.
41. Elizabeth Becker, "U.S. Files a Complaint Against China at the W.T.O.," *New York Times*, March 19, 2004, https://www.nytimes.com/2004/03/19/business/us-files-a-complaint-against-china-at-the-wto.html.
42. Niall Ferguson and Moritz Schularick, "'Chimerica' and the Global Asset Market Boom," *International Finance* 10, no. 3 (2007): 215–39.
43. "Chinese President Hu Jintao Holds Telephone Conversation with U.S. President-Elect Obama," Embassy of the Republic of China in the Democratic Socialist Republic of Sri Lanka, November 8, 2008, http://lk.china-embassy.gov.cn/eng/zgxw/200811/t20081111_1398010.htm.
44. "US-China Joint Announcement on Climate Change," Office of the Press Secretary, White House, November 11, 2014, https://obamawhitehouse.archives.gov/the-press-office/2014/11/11/us-china-joint-announcement-climate-change.
45. Orville Schell, "The Death of Engagement," *The Wire China*, June 7, 2020, https://www.thewirechina.com/2020/06/07/the-birth-life-and-death-of-engagement/.
46. Kurt Campbell, *The Pivot: The Future of American Statecraft in Asia* (New York: Twelve, 2016).
47. Doug Palmer, "Obama Slaps Duties on Tire Imports from China," Reuters, September 11, 2009, https://www.reuters.com/article/us-usa-china-tires/obama-slaps-duties-on-tire-imports-from-china-idUSTRE58B08G20090912.

48. "Remarks by the President on Fair Trade," White House, March 13, 2012, https://obamawhitehouse.archives.gov/photos-and-video/video/2012/03/13/president-obama-speaks-enforcing-trade-rights-china#transcript.
49. Don Lee and Christi Parsons, "U.S. Opens Trade Case Against China Over Rare Earth Export Limits," *Los Angeles Times*, March 14, 2012, https://www.latimes.com/business/la-xpm-2012-mar-14-la-fi-obama-china-20120314-story.html.
50. "Joint Fact Sheet on Strengthening U.S.-China Economic Relations," Office of the Press Secretary, White House, February 14, 2012, https://obamawhitehouse.archives.gov/the-press-office/2012/02/14/joint-fact-sheet-strengthening-us-china-economic-relations.
51. Michael Brown and Pavneet Singh, *China's Technology Transfer Strategy: How Chinese Investments in Emerging Technology Enable a Strategic Competitor to Access the Crown Jewels of U.S. Innovation* (Mountain View, CA: Defense Innovation Unit Experimental, January 2018).
52. Paul Blustein, *Schism: China, America and the Fracturing of the Global Trading System* (Waterloo, Canada: Centre for International Governance Innovation, 2019), 205.
53. "Fact Sheet: Advancing the Rebalance to Asia and the Pacific," Office of the Press Secretary, White House, November 16, 2015, https://obamawhitehouse.archives.gov/the-press-office/2015/11/16/fact-sheet-advancing-rebalance-asia-and-pacific.
54. Chris Buckley, "China Paper Calls Chen a U.S. Pawn; Envoy Is a 'Troublemaker,'" Reuters, May 3, 2012, https://www.reuters.com/article/us-china-usa-paper/china-paper-calls-chen-a-u-s-pawn-envoy-is-a-troublemaker-idUSBRE8430BE20120504.
55. Elizabeth Economy, *The Third Revolution: Xi Jinping and the New Chinese State* (Oxford: Oxford University Press, 2018).
56. David O. Shullman, "Power in China Now Unquestionably Flows Through One Man," Atlantic Council, October 17, 2022, https://www.atlanticcouncil.org/blogs/new-atlanticist/experts-react-what-the-world-needs-to-know-from-chinas-communist-party-congress/#shullman.
57. Minxin Pei, "China: From Tiananmen to Neo-Stalinism," *Journal of Democracy* 31, no. 1 (January 2020): 149.
58. Jennifer Pan, Xu Xu, and Yiqing Xu, "Disguised Repression: Targeting Opponents with Non-Political Crimes to Undermine Dissent," *The Journal of Politics*, forthcoming.
59. Yingdan Lu, Jennifer Pan, Xu Xu, and Yiqing Xu, "Decentralized Propaganda in the Era of Digital Media: The Massive Presence of the Chinese State on Douyin," *American Journal of Political Science*, forthcoming.
60. Erin Carter and Brett Carter, *Propaganda in Autocracies: Institutions, Information, and the Politics of Belief* (Cambridge: Cambridge University Press, 2023), 445.
61. Minxin Pei, *The Sentinel State: Surveillance and the Survival of Dictatorship in China* (Cambridge, MA: Harvard University Press, 2024).
62. Genia Kostka and Lukas Antoine, "Fostering Model Citizenship: Behavioral Responses to China's Emerging Social Credit Systems," *Policy and Internet* 12, no. 3 (September 2020): 256–89.
63. Vivian Wang, "Chinese Citizen Journalist Sentenced to 4 Years for Covid Reporting," *New York Times*, December 28, 2020 (updated on October 8, 2021), https://www.nytimes.com/2020/12/28/world/asia/china-Zhang-Zhan-covid-convicted.html.
64. Yasheng Huang, *The Rise and Fall of the EAST: How Exams, Autocracy, Stability, and Technology Brought China Success, and Why They Might Lead to Its Decline* (New Haven, CT: Yale University Press, 2023), 286.
65. Tony Saich, *From Rebel to Ruler: One Hundred Years of the Chinese Communist Party* (Cambridge, MA: Harvard University Press, 2021).
66. Nicholas Lardy, *The State Strikes Back: The End of Economic Reform in China?* (Washington, DC: Peterson Institute for International Economics, 2019).

67. Michael Alisky, Scott Rozelle, and Martin King Whyte, "Getting Ahead in Today's China: From Optimism to Pessimism," *China Journal* 93, no. 1 (2025), https://www.journals.uchicago.edu/doi/abs/10.1086/733178.
68. Li Yuan, "Beijing Offers Love, but Chinese Entrepreneurs Aren't Buying It," *New York Times*, July 22, 2023, https://www.nytimes.com/2023/07/22/business/china-private-enterprise.html?smid=tw-share.
69. Tiffany May, "Hong Kong Editors Sentenced in Landmark Case," *New York Times*, September 26, 2024.
70. Adrian Zenz, "The Karakax List: Dissecting the Anatomy of Beijing's Internment Drive in Xinjiang," *Journal of Political Risk* 8, no. 2 (February 2020), https://www.jpolrisk.com/karakax/.
71. Cate Cadell, "Exclusive: China Sharply Expands Mass Labor Program in Tibet," Reuters, September 21, 2020, https://www.reuters.com/article/world/exclusive-china-sharply-expands-mass-labor-program-in-tibet-idUSKCN26D0GQ/.
72. "Freedom in the World 2024: China," Freedom House, https://freedomhouse.org/country/china/freedom-world/2024.
73. Nick Gass, "Trump: 'We Can't Continue to Allow China to Rape Our Country,'" *Politico*, May 2, 2016, https://www.politico.com/blogs/2016-gop-primary-live-updates-and-results/2016/05/trump-china-rape-america-222689.
74. "Trump Hails 'Tremendous' Progress in Talks with China's Xi," BBC, April 7, 2017, https://www.bbc.com/news/world-us-canada-39517569.
75. David Nakamura, "At Mar-a-Lago, Trump Welcomes China's Xi in First Summit," *Washington Post*, April 7, 2017, https://www.washingtonpost.com/politics/at-mar-a-lago-trump-to-welcome-chinas-xi-for-high-stakes-inaugural-summit/2017/04/06/0235cdd0-1ac2-11e7-bcc2-7d1a0973e7b2_story.html.
76. "National Security Strategy of the United States of America," White House, December 2017.
77. Marc Santora, "Pompeo Calls China's Ruling Party 'Central Threat of Our Times,'" *New York Times*, January 30, 2020, https://www.nytimes.com/2020/01/30/world/europe/pompeo-uk-china-huawei.html.
78. "United States' Strategic Approach to the People's Republic of China," White House, May 20, 2020, https://trumpwhitehouse.archives.gov/wp-content/uploads/2020/05/U.S.-Strategic-Approach-to-The-Peoples-Republic-of-China-Report-5.24v1.pdf.
79. Robert O'Brien, "The Chinese Communist Party's Ideology and Global Ambitions," White House, June 24, 2020.
80. Christopher Wray, "The Threat Posed by the Chinese Government and the Chinese Communist Party to the Economic and National Security of the United States," FBI, July 7, 2020, https://www.fbi.gov/news/speeches/the-threat-posed-by-the-chinese-government-and-the-chinese-communist-party-to-the-economic-and-national-security-of-the-united-states.
81. George Kennan [X, pseud.], "The Sources of Soviet Conduct," *Foreign Affairs*, July 1, 1947.
82. Bob Davis and Lingling Wei, *Superpower Showdown: How the Battle Between Trump and Xi Threatens a New Cold War* (New York: HarperCollins, 2020); Josh Rogin, *Chaos Under Heaven: Trump, Xi, and the Battle for the 21st Century* (New York: Mariner, 2021).
83. *Findings of the Investigation into China's Acts, Policies, and Practices Related to Technology Transfer, Intellectual Property, and Innovation Under Section 301 of the Trade Act of 1974* (Washington, DC: Office of the United States Trade Representative, March 2018), https://ustr.gov/sites/default/files/Section%20301%20FINAL.PDF.
84. Brown and Singh, *China's Technology Transfer Strategy*.
85. Michael Pompeo, "Announcing the Expansion of the Clean Network to Safeguard America's Assets," US Department of State, August 5, 2020, https://2017-2021.state.gov/announcing-the-expansion-of-the-clean-network-to-safeguard-americas-assets/#.XyskRCepNOE.twitter;

Michael Pompeo, "The Clean Network," US Department of State, https://2017-2021.state .gov/the-clean-network.

86. David McCabe and Raymond Zhong, "U.S. Tightens Restrictions on Huawei's Chip Access," *New York Times*, August 18, 2020.
87. Orion Rummler, "Bolton Alleges Trump Encouraged Xi to Continue with Uighur Detainment Camps," *Axios*, June 18, 2020, https://www.axios.com/2020/06/17/trump -uighur-muslim-bolton.
88. Bethany Allen-Ebrahimian, "U.S. Sanctions China's Paramilitary in Xinjiang," *Axios*, July 31, 2020, https://www.axios.com/us-sanctions-china-paramilitary-xinjiang-xpcc-41e29c92-9649-4e47-9e91-a7f78330d4d8.html; Bill Chappell, "Pompeo Accuses China of Genocide Against Muslim Uighurs in Xinjiang," NPR, January 19, 2021, https://www.npr .org/2021/01/19/958468971/pompeo-accuses-china-of-genocide-against-muslim-uighurs -in-xinjian.
89. "United States' Strategic Approach to the People's Republic of China," 10.
90. *Nomination of Hon. Antony J. Blinken to Be U.S. Secretary of State*, 107th Congress, January 19, 2021, https://www.govinfo.gov/content/pkg/CHRG-117shrg43890/html/CHRG -117shrg43890.htm.
91. Antony J. Blinken, "A Foreign Policy for the American People," US Department of State, March 3, 2021, https://www.state.gov/a-foreign-policy-for-the-american-people/.
92. "National Security Strategy," White House, October 12, 2022, 11, https://bidenwhitehouse .archives.gov/wp-content/uploads/2022/10/Biden-Harris-Administrations-National -Security-Strategy-10.2022.pdf.
93. "Readout of President Joe Biden's Meeting with President Xi Jinping of the People's Republic of China," Office of the Press Secretary, White House, November 14, 2022, https:// bidenwhitehouse.archives.gov/briefing-room/statements-releases/2022/11/14/readout-of -president-joe-bidens-meeting-with-president-xi-jinping-of-the-peoples-republic-of-china/.
94. "Fact Sheet: President Biden Takes Action to Protect American Workers and Businesses from China's Unfair Trade Practices," US Department of Commerce, May 14, 2024, https://www .commerce.gov/news/fact-sheets/2024/05/fact-sheet-president-biden-takes-action-protect -american-workers-and.
95. Rachel Treisman, "Where Do Tariffs Stand? A Look at What's in Place and What's on Pause," NPR, April 10, 2025, https://www.npr.org/2025/04/10/nx-s1-5358929/trump-tariff-pause -china.

3. The End of American Hegemony

1. Josef Joffe, *Überpower: The Imperial Temptation of America* (New York: W. W. Norton, 2006).
2. "To Paris, U.S. Looks Like a 'Hyperpower,'" *New York Times*, February 5, 1999, https://www .nytimes.com/1999/02/05/news/to-paris-us-looks-like-a-hyperpower.html.
3. Michael Mandelbaum, *The Case for Goliath: How America Acts as the World's Government in the 21st Century* (New York: Public Affairs, 2005).
4. John Newhouse, *Imperial America: The Bush Assault on the World Order* (New York: Knopf, 2003).
5. Mikhail Zygar, "To Putin, Trump Is a Harbinger of America's Collapse," *New York Times*, November 19, 2024, https://www.nytimes.com/2024/11/19/opinion/putin-trump-russia -america.html.
6. Joseph Nye, *Understanding International Conflicts* (New York: Pearson, 2009), 61.
7. Robert A. Dahl, "The Concept of Power," *Behavioral Science* 2, no. 3 (1957): 202–3.
8. Joseph Nye, *The Future of Power* (New York: Public Affairs, 2011), 4.
9. Thomas Graham Jr., "World Without Russia?," Carnegie Endowment for International Peace, January 9, 1999.
10. Michael McFaul and Alexandra Vacroux, "Russian Resilience as a Great Power," *Post-Soviet Affairs* 22, no. 1 (January–March 2006): 24–33.

11. Amy Zegart, "The Crumbling Foundations of American Strength: Knowledge Is Power—and the United States Is Losing It," *Foreign Affairs* 103, no. 5 (September/October 2024): 136–47; Paul Scharre, *Four Battlegrounds: Power in the Age of Artificial Intelligence* (New York: W. W. Norton, 2023).
12. President George H. W. Bush, "Address Before a Joint Session of the Congress on the Persian Gulf Crisis and the Federal Budget Deficit," September 11, 1990, https://bush41library.tamu.edu/archives/public-papers/2217#:~:text=But%20our%20policy%20cannot%20change,General%20Javier%20Perez%20de%20Cuellar.
13. George H. W. Bush, "State of the Union Address," January 28, 1992, *The American Presidency Project*, https://www.presidency.ucsb.edu/documents/address-before-joint-session-the-congress-the-state-the-union-2.
14. Michael Boskin, John Rader, and Kiran Sridhar, "The Geopolitical, Military and Fiscal Context for Defense Budget Reform," in Michael Boskin, John Rader, and Kiran Sridhar, eds., *Defense Budgeting for a Safer World: The Experts Speak* (Stanford: Hoover Institution Press, 2023), 15.
15. James M. Cunningham, "Our Military Debt Crisis: Preserving America's Strategy Solvency," in Boskin, Rader, and Sridhar, *Defense Budgeting for a Safer World*, 203.
16. Article 5, North Atlantic Treaty, April 4, 1949, https://www.nato.int/cps/eu/natohq/official_texts_17120.htm.
17. George W. Bush, "Speech at the Chamber of Commerce," Washington, DC, November 6, 2003.
18. "Human and Budgetary Costs to Date of the U.S. War in Afghanistan, 2001–2022," Watson Institute for International & Public Affairs, *The Costs of War*, August 2022, https://watson.brown.edu/costsofwar/figures/2021/human-and-budgetary-costs-date-us-war-afghanistan-2001-2022; "Afghanistan: All You Need to Know About the Country," BBC News, September 3, 2021, https://www.bbc.com/news/world-47391821.
19. "The Iraq War," The Council on Foreign Relations, https://www.cfr.org/timeline/iraq-war.
20. "Freedom in the World 2024: Iraq," Freedom House, 2024, https://freedomhouse.org/country/iraq.
21. Barack Obama, *A Promised Land* (New York: Crown, 2020), 668.
22. Joby Warrick, *Red Line: The Unraveling of Syria and the Race to Destroy the Most Dangerous Arsenal in the World* (New York: Doubleday, 2021).
23. Michael McFaul, *Advancing Democracy Abroad* (Lanham, MD: Rowman and Littlefield, 2010).
24. Peter Beinart, "Why Do America's Liberal Hawks Attack Russia While Giving Israel a Free Pass?," *Guardian*, January 29, 2024.
25. Neta C. Crawford, "The Iraq War Has Cost the US Nearly $2 Trillion," *Military Times*, February 6, 2020.
26. "Human and Budgetary Costs to Date of the U.S. War in Afghanistan, 2001–2022."
27. Anusha Chari, Peter Blair Henry, and Hector Reyes, "The Baker Hypothesis: Stabilization, Structural Reforms, and Economic Growth," *Journal of Economic Perspectives* 35, no. 3 (Summer 2021): 83–108.
28. Michael McFaul, "Why Russia's Politics Matter," *Foreign Affairs* 74, no. 1 (January/February 1995): 99.
29. John Weinberg, "The Great Recession and Its Aftermath," *Federal Reserve History*, November 13, 2013.
30. "Statistical Communiqué of the People's Republic of China on the 2009 National Economic and Social Development," National Bureau of Statistics of China, February 25, 2010, https: www.stats.gov.cn/english/NewsEvents/201002/t20100226_26295.html; "China's Economy Grew 10.3% in 2010," BBC News, January 20, 2011, https://www.bbc.com/news/business-12235625.

31. Karishma Vaswani, "Why Asia Turned to China During the Global Financial Crisis," BBC, September 13, 2018.
32. Henry M. Paulson, *Dealing with China* (New York: Twelve, 2016), 240.
33. Paulson, *Dealing with China,* 240.
34. Lucia Mutikani, "U.S. Economy Contracted 19.2% During COVID-19 Pandemic Recession," Reuters, July 29, 2021, https://www.reuters.com/business/us-economy-contracted-192-during-covid-19-pandemic-recession-2021-07-29/.
35. "COVID Mortality Update—United States, 2022," Centers for Disease Control, May 5, 2023, https://www.cdc.gov/mmwr/volumes/72/wr/mm7218a4.htm.
36. Ivo Daalder and James Lindsay, *The Empty Throne: America's Abdication of Global Leadership* (New York: Public Affairs, 2018).
37. Polling data from Morning Consult's US Foreign Policy Tracker Index from January of 2023 cited in Elaine Kamarck and Jordan Muchnick, "One Year into the Ukraine War—What Does the Public Think About American Involvement in the World?," Brookings Institution, February 23, 2023, https://www.brookings.edu/articles/one-year-into-the-ukraine-war-what-does-the-public-think-about-american-involvement-in-the-world/.
38. Jason McMann, "U.S. Foreign Policy Tracker," Morning Consult, accessed November 20, 2024, https://pro.morningconsult.com/trackers/public-opinion-us-foreign-policy.
39. Jacob Poushter and Laura Clancy, "What Are Americans' Top Foreign Policy Priorities?," Pew Research Center, April 23, 2024, https://www.pewresearch.org/global/2024/04/23/what-are-americans-top-foreign-policy-priorities/.

4. Russian vs. American Power

1. Thomas E. Graham, "Russia's Decline and Uncertain Recovery," Carnegie Endowment for International Peace, 2002.
2. Matt Evangelista, "The Chechen Wars: Will Russia Go the Way of the Soviet Union?," Brookings Institution, 2003.
3. Michael McFaul and Alexandra Vacroux, "Russian Resilience as a Great Power," *Post-Soviet Affairs* 22, no. 1 (January–March 2006): 24–33.
4. Kathryn Stoner, *Russia Resurrected: Its Power and Purpose in a New Global Order* (New York: Oxford University Press, 2021), 4.
5. Hans M. Kristensen et al., "United States Nuclear Weapons, 2025," *Bulletin of the Atomic Scientists* 81, no. 2, 135–60, https://doi.org/10.1080/00963402.2025.2467011; Hans M. Kristensen, Matt Korda, Eliana Johns, and Mackenzie Knight, "Russian Nuclear Weapons, 2025," *Bulletin of the Atomic Scientists,* 81, no. 3, 208–37, https://doi.org/10.1080/00963402.2025.2494386.
6. Hans Kristensen et al., "Status of World Nuclear Sources," Federation of American Scientists, March 2025, https://fas.org/initiative/status-world-nuclear-forces/.
7. Hans M. Kristensen et al., "Chinese Nuclear Weapons, 2025," *Bulletin of the Atomic Scientists,* 81, no. 2, 135–60, https://doi.org/10.1080/00963402.2025.2467011.
8. Kristensen et al., "Status of World Nuclear Sources."
9. Jill Hruby, "Russia's New Nuclear Weapon Delivery Systems: An Open-Source Technical Review," NTI, November 2019, https://media.nti.org/pdfs/NTI-Hruby_FINAL.PDF.
10. Vladimir Putin, "On Arms and Arms Race (Interview to Tass)," interview by Andrei Vandenko, Tass, March 2, 2020, http://en.kremlin.ru/events/president/news/62917.
11. Vladimir Putin, presidential address to the Federal Assembly, Moscow, March 1, 2018; "Russia's Nuclear Weapons: Doctrine, Forces, Modernization," Congressional Research Service, April 2022.
12. Hans Kristensen, "Amidst Nuclear Saber Rattling, New START Treaty Demonstrates Importance," Federation of American Scientists, April 2022.

13. Alexander H. Montgomery and Amy J. Nelson, "Ukraine and the Kinzhal: Don't Believe the Hypersonic Hype," Brookings Institution, May 23, 2022, https://www.brookings.edu/articles/ukraine-and-the-kinzhal-dont-believe-the-hypersonic-hype/.
14. Rebecca K. C. Hersman, Joseph Rodgers, and Bryce Farabaugh, "Deep Dive Debrief: U.S. Nuclear Warhead Modernization and 'New' Nuclear Weapons," Center for Strategic and International Studies, December 2020, https://csis-website-prod.s3.amazonaws.com/s3fs-public/publication/201210_Hersman_US_Nuclear.pdf.
15. "Sentinel Deployment & Minuteman III Decommissioning and Disposal," Air Force Global Strike Command, October 2024, https://www.afgsc.af.mil/Sentinel-GBSD/.
16. John Knox, "The Price of the Sentinel Nuclear Weapons Program Keeps Going Up, but the True Costs Are Even Higher," Union of Concerned Scientists, August 14, 2024, https://blog.ucsusa.org/jknox/the-price-of-the-sentinel-nuclear-weapons-program-keeps-going-up-but-the-true-costs-are-even-higher/.
17. "Department of Energy Fiscal Year 2023 Budget Statistical Table by Appropriation," US Department of Energy, April 2022, https://www.energy.gov/sites/default/files/2022-04/doe-fy-23-budget-stat-by-appropriation-enacted-v2.pdf.
18. Clayton Swape and Tom Karako, "Why a Missile Shield in Space Makes Sense," *Space News*, February 4, 2025, https://spacenews.com/why-a-missile-shield-in-space-makes-sense/.
19. Guy Faulconbridge, "Has Putin Threatened to Use Nuclear Weapons?," Reuters, October 27, 2022, https://www.reuters.com/world/europe/has-putin-threatened-use-nuclear-weapons-2022-10-27/.
20. David E. Sanger, "Biden's Armageddon Moment: When Nuclear Detonation Seemed Possible in Ukraine," *New York Times*, March 9, 2024, https://www.nytimes.com/2024/03/09/us/politics/biden-nuclear-russia-ukraine.html.
21. William Odom, *The Collapse of the Soviet Military* (New Haven, CT: Yale University Press, 1998).
22. Yegor Gaidar, *Days of Defeat and Victory* (Seattle: University of Washington Press, 1999).
23. Stoner, *Russia Resurrected*, 185.
24. Anna Borshchevskaya, *Putin's War in Syria: Russian Foreign Policy and the Price of America's Absence* (London: I. B. Tauris, 2018), 80.
25. Data presented on the Russian military in this table might not be complete, as official statistics do not include roughly $46.3 billion of state funding for security and law enforcement organizations, such as the Rosgvardia (Russian National Guard), which has also been fighting in Ukraine; see Pavel Luzin, "Russia's Skyrocketing Defense Spending, 2022–2023," *Eurasia Daily Monitor* 19, no. 148 (October 2022), https://jamestown.org/program/russias-skyrocketing-defense-spending-2022-2023/.
26. Zoltan Barany, "Armies and Autocrats: Why Putin's Military Failed," *Journal of Democracy* 34, no. 1 (January 2023): 80.
27. Author's conversations with leaders from the Baltic states and Poland in Vilnius, Lithuania, January 2024.
28. "Chapter One: Defense and Military Analysis," *Military Balance* 123:1 (2025), 6–11, https://doi.org/10.1080/04597222.2025.2445473.
29. Data collected from the *Military Balance* includes some approximations of exact numbers of equipment. Approximations denoted by +.
30. "Chapter Five: Russia and Eurasia," *Military Balance* 123:1 (2023): 150–207, https://doi.org/10.1080/04597222.2023.2162717; "Chapter Three: North America," *Military Balance* 123:1 (2023): 16–49, https://doi.org/10.1080/04597222.2023.2162715.
31. Jakub Janovsky et al., "Attack on Europe: Documenting Equipment Losses," *Oryx Spioenkop* (February 2022), https://www.oryxspioenkop.com/2022/02/attack-on-europe-documenting-equipment.html.

32. James Anderton, "Tank Tech: The Abrams and Leopard 2 vs. Russian Tanks," Engineering.com, January 31, 2023, https://www.engineering.com/story/tank-tech-the-abrams-and-leopard-2-vs-russian-tanks.
33. Leonid Nersisyan, "Russian Combat Aviation: Procurement, Modernization, and Future Outlook," Center for Naval Analyses, December 2020, https://www.cna.org/archive/CNA_Files/pdf/iop-2020-u-028810-final.pdf.
34. "B-21 Raider Makes Public Debut, Will Become Backbone of Air Force's Bomber Fleet," US Air Force, December 2, 2022, https://www.af.mil/News/Article-Display/Article/3235250/b-21-raider-makes-public-debut-will-become-backbone-of-air-forces-bomber-fleet/.
35. Bohdan Tuzov, "How in 2 Years Ukraine Crippled the Black Sea Fleet," *Kyiv Post*, February 24, 2024, https://www.kyivpost.com/post/28412.
36. Eliana Johns, "Upgrades to Russia's Nuclear-Capable Submarine Fleet," Federation of American Scientists, February 7, 2024.
37. Keith Crane, Olga Oliker, and Brian Nichiporuk, "Trends in Russia's Armed Forces: An Overview of Budgets and Capabilities," Rand Corporation, October 29, 2019, https://www.rand.org/pubs/research_reports/RR2573.html.
38. Patrick Tucker, "Russian Submarine Tech Could Help China Outpace U.S., Says INDOPACOM Chief," Defense One, November 23, 2024, https://www.defenseone.com/threats/2024/11/russian-submarine-tech-could-help-china-out-pace-us-says-indopacom-chief/401270/?oref=d1-author-river.
39. "Submarine Force Facts," US Navy, 2024, https://www.sublant.usff.navy.mil/About-Us/Submarine-Facts/#:~:text=Today's%20submarine%20force%20is%20the,and%20four%20guided%2Dmissile%20submarines.
40. "Catalog of Russian PMCs," Molfar, accessed November 21, 2024, https://molfar.com/en/blog/catalog-of-russian-pmcs.
41. Jonathan Beale, "Russia-Supporting Wagner Group Mercenary Numbers Soar," BBC News, December 22, 2022, https://www.bbc.com/news/world-europe-64050719.
42. Kenny Stansil, "Pentagon Projected to Hand $407 Billion to Private Military Contractors This Fiscal Year," Common Dreams, December 31, 2021, https://www.commondreams.org/news/2021/12/31/pentagon-projected-hand-407-billion-private-military-contractors-fiscal-year.
43. "Outer Space Treaty at a Glance," Arms Control Association, July 2024, https://www.armscontrol.org/factsheets/outer-space-treaty-glance.
44. Pavel Podvig and Hui Zhang, "Russian and Chinese Responses to U.S. Military Plans in Space," American Academy of Arts and Sciences, 2008, 13, https://fsi-live.s3.us-west-1.amazonaws.com/s3fs-public/militarySpace.pdf.
45. "UCS Satellite Database," Union of Concerned Scientists, updated January 1, 2024.
46. Pavel Luzin, "Russia Is Behind in Military Space Capabilities, but That Only Drives Its Appetite," *DefenseNews*, April 2, 2020, https://www.defensenews.com/opinion/commentary/2020/04/02/russia-is-behind-in-military-space-capabilities-but-that-only-drives-its-appetite/.
47. "A Russian Anti-Satellite Missile Test Puts the ISS in Peril," *Economist*, November 16, 2021, https://www.economist.com/science-and-technology/a-russian-anti-satellite-missile-test-puts-the-iss-in-peril/21806325.
48. Elena Grossfeld, "Russia's Declining Satellite Reconnaissance Capabilities and Its Implications for Security and International Stability," *International Journal of Intelligence and CounterIntelligence* 38, no. 1 (2024): 1–30, https://doi.org/10.1080/08850607.2024.2330848.
49. Steven Lambakis, "Foreign Space Capabilities: Implications for U.S. National Security," *Comparative Strategy* 37, no. 2 (2018): 113, https://doi.org/10.1080/01495933.2018.1459144.

50. Todd Harrison et al., *Space Threat Assessment 2020* (Washington, DC: Center for Strategic & International Studies, March 2020): 22, https://csis-website-prod.s3.amazonaws.com/s3fs-public/publication/200330_SpaceThreatAssessment20_WEB_FINAL1.pdf.
51. Stew Magnuson, "Budget 2021: Pentagon Rolls Out First Space Force Budget," *National Defense*, February 10, 2020, https://www.nationaldefensemagazine.org/articles/2020/2/10/pentagon-rolls-out-first-space-force-budget; "Counterspace Operations," Curtis E. Lemay Center, US Air Force, accessed January 27, 2021, https://www.doctrine.af.mil/Portals/61/documents/AFDP_3-14/3-14-D05-SPACE-Counterspace-Ops.pdf.
52. Tate Nurkin, "What Focus Areas Are Key to America's Future Space Capabilities," *DefenseNews*, April 28, 2021, https://www.defensenews.com/opinion/commentary/2021/04/28/what-focus-areas-are-key-to-americas-future-space-capabilities/.
53. "Fact Sheet: Vice President Harris Advances National Security Norms in Space," *The American Presidential Project*, April 18, 2022, https://www.presidency.ucsb.edu/documents/vice-presidential-pool-reports-april-18-2022.
54. Svetla Ben-Itzhak, "Companies Are Commercializing Outer Space. Do Government Programs Still Matter?," *Washington Post*, January 11, 2022, https://www.washingtonpost.com/politics/2022/01/11/companies-are-commercializing-outer-space-do-government-programs-still-matter/.
55. Raj Shah and Christopher Kirchoff, *Unit X: How the Pentagon and Silicon Valley Are Transforming the Future of War* (New York: Scribner, 2024).
56. SpaceTech Analytics, *SpaceTech Industry 2021 Landscape Overview* (London: Deep Knowledge Group, 2021), 69, https://www.spacetech.global/report.
57. Jonathan McDowell, "Jonathan's Space Report: Space Activities in 2023," Planet4589, January 15, 2024, https://planet4589.org/space/papers/space23.pdf.
58. Thomas G. Roberts, "Space Launch to Low Earth Orbit: How Much Does It Cost?," Center for Strategic and International Studies, September 1, 2022, https://aerospace.csis.org/data/space-launch-to-low-earth-orbit-how-much-does-it-cost/.
59. "Cyber Capabilities and National Power: A Net Assessment," International Institute for Strategic Studies, June 28, 2021, https://www.iiss.org/blogs/research-paper/2021/06/cyber-capabilities-national-power.
60. Ryan C. Maness et al., "Expanding the Dyadic Cyber Incident and Campaign Dataset (DCID): Cyber Conflict from 2000 to 2020," *Cyber Defense Review* 8, no. 2 (2023): 65–90, https://www.jstor.org/stable/48743091.
61. David Sanger, *The Perfect Weapon: War, Sabotage, and Fear in the Cyber Age* (New York: Random House, 2019).
62. "Understanding and Mitigating Russian State-Sponsored Cyber Threats to U.S. Critical Infrastructure," Cybersecurity and Infrastructure Security Agency, March 1, 2022, https://www.cisa.gov/uscert/ncas/alerts/aa22-011a.
63. Andrei Soldatov and Irina Borogan, "Russia's New Nobility—the Rise of the Security Services in Putin's Kremlin," *Foreign Affairs* 89, no. 1 (2010): 80.
64. David Kirkpatrick, "Black Budget Summary Details U.S. Spy Networks' Successes, Failures, and Objectives," *Washington Post*, August 29, 2013, https://www.washingtonpost.com/world/national-security/black-budget-summary-details-us-spy-networks-successes-failures-and-objectives/2013/08/29/7e57bb78-10ab-11e3-8cdd-bcdc09410972_story.html.
65. Mark Lowenthal, *Intelligence: From Secrets to Policy*, 6th ed. (Washington, DC: CQ Press, 2015), 472.
66. "Kremlin-Ordered Assassinations Abroad Will Probably Persist," National Intelligence Council Sense of the Community Memorandum, July 11, 2016, https://upload.wikimedia.org/wikipedia/commons/8/8c/Kremlin-Ordered_Assassinations_Abroad_Will_Probably_Persist.jpg.
67. "Defence Expenditure of NATO Countries (2014–2024)," NATO, June 2024, www.nato.int/nato_static_fl2014/assets/pdf/2024/6/pdf/240617-def-exp-2024-en.pdf.

68. "The Power of NATO's Military," Supreme Headquarters Allied Powers Europe, accessed November 25, 2024, https://shape.nato.int/page11283634/knowing-nato/episodes/the-power-of-natos-military.
69. Siranush Ghazanchyan, "Armenian PM on Possibility of Leaving CSTO," Public Radio of Armenia, March 12, 2024, https://en.armradio.am/2024/03/12/armenian-pm-on-possibility-of-withdrawing-from-csto/.
70. Thomas Ambrosio, "The Collective Security Treaty Organization: A Lifeless, Shambling 'Alliance,'" *Georgetown Journal of International Affairs* (March 4, 2024).
71. "China's Global Security Initiative: Tilting the Balance in Central Asia," US Institute of Peace, August 2024, https://iais.uz/en/outputnew/chinas-global-security-initiative-tilting-the-balance-in-central-asia.
72. "President Resolves to Sign Treaty on Comprehensive Strategic Partnership with North Korea," President of Russia, June 18, 2024, http://en.kremlin.ru/acts/news/74321.
73. Vladimir Milov, *Russian Economic and Sanctions Brief* (Washington, DC: Freed Russia Foundation, November 2024).
74. Anders Åslund, "Russia's Economic Transformation under Putin," *Eurasian Geography and Economics* 45, no. 6 (2004): 397–420, https://www.tandfonline.com/doi/epdf/10.2747/1538-7216.45.6.397?needAccess=true.
75. Polina Devitt, "Russia's Dependence on Exports to Asia Rises as Business with Europe Falls," Reuters, February 12, 2024, https://www.reuters.com/world/russias-dependence-exports-asia-rises-business-with-europe-falls-2024-02-12/#:~:text=Russia's%202023%20total%20exports%20fell,%25%20from%2049%25%20in%202022.
76. Devitt, "Russia's Dependence on Exports."
77. "U.S. International Trade in Goods and Services, December and Annual 2023," Bureau of Economic Analysis, US Department of Commerce, February 12, 2024.
78. Saeed Ghasseminejad, "Trade Between Russia and China Surges in 2024," Foundation for Defense of Democracies, June 15, 2023, https://www.fdd.org/analysis/2023/06/15/trade-between-russia-and-china-surges-in-2023/.
79. Amy Hawkins, "Russia and China Deepen Economic Ties Amid Surge in Trade Since Ukraine Invasion," *Guardian*, May 24, 2023, https://www.theguardian.com/world/2023/may/24/russia-and-china-deepen-economic-ties-amid-surge-in-trade-since-ukraine-invasion.
80. Alexandra Prokopenko, "Is the Kremlin Overconfident About Russia's Economic Stability?," Carnegie Endowment for International Peace, April 10, 2024.
81. "Indian Oil Faces Decline in Russian Oil Imports in 2024/25," Reuters, January 27, 2025, https://www.reuters.com/markets/commodities/indian-oil-faces-decline-russian-oil-imports-202425-2025-01-28/.
82. Temur Umarov and Alexander Gabuev, "Is Russia Losing Its Grip on Central Asia," *Foreign Affairs* (June 30, 2023), https://www.foreignaffairs.com/china/russia-losing-its-grip-central-asia.
83. "Vladimir Putin's Remarks at the Meeting with President Xi Jinping," President of Russia, March 21, 2023, http://kremlin.ru/events/president/news/70750.
84. Igor Logvinenko, *Global Finance, Local Control: Corruption and Wealth in Contemporary Russia* (Ithaca, NY: Cornell University Press, 2021).
85. "SberBank Outside Russia," SberBank, accessed on April 4, 2021, https://www.sberbank.com/about/group-overview; Annual Report 2019, VTB, June 29, 2020, 6, https://www.vtb.com/akcionery-i-investory/raskrytie-informacii/godovoj-i-socialnyj-otchet/.
86. "Sber Net Profit Down 78% to $3.56 Bln in 2022," Tass, March 9, 2023, https://tass.com/economy/1586585/.
87. "Bank of Russia Expands Restrictions for Hard-Currency Withdrawals Until March 2023," Radio Free Europe, August 1, 2022, https://www.rferl.org/a/bank-russia-expands-restrictions-hard-currency-withdrawals/31969013.html.

88. Dan Senor and Saul Singer, *Start-Up Nation: The Story of Israel's Economic Miracle* (New York: Twelve, 2009).
89. Michael McFaul, "The Missed Opportunity of Technological Breakthrough in Putin's Russia," Governance in an Emerging New World, Hoover Institution, Fall 2018.
90. Dmitriy Frolovskiy, "Russia's Innovation Façade," *Diplomat*, February 7, 2017, https://thediplomat.com/2017/02/russias-innovation-facade/; С.Ю., Фридлянова, наука технологии инновации (Институт статистических исследований и экономики знаний НИУ ВШЭ, October 2016), https://issek.hse.ru/data/2016/10/18/1107774820/NTI_N_24_18102016.pdf.
91. Sergey Aleksashenko, *Putin's Counterrevolution* (Lanham, MD: Rowman and Littlefield, 2018), 384.
92. "Research and Development Expenditure (% of GDP)—United States," World Bank, May 2024.
93. "Профиль в цифрах: как будет работать база данных о россиянах в 2023 году," *RBK*, September 20, 2018, https://www.rbc.ru/technology_and_media/20/09/2018/5ba262ef9a7947c2ab193522.
94. Loredana Fattorini et al., "What Countries Are Leading in AI: 2023 Global AI Vibrancy Ranking," Institute for Human-Centered Artificial Intelligence, Stanford University, November 2024, https://hai.stanford.edu/ai-index/global-vibrancy-tool.
95. "Much of Russia's Intellectual Elite Has Fled the Country," *Economist*, August 9, 2022, https://www.economist.com/international/2022/08/09/much-of-russias-intellectual-elite-has-fled-the-country.
96. Phillip Martin, "MIT Abandons Russian High-Tech Campus Partnership in Light of Ukraine Invasion," MIT SkolTech Program, February 25, 2022, https://www.wgbh.org/news/local-news/2022/02/25/mit-abandons-russian-high-tech-campus-partnership-in-light-of-ukraine-invasion.
97. Anders Åslund, *Russia's Crony Capitalism: The Path from Market Economy to Kleptocracy* (New Haven, CT: Yale University Press, 2019).
98. Chris Miller, *Putinomics: Power and Money in Resurgent Russia* (Chapel Hill: University of North Carolina Press, 2018).
99. Catherine Belton, *Putin's People: How the KGB Took Back Russia and Took on the West* (New York: Farrar, Straus and Giroux, 2022); Karen Dawisha, *Putin's Kleptocracy: Who Owns Russia?* (New York: Simon & Schuster, 2014).
100. "Total Population by Sex (Russia)," United Nations Data Portal, May 2024.
101. Marc Bennets, "Putin Appeals to Russians to Accept 'Painful' Pension Changes," *Guardian*, August 28, 2018, https://www.theguardian.com/world/2018/aug/29/vladimir-putin-russia-pension-reforms-retirement.
102. "Russia's Putin Seeks to Stimulate Birth Rate," BBC News, January 15, 2020, https://www.bbc.com/news/world-europe-51120165.
103. "Birth Rate, Crude (per 1,000 People)—Russian Federation, United States," World Bank, May 2024.
104. "Government Expenditure on Education, Total (% of GDP)—United States," World Bank, May 2024.
105. "World Development Indicators, 2025," Gini Index, World Bank Group, 2025, https://databank.worldbank.org/reports.aspx?source=2&series=SI.POV.GINI&country=.
106. Filip Novokmet, Thomas Piketty, and Gabriel Zucman, "From Soviets to Oligarchs: Inequality and Property in Russia, 1905–2016," National Bureau of Economic Research, August 2017, https://www.nber.org/papers/w23712.pdf.

5. Chinese vs. American Power

1. Scott Rozelle and Natalie Hell, *The Invisible China: How the Urban-Rural Divide Threatens China's Rise* (Chicago: University of Chicago Press, 2020).

2. Graham Allison, *Destined for War: Can America and China Escape the Thucydides's Trap?* (Boston: Houghton Mifflin Harcourt, 2017).
3. Hans M. Kristensen, Matt Korda, Eliana Johns, and Mackenzie Knight, "United States nuclear weapons, 2025," *Bulletin of the Atomic Scientists,* 81, no. 1: 53–79, https://doi.org/10.1080/00963402.2024.2441624; Hans M. Kristensen, Matt Korda, Eliana Johns, and Mackenzie Knight, "Chinese Nuclear Weapons, 2025," *Bulletin of the Atomic Scientists,* 81, no. 2, 135–60, https://doi.org/10.1080/00963402.2025.2467011.
4. US Department of Defense, *Military and Security Developments Involving the People's Republic of China 2023: Annual Report to Congress.* Washington, DC: Office of the Secretary of Defense, October 19, 2023, viii, https://media.defense.gov/2023/Oct/19/2003323409/-1/-1/1/2023-MILITARY-AND-SECURITY-DEVELOPMENTS-INVOLVING-THE-PEOPLES-REPUBLIC-OF-CHINA.PDF.
5. US Department of Defense, *Military and Security Developments Involving the PRC,* 66.
6. Zachary Basu, "Top General: China's Hypersonic Missile Test 'Very Close' to a 'Sputnik Moment,'" *Axios,* October 27, 2021, https://www.axios.com/2021/10/27/china-hypersonic-missile-mark-milley-sputnik.
7. Henrik Stålhane Hiim, M. Taylor Fravel, and Magnus Langset Trøan, "The Dynamics of an Entangled Security Dilemma: China's Changing Nuclear Posture," *International Security* 47, no. 4 (2023): 147–87.
8. Christopher Carlson and Howard Wang, *China Maritime Report No. 30: A Brief Technical History of PLAN Nuclear Submarines* (Newport, RI: China Maritime Studies Institute, US Naval War College, 2023).
9. Brad Roberts et al., *China's Emergence as a Second Nuclear Peer: Implications for U.S. Nuclear Deterrence Strategy* (Livermore, CA: Lawrence Livermore National Laboratory, 2023).
10. Mackenzie Eaglen, *Keeping Up with the Pacing Threat: Unveiling the True Size of Beijing's Military Spending* (Washington, DC: American Enterprise Institute, 2024).
11. Michael Boskin, John Rader, and Kiran Sridhar, eds., *Defense Budgeting for a Safer World: The Experts Speak* (Stanford: Hoover Institution Press, 2023).
12. US Department of Defense, *Military and Security Developments Involving the PRC,* 47.
13. Michael Beckley, *Unrivaled: Why America Will Remain the World's Sole Superpower* (Ithaca, NY: Cornell University Press, 2018), 67.
14. Xi Jinping, "Writing a Brand-New Chapter of Strengthening the Army in the New Era," Xinhua News Agency, March 13, 2018, https://www.gov.cn/xinwen/2018-03/13/content_5273525.htm.
15. US Department of Defense, *Military and Security Developments Involving the PRC,* 62.
16. US Department of Defense, *Military and Security Developments Involving the PRC,* 53.
17. Ronald O'Rourke, "China Naval Modernization: Implications for U.S. Navy Capabilities—Background and Issues for Congress (RL33153)," Congressional Research Service, January 30, 2024.
18. O'Rourke, "China Naval Modernization: Implications for U.S. Naval Capabilities," 10.
19. "Chapter Five: Asia," *The Military Balance* 125, no. 1 (2025): 206–311, https://doi.org/10.1080/04597222.2025.2445477.
20. Brendan Rittenhouse Green and Caitlin Talmadge, "Then What? Assessing the Military Implications of Chinese Control of Taiwan," *International Security* 47, no. 1 (2022): 7–45.
21. US Department of Defense, *Military and Security Developments Involving the PRC,* 52.
22. Michael R. Gordon, "China's Newest Nuclear Submarine Sank, Setting Back Its Military Modernization," *Wall Street Journal,* September 26, 2024.
23. Geoffrey Blainey, *The Causes of War,* 3rd ed. (New York: Free Press, 1988).
24. Daniel Deudney, *Dark Skies: Space Expansionism, Planetary Geopolitics, and the Ends of Humanity* (Oxford: Oxford University Press, 2020), 166.

25. Katrina Miller, "China Becomes First Country to Retrieve Rocks from the Moon's Far Side," *New York Times*, June 25, 2024, https://www.nytimes.com/2024/06/25/science/change-6-china-earth-moon.html.
26. "Full Text: China's Space Program: A 2021 Perspective," Xinhua, January 28, 2022, https://english.www.gov.cn/archive/whitepaper/202201/28/content_WS61f35b3dc6d09c94e48a467a.html.
27. Mickey Carroll, "NASA Chief Says 'Secretive' China Is Hiding Military Projects in Space," Sky News, April 18, 2024, https://news.sky.com/story/nasa-chief-says-secretive-china-is-hiding-military-projects-in-space-13117766.
28. "UCS Satellite Database," Union of Concerned Scientists, updated January 1, 2024.
29. Jonathan McDowell, "Jonathan's Space Report: Space Activities in 2023," January 15, 2024, https://planet4589.org/space/papers/space23.pdf.
30. McDowell, "Jonathan's Space Report," 11.
31. Jack Kuhr, "A Look into China's Defense Payloads: Payload Research," Payload, May 29, 2024, https://payloadspace.com/a-look-into-chinas-defense-payloads-payload-research/.
32. Julia Voo, Irfan Hemani, and Daniel Cassidy, *National Cyber Power Index 2022* (Boston: Belfer Center for Science and International Affairs, September 2022), https://www.belfercenter.org/sites/default/files/files/publication/CyberProject_National%20Cyber%20Power%20Index%202022_v3_220922.pdf.
33. "Cyber Capabilities and National Power: A Net Assessment," International Institute for Strategic Studies, June 2021, https://www.iiss.org/blogs/research-paper/2021/06/cyber-capabilities-national-power.
34. David Sanger et al., "Hack by China: Long Unknown, Tough to Expel," *New York Times*, November 24, 2024.
35. "Intelligence Capabilities," *Asia Power Index*, accessed June 13, 2024, https://power.lowyinstitute.org/data/military-capability/signature-capabilities/intelligence-capabilities/.
36. Ellen Nakashima, "Confidential Report Lists U.S. Weapons System Designs Compromised by the Chinese Cyberspies," *Washington Post*, May 27, 2013, https://www.washingtonpost.com/world/national-security/confidential-report-lists-us-weapons-system-designs-compromised-by-chinese-cyberspies/2013/05/27/a42c3e1c-c2dd-11e2-8c3b-0b5e9247e8ca_story.html.
37. Benjamin Jensen, "How the Chinese Communist Party Uses Cyber Espionage to Undermine the American Economy," CSIS, October 19, 2023, https://www.csis.org/analysis/how-chinese-communist-party-uses-cyber-espionage-undermine-american-economy.
38. "Survey of Chinese Espionage in the United States Since 2000," Center for Strategic and International Studies, March 2023, https://www.csis.org/programs/strategic-technologies-program/survey-chinese-espionage-united-states-2000.
39. Jensen, "How the Chinese Communist Party Uses Cyber Espionage."
40. Grant Newsham, "Japan as the 'Swing Vote,'" in Matt Pottinger, ed., *The Boiling Moat: Urgent Steps to Defend Taiwan* (Stanford: Hoover Institution Press, 2024), 187–200.
41. Ross Babbage, "Australia's Job Now," in Pottinger, *The Boiling Moat*, 213–36.
42. "Major Non-NATO Ally Status," Bureau of Political-Military Affairs, US Department of State, January 20, 2021, https://www.state.gov/major-non-nato-ally-status/.
43. Oriana Skylar Mastro, *Upstart: How China Became a Great Power* (Oxford: Oxford University Press, 2024).
44. Zongyuan Zoe Lui, "Tracking China's Control of Overseas Ports," Council on Foreign Relations, last modified August 26, 2024, https://www.cfr.org/tracker/china-overseas-ports.
45. David Autor and David Dorn, "The Growth of Low-Skill Service Jobs and the Polarization of the US Labor Market," *American Economic Review* 103, no. 5 (August 2013), 1553–97; Nicholas Bloom et al., "The China Shock Revisited: Job Reallocation and Industry Switching in U.S. Labor Markets," Working Paper 33098 (National Bureau of Economic Research, November 2024).
46. Jeremy Wallace, *Seeking Truth and Hiding Facts: Information, Ideology, and Authoritarianism in China* (Oxford: Oxford University Press, 2023).

47. "GDP, Current Prices—China, United States," IMF, https://www.imf.org/external/datamapper/NGDPD@WEO/CHN/USA.
48. "GDP, Current Prices (Purchasing Power Parity)—China, United States," IMF, https://www.imf.org/external/datamapper/PPPGDP@WEO/CHN/USA.
49. "Real GDP Growth: Annual Percentage Change—China," IMF, https://www.imf.org/external/datamapper/NGDP_RPCH@WEO/CHN?zoom=CHN&highlight=CHN.
50. David Leonhardt, "The U.S. Economy Is Racing Ahead as the Well-Being of the Nation Lags," *New York Times*, February 8, 2025.
51. "Real GDP Growth: Annual Percentage Change—EU," IMF, https://www.imf.org/external/datamapper/NGDP_RPCH@WEO/EU/EURO/EUQ.
52. "GDP per Capita, Current Prices: US Dollars per Capita—US," IMF, https://www.imf.org/external/datamapper/NGDPDPC@WEO/CHN.
53. "GDP per Capita, Current Prices: US Dollars per Capita," IMF, https://www.imf.org/external/datamapper/NGDPDPC@WEO/OEMDC/ADVEC/WEOWORLD.
54. "Trade in Goods with China," US Census Bureau, https://www.census.gov/foreign-trade/balance/c5700.html.
55. "Trade in Goods with China," US Census Bureau.
56. United States Trade Representative, "The People's Republic of China," https://web.archive.org/web/20220201202329/https://ustr.gov/countries-regions/china-mongolia-taiwan/peoples-republic-china.
57. Iori Kawate and Shusuke Tabeta, "Foreign Direct Investment in China Falls to 30-Year Low," *Nikkei Asia*, February 19, 2024, https://asia.nikkei.com/Economy/Foreign-direct-investment-in-China-falls-to-30-year-low.
58. Milton Ezrati, "American Investors Say No to China," *Forbes*, January 1, 2024, https://www.forbes.com/sites/miltonezrati/2024/01/01/american-investors-say-no-to-china/.
59. "U.S. International Trade in Goods and Services, Annual Revision," US Census Bureau, June 7, 2023, https://www.census.gov/foreign-trade/Press-Release/ft900/final_2022.pdf; Luis Torres, "Mexico Seeks to Solidify Rank as Top U.S. Trade Partner, Push Further Past China," Federal Reserve Bank of Dallas, July 11, 2023, https://www.dallasfed.org/research/economics/2023/0711.
60. C. Fred Bergsten, *The United States vs. China: The Quest for Global Economic Leadership* (Cambridge: Polity Press, 2022), 98.
61. Roland Rajah and Ahmed Albayrak, "China Versus America on Global Trade," Lowy Institute, January 2025, https://interactives.lowyinstitute.org/features/china-versus-america-on-global-trade/#section-analysis.
62. Jared Cohen, "Don't Bet Against the Dollar," *Foreign Policy*, June 10, 2024.
63. "Yuan Overtakes Dollar to Become Most-Used Currency in China's Cross-Border Transactions," Reuters, April 26, 2023, https://www.reuters.com/markets/currencies/yuan-overtakes-dollar-become-most-used-currency-chinas-cross-border-transactions-2023-04-26/; Darrell Duffie and Elizabeth Economy, eds., *Digital Currencies: The US, China, and the World at a Crossroads* (Stanford: Hoover Institution Press, 2022).
64. "Currency Composition of Official Exchange Reserves (COFER)," IMF, March 29, 2024, https://data.imf.org/?sk=e6a5f467-c14b-4aa8-9f6d-5a09ec4e62a4.
65. Matthew Klein and Michael Pettis, *Trade Wars Are Class Wars: How Rising Inequality Distorts the Global Economy and Threatens International Peace* (New Haven, CT: Yale University Press, 2020).
66. "Major Foreign Holdings of Treasury Securities (in Billions of Dollars)," Department of the Treasury/Federal Reserve Board, March 15, 2023, https://ticdata.treasury.gov/Publish/mfh.txt.
67. Jiaxing Li, Summer Zhen, and Li Gu, "China's Bond Market Sees More Economic Pain Ahead," Reuters, December 12, 2024, https://www.reuters.com/markets/rates-bonds/chinas-bond-market-sees-more-economic-pain-ahead-2024-12-13/.

68. Martin Chorzempa, *The Cashless Revolution: China's Reinvention of Money and the End of America's Domination of Finance and Technology* (New York: Public Affairs, 2022).
69. Chris Miller, *Chip War: The Fight for the World's Most Critical Technology* (New York: Scribner, 2022).
70. Jamie Gaida et al., *ASPI's Critical Technology Tracker: A Global Race for Future Power* (Canberra: ASPI, February 2023), https://ad-aspi.s3.ap-southeast-2.amazonaws.com/2023-08/ASPIs%20Critical%20Technology%20Tracker.pdf?VersionId=nVmWySgLSX2FMaS1U.uQVgQvvd_W427G.
71. "World University Rankings 2025," *Times Higher Education*, accessed February 10, 2025, https://www.timeshighereducation.com/world-university-rankings/latest/world-ranking?page=2#!/length/25/sort_by/rank/sort_order/asc/cols/scores.
72. Gary Anderson, "U.S. R&D Increased by $72 Billion in 2021 to $789 Billion; Estimate for 2022 Indicates Further Increase to $886 Billion," National Center for Science and Engineering Statistics, National Science Foundation, January 22, 2024, https://ncses.nsf.gov/pubs/nsf24317.
73. "U.S. R&D Totaled $892 Billion in 2022; Estimate for 2023 Indicates Further Increase to $940 Billion," National Science Foundation, accessed April 10, 2025, https://ncses.nsf.gov/pubs/nsf25327.
74. Xinhua, "China's R&D Expenditure Exceeds 3.3 Trillion Yuan in 2023: Minister," the State Council, the People's Republic of China, March 5, 2024, https://english.www.gov.cn/news/202403/05/content_WS65e6ff4dc6d0868f4e8e4b66.html#:~:text=China's%20R%26D%20expenditure%20exceeds%203.3%20trln%20yuan%20in%202023%3A%20minister&text=BEIJING%2C%20March%205%20%2D%2D%20China's,Technology%20Yin%20Hejun%20said%20Tuesday.
75. United States, "Science and Engineering Indicators 2024: The State of U.S. Science and Engineering": NSB-2024-3, National Science Foundation, 2024, https://ncses.nsf.gov/pubs/nsb20243; China: National Bureau of Statistics of China, "Statistical Communiqué of the People's Republic of China on the 2021 National Economic and Social Development," *National Bureau of Statistics of China*, January 27, 2022, https://www.stats.gov.cn/english/PressRelease/202201/t20220127_1827065.html.
76. Cole McFaul, "Washington's Science Cuts Are a Gift to Beijing," *The Hill*, March 7, 2025, https://thehill.com/opinion/technology/5180183-china-us-innovation-race/.
77. "2024 Research Leaders: Leading Countries/Territories," Nature Index, 2024, https://www.nature.com/nature-index/research-leaders/2024/country/all/all.
78. "Research Leaders 2016: Institutions," Nature Index, 2016, https://www.nature.com/nature-index/research-leaders/2016/institution/all/all/global.
79. "Institution Outputs," Nature Index, accessed November 23, 2024, https://www.nature.com/nature-index/institution-outputs/generate/natural-sciences/global/all.
80. Cole McFaul et al., *Fueling China's Innovation: The Chinese Academy of Sciences and Its Role in the PRC's S&T Ecosystem* (Washington, DC: Center for Security and Emerging Technology, October 2024), 14.
81. Cole McFaul et al., *Fueling China's Innovation*, 20.
82. Beckley, *Unrivaled*, 48.
83. William C. Hannas and Huey-Meei Chang, eds., *Chinese Power and Artificial Intelligence* (New York: Routledge, 2023).
84. "AI Index Report 2023," Institute for Human-Centered Artificial Intelligence, Stanford University, 2023, https://aiindex.stanford.edu/wp-content/uploads/2023/04/HAI_AI-Index-Report_2023.pdf.
85. Nestor Maslej et al., "AI Index Report 2024," Institute for Human-Centered Artificial Intelligence, Stanford University, April 2024, https://aiindex.stanford.edu/wp-content/uploads/2024/05/HAI_AI-Index-Report-2024.pdf, 5.

86. Nestor Maslej et al., "AI Index Report 2024."
87. Ashwin Acharya and Brian Dunn, "Comparing U.S. and Chinese Contributions to High-Impact AI Research," Center for Security and Emerging Technology, Georgetown University, January 2022, https://cset.georgetown.edu/publication/comparing-u-s-and-chinese-contributions-to-high-impact-ai-research.
88. Karen M. Sutter and Zachary Arnold, "China's AI Companies: Hybrid Players," in Hannas and Chang, *Chinese Power,* 19–35.
89. Cole McFaul et al., *Fueling China's Innovation*, 23–24.
90. "Fact Sheet: President Biden Issues Executive Order to Protect Americans' Sensitive Personal Data," Office of the Press Secretary, White House, February 28, 2024, https://bidenwhitehouse.archives.gov/briefing-room/statements-releases/2024/02/28/fact-sheet-president-biden-issues-sweeping-executive-order-to-protect-americans-sensitive-personal-data/.
91. Keely Le, "Chinese Firms Lag Behind US Peers in AI Development 'by Two Years,' Alibaba Chairman Joe Tsai Says," *South China Morning Post,* April 5, 2024, https://www.scmp.com/tech/big-tech/article/3258002/chinese-firms-lag-behind-us-peers-ai-development-two-years-alibaba-chairman-joe-tsai-says?module=top_story&pgtype=section.
92. Eduardo Baptista, "China's Military and Government Acquire Nvidia Chips Despite US Ban," Reuters, January 15, 2024, https://www.reuters.com/technology/chinas-military-government-acquire-nvidia-chips-despite-us-ban-2024-01-14/.
93. Samantha Subin, "Nvidia Sheds Almost $600 Billion in Market Cap, Biggest One-Day Loss in U.S. History," CNBC, January 27, 2025, https://www.cnbc.com/2025/01/27/nvidia-sheds-almost-600-billion-in-market-cap-biggest-drop-ever.html#:~:text=Nvidia%20shares%20plunged%2017%25%20on,from%20Chinese%20AI%20lab%20DeepSeek.
94. Eduardo Baptista, "Alibaba Releases AI Model It Says Surpasses DeepSeek," Reuters, January 29, 2025, https://www.reuters.com/technology/artificial-intelligence/alibaba-releases-ai-model-it-claims-surpasses-deepseek-v3-2025-01-29/.
95. James Andrew Lewis and Georgia Wood, "Quantum Technology: Applications and Implications," Center for Strategic and International Studies, May 25, 2023, https://www.csis.org/analysis/quantum-technology-applications-and-implications.
96. "Quantum Technology Monitor," McKinsey, April 24, 2024, www.mckinsey.com/capabilities/mckinsey-digital/our-insights/steady-progress-in-approaching-the-quantum-advantage.
97. "Quantum Technology Monitor."
98. "IBM Unveils 400 Qubit-Plus Quantum Processor and Next-Generation IBM Quantum System Two," IBM, November 9, 2022, https://newsroom.ibm.com/2022-11-09-IBM-Unveils-400-Qubit-Plus-Quantum-Processor-and-Next-Generation-IBM-Quantum-System-Two.
99. Myungshin Cho, "China's Debt-to-GDP Ratio Rises to Fresh Record of 286.1%," Bloomberg, January 16, 2024, https://www.bloomberg.com/news/articles/2024-01-17/china-s-debt-to-gdp-ratio-rises-to-fresh-record-of-286-1.
100. James Mayger and Fran Wang, "Chinese Are Becoming More Pessimistic About Incomes and Housing," Bloomberg, June 29, 2023, https://www.bloomberg.com/news/articles/2023-06-29/chinese-are-becoming-more-pessimistic-about-incomes-and-housing.
101. Chan Ho-him and Thomas Hale, "Chinese Property Stocks Fall After Evergrande Reveals Restructuring Plan," *Financial Times,* March 23, 2023, https://www.ft.com/content/9e8b0e71-dc12-4c07-b1f0-a203f32d9166.
102. Guanghua Wan, Chen Wang, and Yu Wu, "What Drove Housing Wealth Inequality in China?," *China and World Economy* 29, no. 1 (2021): 32–60, https://doi.org/10.1111/cwe.12361.
103. Briana Sullivan, Donald Hays, and Neil Bennett, *The Wealth of Households: 2021* (Maryland: US Census Bureau, 2023), 3.

104. Hongbin Li et al., "Human Capital and China's Future Growth," *Journal of Economic Perspectives* 31, no. 1 (Winter 2017): 25–48.
105. Yanzhe Zhang Bowen Zou, Huai Zhang, and Jian Zhang, "Empirical Research on Male Preference in China: A Result of Gender Imbalance in the Seventh Population Census," *International Journal of Environmental Research and Public Health* 19, no. 11 (2022): 6482, https://doi.org/10.3390/ijerph19116482.
106. "World Population Prospects," Department of Economic and Social Affairs, Population Division, United Nations, accessed April 7, 2025.
107. "U.S. Immigrant Population and Share Over Time, 1850–Present," Migration Policy Institute Data Hub, accessed August 2, 2023, https://www.migrationpolicy.org/programs/data-hub/charts/immigrant-population-over-time.
108. Yu Bai et al., "Past Successes and Future Challenges in Rural China's Human Capital," *Journal of Contemporary China* 28, no. 120 (2019): 883–98.
109. Andreas Schleicher, *PISA 2018: Insights and Interpretations* (Paris: Organisation for Economic Co-Operation and Development, 2019), 6–9.
110. Arthur Herman, "America's High-Tech STEM Crisis," *Forbes*, September 10, 2018, https://www.forbes.com/sites/arthurherman/2018/09/10/americas-high-tech-stem-crisis/#41741882f0a2.
111. "International Students," Open Doors, 2022, https://opendoorsdata.org/wp-content/uploads/2022/11/Open-Doors-2022_Fast-Facts.pdf.
112. Li et al., "Human Capital and China's Future Growth," 30.
113. Rozelle and Hell, *Invisible China*.
114. Briana Boland et al., "How China's Human Capital Impacts Its National Competitiveness," Center for Strategic and International Studies, June 17, 2024, https://www.csis.org/analysis/how-chinas-human-capital-impacts-its-national-competitiveness.
115. Rozelle and Hell, *Invisible China*.
116. "Adults' Educational Attainment Distribution, by Age Group and Gender," OECD, 2024, https://data-explorer.oecd.org/?lc=en&fs[0]=Topic%2C1%7CEducation%20and%20skills%23EDU%23%7CEducation%20attainment%23EDU_ATT%23&pg=0&fc=Topic&bp=true&snb=6.
117. Abhijit V. Banerjee and Esther Duflo, "Inequality and Growth: What Can the Data Say?," *Journal of Economic Growth* 8 (2003): 267–99, https://doi.org/10.1023/A:1026205114860.
118. World Bank, Gini Index, World Development Indicators, last modified September 19, 2024. https://fred.stlouisfed.org/data/SIPOVGINICHN.
119. "GDP, Current Prices," IMF, accessed May 22, 2024, https://www.imf.org/external/datamapper/NGDPD@WEO/OEMDC/ADVEC/WEOWORLD.
120. Kurt Campbell and Rush Doshi, "Underestimating China: Why America Needs a New Strategy of Allied Scale to Offset Beijing's Enduring Advantages," *Foreign Affairs*, April 10, 2025, https://www.foreignaffairs.com/china/underestimating-china.
121. Matthew Reynolds and Matthew Goodman, *Deny, Deflect, Deter: Countering China's Economic Coercion* (Washington, DC: CSIS, March 2023).

6. The Waning of Democracy as a Universal Value

1. Michael McFaul, "The Fourth Wave of Democracy and Dictatorship: Noncooperative Transitions in the Post-Communist World," *World Politics* 54, no. 2 (January 2002): 212–44.
2. Chris Buckley, "In China, a Little-Known Advisor 'Has the Top Leader's Trust,'" *New York Times*, October 27, 2024.
3. Francis Fukuyama, "The End of History?," *National Interest*, no. 16 (Summer 1989): 3.
4. Michael McFaul, "Democracy Promotion as a World Value," *Washington Quarterly* 28, no. 1 (Winter 2004–5): 147–63.

5. Seva Gunitsky, *Aftershocks: Great Power and Domestic Reforms in the Twentieth Century* (Princeton, NJ: Princeton University Press, 2017).
6. Steven Levitsky and Lucan Way, "The Path to American Authoritarianism," *Foreign Affairs* (March/April 2025), https://www.foreignaffairs.com/united-states/path-american-authoritarianism-trump.
7. Mark L. Haas, *The Ideological Origins of Great Power Politics, 1789–1989* (Ithaca, NY: Cornell University Press, 2007), 5.
8. Judith Goldstein and Robert Keohane, eds., *Ideas and Foreign Policy: Beliefs, Institutions, and Political Change* (Ithaca, NY: Cornell University Press, 1993).
9. John Mearsheimer, *The Great Delusion: Liberal Dreams and International Realities* (New Haven, CT: Yale University Press, 2018).
10. Henry Kissinger, *A World Restored: Metternich, Castlereagh and the Problems of Peace, 1812–1822* (Boston: Houghton Mifflin, 1957).
11. "First Inaugural Address of William J. Clinton," January 20, 1993, https://avalon.law.yale.edu/20th_century/clinton1.asp.
12. George W. Bush, "President Bush Discusses Freedom Agenda," Ronald Reagan Building and International Trade Center, Washington, DC, July 24, 2008, https://georgewbush-whitehouse.archives.gov/news/releases/2008/07/20080724-6.html.
13. Michael McFaul, *From Cold War to Hot Peace* (Boston: Houghton Mifflin Harcourt, 2018), chapter 7.
14. Philip H. Gordon, *Losing the Long Game: The False Promise of Regime Change in the Middle East* (New York: St. Martin's Press, 2020).
15. Tom Porter, "How Do I Love Thee? A Short History of Trump's Praise for Putin," *Newsweek*, November 12, 2017, https://www.newsweek.com/heres-all-times-trump-has-praised-putin-708859; Fiona Hill, *There Is Nothing for You Here: Finding Opportunity in the Twenty-First Century* (New York: Mariner, 2021); H. R. McMaster, *At War with Ourselves: My Tour of Duty in the Trump White House* (New York: HarperCollins, 2022).
16. Michael Crowley, "Trump Says He Avoided Punishing China Over Uighur Camps to Protect Trade Talks," *New York Times*, July 9, 2020, https://www.nytimes.com/2020/06/21/us/politics/trump-uighurs-china-trade.html.
17. Calamur Krishnadev, "Nine Notorious Dictators, Nine Shout-Outs from Donald Trump," *Atlantic*, March 4, 2018, https://www.theatlantic.com/international/archive/2018/03/trump-xi-jinping-dictators/554810/.
18. *Report of the Commission on Unalienable Rights*, Office of Policy Planning, US Department of State, https://2017-2021.state.gov/wp-content/uploads/2020/08/Report-of-the-Commission-on-Unalienable-Rights.pdf.
19. "Remarks by President Trump to the 73rd Session of the United Nations General Assembly," White House, September 25, 2018, https://trumpwhitehouse.archives.gov/briefings-statements/remarks-president-trump-73rd-session-united-nations-general-assembly-new-york-ny/.
20. David E. Sanger, *The Perfect Weapon: War, Sabotage, and Fear in the Cyber Age* (New York: Random House, 2019), 161.
21. "National Endowment for Democracy (NED), NDI, IRI, CIPE and Solidarity Center Welcome Increased Funding from Congress," National Endowment for Democracy, December 21, 2019, https://www.ned.org/national-endowment-for-democracy-ned-ndi-iri-cipe-and-solidarity-center-welcome-increased-funding-from-congress/.
22. "NED's Grantmaking in 2020 Is the Highest in 36-Year History," National Endowment for Democracy, October 19, 2020, https://www.ned.org/ned-democracy-support-continues-october-2020.
23. "Remarks by President Biden," 2021 Virtual Munich Security Conference, February 19, 2021,

https://bidenwhitehouse.archives.gov/briefing-room/speeches-remarks/2021/02/19/remarks-by-president-biden-at-the-2021-virtual-munich-security-conference/.

24. "Remarks by President Biden," address to a Joint Session of Congress, April 28, 2021, https://bidenwhitehouse.archives.gov/briefing-room/speeches-remarks/2021/04/29/remarks-by-president-biden-in-address-to-a-joint-session-of-congress/.
25. Shibley Telhami and Michael Hanmer, "American Public Attitudes on the U.S. Role in Global Human Rights and Democracy, Critical Issues Poll with Ipsos," University of Maryland, February 2024, https://criticalissues.umd.edu/sites/criticalissues.umd.edu/files/UMCIP_February2024_HR-Democracy_Results.pdf.
26. Jacob Poushter and Laura Clancy, "What Are Americans' Top Foreign Policy Priorities?," Pew Research Center, April 23, 2024, https://www.pewresearch.org/global/2024/04/23/what-are-americans-top-foreign-policy-priorities/.
27. Sarah Repucci, "From Crisis to Reform: A Call to Strengthen America's Battered Democracy," Freedom House, March 2021, https://freedomhouse.org/report/special-report/2021/crisis-reform-call-strengthen-americas-battered-democracy.
28. Larry Diamond, *Ill Winds: Saving Democracy from Russian Rage, Chinese Ambition, and American Complacency* (New York: Penguin, 2019), chapter 5.
29. "The United States," Freedom House, 2020, https://freedomhouse.org/country/united-states/freedom-world/2020; James Traub, "The Free World's Leader Isn't Free Anymore," *Foreign Policy* (June 18, 2020), https://foreignpolicy.com/2020/06/18/free-world-america-trump-us-democracy/.
30. Miriam Berger, "U.S. Listed as a 'Backsliding' Democracy for First Time in Report by European Think Tank," *Washington Post*, November 22, 2021, https://www.washingtonpost.com/world/2021/11/22/united-states-backsliding-democracies-list-first-time/.
31. Daniel Ziblatt and Steven Levitsky, *How Democracies Die* (New York: Crown, 2018).
32. "Remarks by President Biden," address to a Joint Session of Congress.
33. Lisa Lerer and Astead W. Herndon, "Menace Enters the Republican Mainstream," *New York Times*, November 12, 2021, https://www.nytimes.com/2021/11/12/us/politics/republican-violent-rhetoric.html.
34. Devan Cole, "34% of Americans Say Violence Against Government Is Sometimes Justified, New Poll Finds," CNN, January 2, 2022, https://www.cnn.com/2022/01/02/politics/january-6-poll-violence-against-government/index.html.
35. Larry Diamond, "Defending Democracy in America: It's Time to Take Action," *Persuasion*, March 24, 2025, https://www.persuasion.community/p/defending-democracy-in-america.
36. Kimiko Hiroto, "Trump Is Repeating One of the Darkest Chapters in US History," *The Hill*, April 11, 2025, https://thehill.com/opinion/white-house/5242442-trump-aliens-enemies-act/.
37. "Budget and Financial Reports, Congressional Budget Justification (CBJ)," U.S. Agency for Global Media, https://www.usagm.gov/our-work/strategy-and-results/strategic-priorities/budget-and-financial-reports/.
38. Anthony J. Blinken, Secretary of State, "The President's Fiscal Year 2025 Budget Request for the Department of State and the U.S. Agency for International Development," March 11, 2024, https://2021-2025.state.gov/the-presidents-fiscal-year-2025-budget-request-for-the-department-of-state-and-the-u-s-agency-for-international-development/.
39. Antony Blinken, "EducationUSA Virtual Forum: Welcoming Remarks," July 21, 2021, https://2021-2025.state.gov/educationusa-virtual-forum-welcoming-remarks/.
40. Michael McFaul, *Advancing Democracy Abroad* (Lanham, MD: Rowman and Littlefield, 2010).
41. "Freedom in the World 2025: The Uphill Battle to Safeguard Rights," Freedom House, 2025, https://freedomhouse.org/sites/default/files/2025-02/FITW_World_2025_Feb.2025.pdf.
42. Sarah Repucci and Amy Slipowitz, "Freedom in the World 2021: Democracy Under Siege,"

Freedom House, 2021, https://freedomhouse.org/report/freedom-world/2021/democracy-under-siege.

43. Larry Diamond, "Democracy's Arc: From Resurgent to Imperiled," *Journal of Democracy* 33, no. 1 (January 2022): 169.
44. Steven Levitsky and Lucan Way, "Democracy's Surprising Resilience," *Journal of Democracy* 34, no. 4 (October 2023): 5.
45. Larry Diamond, "Democratic Regression in Comparative Perspective: Scope, Methods, and Causes," *Democratization* 28, no. 1 (2020): 22–42.
46. Richard Wike et al., "Representative Democracy Remains a Popular Ideal, but People Around the World Are Critical of How It's Working," Pew Research Center, 2024, https://www.pewresearch.org/global/wp-content/uploads/sites/2/2024/02/gap_2024.02.28_democracy-closed-end_report.pdf.
47. Lara Silver and Kat Devlin, "Around the World, More See the U.S. Positively Than China, but Little Confidence in Trump or Xi," Pew Research Center, January 10, 2020, https://www.pewresearch.org/fact-tank/2020/01/10/around-the-world-more-see-the-u-s-positively-than-china-but-little-confidence-in-trump-or-xi/.

7. Exporting Putinism

1. "Meeting with Public Representatives of Crimea and Sevastopol," President of Russia, March 18, 2021, http://en.kremlin.ru/events/president/news/65172.
2. "О Стратегии Национальной Безопасности Российской Федерации," Указ Президента Российской Федерации (Moscow, Kremlin, July 2, 2021), http://scrf.gov.ru/media/files/file/l4wGRPqJvETSkUTYmhepzRochb1j1jqh.pdf.
3. Maria Snegovaya, Michael Kimmage, and Jade McGlynn, "The Ideology of Putinism: Is It Sustainable?," Center for Strategic and International Studies, September 27, 2023, 14, https://www.csis.org/analysis/ideology-putinism-it-sustainable.
4. "Putin Streamlines Immigration Process for Foreigners Opposed to Western 'Neoliberal Ideology,'" *Novaya Gazeta Europe*, August 19, 2024, https://novayagazeta.eu/articles/2024/08/19/putin-streamlines-immigration-process-for-foreigners-opposed-to-western-neoliberal-ideology-en-news.
5. "Meeting of the Valdai International Discussion Club," President of Russia, September 19, 2013, http://www.en.kremlin.ru/events/president/news/19243.
6. Lionel Barber, Henry Foy, and Alex Barber, "Vladimir Putin Says Liberalism Has 'Become Obsolete,'" *Financial Times*, June 27, 2019.
7. Brian Taylor, *The Code of Putinism* (Oxford: Oxford University Press, 2018), 7.
8. Fiona Hill, "The Kremlin's Strange Victory: How Putin Exploits American Dysfunction and Fuels American Decline," *Foreign Affairs* (September 27, 2021), https://www.foreignaffairs.com/russia/fiona-hill-putin-kremlin-strange-victory.
9. Mikhail Ulyanov (@Amb_Ulyanov), "The distinction is evident for me," Twitter, February 4, 2023, https://twitter.com/Amb_Ulyanov/status/1622012391104856065.
10. Qin Gang and Anatoly Antonov, "Russian and Chinese Ambassadors: Respecting People's Democratic Rights," *The National Interest*, November 27, 2021, https://nationalinterest.org/feature/russian-and-chinese-ambassadors-respecting-peoples-democratic-rights-197165.
11. "Путин Назвал 'Национал-Предателями' Граждан, Ориентирующихся На Запад," Радио Свобода, March 16, 2022, https://www.svoboda.org/a/vladimir-putin-zapadu-ne-nuzhna-siljnaya-rossiya/31756201.html.
12. "Presidential Address to Federal Assembly," President of Russia, February 21, 2023, http://en.kremlin.ru/events/president/news/70565.
13. Michael McFaul, *From Cold War to Hot Peace* (Boston: Houghton Mifflin Harcourt, 2018), chapter 15.

14. "Presidential Address to Federal Assembly."
15. "Presidential Address to Federal Assembly."
16. Maria Snegovaya and Jade McGlynn, "Dissecting Putin's Regime Ideology," *Post-Soviet Affairs* 41, no. 1 (2024): 42–63, 2024, 15, https://doi.org/10.1080/1060586X.2024.2386838.
17. Ilya Klishen, "Putin and the 'Distinct Russian Civilization,'" *Moscow Times*, May 25, 2020, https://www.themoscowtimes.com/2020/05/25/putin-and-the-distinct-russian-civilization-a70370.
18. Петр Щедровицкий, "Русский Мир и Транснациональное Русское," Русский Журнал, March 2, 2000, http://old.russ.ru/politics/meta/20000302_schedr.html#3.
19. Snegovaya, Kimmage, and McGlynn, "The Ideology of Putinism."
20. Angela Stent, *Putin's World* (New York: Twelve, 2019), 36–37.
21. Peter Pomerantsev, *Nothing Is True and Everything Is Possible: The Surreal Heart of the New Russia* (New York: Public Affairs, 2015).
22. Anne Applebaum, *Autocracy, Inc.: The Dictators Who Want to Rule the World* (New York: Doubleday, 2024), 74.
23. Felix Light, "Protests in Georgia After Government Halts EU Application Until 2028," Reuters, November 28, 2024.
24. Nikolai Petrov and Andrey Ryabov, "Russia's Role in the Orange Revolution," in Anders Åslund and Michael McFaul, eds., *Revolution in Orange: The Origins of Ukraine's Democratic Breakthrough* (Washington, DC: Carnegie Endowment for International Peace, 2006), 145–64.
25. Tamra Vall, "Putin Claims Victory in Defending Kazakhstan from Revolt," Reuters, January 10, 2022, https://www.reuters.com/world/asia-pacific/kazakhstan-detains-7939-people-over-unrest-2022-01-10/.
26. Agence France-Presse, "Mongolia's New President Earned His Nickname 'Fist' After Punching a Member of Parliament," *South China Morning Post*, June 10, 2021, https://www.scmp.com/news/asia/east-asia/article/3136741/mongolias-new-president-earned-his-nickname-fist-after-punching.
27. Marine Le Pen, interviewed by Andrew Marr, BBC, November 13, 2013, http://news.bbc.co.uk/2/shared/bsp/hi/pdfs/000000.pdf.
28. Thomas Morley and Etienne Soula, "Caught Red Handed: Russian Financing Scheme in Italy Highlights Europe's Vulnerabilities," Alliance for Securing Democracy, July 12, 2019, https://securingdemocracy.gmfus.org/latest-russian-financing-scheme-in-italy-highlights-europes-vulnerabilities/.
29. "Nigel Farage: I Admire Vladimir Putin," *Guardian*, March 31, 2014, https://www.theguardian.com/politics/2014/mar/31/farage-i-admire-putin.
30. Intelligence and Security Committee of Parliament, Russia (London: House of Commons, July 21, 2020).
31. Maia de la Baume, "Orbán, Le Pen, Salvini Join Forces to Blast EU Integration," *Politico EU*, July 2, 2021, https://fidesz.hu/int/news/joint-declaration-on-the-future-of-the-european-union.
32. Jon Jackson, "Russian Textbooks Say Trump Lost in Rigged Election," *Newsweek*, December 27, 2023, https://www.newsweek.com/russian-textbooks-say-trump-lost-rigged-election-1855656.
33. Kathryn Watson, "Hearty Handshake Between Putin and Saudi Crown Prince Goes Viral," CBS News, November 30, 2018, https://www.cbsnews.com/news/vladimir-putin-and-saudi-crown-prince-mohammed-bin-salman-handshake-g20-summit-greeting-argentina-today-2018-11-30/.
34. Clifford Kraus, "Ostracized by West, Russia Aligns with Saudis," *New York Times*, September 15, 2022.

35. "Vladimir Putin Spoke at the Final Plenary Session of the 16th Meeting of the Valdai International Discussion Club," President of Russia, October 3, 2019, http://en.kremlin.ru/events/president/news/61719.
36. Thomas Grove and Georgi Kantchev, "With an Eye on China, Russia's President Putin Blasts U.S. Dominance," *Wall Street Journal*, June 7, 2019, https://www.wsj.com/articles/with-an-eye-on-china-russias-president-putin-blasts-u-s-dominance-11559926052.
37. Chris Miller, *We Shall Be Masters: Russian Pivots to East Asia from Peter the Great to Putin* (Cambridge, MA: Harvard University Press, 2021), 281.
38. Mukhammadsharif Mamatkulov, "Putin Says Xi Has Questions and Concerns Over Ukraine," Reuters, September 15, 2022, https://www.reuters.com/world/putin-xi-set-meet-thursday-samarkand-2022-09-15/.
39. Tessa Wong, "Zelensky Claims 155 Chinese Fighting for Russia in Ukraine," BBC, April 10, 2025, https://www.bbc.com/news/articles/c1wdd228953o.
40. "Modi-Putin Meet: Russia Backs India on Kashmir, Agrees on No 'Outside Influence' in Internal Matters," *Business Today*, September 5, 2019, https://www.businesstoday.in/current/world/modi-putin-russia-backs-india-kashmir-agrees-outside-influence-internal-matters/story/377365.html.
41. Timothy Garton Ash, Ivan Krastev, and Mark Leonard, "United West, Divided from the Rest: Global Public Opinion One Year into Russia's War on Ukraine," European Council on Foreign Relations, February 22, 2023.
42. "Russia Vows to Do 'Everything' to Support Maduro, Criticizes U.S. Sanctions," Radio Free Europe, January 29, 2019, https://www.rferl.org/a/russia-everything-support-maduro-venezuelan-government/29739552.html.
43. Marine Turchi, "Le Front National Décroche les Millions Russes," Mediapart, November 22, 2014, https://www.mediapart.fr/journal/france/221114/le-front-national-decroche-les-millions-russes.
44. "Xi Jinping Holds Meeting with Russian President Vladimir Putin," Ministry of Foreign Affairs, People's Republic of China, October 23, 2024.
45. Andrei Soldatov and Irina Borogan, *The Compatriots: The Brutal and Chaotic History of Russia's Exiles, Émigrés, and Agents Abroad* (New York: Public Affairs, 2019), 218.
46. Miranda Blue, "Globalizing Homophobia, Part 2: 'Today the Whole World Is Looking at Russia,'" Right Wing Watch, October 3, 2013, https://www.rightwingwatch.org/post/globalizing-homophobia-part-2-today-the-whole-world-is-looking-at-russia/.
47. "American Extremists in Russia," Human Rights Campaign, https://assets2.hrc.org/files/assets/resources/American_Extremists_in_Russia.pdf.
48. "American Extremists in Russia," Human Rights Campaign.
49. Franklin Foer, "It's Putin's World," *Atlantic*, March 2017, https://www.theatlantic.com/magazine/archive/2017/03/its-putins-world/513848/.
50. Foer, "It's Putin's World."
51. Jonathan Swan and Andrew Solender, "Tucker Carlson-Fueled Republicans Drop Tough-on-Russia Stance," *Axios*, January 27, 2022, https://www.axios.com/tucker-carlson-fueled-republicans-drop-tough-on-russia-stance-7311d46f-49fc-47b5-af46-f365c4e7809d.html.
52. Tucker Carlson, "The Vladimir Putin Interview," *Tucker Carlson Tonight*, accessed November 27, 2024, https://tuckercarlson.com/the-vladimir-putin-interview.
53. Alex Jones (@RealAlexJones), "Top Russian Strategist Alexander Dugin Says The World Has Just Witnessed The 2nd American Revolution & That The Globalist System Has Been Defeated . . . ," X, February 19, 2025, https://x.com/RealAlexJones/status/1892358438363287664.
54. Alexander Dugin (@AGDugin), "Confirmation of Kash Patel is huge success. Trump shows who is the absolute master in the house. . . ," X, February 20, 2025, https://x.com/AGDugin/status/1892667170544386059.

55. Nadiia Koval and Denys Tereshchenko, eds., *Russian Cultural Diplomacy Under Putin: Rossotrudnichestvo, the "Russyi Mir" Foundation, and the Gorchakof Fund in 2007–2022* (Stuttgart: Ibidem-Verlag, 2023).
56. Anton Shekhovtsov, "Fake Election Observation as Russia's Tool for Election Interference: The Case of AFRIC," European Platform for Democratic Elections, April 10, 2020, https://epde.org/?news=fake-election-observation-as-russias-tool-of-election-interference-the-case-of-afric-2599.
57. "Treasury Escalates Sanctions Against the Russian Government's Attempts to Influence U.S. Elections," Office of Foreign Assets Control, US Department of the Treasury, April 15, 2021, https://home.treasury.gov/news/press-releases/jy0126.
58. Neil Melvin, *Russia's Policy of Passport Proliferation* (London: Royal United Services Institute, May 1, 2020).
59. Soldatov and Borogan, *The Compatriots*; Bill Browder, *Red Notice: A True Story of High Finance, Murder, and One Man's Fight for Justice* (New York: Simon & Schuster, 2015).
60. "Госфинансирование RT и МИА «Россия Сегодня» будет увеличено на 1,4 и 1,7 млрд рублей в 2022 году," RTVI, December 14, 2021, https://rtvi.com/news/gosfinansirovanie-rt-i-mia-rossiya-segodnya-budet-uvelicheno-na-1-4-i-1-7-mlrd-rubley-v-2022-godu/.
61. "Meta Bans RT and Other Russian State Media Networks," Reuters, September 17, 2024, https://www.reuters.com/business/media-telecom/meta-bans-rt-other-russian-state-media-networks-2024-09-17/.
62. "Alerting the World to RT's Global Covert Activities," US Department of State, September 13, 2024, https://2021-2025.state.gov/alerting-the-world-to-rts-global-covert-activities/.
63. Shelby Grossman, Daniel Bush, and Renée DiResta, "Evidence of Russia-Linked Influence Operations in Africa," Stanford Internet Observatory, October 29, 2019.
64. "Background to 'Assessing Russian Activities and Intentions in Recent US Elections': The Analytic Process and Cyber Incident Attribution," Office of the Director of National Intelligence, January 6, 2017, 9, https://www.dni.gov/files/documents/ICA_2017_01.pdf.
65. «Нет никакой объективности» https://archive.is/o/Vy4i0/https://www.kommersant.ru/doc/1911336%23.
66. *Russian Active Measures Campaigns and Interference in the 2016 U.S. Election Volume 1: Russian Efforts Against Election Infrastructure with Additional Views*, U.S. Senate Select Committee on Intelligence, July 25, 2019, https://www.intelligence.senate.gov/sites/default/files/documents/Report_Volume1.pdf; *Russian Active Measures Campaigns and Interference in the 2016 U.S. Election Volume 2: Russia's Use of Social Media with Additional Views*, U.S. Senate Select Committee on Intelligence, October 8, 2019, https://www.intelligence.senate.gov/sites/default/files/documents/Report_Volume2.pdf.
67. United States v. Internet Research Agency, 18 U.S.C. §§ 2, 371, 1349, 1028A (D.D.C February 16, 2018), https://s3.documentcloud.org/documents/4380512/Internet-Research-Agency-Indictment.pdf.
68. Sean J. Edgett, "Testimony of Sean J. Edgett, Acting General Counsel, Twitter, Inc.," *Extremist Content and Russian Disinformation Online,* hearing before the U.S. Senate Committee on the Judiciary Subcommittee on Crime and Terrorism, 115th Congress, Session 1, October 31, 2017, https://www.judiciary.senate.gov/imo/media/doc/10-31-17%20Edgett%20Testimony.pdf.
69. *Social Media Influence in the 2016 U.S. Election, Hearing Before the Senate Select Committee on Intelligence,* 115th Congress, Session 1, November 1, 2017, https://www.intelligence.senate.gov/hearings/open-hearing-social-media-influence-2016-us-elections.
70. *Russian Active Measures Campaigns and Interference in the 2016 U.S. Election Volume* 2, 4.
71. Leo Graiden Stewart, Ahmed Arif, and Kate Starbird, "Examining Trolls and Polarization with a Retweet Network," University of Washington, 2018, https://faculty.washington.edu/kstarbi/examining-trolls-polarization.pdf.
72. Office of the Director of National Intelligence, *Foreign Threats to the 2020 US Federal Elections,*

Intelligence Community Assessment 2020-00078D (Washington, DC: National Intelligence Council, March 10, 2021), 1, https://www.dni.gov/files/ODNI/documents/assessments/ICA-declass-16MAR21.pdf.

73. *Foreign Threats to the 2020 US Federal Elections*, 4.
74. *Foreign Threats to the 2020 US Federal Elections*, 4–5.
75. Steven Lee Myers and Julian E. Barnes, "How Russia Openly Escalated Its Election Interference Efforts," *New York Times*, November 7, 2024, https://www.nytimes.com/2024/11/07/technology/russia-us-election-interference.html; Steven Lee Myers and Julian E. Barnes, "U.S. and Allies Take Aim at Covert Russian Disinformation Campaign," *New York Times*, July 9, 2024, https://www.nytimes.com/2024/07/09/business/russian-bots-artificial-intelligence-propaganda.html.
76. "Russia" (HC632), Intelligence and Security Committee of Parliament, presented to Parliament pursuant to section 3 of the Justice and Security Act 2013, ordered by the House of Commons to be printed on July 21, 2020, https://isc.independent.gov.uk/wp-content/uploads/2021/03/CCS207_CCS0221966010-001_Russia-Report-v02-Web_Accessible.pdf.
77. Luiza Ilie, "Thousands Attend Pro-European Rally in Romania Ahead of Presidential Run-off Vote," Reuters, December 6, 2024, https://www.reuters.com/world/europe/thousands-attend-pro-european-rally-romania-ahead-presidential-run-off-vote-2024-12-06/.
78. Robert S. Mueller, *Report on the Investigation into Russian Interference in the 2016 Presidential Election* (Washington, DC: US Department of Justice, 2019).
79. Eric Bradner, "Hillary Clinton on Emails: 'It Is a Drip-Drip-Drip,'" CNN, September 27, 2015, https://www.cnn.com/2015/09/27/politics/hillary-clinton-emails-meet-the-press.
80. Regina Lawrence, Michael Traugott, and Justin Grimmer, "Discussion of Kathleen Hall Jamieson's Cyberwar: How Russian Hackers and Trolls Helped Elect a President—What We Don't, Can't, and Do Know," *Public Opinion Quarterly* 83, no. 1 (Spring 2019): 159.
81. Renée DiResta and Shelby Grossman, "Potemkin Pages & Personas: Assessing GRU Online Operations, 2014–2019," Stanford Internet Observatory, 2019.
82. US Senate Committee on Foreign Relations, Minority Staff, *Putin's Asymmetric Assault on Democracy in Russia and Europe: Implications for U.S. National Security*, 115th Congress, Session 2, January 10, 2018, https://www.foreign.senate.gov/imo/media/doc/FinalRR.pdf, 123.
83. "Russia," Intelligence and Security Committee of Parliament, 5.
84. US Senate Committee on Foreign Relations, *Putin's Asymmetric Assault on Democracy.*
85. Jack Stubbs and Guy Faulconbridge, "Exclusive: Papers Leaked Before UK Election in Suspected Russian Operation Were Hacked from Ex-Trade Minister—Sources," Reuters, August 3, 2020, https://www.reuters.com/article/world/uk/exclusive-papers-leaked-before-uk-election-in-suspected-russian-operation-were-idUSKBN24Z1UK/.
86. Daniel Bush, Anna Gielewska, and Maciej Kurzynski, "How a Mysterious Website Supported a Disinformation Operation Targeting the Polish Military," Stanford Internet Observatory, May 8, 2020, https://fsi-live.s3.us-west-1.amazonaws.com/s3fs-public/documents/sio_disinformation_polish_military_0.pdf.
87. Mueller, *Report on the Investigation into Russian Interference.*
88. *Foreign Threats to the 2020 US Federal Elections*, 2–3.
89. *Foreign Threats to the 2020 US Federal Elections*, 3.
90. "PM Brnabić Thanks Russian Security Services," N1 Info, November 26, 2021, https://n1info.rs/english/news/pm-brnabic-thanks-russian-security-services/.
91. Peter Apps, "Russia's Suspected Sabotage Campaign Steps Up in Europe," Reuters, October 20, 2024, https://www.reuters.com/world/russias-suspected-sabotage-campaign-steps-up-europe-2024-10-21/.
92. "Russia" (HC632), Intelligence and Security Committee of Parliament, 15.
93. Lucian Kim, *Putin's Revenge: Why Russia Invaded Ukraine* (New York: Columbia University Press, 2024).

94. Nadiia Koval et al., "Rossotrudnichestvo: The Unbearable Harshness of Soft Power," in Koval and Tereshchenko, eds., *Russian Cultural Diplomacy Under Putin* (Stuttgart: Ibidem-Verlag, 2023), 32.
95. Evan Gershkovich, "At Russia's Inaugural Africa Summit, Moscow Sells Sovereignty," *Moscow Times*, October 26, 2019, https://www.themoscowtimes.com/2019/10/26/russias-inaugural-africa-summit-moscow-sells-sovereignty-a67916.
96. Grace Kier and Paul Stronski, "Russia's Vaccine Diplomacy Is Mostly Smoke and Mirrors," Carnegie Endowment for International Peace, August 3, 2021, https://carnegieendowment.org/posts/2021/08/russias-vaccine-diplomacy-is-mostly-smoke-and-mirrors?lang=en.
97. Annette Bohr, "Revolution in Kyrgyzstan—Again," Chatham House, April 2010, https://www.chathamhouse.org/sites/default/files/public/Research/Russia%20and%20Eurasia/0410pp_kyrgyzstan.pdf.
98. Loveday Morris, Ladka Bauerova, and Robyn Dixon, "Accusations of Spying and Sabotage Plunge Russian-Czech Relations into the Deep Freeze," *Washington Post*, April 19, 2021, https://www.washingtonpost.com/world/europe/russia-diplomats-expulsions-czech/2021/04/19/ef7f6178-9fbb-11eb-b2f5-7d2f0182750d_story.html.
99. Dimitar Bechev, *The 2016 Coup Attempt in Montenegro: Is Russia's Balkans Footprint Expanding?* (Philadelphia: Foreign Policy Research Institute, April 2018), 8–10, https://www.fpri.org/article/2018/04/the-2016-coup-attempt-in-montenegro-is-russias-balkans-footprint-expanding/.
100. Nina Iskandarsjach, "The Wagner Scramble for Africa: Assessing the Effectiveness of Russian Intervention in Africa Sahel" (BA thesis, Stanford University, 2024).
101. Moira Fagan, Sneha Gubbala, and Jacob Poushter, "Views of Russia and Putin Remain Negative in Many Countries," Pew Research Center, July 2, 2024, https://www.pewresearch.org/global/2024/07/02/views-of-russia-and-putin-july-24/.
102. Margaret Vice, "Publics Worldwide Unfavorable Toward Putin, Russia," Pew Research Center, August 16, 2017, https://www.pewresearch.org/global/2017/08/16/publics-worldwide-unfavorable-toward-putin-russia/.
103. Ope Adetayo and Hamza Ibrahim, "Nigeria Detains Tailors Who Made Russian Flags for Anti-Government Protests," Reuters, August 6, 2024, https://www.reuters.com/world/africa/nigeria-detains-tailors-who-made-russian-flags-anti-government-protests-2024-08-06/.
104. Garton Ash, Krastev, and Leonard, "United West, Divided from the Rest."

8. Exporting Xi Jinping Thought

1. Rowan Callick, "Helmsman Xi Takes China Back to the Future," *The Strategist* (blog), Australian Strategic Policy Institute, September 6, 2021, https://www.aspistrategist.org.au/helmsman-xi-takes-china-back-to-the-future/.
2. Elizabeth Economy, *The Third Revolution: Xi Jinping and the New Chinese State* (Oxford: Oxford University Press, 2018).
3. Central Committee of the Communist Party of China's General Office, *Communiqué on the Current State of the Ideological Sphere*, translated by ChinaFile, April 22, 2013, https://www.chinafile.com/document-9-chinafile-translation.
4. Michael Pompeo, "The China Challenge," US Department of State, October 30, 2019, https://2017-2021-translations.state.gov/2019/10/30/the-china-challenge/.
5. Gavin Bade, "Biden: U.S. Locked in 'Battle' with China for Global Influence," *Politico*, March 25, 2021, https://www.politico.com/news/2021/03/25/biden-china-press-conference-478052.
6. "About the Committee," U.S. House Select Committee on the CCP, accessed April 20, 2025, https://selectcommitteeontheccp.house.gov/about-committee.

7. Michael Gallagher, "Chairman Gallagher's Opening Remarks," U.S. House Select Committee on the CCP, February 28, 2023, https://selectcommitteeontheccp.house.gov/media/press-releases/chairman-gallaghers-opening-remarks.
8. Marco Rubio, *The World China Made: "Made in China" Nine Years Later* (Washington, DC: Project for Strong Labor Markets and National Development, Office of Senator Marco Rubio, September 9, 2024), 2.
9. Yan Xuetong, "Chinese Values vs. Liberalism: What Ideology Will Shape the International Normative Order?," *Chinese Journal of International Politics* 11, no. 1 (Spring 2018): 1–22, https://doi.org/10.1093/cjip/poy001.
10. Jessica Chen Weiss, "A World Safe for Autocracy?," *Foreign Affairs*, vol. 98, no. 4, June 11, 2019, https://www.foreignaffairs.com/articles/china/2019-06-11/world-safe-autocracy.
11. Richard McGregor, "Exporting the China Model," *American Purpose*, April 6, 2022, https://www.americanpurpose.com/articles/exporting-the-china-model/.
12. Maria Repnikova, *Chinese Soft Power: Elements in Global China* (Cambridge: Cambridge University Press, 2022).
13. Ya-Wen Li, *The Gilded Cage: Technology, Development, and State Capitalism in China* (Princeton, NJ: Princeton University Press, 2023), 4.
14. Julian Gewirtz, *Unlikely Partners: Chinese Reformers, Western Economists, and the Making of Global China* (Cambridge, MA: Harvard University Press, 2017).
15. David Shambaugh, *China's Leaders: From Mao to Now* (New York: Polity Press, 2021), 130.
16. Jean Oi, *Rural China Takes Off: Institutional Foundations of Economic Reform* (Oakland: University of California Press, 1999).
17. Minxin Pei, *China's Trapped Transition: The Limits of Developmental Autocracy* (Cambridge, MA: Harvard University Press, 2006); Yasheng Huang, *Capitalism with Chinese Characteristics: Entrepreneurship and the State* (Cambridge: Cambridge University Press, 2008).
18. Keyu Jin, *The New China Playbook: Beyond Socialism and Capitalism* (New York: Viking, 2023), 3.
19. Steve Tsang and Olivia Cheung, *The Political Thought of Xi Jinping* (Oxford: Oxford University Press, 2024), 63.
20. Yuen Yuen Ang, "The Real China Model," *Foreign Affairs*, June 29, 2018, https://www.foreignaffairs.com/articles/asia/2018-06-29/real-china-model/.
21. Central Committee of the CCP, *Hold High the Great Banner of Socialism with Chinese Characteristics and Strive in Unity to Build a Modern Socialist Country in All Respects*, translated by Xinhua News Agency, October 25, 2022, 18, https://interpret.csis.org/translations/hold-high-the-great-banner-of-socialism-with-chinese-characteristics-and-strive-in-unity-to-build-a-modern-socialist-country-in-all-respects-report-to-the-20th-national-congress-of-the-communi/.
22. "The Global Security Initiative Concept Paper," Ministry of Foreign Affairs of People's Republic of China, February 21, 2023, https://www.mfa.gov.cn/mfa_eng/xw/wjbxw/202405/t20240530_11343274.html.
23. "Initiatives Proposed by China, Fruitful Outcomes Shared by World," Embassy of the People's Republic of China in the Independent State of Samoa, May 22, 2023, http://ws.china-embassy.gov.cn/eng/xwdt/202305/t20230522_11081047.htm.
24. Nadège Rolland, "China's Southern Strategy," *Foreign Affairs*, June 9, 2022, https://www.foreignaffairs.com/articles/china/2022-06-09/chinas-southern-strategy.
25. Eric Li, *Party Life: Chinese Governance and the World Beyond Liberalism* (Singapore: Palgrave, 2023), 241.
26. Daniel Lynch, "The End of China's Rise," in Ying Zhu, Kingsley Edney, and Stanley Rosen, eds., *Soft Power with Chinese Characteristics: China's Campaign for Hearts and Minds* (New York: Routledge, 2019), 49.

27. Nadège Rolland, *China's Vision for a New World Order* (Washington, DC: National Bureau of Asian Research, 2020), 17, https://www.nbr.org/wp-content/uploads/pdfs/publications/sr83_chinasvision_jan2020.pdf.
28. Author's interviews with Chinese scholars, Beijing, April 2024.
29. Robert Lighthizer, *No Trade Is Free: Changing Course, Taking on China, and Helping America's Workers* (Northampton, MA: Broadside, 2023), 89–90.
30. Chun Han Wong, *Party of One: The Rise of Xi Jinping and China's Superpower Future* (New York: Avid Reader Press, 2023), 215.
31. Pjotr Sauer and Amy Hawkins, "'Good Old Friend': Putin Offers Praise for Xi Ahead of First Trip to Russia Since Ukraine Invasion," *Guardian*, March 19, 2023, https://www.theguardian.com/world/2023/mar/20/xi-set-to-visit-russia-in-trip-that-will-reaffirm-ties-with-putin-china.
32. Jason Lemon, "Xi Jinping: President Putin Is My Best, Most Intimate Friend," *Newsweek*, June 8, 2018, https://www.newsweek.com/putin-my-best-most-intimate-friend-chinese-president-xi-says-967531.
33. Xi Jinping and Vladimir Putin, "Joint Statement of the Russian Federation and the People's Republic of China on the International Relations Entering a New Era and the Global Sustainable Development," President of Russia, February 4, 2022, http://en.kremlin.ru/supplement/5770#sel=1:21:S5F,1:37:3jE.
34. Olena Bilousova et al., "Challenges of Export Controls Enforcement," Working Group Paper no. 6, Stanford International Working Group on Russian Sanctions, January 2024, https://fsi9-prod.s3.us-west-1.amazonaws.com/s3fs-public/2024-01/export_controls_-_final_-_1-11-24_update.pdf.
35. "Introduction to the International Liaison Department [中联部简介]," International Department, Central Committee of CPC [中共中央对外联络部], accessed April 28, 2023, https://www.idcpc.org.cn/zlbjj/wbjj/; David Shin and Joshua Eiseman, *China's Relations with Africa: A New Era of Strategic Engagement* (New York: Columbia University Press, 2023), 89.
36. Christine Hackenesch and Julia Bader, "The Struggle for Minds and Influence: The Chinese Communist Party's Global Outreach," *International Studies Quarterly* 64, no. 3 (September 2020): 723–33, https://doi.org/10.1093/isq/sqaa028; Xu Wei, "Xi Calls for Closer Ties with Vietnam," *China Daily*, April 9, 2024.
37. Cole McFaul, "Some Strings Attached: Explaining the Motivations for and Impact of Chinese Engagement in Ghana" (BA thesis, Stanford University, 2021).
38. Bethany Allen-Ebrahimian, "In Tanzania, Beijing Is Running a Training School for Authoritarianism," *Axios*, August 21, 2023, https://www.axios.com/2023/08/21/chinese-communist-party-training-school-africa; Yun Sun, "Political Party Training: China's Ideological Push in Africa?," Brookings Institution, July 5, 2016, https://www.brookings.edu/blog/africa-in-focus/2016/07/05/political-party-training-chinas-ideological-push-in-africa/.
39. He Huifeng, "In a Remote Corner of China, Beijing Is Trying to Export Its Model by Training Foreign Officials the Chinese Way," *South China Morning Post*, July 14, 2018, https://www.scmp.com/news/china/economy/article/2155203/remote-corner-china-beijing-trying-export-its-model-training.
40. Jessica Chen Weiss, "Does China Actively Promote Its Way of Governing—and Do Other Countries Listen?," *Washington Post*, July 14, 2021, http://www.washingtonpost.com/politics/2021/07/14/does-china-actively-promote-its-way-governing-do-other-countries-listen/.
41. Elizabeth Economy, *"Exporting the China Model," Hearing on "A 'China Model?' Beijing's Promotion of Alternative Global Norms and Standards,"* hearing before the U.S.-China Economic and Security Review Commission, March 13, 2020, 3, https://www.uscc.gov/sites/default/files/testimonies/USCCTestimony3-13-20%20(Elizabeth%20Economy)_justified.pdf.
42. Ryan Fedasiuk, "Putting Money in the Party's Mouth: How China Mobilizes Funding for United Front Work," Jamestown Foundation, September 16, 2020, https://jamestown.org

/program/putting-money-in-the-partys-mouth-how-china-mobilizes-funding-for-united-front-work/.

43. Alexander Bowe, *China's Overseas United Front Work: Background and Implications for the United States* (Washington, DC: U.S. China Economic and Security Review Commission, August 24, 2018), https://www.uscc.gov/sites/default/files/Research/China%27s%20Overseas%20United%20Front%20Work%20-%20Background%20and%20Implications%20for%20US_final_0.pdf.
44. Wanning Sun, "Vessels of Soft Power Going Out to Sea," in Zhu, Edney, and Rosen, *Soft Power with Chinese Characteristics*, 88.
45. David Shambaugh, "China's Soft-Power Push: The Search for Respect," *Foreign Affairs* 94, no. 4 (July/August 2015): 99–107, https://www.foreignaffairs.com/articles/china/2015-06-16/chinas-soft-power-push.
46. Joshua Kurlantzick, *Beijing's Global Media Offensive: China's Uneven Campaign to Influence Asia and the World* (Oxford: Oxford University Press, 2022); Brandon L. Van Grack, *Letter of Determination Regarding Xinhua News Agency North America's Obligation to Register Under the Foreign Agents Registration Act*, U.S. Department of Justice, National Security Division, Counterintelligence and Export Control Section, May 18, 2020, https://www.justice.gov/nsd-fara/letters-determination/xinhua/dl.
47. Digital Forensics Research Lab, "How China Funds Foreign Influence Campaigns," Atlantic Council, January 12, 2023, https://dfrlab.org/2023/01/12/how-china-funds-foreign-influence-campaigns/.
48. Kurlantzick, *Beijing's Global Media Offensive*, 22.
49. Sarah Cook, *Beijing's Global Megaphone* (Washington, DC: Freedom House, January 2020), https://freedomhouse.org/report/special-report/2020/beijings-global-megaphone.
50. Peter Martin, *China's Civilian Army: The Making of Wolf Warrior Diplomacy* (Oxford: Oxford University Press, 2021).
51. Samantha Bradshaw and Philip Howard, *The Global Disinformation Disorder: 2019 Global Inventory of Organized Social Media Manipulation* (Oxford: Computational Propaganda Research Project, 2019), https://digitalcommons.unl.edu/cgi/viewcontent.cgi?article=1209&context=scholcom.
52. "Information Operations Directed at Hong Kong," *X Blog*, August 19, 2019, https://blog.x.com/en_us/topics/company/2019/information_operations_directed_at_Hong_Kong.
53. Lilly Min-Chen Lee et al., "Deafening Whispers: China's Information Campaign and Taiwan's 2020 Elections," Doublethink Lab, 2021.
54. Joel Finkelstein et al., "The CCP's Digital Charm Offensive: How TikTok's Search Algorithm and Pro-China Influence Networks Indoctrinate GenZ Users in the United States," Network Contagion Research Institute, accessed December 9, 2024, https://networkcontagion.us/wp-content/uploads/NCRI-Report_-The-CCPs-Digital-Charm-Offensive.pdf.
55. Rebecca Klar, "TikTok Urges Users to Call Congress, Stop 'TikTok Shutdown,'" *The Hill*, March 7, 2024, https://thehill.com/policy/technology/4516261-tiktok-urges-users-to-call-congress-stop-tiktok-shutdown/.
56. David O. Shullman, "Protect the Party: China's Growing Influence in the Developing World," Brookings Institution, January 22, 2019, https://www.brookings.edu/articles/protect-the-party-chinas-growing-influence-in-the-developing-world/.
57. "Xi Jinping: Ideological Work Is Extremely Important for the Party" [习近平：意识形态工作是党的一项极端重要的工作], Xinhua, August 20, 2013, http://www.xinhuanet.com//politics/2013-08/20/c_117021464.htm.
58. "Control, Halt, Delete: Reporting in China Under Threat of Expulsion," Foreign Correspondents' Club of China, March 2020, https://www.fcchk.org/wp-content/uploads/2020/03/control-halt-delete.pdf.

59. Erin Baggott Carter, "When Beijing Goes to Washington: Autocratic Lobbying Influence in Democracies," Stanford APARC, April 23, 2021, https://www.youtube.com/watch?v=gX8nXKN1UKU&ab_channel=StanfordAPARC.
60. Erich Schwartzel, *Red Carpet: Hollywood, China, and the Global Battle for Cultural Supremacy* (New York: Penguin, 2022); James Tager, *Made in Hollywood, Censored by Beijing: The U.S. Film Industry and Chinese Government Influence* (New York: PEN America, 2020).
61. Aynne Kokas, "How Beijing Runs the Shows in Hollywood," in William Dobson, Tarek Masoud, and Christopher Walker, eds., *Defending Democracy in an Age of Sharp Power* (Baltimore: Johns Hopkins University Press, 2023), 54.
62. Josh Feldman, "Judd Apatow Calls Out 'Chilling' Hollywood Censorship: 'China Has Bought Our Silence,'" Mediaite, September 14, 2020, https://www.mediaite.com/tv/judd-apatow-calls-out-chilling-hollywood-censorship-china-has-bought-our-silence/.
63. Falk Hartig, "A Decade of Wielding Soft Power Through Confucius Institutes: Some Interim Results," in Zhu, Edney, and Rosen, *Soft Power with Chinese Characteristics,* 133; "Confucius Institute Annual Development Report," Confucius Institute, Chinese International Education Foundation, 2022.
64. "U.S. Department of Education Launches Investigation into Foreign Gifts Reporting at Ivy League Universities," US Department of Education, February 12, 2020, https://web.archive.org/web/20200213034524/https://www.ed.gov/news/press-releases/test-0.
65. Maria Repnikova, "Rethinking China's Soft Power: 'Pragmatic Enticement' of Confucius Institutes in Ethiopia," *China Quarterly* 250 (2022): 440–63, https://doi.org/10.1017/S0305741022000340.
66. "How Many Confucius Institutes Are in the United States?," National Association of Scholars, June 22, 2023, https://www.nas.org/blogs/article/how_many_confucius_institutes_are_in_the_united_states.
67. *DHS Restrictions on Confucius Institutes and Chinese Entities of Concern Act, H.R. 1516,* 118th Congress (2024), https://www.congress.gov/bill/118th-congress/house-bill/1516.
68. Tim Khang, "Testimony Before the US-China Economic and Security Review Commission," *Made in China 2025—Who is Winning?* Hearing before the U.S.-China Economic and Security Review Commission, February 6, 2025, https://www.uscc.gov/sites/default/files/2025-02/Tim_Khang_Testimony.pdf.
69. Glenn Tiffert, ed., *Global Engagement: Rethinking Risk in the Research Enterprise* (Stanford: Hoover Institution Press, 2020).
70. "Former Harvard University Professor Sentenced for Lying About His Affiliation with Wuhan University of Technology; China's Thousand Talents Program; and Filing False Tax Returns," United States Attorney's Office, District of Massachusetts, April 26, 2023, https://www.justice.gov/usao-ma/pr/former-harvard-university-professor-sentenced-lying-about-his-affiliation-wuhan.
71. "Information About the Department of Justice's China Initiative and a Compilation of China-Related Prosecutions Since 2018," US Department of Justice, March 9, 2021, https://www.justice.gov/nsd/information-about-department-justice-s-china-initiative-and-compilation-china-related.
72. Permanent Subcommittee on Investigations, *Threats to the U.S. Research Enterprise: China's Talent Recruitment Plans,* US Senate Committee on Homeland Security and Government Affairs, November 18, 2019, https://www.hsgac.senate.gov/wp-content/uploads/imo/media/doc/2019-11-18%20PSI%20Staff%20Report%20-%20China's%20Talent%20Recruitment%20Plans%20Updated2.pdf.
73. Ellen Nakashima, "Charges Dismissed Against MIT Professor Accused of Hiding Research Ties to China," *Washington Post,* January 20, 2022, https://www.washingtonpost.com/national-security/mit-gang-chen-dismiss/2022/01/20/912f68aa-786b-11ec-bf97-6eac6f77fba2_story.html.

74. "Forum on China-Africa Cooperation Beijing Action Plan (2019–2021)," Forum on China-Africa Cooperation, September 12, 2018, http://www.focac.org/eng/zywx_1/zywj/201809/t20180912_7933578.htm.
75. Antonio Fiori and Stanley Rosen, "The Sino-African Relations: An Intense and Long Embrace," in Zhu, Edney, and Rosen, *Soft Power with Chinese Characteristics*, 196.
76. Aisi Li, "'One Belt One Road' and Central Asia: A New Trend in Internationalization of Higher Education?," *International Higher Education*, no. 92 (Winter 2018), https://doi.org/10.6017/ihe.2018.92.10279.
77. David Shambaugh, *China Goes Global: The Partial Power* (Oxford: Oxford University Press, 2013).
78. Andrew G. Walder, "The Limits of Socialist Mercantilism: China's Corporate Expansion Abroad," *The China Journal* 94 (July 2025), 6.
79. Julia Bader, "Would Autocracies Promote Autocracy? A Political Economy Perspective on Regime-Type Export in Regional Neighbourhoods," *Contemporary Politics* 16, no. 1 (2010): 81–100, https://doi.org/10.1080/13569771003593904.
80. Cole McFaul, "Win-Win Cooperation for Who? The Political Economy of State-Business Relations in Global China" (MA thesis, Stanford University, 2023).
81. Jude Blanchette, "China Is in Denial About the War in Ukraine," *Foreign Affairs*, August 13, 2024, https://www.foreignaffairs.com/china/china-denial-about-war-ukraine-jude-blanchette.
82. Erin Baggott Carter and Brett L. Carter, "Exporting the Tools of Dictatorship: The Politics of China's Technology Transfers to Africa," Working Paper 122 (Williamsburg, VA: AidData, 2022), https://www.aiddata.org/publications/exporting-the-tools-of-dictatorship-the-politics-of-chinas-technology-transfers-to-africa.
83. S. Custer et al., "Tracking Chinese Development Finance: An Application of AidData's TUFF 3.0 Methodology," AidData (2023), https://www.aiddata.org/data/aiddatas-global-chinese-development-finance-dataset-version-3-0.
84. Dong Wang and Dejun Cao, *Reglobalisation: When China Meets the World Again* (London: Routledge, 2021).
85. Jonathan Hillman, *The Digital Silk Road: China's Quest to Wire the World and Win the Future* (New York: HarperCollins, 2021).
86. US Department of Defense, *Military and Security Developments Involving the People's Republic of China: A Report to Congress,* Washington, DC: US Department of Defense, December 18, 2024, https://media.defense.gov/2024/Dec/18/2003615520/-1/-1/0/MILITARY-AND-SECURITY-DEVELOPMENTS-INVOLVING-THE-PEOPLES-REPUBLIC-OF-CHINA-2024.PDF.
87. Jonathan Hillman, *The Emperor's New Road: China and the Project of the Century* (New Haven, CT: Yale University Press, 2020), 4.
88. "Credit Ratings Reports—AIIB," Asian Infrastructure Investment Bank, accessed December 21, 2021, https://www.aiib.org/en/treasury/_other_content/rating-reports/index.html.
89. Author's interviews with AIIB officials in Beijing, June 2019 and April 2024.
90. "History," New Development Bank, accessed December 22, 2021, https://www.ndb.int/about-ndb/history/.
91. Bas Hooijmaaijers, "Understanding Success and Failure of Establishing New Multilateral Development Banks: The SCO Development Bank, the NDB, and the AIID," *Asian Perspective* 45, no. 2 (Spring 2021): 459.
92. Anna Chuwen Dai, "The International Investment Agreement Network Under the 'Belt and Road' Initiative," in J. Chaisse and J. Górski, eds., *The Belt and Road Initiative: Law, Economics and Politics* (Leiden: Bril, 2018), 220–49; Florian Schneider, "Actors and Agency in China's Belt and Road Initiative: An Introduction," in Florian Schneider, ed., *Global Perspectives on China's Belt and Road Initiative: Asserting Agency Through Regional Connectivity* (Amsterdam: Amsterdam University Press, 2021), 11–32.

93. Stephen Krasner, *Defending the National Interest: Raw Materials Investments and U.S. Foreign Policy* (Princeton, NJ: Princeton University Press, 1978).
94. Muyang Chen, *The Latecomer's Rise: Policy Banks and the Globalization of China's Development Finance* (Ithaca, NY: Cornell University Press, 2024).
95. The Sri Lanka case was complicated and did not necessarily have the outcome that Beijing desired. See Jonathan Hillman, "Game of Loans: Sri Lanka," in Hillman, *The Emperor's New Road*, 151–72.
96. Sylvie Corbet, "Debt-Plagued Zambia Reaches Deal with China, Other Nations to Rework $6.3B in Loans, French Say," AP News, June 22, 2023, https://apnews.com/article/zambia-debt-restructuring-deal-china-a0d14e7af986e2f873555685cedb86b3.
97. Lingling Wei, "China Reins In Its Belt and Road Program, $1 Trillion Later," *Wall Street Journal*, September 26, 2022, https://www.wsj.com/articles/china-belt-road-debt-11663961638?st=2q4c08j3srh0k4d.
98. Sebastian Horn et al., "China as an International Lender of Last Resort," Working Paper. 2244 (Kiel Institute for the World Economy, 2023), 4, https://www.nber.org/papers/w31105.
99. Elaine K. Dezenski, "Below the Belt and Road: Corruption and Illicit Dealings in China's Global Infrastructure," Foundation for Defense of Democracies, May 6, 2020, https://www.fdd.org/wp-content/uploads/2020/05/fdd-monograph-below-the-belt-and-road.pdf.
100. Joe Cash, "Leaders Gather in China for Smaller, Greener Belt and Road Summit," Reuters, October 16, 2023, https://www.reuters.com/world/china/leaders-gather-china-smaller-greener-belt-road-summit-2023-10-16/.
101. Christoph Nedopil, "China Belt and Road Initiative (BRI) Investment Report 2023," Griffith Asia Institute, Griffith University and Green Finance and Development Center, FISF Fudan University, February 2024, https://greenfdc.org/wp-content/uploads/2024/02/Nedopil-2024_China-BRI-Investment-Report-2023.pdf.
102. Evan A. Feigenbaum and Adam Szubin, "What China Has Learned from the Ukraine War," *Foreign Affairs*, February 14, 2023, https://www.foreignaffairs.com/china/what-china-has-learned-ukraine-war.
103. Bethany Allen, *Beijing Rules: How China Weaponized Its Economy to Confront the World* (New York: Harper, 2023), 2–5.
104. Wendy Cutler and Shay Wester, "Resilience and Resolve: Lessons from Lithuania's Experience with Chinese Economic Coercion," Asia Society Policy Institute, April 17, 2024, https://asiasociety.org/policy-institute/resilience-resolve-lessons-lithuanias-experience-chinese-economic-coercion.
105. Rosie Perper and Will Martin, "China and the NBA Are Coming to Blows over a Pro–Hong Kong Tweet. Here's Why," *Business Insider*, October 22, 2019, https://www.businessinsider.com/nba-china-feud-timeline-daryl-morey-tweet-hong-kong-protests-2019-10.
106. Allen, *Beijing Rules*, 29–44.
107. Katja Drinhausen and Helena Legarda, "China's Anti-Foreign Sanctions Law: A Warning to the World," Merics, June 24, 2021, https://merics.org/de/kommentar/chinas-anti-foreign-sanctions-law-warning-world.
108. Feigenbaum and Szubin, "What China Has Learned."
109. Allen, *Beijing Rules*, xix.
110. "In Clinical and Real-World Trials, China's Sinovac Underperforms," *Economist*, April 15, 2021, https://www.economist.com/graphic-detail/2021/04/15/in-clinical-and-real-world-trials-chinas-sinovac-underperforms.
111. Cole McFaul, "Some Strings Attached."
112. Michael Pompeo, "Secretary Michael R. Pompeo Remarks 'Communist China and the Free World's Future,'" US Department of State, Office of the Spokesperson, July 23, 2020, https://cl.usembassy.gov/secretary-michael-r-pompeo-remarks-communist-china-and-the-free-worlds-future/.

113. Michael Froman, "China Has Already Remade the International System: How the World Adopted Beijing's Economic Playbook," *Foreign Affairs*, March 25, 2025, https://www.foreignaffairs.com/china/economics-china-international-system-tariffs-michael-froman.
114. Laura Silver, "More People View the U.S. Positively Than China Across 35 Surveyed Countries," Pew Research Center, July 9, 2024, https://www.pewresearch.org/short-reads/2024/07/09/more-people-view-the-us-positively-than-china-across-35-surveyed-countries/.
115. Yu Xie and Yongai Jin, "Global Attitudes Toward China: Trends and Correlates," *Journal of Contemporary China* 31, no. 133 (2021): 1–16, https://doi.org/10.1080/10670564.2021.1926088.
116. Bernard Condon, "China's Loans Pushing World's Poorest Countries to Brink of Collapse," Associated Press, December 12, 2023, https://apnews.com/article/china-debt-banking-loans-financial-developing-countries-collapse-8df6f9fac3e1e758d0e6d8d5dfbd3ed6.
117. David Dollar, *China's Engagement with Africa: From Natural Resources to Human Resources* (Washington, DC: Brookings Institution, 2016), https://www.brookings.edu/articles/chinas-engagement-with-africa-from-natural-resources-to-human-resources/; Laura Silver, Christine Huang, Laura Clancy, Nam Lam, Shannon Greenwood, John Carlo Mandapat, and Chris Baronavski, "*Comparing Views of the U.S. and China in 24 Countries*," Pew Research Center, November 6, 2023, https://www.pewresearch.org/global/2023/11/06/comparing-views-of-the-us-and-china-in-24-countries/.
118. Laura Silver, Christine Huang, and Laura Clancy, "Views on China," Pew Research Center, July 23, 2023, https://www.pewresearch.org/global/2023/07/27/views-of-china.
119. Repnikova, "Rethinking China's Soft Power."
120. ASEAN Studies Centre, *The State of Southeast Asia 2024* (Singapore: ISEAS-Yusof Ishal Institute, 2024), 50, https://www.iseas.edu.sg/centres/asean-studies-centre/state-of-southeast-asia-survey/the-state-of-southeast-asia-2024-survey-report/.
121. Michael Robbins, Amaney A. Jamal, and Mark Tessler, "America Is Losing the Arab World and China Is Reaping the Benefits," *Foreign Affairs* (June 11, 2024), https://www-foreignaffairs-com.stanford.idm.oclc.org/united-states/america-losing-arab-world.
122. Laura Silver, Kat Devlin, and Christine Huang, "Unfavorable Views of China Reach Historic Highs in Many Countries," Pew Research Center, October 6, 2020, https://www.pewresearch.org/global/2020/10/06/unfavorable-views-of-china-reach-historic-highs-in-many-countries/.
123. Christine Huang, Laura Silver, and Laura Clancy, "Americans Remain Critical of China," Pew Research Center, 2024, https://www.pewresearch.org/global/2024/05/01/americans-remain-critical-of-china/.
124. Silver, "More People View the U.S. Positively."
125. Daniel Mattingly et al., "Chinese State Media Persuades a Global Audience That the 'China Model' Is Superior: Evidence from a 19-Country Experiment," *American Journal of Political Science*, 2024, 1-18, https://onlinelibrary.wiley.com/doi/10.1111/ajps.12887.
126. Kurlantzick, *Beijing's Global Media Offensive*, 267.
127. Bonnie Bley, "Charting China, the (Not Always) Super Power," *Interpreter*, June 3, 2019, https://www.lowyinstitute.org/the-interpreter/charting-china-not-always-super-power.

9. The Decline of the Liberal International Order

1. John Mearsheimer, *The Tragedy of Great Power Politics* (New York: W. W. Norton, 2014), 10.
2. G. John Ikenberry, *Liberal Leviathan: The Origins, Crisis, and Transformation of the American World Order* (Princeton, NJ: Princeton University Press, 2012).
3. This literature in the liberal tradition of international politics dates to founding scholars such as Immanuel Kant and Hugo Grotius. Some of the classics include Robert O. Keohane

and Joseph Nye, *Power and Independence: World Politics in Transition* (Boston: Little, Brown, 1977); Hedley Bull, *The Anarchical Society: A Study of Order in World Politics* (London: MacMillan, 1977); Michael Doyle, "Kant, Liberal Legacies, and Foreign Affairs," *Philosophy and Public Affairs* 12, no. 3 (Summer 1983): 205–25; and G. John Ikenberry, *A World Safe for Democracy: Liberal Internationalism and the Crises of Global Order* (New Haven, CT: Yale University Press, 2020).

4. Stephen Krasner, ed., *International Regimes* (Ithaca, NY: Cornell University Press, 1983), 5.
5. President George H. W. Bush, "Remarks at Maxwell Air Force Base War College in Montgomery, Alabama," April 13, 1991, https://www.presidency.ucsb.edu/documents/remarks-maxwell-air-force-base-war-college-montgomery-alabama.
6. Thomas Friedman, "Soviet Disarray: Yeltsin Says Russia Seeks to Join NATO," *New York Times*, December 21, 1991, https://www.nytimes.com/1991/12/21/world/soviet-disarray-yeltsin-says-russia-seeks-to-join-nato.html.
7. Erik Voeten, *Ideology and International Institutions* (Princeton, NJ: Princeton University Press, 2021), 7.
8. Anusha Chari, Peter Blair Henry, and Hector Reyes, "The Baker Hypothesis: Stabilization, Structural Reforms, and Economic Growth," *Journal of Economic Perspectives* 35, no. 3 (Summer 2021): 83–108, https://doi.org/10.1257/jep.35.3.83.
9. Sungmin Cho, "Why Non-Democracy Engages with Western Democracy-Promotion Programs: The China Model," *World Politics* 73, no. 4 (2021): 774–817, https://doi.org/10.1017/S0043887121000137.
10. Xi Jinping and Vladimir Putin, "Joint Statement of the Russian Federation and the People's Republic of China on the International Relations Entering a New Era and the Global Sustainable Development," President of Russia, February 4, 2022, http://en.kremlin.ru/supplement/5770#sel=1:21:S5F,1:37:3jE.
11. Gita Gopinath et al., "Changing Global Linkages: A New Cold War?," Working Paper 2024/76 (IMF, April 2024), https://www.imf.org/en/Publications/WP/Issues/2024/04/05/Changing-Global-Linkages-A-New-Cold-War-547357.
12. Elizabeth Braw, *Goodbye Globalization: The Return of a Divided World* (New Haven, CT: Yale University Press, 2024); Peter Zeihan, *The End of the World Is Just the Beginning: Mapping the Collapse of Globalization* (New York: HarperCollins, 2022).
13. Barack Obama, "Remarks by the President at the United States Military Academy Commencement Ceremony," White House Office of the Press Secretary, May 28, 2014, https://obamawhitehouse.archives.gov/the-press-office/2014/05/28/remarks-president-united-states-military-academy-commencement-ceremony.
14. "Remarks by President Trump to the 73rd Session of the United Nations General Assembly," White House, September 25, 2018, https://trumpwhitehouse.archives.gov/briefings-statements/remarks-president-trump-73rd-session-united-nations-general-assembly-new-york-ny/.
15. Robert Kagan, *The Ghost at the Feast: America and the Collapse of World Order, 1900–1941* (New York: Knopf, 2023).
16. Kyle M. Lascurettes, *Orders of Exclusion* (Oxford: Oxford University Press, 2020), 3.
17. Ivo H. Daalder and James Lindsay, *The Empty Throne: America's Abdication of Global Leadership* (New York: Public Affairs, 2018).
18. Kristen Hopewell, "When the Hegemon Goes Rogue: Leadership Amid the US Assault on the Liberal Trading Order," *International Affairs* 97, no. 4 (July 2021): 1025–43, https://doi.org/10.1093/ia/iiab073.
19. Ikenberry, *A World Safe for Democracy*, 3.
20. "Indo-Pacific Economic Framework for Prosperity (IPEF)," US Department of Commerce, accessed December 16, 2024, https://www.commerce.gov/ipef.
21. Paul Krugman, "Why America Is Getting Tough on Trade," *New York Times*, De-

cember 12, 2022, https://www.nytimes.com/2022/12/12/opinion/america-trade-biden.html.

22. Adam Hodge, "Statement from USTR Spokesperson," Office of the United States Trade Representative, December 9, 2022, https://ustr.gov/about-us/policy-offices/press-office/press-releases/2022/december/statement-ustr-spokesperson-adam-hodge.
23. Antony J. Blinken, "The Administration's Approach to the People's Republic of China at George Washington University," US Department of State, May 26, 2022, https://www.state.gov/the-administrations-approach-to-the-peoples-republic-of-china/.
24. Diana Smeltz and Karl Friedhoff, "Republicans and Democrats Support US Alliance, but for Different Reasons" (Chicago: Chicago Council on Global Affairs, August 2024), https://globalaffairs.org/research/public-opinion-survey/republicans-and-democrats-support-us-alliances-different-reasons.
25. David H. Autor, David Dorn, and Gordon Hanson, "The China Syndrome: Local Labor Market Effects of Important Competition in the United States," *American Economic Review* 103, no. 6 (October 2013): 2121–68, https://doi.org/10.1257/aer.103.6.2121.
26. Robert Lighthizer, *No Trade Is Free: Changing Course, Taking on China, and Helping America's Workers* (Northampton, MA: Broadside, 2023).
27. Cole McFaul et al., *Assessing South Korea's AI Ecosystem: Data Brief* (Washington, DC: Center for Security and Emerging Technology, August 2023), https://cset.georgetown.edu/publication/assessing-south-koreas-ai-ecosystem/.
28. Elon Musk (@elonmusk), "We should not have any international treaties that restrict the freedom of Americans," X, December 5, 2024, https://x.com/elonmusk/status/1864905121475227712.
29. Jeff Sommer, "This Trade War Is Different from All Others," *New York Times*, April 13, 2025, https://www.nytimes.com/2025/04/11/business/tariffs-trump-markets-history-trade-wars.html.
30. Miranda Bryant and Jennifer Ranklin, "New Opinion Poll Shows 85% of Greenlanders Do Not Want to Join US," *Guardian*, January 28, 2025, https://www.theguardian.com/world/2025/jan/28/85-of-greenlanders-do-not-want-to-join-us-says-new-poll.

10. Russian Global (Dis)Order

1. James Goldgeier and Michael McFaul, "Russians as Joiners: Realists and Liberal Conceptions of Postcommunist Europe," in Michael McFaul and Kathryn Stoner-Weiss, eds., *After the Collapse of Communism* (Cambridge: Cambridge University Press, 2004), 232–56.
2. Andrei Kozyrev, *Firebird: The Elusive Fate of Russian Democracy* (Pittsburgh: University of Pittsburgh Press, 2019), 123.
3. Vladimir Putin, "Expanded Meeting of the Defence Ministry Board," December 16, 2024, http://en.kremlin.ru/events/president/news/75887.
4. "Putin's Prepared Remarks at the 43rd Munich Security Conference on Security Policy," *Washington Post*, February 12, 2007, https://www.washingtonpost.com/wp-dyn/content/article/2007/02/12/AR2007021200555.html.
5. Putin, "Putin's Prepared Remarks."
6. "Presidential Address to Federal Assembly," President of Russia, February 21, 2023, http://en.kremlin.ru/events/president/news/70565.
7. "Statement by the President of the Russian Federation," President of Russia, November 21, 2024, http://en.kremlin.ru/events/president/news/75614.
8. Xi Jinping and Vladimir Putin, "Joint Statement of the Russian Federation and the People's Republic of China on the International Relations Entering a New Era and the Global Sustainable Development," President of Russia, February 4, 2022, http://en.kremlin.ru/supplement/5770#sel=1:21:S5F,1:37:3jE.
9. Dmitry Gorenburg, "Russia and Collective Security: Why CSTO Is No Match for Warsaw Pact," Russia Matters, May 27, 2020, https://www.russiamatters.org/analysis/russia-and-collective-security-why-csto-no-match-warsaw-pact.

10. "Armenia to Quit Russia-Led CSTO," Deutsche Welle, June 13, 2024, https://www.dw.com/en/armenia-to-leave-russian-led-csto-security-bloc/a-69348061.
11. "Putin Agrees with Emperor That Russia's Only Allies Are Army and Navy," Tass, April 16, 2015, https://tass.com/russia/789866.
12. Lolita C. Baldor and Didi Tang, "Chinese and Russian Bombers Patrolling Off Alaska Raise Concerns," Associated Press, July 25, 2024, https://apnews.com/article/china-russia-us-military-planes-norad-alaska-4994b489e75ae636b4a4cd5bb40f91ac.
13. Olena Bilousova et al., "Challenges of Export Controls Enforcement: How Russia Continues to Import Components for Its Military Production," International Working Group on Russian Sanctions, January 11, 2024, https://fsi9-prod.s3.us-west-1.amazonaws.com/s3fs-public/2024-01/export_controls_-_final_-_1-11-24_update.pdf.
14. "Vladimir Putin Meets with Members of the Valdai Discussion Club. Transcript of the Plenary Session of the 17th Annual Meeting," President of Russia, October 22, 2020, http://en.kremlin.ru/events/president/news/64261.
15. Joseph Bermudez, Victor Cha, and Jennifer June, "Major Munitions Transfers from North Korea to Russia," Working Paper (CSIS, February 28, 2024), https://beyondparallel.csis.org/major-munitions-transfers-from-north-korea-to-russia/.
16. William J. Burns, *The Back Channel: A Memoir of American Diplomacy and the Case for Its Renewal* (New York: Random House, 2019), chapter 9.
17. Thomas D. Arnold, "Exploiting Chaos: Russia in Libya," Center for Strategic and International Studies, 2020, https://www.csis.org/blogs/post-soviet-post/exploiting-chaos-russia-libya.
18. Eric Schmitt, "Russia's Military Mission Creep Advances to a New Front: Africa," *New York Times*, March 31, 2019, https://www.nytimes.com/2019/03/31/world/africa/russia-military-africa.html.
19. Grant T. Harris and Michael McFaul, "How Vladimir Putin Is Outplaying the U.S. in Africa," *Washington Post*, September 17, 2019, https://www.washingtonpost.com/opinions/2019/09/17/how-vladimir-putin-is-outplaying-us-africa/.
20. Rocio Cara Labrador, "Maduro's Allies: Who Backs the Venezuelan Regime?," Council on Foreign Relations, February 5, 2019, https://www.cfr.org/in-brief/maduros-allies-who-backs-venezuelan-regime.
21. Dylan Malyasov, "Russia's Notorious Private Military Company Spotted in Venezuela," *Defence Blog*, August 1, 2024, https://defence-blog.com/russias-notorious-private-military-company-spotted-in-venezuela/.
22. "UN General Assembly Demands Russia Reverse Course on 'Attempted Illegal Annexation' of Ukraine Regions," UN News, October 12, 2022, https://news.un.org/en/story/2022/10/1129492.
23. Charles Clover, "Clinton Vows to Thwart New Soviet Union," *Financial Times*, December 6, 2012, https://www.ft.com/content/a5b15b14-3fcf-11e2-9f71-00144feabdc0.
24. Michael McFaul, *From Cold War to Hot Peace* (Boston: Houghton Mifflin Harcourt, 2018), Chapter 23: Annexation and War in Ukraine.
25. "The BRICS Bloc Is Riven with Tensions," *Economist*, August 17, 2023, https://www.economist.com/international/2023/08/17/the-brics-are-getting-together-in-south-africa.
26. Edward Wong, "China Is Increasingly Seen as Playing a Spoiler Role in Diplomatic Discussions," *New York Times*, March 3, 2023.
27. Anton Troianovski, Niraj Chokshi, and Ivan Nechepurenko, "The One Western Company That Russia May Miss the Most: Boeing," *New York Times*, April 13, 2025.
28. McFaul, *From Cold War to Hot Peace*.
29. William E. Pomeranz, "Uneasy Partners: Russia and the European Court of Human Rights," European Court of Human Rights, https://www.corteidh.or.cr/tablas/r29628.pdf.

30. "Russia to Withdraw from International Criminal Court," BBC News, November 16, 2016, https://www.bbc.com/news/world-europe-38005282.

11. China and the Global Order

1. Cristiano Lima, "Trump Calls Trade Deal 'a Rape of Our Country,'" *Politico*, June 28, 2016, https://www.politico.com/story/2016/06/donald-trump-trans-pacific-partnership-224916.
2. Rush Doshi, *The Long Game: China's Grand Strategy to Displace American Order* (Oxford: Oxford University Press, 2021), 262, 281.
3. Doshi, *The Long Game*, 265.
4. Michael Froman, "China Has Already Remade the International System: How the World Adopted Beijing's Economic Playbook," *Foreign Affairs*, March 25, 2025, https://www.foreignaffairs.com/china/economics-china-international-system-tariffs-michael-froman.
5. Alastair Iain Johnston, "China in a World of Orders: Rethinking Compliance and Challenge in Beijing's International Relations," *International Security* 44, no. 2 (Fall 2019): 9–60.
6. Elizabeth Economy, "China's Alternative Order: And What Americans Should Learn from It," *Foreign Affairs* 103, no. 3 (May/June 2024): 12, https://www.foreignaffairs.com/china/chinas-alternative-order-xi-jinping-elizabeth-economy.
7. Nadège Rolland, *China's Vision for a New World Order* (Washington, DC: National Bureau of Asian Research, 2020), 32–35, https://www.nbr.org/publication/chinas-vision-for-a-new-world-order/.
8. Robert Gilpin, *War and Change in World Politics* (New York: Cambridge University Press, 1981), 9–10.
9. Dale Copeland, *A World Safe for Commerce: American Foreign Policy from the Revolution to the Rise of China* (Princeton, NJ: Princeton University Press, 2024).
10. Phillip Lipscy, *Renegotiating the World Order: Institutional Change in International Relations* (Cambridge: Cambridge University Press, 2017), Chapter 4: Japan in the International Monetary Fund and the World Bank.
11. For best attempts to do so, see Doshi, *The Long Game*; Elizabeth Economy, *The World According to China* (Cambridge: Polity, 2022); Bates Gill, *Daring to Struggle: China's Global Ambitions Under Xi Jinping* (Oxford: Oxford University Press, 2022).
12. Steve Tsang and Olivia Cheung, *The Political Thought of Xi Jinping* (Ashland, OR: Blackstone Publishing, 2024), 171.
13. Economy, *The World According to China*, 170.
14. Oriana Skylar Mastro, *Upstart: How China Became a Great Power* (Oxford: Oxford University Press, 2024), 88–92.
15. Gill, *Daring to Struggle*, 173.
16. "UN: Russia and China's Abusive Use of Veto 'Shameful,'" Amnesty International, February 28, 2017, https://www.amnesty.org/en/latest/news/2017/02/un-russia-and-chinas-abusive-use-of-veto-shameful/.
17. Jeffrey Feltman, "China's Expanding Influence at the United Nations—and How the United States Should React," Brookings Institution, September 2020, https://www.brookings.edu/articles/chinas-expanding-influence-at-the-united-nations-and-how-the-united-states-should-react/.
18. Kelsey Davenport, "Russia Ends North Korean Sanctions Panel," Arms Control Association, May 2024, https://www.armscontrol.org/act/2024-05/news/russia-ends-north-korean-sanctions-panel.
19. Stephen D. Krasner, *Sovereignty: Organized Hypocrisy* (Princeton, NJ: Princeton University Press, 1999).
20. Isaac B. Kardon, "China Can Say 'No': Analyzing China's Rejection of the South China Sea Arbitration," University of Pennsylvania, *Asian Law Review* 13, no. 2 (2018), https://scholarship.law.upenn.edu/alr/vol13/iss2/1.

21. Lisa Curtis and Derek Grossman, "India-China Border Tensions and U.S. Strategy in the Indo-Pacific," Center for a New American Security, March 30, 2023, https://www.cnas.org/publications/reports/india-china-border-tensions-and-u-s-strategy-in-the-indo-pacific.
22. Iain Marlow, "Blinken Says China Wants to Seize Taiwan 'on Much Faster Timeline,'" Bloomberg, October 17, 2022, https://www.bloomberg.com/news/articles/2022-10-17/blinken-says-china-wants-taiwan-on-much-faster-timeline.
23. "Full Text of Xi Jinping's Speech at China's Party Congress," Bloomberg, October 18, 2022, https://www.bloomberg.com/news/articles/2022-10-18/full-text-of-xi-jinping-s-speech-at-china-20th-party-congress-2022.
24. Ben Blanchard, Yimou Lee, and Angie Teo, "China's New Tactic Against Taiwan: Drills 'That Dare Not Speak Their Name,'" Reuters, December 12, 2024, https://www.reuters.com/world/asia-pacific/chinas-new-tactic-against-taiwan-drills-that-dare-not-speak-their-name-2024-12-13/.
25. Shi Bin [石斌], "China's View on International Order in the New Era: Cognition, Policy Orientation and Implementation Path [新时代中国国际秩序观：认知、政策取向与实现路径]," Belt and Road Database, March 15, 2021, https://www.ydylcn.com/zjgd/336960.shtml.
26. Economy, "China's Alternative Order," 14.
27. Jinghan Zeng, *Slogan Politics: Understanding Chinese Foreign Policy Concepts* (London: Palgrave Macmillan, 2020).
28. David H. Shinn and Joshua Eisenman, *China's Relations with Africa: A New Era of Strategic Engagement* (New York: Columbia University Press, 2023), 214–17.
29. Peng Bo, *China and Global Governance: A New Leader?* (London: Palgrave Macmillan, 2021), 193.
30. Matthew Southerland, Will Green, and Sierra Janik, "The Shanghai Cooperation Organization: A Testbed for Chinese Power Projection," US-China Economic and Security Review Commission, November 12, 2020, https://www.uscc.gov/research/shanghai-cooperation-organization-testbed-chinese-power-projection.
31. Mastro, *Upstart*.
32. Bonny Lin et al., "Analyzing the Latest Xi-Putin Meeting and China's Belt and Road Forum," Center for Strategic and International Studies, October 20, 2023, https://www.csis.org/analysis/analyzing-latest-xi-putin-meeting-and-chinas-belt-and-road-forum.
33. Olena Bilousova et al., "Challenges of Export Controls Enforcement: How Russia Continues to Import Components for Its Military Production," International Working Group on Russian Sanctions, January 11, 2024, https://fsi9-prod.s3.us-west-1.amazonaws.com/s3fs-public/2024-01/export_controls_-_final_-_1-11-24_update.pdf.
34. "China-Russian 2023 Trade Value Hits Record High of $240 Bln—Chinese Customs," Reuters, January 11, 2024, https://www.reuters.com/markets/china-russia-2023-trade-value-hits-record-high-240-bln-chinese-customs-2024-01-12/; "Trade Turnover Between Russia, China to Reach $240 Bln—Medvedev," Tass, December 14, 2024, https://tass.com/economy/1886533.
35. Brian Hart et al., "How Deep Are China-Russia Military Ties?," Center for Strategic and International Studies, August 4, 2022, https://chinapower.csis.org/china-russia-military-cooperation-arms-sales-exercises/.
36. Simantik Dowerah, "Why China, Russia Are Holding So Many Joint Military Drills and Why NATO Looks Alarmed," October 10, 2024, Firstpost, https://www.firstpost.com/world/why-china-russia-are-holding-so-many-joint-military-drills-and-why-nato-looks-alarmed-13823935.html.
37. Hart et al., "How Deep Are China-Russia Military Ties?"
38. "Joint Statement of the People's Republic of China and the Russian Federation on Deepening the Comprehensive Strategic Cooperative Partnership in the New Era on the Occasion of

the Seventy-Fifth Anniversary of the Establishment of Diplomatic Relations Between the Two Countries (full text)," May 16, 2024, https://www.mfa.gov.cn/zyxw/202405/t20240516_11305860.shtml.

39. Matina Stevis-Gridneff and Steven Erlanger, "E.U. Summons Chinese Ambassador Over Comments on Russia Ties," *New York Times*, April 5, 2023, https://www.nytimes.com/2023/04/05/world/europe/eu-china-embassador-russia-fu-cong.html.
40. Author's conversations with Chinese officials and academics, Fall 2024.
41. "President Xi Jinping Meets with German Chancellor Olaf Scholz," Ministry of Foreign Affairs of the People's Republic of China, November 4, 2022, https://www.fmprc.gov.cn/mfa_eng/zxxx_662805/202211/t20221104_10800546.html.
42. Anya Konstantinovsky and Molly Carlough, "China-Russia Relations: September 2024," Council on Foreign Relations, September 2024, https://www.cfr.org/article/china-russia-relations-september-2024.
43. Brendan Cole, "Chinese State Banks Off-Load Russia Assets in Blow to Putin: Report," *Newsweek*, September 7, 2024, https://www.newsweek.com/russia-china-yuan-ruble-banks-1950254.
44. Max Seddon, Anastasia Stognei, and Henry Foy, "Russia-China Pipeline Deal Stalls Over Beijing's Price Demands," *Financial Times*, June 2, 2024, https://www.ft.com/content/f7a34e3e-bce9-4db9-ac49-a092f382c526.
45. Agathe Demarais, "The China-Russia Trade Friendship May Not Be Quite What You Think," *Financial Times*, April 23, 2024, https://www.ft.com/content/4bc0973c-c1f3-4df7-821d-0c262e506bb8.
46. Bobo Lo, "Axis of Convenience: Moscow, Beijing, and the New Geopolitics" (Washington, DC: Brookings Institution Press, 2008), 3.
47. Paul Stronski and Nicole Ng, "Cooperation and Competition: Russia and China in Central Asia, the Russian Far East, and the Arctic," Carnegie Endowment for International Peace, February 28, 2018, https://carnegieendowment.org/2018/02/28/cooperation-and-competition-russia-and-china-in-central-asia-russian-far-east-and-arctic-pub-75673; Ankur Shah, "Russia Loosens Its Belt," *Foreign Policy*, July 16, 2020, https://foreignpolicy.com/2020/07/16/russia-china-belt-and-road-initiative/?utm_source=chatgpt.com.
48. Niva Yau, "Russia and China's Quiet Rivalry in Central Asia," Foreign Policy Research Institute, September 2020, www.fpri.org/wp-content/uploads/2020/09/cap-1-yau.pdf.
49. Robert E. Hamilton, "China, Russia, and Power Transition in Central Asia," Foreign Policy Research Institute, May 31, 2024, https://www.fpri.org/article/2024/05/china-russia-and-power-transition-in-central-asia/.
50. Author's interviews with Chinese officials, former officials, and think-tank analysts closely connected to China-Russia relations, Beijing, April 2024.
51. Yujun Feng, "Russia Is Sure to Lose in Ukraine," *The Economist*, April 11, 2024, https://www.economist.com/by-invitation/2024/04/11/russia-is-sure-to-lose-in-ukraine-reckons-a-chinese-expert-on-russia.
52. Doshi, *The Long Game*.
53. Chris Ogden, *The Authoritarian Century: China's Rise and the Demise of the Liberal International Order* (Bristol: Bristol University Press, 2022).
54. Scott Kastner, Margaret Pearson, and Chad Rector, *China's Strategic Multilateralism: Investing in Global Governance* (Cambridge: Cambridge University Press; 2018).
55. Dong Wang and Dejun Cao, *Reglobalisation: When China Meets the World Again* (London: Routledge, 2021), 144.
56. "President Hu Jintao's Written Interview with the Korean Press," Ministry of Foreign Affairs of the People's Republic of China, November 10, 2010, https://www.fmprc.gov.cn/mfa_eng/gjhdq_665435/2675_665437/2701_663406/2703_663410/201011/t20101110_511356.html.

57. "G20 Hangzhou Summit Continues, President Xi Jinping Chairs the Meeting and Delivers a Closing Speech, Stressing to Take the Hangzhou Summit as a Fresh Starting Point for the G20 to Embark on a New Journey," Ministry of Foreign Affairs of the People's Republic of China, September 5, 2015, https://www.mfa.gov.cn/eng/topics_665678/2016zt/XJPCXBZCESGJTLDRDSYCFHJCXYGHD/201609/t20160907_704148.html.
58. "Full Text of Xi Jinping Keynote at the World Economic Forum," CGTN America, January 17, 2017, https://america.cgtn.com/2017/01/17/full-text-of-xi-jinping-keynote-at-the-world-economic-forum.
59. Xi Jinping, "Carrying Forward the Five Principles of Peaceful Coexistence and Jointly Building a Community with a Shared Future for Mankind: Address at the Conference Marking the 70th Anniversary of the Five Principles of Peaceful Coexistence," *China Daily*, June 28, 2024, https://www.chinadaily.com.cn/a/202406/28/WS667e6f2ea31095c51c50b638.html.
60. "IMF Executive Board Concludes Quinquennial SDR Valuation Review and Determines New Currency Weights for SDR Valuation Basket," International Monetary Fund, May 14, 2022, https://www.imf.org/en/News/Articles/2022/05/14/pr22153-imf-board-concludes-sdr-valuation-review.
61. Nathaniel Fick et al., *Confronting Reality in Cyberspace: Foreign Policy for a Fragmented Internet* (New York: Council on Foreign Relations, 2022), https://www.cfr.org/task-force-report/confronting-reality-in-cyberspace; Economy, *The World According to China*, 195–99.
62. Economy, *The World According to China*, 199.
63. Tanner Greer, "Xi Jinping in Translation: China's Guiding Ideology," *Palladium*, May 31, 2019, https://www.palladiummag.com/2019/05/31/xi-jinping-in-translation-chinas-guiding-ideology/.
64. Xi Jinping, "Keynote Speech at the Boao Forum for Asia Annual Conference 2021," April 20, 2021, http://www.xinhuanet.com/english/download/2021-04-20/Fulltext.docx.
65. *The United States and Europe: A Concrete Agenda for Transatlantic Cooperation on China, Majority Report*, US Senate Committee on Foreign Relations, November 2020, www.foreign.senate.gov/imo/media/doc/SFRC_Majority_China_Europe_Report_FINAL_P_and_G.pdf.
66. Michael Brown and Pavneet Singh, *China's Technology Transfer Strategy: How Chinese Investments in Emerging Technology Enable a Strategic Competitor to Access the Crown Jewels of U.S. Innovation* (Mountain View, CA: Defense Innovation Unit Experimental, January 2018), https://nationalsecurity.gmu.edu/wp-content/uploads/2020/02/DIUX-China-Tech-Transfer-Study-Selected-Readings.pdf.
67. Doshi, *The Long Game*, 161.
68. Dawn Murphy, *China's Rise in the Global South: The Middle East, Africa, and Beijing's Alternative World Order* (Stanford: Stanford University Press, 2022).
69. Doshi, *The Long Game*, 209, 225–34.
70. Doshi, *The Long Game*, 238–40.
71. Doshi, *The Long Game*, 249–50.
72. Rush Doshi, "China's Ten-Year Struggle Against U.S. Financial Power," National Bureau of Asian Research, January 6, 2020, https://www.nbr.org/publication/chinas-ten-year-struggle-against-u-s-financial-power/.
73. Darrell Duffie and Elizabeth Economy, eds., *Digital Currencies: The US, China, and the World at a Crossroads* (Stanford: Hoover Institution Press, 2022); Martin Chorzempa, *The Cashless Revolution: China's Reinvention of Money and the End of America's Domination of Finance and Technology* (New York: Public Affairs, 2022).
74. Jindong Zhang, Winnie Zhou, and Tom Westbrook, "Yuan Overtakes Dollar to Become Most-Used Currency in China's Cross-Border Transactions," Reuters, April 26, 2023, https://www.reuters.com/markets/currencies/yuan-overtakes-dollar-become-most-used-currency-chinas-cross-border-transactions-2023-04-26/.

75. Rolland, *China's Vision for a New World Order*, 4–5.
76. Sebastian Horn et al., "China as an International Lender of Last Resort," Working Paper 2244 (Kiel Institute for the World Economy, 2023), 2, https://docs.aiddata.org/ad4/pdfs/WPS124_China_as_an_International_Lender_of_Last_Resort.pdf.
77. Jonathan Woetzel et al., *China and the World: Inside the Dynamics of a Changing Relationship* (New York: McKinsey Global Institute, July 2019).
78. Stephanie Segal and Dylan Gerstel, "Degrees of Separation: A Targeted Approach to US-China Decoupling—Interim Report," Center for Strategic and International Studies, February 3, 2021, https://csis-website-prod.s3.amazonaws.com/s3fs-public/publication/210203_Segal_Degrees_Separation.pdf.
79. "Major Foreign Holders of Treasury Securities," Federal Reserve Board, April 2024, https://ticdata.treasury.gov/resource-center/data-chart-center/tic/Documents/slt_table5.html.
80. Erik Gartzke and Jiakun Jack Zhang, "Trade and War," in Lisa Martin, ed., *The Oxford Handbook of the Political Economy of International Trade* (Oxford: Oxford University Press, 2015), 419–38.
81. David H. Autor, David Dorn, and Gordon H. Hanson, "The China Shock: Learning from Labor-Market Adjustment to Large Changes in Trade," *Annual Review of Economics* 8 (2016): 205–40, https://doi.org/10.1146/annurev-economics-080315-015041.
82. Nicholas Bloom et al., "The China Shock Revisited: Job Reallocation and Industrial Switching in U.S. Labor Markets," Working Paper 33098 (National Bureau of Economic Research, November 2024), https://www.nber.org/papers/w33098.
83. Johnston, "China in a World of Orders."
84. "Secretary Antony J. Blinken, National Security Advisor Jake Sullivan, Director Yang and State Councilor Wang at the Top of Their Meeting," US Department of State, March 18, 2021, https://2021-2025.state.gov/secretary-antony-j-blinken-national-security-advisor-jake-sullivan-chinese-director-of-the-office-of-the-central-commission-for-foreign-affairs-yang-jiechi-and-chinese-state-councilor-wang-yi-at-th/.
85. "Transcript of Vice Minister Le Yucheng's Exclusive Interview with the Associated Press of the United States," *Global Times*, April 18, 2021, https://www.globaltimes.cn/page/202104/1221327.shtml.
86. Rolland, *China's Vision for a New World Order*, 11–13.
87. "The Costs of International Advocacy: China's Interference in United Nations Human Rights Mechanisms," Human Rights Watch, 2017, www.hrw.org/sites/default/files/report_pdf/chinaun0917_web.pdf; Ted Piccone, "China's Long Game on Human Rights at the United Nations," Brookings Institution, September 2018, https://www.brookings.edu/wp-content/uploads/2018/09/FP_20181009_china_human_rights.pdf.
88. Rana Siu Inboden, "China at the UN: Choking Civil Society," *Journal of Democracy* 32, no. 3 (July 2021): 124–35, https://www.journalofdemocracy.org/articles/china-at-the-un-choking-civil-society/.
89. Sophie Richardson, "China's Influence on the Global Human Rights System," Brookings Institution, September 2020, www.brookings.edu/wp-content/uploads/2020/09/FP_20200914_china_human_rights_richardson.pdf.
90. Economy, *The World According to China*, 186–87.
91. Simon Denyer, "Europe Divided, China Gratified as Greece Blocks E.U. Statement Over Human Rights," *Washington Post*, June 19, 2017, https://www.washingtonpost.com/news/worldviews/wp/2017/06/19/europe-divided-china-gratified-as-greece-blocks-e-u-statement-over-human-rights/.
92. Economy, *The World According to China*, 193.
93. Aynne Kokas, *Trafficking Data: How China Is Winning the Battle for Digital Sovereignty* (Oxford: Oxford University Press, 2023).

94. "Joint Statement by the Foreign Ministers of China and Russia on Certain Aspects of Global Governance in Modern Conditions," the Ministry of Foreign Affairs of the Russian Federation, March 23, 2021, https://www.mid.ru/en/maps/cn/1418041/.
95. Xi Jinping and Vladimir Putin, "Joint Statement of the Russian Federation and the People's Republic of China on the International Relations Entering a New Era and the Global Sustainable Development," President of Russia, February 4, 2022, http://en.kremlin.ru/supplement/5770#sel=1:21:S5F,1:37:3jE.
96. "Agenda Item 13: Integrated and Coordinated Implementation of and Follow-Up to the Outcomes of the Major United Nations Conferences and Summits in the Economic, Social, and Related Fields," UN General Assembly, 78th Session, March 11, 2024, https://documents.un.org/doc/undoc/ltd/n24/065/92/pdf/n2406592.pdf.
97. "President Xi Jinping Meets with U.S. President Joe Biden in Bali," Ministry of Foreign Affairs of the People's Republic of China, November 14, 2022, https://www.mfa.gov.cn/eng/zxxx_662805/202211/t20221114_10974686.html.
98. "Secretary Antony J. Blinken and People's Republic of China President Xi Jinping Before Their Meeting," US Department of State, April 26, 2024, https://2021-2025.state.gov/secretary-antony-j-blinken-and-peoples-republic-of-china-president-xi-jinping-before-their-meeting-2/.

12. Learning from Cold War Mistakes

1. Hal Brands, *The Twilight Struggle: What the Cold War Teaches Us About Great-Power Rivalry Today* (New Haven, CT: Yale University Press, 2022), 3.
2. "Professor Predicts Soviet Union Growth Will Overtake U.S.," *Harvard Crimson*, October 17, 1960, https://www.thecrimson.com/article/1960/10/17/professor-predicts-soviet-union-growth-will/.
3. Niall Ferguson, "Capitalism, Socialism and Nationalism: Lessons from History," Hoover Institution, January 2020, https://www.hoover.org/sites/default/files/research/docs/mps_ferguson.pdf, 4.
4. Jeremy Friedman, *Ripe for Revolution: Building Socialism in the Third World* (Cambridge, MA: Harvard University Press, 2021), 246.
5. "Energy and the National Goals—A Crisis of Confidence," President Jimmy Carter, July 15,1971, https://www.americanrhetoric.com/speeches/PDFFiles/Jimmy%20Carter%20-%20Crisis%20of%20Confidence.pdf.
6. Michael McFaul, "The Fourth Wave of Democracy and Dictatorship: Noncooperative Transitions in the Postcommunist World," *World Politics* 54, no. 2 (January 2002): 212–44, https://doi.org/10.1353/wp.2002.0004.
7. Kurt Campbell, *The Pivot: The Future of American Statecraft in Asia* (New York: Twelve, 2016); "National Security Strategy of the United States of America," White House, December 2017, https://www.whitehouse.gov/wp-content/uploads/2017/12/NSS-0Final-12-18-2017-0905-2.pdf.
8. Robert Lighthizer, *No Trade Is Free: Changing Course, Taking on China, and Helping America's Workers* (Northampton, MA: Broadside, 2023), 89.
9. Ian Easton, *The Final Struggle* (Manchester: Eastbridge Books, 2022), 238.
10. Thomas Newdick, "China's Monster Amphibious Assault Ship Has Twin Island Superstructures Optimized for Aviation Ops," Warzone, October 7, 2024, https://www.twz.com/sea/chinas-monster-amphibious-assault-ship-has-twin-island-superstructures-optimized-for-aviation-ops; Thomas Newdick and Tyler Rogoway, "China Stuns with Heavy Stealth Tactical Jet's Sudden Appearance," Warzone, December 26, 2024, https://www.twz.com/air/china-stuns-with-heavy-stealth-tactical-jets-sudden-appearance.
11. Peter Robertson and Wilson Beaver, "China's Defense Budget Is Much Bigger Than It Looks," *Foreign Policy* (September 19, 2023), https://foreignpolicy.com/2023/09/19/china-defense-budget-military-weapons-purchasing-power/.

12. M. Taylor Fravel, George J. Gilboy, and Eric Heginbotham, "Estimating China's Defense Spending: How to Get It Wrong (and Right)," *Texas National Security Review* 7, no. 3 (Summer 2024), https://doi.org/10.26153/tsw/54043.
13. Oriana Skylar Mastro, *Upstart: How China Became a Great Power* (Oxford: Oxford University Press, 2024), 197.
14. Kurt Campbell and Rush Doshi, "Underestimating China," *Foreign Affairs,* April 10, 2025, https://www.foreignaffairs.com/china/underestimating-china.
15. Kyle Wiggers, "DeepSeek's New AI Model Appears to Be One of the Best 'Open' Challengers Yet," *TechCrunch,* December 26, 2024, https://techcrunch.com/2024/12/26/deepseeks-new-ai-model-appears-to-be-one-of-the-best-open-challengers-yet/.
16. Ezra Vogel, *Japan as Number One: Lesson for America* (Cambridge, MA: Harvard University Press, 1979); Paul Kennedy, *The Rise and Fall of Great Powers: Economic Change and Military Conflict from 1500 to 2000* (New York: Vintage, 1989).
17. George Friedman and Meredith Lebard, *The Coming War with Japan* (New York: St. Martin's Press, 1991).
18. Yasheng Huang, *Capitalism with Chinese Characteristics: Entrepreneurship and the State* (Cambridge: Cambridge University Press, 2008).
19. Scott Rozelle and Natalie Hell, *Invisible China: How the Urban-Rural Divide Threatens China's Rise* (Chicago: University of Chicago Press, 2020).
20. Daisuke Wakabayashi and Claire Fu, "A Crisis of Confidence Is Gripping China's Economy," *New York Times,* August 25, 2023, https://www.nytimes.com/2023/08/25/business/china-economy-confidence.html; Arjun Neil Alim and Ian Smith, "Chinese Bond Market Grapples with 'Japanification,'" *Financial Times,* November 29, 2024, https://www.ft.com/content/d299727e-41a1-480b-a44d-780b290bc3c0.
21. Michael Alisky, Scott Rozelle, and Martin King Whyte, "Getting Ahead in Today's China: From Optimism to Pessimism," *China Journal* 93, no. 1 (2025), https://www.journals.uchicago.edu/doi/abs/10.1086/733178.
22. Jude Blanchette and Ryan Hass, "Know Your Rival, Know Yourself: Rightsizing the China Challenge," *Foreign Affairs* 104, no. 1 (January/February 2025): 88–101, https://www.foreignaffairs.com/united-states/know-your-rival-know-yourself-china.
23. Jude Blanchette, "Is Xi Jinping a Marxist?," *China Books Review,* October 17, 2024, https://chinabooksreview.com/2024/10/17/xi-thought/.
24. John Garnaut and Sam Chetwin George, "This Unreadable Russian Novel Is Xi Jinping's Spiritual Guide," *New York Times,* December 15, 2024, https://www.nytimes.com/2024/12/15/opinion/china-brics-xi-jinping-trump.html.
25. Robert O'Brien, "The Chinese Communist Party's Ideology and Global Ambitions," White House, June 24, 2020, https://trumpwhitehouse.archives.gov/briefings-statements/chinese-communist-partys-ideology-global-ambitions/.
26. I am thankful to Steve Sestanovich for suggesting this analogy.
27. David E. Sanger, *New Cold Wars: China's Rise, Russia's Invasion, and America's Struggle to Defend the West* (New York: Crown, 2024), 243.
28. Khrystyna Bondarieva and Valentyna Romanenko, "NATO Secretary General Says Losses in Russia's War in Ukraine Exceed 1 Million People," *Ukrainska Pravda,* December 12, 2024, https://www.pravda.com.ua/eng/news/2024/12/12/7488860/.
29. Tim Martin, "Russia Overtakes All of Europe on Defense Spending in Key Metric: IISS Military Balance," *Breaking Defense,* February 12, 2025, https://breakingdefense.com/2025/02/russia-overtakes-all-of-europe-on-defense-spending-in-key-metric-iiss-military-balance/. Quote from Renaud Foucart, "Russia's Economy Is Now Completely Driven by the War in Ukraine—It Cannot Afford to Lose, but Nor Can It Afford to Win," *The Conversation,* February 22, 2024, https://theconversation.com/russias-economy-is-now-completely-driven-by-the-war-in-ukraine-it-cannot-afford-to-lose-but-nor-can-it-afford-to-win-221333.

30. Andrew Roth, "'A Lot Higher Than We Expected': Russian Arms Production Worries Europe's War Planners," *Guardian*, February 12, 2024, https://www.theguardian.com/world/2024/feb/15/rate-of-russian-military-production-worries-european-war-planners.
31. John Lewis Gaddis, *Strategies of Containment: A Critical Appraisal of Postwar American National Security* (Oxford: Oxford University Press, 1982), 25–53.
32. Michael McFaul, "Southern African Liberation and Great Power Intervention: Towards a Theory of Revolution in an International Context" (PhD diss., Oxford University, 1991).
33. Frederik Logevall, *Embers of War: The Fall of an Empire and the Making of America's Vietnam* (New York: Random House, 2012), 218–20.
34. Michael Green, *By More Than Providence: Grade Strategy and American Power in the Asia Pacific Since 1783* (New York: Columbia University Press, 2017), 271.
35. Hal Brands, *The Twilight Struggle* (New Haven: Yale University Press, 2022), 29.
36. Desha Girod, "How to Win Friends and Influence Development: Optimising US Foreign Assistance," *Survival* 61, no. 6 (2019): 99–114, https://doi.org/10.1080/00396338.2019.1688572.
37. Matthieu Olivier, "CAR—Cameroon: An Investigation into the Wagner Group's African Financial Model," *Africa Report*, January 18, 2023, https://www.theafricareport.com/275235/car-cameroon-an-investigation-into-the-wagner-groups-african-financial-model/.
38. Susan Shirk, *Overreach: How China Derailed Its Peaceful Rise* (Oxford: Oxford University Press, 2022).
39. Logevall, *Embers of War*, 222.
40. "Sen. Rick Scott Introduces Bill to Ban U.S. Import of Communist China's Sewage Garlic," Office of Senator Rick Scott, January 16, 2024, https://www.rickscott.senate.gov/2024/1/sen-rick-scott-introduces-bill-to-ban-u-s-import-of-communist-china-s-sewage-garlic.
41. Odd Arne Westad, *The Cold War: A World History* (New York: Basic Books, 2017).
42. Carles Boix, "Democracy, Development, and the International System," *American Political Science Review* 105, no. 4 (November 2011): 809–28, http://www.jstor.org/stable/23275354.
43. David Adesnik and Michael McFaul, "Engaging Autocratic Allies to Promote Democracy," *Washington Quarterly* 29, no. 2 (Spring 2006): 7–26, https://doi.org/10.1162/wash.2006.29.2.7
44. "Remarks of Senator John F. Kennedy in the Senate," Washington, DC, July 2, 1957, Presidential Library and Museum, https://www.jfklibrary.org/archives/other-resources/john-f-kennedy-speeches/united-states-senate-imperialism-19570702.
45. Bennet Freeman and Nataliya Popovich, "Over 300 U.S. Companies Still Operate in Russia—And Risk Being Complicit in the Kremlin's War Crimes," *Fortune*, March 4, 2024, https://fortune.com/2024/03/04/over-300-us-companies-still-operate-in-russia-risk-being-complicit-in-the-kremlins-war-crimes/.
46. Hal Brands, *The Eurasian Century: Hot Wars, Cold Wars, and the Making of the Modern World* (New York: W. W. Norton, 2025), 235.
47. Girod, "How to Win Friends and Influence Development."
48. Seymour Martin Lipset, "Some Social Requisites of Democracy," *American Political Science Review* 53, no. 1 (1959): 69–105, https://doi.org/10.2307/1951731.
49. Brett L. Carter, "Why the New Cold War Will Split Africa," *Foreign Affairs* (September 20, 2023), https://www.foreignaffairs.com/africa/why-new-cold-war-will-split-africa.
50. Daron Acemoglu et al., "Democracy Does Cause Growth," *Journal of Political Economy* 127, no. 1 (2019): 47–100.
51. Joseph Wright and Matthew S. Winters, "The Politics of Effective Foreign Aid," *Annual Review of Political Science* 13 (2010): 61–80.
52. Desha Girod, "The Political Economy of Aid Conditionality," in James A. Caporaso, ed., *Oxford Research Encyclopedia of Politics* (Oxford: Oxford University Press, 2018).
53. A. Malik et al., "Banking on the Belt and Road: Insights from a New Global Dataset of 13,427 Chinese Development Projects," AidData, 2021, https://docs.aiddata.org/ad4/pdfs

/Banking_on_the_Belt_and_Road__Insights_from_a_new_global_dataset_of_13427_Chinese_development_projects.pdf.

54. Michael McFaul, "Post-Communist Politics: Democratic Prospects in Russia and Eastern Europe," Center for Strategic and International Studies, 1993.
55. Michael McFaul, *Russia's Unfinished Revolution: Political Change from Gorbachev to Putin* (Ithaca, NY: Cornell University Press, 2001).
56. Erin Baggott Carter, Brett Carter, and Stephen Schick, "Do Chinese Citizens Conceal Opposition to the CCP in Surveys? Evidence from Two Experiments," *China Quarterly* (2024): 1–10, https://cddrl.fsi.stanford.edu/publication/do-chinese-citizens-conceal-opposition-ccp-surveys-evidence-two-experiments; Vladimir Milov, "How Strong Is Russian Public Support for the Invasion of Ukraine?," Atlantic Council, January 9, 2024, https://www.atlanticcouncil.org/blogs/ukrainealert/how-strong-is-russian-public-support-for-the-invasion-of-ukraine-2/.
57. Michael McFaul, "Choosing Autocracy: Revolution, Institutional Inertia, and Actors in the Erosion of Russian Democracy," *Comparative Politics* 50, no. 3 (Spring 2018): 305–25.

13. Replicating Cold War Successes Today

1. Elbridge Colby, *The Strategy of Denial: American Defense in an Age of Great Power Competition* (New Haven, CT: Yale University Press, 2021), 148.
2. Gil Barndollar and Matthew Mai, "The U.S. Navy Can't Build Ships," *Foreign Policy*, May 17, 2024, https://foreignpolicy.com/2024/05/17/us-navy-ships-shipbuilding-fleet-china-naval-race-pacific/.
3. "U.S. Shipbuilding," United Nations Conference on Trade and Development, last updated June 5, 2024, https://unctadstat.unctad.org/datacentre/dataviewer/US.ShipBuilding.
4. "Assessing and Strengthening the Manufacturing and Defense Industrial Base and Supply Chain Resiliency," US Department of Defense, October 5, 2018, https://media.defense.gov/2018/oct/05/2002048904/-1/-1/1/assessing-and-strengthening-the-manufacturing-and%20defense-industrial-base-and-supply-chain-resiliency.pdf.
5. Michèle A. Flournoy, "How to Prevent a War in Asia," *Foreign Affairs* (June 18, 2020), https://www.foreignaffairs.com/articles/united-states/2020-06-18/how-prevent-war-asia.
6. "Air Force Exercises Two Collaborative Combat Aircraft Option Awards," Secretary of the Air Force, April 24, 2024, https://www.af.mil/News/Article-Display/Article/3754980/air-force-exercises-two-collaborative-combat-aircraft-option-awards/.
7. Seth G. Jones, "Empty Bins in a Wartime Environment: The Challenge to the U.S. Defense Industrial Base," Center for Strategic and International Studies, January 23, 2023, https://www.csis.org/analysis/empty-bins-wartime-environment-challenge-us-defense-industrial-base.
8. "Fact Sheet: Biden-Harris Administration Introduces New Guidance for Missile Technology Exports to Advance Nonproliferation Goals and Bolster Allied Defense Capabilities," White House, January 2025, https://bidenwhitehouse.archives.gov/briefing-room/statements-releases/2025/01/07/fact-sheet-biden-harris-administration-introduces-new-guidance-for-missile-technology-exports-to-advance-nonproliferation-goals-and-bolster-allied-defense-capabilities/.
9. Christian Brose, *The Kill Chain: Defending America in the Future of High-Tech Warfare* (New York: Hachette, 2020), 197.
10. Oriana Skylar Mastro, *Upstart: How China Became a Great Power* (Oxford: Oxford University Press, 2024), 196.
11. Ash Carter, *Inside the Five-Sided Box: Lesson from a Lifetime of Leadership in the Pentagon* (New York: Dutton, 2019), 322.
12. Andrew Lim and James Fearon, "The Conventional Balance of Terror: America Needs a New Triad to Restore Its Eroding Deterrence," *Foreign Affairs* 104, no. 3 (May/June 2025): 131, https://www.foreignaffairs.com/united-states/conventional-balance-terror-lim-fearon.
13. Simone McCarthy, "China Is Practicing 'Dogfighting' with Satellites as It Ramps Up Space Capabilities," CNN, March 21, 2025, https://www.cnn.com/2025/03/21/china/china-space-force-dogfighting-satellites-intl-hnk/index.html.

14. "Space Force Awards Four 'Quick Start' Resilient GPS Agreements," United States Space Force, September 23, 2024, https://www.spaceforce.mil/News/Article-Display/Article/3914829/space-force-awards-four-quick-start-resilient-gps-agreements/.
15. John Plumb, *Tactically Responsive Space: An Emerging New Deterrence Tool* (Washington, DC: Center for Strategic and International Studies, October 31, 2024), https://www.csis.org/analysis/tactically-responsive-space-emerging-new-deterrence-tool.
16. "Transport Layer," US Space Development Agency, May 2024, https://www.sda.mil/wp-content/uploads/2024/05/Transport-Layer_distro-A_FINAL.pdf.
17. Theresa Hitchens, "EXCLUSIVE: First Space Force Civil Reserve 'Pilot' Contracts Go to 4 Space Watch Firms," *Breaking Defense*, March 21, 2025, https://breakingdefense.com/2025/03/exclusive-first-space-force-civil-reserve-pilot-contracts-go-to-4-space-watch-firms/.
18. Roger Brent, Greg McKelvey, and Jason Matheny, "The New Bioweapons: How Synthetic Biology Could Destabilize the World," *Foreign Affairs* 103, no. 5 (September/October 2024): 157, https://www.foreignaffairs.com/world/new-bioweapons-covid-biology.
19. Paul Scharre, *Four Battlegrounds: Power in the Age of Artificial Intelligence* (New York: W. W. Norton, 2023), 304; Mark Milley and Eric Schmidt, "AI Shows That America Isn't Ready for the Wars of the Future," *Foreign Affairs* (August 5, 2024), https://www.foreignaffairs.com/united-states/ai-america-ready-wars-future-ukraine-israel-mark-milley-eric-schmidt.
20. Michael Brown, "The Empty Arsenal of Democracy: How America Can Build a New Defense Industrial Base," *Foreign Affairs* 104, no. 3 (May/June 2025): 143, https://www.foreignaffairs.com/united-states/empty-arsenal-democracy-michael-brown.
21. Raj Shah and Christopher Kirchhoff, *Unit X: How the Pentagon and Silicon Valley Are Transforming the Future of War* (New York: Scribner, 2024); "CDAO Announces New Approach to Scaling Data, Analytics and AI Capabilities," US Department of Defense, May 30, 2024, https://www.defense.gov/News/Releases/Release/Article/3791829/cdao-announces-new-approach-to-scaling-data-analytics-and-ai-capabilities/; and https://www.iqt.org/.
22. Prasanth Aby Thomas, "Meta Offers Llama AI to US Government for National Security," CIO, November 5, 2024, https://www.cio.com/article/3599448/meta-offers-llama-ai-to-us-government-for-national-security.html.
23. US Department of Defense, "Deputy Secretary of Defense Hicks Announces First Tranche of Replicator Capabilities Focused on All Domain Attritable Autonomous Systems," May 6, 2024, https://www.defense.gov/News/Releases/Release/Article/3765644/deputy-secretary-of-defense-hicks-announces-first-tranche-of-replicator-capabil/; Anastasia Obis, "Hicks Presses Congress to Increase Support for Replicator RDER," Federal News Network, August 2024, https://federalnewsnetwork.com/defense-main/2024/08/hicks-presses-congress-to-increase-support-for-replicator-rder/; US Department of Defense Appropriations Act, 2024, https://docs.house.gov/billsthisweek/20240318/Division%20A%20Defense.PDF.
24. Edward Lucas, "Fogged Up: The Muddle in the Gray Zone," CEPA, November 25, 2024, https://cepa.org/article/fogged-up-the-muddle-in-the-gray-zone/; Lara Jakes, "Drones, Exploding Parcels and Sabotage: How Hybrid Tactics Target the West," *New York Times*, January 4, 2025, https://www.nytimes.com/2025/01/04/world/europe/nato-attacks-drones-exploding-parcels-hybrid.html.
25. Author's conversations with senior officials from these frontline countries in Vilnius, Lithuania, January 2024.
26. Johanna Lemola and Lynsey Chutel, "Finland Says Vessel Suspected of Cutting Cable May Be Part of Russia's 'Shadow Fleet,'" *New York Times*, December 27, 2024, https://www.nytimes.com/2024/12/26/world/europe/finland-estonia-cables-russia.html.
27. Steven Erlanger and Jenny Gross, "Europe's New Defense Commissioner: 'A King Without a Kingdom'?," *New York Times*, September 21, 2024, https://www.nytimes.com/2024/09/20/world/europe/defense-commissioner-military-ukraine-russia.html.

28. Mario Draghi, "The Future of European Competitiveness," European Commission, September 2024, 57, https://commission.europa.eu/topics/eu-competitiveness/draghi-report_en.
29. C. Todd Lopez, "U.S. Intends to Reconstitute U.S. Forces Japan as Joint Forces Headquarters," *DOD News*, July 28, 2024, https://www.defense.gov/News/News-Stories/Article/Article/3852213/us-intends-to-reconstitute-us-forces-japan-as-joint-forces-headquarters/.
30. Kurt Campbell and Rush Doshi, "Underestimating China," *Foreign Affairs*, April 10, 2025, https://www.foreignaffairs.com/china/underestimating-china.
31. David Vergun, "DOD Applauds Funding for Pacific's Freely Associated States," Department of Defense, March 24, 2024, https://www.defense.gov/News/News-Stories/Article/Article/3707447/dod-applauds-funding-for-pacifics-freely-associated-states/.
32. Matt Pottinger, ed., *The Boiling Moat: Urgent Steps to Defend Taiwan* (Stanford: Hoover Institution Press, 2024), 3.
33. Michael McFaul, "How to Get a Breakthrough in Ukraine: The Case Against Incrementalism," *Foreign Affairs* (January 30, 2023), https://www.foreignaffairs.com/ukraine/how-get-breakthrough-ukraine.
34. Ivan Kanapathy, "Countering China's Use of Force," in Pottinger, *The Boiling Moat*, 91.
35. John Dotson, "Taiwan Announces an Increased Defense Budget for 2024," *Global Taiwan Brief* 8, no. 18 (Taipei: Global Taiwan Institute, 2024), https://globaltaiwan.org/2023/09/taiwan-announces-an-increased-defense-budget-for-2024/.
36. Lee His-min and Eric Lee, "Taiwan's Overall Defense Concept, Explained," *Diplomat*, November 3, 2020, https://thediplomat.com/2020/11/taiwans-overall-defense-concept-explained/.
37. Jim Timbie and James Ellis, "Large Numbers of Small Things," *Texas National Security Review* (December 2021), https://tnsr.org/2021/12/a-large-number-of-small-things-a-porcupine-strategy-for-taiwan/.
38. Kanapathy, "Countering China's Use of Force," 97.
39. Larry Diamond, James Ellis, and Orville Schell, eds., *Silicon Triangle: The United States, Taiwan, China, and Global Semiconductor Security* (Stanford: Hoover Institution Press, 2023), 373.
40. Robert Haddick, Mark Montgomery, and Isaac Harris, "Sink China's Navy," in Pottinger, *The Boiling Moat*, 140–41.
41. Evan Feigenbaum and Adam Szubin, "What China Has Learned from the Ukraine War," *Foreign Affairs* (February 14, 2023), https://www.foreignaffairs.com/china/what-china-has-learned-ukraine-war.
42. Fareed Zakaria, interview with Marc Liu, *GPS*, CNN, July 31, 2022, https://transcripts.cnn.com/show/fzgps/date/2022-07-31/segment/01.
43. Stephen Burgess, "Confronting China's Maritime Expansion in the South China Sea," *Journal of Indo-Pacific Affairs*, Fall 2020, 112–34, https://media.defense.gov/2020/Aug/31/2002488087/-1/-1/1/BURGESS.PDF.
44. Bill Hayton, "How to Solve the South China Sea Disputes," ISEAS Perspective, March 15, 2022, https://www.iseas.edu.sg/articles-commentaries/iseas-perspective/2022-25-how-to-solve-the-south-china-sea-disputes-by-bill-hayton/.
45. Hans Kristensen et al., "Status of World Nuclear Sources," Federation of American Scientists, March 2023, https://fas.org/initiative/status-world-nuclear-forces/.
46. *Military and Security Developments Involving the People's Republic of China 2024, Annual Report to Congress* (Washington, DC: Department of Defense, 2024), 101.
47. Mastro, *Upstart*, 192.
48. M. Taylor Fravel, Henrik Stålhane Hiim, and Magnus Langset Trøan, "China's Misunderstood Nuclear Expansion," *Foreign Affairs* (November 10, 2023), https://www.foreignaffairs.com/china/chinas-misunderstood-nuclear-expansion.

49. Michael Albertson, "Moving from the Abstract to the Concrete in U.S. Arms Control with Russia and China," in Michael Albertson, ed., *Aligning Arms Control with the New Security Environment* (Livermore, CA: Center for Global Security Research, Lawrence Livermore National Laboratory, May 2024), 66.
50. Alexander George, *Managing US-Soviet Rivalry: Problems of Crisis Prevention* (Boulder, CO: Westview, 1983).
51. George Shultz, *Turmoil and Triumph: My Years as Secretary of State* (New York: Scribner, 1993).
52. Xuetong Yan, "Why China Isn't Scared of Trump," *Foreign Affairs* (December 20, 2024), https://www.foreignaffairs.com/united-states/why-china-isnt-scared-trump.
53. Condoleezza Rice, "The Perils of Isolationism: The World Still Needs America—and America Still Needs the World," *Foreign Affairs* 103, no. 5 (September/October 2024): 11, https://www.gsb.stanford.edu/faculty-research/publications/perils-isolationism-world-still-needs-america-america-still-needs.
54. The United States never recognized Moscow's annexation of Estonia, Latvia, and Lithuania, but other countries did.
55. "As China's Power Waxes, the West's Study of It Is Waning," *Economist*, November 26, 2020, https://www.economist.com/china/2020/11/26/as-chinas-power-waxes-the-wests-study-of-it-is-waning.
56. Elisabeth Braw, "When Knowledge Stops at the Water's Edge," *Foreign Policy* (May 24, 2024); Emily Feng, "American Graduates of China's Yenching Academy Are Being Questioned by the FBI," NPR, August 1, 2019, https://www.npr.org/2019/08/01/746355146/american-graduates-of-chinas-yenching-academy-are-being-questioned-by-the-fbi.
57. Larry Diamond, "Democratic Regression in Comparative Perspective: Scope, Methods, and Causes," *Democratization* 28, no. 1 (2020): 22–42, https://doi.org/10.1080/13510347.2020.1807517.
58. Stephen Krasner, *How to Make Love to a Despot: An Alternative Foreign Policy for the Twenty-First Century* (New York: Liveright, 2020).
59. Maya Wang, "Hong Kongers Are Purging the Evidence of Their Lost Freedom," *New York Times*, March 27, 2024, https://www.nytimes.com/2024/03/26/opinion/hong-kong-law-freedom.html.
60. Daron Acemoglu et al., "Democracy Does Cause Growth," *Journal of Political Economy* 127, no. 1 (2019): 47–100; Thomas J. Bollyky et al., "The Relationships Between Democratic Experience, Adult Health, and Cause-Specific Mortality in 170 Countries Between 1980 and 2016: An Observational Analysis," *Lancet* 393, no. 10181 (2019): 1628–40.
61. Dani Rodrik and Romain Wacziarg, "Do Democratic Transitions Produce Bad Economic Outcomes?," *American Economic Review* 95, no. 2 (May 2005): 50–55.
62. Richard Wike et al., "Representative Democracy Remains a Popular Ideal, but People Around the World Are Critical of How It's Working," Pew Research Center, 2024, https://www.pewresearch.org/global/wp-content/uploads/sites/2/2024/02/gap_2024.02.28_democracy-closed-end_report.pdf.
63. Sergey Guriev and Daniel Treisman, *Spin Doctors: The Changing Face of Tyranny in the 21st Century* (Princeton, NJ: Princeton University Press, 2022).
64. Michael McFaul et al., "Securing American Elections: Prescriptions for Enhancing the Integrity and Independence of the 2020 U.S. Presidential Election and Beyond," Stanford University, June 2019.
65. Sarah Anderson, Daniel Butler, and Laurel Harbridge-Yong, *Rejecting Compromise: Legislators' Fear of Primary Voters* (Cambridge: Cambridge University Press, 2020).
66. Larry Diamond, *Ill Winds: Saving Democracy from Russian Rage, Chinese Ambition, and American Complacency* (New York: Penguin, 2019), 257.
67. Robert Gorwa and Timothy Garton Ash, "Democratic Transparency in a Platform Society,"

in Nathaniel Persily and Joshua Tucker, eds., *Social Media and Democracy: The States of the Field and Prospects for Reform* (Cambridge: Cambridge University Press, 2020), 286–312; David McCabe, "Microsoft Calls for Rules to Minimize Risks of A.I.," *New York Times*, May 26, 2023.

68. Zolan Kanno-Youngs, "El Salvador's Leader Says He Won't Return Wrongly Deported Maryland Man," *New York Times*, April 14, 2025, https://www.nytimes.com/2025/04/14/us/politics/trump-bukele-prison-deported-migrants.html.
69. For more detailed proposals, see Diamond, *Ill Winds*, Chapter 13: Reviving American Democracy; and William Howell and Terry Moe, *Presidents, Populism, and the Crisis of Democracy* (Chicago: University of Chicago Press, 2020).
70. Vivian Lee, *The Long Fix: Solving America's Health Care Crisis with Strategies That Work for Everyone* (New York: W. W. Norton, 2020).
71. "World University Rankings," *Times Higher Education*, accessed January 10, 2025, https://www.timeshighereducation.com/world-university-rankings.
72. Zachary Arnold and Remco Zwetsloot, "Foreign Brains Help America Compete," *Wall Street Journal*, January 29, 2020, https://www.wsj.com/articles/foreign-brains-help-america-compete-11580341875. See also the Editorial Board, "Keeping Talent: America Trains," *Wall Street Journal*, March 4, 2019, https://www.wsj.com/articles/keeping-talent-america-trains-11551741561.
73. Michael McFaul, *Advancing Democracy Abroad* (Lanham, MD: Rowman and Littlefield, 2010).
74. Diamond, "Democratic Regression."
75. "Democracy Delivers Initiative," US Agency for International Development, https://web.archive.org/web/20241226113525/https://www.usaid.gov/news-information/press-releases/sep-25-2024-united-states-and-partners-mobilize-517-million-support-democratic-openings-around-world.
76. Thomas Carothers and Brendan Hartnett, "Misunderstanding Democratic Backsliding," *Journal of Democracy* 35, no. 3 (July 2024): 35.
77. Larry Diamond, "How to End the Democratic Recession: The Fight Against Autocracy Needs a New Playbook," *Foreign Affairs* 103, no. 6 (November/December 2024): 126–40, https://www.foreignaffairs.com/world/how-end-democratic-recession-autocracy-larry-diamond.
78. For the details, see Michael McFaul, "It's Time to Up Our Democracy Promotion Game," *American Purpose*, November 12, 2021.
79. "D-10 Strategy Forum," Atlantic Council, accessed January 10, 2025, https://www.atlanticcouncil.org/programs/scowcroft-center-for-strategy-and-security/global-strategy-initiative/democratic-order-initiative/d-10-strategy-forum/.
80. Thomas Carothers and Frances Z. Brown, "Revitalizing Democracy Internationally," Carnegie Endowment for International Peace, September 9, 2020, https://carnegieendowment.org/2020/09/09/revitalizing-democracy-internationally-pub-82502.
81. Katie Paul, "Meta Bans Russian State Media for 'Foreign Interference,'" Reuters, September 17, 2024, https://www.reuters.com/business/media-telecom/meta-bans-rt-other-russian-state-media-networks-2024-09-17/.
82. Eric Edelman et al., "Linking Values and Strategy: How Democracies Can Offset Autocratic Advances," Alliance for Securing Democracy, October 2020, https://securingdemocracy.gmfus.org/wp-content/uploads/2020/10/Linking-Values-and-Strategy.pdf.
83. Richard Stengel, *Information Wars: How We Lost the Global Battle Against Disinformation and What We Can Do About It* (New York: Atlantic Monthly Press, 2019).
84. Jeffrey Gedmin, "Soft Power, Anyone?," *American Purpose*, December 2, 2020, https://www.americanpurpose.com/articles/soft-power-anyone/.
85. Michael Beeman, *Walking Out: America's New Trade Policy in the Asia-Pacific and Beyond* (Stanford: Stanford University Press, 2024), 1.

86. Kimberly Clausing, *Open: The Progressive Case for Free Trade, Immigration, and Global Capital* (Cambridge, MA: Harvard University Press, 2019).
87. Ngozi Okonjo-Iweala, "Why the World Still Needs Trade," *Foreign Affairs* 102, no. 4 (July/August 2023): 94–103, https://www.foreignaffairs.com/united-states/why-world-still-needs-trade.
88. Liza Tobin, "China's Brute Force Economics: Waking Up from the Dream of a Level Playing Field," *Texas National Security Review* 6, no. 1 (Winter 2022/2023): 82, http://dx.doi.org/10.26153/tsw/44439.
89. Paul Blustein, *Schism: China, America and the Fracturing of the Global Trading System* (Waterloo, Canada: Centre for International Governance Innovation, 2019), 167.
90. Ian Allen, "It's Time for the United States to End Its Bipartisan Attack on the WTO," Just Security, March 4, 2024, https://www.justsecurity.org/93024/its-time-for-the-united-states-to-end-its-bipartisan-attack-on-the-wto/.
91. Miriam Sapiro and Todd Tucker, "How Trade Can Serve the American Worker," *Foreign Affairs* (October 23, 2024), https://www.foreignaffairs.com/north-america/how-trade-can-serve-american-worker.
92. Robert McDougall, "Crisis in the WTO: Restoring the WTO Dispute Settlement Function," Centre for International Governance Innovation, October 2018, 2, https://www.cigionline.org/sites/default/files/documents/Paper%20no.194.pdf.
93. Jennifer Hillman, "The Best Way to Address China's Unfair Policies and Practices Is Through a Big, Bold Multilateral Case at the WTO," *US Tools to Address Chinese Market Distortions*, hearing before the U.S.-China Economic and Security Review Commission, June 2018, https://www.uscc.gov/sites/default/files/Hillman%20Testimony%20US%20China%20Comm%20w%20Appendix%20A.pdf.
94. "The Blue Dot Network Begins Global Certification Framework for Quality Infrastructure," OECD, April 9, 2024, https://www.oecd.org/en/about/news/press-releases/2024/04/the-blue-dot-network-begins-global-certification-framework-for-quality-infrastructure-hosted-by-the-oecd.html.
95. Marietje Schaake, "We Need a New Global Standard to Curb Intrusive Spyware," *Financial Times*, November 9, 2021, https://www.ft.com/content/bdd6581c-96fc-474b-a2f3-8a06b617825e.
96. "General Assembly Adopts Landmark Resolution on Steering Artificial Intelligence towards Global Good, Faster Realization of Sustainable Development," *UN Press*, March 21, 2024, https://press.un.org/en/2024/ga12588.doc.htm.
97. Ali Wyne, "U.S. Hypocrisy in the South China Sea," *Foreign Affairs* (July 14, 2016), https://www.foreignaffairs.com/articles/china/2016-07-14/us-hypocrisy-south-china-sea.
98. James Mattis et al., "Ending China's Chokehold on Rare-Earth Minerals," *Bloomberg Opinion*, September 18, 2020.
99. Dave Lawler, "The 53 Countries Supporting China's Crackdown on Hong Kong," *Axios*, updated July 2, 2020, https://www.axios.com/2020/07/02/countries-supporting-china-hong-kong-law.
100. Samm Sacks and Peter Swire, "A Framework for Assessing U.S. Data Policy Toward China," SSRN, October 13, 2023, https://ssrn.com/abstract=4601794.
101. Charina Chou, James Manyika, and Hartmut Neven, "The Race to Lead the Quantum Future," *Foreign Affairs* 104, no. 1 (January/February 2025): 165, https://www.foreignaffairs.com/united-states/race-lead-quantum-future-chou-manyika-neven.
102. Matthew Goodman, "From TPP to CPTPP," Center for Strategic and International Studies, March 8, 2018, https://www.csis.org/analysis/tpp-cptpp.
103. Peter A. Petri and Michael G. Plummer, "Regional Trade Agreements Will Reorient East Asian Economies Away from the US," Peterson Institute for International Economics, June 16, 2020, https://www.piie.com/research/piie-charts/regional-trade-agreements-will-reorient-east-asian-economies-away-us.

14. New Policies for New Challenges

1. "Remarks by Vice President Vance at the Munich Security Conference," February 14, 2025, https://www.whitehouse.gov/remarks/2025/02/remarks-by-vice-president-vance-at-the-munich-security-conference/
2. "Understanding US-China Decoupling: Macro Trends and Industry Impacts," US Chamber of Commerce and the Rhodium Group, February 17, 2021, https://www.uschamber.com/sites/default/files/024001_us_china_decoupling_report_fin.pdf.
3. Dale Copeland, *A World Safe for Commerce: American Foreign Policy from the Revolution to the Rise of China* (Princeton, NJ: Princeton University Press, 2024), chapter 7.
4. Erik Gartzke, "The Capitalist Peace," *American Journal of Political Science* 51, no. 1 (2007): 166–91; Dale Copeland, *Economic Interdependence and War* (Princeton, NJ: Princeton University Press, 2015).
5. "Fentanyl: China's Deadly Export to the United States," US-China Economic and Security Review Commission, February 1, 2017, https://www.uscc.gov/research/fentanyl-chinas-deadly-export-united-states.
6. "Commerce Strengthens Export Controls to Restrict China's Capability to Produce Advanced Semiconductors to Military Applications," Bureau of Industry and Security, US Department of Commerce, December 2, 2022, https://www.bis.gov/press-release/commerce-strengthens-export-controls-restrict-chinas-capability-produce-advanced-semiconductors-military; "Commerce Implements New Export Controls on Advanced Computing and Semiconductor Manufacturing Items to the People's Republic of China (PRC)," Bureau of Industry and Security, October 7, 2022, https://www.bis.gov/press-release/commerce-implements-new-export-controls-advanced-computing-semiconductor-manufacturing-items-peoples; Keith Bradsher, "China Just Showed Washington How It Plans to Fight the Next Trade War," *New York Times*, December 5, 2024, https://www.nytimes.com/2024/12/04/business/china-us-trade-export-controls.html.
7. Lloyd Lee and Shubhangi Goel, "Nvidia Stock Slides Premarket After Warning of $5.5 Billion Hit from Trump's China Chip Restrictions," Yahoo Finance, April 16, 2025, https://uk.finance.yahoo.com/news/nvidia-expects-5-5-billion-002904173.html.
8. Glenn Tiffert, ed., *Global Engagement: Rethinking Risk in the Research Enterprise* (Stanford: Hoover Institution Press, 2020).
9. "Fact Sheet: U.S. Department of Commerce, U.S. Department of State Launch International Network of AI Safety Institutes at Inaugural Convening in San Francisco," US Department of Commerce, November 2024, https://www.commerce.gov/news/fact-sheets/2024/11/fact-sheet-us-department-commerce-us-department-state-launch-international.
10. Dan Hendrycks, Eric Schmidt, and Alexandr Wang, "Superintelligence Strategy: Expert Version" (2025), https://media.datacenterdynamics.com/media/documents/Superintelligence_Strategy_Expert.pdf
11. Hendrycks, Schmidt, and Wang, "Superintelligence Strategy," 17–23.
12. "Executive Order on Addressing United States Investments in Certain National Security Technologies and Products in Countries of Concern," White House, August 9, 2023, https://bidenwhitehouse.archives.gov/briefing-room/presidential-actions/2023/08/09/executive-order-on-addressing-united-states-investments-in-certain-national-security-technologies-and-products-in-countries-of-concern/#:~:text=(a)%20To%20assist%20in%20addressing,to%20public%20notice%20and%20comment%2C.
13. "Investigative Report on the U.S. National Security Issues Posed by Chinese Telecommunications Companies Huawei and ZTE," US House of Representatives, Permanent Select Committee on Intelligence, October 8, 2012, https://intelligence.house.gov/news/documentsingle.aspx?DocumentID=327.
14. "Secure 5G and Beyond Act of 2020," Congress.gov, March 23, 2020, https://www.congress.gov/116/plaws/publ129/PLAW-116publ129.pdf; "President Donald J. Trump Is Committed

to Safeguarding America's Vital Communications Networks and Securing 5G Technology," White House, March 12, 2020, https://www.whitehouse.gov/briefings-statements/president-donald-j-trump-committed-safeguarding-americas-vital-communications-networks-securing-5g-technology/.

15. Lucy Fisher, "Downing Street Plans New 5G Club of Democracies," *Sunday Times*, May 29, 2020, https://www.thetimes.co.uk/article/downing-street-plans-new-5g-club-of-democracies-bfnd5wj57.
16. Henry Farrell and Abraham Newman, *Underground Empire: How America Weaponized the World Economy* (New York: Henry Holt, 2023), 190.
17. Edward Fishman, *Chokepoints: American Power in the Age of Economic Warfare* (New York: Portfolio, 2025); Farrell and Newman, *Underground Empire*, 204.
18. Michael Mastanduno, *Economic Containment: CoCom and the Politics of East-West Trade* (Ithaca, NY: Cornell University Press, 1992).
19. "The Committee on Foreign Investment in the United States (CFIUS)," US Department of the Treasury, accessed January 9, 2025, https://home.treasury.gov/policy-issues/international/the-committee-on-foreign-investment-in-the-united-states-cfius.
20. Larry Diamond, James Ellis, and Orville Schell, eds., *Silicon Triangle: The United States, Taiwan, China and Global Semiconductor Security* (Stanford: Hoover Institution Press, 2023), 363.
21. "National AI Research Resource," Institute for Human-Centered Artificial Intelligence, Stanford University, accessed January 9, 2025, https://hai.stanford.edu/policy/policy-efforts/national-ai-research-resource.
22. "Executive Order on the Safe, Secure, and Trustworthy Development and Use of Artificial Intelligence," White House, October 30, 2023, https://bidenwhitehouse.archives.gov/briefing-room/statements-releases/2023/10/30/fact-sheet-president-biden-issues-executive-order-on-safe-secure-and-trustworthy-artificial-intelligence/.
23. Daniel Zhang et al., "Enhancing International Cooperation in AI Research: The Case for a Multilateral AI Research Institute," Institute for Human-Centered Artificial Intelligence, Stanford University, May 2022, https://hai.stanford.edu/policy/white-paper-enhancing-international-cooperation-ai-research-case-multilateral-ai-research-institute.
24. Kimberly Clausing, "The Real Reason Trump Pushes Tariffs," *New York Times*, February 21, 2025, https://www.nytimes.com/2025/02/21/opinion/trump-tariffs-tax-cuts.html.
25. Minxin Pei, "To Beat China, US Should Stop Acting Like China," *Bloomberg Opinion*, May 30, 2024, https://www.bloomberg.com/opinion/articles/2024-05-30/us-can-t-beat-china-by-prioritizing-security-over-economy.
26. "US Tariffs: Allies Retaliate With Levies on Jam, Lamps and Sleeping Bags," BBC, June 1, 2018, https://www.bbc.com/news/business-44320727.
27. Chris Miller and David Talbot, "Mexico's Microchip Advantage," *Foreign Affairs*, August 28, 2023, https://www-foreignaffairs-com.stanford.idm.oclc.org/mexico/mexicos-microchip-advantage-semiconductor-china.
28. Gita Gopinath et al., "Changing Global Linkages: A New Cold War?," Working Paper 2024/76 (IMF, April 2024), https://www.imf.org/en/Publications/WP/Issues/2024/04/05/Changing-Global-Linkages-A-New-Cold-War-547357.
29. Zack Budryk, "China Imposes Export Control on Rare Minerals Used to Make Semiconductor Chips," *The Hill*, July 3, 2023, https://thehill.com/policy/energy-environment/4079680-china-imposes-export-controls-on-rare-minerals-used-to-make-semiconductor-chips/.
30. "Will the White House Big Bet on Intel Backfire?," *New York Times*, October 28, 2024, https://www.nytimes.com/2024/10/24/us/politics/intel-chips-biden.html#:~:text=Big%20on%20Intel.-,Will%20It%20Backfire%3F,government%20pushes%20for%20the%20opposite.&text=Ana%20Swanson%20reported%20from%20Washington%2C%20and%20Tripp%20Mickle%20from%20San%20Francisco; Don Clark, "Intel Has a $16.6 Billion Loss,

Its Worst Result for a Quarter," *New York Times*, November 2, 2024, https://www.nytimes.com/2024/10/31/technology/intel-earnings-loss.html.

31. "2023 Annual Report," ASML, accessed January 9, 2025, https://www.asml.com/en/investors/annual-report/2023#environmental; Farrell and Newman, *Underground Empire*, 200–201.
32. Daniel Drezner, "Global Economic Sanctions," *Annual Review of Political Science* 27 (2024): 9–24.
33. Matthew Reynolds and Matthew Goodman, *Deny, Deflect, Deter: Countering China's Economic Coercion* (Washington, DC: CSIS, March 2023), 1, https://www.csis.org/analysis/deny-deflect-deter-countering-chinas-economic-coercion.
34. Adam Taylor, "Two Years After Start of Ukraine War, Russian Titanium Keeps Flowing to West," *Washington Post*, March 21, 2024, https://www.washingtonpost.com/world/2024/03/21/russia-titanium-exports-sanctions/.
35. Madhumitha Jaganmohan, "Leading Countries Based on the Mine Production of Titanium Minerals Worldwide in 2023," Statista, May 3, 2024, https://www.statista.com/statistics/759972/mine-production-titanium-minerals-worldwide-by-country/.
36. Diamond, Ellis, and Schell, *Silicon Triangle*, 354.
37. "DFC Expands Global Impact with Record-Breaking Investments in Fiscal Year 2024," US International Development Finance Corporation, October 24, 2024, https://www.dfc.gov/media/press-releases/dfc-expands-global-impact-record-breaking-investments-fiscal-year-2024.
38. Advait Arun, "What Private Capital Cannot Do Alone: The Future of Global Infrastructure Development," Carnegie Endowment for International Peace, December 20, 2024, https://carnegieendowment.org/research/2024/12/what-private-capital-cannot-do-alone-the-future-of-global-infrastructure-development?lang=en.
39. Cole McFaul and Peter Engelke, "Navigating the US-PRC Tech Competition in the Global South," *Atlantic Council Report*, April 16, 2025, https://www.atlanticcouncil.org/in-depth-research-reports/report/navigating-the-us-prc-tech-competition-in-the-global-south/.
40. Bharatha Mallawarachi, Didi Tang, and the Associated Press, "U.S. Counters China's Belt and Road with Announcement of $553m Investment in Sri Lanka Port," *Fortune*, November 8, 2023, https://fortune.com/asia/2023/11/08/us-dfc-china-belt-and-road-553m-investment-sri-lanka-colombo-port/.
41. Camille Gardner and Peter Blair Henry, "The Global Infrastructure Gap: Potential, Perils, and a Framework for Distinction," *Journal of Economic Literature* 61, no. 4 (December 2023): 1318–58.
42. Michael L. Beeman, *Walking Out: America's New Trade Policy in the Asia-Pacific and Beyond* (Stanford: Stanford University Press, 2024), 283–88.
43. Organisation for Economic Co-operation and Development (OECD), "Measuring Foreign Direct Investment," last modified April 28, 2023, https://www.oecd.org/en/topics/foreign-direct-investment-fdi.html.
44. Larry Diamond and Orville Schell, *China's Influence and American Interests: Promoting Constructive Vigilance* (Stanford: Hoover Institution Press, 2019).
45. "Harvard Failed to Stand Up to CCP Influence on Campus," US House of Representatives Select Committee on the CCP, accessed January 9, 2025, https://selectcommitteeontheccp.house.gov/media/investigations/harvard-failed-stand-ccp-influence-campus-0.
46. Luc Cohen, "US Arrests Two for Setting Up Chinese 'Secret Police Station' in New York," Reuters, April 18, 2023, https://www.reuters.com/world/us/us-charges-two-new-yorkers-with-conspiring-act-chinese-agents-statement-2023-04-17/.
47. Karoun Demirjian, "Senate Targets China, Voting to Restrict Farmland Purchases and U.S. Investment," *New York Times*, July 25, 2023, https://www.nytimes.com/2023/07/25/us/politics/senate-china-farmland-investment.html.

48. See, for instance, S. 1717, the Corporate Transparency Act of 2017, https://www.congress.gov/bill/115th-congress/senate-bill/1717; Anders Åslund, *How the United States Can Combat Russia's Kleptocracy* (Washington, DC: Atlantic Council, July 31, 2018), https://www.atlanticcouncil.org/in-depth-research-reports/issue-brief/how-the-united-states-can-combat-russia-s-kleptocracy/.
49. Erik Jensen et al., *Regulating the Lawyer-Enablers of Russia's War on Ukraine* (Stanford: Stanford Law School, 2024).
50. David Sanger and Mark Lander, "U.S. and Britain Accuse China of Cyberespionage Campaign," *New York Times*, March 25, 2024.
51. Ellen Nakashima, "Top Senator Calls Salt Typhoon 'Worst Telecom Hack in Our Nation's History,'" *Washington Post*, November 21, 2024, https://www.washingtonpost.com/national-security/2024/11/21/salt-typhoon-china-hack-telecom/.
52. Diamond, Ellis, and Schell, *Silicon Triangle*, 361.
53. Alexander Ward and Asa Fitch, "Raimondo Says Holding Back China in Chips Race Is a 'Fool's Errand,'" *Wall Street Journal*, December 22, 2024, https://www.wsj.com/politics/national-security/china-biden-chip-manufacturing-gina-raimondo-b98c2606.
54. Michael W. Doyle, *Cold Peace: Avoiding the New Cold War* (New York: Liveright, 2023), 71.
55. Jared Cohen, "The Rise of Geopolitical Swing States," Goldman Sachs, May 15, 2023, https://www.goldmansachs.com/insights/articles/the-rise-of-geopolitical-swing-states; Oliver Stuenkel, *Post-Western World: How Emerging Powers Are Remaking Global Order* (New York: Polity Press, 2016).
56. Ruth Maclean, Abdi Dahir, and Alian Peltier, "Putting Past Aside Many Africans Look Forward to Trump's New Term," *New York Times*, December 29, 2024.
57. Author's conversations on this issue with Henry Kissinger.
58. Meduza, "Что конкретно Путин изменил в политике РФ в области ядерного сдерживания" [What Exactly Putin Changed in Russia's Nuclear Deterrence Policy], November 19, 2024, https://meduza.io/feature/2024/11/19/chto-konkretno-putin-izmenil-v-politike-rf-v-oblasti-yadernogo-sderzhivaniya.
59. "The Longer Telegram: Toward a New American China Strategy," Atlantic Council, January 28, 2021, https://www.atlanticcouncil.org/content-series/atlantic-council-strategy-paper-series/the-longer-telegram/.
60. Oriana Mastro, "Sino-Russian Military Alignment and Its Implications for Global Security," *Security Studies* 33, no. 2 (2024): 254–90.
61. "Secretary Antony J. Blinken with Daniel Kurtz-Phelan of the *Foreign Affairs* Interview," US Department of State, December 18, 2024. https://2021-2025.state.gov/secretary-antony-j-blinken-with-daniel-kurtz-phelan-of-the-foreign-affairs-interview/.
62. Tim Malloy and Doug Schwartz, "Majority Say System of Checks & Balances Not Working Well, Quinnipiac University National Poll Finds," Quinnipiac Poll, February 19, 2025, https://poll.qu.edu/images/polling/us/us02192025_urxu99.pdf.
63. Shiwei Shen, "Why Is China Not Supporting Russia Nor Ukraine in Drone Conflicts?," *The China Briefing*, February 22, 2025, https://substack.com/home/post/p-157674111.
64. David Ingram, "TikTok Removes Russian State Media Outlets RT and Sputnik, Citing 'Covert Influence Operations,'" NBC News, September 23, 2024, https://www.nbcnews.com/news/us-news/tiktok-removes-rt-sputnik-covert-operations-rcna172358.
65. Yujun Feng, "Russia Is Sure to Lose in Ukraine Reckons a Chinese Expert on Russia," *Economist*, April 11, 2024, https://www.economist.com/by-invitation/2024/04/11/russia-is-sure-to-lose-in-ukraine-reckons-a-chinese-expert-on-russia.
66. "Secretary Antony J. Blinken with Daniel Kurtz-Phelan," US Department of State, December 18, 2024, https://2021-2025.state.gov/secretary-antony-j-blinken-with-daniel-kurtz-phelan-of-the-foreign-affairs-interview/.

67. Joseph Nye, *Do Morals Matter? Presidents and Foreign Policy from FDR to Trump* (Oxford: Oxford University Press, 2020), 4.
68. Charles Kupchan, *Isolationism: A History of America's Efforts to Shield Itself from the World* (Oxford: Oxford University Press, 2020), xii.
69. Bret Stephens, *America in Retreat: The New Isolationism and the Coming Global Disorder* (New York: Sentinel, 2014).
70. Rachel Maddow, *Prequel: An American Fight Against Fascism* (New York: Crown, 2023).
71. Xuetong Yan, "Why China Isn't Scared of Trump," *Foreign Affairs*, December 20, 2024, https://www.foreignaffairs.com/united-states/why-china-isnt-scared-trump.
72. Elon Facts, "@ElonFactsX," X, December 14, 2024, https://x.com/ElonFactsX/status/1864712701852733630.
73. Beeman, *Walking Out*, 6.
74. David Shambaugh, "China's Long March to Global Power," in David Shambaugh, ed., *China and the World* (Oxford: Oxford University Press, 2020), 19.
75. Huiyao Wang, *The Ebb and Flow of Globalization: Chinese Perspectives on China's Development and Role in the World* (Singapore: Springer Publishers, 2022).
76. Kimberly Clausing, *Open: The Progressive Case for Free Trade, Immigration, and Global Capital* (Cambridge, MA: Harvard University Press, 2019).
77. Robert Kagan, *The Ghost at the Feast: America and the Collapse of World Order, 1900–1941* (New York: Knopf, 2023).
78. Steven Levitsky and Daniel Ziblatt, *Tyranny of the Minority* (New York: Crown, 2023), 122.
79. Robert Kagan, *Rebellion: How Antiliberalism Is Tearing America Apart—Again* (New York: Knopf, 2024), 215.
80. Zack Beauchamp, *The Reactionary Spirit: How America's Most Insidious Political Tradition Swept the World* (New York: Public Affairs, 2024), 65.
81. "Poll: Americans Concerned About Honesty, Openness of 2024 Elections," Public Affairs Council, October 10, 2023, https://pac.org/poll-americans-concerned-about-honesty-openness-of-2024-elections.
82. Nick Corasaniti, Ruth Igielnik, and Camille Baker, "Voters Are Skeptical About the Health of U.S. Democracy a New Poll Finds," *New York Times*, October 28, 2024, https://www.nytimes.com/2024/10/27/us/politics/american-democracy-poll.html.
83. Aaron Stigile, "Donald Trump Rallies Arizonans at Mullett Arena," *Cronkite News*, October 24, 2024, https://cronkitenews.azpbs.org/2024/10/24/donald-trump-rallies-arizonans-tempe-mullett-arena/.
84. "State Voting Bills Tracker: 2021," Brennan Center for Justice, updated May 28, 2021, https://www.brennancenter.org/our-work/research-reports/state-voting-bills-tracker-2021.
85. Lisa Lerer and Astead W. Herndon, "Menace Enters the Republican Mainstream," *New York Times*, November 12, 2021, https://www.nytimes.com/2021/11/12/us/politics/republican-violent-rhetoric.html.
86. Emily A. Vogels, "Support for More Regulation of Tech Companies Has Declined in U.S., Especially Among Republicans," Pew Research Center, May 13, 2022, https://www.pewresearch.org/short-reads/2022/05/13/support-for-more-regulation-of-tech-companies-has-declined-in-u-s-especially-among-republicans/.
87. Michael Tomasky, "Why Does No One Understand the Real Reason Trump Won?," *New Republic*, November 8, 2024, https://newrepublic.com/post/188197/trump-media-information-landscape-fox.
88. "Views of the U.S. Political System, the Federal Government, and Federal-State Relations," Pew Research Center, September 19, 2023, https://www.pewresearch.org/politics/2023/09/19/views-of-the-u-s-political-system-the-federal-government-and-federal-state-relations/.
89. Maddow, *Prequel*.

90. Condoleezza Rice, "The Perils of Isolationism: The World Still Needs America—and America Still Needs the World," *Foreign Affairs* 103, no. 5 (September/October 2024): 24.
91. Robert Putnam, *The Upswing: How America Came Together a Century Ago and How We Can Do It Again* (New York: Simon & Schuster, 2020).
92. Francis Gavin, *The Taming of Scarcity and the Problems of Plenty: Rethinking International Relations and American Grand Strategy in a New Era* (London: IISS, 2024), 78.
93. Robert M. Gates, "The Pentagon and Congress Must Change Their Ways," *Washington Post*, September 24, 2024, https://www.washingtonpost.com/opinions/2024/09/24/robert-gates-peril-china-russia-pentagon-congress-defense/.
94. Matt Pottinger and Matthew Turpin, "The Myth of Accidental Wars," in Matt Pottinger, ed., *The Boiling Moat: Urgent Steps to Defend Taiwan* (Stanford: Hoover Institution Press, 2024), 64.
95. Ezra Klein, *Why We're Polarized* (New York: Avid Read Press, 2020).
96. Jan G. Voelkel et al., "Megastudy Testing 25 Treatments to Reduce Antidemocratic Attitudes and Partisan Animosity," *Science* 386, no. 6719 (October 18, 2024), https://doi.org/10.1126/science.adh4764.
97. Larry Bartels, "The Populist Phantom: Threats to Democracy Start at the Top," *Foreign Affairs* 102. no. 6 (November/December 2024): 110, https://www.foreignaffairs.com/united-states/populist-phantom-threat-democracy-bartels.
98. Robert D. Putnam and Shaylyn Romney Garrett, *The Upswing: How America Came Together a Century Ago and How We Can Do It Again* (New York: Avid Reader Press, 2020).

Epilogue: Don't Bet Against America Just Yet

1. Kenneth Waltz, *Theory of International Politics* (Reading, MA: Addison-Wesley, 1979), 191.
2. Hal Brands and Michael Beckley, *Danger Zone: The Coming Conflict with China* (New York: W. W. Norton, 2022).
3. "Remarks by Vice President Vance at the Munich Security Conference," February 14, 2025, https://www.whitehouse.gov/remarks/2025/02/remarks-by-vice-president-vance-at-the-munich-security-conference/.
4. Namrata Sen, "China Steps In to Replace USAID Projects in Asia After Trump Administration Cuts Funding," Yahoo Finance, March 26, 2025, https://finance.yahoo.com/news/china-steps-replace-usaid-projects-233814054.html.
5. Cole McFaul, "Washington's Science Cuts Are a Gift to Beijing," *The Hill*, March 7, 2025, https://thehill.com/opinion/technology/5180183-china-us-innovation-race.
6. Douglass North, John Wallis, and Barry Weingast, *Violence and Social Orders: A Conceptual Framework for Interpreting Recorded Human History* (Cambridge: Cambridge University Press, 2009).
7. Robert Kagan, *Rebellion: How Antiliberalism Is Tearing America Apart—Again* (New York: Knopf, 2024); Edward Luce, *The Retreat of Western Liberalism* (New York: Atlantic Monthly Press, 2017).
8. Michael Froman, "China Has Already Remade the International System," *Foreign Affairs*, March 25, 2025, https://www.foreignaffairs.com/china/economics-china-international-system-tariffs-michael-froman.
9. Jude Blanchette, "China Sees Opportunity in Trump's Upheaval," *Foreign Affairs*, March 27, 2025, https://www.foreignaffairs.com/china/china-sees-opportunity-trumps-upheaval.
10. Graham Allison, *Destined for War: Can America and China Escape Thucydides's Trap?* (Boston: Houghton Mifflin Harcourt, 2017); and Jack Levy, "Preventive War: Concept and Propositions," *International Interactions* 37, no. 1 (2011), 87–96.
11. Matthew Kroenig, *The Return of Great Power Rivalry: Democracy Versus Autocracy from the Ancient World to the U.S. and China* (Oxford: Oxford University Press, 2020).

Index